# SINATRA!
## THE SONG IS YOU
### ◼— A SINGER'S ART —◼

RON

Copyright © 1995, 2018 by Will Friedwald
Foreword copyright © 2018 by Tony Bennett
All rights reserved
Published by Chicago Review Press Incorporated
814 North Franklin Street
Chicago, Illinois 60610
ISBN 978-1-61373-770-5


**Library of Congress Cataloging-in-Publication Data**

Names: Friedwald, Will, 1961- author.
Title: Sinatra! the song is you : a singer's art / Will Friedwald.
Description: Chicago, Illinois : Chicago Review Press, [2018] | Series:
 Revised and expanded edition | Includes index.
Identifiers: LCCN 2017054445 (print) | LCCN 2017055331 (ebook) | ISBN
 9781613737712 (adobe pdf) | ISBN 9781613737729 (kindle) | ISBN
 9781613737736 (epub) | ISBN 9781613737705 (trade paper)
Subjects: LCSH: Sinatra, Frank, 1915-1998. | Singers—United
 States—Biography.
Classification: LCC ML420.S565 (ebook) | LCC ML420.S565 F78 2018 (print) |
 DDC 782.42164092 [B] —dc23
LC record available at https://lccn.loc.gov/2017054445


Cover design: Debbie Berne Design
Cover photographs: Charles L. Granata
Interior design: Jonathan Hahn

Printed in the United States of America
5  4  3  2  1

# DEDICATION

For Patty, my one and only love.

"She loved me for the dangers I had passed,
And I loved her that she did pity them.
This is the only witchcraft I have used."
—Othello: Act 1, Scene 3

"Those fingers in my hair,
That sly, come-hither stare,
That strips my conscience bare."
—Cy Coleman & Carolyn Leigh

# CONTENTS

# FOREWORD

When people hear the name Tony Bennett, they inevitably think of two things. The first is my signature song, "I Left My Heart in San Francisco," which first made me an internationally known citizen of the world fifty years ago, and I've been happily singing it ever since. And the other thing that nearly everybody knows about me is that Frank Sinatra once named me as his favorite singer.

Obviously, I can never communicate completely how much that meant to me—not only to my career, but to me personally. You see, I was one of the original Sinatra groupies. Back when I was in New York's High School of Industrial Art, I used to get out of classes to see the Tommy Dorsey Orchestra at the Paramount. I would stay for seven shows a day at the Paramount, and just watch him over and over again. Just imagine, in those days you had Tommy Dorsey's band, with Jo Stafford, the Pied Pipers, Buddy Rich, and Ziggy Elman, plus a dance team, a great juggler, or a comic. All that plus Frank Sinatra! All these acts in an hour and twenty-five minutes, for seventy-five cents. I didn't even mind having to sit through the movie seven times.

The whole Sinatra saga really just took off from there. Even in the Dorsey days, there was the most incredible furor over Frank. The band's press agent, for instance, would spread the word around that Sinatra was going to be in the Gaiety Music Shop on Broadway at such and such a time, and he would also arrange for news photographers to be there. The place could only hold about seventy-five people, but thousands of bobby-soxers would cram themselves into that little store! Broadway would look like it did on New Year's Eve. No one had ever seen anything like that before, and it was certain to get Frank and the band a two-page spread in the New York papers.

After the war, when I became a singer myself, I was signed to Columbia Records, which, coincidentally, was the same label Frank was under contract to. Although we were both at Columbia for about two years, we never actually met at this time. It wasn't the happiest period in Frank's life, partially because he wasn't happy with the kind of songs Mitch Miller, who was then in charge of pop music A&R at Columbia, wanted him to record. Of course, I had my own issues with Mitch, although he and I created a lot of hits together.

How I finally met Francis Albert Sinatra is one of the great little stories of my life. By 1956, I had had a few hits, like "Rags to Riches" and "Because of You." At this time Perry Como was the biggest thing on television. Perry was nice enough to offer me the chance to take over for him as a summer replacement. However, the various agencies involved sort of left me hanging: where Perry had Mitchell Ayers and his huge thirty-five–piece orchestra, the Ray Charles Singers, and a fabulous roster of guest stars, they wouldn't give me anything—just an empty stage and a cut-down ten-piece band. And no big-name guest stars, which meant I could never get any ratings. Now I'm usually nervous when I hit the stage to begin with, but this time I was at a total loss.*

I was so desperate that for some reason I thought of going to see Frank Sinatra for advice—even though we had never met! I was so impressed by Sinatra and such a fan of his that somehow I felt that he could help me. Fatefully enough, he was back at the Paramount, only by now he was being backed up by Tommy Dorsey's orchestra and sharing the bill with one of his own movies. When I told people "I'm going to go backstage and see Sinatra!" everybody said, "You gotta stay away from him, he's tough! Look out!" But I just said, "No, no, I'm gonna go take a shot at this." So, I just knocked on his dressing room door, and he opened it and said, "Come in, kid." I was surprised that he even knew me!

And we sat down and he gave me the best music lesson that I could ever imagine. I told him how nervous I was. He said not to worry about that, the people don't mind when you're nervous. It's when you're not nervous that it's dangerous. If you don't care, why should the people care? "The fact that you're nervous is to your credit," Frank told me. "People will adore that, they'll see that you really want to go over and they'll support you for that." Frank not only gave me the confidence to make the television show as good as I possibly could, he gave me a great lesson that I follow to this day. Being excited is a very essential part of performing: those butterflies mean that you care about what you're doing. "Is the light gonna work?" "Am I gonna remember the words?" You have to be concentrated on these elements when you do a show.

Through the years Sinatra said wonderful things about me, and really helped build up my audience for me. One of the first compliments Frank

---

* This was *The Tony Bennett Show*, which served as one of the summer replacement series for *The Perry Como Show* in 1956. It ran for five Saturdays beginning on August 11. Sinatra's final run at the Paramount (and his last reunion with Tommy Dorsey), in support of his latest film, *Johnny Concho*, lasted a week, beginning August 15, 1956.

paid me has always stayed with me—he told me, "Tony, you can only be yourself, but you're very good at that."

I feel Sinatra is the best example of the best music that ever came out of the United States. Not only is he a great interpreter, he has a magic voice. Before Frank, Bing Crosby had really invented the concept of singing intimately, and the microphone made that possible. It was a total break from the earlier, more operatic style, where singers like Al Jolson had to hit the back of the house. But Sinatra took it a whole step further in a way that no one could have imagined. What Sinatra did was psychologically communicate precisely what he was thinking at any moment. After Sinatra, there was no longer any wall between performer and audience—he invited listeners under his skin and inside his brain. He perfected the art of intimacy, and that was a big contribution to the art of popular music. No one ever did that before, to tell such vivid and completely believable stories using the popular song.

But what made an impression on me was that Frank was the one who taught me just not to compromise. He said just to do good songs and success will follow. That's the most important thing he taught me. I asked him many years later, "Why do you think you and I have stayed around so long?" He said, "There's no mystery, it's because we stayed with good songs." And he's right: we never compromised, we just stayed with the best music that we knew, and people responded to that.

My final thought about Frank is how he always surprised me by telling everyone that I was his favorite singer—he even would say it in the middle of his concerts. One of my most cherished memories is from 1974, when my mother was bedridden, tragically, and we were watching Frank's televised concert at Madison Square Garden, *The Main Event*. Suddenly, in between songs, he tells the audience that he thinks I'm the only singer to extend his heritage. I looked over at my mom, and her eyes had opened almost as big as her heart—it was one of the great moments in both of our lives. I'll never forget what he did for me that day, and Frank and his musical legacy will never be forgotten.

—Tony Bennett
2017

# ACKNOWLEDGMENTS

So many people have contributed so much to this book that I'm tempted to ape virtually every other author you've ever read and say I don't know where to begin in terms of thanking people.

Actually, I know exactly where to begin: with the musicians. "I've never heard of a book like that," Al Viola said after we had finished talking, "a book on Frank where they talked to guys like me. The people that were really there with him, sweating it out. That's the one book on Frank that hasn't been written. And I think that's the soul of his music."

First, to the following sidemen and women, who worked with Sinatra from his big band days up through his last performance in 1995: Trigger Alpert, Artie Baker, Julius Baker, Milt Bernhart, Joe Bushkin, Pete Candoli, Page Cavanaugh, John Cave, ("the other") Ray Charles, Mahlon Clark, Buddy Collette, Sid Cooper, Jerry Dodgion, Harry "Sweets" Edison, Alec Fila, Frank Flynn, Stan Freeman, Dave Frisina, Chris Griffin, Bob Haggart, Dave Harris, Arthur "Skeets" Herfurt, Jerry Jerome, Deane Kincaide, Harry Klee, Lou Levy, Johnny Mince and Betty Williams, Dick Nash, Ted Nash, Loulie Jean Norman, Bobby Pring, Pete Pumiglio, Emil Richards, George Roberts, Don Ruffell, Paul Shure, Eleanor Slatkin, Paul Smith, Alvin Stoller, Warren Webb, and Zeke Zarchy.

I'm particularly grateful to the following members of Sinatra's touring rhythm sections, truly the backbone of his music, for sharing their time and memories with me: Johnny Blowers, Vince Falcone, Sol Gubin, Tony Mottola, Al Viola, and, in particular, Bill Miller. (I also made use of a 1979 interview with the late Irv Cottler.)

"A good arranger is terribly vital," Sinatra said, and I have also found that to be the case. Thanks to the late Billy Byers, Charles Calello, Robert Farnon, Frank Foster, Neal Hefti, Quincy Jones, Johnny Mandel, Claus Ogerman, Lillian (Mrs. Sy) Oliver, Marty Paich, George Siravo, and especially to Billy May. I was also fortunate enough to obtain a series of interviews with the late

Nelson Riddle and the late Gordon Jenkins; two of Riddle's children, Christopher and Rosemary, were also very helpful (as was Bruce Jenkins, journalist and son of the late Gordon, in the 2017 edition).

Thanks also to the singers who shared their reflections on and experiences with a man whom they all consider one of the dominant influences on their own work: Eileen Barton, Tony Bennett, Rosemary Clooney, Steve Lawrence and Eydie Gormé, Al Hibbler, Peggy Lee, Jo Stafford, Louise Tobin, Mel Tormé, Bea Wain, and Joe Williams.

"And he wasn't singing la-la-la up there," as Sammy Cahn pointed out. Muchos gracias to the late Mr. Cahn, as well as to his fellow songwriters Alan and Marilyn Bergman, Cy Coleman, Betty Comden, Matt Dennis, Joel Herron, Bart Howard, Jack Lawrence, Lew Spence, and Jack Wolf.

"To continue," as Sinatra sings in "Cherry Pies Ought to Be You," my gratitude also to producers George Avakian, Jimmy Bowen, Alan Livingston, Mitch Miller, Phil Ramone, and George Simon, and to engineers Lee Herschberg and Frank Laico. And also to the following musical giants who have all interacted with Sinatra in one way or another: Les Brown, Bill Finegan, Milt Gabler, Skitch Henderson, Red Norvo, Tito Puente, Pete Rugolo, George Shearing, and Paul Weston.

I was also tremendously well served by the army of Frankenmavens (more recently I dubbed them the "Frank Tank") out there who provided reams of data and miles and miles of tape. They are: Richard Apt, Ken Carley, Eric Comstock, Bob Conrad, Bill Denton, the late Gary Doctor (of the International Sinatra Society), Helen Green, Ken Hutchins, Kenny Lucas, Rebecca Hargrave Malamud, Sid Mark, Tony Natelli, Ed O'Brien, Ric Ross, Ron Sarbo, Arthur Schell, Jonathan Schwartz, Bobby Sherrick, Jude Spatola, David Weiner, and Mitch Zlokower. Very special thanks to the incredibly meticulous Michael Kraus, the monarch and majordomo of musical minutiae, for helping me prepare this paperback edition. Other professionals who contributed ideas include Nate Chinen, Stanley Crouch, Nancy Franklin, Gary Giddins, Ira Gitler, Mary Cleere Haran, Stephen Holden, Bob Jones, Peter Levinson, James Maher, Dan Morgenstern, Ben Ratliff, Peter Watrous, and my father, Herb Friedwald.

And to Melissa Berger and Ted Panken, for wearing out several computers in pounding out roughly six million pages of transcripts from over two hundred interviews.

Not to mention my editor at Scribner, Bill Goldstein (and his invaluable assistant, Ted Lee). Very special thanks to all my editors past and present, and to acknowledge all my editors from the years when I was writing the first edition, namely Doug Simmons, Joe Levy, and Ann Powers of the *Village Voice* as well as Gerald Gold and Fletcher Roberts of the *New York Times*. Currently, the main editor who has given me the most chances to write about Sinatra is Eric Gibson of the *Wall Street Journal.*

Then too, I can't imagine having undertaken this deal without the help and Rolodex of Frank Military, Sinatra's longtime right-hand man (and subsequently the president of Warner-Chappell's East Coast operations). Thanks also to three stalwarts in the Sinatra office who all served "the Old Man" faithfully for many decades: Susan Reynolds (the Chairman's public relations manager), Dorothy Uhlemann (his personal assistant), and Sonny Golden (his business manager).

Sinatra's daughters were also very helpful to me, perhaps more than they realize. Thanks to Nancy Sinatra Lambert for inviting me to participate in *Frank Sinatra: The Capitol Years*; and also to Tina Sinatra, who, like her father, is more of a softie than she lets on, and has a gift for saying the right thing at the right time. Nancy's daughter, A. J. Lambert, has also become a good friend over the years.

Most of all to my indefatigable partner in research, Charles L. Granata. Apart from having amassed the most amazing collection of Sinatra material I've ever seen, Chuck has an insatiable desire to know all there is to know about our culture's greatest popular artist. As often as not, his enthusiasm was the spark plug that kept this project going full steam ahead for five years. A few years after this volume was published, Chuck came out with his own book, *Sessions with Sinatra*, an indispensable guide to Sinatra's career with an emphasis on what Chuck has termed "The Art of Recording." To say that it's essential reading for any Frank fan would be an understatement. Chuck is also the coproducer of *Nancy for Frank*, on Sirius XM, which is the only Sinatracentric radio show I regularly listen to.

And, to use a term of which he would heartily disapprove, "megathanks" to Robert Gottlieb. "The smartest man in New York" (as the late Mary Cleere Haran called him) extended to me the greatest gift I could possibly have asked for: a month of his time, in order to prevent me, as Bob says, from telling people "more about penguins than they need to know."

Let me now throw a bone of gratitude to my agents, the late Claire Medney Smith, who helped conceive this book in 1989, and Robert Cornfield. Special thanks to William Clark, my agent of the last twenty years, and to Yuval Taylor, editor at Chicago Review Press, who made this new edition possible.

Thanks once again to Patty Farmer, who has been such a source of joy, beauty, and inspiration to me for these last five years that a major part of my motivation for preparing this new edition is the opportunity to dedicate it to her. (Would that I could do so with all of my books.)

As trumpeter Chris Griffin has pointed out, "Frank always gave musicians the credit that they were due, saying, 'I wouldn't be here if it weren't for these guys.'" I'm also saying that now.

And so, in the famous words of the great Joe E. Lewis, perhaps the single most significant of Sinatra's role models, "It is now post time."

# INTRODUCTION TO THE 2018 EDITION

Between 1990 and 1995, I kept having the same conversation over and over. I would run into a listener at a club or a concert, usually one who knew my previous book, *Jazz Singing*, or was familiar with my early articles in the *New York Times* or the *Village Voice*. They would ask me if I was working on something new, and I would tell them I was doing a book about Frank Sinatra. At this point, they would respond in one of two ways: first they would say, "Oh you can't do that, he'll beat you up!" They were serious too. They seemed to honestly believe that the seventy-five-year-old Chairman of the Board was going around punching out the lights (as Shelley Winters threatens him in "A Good Man Is Hard to Find") of any journalist who dared to write *anything* about him—even as he had done to Lee Mortimer in 1946.

Or they would say, "Another book? What's left to be said about him?"

Either response indicated essentially the same thing: that anything that one could possibly write about Sinatra would provoke him to the point where he would personally go upside my head; in other words, that there was nothing positive that one could say about him. The only books that anyone expected to be written about Sinatra were those wildly irresponsible pathologies like that of Kitty Kelley (who was neither the first nor the last to do so, but holds the distinction of being the worst) that devoted pages after pages to marriages and his alleged Mafia misdeeds without so much as even mentioning a single song title. In 1990, nobody could believe that there was a book to be written about his music; the only way one could write about Sinatra was to scandalize his name. They came not to praise Sinatra, but to bury him.

It seems hard to believe twenty-five years later, especially in the aftermath of the worldwide centennial lovefest of 2015, that there was a time when Sinatra was adored—and, by some, feared—but not respected. To the end of his life, he could fill Radio City for a week, a level of popularity matched by few rock 'n' roll superstars, yet he was, in a very real sense, taken for granted. For nearly all of his career, he was overlooked by the critical elite and the intelligentsia. Even the National Academy of Recording Arts and Sciences and the Grammys paid scant attention to him until very late, and when they did honor him in 1994, they rather ignominiously yanked him off the stage in mid-acceptance speech. He was apparently never considered for recognition as a National Endowment for the Arts Jazz Master, even though it's hard to think of a jazz singer (or even musician) performing today who doesn't cite him as a major influence.

That period seems more like a hundred years ago, rather than a mere twenty. The lionizing of the singer reached a climax during the one-hundreth birthday year, in which there didn't seem to be an arts organization on the planet that didn't commemorate the centennial. That 2015 event made even the mass media grieve-a-thon that followed his death in 1998 seem insignificant—now we had the Internet and social media. When Sinatra was alive, and I was asked to do talks and events about him, nearly every question I fielded from the audience was about the mob, the marriages, or the Kennedys. Today, as I continue to lecture about him in the twenty-first century, I almost never get asked about his nonmusical life. And this centennial state of transcendence shows no sign of abating now that 2015 has come and gone. I wouldn't be so egocentric as to suggest that my book played even the smallest part in helping to achieve this turnaround, but rather, it was part of the zeitgeist of change that began occurring through the artist's final years.

In a way, it all made sense—at every stage of his career Sinatra was a far-from-marginal performer, but one who deliberately avoided positioning himself in the absolute center of the cultural mainstream. As a recording artist he created classic albums and many signature songs, but relatively few hit singles; he was never a chart-dominating monster in the way that his inspiration (Bing Crosby), his contemporary (Nat King Cole), and his successor (Elvis Presley) all were. It's a fact that he was a major movie star for over three decades, but also that he made only a handful of really meaningful, well-remembered films (whether musicals or in straight dramatic roles)—and yet he nonetheless remained popular enough to keep making movies for as long as he felt like making them (and to be paid a lot of money for doing so). And even though as a young man, he had been a major figure in the last era of network radio, for the rest of his life he was largely indifferent to television, with some highly notable exceptions.

As I say elsewhere in the book, Sinatra knew the value of making sure to zig while the rest of the world zagged; in the World War II period, when America's idea of a real man was the strong, stoic type like Gary Cooper or

John Wayne, who never let his feelings show, Sinatra triumphed by embodying a creature of pure emotion, who made every feeling explicit. In the age of the nuclear family, when most of our role models were running home to a two-car garage and 2.5 kids, Sinatra exemplified the ideal of the swinging bachelor. In the 1960s pop music was taken over by the passive aggression of the flower people; that's when Sinatra made a permanent move to the political right—indeed, this is the very moment when the rest of the world started to pick up on the agenda of civil rights that he had put his career on the line for some twenty years earlier.

In the broad strokes of his music, Sinatra paralleled Duke Ellington; during the 1920s and 1930s, when Ellington was at his most popular, no other bandleaders or composers ever tried to imitate his sound or even pay him homage. It was only during the modern era that younger jazz composers like Thelonious Monk, Gerry Mulligan, and Charles Mingus began to show an Ellingtonian influence. Likewise with Sinatra—during the high point of the "Sinatrauma" movement in the war years and immediately after, when he was causing riots in Times Square and both his skinniness and his power over young women were fodder for comedians and cartoonists, he was still too new for anyone to imitate—his closest rivals, like Dick Haymes and Perry Como, still sounded more like Crosby. Sinatra's own progeny, like Vic Damone, Steve Lawrence, and Jack Jones, wouldn't emerge for another generation. Sinatra seemed to be everywhere and nowhere—or that is, everywhere but where you'd expect him to be.

It was in trying to get a bead on Sinatra that I had decided to write this book; of all the major figures of American popular music and jazz, he seemed to be the hardest to understand. I already considered myself a fan and collector of Bing Crosby, Nat King Cole, Mel Tormé, and Tony Bennett (not to mention Al Bowlly), well before I had my Sinatra epiphany. I had seen several of his 1970s TV specials in my teens, and was ostensibly waiting to be hooked. Most of what I knew about music had been passed on to me by my father, but it was my mother's sister, my aunt Mary Lois (raised, like the rest of my mother's family, in Lower Alabama—the family joke was that we were from "L.A."—but a sophisticated urbanite who actually lived in Manhattan) who provided my portal into the realm of Planet Frank; in other words, she knew the right record to play for me.

The album that did the trick was *A Swingin' Affair!*, and in particular the song "I Wish I Were in Love Again." It was, as the album title promised, *swingin'*—Richard Rodgers's melody and Nelson Riddle's 4/4 dance beat were impossible to extricate from one's head. Lorenz Hart's lyrics were a whole other ball game, somehow incredibly sophisticated and yet with a certain optimistic quality that was, somehow, knowingly naive. To a backwards fourteen-year-old who had little idea what any of this meant, the idea of wanting to fall in love *again* seemed irresistible, the idea that you knew what heartbreak and joy, exhilaration and frustration all lie ahead of you, but you wanted it anyway. Plus there was that "faint aroma of performing seals"—what could *that* possibly mean? I had no idea, but I kept hoping it was some kind of reference to the female anatomy. Rodgers and Hart had come up with a song that was many things at once and yet in the hands and tonsils of Sinatra it was all that and much, much more. The first time I heard the track, I had to hear it over and over; and I did, until I was—as the lyrics put it—punch-drunk.

I realized that here was something totally different from any other artist I had experienced. Crosby had taught me, for instance, that we pay for our happiness with pennies from heaven; in other words, that we can't enjoy the good times unless we have experienced the bad times. But only Sinatra seemed to positively revel in the dark side; the darkness was not just to be endured for as briefly as possible—on our way to the good things—but to be celebrated. Crosby was wise and paternal; thus he tended to sing to us as if we were his own kids. Sinatra, conversely, made it plain that he was offering no wisdom, only empathy—because his pain not only matched our own but exceeded it, as did his joy. Even in "The House I Live In," he's never the least bit didactic—he's not merely telling us what makes America great, he's relating what sounds like his own personal experience, and that's what makes the patriotic message of the song become vivid and real. It's a life lesson, not a lecture.

In terms of his relationship with listeners, Sinatra is himself like the luckless drunk he describes in his spoken intro to "Angel Eyes" (most famously during the 1974 *Main Event* concert). His woman left him, and after steadily drinking in his lonely apartment for a few days, he finally stumbles out the door and heads to a nearest bar, not just to drink, but to talk. "This poor soul comes in, fractured out of his skull, and he's looking for somebody to talk to. He doesn't want any answers, he just wants to talk."

Sinatra continually trumpeted his love for both Mabel Mercer and Billie Holiday, yet he's never a guru of relationships like the first, but rather, a fellow sufferer like the second. Whether we're feeling "sadness or elation," as he put it (or at least his ghostwriter, Mike Shore, did in the infamous 1963 *Playboy* "interview") he has us all covered.

Someone once asked Richard Rodgers if his late partner, Lorenz Hart, was waxing autobiographical when he wrote "Glad to Be Unhappy," which Sinatra sang definitively on the 1955 album *In the Wee Small Hours*. Rodgers's response was something along the lines of "No, he was pretty miserable about it"—or to put it another way, he was unhappy to be unhappy. Sinatra, on the other hand, positively celebrates his unhappiness. It seems totally typical of Sinatra that he recorded a song called "Winners," which is dark and somber, highly depressing. The flip side of this is "Here's to the Losers," which is joyful and upbeat—a swinging take on the Sermon on the Mount, with directly biblical overtones. The implication is that winning is something to be taken seriously, something that carries with it grave responsibility; but losing is something that you can have fun with. The real joy of life is in the losing.

There's a story about another singer that helps illuminate Sinatra's attitudes toward the content of his music. Around 1980, songwriter and iconoclast Alec Wilder wrote a song called "I've Been There" for the marvelous baritone Johnny Hartman. As Hartman's pianist, Tony Monte, later remembered, "Johnny didn't like the song, it was a victim song. It was about being down and out." Hartman refused to sing it. "So I told [Wilder] that Johnny doesn't like to sing that kind of song, we'll pass on this one, so he said, 'No you can't pass, I'll write more lyrics!' So he wrote more lyrics, the new set shows up, and they're not much better in terms of concept, so Johnny still wouldn't sing it. So finally, I think there were three sets of lyrics, and Alec finally got bugged enough. So he changed a few of the words, and gave the song to Frank Sinatra, who recorded it." By now the song had been retitled "A Long Night" and is heard on the 1981 album *She Shot Me Down*. The moral of the story is, as Wilder learned, that it was impossible to write a song too dark, too "down," or too nihilistic for Sinatra.

If you were to ask me what my single favorite Sinatra track was, it would probably be a draw between "I Wish I Were in Love Again" and "Same Old Saturday Night," a modest but brilliant single from 1955 and an otherwise unknown song. Both are classic Nelson Riddle arrangements, and the latter is a lyric by Sammy Cahn that is clearly a follow-up to his "Saturday Night (Is the Loneliest Night of the Week)." The music to that 1944 song is by Jule Styne; the melody of the 1955 is credited to one Frank Reardon, but I've always suspected that Jimmy Van Heusen was involved.

"Same Old Saturday Night" is perhaps the most extreme example of Sinatra's skills at mood-mixing: the melody is joyful and euphoric, like a happy-go-lucky love song, but the lyric is, if not totally down, exceedingly melancholy, it's a song about being lonely and missing someone. He sounds both defeated and triumphant at the same time, even enjoying his state of abject loneliness. He expresses both in the timbre of his voice and even uses rhythm as an emotional signifier: for most of the song, he phrases solidly on the beat, with the optimism of a little kid reciting a nursery rhyme (and I'm particularly enamored of the way he turns the beat around at the end of the bridge on the second chorus, "How I wish you'd *lift* the phone"). Then, at the end, following a tag that only appears in the second chorus (and that he probably suggested himself: "Only your face / Can help me erase . . .") he starts to relax his hold on the time, the mood then shifts from staccato to legato, and the singer starts to reveal the amazing storehouse of passion that he's been saving up for the person he's been singing to. It's enough to expect any other singer to offer us either sadness or elation, but no one matched Sinatra at delivering both at the same time, enough to turn even a minor song, virtually never sung by anyone else, into a pop classic, a complex web of emotions that transcends anything else in the realm of popular song interpretation and invites comparison to Verdi, Hart, Porter, or Sondheim.

"When I do the medley of saloon songs, or a single two-o'clock-in-the-morning kind of a song, you get a response from the audience and you know that they have been there," Sinatra told Bill Boggs in 1975. "That's the time that I feel I am fulfilled. That they have been there. These are not all youngsters. These are grown-ups, who have experienced some form of sadness, that they hear in the song, and it brings it back to them."

And it's key that Sinatra only offers the undistilled emotions without commentary or anything like a moral lesson. As stated earlier, he offers no wisdom, only empathy.

Flashback to 1976. Once I had saved up $3.49—and another fifty cents for the subway—I IRTed over to Sam Goody on West Forty-Second Street and plunked down my paper route money for a copy of *A Swingin' Affair!* It was what Capitol then called a "special abridged edition" of the album, which was their market-friendly way of making the deletion of certain tracks appear to be a virtue. Thank God that "I Wish I Were in Love Again" remained on the abridged edition or I might never have purchased another Sinatra record.

By the time I smuggled myself into New York University in the early 1980s, I was severely hooked on Francis, and had amassed every album that could be found in Sam Goody or elsewhere. I didn't get to see him live until about 1984; that year I was working at the new Tower Records on lower Broadway. A Ticketron unit was installed at the front of the store, and being an employee meant that I had access to tickets about fifteen minutes before everyone else. Coached by my first full-on Sinatra guru, Ron Sarbo, I conspired to pick up a pair for Sinatra's appearance at the Nassau Coliseum on Long Island at the very instant they went on sale. We wound up with incredible seats for relatively little money.

The Coliseum experience was essentially a replay of that which can be seen in the *Sinatra—The Main Event* television special of 1974—a boxing ring in the middle of an arena—but we were among the few sitting in seats on the floor (standing for the most part) gazing up at the stage. The ushers kept looking at us as if we were a side dish that they hadn't ordered, but fortunately, Ron, who had amassed a considerable amount of Sinatra-specific street smarts, had the forethought (and resources) to bring a fistful of twenty-dollar bills to hand out and make them happy.

I vividly remember that first concert. I remember his opening act, Buddy Rich (the only time I saw him live), playing like he was determined to give himself a heart attack. I also remember Sinatra singing "I Can't Get Started" in a dedication to another old friend from the Dorsey days, Bunny Berigan. The past seemed to be living all around me (I caught another associate of those years, Harry James, playing at the Bottom Line, of all unlikely venues, that same year) and yet there was never an artist who was more in the moment.

How many more times did I see Sinatra live? I couldn't tell you, but he loomed large enough in my consciousness to occupy a place of honor in my first book on music, *Jazz Singing*, which was published when I was about twenty-seven or twenty-eight. Because of that book, I was lucky enough to make contact with the larger community of Sinatra fans, including Ric Ross, Rick Apt, Ed O'Brien, and, thankfully soon enough, Chuck Granata, and through them the Sinatra family. The next time Sinatra played New York, I presented a copy of *Jazz Singing* to Sinatra himself at the Waldorf Astoria Tower, his home base in the city. No, I didn't get to meet him at that point, I handed off the book to his secretary of many years, Dorothy Uhlemann, and I assumed that would be the end of it.

But a week later a letter arrived—an almost-sacred missive from the man himself, thanking me for the book and stating that he intended to read it at the first opportunity. I like to believe that he actually did. When I finally met him in person, about three years later—backstage at a concert in New Jersey during the period when *The Columbia Years 1943–1952: The Complete Recordings* package was in production (and this book was being written)—our "conversation" (and it's hardly worthy of the word, even in quotes) was so brief that I hardly had the chance to ask him if he'd ever gotten around to reading my chapter on him.

Still, someone read it—shortly after *Jazz Singing* was published, I started receiving opportunities to work on the complete Sinatra sets that were beginning to be produced: *The Capitol Years*; the twelve-CD *Columbia Years* and the huge fourteen-CD *Capitol Records Concept Albums* set, both of which boasted imposing wooden packages; and other sets for RCA (the Sinatra-Dorsey set) and Reprise–Warner Bros.

It was in 1990, after attending Sinatra's Diamond Jubilee tour—Steve and Eydie were the opening acts, and the New York stop was in Madison Square Garden (and tickets were fifty dollars, which seemed a fortune at the time)—that I decided to write this book. I was much encouraged in this endeavor by my agent at the time, the redoubtable and much-missed Claire Smith (who was the mother of my girlfriend in high school, although, if you asked her today, Heidi will probably deny the charge). The idea seemed radical at the time: who would buy a book about Sinatra in which Nelson Riddle was more important than Sam Giancana?

I made the decision early on to start interviewing as many of the major figures in Sinatra's music as I possibly could. Old Man Time was my enemy: he put a very literal deadline in my way—most of Sinatra's key collaborators were his age and most of them didn't have his iron man constitution. In the five years it took me to research and write *The Song Is You*, at least half a dozen prominent figures in Sinatra's life passed (their names are listed in the dedication); thankfully, I was able to interview most of them. I already already missed Gordon Jenkins and Nelson Riddle, and Jimmy Van Heusen died in 1990 (but I doubt that Van Heusen would have consented to an interview in any case). Sammy Cahn, however, gave us a series of interviews that were, as anyone who knew him will attest, more like one-man shows given for an audience of two in his apartment at 215 East 68th Street.

By "us" and "two" I mean Chuck Granata and me. I said that I was unfortunate in that Sinatra's key collaborators were starting to "buy the farm" or "take a cab" in the decade leading up to Sinatra's own death. (Sammy Cahn himself, alas, died in 1993.) But fate smiled upon me in other ways: I was very much blessed to meet Chuck; two years younger than me, he already had amassed a museum-worthy archive of Sinatra recordings and memorabilia, but his greatest assets were his enthusiasm, his energy, and his dedication. We interviewed dozens of Sinatra associates together and separately, and then pooled that material; Chuck eventually drew on them as well for his own excellent book, *Sessions with Sinatra*. I'm proud to say that I helped open doors for him at Sony Music, where he eventually became the de facto producer (along with Didier Deutsch) of all of the excellent reissues of Columbia-era Sinatra tracks on compact disc. I'm even more proud to say that Chuck and I are still close to this day. (I watched his little girls arrive and grow up—and he watched me undergo serial divorces. But that's the way the dice rolls, pally.)

If Chuck helped me to make sure that there was no shortage of new information in the book, it was Robert Gottlieb—Bob to everyone who knows him—who performed the equally valuable service of making sure that there wasn't too much. The way we met has now become part of literary history—ha!—as enshrined in his majestic memoir *Avid Reader* (2016). I found it amazing that the selfsame super editor who worked with Joseph Heller, John le Carré, and Michael Crichton—not to mention such personal heroes as Whitney Balliett and Robert Kimball—took an interest in my work. Because of personnel changes at Simon & Schuster, Bob served as editor and overseer of *Sinatra! The Song Is You.* And then I had the great fortune to write three other books under Bob's genius tutelary at Pantheon: *Stardust Melodies* (2002), *A Biographical Guide to the Great Jazz and Pop Singers* (2010), and *The Great Jazz and Pop Vocal Albums* (2017).

Around 2000, Bob went to work on the most celebrated autobiography of the early millennial era, that of Bill Clinton. So for years I was after him to introduce me to the former president. That is, until I found out that Bob had also been the editor of that literary masterpiece, *Miss Piggy's Guide to Life.* At which point I said, "Bob, you don't have to introduce me to Bill Clinton anymore, but you do have to hook me up with Miss Piggy." That's the way our relationship has been. (Over these last twenty-five years, I watched Bob's grandchildren grow up, and he watched me . . . well, by now you know where this is going.)

The years 1997 and 1998 were not good to me: the most positive thing that happened in this period was my first divorce. My father died at age sixty-two in August 1997, and then so did Sinatra, eight months later—coincidentally, on what would have been my dad's next birthday, May 14. The major difference between the two was that in all the years I had known my father, you could never describe him as "healthy." Somewhere in my heart, I knew that Herb would never live to be an old man; as devastated as I was by his passing, I can't claim to have been surprised by it. Sinatra, on the other hand, was such a fundamental part of the natural order of things that it was impossible to imagine the world without him. Eighteen years later, I still feel the same way. Both deaths left a void in my life that has never been filled (at least until I met Patty).

I can never forget Friday, May 15, 1998: it began with a phone call—the one I had been dreading for years—and me being picked up by a limo to do *The Today Show, Good Morning America,* and from there a long round of news and morning magazine programs. Some friends recorded those appearances, but I never had the heart to actually watch them. About ten years later, I finally steeled my courage to the sticking place and put the tape in the machine. What I saw confirms my memory of that day; I look like I had just lost my best friend. I was inarguably the least cheerful talk show guest in the history of television. Watching the tapes, I see that I am sad, angry, and defensive. Small wonder that Matt Lauer, Katie Couric, and Barbara Walters have never called me again.

My payoff wasn't in doing those shows, but it was in a phone call a few days later. I picked up the receiver and heard a voice that was not entirely new to me, but not one that I knew well. It was Tina Sinatra. "I just wanted to thank you for everything you're doing for my father," she said. Like the letter the Old Man had sent me eight years previously, that too was a badge of honor that I've been proud to carry ever since.

Sinatra and his music have continued to be at the emotional center of my life and always will be; Chuck Granata is still one of my very best friends, but so are Bill Boggs (and his adorable other half, Jane Rothchild, and her mom, Dottie), Cary Hoffman, Jeff Leibowitz, Michael Kraus, Ken Peplowski, Ken Hutchins, Mark Mairowitz, Dan Levinson, Rob Waldman, Jonathan Cohen, Steve Kramer, Mark Cantor, David Garrick, Harvey Kaplan, Burton Kittay, Jim Davison, Jim Burns, Brook Babcock, Anthony di Florio, Michael B. Schnurr, and many other pals in disparate walks of life who are all connected by our shared passion for everything Frankish. It was also both a pleasure and a privilege to be of some assistance to James Kaplan and his monumental and absolutely essential two-volume biography of Sinatra.

To return to the summer of 1995, I remember well the day that Bob Gottlieb and I finally finished work on the original edition of the book that you're now holding in your hands, *Sinatra! The Song Is You*. Just as we were putting it to bed, Bob said to me, "Well, we've done it—for the first time, there is now a serious book on Frank Sinatra."

He thought a second and added, "Can you imagine a time, many years in the future, when Sinatra's work will be regarded as a legitimate course of study in universities?"

I responded, "I can see it now—some kid in the class of 2025 will say, 'I'm majoring in Sinatra Studies.'" Insert a Jack Benny–like pause for comedic effect here. "'And I'm doing a minor in Bob Eberly.'"

—WILL FRIEDWALD
Harlem, New York, 2016

# 1

# "NIGHT AND DAY"

## *The Sinatra Style*

*An artist must create a personal cosmos, a verdant world in continuity with tradition, further fulfilling man's "awareness," his "degree of consciousness," and bringing new subtilization, vision, and beauty to the elements of experience. It is in this way that Idea, powered by conviction and necessity, will create its own style and the singular, momentous structure capable of realizing its intent.*

—LEON KIRCHNER
(American composer, 1919–2009)

"Why is it," one late-night comic asked in the late 1980s, "that when either Frank Sinatra or the president is in New York, all the hookers suddenly get better looking?" The hubbub regarding a visit from the chief executive can be easily understood. But how could we account for the disruptive power of this swinging septuagenarian, especially in the city that's seen it all? Nearing the end of his long career, Sinatra was undeniably a dinosaur. But like those two-hundred-million-year-old brontosauri that are let loose in twentieth-century Manhattan in all those 1950s B movies, he still had the power to trample the city beneath his feet.

The era that spawned Sinatra "is no more," as P. G. Wodehouse wrote of the England of his youth. "It is gone with the wind. It is one with Nineveh and Tyre." If mankind has been around for only a few minutes in the calendar of the cosmos, then the Sinatra epoch flourished and then was finished in a brief, shining microsecond. The concept of something like quality in what we call American popular culture doesn't even amount to a momentary aberration. The idea that music could have substance as well as mass-marketability came into being at the end of World War I. It reached a climax during World War II and slowly fizzled out during the Vietnam War in the 1960s.

1

The dinosaur metaphor falls apart at this point, because Sinatra can't be compared to a lumbering behemoth who flattened the earth for eons, but rather to some magnificent beast whose entire existence came and went in the twinkling of an eye. Sinatra further represents a unique case where the greatest example of a breed happened to be the one to weather the decades as if in his own personal time capsule—one with hot and cold running babes, a private stock of Jack Daniel's, and no photographers.

The mom-and-pop store that was the music industry in Sinatra's heyday had long since been demolished to make room for the superhighway of low-est-common-denominator culture. Still, Sinatra has dominated the last thirty years—the age of digitally-distributed music—perhaps even more completely than he had any previous period. (Even by 1994, there were no fewer than 283 Sinatra entries listed in a database of compact discs then available.) At the time of Sinatra's "Diamond Jubilee," in honor of his seventy-fifth birthday, while the grandchildren of Sinatra's first audience, the World War II generation, prepared for new global conflicts (with the Bosnian War occurring roughly simultane-ously with the first Gulf War), Sinatra product continued to move in quantities that the music industry traditionally describes in terms of precious metals.

As Sinatra's own career arrived at its conclusion and that much-men-tioned "final curtain" became more concrete than mythic, it became increas-ingly clear how much he meant to all of us. So much of our lives have been lived to the soundtrack of Sinatra music, it's hard to tell where our actual experiences end and those we've felt vicariously through Sinatra lyrics begin. Even as early as my thirties, I had long since lost the ability to distinguish whether some event had really happened to me or if I had just experienced it vicariously through a Sinatra song. It's almost as if he had rather liter-ally implanted his narratives into our memories (almost like the Communist brainwashing conspirators do to Sinatra and Laurence Harvey in the 1962 film *The Manchurian Candidate*). The Sinatra-inspired "memories" amount to a collective stock-footage library of shared experiences. Most of us can feel the small-town episode of "It Was a Very Good Year" amazingly vividly even if we've never been in a village more rural than Greenwich. As film direc-tor and cultural commentator Peter Bogdanovich once put it, Sinatra's songs aren't only his autobiography, they are ours as well.

The late Gordon Jenkins once explained: "Frank does one word in 'Send in the Clowns,' which is my favorite of the songs we did together, and it's the damnedest thing I've ever heard. He just sings the word 'farce,' and your whole life comes up in front of you. He puts so much in that phrase that it just takes a hold of you." Where other singers, at best, work with lyrics and melodies, Sinatra dealt in mental images and pure feelings that he seemed to summon up almost without the intervention of composers, arrangers, and musicians, as vital as their contributions were. (In fact, Sinatra was so sure of his relationship with his audience that he gladly acknowledged orchestrators and songwriters in his spoken introductions to each number. How could it take away from what he did to mention the men who put the notes and words on paper when it was he who imbued them with all of their meaning?)

Sinatra was often larger than life, projecting heightened emotions through intensified vocal gestures. At other times Sinatra was whisperingly intimate, underplaying every note and every emotion to extract the most believability out of a text. At still other times Sinatra was dead-on, having reached a point where we could no longer discern between the part of him that was engaged in what was ultimately a theatrical performance and the real-life man himself. In many numbers—such as his 1961 version of "Without a Song"—Sinatra was all three things at different points in the same song.

There were times when Sinatra acted as if the lyric didn't mean anything to him at all, as with a new novelty number (such as "The Hucklebuck") or an archaic throwaway revived as a "rhythm song" (such as "My Blue Heaven") that he just wanted to have fun with and not be expected to take seriously. When Sinatra titled one 1956 album *Songs for Swingin' Lovers!* it wasn't just a marketing hook but an accurate manifestation of his musical-dramatic ambitions; Sinatra showed the world how a singer could be at once romantic and rhythmically playful. His milestone performance of "I've Got You Under My Skin" (on *Swingin' Lovers*) has Sinatra being supremely sensitive to the intimate nuances of Cole Porter's lyric at one moment and then, eight bars later, being swaggeringly indifferent to it. When Sinatra adds an ad-lib line, most famously "it repeats—how it *yells*—in my ear," he's kidding the text even while he underscores it. (These genuinely spontaneous interjections he varied from performance to performance.)

"Frank's appeal is so great and so wide, I think, because it boils down to one thing: You believe that he's singing [directly] to you," explained Frank Military, Sinatra's right-hand man for roughly ten years, beginning in 1951. "If you go to any of the concerts, you'll see truck drivers and prizefighters and all kinds of people, and they just go crazy over him. You'll see people that were there from the beginning, his [original] audience, all those older folks who were there at the Paramount in 1941 and 1942. You can talk to them, as well as to the new audience that he gets, the young kids today, and every one of them swears that Sinatra sang to them personally."

Sinatra's most appealing talent may have been his capacity for emotional expressiveness. As time went on, he played an increasingly finely tuned instrument, not only with a broader range at the bottom and top—sadder sads and happier happies—but with more degrees between the peaks. He could develop fifteen different kinds of post–"I've Got You Under My Skin" climax-building euphoria on *A Swingin' Affair!*, get you to feel pensive and squirmy twelve different ways on *Where Are You?*, splash cold water in your face from twelve surprising angles on *Come Swing with Me!*, or even "kvell" fifteen different finger-snapping ways on the masterpiece *Songs for Swingin' Lovers!* Even more effective are the ways he increased the emotional, no less than the musical, pitch within a single track: "You Make Me Feel So Young" modulates from mere cheerfulness to exalted rapture so overpoweringly it could make a statue want to fall in love.

Sinatra's vocal range extended all the way up to the stratospheric falsetto note that he used to climax the Axel Stordahl arrangement of "The Song Is You"—a very high F (two Fs above middle C). In the Capitol and early Reprise eras, his top note would more likely be the high F he attained on "The Tender Trap," going down to the ultradeep, Jolsonian low G that concluded his show-stopping 1960s treatment of "Ol' Man River." (He also hit sub-terranean basement-level low notes on the 1959 "Cottage for Sale" and the 1969 "Wave.") Taken in toto, this amounts to a span of nearly two octaves, yet as longtime accompanist Bill Miller cautioned, he reserved those extremes purely for occasional dramatic emphasis. His "practical range," as Miller put it, was rarely quite so high or so low.

While Sinatra had a wonderful voice, he was not a vocal virtuoso. There are popular singers whose techniques are superior to Sinatra's, among them Ella Fitzgerald, Nat King Cole, Vic Damone, and Billy Eckstine. Sinatra's spiritual father, Bing Crosby, perhaps had a greater gift for resonant melody, and Sinatra presented himself as a practitioner of pure power-singing only in the mid-1940s, when he was promoted as, appropriately, "The Voice." In his personal and professional upheavals of the early 1950s, he lost a lot of that wind power and, truth to tell, would go on to very gradually lose more and more of it in the decades that followed.

But what he substituted for pure technique in the very good years that followed his youth would prove to be far more meaningful. His ability to tell a story consistently grew sharper even as the voice grew deeper and the textures surrounding it richer. Generally, rhythm and dynamics are discussed as if they are two distinct qualities, but with Sinatra they're inseparable. They amount to the primary tools through which he afforded varying degrees of weight to key phrases. That weight of emphasis can be applied in terms of both duration—the length of time that he held the note (rhythm)—or in the volume level at which he chose to hit it (dynamics). Before Sinatra, loud generally tended to mean long, but The Voice opened up a whole new world of rhythmic-dynamic thinking in which soft notes could be indefinitely extended for greater emotional effect.

The cumulative effect was to make any word sound more like what it was. Sammy Cahn, the lyricist who was closest to Sinatra personally, observed, "When he sings 'lovely,' he makes it sound '*lovely*' as in 'weather-wise it's such a '*lo-ovely* day'" (in Cahn's own lyric to "Come Fly with Me"). Cahn demonstrated to me, caressing and extending the long soft vowel sound at the center. "Likewise, when he sings 'lonely' [in "Only the Lonely"] he makes it into such a lonely word."

We could sum up Sinatra's capacity for rhythm with the word "swing," but in saying that we should stay aware that the term means a lot of things. Count Basie's kind of swing is different from Louis Armstrong's, and Sinatra is no less the creator of his own, unique rhythmic idiom. Particularly in conjunction with his longtime colleague and arranger Nelson Riddle, Sinatra masterminded a rhythmic feeling that the team mutually characterized as the "tempo of the heartbeat."

The basic Sinatra-Riddle beat amounts to a bridge between the four-four time signature, played by most swing-era bands, and the two-four beat that an earlier Sinatra collaborator, Sy Oliver, perfected for Jimmie Lunceford and then brought with him to Tommy Dorsey. "Frank likes the Buddy Rich style," said pianist Lou Levy, "the Tommy Dorsey band style, which he was raised on, you could say. The band had so much talent, I'm sure it affected him and stayed with him. That's where his taste was formulated. He's a swing-era guy: Tommy Dorsey, Benny Goodman, Count Basie, Duke Ellington."

Even if that *Swingin' Lovers* beat is the one we most identify with Sinatra, he mastered other time signatures as well, especially the straight-down-the-middle four-four he utilized in albums with Count Basie, Johnny Mandel, and Neal Hefti. Although he was never completely comfortable with waltzes, Sinatra once made an entire album of ballads, *All Alone* (1962), in three-four time, in which he brilliantly takes advantage of his tentativeness in that time signature and turns it into an asset; that slight hesitation makes these vintage songs of love and loss even more moving.

In one of the few interviews where Sinatra talked about his sense of rhythm, he said, "I think that that's kind of inbred. I think you have or you haven't got it. I'm probably one of the fortunate people to whom it was given. I never thought about it much." Typically, Sinatra then gave credit for his success in this area to his accompanists. "If I do a jump arrangement with a band, either on records or on a stage, I find that if the band doesn't settle down into a proper tempo, then you cannot swing. I don't care how good you are, it just doesn't move."

"Once while I was driving I heard an old record by Frank and Nelson, and I had to get out of the car and call the radio station," trumpeter Zeke Zarchy told me. "It was 'The Way You Look Tonight' [from *Academy Award Winners*, 1964]. The greatest thing I ever heard! I defy any instrumentalist to swing like he does with his voice on that record."

On another occasion, Billy May, the great big-band writer who frequently worked with Sinatra from the mid-1940s to the mid-1980s, was asked if he considered Sinatra a jazz singer. He answered that it depended on how one defines the term. "If your definition of a jazz singer is someone who can approach [a song] like an instrumentalist and get [the written melody] across but still have a feeling of improvisation, a freshness to it, and do it a little bit differently every time, then I would agree that Frank is."

Which isn't to say that Sinatra was strictly a jazz guy all the time, the way Betty Carter was. "I'm not so sure that being a jazz musician is that all-inclusive," trombonist Milt Bernhart, who should know, elaborated. "A jazz musician usually is somebody who refuses to do anything else, like Miles Davis and John Coltrane. But I wouldn't say that Duke Ellington was purely a jazz musician. I mean, when you've got an orchestra and they're all up there playing together and it's so beautiful, I wouldn't necessarily call that jazz. I would call that music. I'll bet if you were to ask Sinatra, 'Do you consider yourself a jazz singer?,' he would probably respond, 'Hey, I'm a singer.' And even when he sings a song exactly the way it's written, that's good enough for me."

Apart from jazz, big bands, and great singers like Ella Fitzgerald, Sinatra's other great musical love is classical music. "He's really interested in good music," May pointed out. "He and his wife and my wife and I have gone to the symphony a couple of times together. He astounds me with how really knowledgeable he is about classical music. We went one night, and he was telling me about how he liked [Soviet composer] Reinhold Glière. Now, Glière was a contemporary of Rimsky-Korsakov and a fairly obscure Russian composer. For Sinatra to have even heard of him shows he knows a lot." Eleanor Slatkin, who with her husband Felix (Riddle's preferred concertmaster and the conductor of the Hollywood Bowl Symphony Orchestra) saw quite a lot of Sinatra socially in the Capitol era, remarked, "Every time we went to his house, he always had classical music on. I don't remember hearing anything but classical and opera. And, of course, he [was] *very* knowledgeable and [knew] many of the artists personally."

While Sinatra may have occasionally employed backdrops that reflected his appreciation of European classical music, in his own singing he owes far more to Crosby than to Caruso. Even on the dozen or so songs based on classical themes that Sinatra recorded (mainly in the 1940s), he constantly altered the material in a way a lieder or opera singer wouldn't. Even when singing the melodic intervals exactly as notated, Sinatra can't help doing creative and interesting things with the rhythm. He never stops playing with the tempo, whether the piece is serious, romantic, or swinging. In fact, it's easier to list the songs where he does sit squarely on the beat—as on parts of "I Whistle a Happy Tune" and his original coda to "Anything Goes" on *Songs for Swingin' Lovers!* ("may I say before this record spins to a close?")—than to cover the endless occasions when he lags behind it or rushes ahead of it for musical and dramatic effect. (In Sinatra's era, jazz and pop singers weren't expected to read music or "sight sing," but it's said that when he saw, for instance, a C next to a D-sharp, he had a definite idea of what that interval should sound like.)

There were only a few singers—even in the pure jazz idiom—who dug as deeply into the groove as Sinatra—and most of them (like Nat King Cole, Louis Armstrong, and, to a lesser extent, Mel Tormé) were also experienced instrumentalists. As bassist David Finck has said, Sinatra is so rhythmically specific that it's possible to isolate one of his vocal tracks and mark every beat, even without actually hearing the rhythm section behind him.

Likewise, the only singer who possibly covered more ground stylistically than Sinatra was one of his key inspirations, the original musical everyman, Bing Crosby. Sinatra worked in a wide range of formats: in the '60s, in particular, he kept his art fresh and vital in his third decade at the top by collaborating with orchestra stylists as individual as Basie, Antônio Carlos Jobim, and Duke Ellington, while using a different orchestrator on almost every new album. "I tried to vary the arrangers," he once said, "so that there's a different quality to the songs."

Still, overall, Sinatra's primary focus was always on consistency rather than diversity, in other words, on doing a smaller number of things extremely well. Sinatra's concerts, essentially, were comprised of two kinds of songs: fast and swinging up-tempo numbers and slow, emotionally intense ballads.

A great many classic Sinatra numbers may fall between those two poles ("Witchcraft," "Young at Heart," "Summer Wind"), but these extremes represent Sinatra's two primary musical colors. We can talk about his technical capacities in terms of both pitch and rhythm, and say how this singer might have better intonation or that one swings more, but no one deployed those resources and put it all together as meaningfully—especially in the service of the narrative—as Sinatra. Earlier, both Al Jolson and Crosby had introduced the idea that a pop performer could be at once a master musician and a great dramatist, but Sinatra brought both ideas to their fruition. His style represents, in every sense, the perfect synthesis of fifty years of influences going back and forth between jazz-inspired and mass-media–motivated popular music. Songwriter and Sinatra confidant Jule Styne famously said that Crosby was one of the few singers before Sinatra to have a distinct sense of style, but Sinatra was the one who took it all the way.

With Sinatra, all vocal considerations—vocal, musical, rhythmic, or whatever—are secondary to his fundamental mission statement, which is to tell a story in the most expressive way possible. His formidable musical and dramatic skills immediately blur together. On the few occasions when he discussed his musical approach, Sinatra spoke of what he called his "long breath" technique, which he identified as the single most essential tool in his kit. "It's important to know the proper manner in which to breathe at given points in a song," as he said in an interview with friend and radio host Arlene Francis, "because otherwise what you're saying becomes choppy. For instance, there's a phrase in the song 'Fools Rush In' that says, 'Fools rush in where wise men never go / But wise men never fall in love / So how are they to know?' Now that should be one phrase because it tells the story right there. But you'll hear somebody say, 'Fools rush in' and breathe [right in the middle], 'Where wise men never go'—breath—'But wise men never fall in love. . . .' But if you do it [in one breath], that's the point, you told the whole story."

While Sinatra occasionally discussed his breathing technique in interviews, he rarely if ever mentioned the other aspects of his artistry. The fact of his singing multiple lines on a single breath (actually, in his 1960 version of "Fools Rush In," he divides the four lines into two breaths) may be the least remarkable thing that he does within that eight-bar phrase. It isn't just breathing but a multilayered process involving dynamics, shading, accenting, twisting of pitch, and vocal color, all within a single long-breath phrase.

He holds the first "fools" and stretches the "ooo" sound in the middle, then catches up by fittingly rushing through the word "rush." Then he makes it sound as if he's going down a tone on the word "in" even though both "rush" and "in" are actually sung on the same note. The next two lines contain an imitative textual-musical device in which the words "wise men never" are heard in each, and Sinatra phrases each occurrence of the three words so differently that they might as well be completely different words. The first time, he puts a slight syncopation on the word "never" by accentuating the first syllable ("*ne*-ver"). The second time, he emphasizes "*wise* men" and then he pauses for roughly half a beat between those two words and the next ("never") so that he not only stresses the parallel construction of a master lyricist, in this case Johnny Mercer, he also makes the lyric seem more immediate, as if it were occurring to him as he's singing it.

Even before this section of the song there's another peerless exhibition of technique, when he connects the end of one word, at the finish of a line, to the start of the next, a device he uses here in the bridge of "Fools Rush In" and more spectacularly in his blockbuster concert piece "Ol' Man River." "Frank [would] do one thing that really freaked me out on my ass," vibraphonist Emil Richards recalled. "He would hold his hands behind his back as if he were handcuffed, pull his shoulders forward, or his chest forward and his shoulders back, to get more air. He would go, 'Tote that barge / Lift that bale / Get a little drunk and you land in *jailllll* . . .' and without a pause for a breath would go right into 'I get weary.' He would go that long without a breath, and then still sing 'I get weary.' And by the time he got there, let me tell you, he was friggin' weary! I tried doing that along with him a couple of times, and it was almost impossible. But he did it with that one breath, and it was so effective, it gave me chills or made me cry every time."

Sinatra's ballads can be intimate, like "Fools Rush In," or larger than life, like "Ol' Man River." In the first, he wants the song to sound like the working out of an extemporaneous mental process, in the second, it resonates like a proclamation from God; but in both, every note, every syllable, every inflection is exactly in place. Contrastingly, on Sinatra's swingers, the singer is just as unflappably informal as he is precise on the "serious" songs. He takes a devilish delight in toying with the tune (not that he doesn't alter melodies on slow numbers, too, though not with the same gleeful audacity), substituting his pet phrases for key words in the lyric, dancing around with it, boxing with it—treating the song like a punching bag. Sinatra can maintain the inherent intimacy of a piece like "I've Got the World on a String" even at a superfast speed; in spite of his apparent refusal to treat the text as sacred, the emotion and passion come through.

The result is total credibility. No popular recording artist has ever been as totally believable so much of the time as Sinatra. "Frank was very attentive to lyrics," explained Alan Livingston, who signed Sinatra to Capitol Records in 1953. "If he was looking at songs, the lyric would be his very first consideration. Frank wanted to know what that song said and whether it appealed to him or not. He said, 'I'll leave the music to somebody else. I pick the lyrics.'"

These priorities are evident especially in an overtly autobiographical text like "My Way." Sung by any other interpreter, including the teenage idol Paul Anka (who wrote his original English lyric to an existing French song), that 1969 hit would sound like an obnoxious joke. In fact, it's a deliberate gag in the messy mitts of Sid Vicious and an unintentional one in the countrified cadenzas of Elvis Presley, both of whom recorded it. Anka's text might be classified as inapposite from the classic works of, say, Irving Berlin and Cole

Porter. Those songs brought out the best from nearly everybody who ever sang them; Anka's self-aggrandizing text, however, brings out the worst in its interpreters, making them all sound like pretentious egomaniacs.

"My Way," Livingston said, "is [absolutely] Frank. He's telling you a story there. And it has to be something that he believes in, like 'In the Wee Small Hours of the Morning.' I know Frank [suffered through] many wee small hours of the morning in his unhappy days. Frank has lived through every conceivable emotion. He's had unhappy divorces, and lost women he didn't want to lose, and experienced his career going down the tubes. He went through everything that could happen to a young man who had been *the* teenage idol from the forties. I think that actually gives him his credibility as well as his ability to interpret a lyric and to phrase it. Because he feels it, he understands it."

Sinatra never liked "My Way"—as he said over and over, virtually every time he ever sang it—and it's not hard to see why. The idea of a deliberately "autobiographical" text was superfluous to him—every song he sang instantly became a kind of autobiography. As he told Bill Boggs in 1975, "I think it has to do with something in your background that comes forth. It comes forward and presents itself and rather than just reading a piece of poetry . . . if it were a poem." He continued, talking specifically about "Send in the Clowns," but in a larger sense, about everything he ever sang, "So I try to transpose my thoughts about the song into a person who might be saying that to somebody else, you know what I mean, he's making his case. In other words, for himself. And I think, I don't know where it started, I have no idea where it started, in my life, but I have worked in that vein always, back with Tommy and before Tommy, when I was a kid it [was] just kind of working from one small joint to another."

Mitch Miller, who at Columbia produced some of the greatest as well as the worst records of Sinatra's career, warned against overemphasizing actual life experiences and undervaluing the technique of a great popular singer. "The ability to bring all your talent together at a certain moment depends solely on craftsmanship," claimed Miller. "Emotion never makes you a hit. I always tell this to singers: Emotion is not something *you* feel. It's something you make the listener feel. And you have to be very cool and know what you're doing. You get a little tear in your voice, you put it there if the lyric calls for it—and little things like that. That's where a good producer comes in. Because now you're going to a nightclub, or you're going to do it on radio or television. What are you going to do? You had a fight with your wife. The kid threw up at you. Comes eight o'clock, you have to go on. You have to put it together! So it's craftsmanship." Miller emphasized that, even in the lowest point of Sinatra's life when his career and his voice were both fading fast, Sinatra always had "craftsmanship."

Irv Cottler, who played drums for Sinatra for nearly thirty-five years, believed that the singer's passionate involvement with his material immediately communicated itself to both the musicians accompanying him and to the audience. "He gets you up emotionally, because that's what you need to be a player. You have to have a lot of emotion, and he's got that, he projects that. If you don't have that kind of feeling, then forget it, you can't play." As orchestrator Robert Farnon corroborated, "Frank is the inspiration. You know when you're writing for him or in anything you do for him, you have to do your very, very best."

One anecdote will illustrate how Sinatra could inspire an orchestra: For one week in the late 1940s, Sinatra served as guest host of a nightly radio musical series. The musicians in the show's house band, some of whom had worked with Sinatra before, quickly discovered the difference between Sinatra and the program's regular star, Perry Como—also a great artist, but a very different one than Sinatra—who was out sick that week with a cold. "We're at a rehearsal," recalled saxophonist Artie Baker, "and we're playing soft, the way we usually played for Perry. Frank had his hat over his eyes and was looking very unhappy. He finally stood up and said, 'I would sure like to hear the band. I want to hear the music. Can you guys play a little louder? When I sing, I want to sing *with* the band. And I want the band to swing! So let's take it from there, guys.' That was beautiful. Frank really got the band to swing, and boy, we were swinging like crazy by the time that Perry came back." When Como returned, he immediately complained that the band was playing too loud and too intense for him. "'Well, I'm back now,' he announced at the next rehearsal, meaning, 'Knock it off.'"

Bing Crosby once told jazz journalist George Simon, "I like making records even more than making movies. That's because you're constantly creating. And the good thing about it is that when you're finished recording, you've got something that's really your own." The Crooner's greatest disciple shared that opinion. "One thing that impressed me so much in talking with Sinatra from time to time during the [*Great Songs from Great Britain*] sessions," Robert Farnon reminisced, was that "he said his favorite method of working was in the recording studio, as opposed to a concert hall or doing films or whatever." No vocalist before Sinatra had so completely fathomed the possibilities of recording and was able to so totally transform the medium.

The first pop singer to bring a consciously artistic attitude to recording, Sinatra cultivated a sound expressly tailored to the acoustic requirements of microphones and disc-cutting machines—to an even more refined degree than Crosby. He also became the first pop singer to perceive possibilities for record making that went beyond individual songs. Even though Crosby's career as a band vocalist and then a solo star preceded Sinatra's by a decade, The Voice beat Crosby to the punch in the development of what has come to be known as the "concept album."*

That first album was *The Voice*, released by Columbia in 1945. Twenty-two years later Sinatra collaborated on the album *Francis Albert Sinatra & Antônio Carlos Jobim* with the Brazilian songwriter Jobim and the German orchestrator Claus Ogerman. Like most of Sinatra's arrangers, Ogerman worked on the charts right up to the last minute. A few hours before the first date, he arrived early at the Western Studios in Los Angeles with the intention of using the time to finish the final arrangement. However, Ogerman recalled, "To my amazement, Frank was already there. He was rehearsing the tunes with [accompanist] Bill Miller, which shows the reason why he's so professional and why he needs only one or two takes—because he works on all the stuff beforehand. I found it remarkable."

Preparation for a Sinatra session, particularly on one of the classic concept albums, always began much earlier. Sinatra typically began planning an album not so much around a "concept" per se or an idea, but a mood, an emotional state of being. (Only later in his career, in the sixties, would Sinatra use an extramusical connecting point, on later works like *Academy Award Winners*.) He would then select a set of songs around a particular feeling, as expressed in both tempo (ballads or swingers and all gradations between) and instrumentation (a brass ensemble, a string orchestra, a chamber group).

Most important, Sinatra selected songs and sequenced them so that music and lyrics created a consistent flow from track to track, affording an impression of narrative, as in musical theater or opera. "The thing about Sinatra," Frank Military explained, "was that he never went into a record session just to do a record session. He sat down and carefully planned his albums, and lyrically they had to make sense. They had to tell a story. He'd spend days and weeks just preparing this album. Each song would be handpicked, it had a reason for being in the album."

---

\* The statement requires a little qualification: Decca Records had collected some of Crosby's singles into eight-song albums on many occasions, but as far as several astute Crosby scholars can determine, the Bingster never actually sat down and planned a true concept album until after Sinatra had done it. Likewise, jazz chanteuse Lee Wiley had recorded several songbook collections of a single composer's work, but she can hardly be considered a mass-market pop star.

Sinatra selected and sequenced these songs occasionally with the expert assistance of his in-house songwriters, Jimmy Van Heusen and Sammy Cahn. Both were fellow music mavens, and although both were close to the singer on a personal level, as Cahn frequently said, "Frank spends his days with me and his nights with Van Heusen." The composer also served as rehearsal pianist on many occasions when Sinatra was learning new material, primarily because he was on hand more frequently than Bill Miller. In addition to helping him organize albums out of other people's songs, Cahn and Van Heusen made many of Sinatra's concept albums even more conceptual by writing new songs based on album titles devised by Sinatra. In the case of *Come Dance with Me!* (1958), the twosome took things a step further by providing Sinatra with a closing number, "The Last Dance."

But the majority of the songs on the iconic Sinatra albums are vintage standards, which the Sinatra concept albums made a point of featuring. Beginning in the mid-1940s, Sinatra concentrated (as much as he could get away with) on classic songs that had usually originated in Broadway shows. This at a time, it should be stressed, when *Your Hit Parade* (a radio series that Sinatra starred in for two different stretches) was dominated by ephemeral novelties.

While Sinatra makes a point of featuring great theater songs, he had an affection for practically any half-decent opus from the '20s and '30s, the years he was growing up and first listening to popular music. He was consistently fond of Walter Donaldson (including three of the jazz-age composer's "oldies" on the *Strangers in the Night* album, a set ironically subtitled "Sinatra Sings for Moderns"), and his catalog also includes a disproportionate number of songs originally introduced by Bing Crosby and Fred Astaire. Still, the songwriters best represented in his canon are Van Heusen and Cahn, both together and with other partners, and not only in the many songs that they wrote specifically for him.

Even as Sinatra selected the songs, he had already chosen his collaborator for any given project. For more than half of his albums it was a given that the arranger and conductor would be Nelson Riddle (just as Sinatra almost invariably relied on Axel Stordahl in the 78 era). While Riddle could handle either ballad or swing sets, Sinatra doled out his other assignments according to each writer's key strengths: Billy May for "up" records, Gordon Jenkins for moody downers. In the post-Capitol years, Sinatra expanded his options to include such specialists as Johnny Mandel (more modern, jazz-styled up-tempos), Neal Hefti (more fundamentally earthy swing, with and without Count Basie), and Robert Farnon (almost cerebrally tranquil love songs).

George Siravo, perhaps the most underrated of Sinatra's partners, felt that the term "arranger" falls short of doing justice to what he—and Stordahl, Riddle, May, and the rest—actually achieved. "We're really more like a musical designer, like Christian Dior. The only thing we don't create is the actual cloth itself. But 'arranging,' like they say, requires the same abilities as a composer—you have to create something that will enhance the original melody. It isn't just taking a bunch of chairs and placing them around a table. These guys—like a Nelson Riddle or a Ralph Burns—are true creators."

"On occasions when we were working [in nightclubs or Las Vegas]," guitarist Al Viola, who frequently played for Sinatra during more than thirty years, explained, "we might be warming up in the back room or having a drink. He would look at a tune or he would look at a bunch of songs and say, 'You know, this fits Gordon Jenkins.' Or he would say, 'This would be a great song to do with Nelson.' The *Come Fly with Me* album was typically Billy May, and Frank knew it. Most big-time singers today and even [back then] usually leave those kinds of decisions to their piano players or their musical directors. But Frank used to say, 'I want Nelson to do this album.' Frank was the man who took total charge; he didn't leave it up to the A&R man or anybody. He really thought about his songs. He knew where he was going to go. That's what made him great."

As Sinatra elaborated in the mid-1980s (using the editorial "we" in a sincerely humble fashion), "In ballads, obviously, in the beginning we went with Axel, and then we went to Nelson and then to Gordon Jenkins. And then, [from] the rhythm things, I moved from Billy May to Johnny Mandel to Neal Hefti and people like that. And then came Don Costa into my life."

At this point, Sinatra continued, "We"—meaning himself and Bill Miller—"would sit down with the orchestrator, and I would give him my thoughts on what the background should be from eight measures to eight measures or four measures to four measures." Sinatra then modestly added, "Then I would say, 'How wrong am I?' And he would say, 'Well, you're about sixty percent all right, but let me explain to you how I think it should be done.' Usually we wind up doing it the way the orchestrator feels it should be done because he understands more than we do about it."

Riddle later gave Sinatra near-total credit for the tempo and general outline of each number. "Frank would have been thinking about songs for days," the arranger recalled, "and I used to sit there and take notes. And he, in a sideways joke which I think had some validity, said that I was the best secretary he ever had because I'd take notes and three months later we might do the album. And you could never depend on him forgetting what he had said three months previously. I took the notes on what we discussed, and that's what he got."

In the beginning of the Sinatra-Riddle relationship, "as often as not, Nelson hated it," Bill Miller recalled, probably because no other singer had ever made such demands. "But that got to be a habit. He began to expect it." Sinatra would also make changes on arrangements right up until the session. Riddle had originally planned for "Ol' Mac Donald" (1960) to commence with an orchestral introduction, but on hearing the chart, Sinatra decided to open more simply with just the rhythm section, sort of like "The Lady Is a Tramp." Riddle wasn't thrilled with anybody making any kind of change on his work ("Nelson didn't like that at all," said Miller) but ultimately had to concede that Sinatra's way was better.

"Frank has the finest musical taste that I've ever run into, and I've been around for 163 years," Gordon Jenkins told Paul Compton in a radio interview. "I wouldn't question this man's ideas of what's good and bad in music because I've never seen him wrong. Every suggestion that he's ever made to me has been an improvement. He has an unfailing feel for tempos in a song. You might be inclined to think that a ballad is slow, but it's never *just* slow."

Sinatra didn't always work as closely with his arrangers as he did with Riddle. May and Jenkins, who were known commercial commodities when Sinatra began working with them, were more often left to their own devices. Riddle, contrastingly, had several hits for other singers to his credit, but, at the time, had no easily identifiable style of his own, even as May and Jenkins already had. In a sense, Riddle was a blank page upon which Sinatra could write, and he helped to inspire the trademark Riddle sound, with its colorful emphasis on flutes and bass trombones, to blossom.

The ideas that Sinatra did pass along to his other collaborators, however, were generally ingenious, such as the outline for the introduction to "Lonely Town" on *Where Are You?* (1957). He would continually make changes even after initial takes were recorded; at times he would implement changes even after the session, in post-production—editing and mixing. If he decided he didn't like an arrangement, he would commission a new one.

Nelson Riddle, only half kidding (in his usual highly caustic fashion), once named *Only the Lonely* his favorite album because he had an entire week, much more time than usual, to work on the arrangements. Arranger Johnny Mandel felt that a month is a respectable interval for the proper writing of an entire album, yet Billy May, in particular, was capable of doing a whole chart in not much longer than it took to play the tune on the piano.

While the arranger was scribbling away, the "contractor," as he was called, would be assembling the orchestra. Riddle hated to record unless Felix Slatkin was available to play first violin, along with his wife, Eleanor, on lead cello; why this was so comes through beautifully in Slatkin's solo on "Close

to You." Contrastingly, Gordon Jenkins preferred a more traditionally classical concertmaster—in particular, Dave Frisina, who served as first violin
with the Los Angeles Philharmonic. When Jimmy Bowen produced a series
of contemporary pop singles with Sinatra in the mid-1960s, he made a point
of using Nashville-style string players, who again brought a completely different intonation and more of a "hillbilly" kind of sound to the proceedings.
Likewise, May and Riddle preferred drummers Alvin Stoller and Irv Cottler,
as did Sinatra himself, whereas Jenkins's percussionist of choice was Nick
Fatool.

In Sinatra's time, movie studios and the major broadcasting networks
had full-time studio orchestras, filled with musicians on weekly salaries, but
record labels hired players on a freelance, session-by-session basis. Still, Sinatra and his collaborators made a point to use many of the same top musicians
from date to date. This was, they maintained, the major musical virtue of the
swing era: namely, bands that played together night after night for months
or years on end made for tighter and more precise ensembles. Sinatra drew
from a relatively small pool of musicians and kept these veteran players working together so frequently that they might as well have been a regular "road"
band. Johnny Blowers, Sinatra's most frequent drummer in the years 1942 to
1952, recalled that the singer's accompanying musicians were usually referred
to as the "Sinatra Band." During the 1950s and '60s, union regulations stip-
ulated that an album generally consisted of twelve songs recorded over three
sessions. Sinatra and his contractors made it a particular point to ensure that
the same musicians would be available for all three dates.

These sessions would be scheduled for three hours, with one ten-minute
break, as per the union. For this, Capitol Records would expect four sides and
the musicians would expect fifty dollars. "And don't forget, we were based in
Los Angeles," Alan Livingston delineated, "where all these great musicians
worked in the film studios. They would be at the film studio all day at Paramount or Fox or MGM, and they would come and play at night for us. Most
of our sessions were at night."

"There were so many sessions in those days," French hornist John Cave
said, "and we'd be playing for the studios all day and then at night working
for Sinatra," who, for his part, was also often making movies all day. "We'd all
be pooped out, and Sinatra would sometimes sense this. So he'd break out a
jug of Scotch or something and start passing it around to the guys. Of course,
we all played better after that."

Nearly all the brass, reed, and rhythm players on Sinatra's dates were
veterans from varying stages of the swing era. Many, such as guitarist George
Van Eps (born 1913) and drummers Nick Fatool (born 1915) and Johnny

Blowers (born 1911), were already at the top of their field at the time of the initial explosion of the swing band boom in 1935. (Both Fatool and Van Eps were associated with Benny Goodman's 1930s groups.) By the Capitol era, many musicians in such modern jazz-oriented dance bands as Woody Herman's, Stan Kenton's, and Claude Thornhill's graduated into Sinatra's studio orchestras. In the 1960s, many outright jazz modernists, such as Marty Paich, Bud Shank, and Don Fagerquist, were getting the calls to do Sinatra sessions.

"The thing about Frank," Blowers explained, "was that he knew about everybody, and he handpicked his men. He knew more about you than you ever knew about him. When I first met him, he knew all the things I had done since I had been in New York. Frank is phenomenal that way." Dave Frisina added, "He just made it his business to know everyone."

Sinatra picked up musicians, arrangers, and songs in the same way: he'd hear something he liked and decide if he could use that sound. An admirer of the great Red Norvo–Mildred Bailey band of the late 1930s, he used that band's distinctive sound as a template for his 1954 *Swing Easy!* and put many of Norvo's key men on his own payroll, including his longtime tenor soloist Herbie Haymer, even longer-tenured pianist Bill Miller, drummer Irv Cottler, and then eventually Red Norvo himself.

A pioneering advocate of racial equality, Sinatra was color-blind in his pursuit of the players he wanted, long before mixed sessions became socially acceptable or even legal, during the long years when the musicians' union was still rigidly segregated. Indeed, the most famous of all Sinatra soloists was the master trumpet-obbligato specialist Harry "Sweets" Edison, who had spent several decades on the road with Count Basie. Sinatra also landed Ellingtonians Willie Smith (alto saxophone) and Juan Tizol (valve trombone, most notably on Sinatra's 1956 "Night and Day"), Plas Johnson (on "That Old Feeling"), and the King Cole Trio's bassist Joe Comfort (who supplies the thunderous bass breaks on the 1956 "Too Marvelous for Words" in a clear nod to Duke Ellington's "Ko-Ko").

"I think Sinatra never gets enough credit for what he did as far as fighting segregation," said background singer Lillian Clarke, wife of the late arranger Sy Oliver. "He was really in the forefront." Like most of Sinatra's musical associates, Mrs. Oliver felt that "he just got publicity for all the bad news but none of the good deeds." Sinatra's musicians, in particular the many who, like him, had been on the road with the big swing bands, were truly "his people." When Sinatra felt particularly close to a musician who happened to share his Italian ancestry (among them Al Viola and Emil Richards, who had been born Emilio Radocchia), he had a common nickname for them, "Dago," which he often truncated to "Dag." In Sinatra's parlance it meant "paisano" or "homeboy," and Viola and Richards regarded the epithet as a badge of honor.

"An electrical something or other seems to shoot into the room when he walks in," producer Sonny Burke wrote in 1965. "The musicians, the fans who might be there, and anyone around senses it. However, the tenseness is dispelled with a joke, a warm greeting, or a humorous comment, and everyone has the feeling that something's about to happen."

As much as he enjoyed playing with Sinatra, trombonist Milt Bernhart was on pins and needles because so many people—apart from the orchestra and engineering crew—were always present to witness whatever went down. "There was always a large crowd," Bernhart remembered. "They should have charged admission. There were a hundred, two hundred people sitting in this audience because the recording studio at Capitol on Melrose had been a radio studio, with a very big auditorium. And the place was packed. You weren't just playing a record date; you were playing a performance. They took a great chance on the people applauding because they could get caught up in this thing and ruin a take. I don't know who kept everyone from applauding, but believe me, the engineers were all sitting on the edge." (This is borne out by what is virtually the only actual film of a Sinatra recording session, the 1965 date in which he cut "It Was a Very Good Year," in which several dozen spectators are crammed into a small studio, as shot by CBS-TV.)

On the mid-1960s dates put together by Jimmy Bowen, the producer ensured that no really big celebrities were present, explaining, "I didn't want Frank competing with anybody. I wanted him to have to turn on a crowd because that's when those guys [Sinatra, Dean Martin, Sammy Davis Jr.] did their best work—in front of people live—and it worked every time.

"I was doing one of the songs with Sinatra, when this real great-looking woman got out of her chair, right while tape was rolling, and walked across the floor in her high heels! You could hear it—click click click click! She opened the door and went out—she had to pee! Well, we lost it, you know. Everybody cracked up, so we had to wait until she came back in and sat down, before we could do the take again. Everybody was laughing too hard."

Typically, the band would play through the chart once, and rarely more than once, to get a feel for it and look for wrongly copied notes or other mistakes in the parts. Sinatra, at this point usually in the control room with the engineer, would be checking the recording balances as well as looking for ways to improve the arrangement—as on the 1949 "It All Depends on You," when he edited sixteen bars out of an instrumental chorus. After hearing the arrangement played through once, Sinatra would then attempt a vocal, sometimes with the recording apparatus turned on, sometimes not.

"I remember just running the orchestra down," arranger-conductor Marty Paich said of his one session with Sinatra, "and he sang along with it and said, 'Okay, let's do it,' and then he just gave sort of like one or two cracks at it, and that was the end of it." Of all the arrangers I spoke with, Paich was the only one who didn't share Sinatra's preference for working this way. (Mel Tormé, who worked with Paich on many classic albums, told me that Paich was unique in jazz and pop circles at this time for his insistence on exacting rehearsals.) Known for his intricate, modern jazz-oriented orchestrations, Paich wished "that I could have had more time with him. When we went into the studio, it all went by so quickly." However, most musicians (particularly those based in the swing era) preferred doing it Sinatra's way. Trombonist Bobby Pring recalled that many bandleaders or pop singers would insist on running through a number over and over "until it sounded really labored. Frank liked to keep a feeling of freshness—which I agreed with."

Sinatra occasionally went for more takes when it was obviously necessary, most famously on "I've Got You Under My Skin."* He found that he could be a perfectionist without sacrificing spontaneity. Bowen remembered, "You'd be going along and he'd say, 'Hold it, hold it just a second. I think there's something "rubbing" there in bar nineteen or twenty.' And sure enough, there'd be something wrong, a mistake in copying or something."

"He's very hip about what goes on with a band," observed Billy May. "He knows what to look for. He can look around in the band, and he can pretty much tell if it's a happy band or if there's some bullshit going on." "Everything was Frank," Eleanor Slatkin explained. "Anything you did with Frank was Frank's idea. To be a producer for him had to be a joke because there was no producing [done by anybody else] to speak of. Anybody who produced with Frank, all he did was announce the takes and say, 'Frank, I think you should hear it.' *That's all.* The input was all Sinatra's. He really ran the session."

"What record producer in the world wouldn't give his right arm to work with Sinatra?" asked Alan Freeman, who received that credit on the 1962 album *Great Songs from Great Britain.* Yet, "I can't really say I 'produced' him because Sinatra really produces himself." Freeman also related [to interviewer Stan Britt] that the act of his that most impressed Sinatra was researching the

---

* While the discographies list twenty-two takes on "Skin," this count must also encompass a high percentage of "false starts" in which a take didn't make it past the first thirty seconds or so. It's impossible to guess the number of complete takes that were actually made.

brand of whiskey that Ol' Blue Eyes preferred and making sure that three bottles of same were within reach between takes.

How did musicians like working with Sinatra? Tenor saxophonist Ted Nash answered that question by comparing three legends with whom he recorded extensively: Sinatra, Doris Day, and Barbra Streisand. Nash described Day, with whom he went back the farthest (they both apprenticed in Les Brown's band) as having the talent to "be a great singer, if only she had been given the right material. But when she started getting big, [Columbia Records] started giving her these crappy songs, which made her a big star, but it took away from her singing ability, because everyone thought of her as a trite 'Que Sera, Sera' type of singer from then on. She just played it lightly, took it as it came. But she never really had the ambition to be that great. She just sort of floated along with whatever came up." (Pianist Lou Levy offered a similar account of recording with the great Ella Fitzgerald: "Ella would just walk in and do whatever they handed her, under orders from Norman Granz.")

Working with Barbra Streisand, Nash insisted, amounted to a 180-degree jump in the opposite direction. "She comes in and takes over the whole scene. From then on, no one has anything to say. She dictates the whole policy of the date." Violinist Dave Frisina agrees. "Streisand is temperamental. She's got her own ideas about music and she's not happy unless it's done exactly the way she wants. I only did a couple of sessions with her because I found her so difficult to work with. But then, so does everybody else."

Sinatra falls right in the middle of the two extremes, being neither too passive nor too aggressive. "Frank was half-and-half," Nash feels. "If he had something going, and it wasn't quite right, all of a sudden he'd stomp down and start laying out the situation. But otherwise, if it was going right, he wouldn't have much to say on some of those dates. He had confidence in his people [whom he had chosen to work with] and let them do their thing, and he did his thing, which was what made him such a success."

Yet while Sinatra had no reservations about changing things that didn't suit him, his first move upon hearing the chart actually played was to figure out exactly what he could do to accommodate it. "He would hear what the arranger had put down, listening while he was thinking and wandering around the studio," producer Dave Cavanaugh told Paul Compton in 1973. "Dean [Martin] used to kid him and say, 'You're wandering around because you don't know the song.' He knew it all right, but he wanted to figure out where he would sing, and where he would breathe. He had the great flexibility to adjust to what the chart was, and to duck out of the way of the accompanying orchestra [when it] had something to say."

He also knew when the musicians were playing well. "Frank will never come right out and tell you that you swung your ass off," Irv Cottler made clear, meaning that swinging and playing to the best of their abilities was the very least that was expected of musicians. When Milt Bernhart played the iconic trombone solo (on "I've Got You Under My Skin"), Sinatra invited the brassman to come into the booth and listen to the playback with him. It was the greatest compliment the Chairman could have paid to one of his fellow board members. When Mahlon Clark played a stunning clarinet interlude on "I Couldn't Sleep a Wink Last Night," he asked the singer, "Frank, was the clarinet okay?" Sinatra replied, "You're asking me? You guys are asking *me?* Of course it was all right!"

"Nothing would embarrass him so much as a compliment," said Bernhart. "Once, I was playing with Frank at the Sands, and it was the first time he had done 'One for My Baby' by himself with just piano. Right before, he had said to Bill [Miller], 'Just stay with me,' and the two of them came up with this arrangement," a reduction of the one Riddle had written for *Only the Lonely.* "So he did his little acting bit, trembling as if he'd had a few drinks. It was a masterpiece. Afterward, everybody held their breath, and there was a count of about five before they applauded, and then the house came apart.* After the show I was still shaking a little bit, it was that moving. So I went up the stairs to his dressing room. Frank was sitting by himself and looking into the mirror, which he rarely did. He was sitting alone, and I just stuck my head in and said, 'That was unbelievable! I'll never forget that, Frank.' And his response was, 'Aah!' He didn't want to hear it."

Bernhart got a sample of Sinatra's idea of high praise when the singer was describing a date on which French hornist Vince DeRosa played beyond even his usual impeccably high standards. "I wish you guys could have heard Vince last night," Sinatra said to a small group of brassmen. "[He sounded so good that] I could have hit him in the mouth!" "And believe me," Bernhart elaborated, "he reserved [such accolades] for only special circumstances. That's Sinatra. He sings with the grace of a poet, but when he's talking to you, it's New Jersey. It's remarkable."

Bernhart's favorite personal experience with Sinatra occurred at a more formal affair that the singer threw in his legendary Coldwater Canyon compound in 1957. The joint was crawling with luminaries: movie stars, producers, and

---

* Unbeknownst to Bernhart, Sinatra and Miller had already recorded their duet version of "One for My Baby," although it wouldn't be released until 1990. The Sinatra-Miller duo version had its origins in a treatment Sinatra performed with pianist André Previn in the 1955 film *Young at Heart.*

assorted Tinseltown *glitterati*. Still, the biggest celeb of all, the blue-eyed one himself, spent the entire evening ignoring the Hollywood A-list crowd in order to split a pizza with a handful of studio musicians and their wives, whom he'd also invited.

"Let's face it. That's his great pleasure in life, the music," said Lou Levy. "All the other pleasures are second to that in the long run. Music, that's his great love." The one individual who shared this great love with Sinatra more than any other partner is not an arranger or producer or songwriter but Bill Miller, Sinatra's accompanist and occasional conductor for over forty years. "Bill is the best," said Al Viola, expressing the opinion of every musician to ever play with the two men. "If you listen to the few records they did without any orchestra, like 'Where or When,' where it's just the two of them alone, you can hear the strong structure of his harmonies backing Sinatra. It's perfect." (Sinatra also performed "One for My Baby" and "Angel Eyes" as voice-and-piano duets with Miller, the latter on a 1965 *Tonight Show*.) Yet as adroit as Miller was at minor-mood "saloon piano," let us not forget what a swinging soloist he was on such up-tempo classics as "The Lady Is a Tramp," "Ol' Mac Donald," and "The Lonesome Road" (the latter with a distinctive left-hand bass figure), all of which open with Sinatra and rhythm trio only, with the orchestra gradually joining in.

Miller was born in Brooklyn on February 3, 1915, making him almost a year older than the Old Man himself. He landed his first job with a "name" band around 1933, that name being "Larry Funk and His Band of a Thousand Melodies." In 1935 and 1936, sometimes being listed as "Billy Miller," the pianist played for the ahead-of-his-time arranger-bandleader Joe Haymes in a group that included three of Sinatra's future favorite trumpeters: Chris Griffin, Zeke Zarchy, and Lee Castle. From Haymes, Miller moved on to an even more progressive group directed by Red Norvo. In fact, Norvo's music seemed so beautiful and uncommercial (due in no small part to the sublimely musical orchestrations of Eddie Sauter) that Miller seriously doubted that such an ensemble could actually sustain itself as a working dance band.

"When Red first offered me the job, I thought he was kidding," said Miller. "I had earlier worked with Red in a couple of pickup bands, and then he comes out of nowhere and sends me a wire offering seventy-five dollars a week. That was a lot of money then, and I figured, 'How could Red possibly afford to pay seventy-five dollars a man?' Then, a couple of weeks later, some of the Haymes guys and I were listening to the radio, and we heard this great band. We couldn't figure out who they were, and the announcer didn't come back for a few numbers. When they finally announced that it was Red Norvo, I called him right after the show. I lied and said that his wire had just reached

me, which wasn't that unusual since we were on the road, and asked if the job
was still available."

Beginning in early 1937, Miller served as pianist in the classic edition
of the orchestra that was billed as "Mr. and Mrs. Swing," in which the most
commercial feature was the excellent singing of Norvo's wife and star attraction, Mildred Bailey. Miller, Norvo, and tenor saxophonist Herbie Haymer
were all among Sinatra's favorite musicians (as was Bailey herself) who would
all work with him later on.

Around 1939, Miller took another step down the path that led him to
Sinatra when he captained the rhythm section of another of the swing era's
legendary bands, Charlie Barnet and His Orchestra. By that time, Mr. and
Mrs. Swing's marriage and their band were both on the rocks, while Barnet's
star, in the aftermath of his breakthrough hit, "Cherokee," was on the rise.
"Charlie was kind of a nutty guy off the bandstand," Miller observed, "like all
those marriages—he was married eleven times to nine different women—but
he was great to work for." As one of Barnet's key men from 1939 to 1942,
Miller shared the leader's love for Basie and Ellington, and was called upon to
pay homage to their keyboard styles in two 1939 instrumentals, "The Duke's
Idea" and "The Count's Idea," both written by future Sinatra arranger Skippy
Martin. Most of the band's charts, though, were the work of trumpeter Billy
May. Miller himself also contributed several charts to the library, but only one
of which, the excellent "Southern Fried," based on a riff by Kansas City's Har-
lan Leonard, has been identified among the band's RCA Victor recordings.

"In [the summer of] 1940, when we were working the World's Fair, I was
driving back into the city with a showgirl that I was dating," Miller recalled.
"We turned on the radio, and they were playing 'All or Nothing at All,' the
record that Frank made with Harry James. And she said, 'Hey, listen, doesn't
that sound good? That's Dick Haymes.' I said, 'No, it's not Dick Haymes.
Dick Haymes doesn't sing that good.' I didn't know who it was." Haymes was
singing with James then, but "All or Nothing at All," although not released
until 1940, had been cut a year earlier when Sinatra was still James's male
singer. "And then they announced that it was Frank," Miller said. "That was
the first time I was aware of his talent. I thought he was great."

Miller spent World War II with several army bands, although he didn't
work in any of the "celebrity service" units like Glenn Miller's Army Air
Force or Artie Shaw's Navy bands. Although Barnet had temporarily replaced
Miller with early bop pianists like Dodo Marmarosa and Al Haig, the pianist
reclaimed his chair in the spring of 1946, but only briefly. The band business,
if not quite on its last legs, certainly didn't have many limbs on which it could
stand. Barnet's plans for a band that would stay on the West Coast didn't pan

out, and Miller left in the fall of 1947. In the late 1940s he subbed with a number of groups, including Tommy Dorsey and Benny Goodman, and then began playing more frequently for Martha Raye, with whom he had worked when she made an anonymous guest vocal on a 1946 Barnet recording session. By 1951, Miller was working in Vegas.

Frank Sinatra played Nevada for the first time in 1951, working the Riverside in Reno in August and Moe Dalitz's Desert Inn in Vegas in September. He had recently parted company with accompanist Graham Forbes, who (the pianist later told maven Bob Sherrick) elected not to travel to the West Coast. Sinatra couldn't have been easy to work with in 1951, when his personal and professional lives had hit correspondingly low notes. He was doing little on records or in pictures, and his major venture of the time, his CBS-TV show, was also on the rocks. "You should keep it in mind that Frank was having a rough time," said Al Viola. "His piano players were quitting on him because he didn't have the bucks." According to several sources, it was Jimmy Van Heusen who first "discovered" Miller playing piano in the lounge at the Desert Inn when Sinatra was working in the main venue, the Painted Desert Room. As Viola heard the story, Van Heusen reported to Sinatra, "Frank, I just heard a great piano player. He plays great chords and everything, and he's right here."

Although they had never met, Sinatra knew Miller from his work with Barnet and Norvo. Miller later told friend Mahlon Clark that when he spotted Sinatra, "I immediately started playing solos on songs he liked, and playing the notes that I knew he would like—the pretty notes. And then Frank came up to me and said, 'How would like to work with me, kid?'" Miller began playing for Sinatra at the Desert Inn and soon began accompanying him on the CBS show as well. Miller first recorded with Sinatra on all four of the singer's sessions in 1952, his final year with Columbia Records.

Miller had gone to work for Sinatra when the career of The Voice was at a low ebb. He was thus in the right place when the tide came back in and swept the Chairman of the Board to new heights. Miller remained the Sinatra pianist through the great years of live appearances across the globe and the masterpiece Capitol and Reprise albums. According to Al Viola, "Frank loved Bill because he was a real character." As Irv Cottler, who played drums next to Miller for so many years, put it, "Bill always looked as if he was falling asleep, but he sure knew what he was doing."

Sinatra initially nicknamed his accompanist "Moonface" Miller and eventually began directing even more attention to the pianist's bleached-white prison pallor. For example, here's how Sinatra introduces Miller at the Royal Festival Hall concert of June 1, 1962: ". . . and of course my old chum, my right arm, you might say, my accompanist who is the leader of this infamous group. We affectionately call him 'Suntan Charlie,'"—yes, the nickname was ironic—"and his complexion will explain why we call him that. We suspect he lives under a rock and comes out at ten o'clock every evening, but he's a marvelous pianist and a fine accompanist, Mr. Bill Miller."

By 1988, things hadn't changed much: "Our pianist is a man who loathes the sun. You'll see when he gets up. I call him 'Suntan Charlie' [because] he has never had a suntan as long as I've known him. Mr. Bill Miller from Burbank, California." As Miller stood and the audience applauded, Sinatra continued, "See what I mean, folks?" Yet by 1994, Sinatra in concert was introducing Miller with words that were considerably warmer than anything he was saying about his conductor and son, Frank Sinatra Jr.; by then, he was describing Miller, accurately, as "a fine musician, a wonderful man, and he's my partner at the piano."

Miller was not without his resources, however, if Sinatra took his kidding too far. "Bill always took a lot of flak from Frank, but he had a way of getting back at him," said Emil Richards. "If Frank said, 'Bill, give me a tone,' then Bill would just hit one note. One little-bitty 'boop,' and that would be it. He'd give him just the dinkiest little tone. It's as if Bill were saying, 'Come on, bitch, find it! You've had it over me all this time, now I got you!'" In fact, such a moment is preserved for posterity during one of the sessions (on an outtake reel) for the Sinatra-Basie albums. Miller deputized for Basie on several tracks of *Sinatra-Basie* and *It Might as Well Be Swing*, and at one point on the session tapes, Sinatra asks Miller to help him with a note. The pianist then responds by feeding him the most minuscule and appropriately Basie-esque little "plink" that could possibly be imagined. Without missing a beat, Sinatra immediately drops into his *Amos 'n' Andy* voice and declaims, "Man, you economical!"

In November 1964, a few months after the release of the second Sinatra-Basie album, Miller's house, on a hillside in Burbank, was decimated in a mudslide. His wife, Aimee, was killed, but fortunately both Miller and their daughter were rescued. While Miller was hospitalized, Sinatra took it upon himself to identify the body at the Los Angeles morgue. ("If it's any consolation," Sinatra told Miller, "there wasn't a mark on her." Miller later told the *Washington Post*, "It wasn't.") Within a few months, Miller was playing for Sinatra again. Bill Boggs caught Sinatra and Miller at the Eden Roc in Miami and remembers the pianist with a cast on his leg. "After the accident," said Viola, "Frank picked up all the medical bills, and he bought Bill a new set of clothes and a new apartment."

The most visceral document revealing the extent to which Miller contributed to Sinatra's music is, paradoxically, a concert upon which Miller doesn't play. This is a 1963 benefit concert held at the United Nations (included in the *Sinatra: New York* boxed set, released in 2009), in which the accompanist is Skitch Henderson. Henderson was never a jazz player, nor a particularly skillful accompanist, and it's rather amazing to hear Sinatra, for once, completely defeated by his musical circumstances; Henderson's piano is uninspired, downright plodding, and Sinatra finds it impossible to settle into a swinging groove.

In 1967, Miller became Sinatra's regular road conductor, and he alternated between the piano and the podium for the next decade. In that same year, Sinatra and Miller recorded another of their saloon song spectaculars, the exquisite "Drinking Again," in which arranger Claus Ogerman, Riddle-like, drapes a light sheen of strings behind what is otherwise all voice and piano. In February 1976, Sinatra and Miller recorded "Empty Tables, " which, with "One for My Baby," completed a three-song cycle of Johnny Mercer saloon songs reconceived as duets for the two men.

At that 1976 session, right after doing "Empty Tables" with Miller, the two next tackled a similar voice and piano treatment of "Send in the Clowns"; both songs had previously been recorded by Sinatra with full arrangements by Gordon Jenkins, who considered "Clowns" the best chart he had ever written for Sinatra. The difference between the Jenkins and the Miller versions is every bit as staggering as you'd expect. As good as Jenkins was, there's always an overt formality to his work, whereas the interpretations with Miller (Sinatra introducing "Clowns" with a spoken monologue) resonate as pure drama and emotion.

The only major rupture between the two men occurred in 1978. "We just had a falling-out," as Miller put it to me, as casually as he said everything else. "What happened was we had been like bucking heads for a little while, six months or a year. I think I was there too long, and so I took him for granted, and he took me for granted." Miller missed Sinatra's last two classic albums, *Trilogy* (1979) and *She Shot Me Down* (1981): however, the two were reconciled by 1985. For two years, Miller conducted while Lou Levy, Bernie Leighton, and others sat at the piano (at different times Mike Renzi and Russ Kassoff also played). When Frank Sinatra Jr. took over the baton in 1988, Miller went back to playing, which he preferred anyhow.

After the "Old Man" gave his last public performance in 1995, Miller, who was eighty at the time, retired; temporarily, it turned out. At the end of 1998, six months after Sinatra had died, Sinatra Jr. hired Miller to join his own touring group. Miller continued to play for the younger Sinatra for another seven years. He was on tour in Canada with Junior's group at the time of his death at Montreal General Hospital on July 11, 2006. He was ninety-one.

The papers that covered Miller's death generally acknowledged that "One for My Baby" was the masterpiece of the Sinatra-Miller collaboration. Sinatra kept the Arlen-Mercer song out of his shows, for the most part, during the seven years (1978–1985) when Miller wasn't playing for him. (He had actually first recorded the tune in 1947, a track that sorely lacks Miller's input.) Upon the pianist's return, Sinatra not only reinstated the tune in his repertoire, he and Miller recorded it for the third time together in the summer of 1993. It's appropriate that their most celebrated latter-day effort together should appear on an album called *Duets,* but perhaps ironic that the most worthwhile duet on the two so-named albums isn't with a singer at all. The track actually starts with "All the Way" played by smooth jazz electro-wood-wind player Kenny G (who, unlike Miller, is given credit on the CD back tray), which is quickly and gratefully forgotten. This then leads into a super-lative duo by the two old campaigners.

Sinatra's vocal here is one of the most painfully moving of his career. Even at seventy-eight or seventy-nine years of age, Sinatra's ability to tell a story and move an audience within the framework of a saloon song hasn't diminished. And Miller's accompaniment, as so many of his fellow musicians have said, can only be described as "perfect." Miller plays two roles at once: first, he's providing Sinatra with musical support, harmonies, and rhythm. As engineer Lee Herschberg put it, "Bill has always had a great sense of what Frank [is] going to do. He always knew exactly where he was going to be, and he was always in the right place."

Second, Miller is a fellow actor "playing," if you will, the role of a piano player in the saloon that Sinatra's character has wandered into and where he's now telling his story. Ostensibly, the Sinatra character is spilling his troubles to a bartender, but in this moral universe, the guy listening to Sinatra is some combination of barkeep and saloon pianist. Yet part of Miller's brilliance is the way he plays the melody while pretending to ignore Sinatra. The great pain that Sinatra communicates comes through so strongly partly because it's delivered against such a spare background. What does the guy who is playing the piano in the back care about the drunk who is unburdening himself in the foreground? Miller somehow manages to support Sinatra while all the time sounding as though he's not even noticing him; Miller plays Harold Arlen's saloon piano riff as if it doesn't make any difference what Sinatra is doing, but at the same time he's supporting him on an almost transcendental level. If your heart doesn't stop by the time Sinatra gets to the last line, "that long, long road," then, in the immortal words of Louis Jordan, "Jack, you're dead!" Sinatra lengthens the road by repeating the penultimate phrase over and over—"it's long, it's so long." Every time you think it's going to end, it goes on again until you're dying for Sinatra to resolve the dramatic tension and put himself out of his misery. It's one of the most moving things you'll ever hear, because if there are two guys in the world who know how long that road is, it's Frank Sinatra and Bill Miller. Sinatra's genius was that he could make you think that he was the loneliest man in the world, but he was never truly alone.

One of Milt Bernhart's all-time favorite records was Sinatra's original Bluebird 78 of "The Night We Called It a Day," cut in 1942. Bernhart's future wife bought it when they were dating, and it became "their song." Bernhart told this to Sinatra at that 1957 party, and, the trombonist recalled, "I expected him to brighten up a little." But instead "his face darkened." Sinatra took out a test pressing of the yet-unreleased album *Where Are You?* that included a remake of "The Night We Called It a Day" and played it for Bernhart.

For Sinatra, as Duke Ellington once said of his own work, "the new baby is always the favorite." It was quite beyond Sinatra to fathom why anybody would be sentimentally attached to or even interested in his old recordings. He personally had no use for his records after he finished making them. When Washington, DC, deejay Ed Walker asked Sinatra in 1983 to name his favorite albums, he answered, "The ones that stick in my mind are the ones where I think the orchestrator's work and my work came together closely, for instance, *Only the Lonely*, *Wee Small Hours*, and one of the jazz things with Billy May." At this point Sinatra paused while he tried in vain to remember more album titles. Sinatra junkies, musicians, singers, and civilians of every stripe have memorized these albums from the first downbeat to the final coda, yet the man who made them hadn't thought about them enough in the years since he finished them to even remember the album titles.

"To me, that's the mark of a creative soul," Bernhart said. "It could be a composer, a Rembrandt, or a sculptor. As soon as they're finished with it, they're really through with it. They're finished. They're on to another thing. They'll say, 'Those things are gone, and I am now looking at the next thing to do.'" It has never bothered Sinatra to record some songs two and three times; it has never occurred to him that one reason not to do a song is that he has done it before. Had he not been practically the only one picking his songs, he might have come up with a more varied repertoire, as opposed to so many versions of "The Song Is You." But that seems a small price to pay for the body of work that he has given us. Which isn't to say that Sinatra ever repeats himself—even by recording multiple versions of the same song. "Frank's the only singer who would take a tune he had already done and completely rework it," Frank Military pointed out. "If he had sung it as a ballad, ten years later he might take it out again and make it a swinger. Or if it had been a fast number, he might redo it into a love song."

Perhaps the single most distinguishing characteristic of the American popular song is its inherent flexibility. The great theater songs by Cole Porter, the Gershwins, Harold Arlen, and so forth lend themselves to diverse interpretations. They can be played fast, slow, or medium, reconfigured as waltzes, two-steps, or marches, done as bossa novas, mambos, doo-wop, or operetta. However, as Military suggests, when most pop singers are satisfied with one approach to a particular tune, they tend to stick with it. For instance, more than thirty years ago Tony Bennett discovered that there actually was a way to do "One for My Baby" so that it wouldn't make his listeners think of Sinatra's devastating ballad rendition—by belting it as a rock-'em, sock-'em romper. It worked for him in the mid-1950s, and he was still singing it that way forty, fifty, sixty years later. Likewise, Sinatra had a handful of signature hits that he never messed with, songs that were associated with him and no one else—such as "Strangers in the Night," "Witchcraft," and "New York, New York." In these few cases, he rarely tried to second-guess his own success; audiences may not want to hear a new treatment of "My Way."

But such songs are the exception, rather than the rule. Sinatra's more general policy, particularly with classic show and film tunes, was to tinker with them endlessly. For instance, he sang "Day In, Day Out" and "The Song Is You" more ways than you or even he can shake a cocktail at. The record holder, however, would have to be "Night and Day," which he treated in nearly all tempos and moods and in every era of his seven decades of performing. By examining the different ways Sinatra handled the Cole Porter classic, we can learn a great deal about the singer's working methods and how his artistry evolved from the 1930s to the 1990s.

Porter wrote "Night and Day" in 1932 as a vehicle for Fred Astaire in the Broadway musical *Gay Divorce*. When that show became the basis for Astaire's first starring film, *The Gay Divorcee* (1934), "Night and Day" became the sole song from the original score to be retained in the picture. It's not too much of an exaggeration to claim that "Night and Day" represents the centerpiece of both Astaire's and Porter's movie careers. The image of Astaire and Ginger Rogers entangling with both passion and sophisticated formality in time to this amazing tune cemented the team as a major box-office attraction. The song itself was heard in at least four other films (including a wartime short with Dinah Shore warbling special anti-Axis lyrics), not the last of which (if inarguably the least) was *Night and Day*, Warner Bros.'s lovingly ludicrous 1946 Porter biopic.

Two factors affected the musical shape that the tune eventually took. First, like Duke Ellington, Porter wrote music for specific "voices," and in devising a song for Astaire, Porter knew not to come up with anything that would require a multi-octave range. Astaire was a great singer (and, like Sinatra, a supremely musical one) but not a great voice, and in writing for him, Porter relied heavily on short, repeated pitches with an infectious rhythmic quality rather than a lot of sustained notes.

Second, in a statement apparently doubted by some scholars, Porter, a noted world traveler, claimed to have been inspired by an Islamic religious chant he had heard in the Middle East. In a conversation with Richard Rodgers, Porter also claimed that he was deliberately trying to concoct tunes that had a "Jewish" feel to them. To Rodgers, "Night and Day" did sound "unmistakably Mediterranean."

It's easy to see why "Night and Day" would be a standard of lasting value, particularly to jazz-oriented performers: its repeated notes (rather like a Gershwin piece) and bouncy rhythms could swing even though the song is normally done as a ballad (especially before Sinatra swung it in 1956). Likewise, its intriguing harmonic pattern, which not only continually shifts from minor to major but cleverly uses major chords as part of minor harmonic contexts, also holds great appeal for improvisers. The song is at once complicated and simple. Ten of the sixteen bars of the verse are sung on one and the same note (emphasizing the "beat, beat, beat" and the "tick, tick, tock" Astaire-style), yet the melody moves primarily in chromatic half steps, a most unorthodox approach in 1932. Structurally, the piece has an AABA feel, with a clearly defined bridge, yet it actually breaks down into something more like ABABCB, because it doesn't exactly return to the original melody after the bridge but rather to a variation on the second half of the initial opening section, for a total of forty-eight bars.

Sinatra's personal association with "Night and Day" goes back years before he first recorded it in 1942 and even before the singer himself was "discovered" in 1939 by Harry James. "The song had been written about a couple of years before I decided I'd like to become a vocalist," Sinatra recollected. "And it was written by Cole Porter. I really believe he was the greatest ever, ever! It's one of the first songs I sang when I was a young, rising singer. I didn't get very far in those days, it took a little while, but as years went by I was using 'Night and Day' a lot wherever I worked."*

---

* Sinatra has told the story several times in public (while tape was rolling), and this account is pieced together from several sources, including Sinatra's Yale interview-seminar with Sidney Zion, taped in May 1986, and a concert, also from 1986, privately issued on the two-LP set *Saloon Singer.* (In that particular concert, Sinatra demonstrated how he sang "Night and Day" on the long-ago original night in question, with the aid of the orchestra and the 1956 Nelson Riddle chart.)

Around 1937 or 1938, Sinatra was singing with a "club date"–style septet at the Rustic Cabin, a roadhouse near Englewood Cliffs, New Jersey. "On Sunday evenings during the summer months," Sinatra elaborated, "people would come back from the countryside and come through and stop and have a little nip before they went over the [George Washington] bridge to go back into New York." On one such evening "there were about seven people in the audience, and we had a six-piece 'orchestra.' The trumpet player, named Johnny Bucini, said to me, 'Do you know who's sitting out there?' I said, 'Yeah, I know that face. It's Cole Porter!' I couldn't believe it, but he was sitting out in the audience with four or five people. And I said to the orchestra leader, 'I'd like to do one of Cole Porter's songs. Let's do "Night and Day" for him, and I'll talk about it.'

"So I went out and said, 'Ladies and Gentlemen, I'd like to sing this song and dedicate it to the greatly talented man who composed it and who may be one of the best contributors to American music at this particular time in our lives.' I said that Mr. Porter was in the room and I introduced him, and he got up and took a bow. Then the orchestra played the introduction, and I did the first four bars and then proceeded to forget *all* the goddamn words, swear to God. I couldn't think. I just kept saying, 'Night and day, night and day,' for fifteen bars!"

The punch line to the story arrived roughly twenty years later when MGM cast Sinatra as one of the leads in *High Society*, a musical version of *The Philadelphia Story*, for which the studio commissioned a score from Cole Porter. One evening the composer invited the three principals—Bing Crosby, Grace Kelly, and Sinatra—over to his house to hear the newly written numbers. "He called me inside and said, 'It's been a long time since we met. I don't know if you remember an evening with me at some nightclub where you worked.' And I said, 'Oh, yeah, I remember very well.' He said, 'So do I. That's about the *worst* performance I ever heard.' But we kidded about it."

Considering his even-then longtime fondness for the song, it's not surprising that Sinatra would choose to include it on his debut session as a solo vocalist in 1942. (What is surprising is that RCA Victor Records allowed him to choose his own material and a ten-year-old tune to boot.) This first of six commercially released Sinatra recordings of "Night and Day," like the second and third, consists of a chorus and a half, the half of the refrain that he returns to after a brief instrumental break known as the "outchorus."

Like other songs, "Night and Day" has been published in many keys, including C-major and D-flat; the 1942 version is sung in E-flat. This great orchestration by Axel Stordahl also introduces the great arranger's equally classic countermelody, which pivots on a five-note phrase that the arranger repeats at various intervals and rhythmic durations, generally phrased on the strings. During the years Sinatra used "Night and Day" as his radio theme song, Stordahl's original contrapuntal line became as familiar to listeners as Porter's central melody.

Many of the trademarks of Sinatra's great Columbia period are already here: the "long" phrasing—often eight or even sixteen bars to a breath—the tenuous, breathlessly romantic sound, and the deeply felt and communicated recital of the lyrics. He achieves this partly with the aid of slight alterations, at once jazzy and incredibly personal, making the decade-old song sound spontaneous. The outchorus includes subtle grace notes and word painting, such as "way *down* inside of me" and "this torment won't *ever* be through," both of which Sinatra would keep in the arrangement for years to come. This 1942 disc also includes an extra twist that occurs only here: when the singer gets to "traffic's boom / *or* in the silence" in the first chorus.

The orchestration concludes with another significant melodic alteration. Porter originally set the final three words ("night and day") on the same note—the tonic note, in fact. Sinatra takes the melody down; he sings this climactic "night and day" on three different notes in a descending pattern. Where, in this key, they should be E-flat, E-flat, and E-flat, he makes them D-flat, B, and B-flat. Sinatra would continue to treat the last notes of "Night and Day" in this fashion until the 1956 Riddle arrangement.

The Voice is clearly being pulled in two directions throughout the Bluebird session, his initial impulse being to move beyond the swing band sound. At fifteen pieces, the orchestra is considerably smaller than those Sinatra would use later on a ballad session, yet its combination of strings, woodwinds, and understated rhythm (no drums) is very different from anything any singer was using for accompaniment during this period. At the same time, this especially lilting first rendition of "Night and Day" is clearly part and parcel of the dance band era; the proof lies in the Crosby-like syncopation Sinatra employs on the hard "d" sound at the start of the very final "day." More important, Victor issued this "Night and Day" and the three other tunes from this January 13 session as part of their "Vocadance" series (on the Bluebird subsidiary), which spotlighted star singers from the big bands in vocal recordings designed for dancing. The budding star is therefore obliged to stick to a fairly rigid dance tempo.

Those restrictions gradually diminish with further readings of the classic Stordahl chart, of which more than a dozen additional Sinatra performances have been documented between 1942 and 1950. The second known rendition dates from eight months later, in September 1942. Only two weeks after leaving Tommy Dorsey (their parting performance was another reprise from the Bluebird session, "The Song Is You"), Sinatra prerecorded and then filmed this one song for Columbia Pictures' *Reveille with Beverly*, a B-movie musical, released in 1943, spotlighting mostly star bandleaders of the period, all playing their signature hits and theme songs: Duke Ellington ("Take the 'A' Train"), Count Basie ("One O'Clock Jump"), Bob Crosby ("Big Noise from Winnetka"), Freddie Slack ("Cow-Cow Boogie"), and others. The numbers are great—very valuable footage of the leading big bands of the WWII era—and are only connected by the wispiest excuse for a plot, with Ann Miller as a tap-dancing disc jockey entertaining her serviceman audience with both her tunes and her taps.

Sinatra appears in the picture for only one number, which, considering how absurdly it's staged, may be something of a blessing: the ultrathin crooner, clad in what amounts to half a tuxedo with tails (or, as he once said, "three sleeves"), sings Porter's classic melody in Stordahl's exquisite orchestration for all it's worth while surrounded by a sorority of actresses in formal gowns all pretending to play pianos and violins. This visual inanity unfortunately compromises the sanctity of the audio track; the chart is cluttered up with too many pianos, and, unfortunately, all the *pianos* are much too *forte*.

The arrangement really begins to change over seven performances documented over 1943 (Sinatra's first year of major-league celebrity) and 1944. The lilting, atavistic fox-trot feeling of the 1942 Bluebird slowly fades away, and Sinatra's interpretation of the orchestration starts to sound more and more like a concert piece. The backdrop gradually assumes the characteristics of a tone poem. It's still the same orchestration on paper, with the familiar countermelody and the "way *down* inside" and "torment won't *ever* be true," but it feels completely different. With each successive rendition, the "roaring traffic's boom" gets boomier and "the silence of my lonely room" gets quieter, as the performance as a whole becomes ever more dramatic.

Sinatra "consummated" his relationship with "Night and Day" when he chose it as his opening theme on radio (the closing song was "Put Your Dreams Away"). Each week of *Old Gold Presents Songs by Sinatra* commenced with Sinatra singing the first two lines of the lyric, usually starting the first note by himself, a cappella. Earlier versions also exist that utilize the song as both an opening theme and a stand-alone number. Sinatra continued to use "Night and Day" as the opener for both seasons (1945–46 and 1946–47) and returned to it occasionally on later programs. By 1947 the transformation from "vocadance" disc to concerto was complete—not least because "Night and Day" had by this time highlighted two Sinatra appearances at the Hollywood Bowl; even the radio theme readings are taken much slower than the 1942 version. In 1947, Sinatra rerecorded three of the four tunes from his original Bluebird date for Columbia, including "Night and Day." At the time, none could be released, for contractual reasons: "The Song Is You" was first heard in 1958 and the other two, "The Night We Called It a Day" and "Night and Day," lay unissued and even undocumented in Columbia's vaults until 1993.

The 1947 "Night and Day," released at last forty-six years later, uses more than twice as many musicians as the 1942 reading. Again essentially the same arrangement, it now takes thirty-six seconds longer (from 3:03 in 1942 to 3:39 in 1947) to get through the same chorus and a half. Thirty-six seconds is an eternity in the pop single business, and that extra half minute may also help explain why Columbia kept it in the can. (Sinatra recorded a second "Night and Day" for Columbia that same day, October 22, 1947, this time with a truncated arrangement. The shorter take, which times at 3:18, was issued on the 1997 double-CD set, *Portrait of Sinatra: Columbia Classics*, and is also on the 2008 *Sinatra Sings Cole Porter*.)

Sinatra's style is even more mature by this time; now when he gets to the "boom," the beat is all but entirely suspended, and "the silence" is extended long enough so that we can hear not just the familiar harp but also a celesta in the mix. Where Sinatra was impeccably in tune in 1942, he now sounds more like his older self in that he bobs slightly under the pitch in spots, though it's entirely likely that he was deliberately bending the pitch for emotional effect. He quivers on "spend my life" and bends the notes on the repetition of "under the hide of me" to express his feelings of longing and yearning that much more longingly and yearningly.

Oddly, Sinatra seems not to have sung a complete run-through of "Night and Day" during the entire 1945–47 run of *Songs by Sinatra*. When he returned to star on *Your Hit Parade* in 1947–49, the advertising agency seems to have insisted on using the Lucky Strike theme ("My Lucky Day") and nothing else. In 1949, Sinatra switched from *Your Hit Parade* to *Light-Up Time*, a program closer to his own taste, also sponsored by Lucky Strike. Now the Sinatra theme, "Night and Day," could be heard very, very briefly after a line or two of the "Luckies" intro. Since *Light-Up Time* rarely used a string section on its nightly fifteen-minute spot, the Stordahl chart had to be rethought once again. For the premier broadcast, the familiar violin countermelody is gone and a trumpet obbligato follows the singer. (Sinatra apparently did perform a full treatment of "Night and Day" at least once on *Light-Up Time*, but I have not been able to hear it.)

Though "Night and Day" was never a career-making song for Sinatra the way "I Left My Heart in San Francisco" was for Tony Bennett, this is only the first installment of the multigenerational connection between song and singer. Sinatra next tackled "Night and Day" at several junctures in his transition from his young sound (that is, Stordahl) to his mature sound (that is, Riddle). The first is an extremely disappointing rendition from a generally unfortunate concert given in Blackpool, England, in July 1953.

In 1954, Sinatra exhibited an entirely new "Night and Day." This treatment is unique in many aspects, particularly in terms of its breakneck speed, representing the fastest that he would ever attempt the Porter piece (or practically anything else). Then there's also its Latin jazz format, via a small group with bongos and flute, probably the only time Sinatra ever worked in such a context. (He did do a Latinate session with bandleader Xavier Cugat in 1945, and in the mid-1980s there was talk of an album with the titan of the timbales, Tito Puente—too bad that never happened.) The 1954 arrangement of "N&D" is also unique in the literal sense in that Sinatra is known to have performed it once and only once, on his final radio series, *To Be Perfectly Frank* (various sources claim the track is from either June or October 1954).

Like the Stordahl treatment, the Afro-Latin version has Sinatra ending on three descending notes; he here includes the verse after the first chorus, before going into the outchorus. This marks the first time we've heard Sinatra sing said verse, which is included on only one of the five issued studio recordings (the 1961). (Steve Lawrence later recorded an up-tempo treatment of "Night and Day" in which he, with a slightly less Latin feel, phrases the verse over bongos in almost exactly the same fashion.) Sinatra's other up-tempo readings pointedly omit these sixteen introductory bars.

With this particular performance, Sinatra indicates to us, in hindsight, that he already was well aware that up-tempo numbers were going to be a big part of his future. As it happened, this particular outline for a swinging number was not for him: the pace was too fast for Sinatra or anyone else to deploy the emotional expression necessary to get the most out of a Cole Porter love song. Ella Fitzgerald would do only a scat or a nonsense number ("A-Tisket a-Tasket") at this clip, and Jimmy Rushing might do a really fast blues at this metronome reading, but the only way to make the melody move this fast is to totally trash the words (he also has to fudge some of the notes). There are times when Sinatra was willing to do that—a few numbers on the Basie albums, for instance—but on most occasions, his specific brand of jazz or rhythm singing was entirely different from anyone else's.

The great Nelson Riddle treatment of "Night and Day," introduced in 1956, illustrates precisely that point. Earlier that year Sinatra had brought his newly minted rhythmic and romantic style to a boil with the appropriately titled breakthrough album, *Songs for Swingin' Lovers!* He then revived "Night and Day" for *A Swingin' Affair!*, the album that today would have been called

*Swingin' Lovers II.* Here's why the "heartbeat" tempo worked so well: it offers all the oomph of a fast jazz number without Sinatra's having to sacrifice any of Porter's poetry to a horse-race tempo.

Which brings us to the central paradox of Sinatra's two best-known records of "Night and Day": The Stordahl/Bluebird is best summed up as a ballad and the Riddle/Capitol as strictly a swingin' affair. In actuality, the first is a concert piece sped up to something close to dance tempo, while the second is a swinger slowed down to a heartbeat. The Capitol is certainly much more of a jazz performance; Sinatra swings a lot more in his phrasing, and the beats are more clearly demarcated, making it easier to dance to, but ultimately the 1956 track is only marginally faster than the 1942.

The Riddle "Night and Day" exists in two key performances, on the *Swingin' Affair* album and as the opener of an episode of Sinatra's weekly ABC-TV series (November 29, 1957; this has been issued on the DVD *Vintage Sinatra*). Both readings commence with a fanfare: a brief orchestral intro, Sinatra singing "Night and day . . .", and then the orchestra reentering with a "POW!" before Sinatra gets to the next line ("you are the one!"). However, the television version hits you even harder than the record because, while the commercial recording contains a very brief pause after the initial "Night and day," the TV performance amplifies it into a true fermata (of a duration to be determined by the conductor), and by waiting just half a beat longer, the opening becomes even more suspenseful.

The television version makes one other crucial change from the Capitol. In the *Swingin' Affair* cut, Sinatra and Riddle drolly refer to the song's allegedly Middle Eastern inspiration by including a solo by valve trombonist Juan Tizol. A major voice in Duke Ellington's orchestra, Tizol had established himself as a specialist in exotica as both a soloist and a composer of such Eastern- and Latin-oriented items as "Bakiff," "Pyramid," and the pivotal "Caravan." Tizol's presence in "Night and Day" logically refers to the trombonist's own career.

However, the 1956 "Night and Day" is also a direct outgrowth of the 1955 Sinatra-Porter-Riddle milestone "I've Got You Under My Skin" on *Swingin' Lovers*, which also employed a rough-and-ready trombone solo in much the same fashion in the instrumental midsection. Riddle also reemploys the same kind of bouncing brass, swinging strings, and overall orchestral coloration that he had pulled off so spectacularly in "Skin." This "Night and Day," then, could have been called "I've Got You Under My Skin II."

The nonvocal passage is crucial to the Riddle orchestration because between the first full chorus and outchorus, instead of doing the verse (as in the 1954), Sinatra changes keys, starting half a step higher in E-natural.

Sinatra concludes with the tonic note as written and goes for a big ending, stretching that last note for dramatic impact. Overall, the TV version packs a bigger wallop than the Capitol (even if the audio quality on the commercial version is far superior), although it lacks the Tizol instrumental center, which presents us with a quandary: this exotic interlude in the middle is quite an entertaining halftime show in itself, but the chart and Sinatra swing harder without it. (A further live version of the Riddle chart exists from a concert in the early 1980s, in which the orchestra plays yet a third variation on the midsection.)

Perhaps the most exciting variation on the Riddle arrangement of "N&D" uses the interchorus portion for an even more eventful transition: from small group to full orchestra, in what might be called a *concerto grosso* format. In 1959, Sinatra played a pair of concerts (on March 31 and April 1) in Australia with Red Norvo's quintet—or rather, Norvo's group plus Bill Miller. They open "Night and Day" with an instrumental chorus by Norvo and rhythm trio; here, the canny vibrapharpist builds up suspense rather like Erroll Garner, by avoiding any hint of the melody, and letting the crowd try to figure out exactly what tune he's playing. Therefore, when Sinatra unexpectedly appears singing "Night and Day," it exponentially amplifies the drama of his entrance. On both nights, Sinatra went through two full and fast choruses (as opposed to one and a half) to further build up the momentum.

Sinatra's 1959 Australian vocal is even jazzier and packs more punch than the 1957 ABC-TV reading. Even before he enters on the March 31 performance—the more dynamic of the two—Sinatra can be heard commenting favorably on Norvo's solo ("Marvelous!"). He's like a fan who can't contain his enthusiasm, and that excitement immediately comes through in his singing. He's enjoying everything so much that he has to force himself to stifle his contagious cackling. He shares an infectious ecstasy with both the musicians and the audience. This contagious euphoria comes through in the singer's especially playful treatment of rhythm. In his most pronounced use of "breaks"—a prominent device used by jazz soloists—Sinatra shoots notes back and forth with Norvo, delighted, for once, to break his cardinal rule about interrupting a sentence or thought so that the mallet man can zing a few hot licks his way during the fills. The exchange is overall more similar to the work of Ella Fitzgerald or Louis Armstrong than Sinatra.

In Australia, Sinatra continually accentuates unexpected notes and speeds up and slows down in unpredictable places, particularly in the second chorus when he stretches "why" (as in "why is it so?") and "hide" (as in "under the hide of me") for multiple measures. He spontaneously invents whole new melodies for the phrases "only you beneath the moon" and "in the silence of. . . ." Each time he comes to the three words "night and day," he phrases them differently. At times he chomps down hard on "night" and then pauses before the "and day"; elsewhere he accentuates the "and" for absolutely no reason other than that it swings, and he refuses to repeat the pattern he had employed only a few measures before. He throws in classic Frankisms, such as "'neath *that* moon" and "baby" (rather than "darling"), and he uses the "roaring traffic's boom" as a clever excuse for drummer John Markham to "drop" an unforeseen bebop "bomb." He has to clear his throat in the middle of the second B, mistakenly transposes "night and day" ("day and night") in the outchorus, and drops the "my" in "spend my life." You might say that he sacrifices them to the amazing momentum. But these minor missteps only endear him to us all the more.

In 1961 and 1962, Sinatra concocted yet another two entirely distinctive ballad readings of "Night and Day." The 1961 track amounts to one of twelve superlative charts on *Sinatra & Strings,* Sinatra's first and greatest collaboration with Don Costa. The Costa take on "Night and Day" may not rank as high as that of Stordahl or Riddle, but it's excellent just the same. For the first time Sinatra includes the verse on a ballad treatment of the tune (this on the same album where he sings the verse—and nothing else—of "Stardust"). Costa's setting of this introduction slowly mounts in dynamics and tension, using the strings of the album's title to voice lots of austere, slow-to-resolve chords. Costa concludes the verse with a device suggesting what Sinatra might have done with Gordon Jenkins: by now far beyond the range of any tempo, each of the three occurrences of "you!" is followed by a very dramatic and dour string flourish.

Costa never had a trademark sound as individual as Riddle's, Jenkins's, or May's, but the soft and flowing use of the guitar (Costa's own instrument as a player) behind the singer signifies a break from anything his predecessors might have written. In this one-chorus orchestration, Sinatra's phrasing on "torment" recalls the Stordahl version, but that's about it, and the new way he finds to sing the notes behind "inside of me" (stretching the "side" syllable) is particularly impressive. The only questionable aspect of the Costa chart is the surprising heaviness of the ending, which sledgehammers its point home with movie-title–music bombast. The idea may have been, however, to return to the austerity of the verse. Whatever the case, this marks a worthy addition to the ever-increasing pantheon of Sinatra "Night and Days."

For his 1962 world tour (done on behalf of children's charities), Sinatra visited six continents with six musicians. He included "Night and Day" from the beginning, initially via a sextet transcription of the Riddle (chorus-and-a-half) arrangement. Two renditions performed in Tokyo on April 20 and 21 are unremarkable; the tune doesn't stand out that much from the rest of the concert. In London, at the Royal Festival Hall concert (June 1, 1962), "Night and Day" is performed stunningly as a duet with guitarist Al Viola. "Instead of doing it with the band," Sinatra said to Viola just before the concert, "we might as well do it with just the guitar. It'll be fresh that way."

Sinatra had begun doing "Night and Day" as a duo (with verse and one chorus only) at least as early as May 25 (at the Ice Palace in Milan). He taped the two best-known performances of the duet a few days later, at the Royal Festival Hall and at the Lido in Paris on Tuesday, June 5. While the Paris show was to become the first historic (and previously unissued) Sinatra concert officially released by a major label (in 1994), the London show is much superior. Both occurred at the very end of a long and exhausting tour, and by June 5 Sinatra's voice was completely shot. Somehow, those few days (which included two more concerts in England) were the last straw that broke his voice. Sinatra was laboring hard at the Paris concert.

Fortunately, this didn't affect "Night and Day" all that much, although the London rendition still has the edge, primarily because he played it fairly close to the vest. Throughout the concert, he is very careful, and doesn't start anything he knows that he can't finish. He stays very close to the melody, which he states directly and with great, though not overdone, feeling. Even here, he's not afraid to climb out on the occasional limb, as in the very boomy way he emphasizes the activities of the roaring traffic. Throughout this mano-a-mano rendition, Viola more than holds his own, with graceful and uncomplicated chordal support.

In this effectively minimalist reading, every time Sinatra holds a note a hair longer than we expect, it has a tremendous impact. It's also a tour de force of Sinatra dynamics, as in the way he sings the first line of the verse ("beat, beat, beat") very quietly and the second ("tick, tick, tock") just a few cubic centimeters of pressure more forcefully. As with the best of Billie Holiday, each little pause (as between "stands" and "against" in the verse) and every minute inflection carries with it significant meaning. And, as Viola suggested, if the idea was to help his longtime fans in Europe to recall his original recording, he underscores that idea by reviving the "way *down* inside of me" embellishment of twenty years earlier.

We may wish, however, that he had concluded his reimagining of "Night and Day" right then and there, because his final recording of the song is downright embarrassing. In the 1990s, Sinatra sold records by bartering his vocal tracks to be electronically manipulated into artificial duets; in the 1960s and '70s, when he tried to reach the youth market, he occasionally stooped to conquer by dabbling in ephemeral forms that were well beneath his taste and talent. His mercifully brief dalliance in "disco," as it used to be called, represents by far his most lamentable exercise in trying to be contemporary.

Perhaps in deciding to remake two standards long associated with him rather than a new potential hit or a cover of someone else's chart-topper, Sinatra may have been looking to do damage control even before any actual damage could be done. On February 16, 1977, he and arranger Joe Beck recorded vocal tracks on "Night and Day" and "All or Nothing at All" on top of disco orchestral backings that the producer-arranger had laid down the day before. While "All or Nothing at All" was wisely withheld (released only in 1995 on the *Complete Reprise Studio Recordings* suitcase), "Night and Day" made it out as a single. (Sinatra also performed this version live, even as late as March 1979, at a concert in Valley Forge, Pennsylvania.)

"Night and Day," unlike "Mack the Knife" or "Come Rain or Come Shine," was not one of the songs you could pretty much count on hearing at many '80s and '90s Sinatra concerts. In 1982, Sinatra and pianist Vinnie Falcone revived and revised the *Perfectly Frank* small-group version, eschewing the Latin elements but retaining the jazzy tempo and the verse in the middle. Sinatra also included the Riddle arrangement in a few performances.

In one October 1986 show (issued privately on the *Saloon Singer* double LP), Sinatra makes his peace with "Night and Day" and brings his relationship with the song full circle. He starts by recapping the story of how he screwed up the tune in the presence of its composer nearly five decades earlier and then uses the first eight bars or so to reenact the screw-up, to the audience's delight. He then gets it more than right for the remaining forty measures. It's a bang-up version; you cannot resist its passion and swing. And yes, this rendition of the Riddle arrangement includes yet another middle instrumental section.

Make no mistake, Sinatra's interpretations of standard tunes were always living, breathing organic entities. He couldn't help relentlessly fiddling with the arrangements, much the same way he continually came up with new ways to phrase the individual lines in the best jazz tradition. As long as he was singing, the music of Frank Sinatra would never stop developing and evolving, even to the last note that he ever sung.

The men who forged the fashion and form of American popular music, colossi such as Louis Armstrong, Bing Crosby, Duke Ellington, Fred Astaire, and Benny Goodman, who were all born between 1899 and 1909, conceived the American aesthetic in terms of new vocabularies for instrumental, vocal, and orchestral expression. Although many key members of the second generation (generally born between 1910 and 1920), especially Billie Holiday and Ella Fitzgerald, had achieved prominence before Sinatra began attracting attention in 1939, he immediately established himself as the acknowledged leader of the movement to win recognition for this music as an art form. Sinatra and his collaborators mapped out the territory and demonstrated the difference between the one-shot songs that made up Tin Pan Alley's daily bread—served, consumed, and quickly forgotten—and the rich three-layer cakes created by such master chefs as Cole Porter and Harold Arlen.

In a sense, Sinatra was willfully out of touch with American culture as it evolved from Mitch Miller's era onward. As he consistently achieved higher and higher quality in his recordings, he defied a dichotomy even then encroaching on the American lively arts. Our standard of living rose, and our standard of culture generally plummeted. This was nowhere truer than in pop music, not only in the debasements of the blues that were being packaged for kiddie consumption, but also in the older styles of American pop that were being beaten to death by overpowerful, hit-happy producers. Only Sinatra seemed actually to be getting better with each subsequent release, and was truly seeking to attain the highest possible brackets of popular music. He rarely underestimated the intelligence of his audiences or talked down to them, and he triumphed commercially over those who did.

One couldn't ask for a body of work that more completely fulfills the potential of twentieth-century popular music than that created by Frank Sinatra, or for more variety within the clearly defined stylistic parameters that Sinatra has established. It upsets all known critical theory when a successful and highly stylized artist doesn't descend into self-parody once he passes beyond a certain point. No other performing artist—in any generation—was able to keep his career snowballing so overwhelmingly; even in those periods when his career went downhill, he grew as an artist. In Sinatra's lifetime, long before he rolled himself up in a big ball and died (shot down in May, as it were) his celebrity tended to overshadow much of his musical accomplishment. Yet twenty years later, and going forward, the work stands on its own. The ways he gets under your skin are legion—they repeat, how they yell, in your ear.

## EXHIBIT "A": TABLE OF SINATRA PERFORMANCES OF "NIGHT AND DAY"

1. The original Axel Stordahl ballad arrangement:
   a. Commercial recording for Bluebird, January 19, 1942 [CD: RCA 2269-2].
   b. Sung by Sinatra in the 1943 Columbia Pictures film *Reveille with Beverly*; Sinatra's track recorded on September 17, 1942 [issued commercially on *Frank Sinatra in Hollywood 1940–1964*, the six-CD Rhino/Reprise box, 8122-78285-2].
   c. Special broadcast presented by the March of Dimes, *America Salutes the President's Birthday*, January 29, 1943.*
   d. Concert, the Hollywood Bowl, August 14, 1943.
   e. Armed Forces Radio Service broadcast transcription, *Command Performance #80*, September 5, 1943 [CD: Meteor CDMTBS 001].
   f. Commercial broadcast, *Songs by Sinatra*, December 19, 1943 (sustaining-unsponsored) [CD: Jazz Hour JH 1020].
   g. March of Dimes fundraiser transcription, circa December 1943 (made for broadcast in January 1944) [CD: VJC 1051].
   h. AFRS program, *Front Line Theatre*, March 6, 1944.*
   i. Commercial broadcast, *Vimms Vitamins Presents the Frank Sinatra Program*, undated, circa spring 1944.
   j. Commercial broadcast, *Vimms Vitamins Presents the Frank Sinatra Program*, October 4, 1944.
   k. Commercial broadcast, *A Date with Judy*, February 20, 1945.*
   l. From September 1945 to June 1947, Sinatra used the first two lines from the Stordahl arrangement of "Night and Day" as the opening theme for both seasons of his show *Old Gold Presents Songs by Sinatra*. Sinatra had used "Night and Day" as his program opening music (along with "This Love of Mine") for earlier broadcast appearances, but this is his most celebrated series and use of the Porter song as a theme. (Sinatra further used a different treatment of "Night and Day" as his theme music for an appearance on the Treasury Department *Music for Millions* show of September 5, 1945.)
   m. Concert, the Hollywood Bowl, September 29, 1945.*
   n. Commercial recording for Columbia, October 22, 1947, "long version." First released in 1993 [CD: CXK 48673, CK 52872].
   o. Commercial recording for Columbia, October 22, 1947, "short version." [most easily available on the recommended CD: *Sinatra Sings Cole Porter*, Legacy 507877-2].
   p. Sinatra again used "Night and Day" as his opener on *Lucky Strike Light-Up Time* in 1949–50, using a variant on the Stordahl arrangement, dropping the strings and adding a trumpet obbligato.
   q. Sinatra also performed a "full" version of "Night and Day" on *Light-Up Time* in April 1950 (exact date unknown).*
   r. Concert, The Opera House in Blackpool, England, July 26, 1953.*
2. a. The *To Be Perfectly Frank* "one shot," radio version, circa June or October 1954 (up-tempo with verse) [*Perfectly Frank*, Bravura BCD-103].

      b. Concert (audience tape), Buffalo, New York, May 8, 1982, de-Latinized version of small group treatment (with verse in middle). [Issued semiprivately on CD: NSF 027].

3. The Nelson Riddle up-tempo arrangement:

      a. All-orchestral version (with at least three different instrumental middle sections):

          i. Commercial recording for Capitol, featuring Juan Tizol, valve trombone, November 26, 1956, for album *A Swingin' Affair!* [CD: Capitol CDP 7 94518 2].

          ii. ABC-TV performance, probably broadcast November 29, 1957 [CD: Bravura CD-105; also on the DVD *Vintage Sinatra*, currently available in *The Concert Collection* package, Shout! Factory 12220].

          iii. TV telecast, *The Dean Martin Show*, November 1, 1960.*

          iv. Concert, Golden Nugget, October 1986 [private double LP: *Saloon Singer*, unnumbered].

      b. Concerto grosso: Combined small group (quintet) and big-band version, with Red Norvo:

          i. Concert, West Melbourne, Australia, March 31, 1959 [CD: Bravura CD2-104].

          ii. Concert, West Melbourne, Australia, April 1, 1959 [CD: Bravura CD-102].

      c. All small group (sextet) version, 1962 World Tour:

          i. Concert, Hibiya Park, Tokyo, April 20, 1962.

          ii. Concert, Mikado Theater, Tokyo, April 21, 1962.

4. The Don Costa *Sinatra & Strings* ballad arrangement, with verse, commercially recorded November 22, 1961 [CD: Reprise 9 27020].

5. As a duet with guitarist Al Viola, ballad with verse (all from the 1962 World Tour):

      a. Concert, Ice Palace, Milan, May 26, 1962 [part of three-CD set, Drive CD- 534].

      b. Concert, Royal Festival Hall, London, June 1, 1962 [on DVD in the *Sinatra: London* package, Universal Music 4703568].

      c. Concert, Lido, Paris, June 5, 1962 [CD: Reprise 45487-2].

6. The Joe Beck "disco" arrangement, commercially recorded February 16, 1977 [originally issued on 45 single Reprise RPS 1386 and then on an Italian Reprise LP (W54101). The major CD issue is part of the twenty-CD "suitcase set," *The Complete Reprise Studio Recordings*, Reprise 46013-2].

*Asterisked entries were not available to be auditioned for the purposes of this study, although some may exist in the hands of private collectors.

    In addition, Sinatra renditions of "Night and Day" were released on several sixteen-inch Armed Forces Radio Services BML (Basic Music Library) transcriptions. It's presumed that these duplicate one or more of the performances listed above—but you never know.

# THE SKINNY YEARS

■—■—■—■—■—■—■—■—■—■

*"Of Love and Youth and Spring"*

# 2

# "FOR OLD TIMES' SAKE"
## Hoboken and Harry, 1915–1939

*Police Detective: "What is that dingus?"*
*Spade: "The stuff that dreams are made of."*
　　　　—JOHN HUSTON,
　　　　　*The Maltese Falcon* (film)

As writer and cultural commentator Stanley Crouch once observed, the pre-modern jazz world welcomed innovation with open arms; in the 1920s and '30s, Louis Armstrong, Coleman Hawkins, Art Tatum, and other style-setters were seen as making the music more rewarding for players and audiences alike. So it was, too, in jazz's sister kingdom, mainstream popular music. Once Sinatra had honed his technique (and this occurred fairly early), it's astonishing how quick his rise was. Even before anyone had heard of him, at least four major bandleaders tried to plant him on their bandstands. Once he had achieved a modicum of exposure with a major band, the public went for him in a big way.

　　Francis Albert Sinatra first opened his peepers on the planet on December 12, 1915, in Hoboken, New Jersey. Though considerably sheltered and protected as the son of comparatively affluent, powerful parents, Sinatra nevertheless grew up exposed to his share of violence and hardship in that ethnically dense, blue-collar town. There were, however, compensating kindnesses as well: Sinatra once told Manie Sachs (the Jewish godfather of his son, Frank Jr.) that he was raised as much by a "kindly old Jewish woman" named Mrs. Golden as he was by his own mother (who wasn't home much). Sinatra continued to visit his "Yiddishe Momme" until her death in the early 1950s.*

---

\* It's always seemed, to this biographer in any case, like Sinatra had a spiritual connection with the Jewish people (and later the nation of Israel) that was at least as strong and as meaningful

**47**

Sinatra told Bill Boggs (in 1975) that his earliest ambition, before he discovered pop music, was to become a civil engineer, which was encouraged by his father. "He could neither read nor write his name, but his big point was education, complete and full education. And I had planned to go to Stevens Institute, which is in Hoboken, and is considered one of the finest engineering schools, and I was going to be a civil engineer, in fact I had a great desire to be one, until I got mixed up with vocalizing."

All Sinatra chroniclers, whether seeking to vilify him or deify him, praise him or bury him, agree that the turning point of his young life was catching a Bing Crosby performance and deciding that he could "do that." They don't agree on whether it was a live theater gig or a movie in Jersey City or Manhattan, and whom he was with, but we know that sometime in 1931 or 1932, Sinatra had made up his mind that he was going to be the next Bing Crosby. In the very earliest days, he sang with a megaphone, like Rudy Vallée. As he told Boggs, "I actually had a megaphone! Guys would throw pennies to see if they could get me to swallow them! A lot of fun in those days! I used to move a great deal, so they couldn't hit me."

Sinatra graduated from David E. Rue Junior High School in 1931 but made it through only forty-seven days of high school, and even fewer than that at his first potential career, working on a delivery truck for the *Jersey Observer* newspaper. Early in 1932 the Sinatras moved to their first house, at 841 Garden Street, where he met his "Garden Street girlfriend," Marian Bush Schrieber. Between 1932 and 1939 he took occasional manual labor jobs (at various shipyards), but his main focus was on singing whenever and wherever he could. As Schrieber told researcher Herb Kurtin, in order to find an orchestra to sing with, the young aspiring crooner often had to put it together himself and create his own opportunities.

Martin Sinatra was disappointed, to put it mildly, in his son's decision not to stick with his education or try to get into an engineering program at Stevens Institute, to the extent that one morning he ordered his son out of the house and not to return. "I was shocked! Absolutely shocked! I didn't know that I had to go. I remember the moment we were having breakfast. I was supposed to go out that morning and look for a job. Because I had decided

---

to him as that of his connection to Italy or Sicily. Furthermore, his canon is rife with Yiddishisms: In 1955, Sinatra nailed every nuance of "Sue Me" from *Guys and Dolls* ("so *nu?*"), one of the most *Yiddishkeit* songs in the history of Broadway, and at his great Seattle concert from 1957 Sinatra addresses his musicians collectively as "*klezmer.*" Then there's a 1965 concert, not long after filming *Cast a Giant Shadow* (a 1966 war drama about the founding of Israel, costarring John Wayne), in which Sinatra "kvells" with the audience about how the goyish "Duke" tried to "drink a matzo."

that I didn't want to go to college and he wanted me to go to college," Sinatra told Boggs. "I just was not going out looking for work but at night I was working with little combinations, for nothing, singing with the bands so I could get the experience."

Schrieber picks up the story: "[Frank] didn't have a job at the time, but he loved hanging around musicians, so I suggested that he get an orchestra together for our Wednesday night dances. In exchange for hiring the musicians, he'd get to sing a few numbers with the band. I'd take the money at the door, and when we got enough, we all went to the Village Inn in New York so that Frank could sing with the orchestra there. We'd go in to ask the manager beforehand to let Frankie sing. We said that was the only way we would come in, being underage, and so he usually said yes. Frank did such a good job for our school dances on Wednesday that he wanted to take the orchestra to Our Lady of Grace for their Friday night dances, but the Irish Catholics wouldn't let him in."

Why not? "Because of the scandals involving his mother, Natalie. They would have nothing to do with him." Schrieber is referring to the ambitious and occasionally illegal career of the woman known as Dolly, easily the dominant influence in her son's personal and professional life. In addition to playing a huge role in local Democratic politics, she also worked as a midwife, and as such, performed abortions, for which she was arrested several times.

Irish Catholics aside, this hardly alienated Sinatra from the larger pool of musicians and bandleaders in the area, especially when the young singer began assembling an arsenal of ephemera essential for club dates, namely a library of stock dance band orchestrations (with vocal parts, naturally), an early portable sound system, and that most indispensable item in the bandleader's bag of tricks, an automobile. On the more typical lesser-budget dates, Sinatra sang with just the guitarist Matty Golizio (who would later play on some of his Columbia sessions), his most frequent accompanist for several years beginning in 1934.

Throughout the "golden age of radio," local stations, even though they constituted the country's most profitable medium, frequently had off-hours airtime that they couldn't sell, which they often turned over to young performers willing to work for nothing or next to it. "I didn't have the experience, to warrant radio stations paying me," Sinatra recalled in 1955. During the evening hours the competition was considerably stiffer even for pro bono spots; for instance, Glenn Miller and his orchestra might do a sustaining broadcast for the minimum scale from 11:30 to midnight but that same week would do three well-paying fifteen-minute shows for Chesterfield cigarettes during prime time.

Long before anyone had ever heard of him, Sinatra sang often on local NYC-area radio, especially on station WAAT in Jersey City. Herb Kurtin uncovered a clip from a 1935 radio guide of a listing from Tuesday, April 16, 1935, of Sinatra appearing on WAAT from 5:15 to 5:30. Kurtin also believed Sinatra went on the air on that station under the nom de plume of "The Romancer." Tony Mottola, three years younger than Sinatra, recalled working with the singer both at WAAT, where Sinatra had his own show (possibly as early as 1932) with a five-piece group, and on club dates.

Occasionally, amateurs and newcomers were able to penetrate the commercially controlled prime-time hours, thanks primarily to Major Bowes. The red-nosed Major launched his *Original Amateur Hour* on local New York radio in 1934 and went national with it a year later. Not long after, Sinatra hooked up with a group of Hoboken harmonizers who sang locally and became part of the Major Bowes radio-based amateur circuit. In addition to his widely heard program, the Bowes empire (later inherited by Ted Mack) consisted of vaudeville appearances, which took the group as far away from home as Vancouver, and several one-reel movie shorts filmed in the Bronx (Hollywood on the Hudson).

His mother, at last, had resigned herself to the idea that Frankie was determined to make it in the music business. According to some accounts, Dolly Sinatra pressured the other three Hobokenites to let "Frankie" join, but he soon became their lead singer and star, and female hearts were already starting to flutter during his solo spots. In all of its appearances with Bowes, the group kept changing its name, most humorously to "The Secaucus Cockamamies" (as Sinatra claimed thirty years later in a reminiscence on his *Sands* album) so no one would question their amateur status. It's hard to imagine, however, that that would have been a problem once anyone had heard them sing.

Bowes had many performances preserved, including three items by the Hoboken Four: two audio airchecks—a complete "Shine" and "Curse of an Aching Heart"—as well as a film of the group doing "Shine," which is not known to have survived. "Shine," broadcast September 8, 1935, reveals a spirited if ragged remake of the then-famous 1932 Bing Crosby–Mills Brothers arrangement of this ancient and even then politically incorrect piece. After ninety awkward seconds of banter with the condescending Major (in which Sinatra is introduced as "this fella here" who "never worked at all"), Sinatra can clearly be heard aping Crosby in the solo spots. Overall, the performance bears out Sinatra's statement from 1955 that he "believed, because of [Crosby's] leisurely manner of working, that if he could do it, I could do it. The funny switch is that I've never been able to do it. It's just a trick that he has, a wonderfully relaxed feeling about performing." Overall, the value of the two Bowes airchecks is more historical than musical as the earliest surviving documents of this soon-to-be-famous voice.

Sinatra returned home to New Jersey after growing disillusioned with the good Major, who was as famous for consuming whiskey that, as Sinatra later quipped, "would take the paint off a boat," as he was for his slogan, which cited "the dizzy spin of the wheel of fortune." For a time Sinatra went back to singing at WAAT, where he played badminton in the record library stacks with future jazz producer Gus Statiras. "It didn't take a genius to see that this guy was going to be somebody," Statiras remembered in 1993. "All the girls around Newark were already crazy about him."

In one of his incarnations as a club date (read: bar mitzvah), bandleader, and contractor, Sinatra even appeared on Fred Allen's *Town Hall Tonight* show. Unfortunately, Sinatra did not sing on this May 1937 broadcast, although he does banter with Allen and "conduct" an instrumental quartet identified as "The Four Sharps" in a medley of "Exactly Like You" and "Powerhouse" (a composition by future *Your Hit Parade* compadre Raymond Scott).

If Sinatra ever actually sang in anything that could be called a "saloon," it was only in the most liberal sense of the word. Alcohol was sold, certainly, but even when he was singing in local "joints," these were relatively upscale establishments; though sometimes called "roadhouses," they were more like regional equivalents of the posher clubs that were starting to emerge around the country in the wake of the repeal of Prohibition, like the Persian Room in New York (later the Copacabana) and Ciro's and the Mocambo in Los Angeles.

In working in these Jersey roadhouses, advancing his career at first meant gradually lowering his income, from fifty dollars a week with Bowes to forty dollars a week at the Union Club (where he worked before and after his stint with the Hoboken Four) to thirty-five a week at the Rustic Cabin, to whatever he could get at weddings and dances. "Professionally, and I use the word loosely," Sinatra reminisced years later, "I was working in a roadhouse in Englewood Cliffs, New Jersey, which is about two miles north of the George Washington Bridge, and it was called the Rustic Cabin. I was there for about a year and a half or two. Oh, I was the head waiter and the chief bottle washer and sweep-up man and everything. It was a great experience, I must say."

According to Harry Zinquist, drummer with the Rustic Cabin band (led by Henry Jacobs, aka "Bill Henri"), if Sinatra had ever done anything at the Cabin other than sing, he certainly had stopped long before Harry James made his epochal appearance at the Cabin in late spring 1939. The Rustic Cabin, the most famous of Sinatra's Jersey stints, had figured in his life long before he worked there as a single: an early incarnation of the Hoboken Four (then known as "The Three Flashes") had played there several years earlier.

The Cabin had one major advantage over the better paying Union Club: the owner had a direct line to New York City radio station WNEW, which broadcast all over the tristate area, whereas the owner of the Union Club refused to spring for such a wire.

By the end of 1938, Sinatra was also doing between three and five quarter-hour shows a week from WNEW's New York studio, including one spot with organist Jimmy Rich that ran "about fifteen minutes apart," in Sinatra's words, from a similar show by fellow future star Fannie Rose Shore, already working professionally under the stage name "Dinah." At the same time, he was doing a spot at eight in the morning on WOR in Newark. Both stations paid him little more than carfare, but the Jersey station afforded a compensating benefit. In his 1980 interview with Arlene Francis, Sinatra explained: "I got a job during that period at the WOR Bamberger station in Newark, and I did one show a week with the orchestra there, because they had strings and I wanted to work with strings. I got thirty cents a week for carfare from Hoboken to Newark and back, and that was it, nothing. There was no union, none of that stuff. But out of a half-hour program, I had three songs that I did with a string section, which to me was a very important thing."

At least one musician who would be important in Sinatra's subsequent career first encountered the singer in 1938 or 1939. "The first time I ever met Frank was when I was playing at the Commodore Hotel with Tommy Dorsey," remembered Arthur "Skeets" Herfurt, who would play lead alto on nearly all of Sinatra's Capitol dates a generation or two later. George "Bullets" Durgom, then an "alligator" or band fanatic who later worked in both Miller's and Sinatra's offices, "was a fan of the Dorsey band, and he'd spend most of his nights at the Commodore listening to us. One night he got me a date with a girl in New Jersey, and we went out to Frank Dailey's Meadowbrook on Route 9W. There was a little local band playing there, and guess who was singing? Frankie boy! That's when I first heard him. He sounded just like Frankie. He sounded great."

Sinatra's career began to step up shortly after he married his longtime girlfriend Nancy Barbato, on February 4, 1939. While the earlier documented performances were taken off the radio, Sinatra made his first actual recording (although it was a demo, not a commercially released side) on March 18, 1939.* This was a recording session led by a local saxophonist and bandleader, Francesco Mugnolo, who had been born in Naples in 1904, immigrated to the USA as an infant, and worked under the name "Frank Mane." Around 1937, Mane was playing in the house orchestra at the Jersey City station

---

* This info is from an interview with Frank Mane and his wife Mary, July 1998.

WAAT, where Sinatra was also hanging around, looking for opportunities to sing; at that point Mane owned a car and Sinatra didn't, so Mane would often drop Sinatra off at the Barbato home on Audubon Avenue on his way back to Bayonne (where he lived his whole life, except for a few periods on the road).

In the Spring of 1939, Mane had an offer to join a national band, Clyde Lucas and his California Dons. Because of logistics and technology, Mane couldn't audition for the Los Angeles–based trombonist in any convenient way, so he decided to make a recording of himself playing with a dance band that he put together just for the occasion. Now needing other musicians, he put the word out at his local fraternal organization, the Sicilian Club (as he often did when putting together bands for private parties and "club dates"), and pretty soon he had assembled nine other local players. Word reached Sinatra, who informally asked if he could "come along." Mane hadn't planned on including a vocalist, but he said, "Sure, why not?"

The eleven men, including Mane and Sinatra (and drummer Don Rigney, who had been best man at Sinatra's wedding six weeks earlier), assembled the next day on March 18, 1939, at the Harry Smith Recording studios at 2 West 46th Street in Manhattan. The session cost Mane a total of twenty-seven dollars for the use of the space, the equipment, and the raw materials; it's likely that his musician pallies played as a favor for him without asking to be paid. On the date, Frank Mane and the ten-piece ad-hoc orchestra played three old favorites: two famous pieces adapted from traditional Russian classical music, Rimsky-Korsakov's "Flight of the Bumblebee" (from the opera *The Tale of Tsar Sultan*) and "Our Love" (based on Tchaikovsky's "orchestral fantasy" *Romeo and Juliet*), followed by "Girl of My Dreams," a 1927 waltz hit by territorial bandleader Sunny Clapp. The other piece was something called "Eclipse"—either an original by Mane or possibly a published semiclassical saxophone "study."

The arrangement on "Our Love" sounds like it was written to make ten musicians sound like more—by 1939, regulation dance bands were averaging fourteen or fifteen players plus vocalists—and to make the reeds blend with the brass in a way that suggested a string section, fitting to the semiclassical oeuvre. Coincidentally, the piece had been adapted by Larry Clinton, long one of Tommy Dorsey's arrangers, and recorded by Dorsey and vocalist Jack Leonard (three days earlier on March 15). Generally, when a classical piece was reworked into a pop song, part of the job was compressing it into the standard thity-two–bar (4 x 8) AABA format; however, Tchaikovsky's round peg just refused to conveniently fit into that square hole, so Clinton made each A section ten bars (the B section is still eight) with the overall result that the total piece is thirty-eight bars.

Even at age twenty-three, Sinatra sounds more confident and assured than Leonard, and Tchaikovsky's long, legato lines suit Sinatra's nascent vocal style superbly well—as Mane doubtless realized. He's already holding notes and shading pitches like a much more accomplished and experienced vocalist. He stretches out the words "and so you're *always* near to me" to make that key word sound longer, and then holds the last note, "our *love*" to make that word "love" sound much more eternal.

The orchestration of "Our Love" is in dance band fox-trot 4/4 tempo all the way, but it's also something like a "concert" arrangement, in that it lasts nearly four-and-a-half minutes (like a twelve-inch disc) and has Sinatra returning to reprise the last eight bars at the end, and the way he holds that last "love" anticipates the big note at the end of "All or Nothing at All" a few months later. Sinatra sings with remarkable confidence and assuredness. He's especially smooth on the two-note title phrase. The interval goes from C-sharp to D-natural (in the published key of G) for the first two times the phrase is heard, at the start of the first and second "A" section. When the title phrase is repeated at the wind-up, Clinton has lowered the first note ("our") to the lower D, so that in going from "our" (low D) to "love" (high D) Sinatra has to climb a whole octave. At both points when he sings the final "A," Sinatra pulls it off with both aplomb and considerable drama.

It's significant to compare Sinatra's performance with that of Jack Leonard on the Dorsey disc—Sinatra is already much more urgent and yet relaxed, aggressive, and sensual, and altogether more convincing than Leonard, who was one of the superstars of the dance band world in 1939. He sings well enough on the "Our Love" disc that it would have gotten him work with a leading band if anyone had heard it, but apparently no one did. The one copy in existence sat in Mane's dresser drawer for forty years at least, until at some point Mane exhumed the twelve-disc, and made a tape that he passed along to Sinatra, after which the two enjoyed a reunion. And from that point in the early 1980s, Sinatra himself made numerous copies that he handed out to friends. As well he should: it's an amazingly advanced bit of singing for a twenty-three-year-old newlywed. In everything he was doing, even at this early stage, Sinatra had a plan, an outline of his career, a destination. In the words of Mitch Miller, "He had a direction. He knew where he was going, come hell or high water."

The two most radical, world-changing discoveries of the high swing era were made via listening to local radio. The first occurred when John Hammond heard Count Basie broadcasting from the Reno Club in Kansas City in the spring of 1936. (Coincidentally, Lester Young had himself discovered the

Basie Reno Club band in the same fashion a short while earlier.) In June 1939 Harry James, who had only recently set forth with his own band after first coming to fame with Benny Goodman, was taking a nap in his room at the Hotel Lincoln. The radio was on, and James's wife, singer Louise Tobin, was getting dressed to leave for Boston where she had a gig with Bobby Hackett's band. "I heard this boy singing, and I thought, 'There's a fair singer!' Now I didn't think he was fantastic, I just thought, 'Well, now that's a good singer.' So I woke Harry and said, 'Honey, you might want to hear this kid on the radio. The boy singer on this show sounds pretty good.' That was the end of it as far as I was concerned."

Apparently concurring with the judgment of Mrs. James, the next night, the trumpeter drove out to Route 9W in Englewood Cliffs. "I asked the manager where I could find the singer," James related to George Simon, "and he told me, 'We don't have a singer. But we do have an emcee who sings a little bit.'" As Sinatra recalled, the Rustic Cabin was "where Harry James heard me. He actually heard me on the radio. They used to have a dance band pickup on WNEW five nights a week, for different clubs around the metropolitan area including Jersey and Connecticut. When he left Benny Goodman and started his own band and came over to see me, I almost broke his arm so he wouldn't get away 'cause I was dying to get out of that place!"

Although James and Sinatra effectively corroborated each other's stories, theirs is not the only account of the "discovery." Manie Sachs, who in 1939 was "in charge of artists" (in his words) at the MCA talent agency, maintained that he had actually first heard of "the singer at the Rustic Cabin road house" by reputation. After hearing Sinatra (who, Sachs also recalled, was waiting tables) for himself, Sachs recommended him to James. "He wasn't the most beautiful guy in the world," Sachs said in 1955, "but something about his face was appealing—and he could sing." Within a few months, Sachs would make a lateral professional move from MCA to CBS Radio, which now controlled the newly reorganized Columbia Records, where he would be the first to record the new singer commercially.

Several executives of station WNEW also claimed credit as Sinatra discoverers. But one thing seems certain: however James came to enter the Rustic Cabin, he was impressed and invited Sinatra to audition for him. "Harry was auditioning singers at the Lincoln Hotel," said Skeets Herfurt, who heard this story shortly afterward, "and Frank walked in with no arrangements. The other guys who were auditioning for Harry had charts and everything. But Frank just walked in, walked over to the piano player, told him what he wanted to sing, what key he wanted to sing in, and stood up and sang—and knocked everybody out. They were auditioning a lot of people that day, but the musicians said that when they heard Sinatra, that was it. There was no doubt about it."

As far as Sinatra was concerned, however, James was only the front-runner and the leading contender for his contract. A number of other bandleaders, both established and fledgling, were also interested. The second most likely to sign Sinatra was Bob Chester, who was just organizing his first band—heavily influenced by Glenn Miller—in the spring of 1939. Although Chester had come from a Detroit family rich with big auto bucks, he made up his mind to succeed without benefit of his parents' nest egg, and he had convinced Tommy Dorsey, a considerably more established bandleader, to slip him the necessary bankroll.

Coincidentally, Miller himself had already passed up the chance to hire Sinatra. "I first heard the Miller band sometime between '38 and '39," Sinatra told Dave Garroway in a radio interview conducted not long after Miller's death in 1945. "I was segueing between Jersey and New York, trying to make a buck here and there. Glenn was starting that new-sounding band that he had, and I believe at the time he was at the Grand Island Casino. The first time I heard the Glenn Miller band, I walked up to him and said, 'Glenn, I want a job!' I really did. But he was busy hiring Ray Eberle at the time, and he said to me, in essence, 'Don't call me, I'll call you.' But I did get to meet Glenn quite early in my career, and we became great friends, as a matter of fact. Every time I heard the band I got a big boot out of it, and I still do when I hear some of the records that they made in those days."

Sometime in early 1939, Chester and seventeen-year-old trumpeter Alec Fila (who had just left Jack Teagarden's band) visited the Rustic Cabin. Fifty-five years later, Fila couldn't recollect why they were there, whether by coincidence or if they had gone expressly to catch Sinatra, but Chester was taken enough by the singer to offer him a job with his embryonic orchestra. Fila also recalled that Sinatra did sing with the band at the New Yorker Hotel. "They had a year-round ice show there, with a retracting floor," said Fila. "I have a very vivid [mental] picture of Sinatra at the mic and the ice skaters on the floor. But I couldn't say whether it was a rehearsal or if it was one of the evening shows, or how long he was with the band. That might have been his only night."

Other accounts depict Sinatra as rehearsing with Chester's men in late May 1939, even helping to tote their library up to the fourth floor of New York's Steinway Hall. Saxophonist Ed Scalzi told Herb Kurtin that Sinatra actually cut two "test" sides with Chester, "My Love for You," which he would keep singing into his tenure with James (and record ten years later for Columbia), and the Mexican novelty "Alla en Rancho Grande." (These sides, if they were ever made, have never been found.) The Chester episode indirectly brought him to the attention of Tommy Dorsey, who by the end of the year would deem him ready for his organization's number one "A" band. (Sinatra also used Chester on his resume: a late 1942 solo radio program stated that the newly liberated Sinatra had sung with Harry James, Tommy Dorsey, and Bob Chester.)

Xylophonist Red Norvo, long admired by Sinatra, had a better shot at planting Sinatra on his bandstand. Unlike the James and Chester orchestras, however, the Red Norvo–Mildred Bailey Orchestra had already passed its peak in 1939, although this would conclude only the second phase in Norvo's long career as one of jazz's most thoughtful soloists and innovative ensemble leaders. "When I was married to Mildred," Norvo recalled in 1994, "her brother, Al Rinker [previously a member of Paul Whiteman's Rhythm Boys and partner of Bing Crosby], lived up in the Nyack area. To get there we used to go over the George Washington Bridge and through Jersey. We went up there one Sunday, and coming back we stopped at the Cabin for a drink. That's when we first heard Frank. I hadn't paid much attention to him, singing with this little band. But Mildred remarked right away, 'That kid can sing!'

"Mildred picked Frank out right away.* It was just like when we heard Billie Holiday for the first time with John [Hammond], Mildred said, 'She's great,' and then John went and discovered her. There were so many great songs coming out at that time," Norvo continued, "and we needed a male singer to help Mildred out. We called Frank, but he had just accepted a job with Harry James."

Frank Sinatra began his career—in the major leagues at least—when he joined Harry James and His Orchestra, then barely three months old, at the Hippodrome Theater in Baltimore on June 30, 1939. For most of the next sixty years, Sinatra most consistently named Tommy Dorsey as his major musical inspiration. The Voice should know, but clearly James, whom he called "a dear friend and a great teacher," resounds as a hugely important influence on the technique as well as the emotional content of Sinatra's music. "In six months with Harry," Louise Tobin explained, "Frank learned more about music than he'd ever known in his life up to that point." Certainly Dorsey's long-breath method of extending notes became extremely useful to Sinatra,

---

* Sinatra famously worked with Norvo, at least twenty years later, in 1959–60. Although he never had any actual professional involvement with Mildred Bailey, he and Bing Crosby were the all-important benefactors who paid for her hospital bills at the time of her final illness in 1951.

but the restrained Dorsey could get neither as blisteringly hot nor as swaggeringly sentimental as James, and as Sinatra later could and did. If Dorsey suggested methods of carrying or phrasing a tune, James provided a working model of how to pack an emotional wallop.

From James, too, Sinatra learned much about how to intermingle pop song tenderness with blues-like invective, how to swing, how to give and take with an orchestra, how to personalize a melody, and how to mesmerize an audience. Like Dorsey, James's group was more than a swing band; as one press pundit wrote in 1943, the Harry James Orchestra "features ten strings and turns out a good deal of the sweet stuff which narcotizes teenagers."

No one quite handles a note like Harry James. He pushes them and pinches them, squeezes them and caresses them, tempers each iota of sound in every possible way. Even when he's being delicate, James swings and swaggers with such force that his lines threaten to jump right out of the groove. And there's a brave voice in his head, which would in time speak to Sinatra as well, telling him to be not afraid of schmaltz. It's okay when it's honest, and especially when, as with jazz's greatest sentimentalist, Johnny Hodges, it's leavened by a touch of the blues.

James and Sinatra took their first crack at achieving big-name status together, then went their separate ways, but remained friends for life. Coincidentally, both reached the higher echelon of celebrity at the Paramount Theatre in 1943. The world had already witnessed throngs of post–Depression-and-repression youth working themselves into a lather over Benny Goodman, Glenn Miller, and a few others, yet no one had ever seen anything like the James phenomenon. Even more restrained commentators were comparing him to Dionysus and Gabriel, paralleling the Sinatra phenomenon to a remarkable degree.

While the Paramount Theatre was an impressive place for a band to make its local debut, the Paramount Hotel, where James's band hung their hats in between shows, was far from equally respected. Louise Tobin recalled how these hotels reflected the fortunes of a working band in 1939: "If you were doing pretty good, you stayed at the Piccadilly. If you were doing fair you stayed at the Forest. And if you were doing terrible you stayed at the Paramount. Needless to say, at that point we were at the Paramount." (The Times Square hotel became precisely the opposite when it was refurbished into an exclusive upscale boutique hostelry in the twenty-first century.)

The few recorded James-Sinatra songs, while constituting a declaration of their compatibility and the possibilities of their relationship, sadly also amounted to a musical coitus interruptus since the two performers were separated before the inevitable climax could be achieved. Still, they made a telling case that The Voice and The Horn could have continued making beautiful music together indeed.

Of the ten songs commercially recorded, eight are believed to have been arranged by Andy Gibson, who also wrote for Duke Ellington, Count Basie, Charlie Barnet, and Cab Calloway, and later received credit for the rhythm and blues hit "The Hucklebuck" (which Sinatra recorded for Columbia). The remaining two, "It's Funny to Everyone but Me" and "My Buddy," are believed to be by Jack Mathias, who had written for Jerry Blaine's orchestra in 1937 and who attracted more attention at the time for such instrumental specialties as James's "Night Special" and "Trumpet Rhapsody." Several of the ten also exist in alternate takes, and an additional ten tunes have surfaced in the form of live airchecks.

The first Sinatra-James item, "From the Bottom of My Heart" (which both Gibson and James got their names on as composers), opens with James stating the melody and then Sinatra doing the same (and, naturally, the lyrics besides). Perhaps inspired by the vote of confidence in having been awarded that extra "tag" chorus, Sinatra sounds even more assured than on the more classically styled "Our Love," flowing smoothly over both refrains in two takes. Sinatra makes the most of a minimal lyric, "From the bottom of my heart, I love you / What more can I say?" The lyricist spends altogether too much time telling us that he doesn't have anything to say, which is not an ideal message for a song. Yet Sinatra turns it into a statement, just by the force of his personality and his very Sinatraness, which is already apparent even here, on his very first commercial recording.

"Melancholy Mood," by Walter Schumann (who later composed the theme to *Dragnet)*, is the other Sinatra vocal out of the four tunes James recorded at the first session with the new singer (made on July 13, after the band returned to New York to play the Roseland Ballroom), and changes texture completely. As the title indicates, Sinatra explores a self-pitying state of mind that serves as a twenty-year forerunner of the *Only the Lonely* atmosphere. The leader states the tune growling like a Duke Ellington plunger specialist, in a series of "jungle style" wah-wahs. Similarly, a tenor break later in the chart, identified by Phil Schaap as being by the great future Ellington star Al Sears (whose only pop hit, "Castle Rock," was much later recorded by the Sinatra-James combination), anticipates Ben Webster, then still with Cab Calloway's band.

If the first two Sinatra records seem forward-pointing triumphs, others come off like odd glimpses backward; Sinatra and James are sitting side by side in the back of the caboose, looking to see where they have been. Gibson's arrangement of Walter Donaldson's 1922 "My Buddy," Sinatra's first "oldie" (not counting "Shine" and "Curse of an Aching Heart" with the Hoboken Four), utilizes a schottische tempo of the sort Crosby and Dorsey were independently bouncing along around 1937. Sinatra sounds uncomfortable in the first eight lines and then tries to cover it up by playing with the time in the second, but his rushing and lagging illustrate his increasing ability to bring a lyric to life; newly added trombonist Dalton Rizzotto and leader James come off well, using their mutes not to growl but to turn in a peppy middle-register chorus reminiscent of James's predecessor with Goodman, Bunny Berigan.

Still, the James-Sinatra sessions, in a sense, began with an edge over the Dorsey ones in that leader, arranger, and singer tried at the outset to create a style of their own; contrastingly, the Sinatra-Dorsey collaborations would start with an attempt to squeeze the new singer into a mold that had already been established. "It's Funny to Everyone but Me" looks for a new band-vocal trick in a variation of the Tommy Dorsey "Marie" routine. Sinatra would participate in the "Marie" cycle during his Dorsey years, in which the sidemen would chant a steady stream of song titles behind the male singer up front, always doing a standard. With Jack Lawrence's "It's Funny to Everyone but Me" the band tried to come up with a worthy variation idea, only this time they used a new song and the bandsmen would just chant one song title at the end of the first ("It's the Talk of the Town") and the last eight bar phrases ("I Gotta Right to Sing the Blues"). Lawrence, who wrote no fewer than four of the James-Sinatra numbers, felt that the chanting routine may have also been inspired by the Ink Spots. Whatever the case, the longer lines of the bridge bring out a little more oomph from Sinatra, but the band-chant routine still falls flat.

"All or Nothing at All," by far the best known of the ten James-Sinatra tracks, experiments more successfully with unconventional band-vocal structures. "It's Funny to Everyone but Me" and "From the Bottom of My Heart" use brief vocal reprises, and "Ciribiribin" even opens with Sinatra singing the verse; you won't hear anything like that on a Benny Goodman record. But in even greater contrast to the usual band-vocal-band format, Sinatra dominates all of "All or Nothing at All." Assisted by a brief intro and an instrumental interlude saturated with James's distinctive lead horn, this might as well be a vocal record (i.e., "vocal with accompaniment"). In a sense, it points to the future careers of both men: James would always be more predisposed toward featuring singers than most of his fellow bandleaders (many of his biggest hits were vocal features for Helen Forrest) and, likewise, "All or Nothing at All" presages many Sinatra sides from the Dorsey era and beyond.

Although lyricist Jack Lawrence and composer Arthur Altman were already friendly with James, they didn't write "All or Nothing at All" specifically for Sinatra. This is something you could never tell from listening to it; the long-meter format of the song, cast in sixty-four bars, and the general attitude (the "All the Way" kind of stance) make it seem like the song comes from a much later period in the evolution of American pop. The song would be a key element that Sinatra would incorporate into his performance persona. Jack Lawrence remembered the recording well when we talked to him in May 1995, pointing out that Sinatra would come back to the song many times (there are later arrangements by Axel Stordahl, Don Costa, and Nelson Riddle). "But it's interesting to listen to that young voice when he first started and the way he attacked that song and what he did with the breath control, with all of the wonderful phrasing that he did even in those early days. Later as he went along he learned a lot more and added a lot more interpretation. Every time he rerecorded it, there would be another great lush arrangement, but I still prefer to listen to that young voice singing that song."

"All or Nothing at All" was not released until the summer of 1940 and did not hit the charts until Sinatra's *Your Hit Parade* phase three years later. Nonetheless, the song seems to have been Sinatra's biggest number with James—at least three live versions of it exist, including one from the band's best-remembered gig, at the 1939 World's Fair. Appropriately, the minor-mooded "All or Nothing" also harkens to both past and future vocally, as Sinatra suggests the long lines that would comprise his most radical break with tradition. Yet traces linger of some 1930s square jawed *popera* baritone like Nelson Eddy, ending on a Romberg-type high note that could wear a Viking helmet or a Mountie hat. ("My Love for You," one of the tunes he sang on the radio with James, ends on an even higher, more stratospheric note.)

Sinatra clearly wanted to expand the rhythmic base of the music, but for the time being was only eliminating possibilities and learning what he *didn't* want to do. And although it alluded to the Italo-American machismo we associate with Sinatra, the disc's heavy-footed melodrama lacks the tenderness he would later bring out in similar though subtler performances. All in all, it justifies James's later remark that Sinatra was "a very serious singer [even] then. There was no kidding. When he sang, he sang."

Other James sides peer into directions Sinatra would never explore again. One in a long line of intercultural, interracial-romances-that-can-never-be, "On a Little Street in Singapore" comes out of the pop song equivalent of what African American–film historian Donald Bogle calls "the tragic mulatto syndrome." From *Madame Butterfly* onward (as heard in such 1920s pop pieces as "Poor Butterfly" not to mention "Japanese Mammy"), East and West may meet, but in terms of sustaining a long-term relationship, they don't stand a Chinaman's chance.

"On a Little Street in Singapore" opens like a movie, with Sinatra and James as two American sailors in a Far East opium den. The trumpeter, anticipating Gene Kelly's wolf act from *Anchors Aweigh*, brags audaciously through his horn that he intends to take on every trollop from Tokyo Rose to Shanghai Lil. The timid young crooner, however, seems dazed and confused by the joint's elegantly exotic trappings. Perhaps fearing that the underpinning bolero motif will throw him off, Sinatra plays it cautiously, sticking very close to the melody and the basic 4/4 beat. Sinatra would never seriously return to this genre. The only way he could take on texts on similar subjects, such as "South of the Border" and "Isle of Capri," was to de-melodramatize them into rhythm numbers with near-nonsense lyrics.

"Ciribiribin" was adapted by James and Lawrence from an Italian song, but it's the swinging beat that both the leader and crooner latch on to. Bing Crosby, flanked by hot violinist Joe Venuti and the Andrews Sisters, recorded an even zingier version of this Italian air, but Sinatra also turns in a respectable showing. James had already selected "Ciribiribin" as his theme song and recorded it in January as an instrumental, in a full-length treatment of the way it would open all Harry James sets over the next forty years. On Sinatra's final session with the band, James rerecorded the 1898 aria with the departing singer, thereby making it the closing theme for the James-Sinatra saga.

If the stack of numbers recorded by the James orchestra, both with and without Sinatra, seems somewhat random, such was the custom of the time. Generally speaking, the more established bands had first pick of the new songs, and labels made a point of only having one version of each new song; i.e., if James recorded "All or Nothing at All," then no other band would do it on Brunswick, although Jimmy Dorsey recorded it for Decca as did Count Basie for Okeh. However, bands were much freer in what they could play at public appearances and on the radio; seven additional songs were issued via airchecks (off-the-air recordings) by Sony Music's Legacy in 1995, and generally these are much higher up the food chain. "If I Didn't Care" was Jack Lawrence's big hit of the era, associated with the Ink Spots, but James and Sinatra render it beautifully; and "Wishing (Will Make It So)" is a rather corny contemporary ballad, but James and Sinatra make it memorable, unexpectedly, by swinging the pants off of it. "The Lamp Is Low" and "Moon Love" (which he returned to in 1965) are two classical adaptations (based on Ravel and Tchaikovsky, respectively) that are precisely Sinatra's meat, and again are superior to most of what the team cut commercially for Brunswick.

The James-Sinatra "Stardust" (taken from a Roseland broadcast on July 8) is a major find, considering Sinatra's long-standing future relationship with the song; he sang bits and pieces of it with the Pied Pipers and Tommy

Dorsey and then again in 1961 (wherein he only sang the verse). Here he sings the whole Hoagy Carmichael classic by himself in a completely copacetic medium fox-trot tempo, extending notes as necessary, warmly buffeted by the James reed section. This is a mature and majestic vocal, better than any of the commercial cuttings; if, by any chance, Dorsey happened to have been listening, it's not surprising why he would be keen to snag Sinatra for his team. In fact, Sinatra directly patterned his phrasing here after Dorsey's own reading of the melody on the trombonist's 1936 recording. What happens after Sinatra's vocal is even better: first the reeds play a rapturous chorus on their own, then James himself takes off in one of his best solos of the period, transforming the bridge into a series of bluesy, stop-time breaks, and overall full of the spirit of both Bunny Berigan and Louis Armstrong. The King James edition "Stardust" version is four minutes long, meaning it could have been a twelve-inch 78 RPM disc, and may be the single best document of the Sinatra-James collaboration.

Though they were making progress musically, not much was happening for the band at the box office. After leaving the Paramount Theatre in June, it got little attention at the Roseland Ballroom in July. Despite valuable exposure in broadcasts from the Steel Pier in Atlantic City in August and the 1939 World's Fair in late August and early September, this extremely spirited first James band failed to make an impression on the public.

Business was bad in Chicago in late September; and then business was bad in Denver. Chris Griffin (who had played with James in the Goodman trumpet section) heard the band with Sinatra in Chicago during this westward swing and confirmed, "There was nobody there!" The James men were collectively enthusiastic about their upcoming engagement at the Los Angeles Palomar Ballroom, where many other hot bands had made good. Unfortunately, their hopes were burned to the ground along with that ballroom on October 4, when Charlie Barnet's band apparently got too hot.

James considered himself lucky to find a substitute gig at a restaurant called the Victor Hugo in Beverly Hills, but he got an early indication of what a disaster that would be when the band's salaries were immediately attached. James's faith in Sinatra was such that when he realized he couldn't afford both of his singers, he let his female singer (Connie Haines) go, and this in an age when bandleaders considered canaries a necessity and crooners could be easily replaced by some guy from the sections, the way Bob Chester did it. Sinatra later said, modestly, that the starving sidemen valued and depended on his wife's cooking as much as they did his singing.

The band was so demoralized at the Victor Hugo that when a drunk shoved Sinatra's mic into his face, apparently for a cheap laugh, "Sinatra took it without comment," according to a *Time* reporter. Sinatra was already developing other aspects of his personality by this time: as he reflected in his scripted commentary to the 1965 *A Man and His Music* album, "I was young and full of zip, zap, and zing, and I was also full of myself." "I thought he was a good singer," said Billy May, who first met Sinatra around this time (while he himself played in Charlie Barnet's great band). "But the musicians in Harry's band, and later in Tommy's band, had the opinion that he was a smart-ass Italian kid. He kind of bugged all the guys in the band [at first]. But he soon learned how to get along with them." However, other observers closer to the source feel differently. "Offstage, Frank was a very quiet kid, not at all a braggart," clarinetist Drew Page later put it. "I never noticed any cockiness in his attitude. Mostly a loner on the bus, he dozed, read magazines, and seldom said anything. But he readily responded to humor—he was easy to break up, especially on stage."

Heading back east again, while playing Chicago's Hotel Sherman, the James band shared a benefit for the musicians' union with Tommy Dorsey and other, more established bands; it was there that Dorsey, in search of a replacement for the recently departed Jack Leonard, hired Sinatra away from James. The singer and the trumpeter, several months his junior, were more like brothers than leader and sideman; besides, Sinatra had faith in James and his band, and felt like a rat deserting a sinking ship. In a much-quoted line, the singer said he would have been happier opening a vein. Still, he knew he was making the right move for his career and his forthcoming family; "Big Nancy," as she would be known for the rest of her life (and she was around to enjoy the Sinatra Centennial in 2015) was due to give birth to Little Nancy in June 1940. As James later told radio interviewer Fred Hall, "Nancy was pregnant, and we weren't even making enough money to pay Frank the seventy-five dollars he was supposed to get. So he went with Tommy Dorsey, and I said, 'Well, if we don't do any better in the next six months or so, try to get me on, too.'"

As a barometer of their individual fortunes, the team's most memorable collaboration, "All or Nothing at All," in its original release sold a mediocre eight thousand or so copies over many months of gathering dust in stores (at the time, ten thousand was acceptable and fifteen thousand was news). At the Victor Hugo, when Sinatra was halfway through the number, the manager decided it was going to be nothing at all and sacked the entire band on the spot. But four years later, when both James and Sinatra were considerably hotter, publisher Lou Levy persuaded Columbia to rerelease "All or Nothing at All" as a means of sidestepping the musician's union's ban on recordings. They moved a million pieces in no time. Because of its vocal-dominated structure, younger fans never even questioned that the disc was anything but an all-star pairing of a great band with the number-one singer in the country (Sinatra's tenure with James being generally forgotten even by Sinatra fan club members by that time).

Sinatra later summarized his time with James as "a wonderful six-month experience," describing his former boss as "a real nice guy with real know-how as a musician." Louise Tobin elaborated, "Sinatra learned a lot from Harry. He learned a lot about conducting and a lot about phrasing. And I know they had a lot of mutual admiration for each other. Harry always knew he was going to be a star because of his great ability. There was never any question about that in his mind. And that's also true about Frank. I remember Frank as a very young boy always exuded that confidence. He didn't have to say, 'I'm a great singer,' but you just knew he was. And I think Frank's little comments along the way were helpful to Harry. They had a good relationship until Harry died."

The Sinatra-James story has had a particularly happy afterlife. The two made a wartime propaganda movie short in 1945 (*All-Star Bond Rally*) and occasionally played concerts together over the years, including a show at Caesars Palace in Las Vegas in November 1968, and another in 1979. In 1976, Sinatra and James both guested with Count Basie on a television special hosted by John Denver—okay, so Denver wasn't the jazziest pop star of the era—but that show contains a brilliant, fiery reprise of the 1939 classic "All or Nothing at All."

But their most remarkable reunion occurred in 1951. They were both still under contract to Columbia, and Mitch Miller reteamed them for three sides. (Although Miller never took credit for the idea, the juxtaposition of this combination with these songs could have come from no one else.) Ray Conniff, a former swing band trombonist and later a middle-of-the-road superstar on Columbia, arranged and conducted on all three pieces in his role as James's main writer. The previous year Sinatra had recorded his first LP, *Sing and Dance with Frank Sinatra*, using a process known then as "tracking" and today as overdubbing. Perhaps because of a scheduling conflict, the 1951 Sinatra-James session, Conniff told me, was done in the same fashion. The tracking process isn't the only factor that links these cuts to the *Sing and Dance* sessions of the previous year; Sinatra's rhythmic energy also made these three cuts worthy follow-ups to that extraordinary LP. James is also a veritable dynamo here, giving out gloriously as if to show Sinatra what he had been missing the previous twelve years.

Sinatra's former boss was having problems with his own current one. "Mitch wanted me to do some real corny things—gimmicks and all of this stuff—and I refused to do them," James told deejay Fred Hall, "so I left the company. It was that simple." James added that he considered the "Castle Rock" track from that session with Sinatra "the worst thing that either one of us ever recorded. You ask Sinatra, and he'll tell you the same thing." James is exaggerating; the song, an R&B hit for Johnny Hodges (with a melody by James and Ellington associate Al Sears) is hardly "All or Nothing at All," nor is it "It Was a Very Good Year" (even though its words were by the self-same Ervin Drake who would go on to pen that 1965 Sinatra classic). Still, there's an undeniable energy to the disc; if James actually hates the song, you couldn't prove it by his playing here. Sinatra, in particular, absolutely nails down the mood of this superfast dance extravaganza. At the conclusion of his first vocal, Sinatra exhorts his former boss, "Go get 'em, Harry—for old times' sake!"

James plays a seductive, muted solo on "Deep Night" (co-credited to Rudy Vallée), making it the closest thing to a romantic number here. Elsewhere in the piece, James blasts wide open with a sixteen-bar statement that climaxes in a crescendo that sounds like five gloriously schmaltzy Harry Jameses exploding at once. "Farewell, Farewell to Love" was arranged by either George Siravo or Conniff, but in any case, was based closely on a Siravo instrumental titled "Barbecue Riffs"; here, the old torch becomes a bonfire.

I was fortunate enough to see Harry James once, about 1981, at the Bottom Line, which was essentially an upscale folk-rock club on the periphery of New York University, which I was then attending. I vividly remember two things: that he was playing far better than was expected of a sixty-five-year-old trumpeter at that time (in fact, he sounded better than either Dizzy Gillespie or Roy Eldridge, whom I had heard recently), both his power and his finesse were overwhelming. And second, that this was the closest I would ever come to hearing Louis Armstrong in person. At that time I also thought that he was the greatest trumpet player I'd ever heard; I still think that.

Harry James kept playing through changing times and changing tastes, and didn't live long enough to see his playing deteriorate. He was diagnosed with lymphatic cancer in April 1983, but kept playing for another two months, until his final gig, on June 26. He died only a week after that, on July 5, 1983; Frank Sinatra gave the eulogy at his funeral. There was one aspect of James that imprinted itself on Sinatra, and that was the notion that the proper balance of testosterone, technique, sheer musical muscle, and masculine energy could empower a performer to be as romantic and even sentimental as he wished. Case in point: Sinatra told the mourners on July 8 that when James knew he was dying, he said goodbye to his five children by telling them, "May it be simply said of me, 'He's gone on the road to do one-nighters with Gabriel.'"

# 3

# WITH TOMMY DORSEY

*1940–1942*

*Have we not all about us forms of a musical expression which we can take and purify and raise to the level of great art?*
—RALPH VAUGHAN WILLIAMS

In 1951, Frank Sinatra—then thirty-five—could sing "Hello, Young Lovers" and mean it. The *King and I* ballad is about offering one's own experiences as example to budding romances. Later in the 1950s, Sinatra would expand on that idea as the connecting peg for his pivotal "concept" albums *Songs for Young Lovers* and *Songs for Swingin' Lovers!* As we've seen, he would always show by example, and never offer anything that could be regarded as "advice." In 1940, however, Sinatra was too much the naive young lover himself to be able to do that. The sound of Sinatra in his three years with Tommy Dorsey is that of a sage-to-be experiencing the thrills of first romance. He cannot yet step back and observe the action from a broader perspective; the Sinatra of the Dorsey years is a virginal Sinatra, if such a thing is imaginable.

The only way that Sinatra could process the wide range of songs that were thrown at him in the Dorsey years—the last period when he would have relative control or choice over what he sang—was to take them at face value. It was too early in the game for Sinatra to be able to take a song and look for the deeper meaning therein, the way he did with virtually everything he sang from the mid-1940s on. This Sinatra may not yet be able to extract all the wry ironies from "How About You"; and, similarly, in Jimmy Van Heusen's "Looking for Yesterday," he leaves us unconvinced that he has all that many yesterdays to look for. However, the Sinatra of the Capitol era, for instance, never could have put over such delightfully naive texts as "Pale Moon (An Indian Love Song)" or "Our Love Affair" so earnestly and effectively.

The Sinatra of 1940 to 1942 is a completely different animal from the Sinatra who went on to conquer the world several times over (and even, as we shall see, very different from the Sinatra of 1939), but he's no less worth listening to. Though he quickly became the Dorsey band's biggest drawing card, he was still, after all, only one of many cards in the deck, attractions that the leader presented in an evening's worth of dancing and entertainment.

Sammy Cahn, who was already one of Sinatra's closest personal and professional associates, vividly remembered the Dorsey "stage shows" (as they were called) at the Paramount Theatre. It would start with the band rising up out of the pit on a moving platform, "and Dorsey would be playing his theme song, 'Getting Sentimental over You.' When the pit went up, he went into 'Marie,' and he would stop the show with that. Then he would introduce Connie Haines. Big hit. Then he would introduce Jo Stafford with the Pied Pipers. Big hit. Then he'd introduce Ziggy Elman on the trumpet. Big hit. Then he would introduce Buddy Rich, who would really shatter the theater.

"When all this was finished, out came a thin, frail human being. And I mean the word *thin* in its purest sense, thinner than my pinky. He sang, I'll never forget it, 'South of the Border.' And he just topped the whole show." Within a few years, Sinatra would be filling all these functions by himself—singing love songs, up-tempos, novelties, and theater-shatterers—but for now his goal was to master the craft of ballad singing, to just be one part of a show, rather than to be a whole show by himself.

The final document of the Dorsey-Sinatra relationship is "The Song Is You" (a major mantra of Sinatra's career), performed live on the radio as part of Sinatra's farewell appearance with the band on September 3, 1942. The Jerome Kern love song had marked the most striking performance of Sinatra's first session under his own billing (and without Dorsey), done on January 14 of that year. Eight months later he reprised it on the air with the Dorsey orchestra itself for his final broadcast with the band.

The amazing growth between the two versions, the confidence and cool assurance of the September version as measured against the tenuousness of the January reading, is impossible to miss. It could serve as a microcosm of Sinatra's remarkable artistic development during his three years with Dorsey. And much of that, all evidence indicates, was directly attributable to the fortitude and personality of Tommy Dorsey, as both a man and a musician, as well as to the young Sinatra's ability to take full advantage of one of the most remarkable opportunities for artistic growth ever afforded a popular performer.

Ten years older than Sinatra, Tommy Dorsey (who at thirty-five was known to his employees as "The Old Man") provided Sinatra with a role model, in both a musical and a personal sense. In spite of a fiery temperament and a fondness for alcohol, Dorsey inspired awe throughout the industry for his incredible personal and professional discipline. Internally, Dorsey was strong enough not only to suppress any urges that might come between himself and the advancement of his fortunes, but, more important, to ignore any obstacle that might get in the way of his making the best music possible. As those who have been close to both men testify, all these characteristics would eventually also become part of Sinatra's own personality. "Frank is like Tommy," drummer Alvin Stoller told us, "very demanding."

On any Tommy Dorsey record, including the eighty-three with vocals by Frank Sinatra (a series bookended by two of its least spectacular titles, "The Sky Fell Down" and "Light a Candle in the Chapel"), inevitably the first noise that catches one's ear is the sound of the leader himself; the first thing you always heard was the trombone. The way Dorsey played the "sliphorn" (as hepcats called it) and the way his arrangers molded the band's music around it had far more to do with the fashion and form of popular singing than anything the jazz tradition would lead you to expect. Dorsey's trombone always occupied the center of attention. It didn't matter whether the number was a business-as-usual dance arrangement of a current ballad, a hot jazz up-tempo instrumental (then known as a "flagwaver"), or one of the band's movie-style production numbers—three-ring circuses (like "Let's Get Away from It All") that involved several spotlighted singers, a vocal group, and any number of instrumental soloists. Dorsey's mesmerizing horn pulled at you, pleaded with you, entranced and entreated you into listening to the story it told. Dorsey stands as one of the greatest virtuoso players of all time. Not exclusively a jazzman in his own playing—although his band recorded acres of the finest big-band jazz numbers ever conceived—in the nearly forty years since his death, Dorsey continues to reign as one of the supreme instrumentalists in all of vernacular American music.

In Dorsey's day, big-band swing was so intrinsically close to pure jazz that the major jazz and pop instrumentalists barely bothered to keep a scorecard of which was which. The public couldn't necessarily distinguish between Dorsey or Charlie Barnet, both of whom could swing but didn't necessarily improvise, and Benny Goodman or Harry James, who did both. The difference was strictly academic. Dorsey's own enjoyment of jazz, like Sinatra's, was surpassed by no one's, but improvisation was probably the least of his abilities as a player. He consistently denigrated his own soloing abilities in deference to his contemporary Jack Teagarden (and even, as he told friend Walter Scott, to Les Jenkins and other trombonists in his own band).

Dorsey can best be appreciated as one appreciates a singer: he leaves the substance of the original melodies intact but remolds it to his own image.

He doesn't dramatically reshape a tune the way an all-out jazzman like Dexter Gordon would—as if he were spontaneously composing the melody (although based on predetermined chord changes). Instead, the tune is a friend of his that he wants you to meet, and to make a good impression he's dressed it up in one of his good suits. In the words of ex-sideman Buddy Rich (who couldn't stand Dorsey personally), "He was the greatest melodic trombone player that ever lived. Absolutely." Since Dorsey essentially sang with his trombone, it's easy to see how someone who sang with his own vocal instrument would have much to learn from him.

Dorsey's legato style, which empowered him to play beautiful melodies in remarkably long phrases, had long-term ramifications on music, even on some of what was not yet known as "modern jazz." Dorsey was one of the first to think in terms of melodic lines longer than what human breath could traditionally support, like Charlie Parker and Bud Powell after him. (Which is ironic when you consider Dorsey's opinion of that music: "Bopsters! They're musical communists!") Dorsey's success encouraged singers and musicians to employ longer and smoother phrases and, eventually, slower and more romantic tempos.

Dorsey's tone is no less remarkable. In the words of contemporary jazz trombonist Steve Turre, "Just beautiful!" Like any of the great musicians, from Louis Armstrong to Sonny Rollins, Dorsey could alter his tone to stomp on one solo and moan on the next, and still no one would ever confuse him with anyone else. That tone could be supersmooth on the ballads, then increasingly buzzier as the tempo picked up, and then downright smeary on a hot number like "Well, All Right." Though "the sentimental gentleman of swing"—as he was billed—was best known for his ballads, his up-tempo playing was no less brilliant.

Dorsey was too often unfairly compared to Teagarden, most of all by himself, and to the major improvising swing trombonists who had worked with Count Basie, such as Dicky Wells, Benny Morton, and Vic Dickenson. But he was an ensemble player as much as a soloist; Dorsey would gladly sacrifice his spotlight or his ego for the greater glorification of the tune or orchestration. On exotic works like "Dawn on the Desert" or the more famous "Song of India," Dorsey proved himself capable of competing with Duke Ellington's entire trombone team. All three major members of that greatest unit—Lawrence Brown, Tricky Sam Nanton, and Juan Tizol (who referred to themselves as "the pep section") idolized TD; Brown often described himself as a "Tommy Dorsey man."

The trombone man may be the best man in the band, but with Dorsey it was as much a matter of concept as technique. In June 1939, several months before Sinatra came on board, Dorsey recorded his most famous solo on trumpet on Irving Berlin's "Back to Back." Dorsey hereby made the point that his development as a melody-oriented trombonist was deliberate and not due to any deficiencies as an improviser since, it turned out, as a trumpeter Dorsey sounded more spontaneous but less distinctive and ultimately, less interesting. (He had doubled on the trumpet at the start of his career and made his first records as a leader playing it.)

At various points in his career, Dorsey's demeanor and deportment received more press attention than his music. When he and his wife bashed a lesser-known film actor with a chair in a barroom brawl, all three of them well under the influence, the event and the trial that followed were covered in far more papers than had ever reviewed Dorsey's records or even reported on the boffo box office his band always did. But in other kinds of fights, as in many kinds of music, Dorsey knew when to play it cool. I'm not enough of an armchair psychologist to offer an analysis of the love-hate relationship between Tommy Dorsey and his brother Jimmy. Let's just say that by the time Jimmy was thirty-one and Tommy a few months away from turning thirty, it had festered to the point where either brother could instantaneously piss off the other one merely by looking at him in the wrong way.

Which was what happened several nights after the Dorsey Brothers Orchestra debuted at the Glen Island Casino in New Rochelle, New York, on May 23, 1935. Tommy was conducting, Jimmy let slip a minor crack about the tempo he had set, and that was it. Without even looking at his brother, Tommy packed up his horn and walked off the stand. (The younger Dorsey had other reasons to be upset for, as guitarist Roc Hillman later told researcher Raymond Hair, the older brother had shown up on the bandstand completely soused.) The gig that was to be the band's big breakthrough turned out to be their big breakup. This would become as much a landmark event heralding the swing era as Benny Goodman's epochal opening at the Los Angeles Palomar three months later.

In the band's early years, between 1935 and 1939, Dorsey consistently had room for improvement in the vocal department. The band's first resident crooner and canary were Jack Leonard and Edythe Wright, neither of whom had much to offer in the way of style. After years of getting Wright as a side you hadn't ordered on her dozens of discs with Dorsey, it's possible, with effort, to gradually warm up to her sound and personality. She was loved by the band's musicians and by TD himself (in both the professional and personal senses), but it's not surprising she had virtually no career after Dorsey.

Leonard, for his part, anticipated Sinatra in two key respects. Even as local girls were beginning to swoon over Sinatra when he sang with the

Hoboken Four in 1935, Leonard's own smooth-styled singing was likewise upsetting delicate distaff nervous systems at Dorsey dances and theater gigs. And that was because, as Leonard himself rightfully claimed long after he had stopped performing, he, and not Sinatra, had been the first vocalist to absorb Dorsey's musical influence. "Tommy didn't tell me to do it," Leonard later said. "It was an automatic thing. Sitting there on the bandstand night after night, you had to be influenced. It rubbed off on you whenever you sang." Yet ultimately Leonard only hinted at the long-breath style that did so much to elevate Sinatra to superstardom.

If the shrill texture of Leonard's piercing pipes didn't turn you right off, his blasé attitude would. "Josephine," Leonard and Dorsey's campy retro hit from 1937, features the singer at his most adenoidal—more like a descendent of Rudy Vallée than a forerunner of Frank—but it's one of the few records where Leonard displays any personality of any kind. The one well-remembered Dorsey-Leonard record, "Marie," succeeds by casting the singer as an oblivious straight man, whose very lack of humor makes the silly antics of the band behind him seem that much funnier. (Sinatra would later turn that formula completely around.) Dorsey and Leonard may have made "Our Love" a hit in 1939, but Sinatra, even on his demo disc of the Tchaikovsky-based piece, puts the number over much more convincingly than his Dorsey precursor, who even had the benefit of an Axel Stordahl arrangement.

Leonard's and Sinatra's emulation of Dorsey was hardly unique at this time. "All the band singers with the bands would listen to these great musicians play all night long, and they were all very affected by jazz musicians," as arranger Quincy Jones remembered the big-band era. "Peggy Lee, Ella Fitzgerald, Sarah Vaughan—they were all very jazz-oriented because they were playing with these great jazz instrumentalists, and the instrumentalists were the focal point. In those years the players were the ones getting all of the attention, so naturally the singers emulated them, and that's why their phrasing is so good and so instrumental-like."

Dorsey's radio producer and confidant Herb Sanford thinks that the first time Dorsey may have heard the name Frank Sinatra occurred when Jack Leonard asked Dorsey if he had heard Harry James playing of "All or Nothing at All." It's unimportant that through the Bob Chester association and a possible earlier audition for TD himself, Dorsey doubtlessly already knew who Sinatra was long before the James-Sinatra discs were circulated.* What's worth noting is Leonard's own first reaction to Sinatra. Leonard was in some

---

* Also, as we know, the James record of "All or Nothing at All" wasn't released until Sinatra had already joined Dorsey.

sense speaking for the entire profession of band singers in 1939. "There's a guy on 'All or Nothing at All' who does the vocal, and he scares the hell out of me," Leonard reportedly told Dorsey. "He's that good."

"The first time I heard him," recalled Dorsey's star clarinetist Johnny Mince, "we were standing in front of a hotel before going in for a one-nighter. Tommy said, 'Come here, Johnny, I want you to hear something.' Sinatra was singing 'All or Nothing at All' with Harry James on the radio, and Tommy asked me, 'What do you think?' I said, 'Boy! He really sings well. He really does.' Even though I used to like Jack Leonard, Frank Sinatra had it all over him."

After officially leaving Harry James at the end of 1939, Sinatra took a few weeks off in late 1939 into early 1940, to spend time with his family, his in-laws, and his pregnant wife. A private recording exists, believed to have been made in this interval, of Sinatra accompanied only by a Hoboken accordionist named Walter Costello, singing the WWI British art song "Roses of Picardy." He would later return to the piece in a more ambitious orchestration on the 1962 album *Great Songs from Great Britain*, but this informal home recording—just voice and accordion—is unsurpassed in its low-key charm.*

Tommy Dorsey had long since realized that Allan DeWitt, his first replacement for Jack Leonard, wasn't going to work out. According to the band's press agent, Jack Egan, Sinatra began traveling with the band and stood by in the wings while DeWitt finished out his two weeks' notice (as per union rules). Dorsey and his crew were then in the middle of a midwestern stretch, and Sinatra might have first sung with the band at the end of a week-long run at the Riverside Theater in Milwaukee (January 25, 1940) or the Coronado Theater in Rockford, Illinois.

So even on the first night he sang with the band, he was already one of the guys, having spent the afternoon playing baseball with them (he later remembered that he couldn't hold the mic that night because his hands were covered with blisters). He immediately impressed Dorsey's other singers, the vocal group the Pied Pipers, who had only joined a month or so earlier. There had also been a rehearsal that day, but the quartet didn't attend since it was only for Sinatra. The Pipers got their first look at Sinatra at the show that evening. Jo Stafford, later a great pop-jazz hitmaker and a longtime Sinatra favorite, remembered distinctly that the first time she saw him, her reaction

---

* The disc, which resides in the Hoboken Historical Museum, has not yet been definitively dated, but in the opinion of Chuck Granata and me, it originates from the brief period between Sinatra's tenures with James and Dorsey. And, like the "Our Love" disc from early 1939, it too has yet to be commercially issued.

was more visual than musical. "I thought, 'Hmmmm . . . kinda thin!'" But her opinion changed after he opened his mouth. "Tommy introduced him as the new boy singer. He walked out and started singing, and it didn't take more than eight or ten bars to know that you were listening to something entirely unique and different. You know, nobody had ever sounded like that before. And it was something very, very good."

On February first in Chicago, Sinatra made his first recordings with the band, and from February second to the ninth, he played his first full run with them at the Lyric Theater in Indianapolis. Were the other Dorseyites worried that the newcomer wouldn't be able to fill Leonard's shoes? Deane Kincaide, who was then the band's premier jazz arranger, before he left a week or so later and that position went to Sy Oliver, said that from the very beginning, Sinatra "was far and away the top guy as far as that's concerned."

He made an even bigger impression on the general public. As Jack Egan later told big-band chronicler George Simon, "So when Frank made his first appearance with the band he only had two songs. First he did a ballad, it might have been 'My Prayer.' Then he did 'Marie,' which was still our big number. Well, he broke it up completely. And that was tough to do, because a lot of the kids were big Jack Leonard fans. They kept yelling for more, but Frank had no encore prepared. So right onstage he and Tommy went into a huddle and Frank suggested they fake 'South of the Border.' Well that broke it up even more, especially when Frank started slurring those notes. You know, right then and there, when he went into the slurring bit the kids started screaming, just the way they did later at the Paramount."

In mid-February, the band was set to play a prom at the University of Virginia in Charlottesville. Apparently, it was a multinight affair; Dean Hudson and His Orchestra were booked for February 15, and Dorsey on the 16th and 17th. Mahlon Clark, then a high school music student in Portsmouth (who would later become the star clarinetist of the Sinatra–Nelson Riddle sessions) attended the first night; he later remembered very vividly that Sinatra had arrived a day early and informally did a few numbers that night with the Hudson band. "Dean got up and made an announcement that we had in the audience the new singer with the Tommy Dorsey band, and it was Frank. He came up and sang 'South of the Border.' I remember it very well because it knocked us all out. We thought, 'Who is this?' It sounded beautiful."*

---

* Multiple observers remembered Sinatra doing "South of the Border" as his big number during the first few months with Tommy Dorsey—over a dozen years before the famous Capitol single; alas, no recordings or airchecks of that number are known to exist.

The next stops on the tour brought Sinatra back home; on February 20, they began three weeks at Frank Dailey's Meadowbrook, where Sinatra made his first batch of live remote broadcasts with the band. They would also do a steady series of commercial recording sessions for RCA Victor that spring, starting on March 12 (these would climax in the biggest of all FS-TD hits, "I'll Never Smile Again," in May). On that same evening they opened at the New York Paramount Theatre—this was ground zero for the big-band business, and the kind of big-time engagement that the young Sinatra had been dreaming about for a decade by that point. The "bobby-soxers," as they would later be called, were already out there screaming in full force. "And there was nothing rigged about it either," said Jack Egan. "I know, because I was the band's press agent. And I was also Jack Leonard's close friend, and I wasn't inclined to go all out for any other singer. No, those screams were for real!"

Two other impartial observers were Pee Wee Erwin, a jazz trumpeter who had worked for many years with Dorsey, and pianist Joel Herron, who would later compose "I'm a Fool to Want You," both of whom were then playing in Johnny Green's radio orchestra. Herron told this story: "One day Pee Wee asked me, 'Do you wanna go to the Paramount?' I asked what for, and he said, 'Jack Leonard's outside. He's in his soldier's suit. He's been hauled into the army, and he wants to go over and hear the new kid with Dorsey.'" (Leonard was, at the time, also singing on a CBS radio program called *Concert in Rhythm*, from January to April 1940.)

"We went backstage at the Paramount where they knew Pee Wee and Leonard, and we sat down in front with [me in the middle]. We went there essentially to see this kid get killed. The band came on and did 'Sentimental over You,' the theme, and Dorsey came forward and said, 'Without any further ado we'd like to introduce our new boy singer, Frank Sinatra, singing our hit record 'Who,' which Leonard had recorded [in 1937]. When this new kid came running out, we all were sure that he was gonna fall on his ass. But when he started to sing, I sunk down in my seat. I felt humiliated for the guy who was sitting next to me [Leonard], who had just become the oldest kind of news that there was in the world."

Inspired by this initial success, Sinatra later said, "I began to work harder than ever. The audience reaction meant they liked me. I didn't know what was causing the reaction exactly. I was experimenting with singing and different forms of phrasing and picking songs better." The first ambition, however, was to bring the Sinatra-Dorsey partnership up to the level of the best of the Sinatra-James sides—the live version of "All or Nothing at All" (from the 1939 World's Fair) was a hard one to beat, as was the "Stardust" from Roseland in July.

Some of the first extant Dorsey-Sinatra broadcasts are notable mainly because Sinatra does not steal the show from the rest of the band. The earliest documented shows originate from the Meadowbrook on February 21 and 24. Here, the first "voice" we notice is the trombone man himself, on nearly every song; Babe Russin also attracts attention with his lengthy clarinet solo on "So What!" (no connection with the Miles Davis number). To a certain extent, the James team had an outsider's advantage (as Malcolm Gladwell would say) in that they were starting from zero, which gave them more freedom—albeit more of a challenge—to create something new, rather than trying to fit Sinatra into an existing template, as the Dorsey team was now trying to do.

What did Sinatra hear in Dorsey? If Harry James instilled in Sinatra a greater feeling for jazz, Dorsey imparted to the young singer something even more meaningful than his own prodigious technique. This was the notion of personalizing an existing song, changing it into something unique to the performer, but without altering so that the listening crowds could still always recognize it.

Dorsey billed himself as "The Sentimental Gentleman of Swing," taking the name from Mitchell Parish's 1932 song, "That Sentimental Gentleman from Georgia." His radio theme song was "I'm Getting Sentimental Over You" (which peeved Parish; it amounted to Dorsey using his phrase but without using his song). Still, Dorsey was probably the least sentimental of all bandleaders. There's nothing the least bit maudlin or mawkishly cloying in any of Dorsey's hundreds upon hundreds of records. The trombonist specialized in what are better classified as intimate and eternally danceable ballads. The vast majority of swing-band leaders, like Bob Crosby, who played as hot as they could get away with and indulged in the love songs only begrudgingly, were far more prone to excess sentiment than Dorsey. With his trombone and his band, Dorsey illustrated to Sinatra that if you get into a tune so that you really feel it when you tell its story to an audience, you needn't get sentimental over it. As Sinatra sings in "This Is the Beginning of the End," all you need to do is read the writing in your heart.

Within a few months, it was clear that Sinatra was learning his lessons well from Dorsey. From the beginning, Sinatra was obsessed with the idea of increasing his ability to communicate the lyrics of a song to an audience; to be more effective dramatically, he sought to make his singing sound less artificial and more natural—more conversational. The key, Sinatra realized, was in what he came to refer to as "phrasing." Musicians and singers had used the term before, of course, but Sinatra meant something very special by the expression. "Phrasing" referred to the way he started with a song's lyric and broke it up into shorter individual phrases, it was essentially a combination of breathing and rhythm, with the goal always being to make the narrative more believable.

The first specific cue that the young man picked up from the Old Man involved extending individual phrases so that an entire lyric idea—which he estimated to average at about eight bars—could be sung in a single breath. In other words, to breathe where it made sense logically in the story, rather than being forced to breathe in an awkward place just because he had run out of wind. "You see, any brass instrument player has the same breathing and lung-power problem as a vocalist," Sinatra told Sidney Zion. "They have it a little easier because they blow through a small aperture, and they can cover their mouth with their hands, while a singer couldn't possibly sing like that all the time. You have to get up and sing but still have enough wind down here to make your phrases much more understandable and elongated so that the entire thought of the song is there."

"Dorsey was my teacher, and he was Frank Sinatra's teacher, too. He taught me how to phrase," remembers Arthur "Skeets" Herfurt. "Frank mentions the same thing—that Tommy is the one who taught him to phrase. Tommy sometimes used to make the whole orchestra (not just the trombones) play from the top of a page clear down to the bottom without taking a breath. It was way too many bars! But I sure developed lung power, which I still have at the age of eighty. Everybody in the band would learn to play like Tommy did."

Dorsey-style phrasing seems to have been exactly what popular music needed in the early 1940s. Remember that the mainstream of pop singing had received little fresh input since Bing Crosby and Louis Armstrong a decade earlier: Ella Fitzgerald was years away from her prime, and Billie Holiday was still largely an esoteric influence. The male singers in the big bands had assumed Crosby's rich baritone register (Ray Eberle and Leonard are exceptions) but by and large continued to put a song over in a stiff, unreal way. Crosby's jazz influences were beyond them, and Armstrong was not taken nearly as seriously as a vocalist as he would be in the 1950s, his greatest era of pop success.

Sinatra experimented to discover how technique and interpretation could work together to reach a higher level of artistic credibility. The belter-crooners would blast through a song, taking a breath, gasping right in the middle of a line, shattering both the rhythmic momentum and the mood. By extending the line, Sinatra could put over both the lyrical idea and the melody that much more convincingly. To do so meant developing the chops to hit high notes without blinking—even a toughie like the one that comes out of nowhere at the end of "I'll Be Seeing You" (1940). But more important than hitting them, Sinatra managed to hold them, developing both the physical lung power and the dramatic ability to set up a line of lyrics so that it made sense.

"So I began using the pool at Stevens Institute of Technology whenever I had a chance, and I would swim underwater," Sinatra continued to Sidney Zion. "The guys there would say to me, 'Don't you ever swim on top of the water?' I said, 'No. There's a reason for it. I don't want to explain it.' But it did help me develop. I was very small. I weighed about 130 pounds, and I just had to grow a little more. I did lots of exercises. I did running and that kind of stuff." The reference to the Stevens pool indicates that Sinatra was building up his breath control when he still lived in Hoboken, well before joining James or Dorsey.

"And then when I joined Tommy's band, and even prior to that, I wondered what it was that enabled him to execute sixteen measures of a song. If you count fairly slowly and you count four to a bar, that's a long time. It took me a year and a half to figure out that he was breathing in the corner of his mouth because, the fink, he had his mouth covered, you see, and I couldn't see him doing that most of the time." As Sinatra told Bill Boggs in 1975, "I used to watch his back, his jacket, and I would never see the jacket move, I would think, 'He's got to be breathing someplace!' I used to kind of lean around to see if I could see. But you see in holding the instrument, he covered his mouth, and then cover the rest of his face with his hand and his slide, and on this particular night, he put the horn down, and he walked over to me and he said, haven't you seen it yet? He knew that I had been watching him for about a year, trying to figure it out." Sinatra continued to Zion, "But he could [extend a phrase] for eight measures or maybe ten full measures without breathing, actually without breathing. And I watched him for two years, and I realized that I was learning a great deal, I was growing again."

Dorsey himself was once asked, in the early 1950s (by record producer Arthur Shimkin), "Is it true that Sinatra learned how to breathe from you?" The trombonist answered in his usual sensitive diplomatic fashion, "It's a load of crap!" Dorsey meant that Sinatra was already breathing in this fashion— that was probably one of the main features that attracted Dorsey to Sinatra to begin with. For years before the two men even met, Dorsey had long been one of Sinatra's key musical inspirations; as we saw in Sinatra's July 1939 radio performance of "Stardust" with Harry James, his phrasing was already amazingly Dorseylike.

Dorsey's desire for perfection affected not only Sinatra but the entire band. Dorsey pushed everybody "all the way" to the limit, as Alvin Stoller (who replaced Buddy Rich) recalls. "He was a very demanding man. It wasn't a matter of *can* you do it, or *should* you try it, it was just *do* it! I learned a lot just by following him and watching how he worked. When I got in the band, Tommy wanted this and he wanted that. Eventually you find yourself capable of doing things that you didn't know you could do. If you don't try, you won't make it—talking about it isn't going to make it happen. Tommy would just force you to do it. It hardened me as far as playing is concerned, it gave me an assurance that I didn't know I had."

As Sinatra elaborated for Arlene Francis, "I began listening to musicians, both jazz and classical musicians; for instance, I was fascinated by Jascha Heifetz, who could make a change of his bow in a phrase and get to the end of the bow and continue without a perceptible missing beat in the motion. I thought if that could be done on an instrument—and the violin and the flute are two good examples—why not do it with the human voice? It was very tough to do it. It took a lot of calisthenics and physical work to get the bellows—the breathing apparatus—built up."

If "The Sky Fell Down," the first Dorsey-Sinatra item, and "Moments in the Moonlight" are on the choppy side, "Say It" shows Sinatra beginning to connect notes into long, virtually seamless breaths. Here he also achieves a singular unity with Dorsey's trombone, Dorsey, in this case and others, further accommodating the new singer by muting his bell to produce a sound even closer to a human voice than usual. "The Call of the Canyon," composed by Billy Hill (who brought a pronounced hillbilly feel to Tin Pan Alley in songs like "The Last Roundup" and "The Glory of Love"), sets the long-breath lines of both Dorsey and Sinatra against a contrasting background in which out-of-tempo brass play a countermelody depicting the clip-clop of a canyon pack mule in the fashion of Ferde Grofe's *Grand Canyon Suite* all supported by a waddling arco bass fiddle.

"This Is the Beginning of the End," "Where Do You Keep Your Heart?," and "The World Is in My Arms"(from Al Jolson's comeback show, *Hold On to Your Hats*) find Sinatra extending phrases over a shuffle rhythm in three charts wherein Sy Oliver (or possibly Jimmy Mundy) revives the two-beat rhythm that he perfected for Jimmie Lunceford's orchestra a few years earlier. These are graceful dances, not hell-for-leather flag-wavers; you can easily imagine Ray Bolger or John Bubbles doing a soft shoe or sand dance. Buddy Rich's drumming is perfect here, more like his understated predecessor Dave Tough than the relentless rhythmic juggernaut he became known as years later.

In later years, when Sinatra mostly recorded standard songs, the singer enjoyed the advantage of having lived with much of his repertoire for decades before committing it to shellac. During the Dorsey days, Sinatra's longtime personal manager Hank Sanicola, who doubled as capable if unspectacular pianist, would run over tunes with the singer before a date. In later years that role was largely assumed by composer Jimmy Van Heusen, probably Sinatra's closest friend, and occasionally by his more accomplished regular accompanist, Bill Miller. If Sinatra was prepared, the band usually wasn't—which wasn't necessarily a bad thing. "Whenever we went to a recording studio, we'd almost always get new arrangements that we had never played before," explained pianist Joe Bushkin, "so the guys would get really on top of it. We would put more energy into getting it to sound tight. Tommy didn't do it purposely, but that's what made the hit records. The listeners could pick up on the enthusiasm of the band. We never got anywhere with the goddamn stuff that we were already familiar with. It just so happened that whatever we played on the road had already been recorded. Then we could play our record numbers on the job. Which made sense because if you're traveling three hundred miles a night and just barely making the gig, you sure can't call a rehearsal."

Another point that Dorsey demonstrated to Sinatra was that the improvisatory skills of the more jazz-oriented players could be especially useful in such situations. "Tommy might give a little heat to any lead player who was strictly a technical player," added Bushkin. "But he never bothered any of the guys who could improvise, like [trumpeter] Bunny Berigan or [saxophonist] Don Lodice."

"Tommy became almost a father to me," Sinatra often said, and he selected TD as the godfather of his first child, Nancy Sandra Sinatra (born on June 8, 1940). Many of Sinatra's friends claimed that the iron-fisted Mr. Dorsey supplied a stronger paternal image than the singer's own father, the very passive Marty Sinatra. As with any familial relationship, the course was not always smooth. During the entire first year of their relationship, Dorsey held Bob Allen, a talented crooner then working with Hal Kemp's orchestra, over Sinatra's head; when Sinatra would act up, Dorsey would threaten to call Allen. Once Sinatra walked into the band's dressing room (as Allen later told researcher Bob Conrad) and discovered the other singer's tuxedo draped over the chair. After another session of pleading and shouting with Dorsey, Sinatra went on that night. (Years later, Allen and his wife bumped into Sinatra in a bar. Obviously pie-eyed, he growled to Allen, "So you're the fucker who thought he could replace me!" Eventually Allen did tour as Dorsey's star vocalist, in 1944–45.) On another occasion, Connie Haines recalled, Dorsey canned Sinatra and replaced him with Milburn Stone (later of *Gunsmoke* fame) until Young Blue Eyes came crawling back to him.

Listening only to the Dorsey-Sinatra numbers, especially the earlier 1940 titles, does the band a disservice. You have to hear the band's entire output, the instrumentals, and the other vocalists, the radio show banter and "Memory Medley" numbers, to appreciate the full range and versatility of the Dorsey orchestra. Apart from the sentimentalist sessions, which we'll come to shortly, Sinatra was initially assigned only the basic bread-and-butter fox-trots, the new product being turned out steadily by Hollywood, Broadway, and Tin Pan Alley. And listening only to these tends to paint an unbalanced picture of this band whose leader was dedicated, he declared in radio announcements, "to the proposition that every tune deserves its own style." "No two arrangements are alike. Each one is tailored to fit the mood of the tune," Dorsey said, tying the individual numbers together only with the sound of his own trombone and his standards of excellence.

More than half of the Dorsey-Sinatra recordings use the same format: three choruses in a medium-slow fox-trot tempo. First there's an introductory chorus, usually by Dorsey himself and the ensemble, introducing the melody; then a full vocal by Sinatra; then a jazzier, and often slightly louder, third chorus to make things interesting for the dancers—this is often called the "shout" chorus. Dorsey always dominates the first chorus, although he rarely plays all thirty-two bars of it strictly by himself. Occasionally he divides the responsibility, in search of a little variety, by having something else happen in the bridge, another horn soloist, or the whole ensemble. Then too, in many cases, Dorsey will keep playing up through the bridge, and let something different happen in the last eight bars; this then serves as a transitional passage wherein the main melody gets restated immediately prior to the entrance of the vocalist (frequently with a key change). Thus, on virtually every record, Dorsey claims the first sixteen (or twenty-four) bars, the AA (or AAB) of the first chorus, for himself, making sure the trombone playing the major strain of the melody is the first thing that hits you—which partially explains why it was so crucial that Dorsey play sixteen bars without stopping for a breath.

The shout chorus often includes brief solo statements from various horns, Dorsey wisely not saving his hot men exclusively for the more jazz-oriented instrumentals. Clarinetist Johnny Mince supplies greater warmth than the young Sinatra on some of the earlier tunes, especially "I'll Be Seeing You," "Moments in the Moonlight," and "April Played the Fiddle." Bunny Berigan, the major trumpet legend—and epic lush of the 1930s—who reassumed his old chair in the Dorsey aggregate after his own orchestra went belly-up, gets to blast a bit in the third chorus of "I Haven't Time to Be a Millionaire" and elsewhere. Berigan also reassumes his old role in several Sinatra-Dorsey readings of "Marie," a classic solo that sounds even better following Sinatra than it did Leonard, and reprises this role in the many performances of the "Marie" sequel, "East of the Sun (and West of the Moon)." Much later, in several concerts from the 1980s, Sinatra would sing Berigan's theme song, "I Can't Get Started," and he often introduced it as a dedication to his onetime roommate on the Dorsey tours. "He was the greatest trumpet player in the world," Sinatra would announce with complete and total earnestness. "Then, one day, we couldn't find him."

The majority of the Sinatra-Dorsey sides are in the familiar three-chorus dance band template, although the band's arrangers occasionally utilized other formats, such as "concert"-style numbers, more ambitious production-type numbers, and the "Sentimentalist" format. Even from the beginning, as Sinatra was rapidly establishing himself as the band's most popular attraction, Dorsey was already willing to bend the rules in favor of his new star singer. In March 1940, the band recorded "Polka Dots and Moonbeams"; the record consists of a one-chorus trombone solo (here the bridge is played by tenor champ Irving "Babe" Russin), followed by Sinatra's vocal, then coda. (But in a few live airchecks, some of which are as long as four minutes, there is a full third chorus by the band, featuring clarinetist Johnny Mince, that got truncated because of the playing time of a ten-inch 78 in 1940.)

Even by May, it was clear that Sinatra was bringing something special to the band. In the March and April sessions, Sinatra and the band had already recorded a number of their greatest pieces, such as "This Is the Beginning of the End," "The World Is in My Arms," "East of the Sun," and the blockbuster, "I'll Never Smile Again." Dorsey's widely anticipated engagement at the Astor Roof in May was set to be a big deal, marking the band's New York nightclub debut with their new vocalist as well as the grand reopening of a once and future prime after-theater hotspot. On opening night numerous luminaries such as Benny Goodman and Oscar Levant could be spotted in the audience.

Pianist Joe Bushkin, who had joined the band five or six weeks earlier, recalled that Sinatra's first vocal on that premiere night called for him to sing with the Pied Pipers, while his second, "Begin the Beguine," was strictly a solo feature for him. As Bushkin told us in June 1992, "Beguine" (which unfortunately wasn't preserved in either a live or a studio recording) marked the first Dorsey number to feature Sinatra throughout, with just a brief eight-bar instrumental interlude for the band. "He wound it up with a nice big finish," said Bushkin, "and the place went bananas!" The singer had stopped the show, something that rarely happened during a program of dance music. It was a bonus that Dorsey was immediately keen to take advantage of. The crowd wouldn't let Sinatra off without an encore, and Dorsey wanted to oblige. But "Beguine" represented the total of Sinatra features that Dorsey had in his band book.

Dorsey instructed the band to play "Polka Dots and Moonbeams," but because it wasn't a vocal feature, he took the four-bar transitional passage that precedes the vocal and from there went right into Sinatra's "middle" chorus. After "Polka Dots," "the people were still going nuts," Bushkin continued, so rather than force a dance number into a vocal feature, Dorsey told Sinatra, "Just sing whatever you want with Joe." The two began an impromptu voice and piano duo. Bushkin remembered that Sinatra's confidence was unshakable. He simply went on singing to the wild delight of the crowd, now no longer dancing but just standing and listening. The twenty-three-year-old pianist, however, was completely taken aback. "As we were playing, I was trying to figure out his range," said Bushkin. "I was thinking quickly, 'Where is his top note?' If I can get to the top note, the bottom will take care of itself."

Three or four tunes (including "All the Things You Are") later, a much ruffled Bushkin was still trying to follow Sinatra as best he could. "Then he turned around and said, 'Smoke Gets in Your Eyes.' Well, if you know that tune, man, you know that you can really get lost in the middle part [the bridge]. Unless you really know what you're doing, that chord change will just lose you. I'm right out there without bread and water, man! The next thing I know, Frank was out there singing it all by himself. He was singing the bridge, a cappella. I was so embarrassed. I mean, Jesus, all the guys were looking at me, so I just turned around and walked away from the piano! I went to the side and then ran back to the piano and finished up the tune. And that was the last song we did. I thought Tommy was going to kill me, but he thought it was so funny!

"And that," Bushkin concluded, "is the night that Frank Sinatra happened."

Other attendees concurred. When announcer André Baruch and singer Bea Wain—known to history as radio's leading couple—came down to dance to the band, Dorsey asked them what they thought of the new vocalist. Baruch was less than enthusiastic ("It'll never happen!"), but Wain spoke for most of those present when she told TD, "He's wonderful. He's just electric!"

On the aforementioned "Polka Dots," Sinatra's early uneasiness effectively conveys the interior Sturm und Drang of a nervous young wallflower at a prom. The song is already the third (after "Shake Down the Stars" and "Too Romantic") that Dorsey and Sinatra would do by Jimmy Van Heusen, who was soon to become Sinatra's closest drinking companion and running mate. (Van Heusen would write no fewer than nine songs recorded by Dorsey and Sinatra on Victor.) In 1940, Van Heusen and his new partner, the highly-storied lyricist Johnny Burke, were quickly establishing themselves as the premiere songwriting team for Bing Crosby's movies at Paramount Pictures. In fact, Crosby hangs over Sinatra's Dorsey years rather like the ghost of Hamlet's father; Sinatra is simultaneously learning from the great crooner even while he tries to find his own way.

Crosby had been closely associated with both Dorsey Brothers back to their joint tenure in Paul Whiteman's orchestra fifteen years earlier, and he had been the one to inspire Sinatra to take the art of popular singing seriously to begin with, almost ten years earlier. "Crosby's the only one who knows how to have a career," Sinatra told friend (and PR guy) Gary Stewart. In 1940, Crosby was by far Hollywood's greatest musical hitmaker, and since Dorsey was Victor's number-one band, it was inevitable that the Dorsey unit would be expected to deliver dance arrangements of the songs that Crosby was introducing. In the three years of Sinatra's tenure with the band, Victor assigned Dorsey the task of devising dance-band versions of songs from four Crosby movies, and the results of those assignments offer an accurate barometer of Sinatra's progress. On April 10, 1940, Dorsey recorded the two "plug" songs from Crosby's current release, *If I Had My Way*: "April Played the Fiddle" and "I Haven't Time to Be a Millionaire." "Polka Dots," with its references to an Irish-American "pug-nosed dream," was clearly from the wheelhouse of Mr. Crosby and Mr. Burke. But the typical metaphorical conceits and allusions that made Burke and Crosby so perfect for each other are lost on Sinatra at this early stage; Sinatra would have looked equally silly in Crosby's hat, pipe, and Hawaiian shirt.

Burke's optimism, ironic but devoid of all sarcasm, was perhaps too specific a target for Sinatra to hit in 1940. (So too was the "pug nose": as was already well known, Sinatra liked all kinds of noses on all kinds of pretty faces.) He got around the problem on Burke's "Too Romantic," from *Road to Singapore*, the first of Crosby and Bob Hope's *Road* movies, but that song portrays an exasperatedly nervous would-be Romeo. Dorsey, who had been a sideman on Crosby sessions in the 1920s and '30s, enthusiastically encouraged Sinatra to study the singer, exhorting Sinatra that there was "only one singer, and his name is Crosby."

The Dorsey period afforded Sinatra ample opportunity to study Crosby: both on screen, when the Dorsey band played the same bill at the New York Paramount with that premier *Road* picture in March 1940; and, unexpectedly, in person when the Dorsey band arrived in Hollywood in November 1940. While Dorsey was making his first feature film appearance in Paramount's *Las Vegas Nights* (Sinatra sings "I'll Never Smile Again" with the Pied Pipers), musical director Victor Young also used some of Dorsey's sidemen, including Joe Bushkin and Buddy Rich, to record some music for the second Hope-Crosby caper, *Road to Zanzibar*.

Sinatra's and Crosby's personal paths crossed again a year later when the band returned to Hollywood, this time to participate in what MGM later released as *Ship Ahoy*. "Frank had never met Bing," recalled trumpeter Yank Lawson, who had recently returned to the Bob Crosby band after a season with Dorsey. "We were doing the music for a picture called *Holiday Inn*"—like *Road to Zanzibar*, this was another Crosby Paramount picture in which the star pressured the studio to use real jazz musicians on the soundtrack—"and he asked me if he could go out and see the filming. He wanted to watch Bing work because Bing was his idol. Crosby was the big star of that time, and Sinatra was still just the singer with the band. Frank met me out at the Paramount lot, and I took him in. He just loved it, watching Bing."

Several months after "Too Romantic," Sinatra pulled off the real thing in Dorsey's January 1941 versions of the songs from *Road to Zanzibar*. That second *Road* show opened with Crosby's rapturous baritone bouncing through one of Burke's all-time greatest moonbeams-and-metaphors opuses, "You Lucky People, You," over the main titles. Dorsey similarly commenced his version of "You Lucky People, You" with Sinatra singing, making it one of the earliest Dorsey sides to start with Sinatra in the first chorus rather than the second, and also giving the singer an extra outchorus at the end. Sinatra more than justified the temporary promotion, coming on with such contagious cockiness and charisma that he vividly brings Burke's wraparound skies and green velvet landscapes to life.

He did just as well with the romantic, yet not too romantic, "It's Always You" (later revived, like many other early Sinatra numbers, by Chet Baker) and made one wish that Dorsey had given the other two *Zanzibar* songs, "Birds of a Feather" and "You're Dangerous," to Sinatra instead of Connie Haines, good as she was in this period. By the time of his next reworking of a Crosby song, Irving Berlin's "Be Careful, It's My Heart" from the final season of his Dorsey tenure, in June 1942, Sinatra hadn't exactly caught up with Crosby, but he had considerably narrowed the gap between them.

Dorsey's two chief arrangers on the Sinatra numbers, Axel Stordahl and Sy Oliver, dispensed with the standard three-chorus format more frequently after "You Lucky People, You." Though the standard dance band formats suited Dorsey most of the time, he still got his biggest personal kicks by experimenting with loose, small-group sounds, as he had with the Dixie-land-styled Clambake Seven from December 1935 to August 1939. By the end of 1939, when Dorsey wanted to branch back into settings smaller than the full orchestra, he again stressed intimate vocals but dispensed with the dogged Dixie two-beat.

Dorsey dubbed this new small group "The Sentimentalists." Their first sessions took place in April and May 1940 and immediately gave Dorsey and Sinatra their biggest hit together, "I'll Never Smile Again," thus ensuring that Dorsey would maintain the Sentimentalist format for the rest of Sinatra's stay with the band and beyond. The Sentimentalists presented more intimate music for listening (or dancing very slowly) in contrast to the standard three-chorus fox-trot. (In the beginning Dorsey also applied the Sentimentalist handle to several instrumental jazz numbers recorded by the full orchestra; as with "I'll Never Smile Again," they're also a departure from the standard pop-song/three-chorus format.)

The first two Sinatra Sentimentalist titles, "East of the Sun" and "Head on My Pillow," boast enough jazz solo space to suggest a direct extension of the Clambake Seven series. In format and overall quality, "Pillow" comes very close to the classic Teddy Wilson–Billie Holiday sessions. Trumpeter Bunny Berigan, who played on many Lady Day dates, here underscores that feeling, as does Sinatra himself, fashioning his most relaxed, Holidayesque chorus yet. (*Down Beat* magazine had recently published a photo of the young Sinatra digging Miss Holiday, like everyone else, at Chicago's Off-Beat Club, taken the previous September.)

After the unprecedented success of "I'll Never Smile Again," the Sentimentalist label was reserved for further slow vocals by Sinatra, with the Pied Pipers weaving in and out, and backed by the band's rhythm section with Dorsey himself and one or two other horns. The song had been written in 1939 by Ruth Lowe, a Canadian pianist, in reaction to the tragically young death of her husband. Lowe had played in Ina Ray Hutton's all-female band, and the song had reached Dorsey via the musicians' grapevine. (Later, there would be further connections between the Huttons and the Dorseyites: Ina Ray's sister June would sing with Sinatra on radio and television and eventually marry Axel Stordahl.)

"We were rehearsing on a Saturday afternoon, up at the roof of the Astor Hotel," Sinatra recalled, "and Tommy asked Joe Bushkin to play the song. I noticed that everybody suddenly was very quiet, the whole orchestra sat quietly when he played it. There was a feeling of a kind of eeriness that took place, as though we all knew that this would be a big, big hit, and that it was a lovely song."

Dorsey was impressed enough with the song's effect to commission an arrangement by Stordahl and alto and baritone saxophonist Fred Stulce, and Sinatra took it upon himself to learn it. Stordahl had earlier written some charts that anticipate the Sentimentalist sound for the band's earlier vocal group, The Three Esquires, in which the arranger himself served as one of the singers, including the original hit version of the standard "Once in a While" (a number redone on the radio with Sinatra and the Pipers).

On April 23, 1940, Joe Bushkin remembers, "we were in the studio, and we had already done our sides. We still had about twenty minutes left, so Freddie said, 'Well, I wrote that chart for that gal in Canada, and Tommy said, 'Let's give it a try.' So we do a take, and it was kind of empty. Then, Frank sees a celesta in the studio and has them shove it over by me at the piano. He says, 'Just fill it in.' When they finally orchestrated it, my ad lib became part of the arrangement." Sinatra added, "We made the song with the Pied Pipers and myself, and it was not a very good record. So [a month later, on May 23] we remade it, we did it a second time, still with Tommy. It was strange that it had to be made three times [once by Glenn Miller and twice by Dorsey] before we got it right."

"Smile Again" is heartbreakingly languid, some of the un-fastest popular music ever recorded, tepidly crawling through the super-slow tempos pioneered, again, by Billie Holiday. Sinatra and the Pied Pipers function as equals, neither side of the equation attracting more attention than the others. Sinatra only occasionally arises out of the ensemble to stress key lines in solo, including virtually all of the bridge, almost like the leader of the vocal group rather than a featured star.

No less than Sinatra, the Pipers themselves had collectively absorbed much of Dorsey's legato style, and all five voices harmonize exquisitely with Dorseysque extended notes that amplify the sense of loss in the narrative. Bushkin's celesta provides the only instrumental sound we are conscious of behind the voices, although there's a small and barely noticeable horn ensemble audible here and there. Dorsey himself plays an indescribably mournful eight bars of the main theme before Sinatra and the Pipers cap the piece with a brief outchorus.

Lowe's song became more than a game-changer hit for all concerned: when *Billboard* magazine, already the "Bible" of the music industry, launched the first national hit records chart on July 27, 1940, the first number-one song on the new chart was "I'll Never Smile Again." It remained in the number-one spot until October 12, and therefore can be considered the first blockbuster *Billboard* chart hit. Still, because the number was so unusual, and so difficult to perform, Dorsey rarely featured it in his live broadcasts. "There was practically no band," recalled Jo Stafford. "It was very, very sparse. It was a very tough idea. It was hard to hold the pitch because there was so little background from the band. You really had to mind your p's and q's keeping it in tune."

The big-band era was a period, if not necessarily of formulas, then certainly of successful templates that would be repeated—most famously Tommy

Dorsey's "Marie" cycle, about which more later. It was inevitable that Dorsey would also try to repeat the triumph of "Smile Again." On June 5, the Sentimentalists returned to the studio with "Funny Little Pedro," another, far less successful song by Lowe, with vocal by the Pied Pipers. Then came "Whispering," which reused elements from both "East of the Sun" and "Smile Again": the mix of Sinatra and the Pied Pipers, a slightly more oomphy tempo, a Bunny Berigan trumpet interlude, all applied to a familiar old tune—one that the Dorsey Brothers had played many times with Paul Whiteman and that Sinatra had already sung with TD as part of a radio "Memory Medley." It didn't quite re-create the sensation of "Smile Again," but "Whispering" remains a lovely record; even its title is a mantra for what Sinatra was trying to achieve.

Another standard, "Stardust" returns to the same format as "I'll Never Smile Again": the crawl tempo, the tight harmony vocal, the intimate small group. And very effectively, too, judging by its effect on the band's drummer, Buddy Rich, hardly the band's sensitivity specialist. Rich, who prided himself on being hypermasculine and downright antisentimental, later confided to friend Mel Tormé that Sinatra's rendition of "Stardust" had him hiding his face so that no one would catch a glimpse of his tears. "Do I Worry?" also comes very close tempo-wise, although it's by the full band with Sinatra solo, sans Pipers. A hit for the Ink Spots, "Worry" might have been better off left to them, what with Sinatra trying to suggest one of the Spots' signature musical monologues generally delivered by the talking basso, Hoppy Jones.

More imaginatively, the 1924 "The One I Love Belongs to Somebody Else" and the newer "Dolores" (by Frank Loesser) further desentimentalize the Sinatra–Pied Pipers combination, opening up new possibilities for the five voices in the realm of groovier tempos. "The One I Love" is perhaps the first classic chart arranged for Sinatra by Sy Oliver, a pioneering orchestrator who had already established himself as a master of the large-format jazz ensemble via his breakthrough work with Jimmie Lunceford's orchestra. In particular, Oliver used voices brilliantly by fashioning three or four of the band's more extroverted instrumentalists (including himself) into ad-hoc vocal groups, creating classic charts (like "My Blue Heaven") that would exert a profound influence not only on Sinatra but on both of his two greatest collaborators of his mature years, Nelson Riddle and Billy May. The Oliver-Lunceford tempo is just a philosophical degree of separation away from the "heartbeat" tempo favored by Sinatra on such iconic albums as *Songs for Swingin' Lovers!*

Proving that turnabout is fair play, Sinatra hums behind the Pied Pipers, rather than the other way around (as on "Smile Again"), on the first part of the b sections on "The One I Love." "Dolores," with its super-catchy internal rhyming scheme, is a perfect period piece, which not only reestablishes the Sinatra-Piper hierarchy but boosts his billing, since here, more than previously, he's clearly the star and they're his backup. That role amounts to a show of faith on Dorsey's part since Sinatra had not yet established himself on the more rhythmic numbers. Sinatra proves he's just as adroit at putting over one of these snappy, catchy ones as any love lament, as does Dorsey in a sprightly spot propelled by Buddy Rich's *chinka-chinka* cymbals. Both restore the damage done to the song by baggy-pants comic Bert Wheeler in Paramount's *Las Vegas Nights*, which marked not only Sinatra's first feature film appearance but, surprisingly, also Dorsey's. The record is too short: we could go on listening to Sinatra, the Pipers, and TD serenade "Dolores" chorus after chorus. It gave the Sinatra-Pipers series its sole up-tempo number-one hit. "I Guess I'll Have to Dream the Rest," from June 1941, again follows the same path as "Smile Again," but with the full orchestra and Sinatra securely in the spotlight. The lyric has more of a sense of humor than "Smile Again," and the melody merits a livelier bounce.

What it took to revive the original "Smile Again" sound was strings.* As it happened, Sinatra's first date with strings (since his 1939 demo of "Our Love") turned out to be his own premiere solo session, the Bluebird date of January 1942. In fact, according to a *Down Beat* clipping from early 1942 ("Dorsey Will Sweeten Brass with Fiddles"), the results of the Sinatra-Stordahl session put the idea in Dorsey's mind; and when Artie Shaw broke up his band to join the service, Dorsey seized the opportunity to annex his former rival's entire violin section en masse. The strings support the Sinatra-Pipers combo suitably on their last four outings, "Just as Though You Were Here," "Street of Dreams," "It Started All Over Again," and what was to be both their last number-one hit (as well as Tommy Dorsey's), "There Are Such Things."

The strings, at last, give the Sentimentalists a sound that is inarguably Sentimental; those who know the normally snappy "It Started All Over Again" will be surprised by the stateliness of this ballad reading. Dorsey was taking the fiddles very seriously, even bringing in light-classicist David Rose to score "By the Sleepy Lagoon" and "Melody in A" for the enlarged band. The sound of the strings dominates much more than Dorsey's trombone, heard only in brief instrumental breaks between the vocal choruses. Still, the lightness the strings and voices apply behind Sinatra on "Just as Though You Were Here" is appropriate, considering how that song was to be treated with

---

* Sinatra would later claim that he might never have left James for Dorsey if the latter didn't have a string section. Time plays tricks on memory: Dorsey didn't actually add strings until 1942, two years after Sinatra joined, and James would add strings a whole year earlier than Dorsey, in 1941.

increasing dramatics as the war went on. The strings have the opposite effect on "Street of Dreams," treating the melody grandly, but making the text seem naively light-headed.

In ballrooms (from which the remote broadcasts originated) the band played almost exclusively for dancers, and virtually everything Sinatra did with the Pipers could be danced to. Dorsey and all the major bands worked just as frequently in theaters, however, playing stage shows up to an hour long between movies, where dancing was not encouraged; thus the band was also expected to come up with numbers that were more theatrical in nature, for listening rather than dancing.

To compete for theater gigs, the band had become, like that of Dorsey's rival Glenn Miller and innumerable other bands, a jazz-tinged variety show. In Sinatra's words, "Every band had a million singers back then." In addition, to keep the flow of variety going, the Dorsey entourage occasionally introduced its own "in-house" novelty acts, such as dancing saxist and comic singer Skeets Herfurt.

Sinatra's three central duets with Connie Haines, "Oh! Look at Me Now," "You Might Have Belonged to Another," and "Snooty Little Cutie," which also utilized the Pied Pipers, were doubtlessly crafted with radio and theater audiences in mind. Haines, whose tenures with both James and Dorsey paralleled Sinatra's almost exactly (although she later confessed that the two of them were hardly best buds away from the bandstand), is something of an enigma. Her singing from both before and after her Dorsey period can be so sugary cute it threatens to leave audiences begging for insulin. But apparently the un-Sentimental Gentleman helped Haines restrain her refrains, since her three years with Dorsey resulted in the best work of her long and formidable career, in which she delivered some irresistibly perky and personable band-chirping. She teamed with Sinatra and Pipers for the first time on the ballad "That's How It Goes," performed memorably on the radio but never recorded.

In their very successful duets, Sinatra and Haines come on like spunky siblings rather than singing sweethearts à la Nelson Eddy and Jeanette MacDonald, giving each other as many elbows to the ribs as adoring glances, landing somewhere in the long stretch between Burns and Allen and, in their more overtly comedic moments, Steve Lawrence and Eydie Gormé. Their pinnacle, "Oh! Look at Me Now," has the two of them trading lines for the first chorus, with the Pied Pipers predominating in the second. The less spectacular "You Might Have Belonged to Another" has Sinatra singing the entire first chorus in solo, and Haines and the Pipers getting more to do in the second. Bobby Troup's "Snooty Little Cutie" opens with the Pipers, and in the second chorus the decision goes to Ms. Haines, who comes off like an updated swing-era Betty Boop; here it's Sinatra who sounds slightly uncomfortable. "Snooty" sounds better, however, on an August 1942 aircheck with (in addition to a second half-chorus of Dorsey trombone) Stafford replacing the departed Haines.

Although, as it happened, Dorsey and Sinatra recorded more songs by Jimmy Van Heusen than any other composer (a track record Sinatra would maintain for the rest of his career), the four songs that the singer-bandleader team did by Matt Dennis and Tom Adair, who were hired by Dorsey to write songs for the bandleader's publishing company, are virtually the leitmotifs of The Voice's early career. In fact, Sinatra considered "Violets for Your Furs," "Everything Happens to Me," "Let's Get Away from It All," and "The Night We Called It a Day" such essential career milestones that he remade all four within a few years of signing to Capitol Records in the mid-1950s. Dorsey also recorded four other Dennis-Adair tunes around this time, including "Let's Just Pretend," and a dance arrangement of "The Night We Called It a Day" with Jo Stafford. Sinatra and Dorsey scored their last major hit together with "In the Blue of Evening," Tom Adair's lyric to a theme by New York bandleader Alfred A. D'Artega.

The Dennis and Adair story essentially begins one evening in late 1940 or early 1941 when Dennis, an accomplished (and later widely recorded) pianist and singer, was performing in a Hollywood nightclub. "Tom [Adair] came in one night to hear me play and sing some of my things," Dennis remembered, "and he said to me, 'I'd like to write a song with you.' And I said, 'Let me see what you have.' And the first thing he showed me was the lyric to 'Will You Still Be Mine?' It was a hell of a lyric, you know. That kind of thrilled me, so I wrote the music to that very shortly. And a few days later, working over the phone, we wrote 'Let's Get Away from It All' in one afternoon, and then we did 'Everything Happens to Me' a couple of days after that. All in all, it was a hell of a week."

Jo Stafford remembered what happened next. "I was instrumental in bringing Dennis and Adair into the [Dorsey] organization. I had known Matt since 1936 or 1937. He used to work clubs out here [in Los Angeles], and I was a big fan. At that time, Tommy had a publishing company also. And when I came back out here, we were having a record date, and I asked him to hear Matt and Tom, and let them do some of their songs. And he hired them then and there as part of his organization. Their stuff was awfully good." Her good turn was rewarded in kind: originally hired as a member of the Pied Pipers, Stafford had sung a few solo vocals with the band on radio only before Dorsey had brought in Connie Haines as a longer-term replacement for Edythe Wright. When Dorsey finally decided to let Stafford take a hack at a solo vocal on a record, the tune was Dennis and Adair's "Little Man with a Candy Cigar" (a memorable if sentimental air later surprisingly revived by the Dave Brubeck Quartet).

Dorsey then proceeded to employ his other two star singers to sing his star songwriters, Connie Haines on "Will You Still Be Mine?" and Sinatra, as we'll see, on deluxe, extended vocal features of "Everything Happens to Me" and "Violets for Your Furs." "I'd play my new songs for Tommy," said Dennis, "and I'd say, 'This might be good for Connie,' or Frank or whoever, and usually Tommy would agree." But what Dorsey did for Dennis and Adair's "Let's Get Away from It All" would have been better than a month of Hanukkahs for any songwriter: an extra-long two-sided extravaganza featuring not only every singer in the unit—all seven of 'em—plus a gaggle of the band's best horn soloists. "Tommy thought it would be very entertaining to do it as a [musical comedy–style] production number," said Dennis. "Tom wrote two sets of lyrics, which gave them a little more material, so that everybody could join in. And, of course, the instrumentalists played some wonderful solos."

Sidestepping the possibility that just repeating a thirty-two–bar AABA number for two sides might get repetitious, the Dorsey crew beefed it up with extended transitions and other additional material. The record opens with an instrumental chorus of the tune heavily featuring TD. Next, Jo Stafford and the Pied Pipers sing the verse and refrain once through. A reed passage bridges the gap between the two sides of the disc, and then Sinatra and Haines appear with another chorus's worth of additional lyrics, bantering and one-upping each other more perkily than ever, making the most of the text's snappy attitude and witty rhyme combinations. The instrumental ensemble, spotlighting an enthusiastic trumpet solo from Ziggy Elman, and the vocal sextet, heavy on the Sinatra, divide the last chorus. They don't have to hammer it into your head with a spike and a pile driver: after just one hearing, the tune will stay in your head for the rest of your life.

"It was almost like a production number," says Stafford. "We did quite a few of those things after that." Oliver's "I'll Take Tallulah" didn't get as much attention, as it seemed too tied to its movie origin, MGM's *Ship Ahoy*, a lamentable script redeemed primarily by the generous amount of footage devoted to the Dorsey troop, although Red Skelton, Eleanor Powell, and Bert Lahr also have plenty of moments. The song's title combined a familiar radio comedy tagline, "I'll take vanilla" (in fact, the movie's working title was *I'll Take Manila*) with the name of the picture's protagonist, played by Miss Powell, "Tallulah Winters."

The MGM number excludes Sinatra entirely, but the RCA Victor version makes him its lead voice. It remains one of the most ingenious works in the Dorsey-Sinatra canon, for it's a genuine butt-kicker with a truly humorous text. Not just another rhythm tune with nonsense lyrics to be quickly sung and gotten over with (the sort of thing that the Dorsey-Oliver "Opus One" makes fun of), it incorporates solo and group voices with considerable humor and swing into the true spirit of the big-band flag-waver. "Tallulah" contains all the witty rhymes and puns of "Get Away from It All" and adds two elements, leader Dorsey's harsh but friendly squawking, long familiar to radio listeners, and a Latinate rhythm base ground out by percussion master Rich. Starting with a Cuban clave beat, the piece sets witty wordplay against a rumba backdrop, exchanges between star Sinatra and various guest vocalists: Dorsey, Stafford, and Haines, backed by the Pipers as a swingin' Greek chorus.

By the time the vocal is done, the conga-line routine has been forgotten and the piece is a straight swing up-tempo instrumental; to enforce this, Oliver sets up a shouting match between Dorsey and Ziggy Elman that looks backward to the two-trumpet battle of Ellington's "Tootin' Through the Roof" and forward to Oliver's innovative use of the device in the Dorsey classic "Well, Git It!" "Tallulah" ends with blaring, loudly dissonant brass, making you wonder what is Oliver's greater achievement—making the five-minute "Let's Get Away from It All" seem like half that length or cramming more stuff into "Tallulah" than you would ever believe could fit into three minutes. It's a comedy number, a flag-waver, and a conga all in one.

"Tallulah" had come from E. Y. Harburg and Burton Lane, two songwriters bigger than Dorsey could bag for his publishing concerns. However, the bulk of the band's remaining "production numbers" had been generated specifically by the trombone man's publishing machinations. Around May or June of 1940, Dorsey began a new series of commercial programs, sponsored, for once, not by one of the cigarette companies that bought and sold popular music, but by Nature's Remedy, a laxative manufacturer. Joe Bushkin, expressing the sentiments of the sidemen as a whole, says, "That was a great idea for an advertiser: to take a band that appeals to young people and have them try and sell a laxative! It was pretty stupid."

· Dorsey's broadcasts of the Sinatra years and afterwards utilized several different kinds of programming gimmicks. The "Memory Medley" served as Dorsey's response to the "Something Old, Something New" medley hook that his competitor, Glenn Miller, had been using for over a year. After concentrating on college songs (of all things) in the spring of 1940, Dorsey settled on a format of three songs per medley; the first and last would use different vocalists, while the middle would be an instrumental, often featuring Dorsey, Ziggy Elman, or (from 1942 on) the string section. Sinatra seems to have starred as the opening act of each of the medleys that featured him.

The very existence of the "Memory Medley" idea underscores how the idea of doing old tunes was itself little more than a novelty in the early 1940s. There was still considerably more money in the present than the past. Inspired by the boffo business Dorsey was doing as both publisher and recording artist on "I'll Never Smile Again," Nature's Remedy's ad agency concocted a gimmick to bring its radio program both promotional attention and material. Each week, on what came to be called the *Fame and Fortune* program, Dorsey encouraged amateur songwriters to send in their wares. Dorsey would choose a first-, second-, and third-place winner every week, the top prize being a publishing contract and an advance royalty check for one-hundred dollars. Dorsey didn't mention it on the air, but although the sponsor ponied up the prize loot, the copyrights went into Dorsey's "pubberies."

The Dorsey staff "gussied up" the avocational product considerably. The two runners-up (songs such as "At Least a Little in Love" and "It Came to Me") would receive only rudimentary orchestrations, just one chorus by one of the singers accompanied by a plain-vanilla background; however, the week's big winner received the deluxe treatment. First-placers, such as "You're Part of My Heart," "One Red Rose," "When Daylight Dawns," and "When Sleepy Stars Begin to Fall," all featured first choruses sung solo by Sinatra—in itself enough of a prize for any songwriter. The second chorus consisted of a mixture of Connie Haines and the Pied Pipers, with Jo Stafford heard in occasional solo spots and Sinatra always returning for the coda. While occasional *Fame and Fortune* songs like "You Got the Best of Me" showed Sinatra struggling with obviously inferior material, most of the songs were at least competent. Two songs even made it onto the Dorsey-Sinatra recording schedule, and one, "Oh! Look at Me Now"—written by Joe Bushkin with Johnny DeVries—became a standard.

The best remembered of the Sinatra-Haines duets (even more than the epic "Let's Get Away from It All"), "Oh! Look at Me Now" also represents Sinatra's most successful up-tempo number so far. Not to worry, Francis takes to swinging the way King Kong takes to climbing skyscrapers. Following his example, the Pied Pipers are also immediately in the groove, making this about the snazziest band and vocal group outing since arranger Oliver's great days with Lunceford.

Bushkin and DeVries wrote one other song recorded by Dorsey and Sinatra, "How Do You Do Without Me?" While the mood of that jaunty little number is mock-egotistical, the atmosphere of Frank Loesser's "Love Me as I

Am" is vaguely self-deprecating, anticipating "Why Try to Change Me Now?" Burke and Van Heusen's very hip and subtle "Do You Know Why?" also calls for some extremely accurate pinpointings of attitude. At twenty-five, Sinatra could already hit these very precise and distinct emotional targets with astonishing accuracy. It's hard to imagine anybody else who was singing with a band in 1940–42 or even later doing this—not Ray Eberle, or Herb Jeffries, or Dick Haymes, or Johnny Desmond, or Cab Calloway, or Ella Fitzgerald, or Helen Humes, or Jack Leonard, or anybody. Only Bing Crosby or Billie Holiday could have come close.

Sy Oliver deserves a great deal of the credit for Sinatra's early success as a swinger. "Sy was the man who had made Jimmie Lunceford," said Sammy Cahn, "and Sy was a true genius. I don't use the word lightly. And Tommy Dorsey, who was always an incredibly wise musician, knew that that band was Sy Oliver, and he wouldn't rest until he got Sy." Sammy Cahn had, in fact, already cowritten the theme song of the Lunceford band, "Rhythm Is Our Business," with Oliver. Melvin James "Sy" Oliver was born in Michigan in 1910. Like Stordahl, Oliver started as a trumpeter in a series of territory bands. By the time he graduated to the national scene in Jimmie Lunceford's band, his horn work had taken a backseat to his writing. Between 1933 and 1939, Oliver served as the central architect behind the sound and style of Lunceford, one of the most swinging and distinctively individual big bands of all time.

Dorsey didn't steal Oliver away from Lunceford, as some have claimed, but rather gave the arranger the chance he wanted to leave behind the low pay and other indignities foisted on the black bands of that racist era. While under Dorsey's employ, Oliver could at last escape the tribulations of the road altogether: no longer obliged to sit in the section, he could do his writing in New York. Still, when Dorsey gave him the call, he initially hesitated. "Sy was very ambivalent about joining the band," says Paul Weston. "Tommy wanted him, and made him a nice deal. But he didn't know if he'd be comfortable, being the only black guy around." Oliver arranged most of the band's up-tempo numbers from that point on, a responsibility he shared briefly at first with Deane Kincaide and later with Bill Finegan.

Oliver also presided over the most enjoyable subseries of the Dorsey-Sinatra years, the extension of what one 1939 radio announcer referred to as "The 'Marie' Cycle." With supreme cheekiness, the arranger and vocalist took an idea that had been firmly established by their predecessors and proceeded to do it so well that folks all but forgot it had ever been done before. History generally credits the original idea behind "Marie" to pioneer swing arranger Don Redman, and from him it trickled sideways to a lesser known and as yet unrecorded territory band, Doc Wheeler and the Sunset Royals (also sometimes known as the Sunset Royal Serenaders). Dorsey, as the trombonist himself later wrote, heard the Royals doing it and acquired the chart and the idea from them. The concept was simple enough: if an instrumental ensemble could riff behind a horn soloist, why not have a vocal group sing a countermelody in the background while the solo vocalist in front sang the main tune and lyrics? Along the way someone decided it should be the members of the band chanting behind a solo singer. It had the rough-and-ready sound of a saloon full of crocked "crooners" rather than a professional choir. The background lyrics, on the original "Marie" at least (less so on the sequels), consisted primarily of titles of other songs. The main song itself was an older standard rather than a new number.

Irving Berlin's relatively obscure waltz of 1928, "Marie" provided a perfect vehicle for the device, with its ambiguous lack of traditional distinction between the main (A) sections and the bridge (B), as well as its breathless, single-sentence lyric. Dorsey's 1937 Victor single of "Marie," with an arrangement credited to Fred Stulce, and its flip side, "Song of India," was easily one of the most successful records of the swing era. Dorsey continued to keep "Marie" alive in the band book, and he also extended the pattern by fitting other old, generally better-known standards to that model.* After "Marie" came "Who?" (1937), "Yearning" (1938), "Sweet Sue" (1938), "How Am I to Know?" (1939), and Leonard's final disc with Dorsey, "Deep Night" (1939).

Sinatra's earliest documented appearances with the band include readings of the by-now-classic original-recipe "Marie" itself as well the band's then-current "Marie" sequel, "Deep Night." In the Dorsey years, Sinatra would also eventually get around to "Yearning," "Who?," and "How Am I to Know."† Jack Leonard deserves credit for launching the series with Dorsey, and when he sang a "Marie" variation, the amusement largely derived from the way the chanting band seemed to be putting him down, making musical rabbit ears, as it were, behind the singer for the camera. He's the straight man, and they

---

* In 1954, the Dorsey Orchestra (which now included brother Jimmy) made a new record of "Marie" for Arthur Shimkin's Bell Records. When the producer told Irving Berlin about the new recording, the songwriter told him, "You tell that Irish bastard not to f**k with my song!" When Dorsey learned of this, his reaction was, "You tell that Jew bastard that if I hadn't f**ked with it, there wouldn't be any song!"
† One indirect inspiration for the "Marie" cycle may have been the pioneering radio crooner Rudy Vallée. He had been one of the few singers (or bandleaders) to record Berlin's "Marie" when it was new; Vallée also was the coauthor of the later "Marie" cycle entry, "Deep Night." Vallée once himself sang "Marie" on a guest shot on Dorsey's radio show; I'll take his vocal over Jack Leonard's—he may be more nasal, but he has a lot more personality and warmth, along with a self-mocking sense of humor.

are the comic cutups; he is square and they are hip. But when Sinatra moved up to the mic, he wasn't just hip, he was immediately hipper than all of them put together. At once the band was having fun *with* him rather than making fun *of* him. He comes on strong with the first utterance of the word "Marie," which opens the song. Then when he gets to the next "Marie" at the start of the second line, he glides into it. Throughout all sixteen bars Sinatra is relaxed and affable, going with the grain of the surroundings rather than against it, as Leonard did. With Leonard we quickly want the crooner to shut up so we can hear the cool counter-chorus, but with Sinatra it's the other way around.

"I was trying to get Frank to fall in with the lazy sort of two-beat feeling—the Lunceford beat," Oliver later explained to George Simon. "All kid singers tend to push too hard, and so one day I suggested, 'Lay back on it, Frank.' And you know what? He literally laid back with his body. Then I explained to him what I really meant, to lay back on the beat, not to push but to let the beat sort of carry him along. . . . must say he caught on right away."

Sinatra did not commercially record "Marie" with the band, but RCA subsequently issued several live performances of the song, one from the Hollywood Palladium on October 17, 1940 (issued in the 1950s on the *That Sentimental Gentleman* double album), and another, done at the Hotel Astor a few months earlier on June 12 (issued much later on RCA's subsidiary Buddah Records), that spotlighted a "mother" (as Sinatra would say) of a spectacular tenor sax solo by Don Lodice that brings the piece up to over four minutes—and makes this the "Marie" to end all "Maries."

The two "Marie" clones that Oliver conceived specifically for Sinatra were both "stellar" numbers—"East of the Sun" and "Blue Skies." On the small-group Victor version of "East of the Sun," Sinatra sounds a bit tentative throughout, although he really grooves on the last repeat of the title phrase at the end. Sinatra also had the difficult task of filling the gap between one of TD's exquisite cup-mute choruses and a particularly excellent Berigan bit, the trumpeter's entrance heralded by the band chanting, "Take it, Bunny!" Zeke Zarchy later remembered, "Frank made a great splash when he sang 'East of the Sun' at the Riverside Theatre in Milwaukee when he first joined the band. When you sing 'East of the Sun,' normally you would sing it like very straight (à la Jack Leonard), well Frank would swing it, just like a horn player would do. Everybody in the band got a big kick out of that. Instead of singing it like a ballad, he really swung it."

For "Blue Skies," Oliver creates a slyly minor-key mood for this Berlin ballad, opening with a riff that suggests his later "Swingin' on Nothin'," Dorsey piercing through the ensemble with his trombone like a sunbeam searing through the clouds. Sinatra has never been looser, and is looser still on several aircheck versions; he's not even competing with the background chanters anymore. He fearlessly sits out most of the bridge and gleefully plays with words like *bluebirds*. Sinatra also teasingly extends the final "from . . . now on" before the band declaims, "Mr. Elman, go ahead, go ahead." Oliver brings the thing home with crashing brass, and Elman zigs even higher over them, with Bushkin's piano solo providing a brief breather. Never before or since would Sinatra so completely capture the inner essence of a Dorsey trombone solo, absolutely nailing down TD's phrasing, tone, and conception. He comes even closer to TD's essential spirit than the singing of Louis Armstrong or Jack Teagarden does to their own horn work.

The very best of the Sinatra-Dorsey sides, among them "Pale Moon" and Oliver's "The One I Love," "Oh! Look at Me Now," and "Blue Skies," have a perfection to them that makes them as valid as any of Sinatra's later recordings. By 1941, Sinatra, Stordahl, and Oliver were able to take the ingredients of a no-frills, three-chorus bread-and-butter chart and cook them into a special dish indeed. "Without a Song," widely regarded as a major achievement in both Sinatra's and Oliver's careers, shows Sinatra tempering storytelling with swing in a way that points directly to *Songs for Swingin' Lovers!*

Similarly, "Love Me as I Am," "Where Do You Keep Your Heart?," and many others have Sinatra finding nuances in texts that other vocalists might have easily written off as grade-B Tin Pan Alley material; he alone could turn them into moving, thoroughly felt experiences. He would later describe his singing to Arlene Francis as "a combination of [elements from] musicians and singers that I had heard and was influenced by. Certain nuances that Billie Holiday used to use, and shortly after that it was Sarah Vaughan and Ella Fitzgerald and Louis Armstrong had a great deal to do with it."

He had also risen in Dorsey's trust and became, with Ziggy Elman and Bunny Berigan, that rare deputy Dorsey trusted to conduct the band at rehearsals; when Dorsey missed a broadcast on July 13, 1942, to attend his father's funeral, Sinatra conducted and also took over the leader's role as radio host. Still, he was beginning to feel cramped by Dorsey personally and by the limits of the dance-band format. "Tommy wanted him to be a little more strict with the beat," trombonist Dick Nash explained. "Tommy was always straight up and down, and with that quick vibrato and underneath that good sound. So when Frank sang, he always wanted to be more expressive and bend things around, and maybe delay the beat a little bit and phrase a little more. And of course Tommy would come up behind Frank: 'Hey! Get on the beat, kid. Come on.'"

Sinatra had become, along with the sublime "canary" Helen Forrest (of the Artie Shaw, Benny Goodman, and Harry James bands) and the blues-based Jimmy Rushing (Count Basie's sidekick for many years), one of the recognized masters of the thirty-two–bar vocal refrain. But by the summer of 1942 the time had come to grow again. As the girls started swooning around Dorsey's star crooner, the Sentimental Gentleman was less jealous of Sinatra's position as the band's *voce numero uno* than he was ecstatic to have such a popular attraction under contract. "Tommy knew he had something hot," said lead trumpeter Zeke Zarchy, "because Frank was far and away the best band vocalist of the day when he was singing in bands." On a July 1942 broadcast Dorsey even emitted a sarcastic mock-swoon as he introduced Sinatra on "Just as Though You Were Here." Dorsey did not feature Sinatra on a greater number of discs than Leonard—he had to divide up space among at least four separate vocal acts in 1940–42—but he gradually allocated more space per disc to Sinatra. A significant portion of the Dorsey sides from 1941 on feature at least a chorus and a half of the singer, often opening with him, something unheard of for a boy singer–bandleader relationship of the time. (Sinatra said that James had also started to feature him in this fashion, but unfortunately only "All or Nothing at All" was recorded.)

Unlike the many band singers who failed to make the transition from dance-band cog to center-spotlight attraction, Sinatra was rapidly proving himself an outstanding dramatic actor as well as a musician and instantly knew how to use his additional time. "Shadows on the Sand," a narrative that would still seem dopey even if it didn't turn out to be a dream in the end, offers an early example of a Dorsey record that opened with Sinatra and then had him return for an outchorus at the end. The more conventional love song "This Love of Mine," written by Sinatra, Hank Sanicola, and song-plug-ger Sol Parker, is a thoroughly effective side that applies the Sentimentalist "Never Smile Again" sound to Sinatra in solo, minus the Pipers and customary celesta. Unlike many stars at the time who claimed cowriter status on various songs (a charge that has been leveled at both Rudy Vallée and Al Jolson), Sinatra apparently actually did participate in the writing of this tune rather than merely being "cut in" (in vintage music publishing lingo) for a piece of the royalty action.

Sol Parker (né Solomon Peskin) had originally written the song as a for-ty-eight–bar melody with a title borrowed from Hemingway, "For Whom the Bell Tolls." Parker once told me, "I played it for Hank Sanicola and we went up to the Paramount Theatre. Within minutes, Frank was listening to me sing this song. He's rubbing his chin with his two skinny little fingers, and he immediately said, 'Let's make it more commercial.'" Within two days, Sinatra and Sanicola reworked it into a thirty-two–bar song now titled "This Love of Mine."

"Frank asked me if I wouldn't mind checking out the melody and lyrics [of 'This Love of Mine']," Matt Dennis remembered, "so I got a hold of Tom [Adair] one day and we sat down, and in a couple of hours, we made some minor, minor changes. I remember changing the melody for two or three measures, and Tom did make some minor alterations to the lyric. Anyhow, Frank liked what we did, and that's how they recorded it. Frank was so proud. And the strangest thing happened, for all these years, every time I hear 'This Love of Mine' I feel like I'm hearing one of my own songs. And all I did was change a little bit of it, as a favor to Tommy and Frank." Sinatra would later record the song again, to even greater effect, with Nelson Riddle in the classic 1955 album *In the Wee Small Hours*.

"Pale Moon (an Indian Love Song)" also affords the vocalist more space than was customary in 1941. Along with "Neiani" and "Trade Winds," "Pale Moon" constitutes his major Dorsey-era voyage into the realm of the exotic. This 1920 opus (by Frederick Knight Logan and Jesse Glick) refers not to genuine American (or even Hindu) Indians, but to the stereotypical depiction of Native Americans in literature and poetry. In the tradition of Longfellow—as later parodied by the Shakespearian savage in Huxley's *Brave New World*—"Pale Moon" ascribes King Jamesian *thee*s and *thou*s to its honest injuns. Further, the ensemble plays a brief instrumental passage between all the sung lines, to make the whole thing seem even more like a musical setting for a poetry recitation; the spacing gives the number an unusual structural feel, even though it uses the standard AABA format. Note that when white Americans reflect on the romances of exotic races within their own borders, generally these relationships are intraracial as opposed to interracial; it wouldn't do to suggest that the protagonist could enjoy any liaison—even a doomed one—with someone of another skin color so close to home. The idea is the same in the island flirtations of "Trade Winds," or the Hawaiian-guitar–tinged "Neiani" (coauthored by Stordahl and Oliver).

Two Dennis and Adair standards, Stordahl's treatment of "Everything Happens to Me" and reedman Heinie Beau's chart on "Violets for Your Furs," presented Sinatra with two of his earliest opportunities to sing a verse. "That was interesting because that was not the practice at that time," observed Matt Dennis. "Verses were common in the '20s and early '30s, with famous standards and show tunes. Today also, everybody sings those kind of verses. But nobody ever sang them in the big-band era because they were only interested in the melody of the chorus. But I enjoyed writing verses, and I told Tom, 'Let's write a verse whether anybody does it or not.'" In general, Sinatra was not a believer; relatively few of his recordings, from the big-band era or afterward, actually use the verse, though many of the ones that do (like "Glad to Be Unhappy" on *Wee Small Hours*) are all the more effective because of it.

From start to finish, "Everything Happens to Me" features not hint one of Dorsey's presence, or even the slightest indication that this is a big-band record rather than what were then called "personality" records. It opens with sympathetically sighing brass and ominous baritone sax (somewhat tongue-in-cheek); here, Stordahl's arrangement shows the influence of Oliver. Sinatra's part encompasses a full verse ("black cats creep across my path") and chorus ("I make a date for golf") and a half, followed by a tag.

Likewise, "Violets" opens with a brief trombone teaser before Sinatra's plaintive verse ("It was winter in Manhattan"). Dorsey takes one of his finest trombone solos, yet what's remarkable is that he does so in between Sinatra's two choruses. Both songs have very specific stories that need to be told precisely—the bullseye needs to be hit exactly in the middle—and Sinatra later took the opportunity to take another swing at each with Nelson Riddle at Capitol. Certainly the 1956 "Everything Happens to Me" is a more moving experience. Sinatra is now able to delineate the full ironic range of the text. Sinatra takes the *Close to You* album version considerably slower: the two readings are equally long, but the original still has time for an extra outchorus worth of lyrics ("I've never won a sweepstakes . . ."). However, Sinatra would never quite improve on the original "Violets for Your Furs," which requires a certain amount of wide-eyed prom-date youthfulness. This the prewar Sinatra had in abundance.

Paradoxically, after Dorsey added the strings in March 1942, he wanted to feature the new section as much as he could, and, perhaps to Sinatra's chagrin, the singer found himself both backed by and competing for space with the fiddles. In fact, Dorsey was more likely to give Sinatra almost a whole disc to himself, as on the otherwise unspecial "I Think of You" in late 1941 or early 1942 than after March of that year. Tracks such as "Take Me," "Be Careful, It's My Heart," and "In the Blue of Evening" make it clear that it was becoming impossible even to consider confining Sinatra to a humble thirty-two bars. The Dorsey orchestra with Sinatra by now represented a flagrant and excessive abundance of riches.

It was almost time for Sinatra to "graduate" from the Dorsey orchestra into a solo career of his own. He was still experimenting with various formats. If the full Dorsey orchestra, plus strings, plus Sinatra, was kind of overwhelming (as on "Daybreak"), he and Stordahl would have to find a way to tone that down a bit, and come up with an accompanying sound that would empower Sinatra to go off on his own. On January 19, 1942, he found it.

In 1942, nearly all pop records released were big bands playing for dancing, but some of the major labels had a small precedent of recording well-known band vocalists in solo dates. RCA Victor had done such sessions with Lena Horne, Maxine Sullivan, and Bea Wain in featured roles without their bands, and issued the results on Bluebird, its thirty-five-cent "budget" label. (Wain's tracks were released by Victor on what the label dubbed its Vocadance series, which meant exactly what it sounded like.) Sinatra, ambitious, talented, and already a major asset for the label through his work with Dorsey, was a natural for the project; given the opportunity, he was determined to "make good," in the parlance. Even his rival Connie Haines gave him props for his commitment: "Frank rehearsed day and night for that project."

The numbers were arranged and conducted by Axel Stordahl, who had already established himself as Sinatra's musical director within the Dorsey ranks, and the producer (or "A&R representative," as they said back then) appointed by RCA was Harry Meyerson. The personnel consisted of an amalgam of West Coast studio players, particularly among the seven strings and woodwinds, including Charles Strickfaden (who had played the same role fifteen years earlier on Crosby's breakthrough records with Paul Whiteman), and Dorsey men (mostly the saxophones), as well as guitarist Clark Yocum. Conspicuously absent were pianist Joe Bushkin, replaced by NBC staff pianist Lyle "Skitch" Henderson, and Buddy Rich, as the date went *sans batterie*.

Twenty years before he would become world famous as the conductor on the *Tonight Show*, Henderson had already begun his career-long relationship with NBC, and was, at the time, on staff at the conglomerate's West Coast operation. He was already a known quantity to Sinatra and Stordahl, having already subbed for Bushkin on at least one occasion in the Dorsey rhythm section. Henderson recalled that although Dorsey knew Sinatra was going to do a solo session, the participants were careful not to throw this fact in the boss's face: "When I had become part of that fraternity with Axel and everything, they [only] talked undercover about how they were going to do this record. It was said that we should keep our mouths shut about the date because the Old Man, as we called him, wasn't too happy about it."

Far from being nervous at this critical first solo session, Sinatra, Henderson added, "was always very confident of his skill." Stordahl has his act together no less than Sinatra at this point; one can see the basic evolution from these fairly concrete sketches to the masterpiece Stordahl-Sinatra charts of the mid-to-late 1940s. In fact, this orchestration of "The Song Is You" has only a few additional strings between it and the classic "Song Is You" of 1944 and '45 airchecks and the definitive Columbia 1947 version.

Though the 1942 "Night We Called It a Day" lacks the vocal majesty of the Capitol remake, the original rings truer. Dorsey had intended to record the song, another of his own publications, with Sinatra and the Pied Pipers, and asked composer Matt Dennis to prepare an arrangement similar to "I'll Never Smile Again." When Sinatra cut the song without Dorsey, the leader retaliated by recording it with Jo Stafford, but Victor didn't issue the Dorsey-Stafford version for several seasons. Stordahl's string arrangement of "The Night We Called It a Day" thereby became the property of Dorsey and Sinatra simultaneously. Dorsey kept it in his book with Skip Nelson and other crooners in Sinatra's spot, and it also stayed in Sinatra and Stordahl's repertoire.

One song that shouldn't be overlooked is the one Sinatra never remade and no one else ever bothered with after 1942, "The Lamplighter's Serenade." One of many obscure minor gems by the brilliant Hoagy Carmichael, the tune was also done by Bing Crosby, whose well-established paternal identity it suits better. Reflecting Carmichael's and Crosby's compatible backgrounds, the melody has a Bingish device written right into it, a trill on the last word of the line "he sprinkles their hearts with his *ma-agic*" that Sinatra was duty-bound to honor. It's almost as if some Warner Bros. screenwriter had done a story with Jimmy Cagney in mind but at the last minute the role went to Humphrey Bogart.

The results of the Bluebird session were conclusive: three masterpieces ("The Song Is You," "Night and Day," and "The Night We Called It a Day") and a lesser-known delight ("The Lamplighter's Serenade"). There was no avoiding the conclusion that the good ship Sinatra was ready to sail forth. Sammy Cahn remembered that about this time, "I was sitting with Sinatra, and we were talking, and he says, 'I'm going to be the world's greatest singer.' And I looked at him, and I'll never forget it, I said, 'There's no doubt in my mind. You are the world's greatest singer.' He said, 'Do you mean it?' I said, 'What do you mean, do I mean it? You're the best. You're the *best*. There's nobody better than you. You're the best.'"

Sy Oliver remembered telling Sinatra, "Well, maybe you're not ready yet." Sinatra then contended, "Look at Crosby, look at how he just went out on his own." Oliver insisted, "Well, I think maybe it'd be better if you stayed a little while longer, get more experience." But Sinatra was firm: "No, I'm ready." Oliver concluded the anecdote: "I was wrong! He was ready!"

Sinatra later claimed that as early as the fall of 1941 he realized the time to strike was well-nigh. (Bea Wain recalled that she supported Sinatra in this decision as early as December 1941, shortly after the outbreak of the war.) Around that time, Sinatra met with CBS's Manie Sachs on the West Coast. The A&R head found Sinatra "impatient to get out on his own, and I said I would take him for Columbia."

Even by the end of the 1940s, it had become obvious than Sinatra's departure from the Dorsey organization had already radically altered the power structure of American popular music. Up to World War II, it had been a band-leaders' game; following the wave of "Sinatrauma" that hit the world in 1943, singers were now the focal point.

But Sinatra, visionary that he was, had no way of knowing that in February 1942 as he listened to his test pressings from the January 1942 Bluebird date and planned his next move. "The reason I wanted to leave Tommy's band was that Crosby was number-one, way up on top of the pile," as Sinatra recollected for Sidney Zion. His goal was never to challenge Crosby, but rather simply to stand on his own: thanks to Manie Sachs, Sinatra was relatively sure he could land some sort of recording contract with Columbia Records and, much more important, get work singing on some CBS radio program. There was also reason to hope that a motion picture contract might be in the offing, but that was a longshot. No artist had ever managed the three-media parlay—radio, recordings, and movies—since Crosby had pioneered it a whole decade earlier.*

Sinatra was betting his future on the idea that there might be room for one other male singer to make it on his own in the band-dominated world of 1942. But he was worried; there was also considerable competition for that one "position." As he said in 1986, "In the open field, you might say, were some awfully good singers with the orchestras. Bob Eberly, with Jimmy Dorsey, was a fabulous vocalist. Mr. Como, with Ted Weems, is still such a wonderful singer." However, the main rival that gave Sinatra cause for concern wasn't Como or either one of the brothers Eberly-Eberle. In the spring of 1942, Dick Haymes (who had earlier replaced Sinatra with Harry James) was already doing solo spots in nightclubs as well as serving as Benny Goodman's boy singer. Good-looking, affable, and young enough that he had, in fact, already been able to learn a few tricks from Sinatra, Haymes was the one that Sinatra was really worried about. Watching Haymes's career from the sidelines, Sinatra felt he had to act quickly.

"I thought, if I don't make a move out of this band and try to do it on my own soon, one of those guys will do it, and I'll have to fight all three of them to get a position. So I took a shot and I gave Mr. Dorsey one year's notice. It was in September [1941]. I told him, 'Tom, I'm gonna leave the band one year from today.' Beyond that year I had another six months in the contract. [That contract was probably from January 1940 to January 1943.] Tommy said, 'Sure.' That's all."

---

* Remarkably, there would never be a female popular singer who was equally successful in all three media. By the 1950s, no one, male or female, was achieving the three-way parlay; a top singer had to choose between either movies, like Doris Day, or television, like Dinah Shore.

"Now, when I had left Harry James," Sinatra continued, "I told Harry that I had heard a boy named Dick Haymes. I said, 'He's a hell of a singer, he's great!' Sure enough, Dick Haymes went over with the James band.* Well, time went by, and finally it got to be about three more months left in the year, and I said, 'Tom, do you want me to find a vocalist?'" Sinatra again recommended Haymes as an obvious replacement, but Dorsey responded, "No, no, no, you're not gonna leave this band, not as easy as you think you are."

Fast-forward to a few months later. It is now September 3, 1942, at the Circle Theater in Indianapolis, and the occasion is the "final" radio appearance by Sinatra with the Tommy Dorsey orchestra. Dick Haymes has already filled in for Sinatra on at least one previous Dorsey broadcast (a few weeks earlier, August 13, 1942, when Sinatra supposedly had come down with laryngitis) and Dorsey has made the rather obvious move of hiring him as Sinatra's permanent replacement—once again, Haymes was stepping into Sinatra's immaculately-buffed shoes. On the show, Sinatra and Dorsey banter warmly, with no trace of the acrimony that was to follow; they introduce Haymes, who even then was hardly a new name to Dorsey's listeners, and then, just as quickly drop him so fast you'd think he had fallen through a trap door. Sinatra then performs an absolutely riveting run-through of the Stordahl arrangement of "The Song Is You." As great as the orchestration sounded in January on the Bluebird session, it sounds even better here as played by the Dorsey band proper. Sinatra himself has never sounded more enraptured. Sinatra is still only twenty-six, and this is already one of the major moments of his career, a perfect time capsule that captures the past, present, and future of his art.[†]

Skitch Henderson wasn't actually there, but he remembered it well. He was hanging out with Jimmy Van Heusen one night, and the phone rang with a long-distance call from Indianapolis. "It was Frank saying, 'I'm leaving the band. The Old Man goosed me with his trombone for the last time.'"

Dorsey had come to grips with the inevitable: that Sinatra was too big an attraction to remain with the band, and that it was a better utilization of an

---

*   Sinatra's version of how Haymes joined the James band is at odds with most other accounts. The standard story is that Haymes, who was also a songwriter, initially approached James with the goal to demonstrate his tunes for the bandleader. After listening to him sing his own songs, James wound up hiring Haymes as a replacement for the departing Sinatra.

†   "The Song Is You" and the banter between Sinatra, Dorsey, and Haymes was later issued by RCA (originally on the 1957 double-LP package *That Sentimental Gentleman*) as "the last broadcast." However, Sinatra stayed on the bus for a few more days, and he may be on the broadcast of September 8, which is not known to have survived.

asset to let him go off on his own and then collect a share of the profits. The contract Sinatra had signed with Dorsey entitled the bandleader to a third of his earnings—apparently for life—and he did not intend to let Sinatra off the hook.

Cultural commentator Wilfrid Sheed later observed that Dorsey showed Sinatra how to hold three things: a drink, a note, and a grudge. Especially the latter. Some of his sidemen recalled, not always in a humorous vein, Dorsey's vengeful nature. Skeets Herfurt remembered that Sinatra quickly began referring to his ex-employer as "Boss Tweed," explaining that if you were in Tommy's band you were his "fair-haired boy," but once you left, "you were on his blacklist."

Drummer Alvin Stoller recalled one of the more dramatic examples of Dorsey's temper: "One day Tommy was mad, and he was firing everybody again. He said, 'You don't like it, get your tail out!' So I said, 'Well, I quit!' He said, 'You can't quit!' Then he said, 'There's three real sons of bitches in this world—you, Buddy Rich, and Hitler! And *I* had to be stuck with two out of the three of you in my band.' I told that to Buddy, and he just fell over laughing. He said, 'How'd we get to Hitler?' I don't think Hitler could play drums, but if he could, I still don't think he would have worked for Tommy!"

For the next year or so, the theme song of the Sinatra-Dorsey relationship was "I'll Be Suing You." Dorsey continued to collect a share of Sinatra's earnings—a fact that Sinatra's radio writers turned into a running gag on his early solo shows. On a 1943 *Broadway Bandbox* sketch, when Sinatra and resident comic Bert Wheeler, expecting to hear a hunting call, instead get an out-of-tune trombone moaning "I'm Getting Sentimental Over You," Wheeler yells, "It's Dorsey, coming to collect his commission!" Sinatra responds, "Again?" When a few months later on a *Vimms* show, guest Alan Ladd offers to take "Frankie" to a Philharmonic concert, Wheeler wonders if Dorsey will be there since "he owns 10 percent of Beethoven." Sinatra continued to rib his would-be owner as late as January 1945 when he appeared on the Edgar Bergen and Charlie McCarthy program. When the wooden one offered to become Sinatra's manager, The Voice responded, "Why shouldn't you be? Everybody else is!"

Publicizing the situation encouraged Sinatra's young fans to start a mail campaign against Dorsey—this was apparently the WWII equivalent of social media. After George Evans started handling Sinatra's public relations in early 1943, the press agent organized Sinatra's fan club in Philadelphia into picketing Dorsey's opening at the Earle Theatre. Evans's assistant, Budd Granoff, later told me, "They picketed the theater with signs like 'Dorsey unfair to our boy Frankie!' and 'Dorsey cutting up Frankie!' And George got pictures of this all over the Philly papers. I think that made Tommy change his mind more than anything."

It ultimately took months and months of expensive negotiations, involving the talents of two of the country's top talent agencies, but Sinatra was finally extricated from the contract.* He was partially guided by fatherly advice from Bing Crosby, who warned him it would be smarter to buy off all claims on him as early as he could.

When Sinatra talked about the matter in the 1986 "Yale interview" with Sidney Zion (himself a lawyer), in his recollection the final straw that broke Dorsey's back was provided by an attorney named Sol Jaffe, who also represented the American Federation of Radio Artists. It was AFRA that gave permission for sustaining radio broadcasts, which were done without a sponsor, and for which musicians would not be paid anything other than their usual weekly salary. Jaffe played a card that Dorsey couldn't argue with: if he didn't release Sinatra from the contract, then AFRA wouldn't give Dorsey permission to do these sustaining remotes. Dorsey knew he was licked.[†]

Remarkably, Sinatra and Dorsey eventually became friends again. And they would even work together on several occasions, generally on the radio: in September 1944, Sinatra guest starred on Dorsey's program, *Your All-Time Hit Parade*, and in October 1945 Dorsey appeared on Sinatra's *Old Gold* show. In 1945, Sinatra joined his ex-boss at the 400 Restaurant in New York City to celebrate the tenth anniversary of the Tommy Dorsey Orchestra and sang "Blue Skies" with the band. He did the same in 1955, honoring the twentieth anniversary; on that occasion, he volunteered to sing even before Tommy could ask him, and wound up doing three numbers with the reunited Dorsey Brothers orchestra. (The 1955 reunion was included on the 2009 boxed set *Sinatra: New York*.)

But even after Dorsey and Sinatra stopped working together, theirs was a complicated relationship. After Dorsey died in his sleep in 1956, two of Sinatra's oldest pals, Jackie Gleason and George Simon, produced a television tribute to him in memorial. Yet when they approached Sinatra to appear on the show, he must have been in a foul mood that day: he turned them down, stating that in saying anything nice about Dorsey he would "feel like a hypo-

---

* According to Peter J. Levinson, in his 2006 biography of the bandleader, *Tommy Dorsey: Livin' In a Great Big Way*, the final agreement was reached in the summer of 1943.

† This is mostly Sinatra's own account of why Dorsey released him from the infamous "one-third for life" contract. For more of the specific business details, the reader is referred to both *Tommy Dorsey: Livin' in a Great Big Way* (2006) by Peter J. Levinson and *Frank: The Voice* (2011) by James Kaplan.

crite." But Sinatra himself produced and starred in his own television tribute to Dorsey, costarring Jo Stafford, two years later in 1958, as part of his weekly ABC-TV series.

Around this time Sinatra described Dorsey to George Simon as "a guy who was a real education to me in every possible way. I learned about dynamics and phrasing and style from the way he played his horn, and I enjoyed my work because he saw to it that a singer is always given a perfect setting." In 1955 he elaborated: "Tommy set me up beautifully in the band—the arrangements featured me. Tommy's tempo was always right for singing, never too fast or too slow."

In an interview with Ben Heller in 1950, the disc jockey told Sinatra of a recent chat he had had with Dorsey in which the trombonist declared, "'What is there to say about Frank? It's been done innumerable times—anything I could say would be superfluous.' And he went on for an hour and a half, and all he did was talk about you." Sinatra replied, "I really think that there'll never be a trombone player or a musician who knows his instrument like Dorsey knows that horn. He's just the end of the world."

Sometime between 1953 and 1956 Dorsey visited two of his illustrious alumni, Sinatra and Nelson Riddle, at one of their Capitol sessions. The event was captured by a photographer, though unfortunately not by a recording engineer. Sinatra related to Heller in 1950 that "I went to see [Dorsey] at the Astor [hotel in New York] a couple of weeks ago, and he just knocked me out. I went up and sang a few songs with the band; I sat next to the brass like I used to. It was a big kick, but listen, I ran right away when I heard him call for the bus!"

Sinatra kept a great many of the songs associated with his Dorsey tenure in his act and on his recording schedule. With the Dorsey originals still green in memory, Sinatra rerecorded "Fools Rush In," "Blue Skies," and "When You Awake" in new arrangements. He also kept "I'll Be Seeing You," "There Are Such Things," his own "This Love of Mine," and others alive on the radio, and "Without a Song" in concerts up through the late 1980s. In 1951, Sinatra also waxed a beautiful reading of "I Guess I'll Have to Dream the Rest" that comes fairly close to the original of ten years earlier, with a new, otherwise unknown group, the Whippoorwills, replacing the Pied Pipers. The star appropriately amplifies his own role here, and his singing, so much more emotionally aware, reaches both heights and depths of feeling he could only aspire to in the Dorsey days. In 1941, Sinatra fans had to dream the rest; in 1950, he does it for them.

Over the years Sinatra also revived "How About You?," "Oh! Look at Me Now," "Violets for Your Furs," "Everything Happens to Me," "Stardust" (this too was a complicated subject), "Let's Get Away from It All," "Street of Dreams," "Just as Though You Were Here," and "Be Careful, It's My Heart" in new Capitol and Reprise arrangements. The groundbreaking "I'll Never Smile Again" came to life in many guises: a duet with former bandmate Jo Stafford on their joint television tribute to TD in 1958; with the Hi-Lo's standing in for the Pied Pipers on a 1959 Sinatra show; in a full-blown Gordon Jenkins treatment on *No One Cares* in that same year; in a medley with Dean Martin on the latter's program in 1960; in an exact Sentimentalist-style remake for the *Man and His Music* album in 1965; and in a 1971 concert.

Sinatra further employed echoes of the Dorsey sound throughout the 1940s, primarily in his radio closing theme, "Put Your Dreams Away," another song by Ruth Lowe, which was about as close as one could come in melody and mood (and even trombone solo) to her "Smile Again." It would be played at Sinatra's own funeral in 1998.

For his part, Dorsey kept something of the Sinatra-Dorsey legacy alive in occasional revivals of some of their biggest hits, such as "Smile Again." In 1952, Dorsey also rerecorded "There Are Such Things" as a trombone solo with Gordon Jenkins's orchestra and choir. That same year Dorsey also came up with the most obvious "Smile Again" rehash in a tune titled "You Could Make Me Smile Again" (also recorded by the young Tony Bennett).

From "Put Your Dreams Away" onward, the celeste and super-slow phrasing were to be keynotes of Sinatra's later Dorsey-style numbers, including the series of "chamber" recordings he made beginning in 1945. That same year, Sinatra renewed his acquaintance with the Pied Pipers, within whose ranks June Hutton, later to marry Axel Stordahl, had replaced Jo Stafford. The former Dorseyites became regulars on the *Old Gold Songs by Sinatra* show, and also occasionally appeared on some of his Columbia sides, most sentimentally on Stordahl's tune "Ain'tcha Ever Comin' Back" (1947). The 1949 "If I Ever Love Again" uses a celesta background and super-close harmony between Sinatra and the vocal group the Double Daters. As late as 1954's "Don't Change Your Mind About Me," Sinatra's last recorded meeting with the Pied Pipers, he was still singing variations on "I'll Never Smile Again."

Perhaps the best tribute Sinatra could pay to Dorsey was in the number of veterans of that band who eventually went to work for their former fellow sideman, starting with both of his most important musical directors, Axel Stordahl and Nelson Riddle. Sinatra maintained decades-long relations with arrangers Sy Oliver, Heinie Beau, and Richard Jones, who said "Sinatra's musical taste was developed at Tommy's elbow," as well as with Buddy Rich, Johnny Mince, Jo Stafford, Joe Bushkin, Zeke Zarchy, Lee Castle, Don Lodice, Ziggy Elman, and the Pied Pipers (as well as vocalist-guitarist

Clark Yocum's brother Verne, who for many years worked as Sinatra's music librarian).

If there's one major disappointment regarding Sinatra's later work with his fellow Dorsey veterans, it's that his post-1942 collaborations with Sy Oliver were neither as frequent nor as rewarding as they should have been. Oliver continued to write occasionally for Sinatra even while in the service, turning in a treatment of the spiritual "Swing Low, Sweet Chariot" for him to sing on the 1944 *Vimms* show as well as a remake of his equally gospelly Dorsey classic "Yes, Indeed." But he seems to have arranged only three commercial sides for Sinatra between 1942 and 1961: "Sweet Lorraine," the minor hit "Don't Cry, Joe," and the less successful "A Little Learnin' Is a Dangerous Thing." (The arranger's widow, Lillian Oliver-Clarke, was of the opinion that there were more Oliver-Sinatra charts in these years, but these have not yet been identified.)

The 1946 "Sweet Lorraine" positioned Sinatra with the "Metronome All-Stars," consisting of pianist Nat King Cole and an indisputably stellar group drawn largely from the Dorsey (Charlie Shavers and Buddy Rich) and Ellington bands. Sinatra's vocal is just one of many virtuoso solos, and this Billie Holiday–like chart showcases Sinatra at the height of his late-1940s jazz-singing abilities. The 1947 "A Little Learnin'" with Pearl Bailey, a none-too-funny comedy blues song by Oliver and fellow arranger Dick Jacobs, also published by Sinatra, is notable only as an early interracial duet. The material, thin to begin with, gets stretched beyond the snapping point when the two-sided performance lingers on into the six-minute range.

Thankfully, "Don't Cry, Joe" (1949), a blues-tinged lament penned by Chicago clarinetist Joe Marsala, represents a significant improvement. As Sinatra said in a radio interview from the night after the session, "'Don't Cry, Joe' is a great song and should be a big hit." The hit went to future Sinatra cohort Gordon Jenkins, but Sinatra's version successfully combines the strengths of both blues and ballad singing, and the Pastels vocal group again blends in superbly. Even the odd way Sinatra bends the note on the line "Don't Cry, *Joe*" actually works, and Oliver cleverly borrows the Dixieland coda from Duke Ellington's "I Ain't Got Nothin' But the Blues" as a tag. Sinatra attributed the spirit of the disc to "the fact that we were in a new studio and it was a wonderful Sy Oliver arrangement. Everybody was kind of all excited about it, that may be the answer too. But I will say that because of the song being so good, we couldn't miss with it last night."

Three years after staging a tribute to Dorsey for ABC television, he decided the time was right to do the same for his own new label, Reprise Records. In a sense, the first three Sinatra Reprise albums directly prefigure the 1979 *Trilogy* LP, although in reverse order: *Ring-a-Ding-Ding!* with modernist arranger Johnny Mandel suggesting the future, and *Sinatra Swings* with Billy May being very much in the present.*

As the capper for this early trilogy, Sinatra then invited Sy Oliver to join him in a mutual recollection of their collective past with *I Remember Tommy.* As Sinatra did with most of his 1960s albums, he gave Oliver freedom to do what he wanted with the charts—and on this one he sought the arranger's suggestions on repertory as well. "So many singers worry an orchestra to death," Oliver told Simon, "but never Frank. We picked the tunes together, and then he just let me go. He and Tommy Dorsey were two of the few people who've hired me and never told me what to do."

Sinatra and Oliver attempted the recording of *I Remember Tommy* in two sessions from March 1961, which transpired on the same days that Sinatra recorded his penultimate Capitol album, *Come Swing with Me!* with Billy May. "Frank had been working very hard before [those dates]," Oliver recalled, "and after he listened to the tapes, he realized it wasn't what he wanted." Oliver later told Sinatra researcher Ed O'Brien that they had come too close to the original Dorsey sound—a dance band with a small string section. At forty-five, Sinatra was afraid that his voice was thinning as fast as his hair and that he required the crutch of a lush violin section to cover up any technical shortcomings. "He did sound kind of hoarse," Oliver said to Simon, "and he also decided we should use more strings."

Whether or not Sinatra actually sounded rough on the original dates, Oliver added considerably more fiddles on the remake sessions. In May, Sinatra and Oliver redid seven of the eight March titles (adding another five charts), and the eighth, unremade title, "In the Blue of Evening," eventually found its way onto the expanded CD edition of *I Remember Tommy* in 1992. Far from sounding frail, "Blue of Evening" constitutes the best ballad performance on the disc. In fact, one wishes that Sinatra and Oliver had stuck with that original, more authentically Dorsey-licious sound and the lighter twelve-man string team rather than the very imposing fiddlers twenty. Opening with a vaguely Dorseylike cadenza played by James Decker on French horn, "Blue of Evening" evidences a persuasive sense of economy that TD himself would have been proud of.

Although it contains four or five killer-strong tracks, the completed *I Remember Tommy* does not amount to a classic Sinatra album. By and large,

---

* In early 1961, Sinatra also announced his intentions to produce and star in a film about the big-band era that would feature all the Dorsey sidemen, most of whom, apart from the brothers themselves, were still alive. Alas, it was never made.

Oliver, the teacher, had been surpassed by his pupils—particularly Riddle and May. Much of the album's texture resembles lesser Riddle; add a few more flutes, bass trombones, and Sweets Edison, and it would sound exactly like Riddle. In fact, Oliver does employ Kenny Shroyer's bass trombone on "Without a Song" and unfortunately illustrates why Riddle used the instrument only for color here and there. Oliver has the thing grunting throughout, and it quickly becomes repetitive.

But not even factoring in the disc's two top-heavy dramatic pieces, "Daybreak" and the hugely overdone "Take Me," little on *I Remember Tommy* succeeds as an improvement over the classic Dorsey-Sinatra recordings. Much of the disc seems redundant, not only in comparison to the originals ("Polka Dots and Moonbeams" is decidedly inferior to Axel Stordahl's 1940 arrangement), but in light of the excellent remakes Riddle had already done of "Oh! Look at Me Now," "How About You?," "Violets for Your Furs," and "Everything Happens to Me."

It's sad to report that Sy Oliver actually sounds square in spots. And it's not the Gordon Jenkins kind of old-fashionedness that works because it matches the mood. It sounds doubly out of place in comparison to the high-powered hipness of "The One I Love Belongs to Somebody Else." It's also a rare case of Sinatra exercising questionable judgement—why would he choose a forgettable song like "Take Me" over such gems as "This Is the Beginning of the End" and "The World Is in My Arms"? In general, much of *I Remember Tommy* lacks the freshness of the 1940–42 originals while also not matching the consistently high quality of his other 1961 albums.

Still, the good tracks on *I Remember Tommy*—the ones included in the *Reprise Collection* especially—are about as good as it gets. "East of the Sun" has an instrumental choir following the same lines that the band chorus sang in the original and excitingly builds to a series of multiple false endings patterned on Glenn Miller's "In the Mood." The very danceable "Imagination" has Sinatra offering another variation on the mock closer idea, repeatedly uttering the penultimate phrase before thrillingly resolving it with the final two notes. "Without a Song" doesn't quite come up to the 1941 Victor or the 1965 reading that opened the first *Man and His Music* TV special but remains majestic just the same; the patented Sinatra-Dorsey celeste tinkles against a monstrous brass crescendo and concludes on a haunting and unexpected final chord in the manner of the Nat Cole–Billy May "You'll Never Know."

"It Started All Over Again," boasting a Bushkiny break by Bill Miller, sounds as good as ever in a suitably simple chart that parallels the original. In contrast, Burke and Van Heusen's "It's Always You" finds new life as a Luncefordian bouncer in a two-beat chart that challenges the original. "I'll Be

Seeing You" similarly revamps that hit World War II ballad into a rollicking rocker, following Dorsey's own 1943 rearrangement of the piece with that jivey vocal group, the Sentimentalists.

Sinatra would follow *I Remember Tommy* with two subsequent tributes: the *Man and His Music* album version of "I'll Never Smile Again" (unaccountably left off *I Remember Tommy*) and, for the 1979 *Trilogy*, the Gershwin standard "But Not for Me," stunningly reimagined by Sinatra and Billy May as a Sentimentalist number in the "Never Smile Again" format; Sinatra herewith called upon trombonist Dick Nash (as he had in 1961) to do, as Sinatra put it, "his Tommy Dorsey shit."

Sinatra's most frequent remembrances of Tommy, however, were more personal than professional. It seems as if at least half of every interview Sinatra ever gave was devoted to Dorsey. Saxophonist Jerry Dodgion has said that when he played Australia in 1959 with Red Norvo and Sinatra, the singer spent a lot of time with the musicians and that he "talked mainly about Tommy Dorsey." On Irv Cottler's birthday (circa 1977), the drummer happened to mention that he had also spent some months with the Dorsey band, a fact that Sinatra had forgotten. "We stayed up talking from one AM to about seven in the morning," said Cottier, "all about Tommy." During the writing of this book, around 1990, I asked Sinatra's press agent, Susan Reynolds, if the Old Man (yes, Sinatra was the "Old Man" by then) ever reminisced about the old days. "Yes, he does all the time," she responded. "He especially likes to talk about Tommy Dorsey."

"The Voice That Is Thrilling Millions" and the "Sentimental Gentleman of Swing" worked together for the last time in the summer of 1956, a few months before Dorsey died, on the same bill with Sinatra's new movie, *Johnny Concho*, at the New York Paramount. Although the picture itself was forgettable (the star himself incessantly put it down in the stage show, and for many years thereafter), the engagement marked a triumphant reunion of the bandleader and singer at the venue of their greatest triumphs. For the trombonist, the gig also extended the unfortunately brief reunification of the Dorsey Brothers Orchestra. Far from holding a grudge against Dorsey, Frank Military recalled, "Frank insisted on using Tommy and his band. They were very close."

That engagement also marked a touching reunion between Dorsey and Nelson Riddle, who had played in TD's band in the mid-1940s and, ten years later, was Sinatra's most important collaborator at Capitol Records. Since Riddle had written most of the charts that the Dorseys were playing behind Sinatra, the singer flew him out to New York to run over them with TD, who invited Riddle to come to Connecticut as his guest for the weekend. "The reason I went was that I had never seen him other than as an employee," Riddle told Robert Windeler on a radio profile. "I wanted to see what he was like just as a fella. I went up there and found that things were not too swell between him and his wife [the former Jane Carl New]—things were very tense.

"We had dinner in this formal dining room, and there were just the three of us. And Tommy said, 'I like the things that you've been doing with Frank very much.' I said, 'To tell you the truth, much of the skill and ability to do these came from you.' And you know, that touched him. He started to cry. Maybe it was the rather jagged emotional times he was going through, but that touched him. I went over and put my arm around him and said, 'That's true, you're the one that steered me.' At that moment the very romantic Mrs. Dorsey piped up and said, 'I hope you mean it.' I said, 'Yeah, I mean it.'"

The gentleman, it seems, was sentimental after all.

It was September 1942. Sinatra had won his freedom, but now that he was out, where would he go? He was young but already quite experienced and with something of a name for himself, and, as it happened, lousy with talent. A million possibilities for growth lay ahead of him, but also a million chances to fail. For better or worse, his career and his destiny were now entirely in his own hands. The apprenticeship was over.

# 4

# WITH AXEL STORDAHL

## *1943–1948*

*Great art puts everything else to shame, and makes you wonder what else we could have done that was so marvelous and so unpresumptuous. It makes you feel that maybe we too can create something that will last and be beautiful.*

—ARTHUR MILLER

In the fall of 1942, Frank Sinatra, then recently liberated from Tommy Dorsey's orchestra, met a young future PR agent named Gary Stevens, at a time when both were hanging around the offices and studios of CBS Radio in New York. "I was amazed that Frank knew everything that he wanted to do—he had his whole future laid out for him. He wanted to make records, have his own program, and get into pictures. He even told me, 'Someday, I want to win an Oscar!' And he meant it too." Big dreams for an ex–band singer whose name no one could even spell.

For all of Tommy Dorsey's wailing and gnashing of teeth, the launch of Sinatra's solo career hardly sent shock waves through the music industry; not all at once, anyway. It's almost as if only Sinatra and Dorsey themselves realized the implications of the event. Dorsey replaced Sinatra with Haymes, and that was the end of it. Sinatra had merely been one voice among many in the Dorsey entourage, and in the fall of 1942, he might well have seemed to be heading for the purgatory of ex–band singers (Jack Leonard, Edythe Wright, Ginny Simms, Ray Eberle) who made a few records, landed a guest shot on a radio show or a B movie, but essentially went nowhere. During the swing era, a star trumpeter like Ziggy Elman or Bunny Berigan jumping ship from one band to another rated a headline in *Down Beat*, the Bible of the band biz, but even the music industry press paid little attention to Sinatra's departure from the Dorsey fold.

As Sinatra acknowledged until the end of his days, it was Manie Sachs who became his all-important "rabbi" at this point. Sachs was a hip and savvy broadcasting and recording executive who, impelled by the reunification of CBS Radio and Columbia Records, was assembling a formidable roster of talent for CBS megamogul William Paley; by the war's start, Columbia was releasing records by the King of Swing, Benny Goodman (whose sessions were supervised by the clarinetist's brother-in-law, the redoubtable John Hammond), Count Basie (ditto), Dinah Shore (by far the most popular female singer of the era, not to mention Billie Holiday and Mildred Bailey through 1942), Harry James, and Les Brown (and soon enough, Doris Day). After the war, Columbia was one of the few labels with two star female singers, Shore and Day, and two major males, Sinatra and Buddy Clark. Sachs wasn't a "hands-on" A&R man. He had little to do with picking individual songs or running sessions; rather he signed the talent, from the top down.

But in 1942—and for the next two years—it was almost impossible for Sinatra to make a record, even with the support of Manie Sachs. From summer of 1942 to fall of 1944, the American Federation of Musicians had called a strike that prohibited their members from going into the recording studio. The first labels to make an acceptable deal with the AFM were those lean startups Decca and Capitol—both essentially feisty independents and not connected to recording empires, like RCA Victor to NBC and Columbia Records to CBS. *Down Beat,* in its October 15 issue, mentioned that "Sinatra, rumored set to make a cappella recordings, said that he has no plans along that line."

Recordings were an afterthought in any case; commercial broadcasting was the medium where a singer could really make a killing (even the movies weren't nearly as lucrative, at least for singing talent). The recording industry had peaked and plateaued years earlier, slowed down considerably by the Great Depression and the coming of radio, and as late as WWII it was still a mom-and-pop enterprise. When Glenn Miller's "Chattanooga Choo Choo" reached sales of a million copies in 1942, it marked the first disc to ring in those numbers in fifteen years; even the mighty Crosby hadn't hit the million mark in all of the 1930s.

Well before he could make a record for Columbia, Sinatra was popping up wherever he could on CBS Radio: a few weeks after leaving Dorsey, he began a run as one of the featured vocalists on the sustaining Thursday night show *Reflections*; it wasn't sponsored, so the pay was low, but it was prime time. (Sinatra appears to have appeared on the program from October 1 to December 31, 1942.) Also in October, Sinatra, passing through Chicago, sang a guest appearance on a show called *Your Broadway and Mine,* with

CBS's house conductor, Walter Gross (the future composer of "Tenderly"). (His sole number was "A Touch of Texas," of all unlikely song choices.)

Something had to happen. He not only had a family to support—and already something of an entourage—he was now personally responsible for the salary of Axel Stordahl, who had left the Dorsey organization to serve as his full-time musical director. In essence, he had to pay Stordahl more money in order to get him to accept less security. "After I left Tommy, things were quiet for about six months," Sinatra told Arlene Francis in 1977. "I had an agent. I decided maybe the action was in California, and I packed up my family and we came out." The first significant payoff from the Hollywood relocation was, as Sinatra put it, "I got a little role in a movie at Columbia Pictures"; this was *Reveille with Beverly*, Sinatra's first post-Dorsey cinematic appearance. (Sinatra's vocal was recorded on September 17, only a week after his last appearance with Dorsey.) The musical lineup of the picture shows how ahead of his time Sinatra was: all the other acts are big bands, Sinatra is the sole star singer; the only other vocal act is those old favorites, the Mills Brothers.*

He was finding more work in front of live audiences back east, particularly in his native New Jersey. He "happened," as he later said, to get a week's work at a local vaudeville theater, either in that town or Passaic (probably both at different times). The girls were already swooning, and, as Sinatra remembered, the grapevine of theater managers started buzzing in an attempt to learn "what all the noise was about. Why were the kids screaming and yelling and running up and down the aisles?" His representatives at General Amusement Corporation kept bringing over bookers from ever more important venues; finally he made it to a major theater—the Mosque, in the state's most important city, Newark. His agent then dragged over Bob Weitman, manager of the New York Paramount, which was to 1940s pop music what the Palace had been to vaudeville.

As Sinatra told Sidney Zion, "One day they told me that Bob . . . whom I knew, was coming in to catch the last show. This was on my birthday, December 12. He came in and caught the show, but I didn't see him. I went home, and he rang me at the house and said—it was a famous phrase—'What are you doing New Year's Eve?' I said, 'Not a thing. I can't even get booked anywhere. I can't find anywhere to work.' He said, 'I mean the morning of December 31 and for a couple of weeks after that?' I said nothing. He said,

* For his part, Skitch Henderson distinctly remembered that around this time, "for a very brief period, he was a sustaining singer on the local NBC station in Hollywood, and I was the house pianist there." This seems unlikely; Sinatra was fiercely loyal to Manie Sachs and CBS, but one never knows, does one?

'I'd like you to open at the joint.' He used to call the Paramount 'the joint.' I said, 'You mean on New Year's Eve?' He said, 'That's right. That morning. You got Benny Goodman's orchestra and a Crosby picture.' And I fell right on my butt! I couldn't believe what he said to me, to be put in a position like that. In those days they called you an extra added attraction. I went to rehearsal at 7:30 in the morning. I looked at the marquee on Broadway, and it said, 'Extra Added Attraction: Frank Sinatra,' and I said, 'Wow!'"

That Sinatra received only tiny billing as an "extra added attraction" is verified by copies of contemporary newspaper ads, which ballyhooed the film, *Star Spangled Rhythm* (actually an all-star production with Crosby as top-billed guest star), and not the stage show. The Goodman aggregation got next highest billing, including the acts within the band—the Goodman small group (BG was sporting a sextet that fall) and budding singer Peggy Lee. Next, two nonmusical novelty acts were billed, the Radio Rogues (who, coincidentally, also appeared in *Reveille with Beverly*) and Moke and Poke; finally, way down on the bottom of the ad, Frank Sinatra was billed as the marquee equivalent of a bonus track.

Opening night at the Paramount, New Year's Eve, 1942. This was the engagement that could make or break him; if he didn't go over, it would be unlikely that he would ever be given another chance. In spite of considerable experience by that time, the twenty-seven-year-old Sinatra was mind-numbingly stage-frightened. His tension was unexpectedly broken by Goodman himself. According to Yank Lawson, trumpet soloist in this particularly Olympian BG band, "Benny didn't know who Sinatra was." Goodman, with his characteristic combination of absentmindedness and total tact, took one look at the shaking, sweating crooner (who weighed about 120 pounds soaking wet—twenty pounds of which was hair, as he later quipped), heard the deafening ovation from the audience, and demanded, "What the heck was that?" (And no, according to eyewitnesses, "heck" was not the word that Goodman actually used.)

Goodman's exclamation served to send both Sinatra and the band into hysterics—and diffuse Sinatra's nervousness—even as the swoons and screams from the audience overwhelmed the music (as well as Mr. Goodman's unmiked asides). What they were witnessing was the all-important birth of the cultural explosion that pressmen of the day were soon to label "Sina-trauma." "I didn't know why the hell they were doing it," the singer said later of the swooners and bobby-soxers, "but they were doing it."

And they kept doing it. By the next day, January 1, 1943, Sinatra was the hottest act in the country. Not only were trade magazines like *Down Beat, Metronome,* and *Variety* heralding his supremacy, but, more important, lines of kids, mostly girls, stretched around the block. "I was very confused. I had never seen it. . . . Nobody had ever heard that kind of reaction before," Sinatra said later. Inside the theater, massive crowds of teenagers screamed at the top of their lungs; outside, an even bigger mob of girls launched an epidemic of mass truancy and motionless traffic that transformed Times Square into the world's largest parking lot.

As Lawson remembered, "Frank stopped the show every time. The lines were four-deep clear around the block with people trying to get in the theater." He also recalled that the overworked BG bandsmen, who were doing nine shows at the Paramount every day besides playing for dancers at the New Yorker Hotel each night, found Sinatra and the initial reaction to his music exhilarating: "The applause was so great, and all those kids were dancing in the aisles. We thought it was great!"

"What he was doing at the Paramount was by itself beyond belief, and he was doing it for six shows a day," remembered Sammy Cahn. "And the bobby-soxers, the screaming and the hysteria—it was not to be believed!" Sinatra added, "I was also confused because it was very difficult working in the theaters in those days. If I moved, everybody would scream or squeal . . . and I was afraid to move after a while."

The architect Louis Kahn (1901–1974) once observed that great art creates a need for itself. "The world never needed Beethoven's Fifth Symphony until he created it. Now we could not live without it." The same applies to Sinatra: with World War II escalating, nobody realized the world wanted a new singing star or a new vocal style. Inspired by the female swooning that he had been causing to some degree since the 1930s, however, Sinatra understood that the wartime era was the perfect moment to launch a new, intensely romantic sound.

He had also realized that Axel Stordahl was best equipped to help him develop it. By way of example, Billy May (who served as one of Stordahl's deputies for several years) pointed out that Bing Crosby, then by far the biggest singer in the country, used only four strings; Sinatra insisted on employing twelve. The heavy reliance on "strads" (in *Down Beat's* parlance) helped Sinatra create a strongly sensual atmosphere—you heard all those violins, and you knew you were listening to something other than a regulation crooner or a dance band.

It was time for a new vocal-sound singer: by vacating his steady spot with Dorsey, Sinatra was gambling his entire future on that long shot of an idea. No earth-shattering new voice had captured the public's imagination for a decade. For a few years in the early 1930s, the radio actually featured three star crooners: Bing Crosby, Russ Columbo, and Rudy Vallée. By World War

II, Columbo was long dead, the victim of an accidental gunshot wound in 1934, and Vallée had slowly slid from heartthrob to second banana. Crosby had experienced comparable swoons from female fans at the moment he arrived at the top; in fact, both his and Sinatra's first starring feature films (*The Big Broadcast* and *Higher and Higher,* respectively) cast the crooners in identical roles; playing themselves under their actual names (with fictitious love interests) as radio stars dodging femme fans. Once at the top, however, Crosby downplayed the swooning angle, gradually cultivating a patriarchal image, as familiar as your next-door neighbor and as comfortable as a pipe and pair of slippers.

Then Sinatra came on singing about love, marketing his musical romance initially to teenagers, a new demographic group that had been created by the swing era and then the war. "I think that he just had a very appealing, very personal sound that young girls my age certainly adored," was how Rosemary Clooney, who was fourteen in 1943, described it. If his image was cultivated to attract bobby-soxers, his music was directed at the highest possible mindset. The first major teen idol was also the last one not to pander to his audience.

His very newness made him attractive, and the kids who had grown up listening to big bands in the Depression considered him one of their own— an idea stressed in Sinatra's official publicity biographies of the 1940s, which often made him two years younger than he was. "I think it was a time period that was important for them to have somebody to root for during the war years," Sinatra observed in a 1977 interview. "I always felt that I was, in their minds, one of the kids from the neighborhood who grew up and became a success."

The whole of that first Sinatra film, *Higher and Higher,* functions as a paean to this newness. The freshness of his approach and his sound still seem astonishing fifty years later. Most of Sinatra's successors, the baritones who followed him out of the bands and into solo spots, were still basing their styles on Crosby (similar to the way most of Crosby's competitors in the 1930s, such as Dick Powell and Rudy Vallée, had come from the previous generation, stylistically speaking). Sinatra imitators (Ronnie Deauville, who sang with Tex Beneke and later Ray Anthony, was among the first) would not come along until the first phase of his mass popularity had passed. Dick Haymes, Perry Como, Buddy Clark* (and even those like Bob Eberly whose

---

* "Crosby, Columbo, and Vallée" was a popular novelty song from 1932 that was also made into a Merrie Melodies cartoon. On a 1944 *For the Record* radio show, Sinatra sang a parody of his hit "Sunday, Monday, or Always" with special lyrics depicting his competition with "Dick Todd, Dick Haymes, and Como," which concludes with the aside, "There's just one

solo careers never quite got off the ground) were all, to a degree, men who would be Bing.

Musically, the most striking feature of Sinatra's singing was his use of sustained notes, which helped establish him as the first major voice to build something new on Crosby's foundation. The bobby-sox–wearing young girls were clinging to his every note; "If I did what they call bending a note, if I just kind of looped the note, well, they would wail," he observed.

Sinatra also usually sang slowly, with a patience and a willingness to take his time as well as a sensuality that must have sounded like forbidden fruit to this repressed, post-Depression generation. Compared to Crosby, explained Rosemary Clooney, Sinatra invested much more in his emotional interpretation, "at a deeper level. And I also think Frank showed a vulnerability that perhaps was not in Bing's makeup. Bing wasn't able to come out and sing 'I love you' in a song. It had to be 'if I loved you' or 'if I say I love you' [as in "Moonlight Becomes You"] or something like that. Whereas Sinatra would be more vulnerable and feel very comfortable showing that vulnerability. Therefore, you, as a listener, are more comfortable hearing it." On a piece like "What'll I Do?," Sinatra saturates his performance with the strength required to show vulnerability.* Never in a hurry, yet always in a tempo you could dance or pat your foot to, Sinatra exuded an erotic warmth that implied slow lovemaking.

It's in that most romantic use of time that Axel Stordahl played his biggest role in the Sinatra success story. In the Dorsey period, it had largely been up to Stordahl to develop the slow-ballad side of the band—and Sinatra in particular—at the same time the Oliver rhythm numbers turned TD's orchestra into one of the great jazz organizations of all time. Alternating between the two men, Sinatra, like the band itself, could go either way; by the end of the Dorsey tenure he was as adroit a rhythm singer as he was a balladeer. On Oliver's "Without a Song," he was both at the same time. Sinatra realized that Stordahl could help him develop the strong, new romantic sound he was looking for. Even in the Dorsey period, clarinetist Mahlon Clark expounded, Stordahl was known for "writing *beautiful* countermelodies and using the

---

Crosby." In a 1949 Looney Tunes cartoon, *Curtain Razor*, the trio of competing crooners is identified as "Bingo, Frankie, and Al," the latter being the recently resurrected Jolson.

* At least one unknown cultural commentator at the time accused him of being subversively pansexual. His "style [is] very dangerous to our morale, for it is passive, luxurious, and ends up not with a bang but with a whimper." (As quoted by E. J. Kahn in *The Voice: The Story of an American Phenomenon* [1947], and then again by David Hajdu in *Love for Sale*, some seventy years later.) This has always been my personal theory as to why Sinatra acted like such a badass offstage—to counterbalance the sensitivity and vulnerability that was so present in his music.

right, pretty notes. Frank immediately saw that, so when he went on his own, he took Axel with him."

As the first singer to break out of the dance orchestras into an all-media career, Sinatra released the pivotal stone that caused the avalanche that buried the big bands. "Frank wouldn't want to hear this," said Ted Nash (Sinatra's primary tenor sax soloist in the 1950s), referring to the irony that Sinatra was the catalyst for the demise of his favorite kind of music, but he "put the kibosh on the big bands. Before, people went to see the band, and then they'd listen to a solo now and then or a singer here and there. The singers were strictly secondary. But when Frank hit that screaming bunch of kids, the big bands just went right into the background. From then on, [the idea] was to feature the singer completely, and then everyone else jumped into it. So the bands just died after that." As Mel Tormé put it (in 1950), "Just as Benny Goodman's 1935–36 band made the public orchestra conscious, so did Frank's rise to fame usher in a new era in popular music, a vocalist's era."

The first, most visible result of the Paramount Theatre explosion was that Sinatra was at last signed to a big-money commercial radio program. In fact, it was no less than CBS's flagship series, *Your Hit Parade.* Since its inception in 1935 (coincidentally, Ray Sinatra, who is sometimes described as Sinatra's cousin, had conducted the show's musicians in 1936), the program presented a regular cast of singers—in 1943 they were Sinatra and Joan Edwards (and later, Bea Wain)—doing the ten most popular songs of the week. Stentorian announcer André Baruch (who was also married to Wain) informed us that the weekly list was "determined by *Your Hit Parade*, which checks the best-sellers in sheet music and phonograph records, the songs most heard on the air and most played in the automatic coin machines, an accurate, authentic tabulation of America's taste in popular music."

The orchestrations and, usually, the singing, on *Your Hit Parade* were so devoid of personality that, although it drew ratings in the same league as Bing Crosby's *Kraft Music Hall,* the most popular musical show in the country, it did almost nothing for the careers of its stars. Sinatra's immediate predecessor on the program, Barry Wood,* all but disappeared after leaving

---

* Later an industry executive, Barry Wood had an interesting voice, gray and appropriately woody, with a tinge of a raspy sound somewhere in the area of Al Bowlly and Jack Teagarden. While he had sort of a robust charm, rather like one of movieland's stocky baritones (Dick Foran, anybody?), his rather stiff rhythm makes him tough to listen to today. Although Wood had his own NBC series in the summer of 1943, costarring with Benny Goodman, few of his records have ever been reissued, and he remains but a Trivial Pursuit question as the singer who preceded Sinatra on *Your Hit Parade.*

the show despite his visibility as RCA Victor's number-one male vocalist in the pre-Como period. The same fate befell Joan Edwards, a talented vocalist who was never permitted to display any glimmer of personality that might distract from the songs themselves. Even for Bea Wain, herself one of the most popular singers of the big-band era, *YHP* proved to be an ending rather than a beginning.

Sinatra could not escape the agency's dictatorship of taste even after he became the program's premier ratings asset. Nor did traveling several thousand miles away help: when Hollywood beckoned to Sinatra beginning in the summer of 1943, he petitioned the producing agency, Batten, Barton, Durstine, and Osborn, to let him broadcast his portion of the program from the coast. Lucky Strike's dictatorial president, George Washington Hill, labeled a "tyrannical mastermind" by *Newsweek* after his death in 1946, who called the shots down to the smallest harp glissando, agreed to the arrangement if the cost of the requisite wirings and extra orchestra were deducted from Sinatra's salary. (Hill was the obvious inspiration for Evan Llewellyn Evans, the megalomaniacal sponsor in Frederic Wakeman's novel *The Hucksters*, portrayed marvelously menacingly in the 1947 movie version by Sidney Greenstreet.)

The "West Coast Frank Sinatra *Hit Parade* Orchestra" included Billy May as section trumpeter (Zeke Zarchy played lead) and assistant arranger, marking his earliest professional association with Sinatra; Stordahl also commissioned occasional up-tempo arrangements from George Siravo. The Hollywood portions also afforded Axel Stordahl his first important, albeit unbilled, chance to conduct, although the musical direction credit went to Mark Warnow, who conducted everything except the Sinatra numbers.

Sinatra began on the series in February 1943, and one of the earliest extant Sinatra vocals from *Your Hit Parade* (which actually comes from a rehearsal, not a broadcast) dates from the twenty-seventh of that month. Again, the notion of the solo singer seems so alien that even after the uproar at the Paramount, Sinatra was hardly treated as a "star" but was still singing a brief thirty-two-bar vocal refrain, big band–style (there's even a vaguely Dorseyesque trombone passage near the end). The audience seems to resent the three-chorus formality and applauds after the vocal, effectively drowning out the third chorus. Within a short time, however, the announcer was saving Sinatra's name for last in the weekly lineup, as in "And starring Frank Sinatra!" Within six months he was given the top spot—the number-one song.

When Bea Wain replaced Joan Edwards for four months beginning in July, she quickly realized that Sinatra was at war with the sponsors: G. W. Hill wanted every song delivered with the romance and tenderness of machine-gun fire, and Sinatra, understandably, wanted to employ some of the more sensual sounds that were making him a star. "On that show," Wain recalled, "the tempos were the format. No matter what the ballad was, it had to stay in a certain tempo. And I must say that Frank broke that whole format because when he sang a ballad, it was a ballad. And then I was able to get away with it because he got away with it. We were able to sing slowly and with feeling, instead of just knocking it out."

In spite of the changes and improvements he was able to bring about, Sinatra seems never to have thought of *Your Hit Parade* as "his" show. When the V-Disc project, which supplied specially produced records to servicemen, began "requisitioning" Sinatra performances, he offered them selections from all his other shows, but never *Your Hit Parade.*

Having proven himself on *Your Hit Parade,* Sinatra was given the opportunity to be more broadly featured in his own costarring series. Titled the *Broadway Bandbox,* the program was sustaining (nonsponsored) but national. Sinatra was thus one of the few singers on the air to be featured on two distinct series running simultaneously: the smaller, Friday night *Broadway Bandbox,* which debuted on May 14, 1943, and the big-time, big-money, *Hit Parade* on Saturday night.

Much about *Broadway Bandbox* seemed like a spinoff of *YHP,* or, in the parlance of the show, a "Lucky Strike Extra." (The phrase refers to those rare moments on *YHP* treasured by Sinatra but loathed by the agency when *Your Hit Parade* actually presented a classic song not in the current top ten.) The other featured performer on the show was composer and bandleader Raymond Scott, whose older brother was Mark Warnow, conductor on *YHP.* (Scott would eventually succeed him as conductor on the television *YHP.*) The show felt like *YHP*'s little brother, with announcements delivered over harp glissandi. "The show was a combination," reedman Artie Baker explained. "We would do a Raymond Scott thing, and then when it was time for Frankie to sing, Axel took over because Axel was writing for him all the time."

Guitarist Tony Mottola recalled that initially Scott was expected to conduct the entire program. The producers soon saw the wisdom of bringing in Stordahl to conduct on Sinatra's numbers. "Quite frankly," Mottola elaborated, "in those days Raymond didn't much care for anything but his band. He wasn't too enthralled with being an accompanist for a singer or anything like that, so there wasn't much rapport between Frank and Raymond. That didn't last long, because, in a couple of weeks, Axel was brought in." (Another Scott reedman, clarinetist Pete Pumiglio, added, "Of course, when he fell in love with Dorothy Collins, that's when he got interested in working with singers." Collins would be one of the featured stars on the televised *YHP*.) In July, Sinatra and Scott parted company; in the fall the singer would shift from the *Broadway Bandbox* to the second series of *Songs by Sinatra*, again fifteen minutes and unsponsored, while Scott remained in the same time slot but with a new program title.

While his radio career was burgeoning, Sinatra was also being canny about his choice of "personal appearances." On Saint Patrick's Day, two months prior to the launch of *Broadway Bandbox* (on May 14), he made his night-club debut at the Riobamba, a midtown boîte very deliberately modelled on the highly popular Copacabana. Joel Herron, who occasionally played piano there, described the joint: "This management wanted whatever the Copacabana had, with an imitation Copa (chorus) line and imitation of the whole Copa idea." It was a gamble for Sinatra: he had to accept less money than he could have gotten for a movie theater gig and, as Sammy Cahn (who was in attendance on opening night) recalled, "the audience was not [a bunch of] bobby-soxers. This was an *adult*, mature, *sophisticated*, two-o'clock-in-the-morning Manhattan audience."

Herron remembered that Sinatra was, again, rather nervous on opening night, but this had the effect of actually quieting the audience. Before he could get any words out of his mouth, he began to back up slowly into the curve of bandleader Nat Brandwynne's piano. As soon as Sinatra emitted the first notes of "Night and Day," he heard feminine sighs and knew that he was in the right place. Long before the first set was even over, press agent George Evans had phoned the news of Sinatra's latest triumph to every columnist who wasn't already present.

As at the Paramount, Sinatra had begun as an "extra added attraction" after monologist Walter O'Keefe (whose primary shtick was an exaggerated delivery of the ancient vaudeville number, "The Man on the Flying Trapeze"), comic "songstress" Sheila Barrett, and a dance team, as well as the chorus line. The next week, Herron recalled, the management wanted to bill Sinatra over Barrett, and she decided to leave. The week after, while it would have broken a nightclub taboo to put Sinatra's name above the headliner, the club billed them equally, and O'Keefe left shortly after that.

By May, Sinatra's confidence had soared, together with the club's profits. "A voice would announce, 'And now, brrr . . . the Riobamba *prrroudly* presents, Frank Sinatra!'" Sammy Cahn recalled, miming a drum roll. "Instead of coming out from behind the band, he came walking through the tables. And when he got to the center of the club, he had to do his number. And I say to you again, he was thinner than my finger. And he had them in the grip of his hand. One of my vivid memories is, while he was singing, some gorilla coughed. A giant guy, like 250 pounds. He turned and looked at this guy, and the guy didn't know what to do with himself. Do you understand what I'm trying to say? Frank had power, menace! It was an incredible experience."

The Riobamba gig was also significant in that it may have marked the first of a scant few times when Sinatra crossed paths with Leonard Bernstein. Not yet established as a conductor or composer, Bernstein wrote incidental music for at least one of the club's shows, including a song called "Riobamba" (which Sinatra may well have sung), which the composer later "cannibalized" as one of the themes in his ballet *Fancy Free* (which led to the show *On the Town*, which in turn became one of Sinatra's most memorable films).

The Paramount Theatre kept Sinatra busy for most of June. He then spent the summer conquering two more mediums: Hollywood, with his first starring feature, RKO's *Higher and Higher* (shot mainly in September), and the concert stage. The former was an obvious career goal for any entertainer; the second was entirely unprecedented. Pop singers sang with dance bands or occasionally appeared in musical comedies; they did not perform in sit-down concert halls with philharmonic orchestras. As he had at the Paramount a season earlier, Sinatra was once again billed on the program as a "guest attraction." He took part in a concert series billed as "Music for the Movies," in which classically styled film composers conducted their major works.

The most notable stops on the tour were at Lewisohn Stadium in New York, with Max Steiner and the New York Philharmonic (August 3), and the Hollywood Bowl with Vladimir Bakaleinikoff, Morris Stoloff, and the Los Angeles Philharmonic (August 14). Both the classical critics and the popular press resoundingly disapproved; there was one surprisingly sneery write-up in *Life* magazine, which deemed it deplorable that Sinatra actually had the temerity to inform these great classical musicians what tempo he wanted to sing in.

Sinatra's uneasiness can be detected at the Hollywood Bowl (the only one of the four concerts known to have been recorded); he stayed fairly conservative for most of his eleven numbers, avoiding dramatic high notes. Still, there's little doubt that the concerts represented a big step for Sinatra personally and a giant leap forward for the respectability of popular music. He would play the Hollywood Bowl three or four more times in the 1940s and make such "big rooms" his bread-and-butter from the 1970s onward.

By the time Sinatra returned east in the fall of 1943, he had established his pattern for most of the rest of the decade: he would do two radio shows each week, *Your Hit Parade* and his own starring show, until the start of 1945, when he temporarily quit *YHP* to concentrate on *Max Factor Presents Frank Sinatra* (also known more simply as "The Frank Sinatra Show"). That show would be succeeded by *Old Gold Presents Songs by Sinatra*, sponsored by the same cigarette company that produced *Lucky Strike Presents Your Hit Parade*, for two seasons beginning in September 1945. His primary focus would continue to be movie theaters like the New York Paramount; during November and December 1943 he played up and down the East Coast as headliner of a package that also included Jan Savitt's orchestra.

After singing for his core audience of bobby-soxers in the daytime, most evenings he would play for their better-heeled parents in nightclubs. Beginning in October 1943, his most notable nitery conquest was the pricey Wedgwood Room at the Waldorf Astoria, so named, as Sinatra quipped in a 1945 radio gag, because if they could *wedge* one more person in, they *would*. For really big charity occasions he played the concert stages, and he also made at least one film every year. In 1943 the Sinatras bought their first home, in New Jersey, and in 1945 they permanently settled in Hollywood.

By mid-1943, there was only one major entertainment medium that Sinatra had not yet conquered: commercial recordings—and this was due to circumstances beyond his control. The American Federation of Musicians strike was about to enter its second year in June; Decca and Capitol Records were almost out of it, but Columbia and Victor weren't about to back down. The two most major of the major labels were convinced that Congress would declare the strike unconstitutional during a time of war. They were wrong; Congress had enough on its hands without worrying about a bunch of striking musicians and the fate of a new crooner. And thus the strike dragged on for another year and change.

All sorts of dodges were attempted to get around the musicians' union between 1942 and 1944. Some labels, particularly independents in far-flung Los Angeles, went ahead and recorded anyway, resulting in some of Nat King Cole's best sides as a jazz pianist. Rising musical comedienne and future Sinatra costar Vivian Blaine introduced the oddest record in or out of the ban, "The Air Battle," in which an accordionist (apparently not a member of the union) depicts the sounds of a bombing raid, complete with screams of death and destruction, all as re-created on his squeeze box.

As we have seen, Columbia, following the suggestion of publisher Lou Levy, came up with the lucrative idea of reissuing the Harry James–Sinatra disc of "All or Nothing at All" from 1939, which, fortunately, so heavily featured the boy singer that it was easily passed off as a genuine Sinatra record. The four-year-old master climbed to the top of the *Billboard* best-selling record charts and was treated like a contemporary Sinatra hit. Sinatra

commissioned a new arrangement of the song from Stordahl, which he introduced on the premiere episode of the *Broadway Bandbox* show. The 1939
version was advanced enough for its day, but it was significantly updated for
1943, using strings and ending on a soft and subtle long note instead of the
belting, dramatic closer of the 1939 chart. "All or Nothing at All" became the
first of his own hits that Sinatra would sing on *Your Hit Parade*.

Apparently the labels were collectively considering resorting to a cappella
recordings as early as October 1942 (as *Down Beat* had implied). Bing Crosby,
still very much the industry leader throughout World War II, attempted four
a cappella sides in July and August of 1943, but was not happy with the
results and decided to wait until live musicians were again available. However,
the contenders and would-be contenders to the Crosby throne couldn't afford
to wait. By 1943 these included Ginny Simms, the former Kay Kyser thrush
whom Sachs had signed to Columbia even before Sinatra, as well as Dick
Haymes (who had succeeded Sinatra with both James and Dorsey) and Perry
Como (late of Ted Weems). Following Sinatra's example, they had all struck
out on their own.

Neither Sinatra nor Sachs wanted the singer's first new solo releases on
Columbia to be anything less than the best, and thus they were determined
to wait for the end of the ban. "I was a holdout," Sinatra reminisced in 1970.
"I really held out. I think the strike went on for a couple of years, and I came
in at the end of it with these things. I got a lot of pressure from the people at
Columbia Records to do [the a cappella sessions]. I didn't want to cross the
lines, in a sense."

Jack Kapp, Sachs's equivalent at Decca Records, forced Sinatra to change
his mind. In May and July 1943, Decca had produced a capella sessions with
Dick Haymes. The newly liberated Haymes posed a potential threat to Sachs's
own star attraction, so "in desperation," as Mitch Miller put it, Sachs turned
to Alec Wilder for a cappella arrangements for Sinatra and the Bobby Tucker
Singers (Sinatra's radio backup choir), nine of which would be recorded
between June and November 1943. Wilder, who had been Miller's classmate
at the Eastman School of Music, would be a peripheral if persistent figure
over the years in the Sinatra saga.

As choral singer Ray Charles (who would later bill himself as "The
Other Ray Charles," to distinguish himself from the more famous R&B
singer-pianist) remembered, Axel Stordahl contributed several of these
all-vocal charts, although as a member of the AFM he could not be credited
at that time. "It was like a vocal orchestra," Charles explained. "You wrote
it the way that you would for a band: the bass voices would keep time like
a bass would, and you would write sections on top of that. The girls could

be the equivalent of either the trumpets or strings, depending on what your orchestration was."

Charles made the comparison to Ray Conniff's early choral recordings. "He doubles everything the orchestra does in the voices. Only [in 1943] there wasn't a band. You don't have a drum sound and you don't have a guitar sound, but it's written so that you have an equivalent of a rhythm section. Then you have what the brass would play, what the strings would play, what the saxes would play." Despite how some charts had to be tried and retried on session after session, Charles maintained that recording them "wasn't at all difficult." He added, however, "When I listen to them now, I think they're terribly out of tune."

There's a sense of urgency to the a cappella sessions made by the three big upstarts of 1943, Sinatra, Haymes, and Como, that's missing in Crosby's four musicianless titles. It seems more fitting that these three newcomers should show their mettle by contending with such unmusical circumstances. On the other hand, it was damned annoying for Crosby to be subjected to them; he had already proven himself time and again. Haymes, Como, and Sinatra worked as hard on these dates as new stand-up comics do on their first *Tonight Show* spot, their enthusiasm often compensating for the lopsided accompaniment.

In getting the dozen background voices strong enough to approximate an orchestra, Sinatra and Sachs apparently decided the important thing was to sound credible even at the cost of excitement. The energy it took to record those a cappella charts (fourteen takes have survived of nine separate songs) was only worth expending on surefire material. The nine 1943 masters encompass the much-plugged tunes from three current hit films (among them Sinatra's *Higher and Higher*), and the Broadway sensation *Oklahoma!* Only the very first Sinatra Columbia item, "Close to You," was an unaffiliated song, and Sinatra had a special reason for recording it. Earlier that season, "Close to You" (the same song that would later title one of his best albums for Capitol Records) had initiated the multidecade personal and business relationship between Sinatra and Ben Barton. An ex-vaudevillian determined to get into music publishing, Barton had brought the newly written "Close to You" backstage to Sinatra at the Paramount. The singer took to both Barton and the song so much that he decided to publish it as the first copyrighted work for Barton Music.

Columbia recorded "Close to You" and the other eight choral titles primarily to have something to offer Frank's millions of (mostly) female fans. Unfortunately, the nature of the a cappella beast cornered Sinatra into curtailing the finely caressed notes that made the teenyboppers swoon so. Manie

Sachs once suggested another reason why he temporarily abandoned this device: "The only thing that he minded was the squealing," Sachs recalled in 1955. "They'd do that when he bent his notes. If you follow Frank's history, you'll see that he stopped bending notes for a while."

Sinatra sings beautifully on the nine 1943 titles; still, they are but faint echoes of what Sinatra really sounded like in the theaters at this, the first moment of his impact. Fortunately, many live airchecks survive, a few of which have been issued by Columbia's corporate heirs over the years (most rewardingly on the 2015 boxed set *A Voice on Air*). Among them, Sinatra's *Your Hit Parade* rendition of "Oh, What a Beautiful Mornin'" is so convincing that even the ludicrous image of Sinatra as a bronco-busting, ten-gallon–hatted cowboy (less *Okie* than *Hobokie*) doesn't detract from it. A season later, on a March 1, 1945, broadcast, Sinatra revived "Beautiful Morning" and improved it with a lightly swinging up-tempo version that moves deftly. On the a cappella Columbia master, however, the high-pitched voices are aggravating. All in all, you may find the twelve-voice pseudo-orchestra numbing, but Sinatra sings even more precociously than he did with a genuine string section.

Sinatra would return to two of the nine numbers, "The Music Stopped," in 1947, at which time the 1943 a cappella version of which had not yet been released. (Then much later, in 1956, he made his classic recording of "Close to You" with Nelson Riddle.) The more fully realized, fully orchestrated rendition of "The Music Stopped" contains one of his most moving glissandi (in the first line of the outchorus). Since the lyrics are all about music stopping, he interprets it as a tour de force of pauses, rests, and fermatas, with Sinatra alternately deciding to either extend or cut short the crucial note on "stopped." The lovely way he goes up on "lights" and down on "low" in the same phrase is also particularly compelling; contrastingly, the effectiveness of these vocal effects is severely curtailed on the 1943 reading. (This was a particularly poor song to select for the a cappella process—how can he sing about the music stopping when the music isn't even there to begin with? In that sense, "The Music Stopped" is a theme song for the whole AFM ban period.)

Likewise, the 1943 live orchestral versions of "Close to You" (including one very different treatment in which Sinatra not only includes the verse but also scats for a few bars) as well as the 1956 Nelson Riddle remake paint a similar picture. Here, Sinatra underscores that the title of the song that launched his solo recording career could have served as a perfect metaphor for his developing style: it's all about intimacy and closeness.

Then, at the end of 1944, suddenly the music starts. By the end of the ban, Sinatra had made more of these a cappella records than any other artist, while

Perry Como came in a close second with eight. Still, Columbia gave up before the end of 1943. It's fully a year from "Music Stopped," the last a cappella title, to "If You Are But a Dream," the first true Sinatra-Stordahl recording. If you listen to the Columbia sessions chronologically, the transition is overwhelming; done only three days after Columbia made peace with the union, the song seems to be Stordahl's attempt to make up for lost time. How better than to start with an adaption of the classical piano masterwork *Romance in E Flat Major, Op. 44* by Anton Rubinstein? For what was previously known as a piano solo or a string quartet work, Sinatra employs a full chamber symphony orchestra, including strings and woodwinds, not to mention eight Bobby Tucker Singers for good measure.

The Sinatra-Stordahl sound is so perfected by the time of those November 1944 sessions that it's difficult to trace its development. The 1942–44 AFM ban, apart from lighting the long fuse leading to the explosion that would change the course of pop music, thwarts historians in divining the origins of stylistic evolutions in both the jazz and pop worlds. In roughly two years, between the last Dorsey sides of 1942 and the first Stordahl-Columbia sessions, Sinatra had evolved tremendously; if you were following his career on recordings alone (without having heard any of the interim radio performances) you would find the difference overwhelming. (Almost as much as the concurrent evolution in jazz from swing to bebop.)

Many jazz fans who had served in World War II were astonished to find out how much that music had changed during the duration. Yet those same music-conscious servicemen had been the only ones able to follow, on recordings at least, the equally startling developments in pop music. The sole records released during the ban were V-Discs, distributed among the armed forces exclusively, and they offer a fascinating sideways glance into Sinatra's evolution. These document full orchestral versions of many of the songs he otherwise recorded only a cappella, live versions of songs, and many numbers and arrangements that he never otherwise documented. For instance, the earliest original Sinatra V-Disc contained three numbers: "I Only Have Eyes for You," "Kiss Me Again," and "(There'll Be) A Hot Time in the Town of Berlin." Only the second title, a particularly lovely adaptation from a Victor Herbert operetta, has a close commercial equivalent. The first would be broadly truncated on the 1945 Columbia version, and the third, a wildly jingoistic war anthem by former Dorsey pianist Joe Bushkin, wouldn't be recorded at all.

The Sinatra V-Discs were at last legally issued for commercial consumption in 1994; one thing they make clear is that the mature Sinatra-Stordahl style was completely perfected even by the fall of 1943. The classic early-Sinatra ballad sound is unmistakable in such early V-Disc–only arrangements (none recorded commercially) as "She's Funny That Way," "The Way You Look Tonight," "Speak Low," and Alec Wilder's "I'll Be Around." The only thing that could have improved "The Way You Look" would have been to have Sinatra himself (rather than the background singers) fill in composer Jerome Kern's very romantic, interstitial humming passages. Otherwise, no one else before or since could make a smile seem so warm or a cheek so soft. A big chunk of the credit for that sound has to go to Axel Stordahl—it's impossible to overestimate his contribution.

"Axel and Frank were really pioneers," Billy May put it. "Axel was really ahead. They were really going in the right direction and doing something new, and finally the industry caught up with them." Of Sinatra's four major collaborators we know the least about Stordahl. Unlike Nelson Riddle, Billy May, and Gordon Jenkins, he rarely received cover billing on a Sinatra album, primarily because his Sinatra sessions found their way onto LPs years after the fact. Stordahl also had far less of a career apart from Sinatra than the others.

Sinatra himself once illustrated the awe with which musicians regarded Stordahl. When the young Don Costa first met Stordahl, as Sinatra later related to Sid Mark, he was actually terrified at the prospect of encountering his original idol in the flesh. "In those days I must say that Axel was writing things. . . . Nobody wrote ballads as pretty as he did until many years later when Nelson came along. I think that Axel Stordahl was the 'daddy' that people began to learn from in the sense of writing orchestrations. He was the most prolific of his time."

The one fact that comes through overwhelmingly from those who worked with Stordahl was that he was the ultimate pussycat, perhaps the most beloved man ever to work in Sinatra's circle. Riddle, May, and Jenkins were all adored by their former sidemen, but Stordahl is spoken of as if he qualified for sainthood. "He was one of the single most beautiful men I ever met," said Sammy Cahn. "I tell people that the trouble with Christianity is that I meet so few Christians. When I call a man like Axel a Christian, it's a great compliment. And I don't give out too many compliments."

This is truly remarkable when you consider the responsibilities on Stordahl's shoulders—the pressure of handling all the music for the number-one personality in films and recordings as well as, for a long time, two radio shows simultaneously. Somehow, Stordahl managed to please everybody. "Axel was the consummate craftsman," said Mitch Miller, who worked both under Stordahl as a sideman and later above him as a producer. "He came in with no temperament, no nothing. He just brought [his work] in and did it."

"Axel was a wonderful guy," said Billy May. "He had a very low fuse, which is unheard of in the music business. People would explode, and Axel would just stand there, lighting and then smoking his pipe [generally upside down, in the best Norwegian sailor tradition]. Then, after everybody got their egos out of the way, Axel would go ahead and do his job." Perhaps the most surprising personal tribute to Stordahl came from cellist Eleanor Slatkin. Although both she and her violinist husband, Felix, appear on several Stordahl-Sinatra sessions, Mrs. Slatkin recalled that the conductor was one of many (most, in fact) who exhibited what today would be classified as a "sexist bias" against female musicians. As she put it, "Stordahl wouldn't have women" in the orchestra. Nonetheless, Slatkin describes Stordahl as "a wonderful, *wonderful* person."

Two years older than Sinatra and also apparently a first-generation American, Stordahl was born in Staten Island on August 8, 1913. Originally the youngster sported the more formal old-world Scandinavian name "Odd Stordahl" and just as briefly a head of wavy blond hair, this being long before his most capital dome became one of the more familiar images to the studio audiences of *Songs by Sinatra*. Stordahl joined his first musical group of note around 1933 or 1934 as trumpeter and arranger in Bert Block's rather middle-of-the-road dance band. There, he shared the brass section at different times with the two key trumpeters who would play lead on both his East Coast and West Coast orchestras a decade later, Rubin "Zeke" Zarchy and then Gordon "Chris" Griffin. He also met the first star vocalist he would write for, Jack Leonard.

Stordahl, Zarchy remembered, "wrote the whole book for Bert Block, the whole library, and he also played trumpet in the band, although he was never much of a player." Griffin remembered that "Axel was writing things for Jack Leonard at the time, [and even then] his arrangements were always simple and melodious and in good taste." While Zarchy or Griffin played lead, Joe Bauer served as second, and Stordahl sat in the third trumpet chair. The band recorded six titles for the American Recording Corporation in October 1935, and while it's not known if Stordahl was still in the band at that time, they were certainly his arrangements.

Thanks to Stordahl, Zarchy pointed out, "Bert's band was not a high-note band. It was a very musical, melodic, 'soft-type' band, swinging. [It was] a perfect band for a restaurant, not with loud brass playing high. [And it wasn't] really a sweet band per se because the sweet bands in those days had three tenor saxes and fiddles, so it wasn't Mickey Mouse. All of Block's music was Axel's, and it was a very hip band. Axel wrote the whole book [without first making] a score. He wrote each part individually and kept them all in his head."

As Dorseyite Paul Weston recalled, national-level bandleaders routinely raided local groups for talent, and Tommy Dorsey, who had recently swooped up the Joe Haymes band en masse, hired three of Block's key personnel in a similar coup in late 1935: Bauer, Leonard, and Stordahl as arranger and fill-in trumpeter. "Joe, Axel, and Jack Leonard were also a singing trio," said Zarchy, "so Tommy got a big package: two trumpet players, an arranger, a vocalist, and a singing group, all out of the same three guys." Stordahl, Griffin remembered, "had a terrible lip!" He knew his limitations as a brassman and did everything he could to avoid playing. Stordahl soon became Dorsey's number-two arranger (behind Weston) and also occasionally doubled, Zarchy said, as one of the voices in the band's vocal trio, The Three Esquires.

"But when Tommy got mad at somebody or somebody did something and got fired or quit, then sometimes Axel would have to play [third trumpet] for a couple of nights," said Weston. The first trumpeter played the lead that the whole brass section had to follow, the second normally took the jazz solos, while "the third trumpet really doesn't do anything, he just fills out the section," said drummer Johnny Blowers. Even so, Stordahl dreaded fighting his way through those third-trumpet parts because, or so he claimed, playing made him abnormally hungry. "That was the big joke in the band," recalled section mate Yank Lawson. "Somebody always had to send Axel a sandwich." "He was a hypochondriac," said Griffin. "He used to get weak when he played the trumpet. They had to feed him every fifteen minutes to keep him from fainting."

Dorsey encouraged Stordahl's ambition to arrange full-time, and in 1938 the leader described Stordahl as his principal writer of "sweet arrangements." A ballad man at heart, Stordahl was never at home working on flag-wavers or even danceable fox-trots. Leonard-era items such as "I Hadn't Anyone till You" and "I Can Dream, Can't I?" reveal Stordahl working toward what would, by 1943–44, become one of the great orchestral sounds in all of pop music, albeit hampered by a lesser vocalist. "Axel," said saxophonist and arranger Sid Cooper, "was a revolutionary. He taught a lot of people that strings and harp, and so forth, could be used very nicely in a dance band. And he knew how to do it. Looking back, I can still hear a lot of things that Axel wrote that were unique."

In 1939 and 1940, Stordahl's stock rose substantially in the Dorsey band after the departure of Paul Weston, which increased his responsibilities to the band book. Soon after, the arrival of Sinatra sparked his imagination and gave him a supreme ballad instrument to work with. Within a short time, the Sinatra-Stordahl combination became a formidable commercial-artistic force even within the parameters of the Dorsey aggregation.

"Axel had a gift for making beautiful arrangements," said Zarchy. "That's why Frank wanted him to go with him when he left Dorsey." Sinatra himself later quipped that he took a great pride in offering Stordahl $600 a week to come with him when he had been making $150 with Dorsey.

In January 1943 (the date is approximate), Sinatra prerecorded a series of songs for a wartime-era radio series titled *Treasury Song Parade*; the majority of these tracks use a small house orchestra, with no Stordahl input. In fact, in spite of the fullness of the singer's voice, the group, led by an accordion, would have been at home at any bar mitzvah. It isn't just that Sinatra, as a star attraction, depended on a good band to put him over; rather, hearing Sinatra with just a generic group like this is tantamount to experiencing half of a musical vision. Sinatra was never just a voice or even *The* Voice; he was always a musical auteur, and here he is without his tools.

Sinatra and Stordahl had introduced an embryonic version of their "sound" at the January 1942 Bluebird date, and perfected their approach over the singer's consistent and fairly constant radio appearances throughout 1943 and 1944: *Broadway Bandbox, Songs by Sinatra,* and, later in 1944, Sinatra's first starring half-hour series, *Frank Sinatra in Person,* sponsored by Vimms Vitamins through 1944 and then by Max Factor in the spring of 1945. Virtually all the Sinatra-Stordahl charts recorded by Columbia, especially the classic 1944–5 titles, were initially premiered, tested, and polished on this show.

Axel Stordahl was Sinatra's primary collaborator during the entire eleven years in which he recorded for Columbia Records, and even the first of his Capitol sessions as well—and then, still later and not entirely coincidentally, the last of his projects for Capitol Records, in 1961. Sinatra's Columbia period itself is demarcated by the two AFM recording bans: the first strike, 1942–44, begins it, while the second, in 1948, signified the halftime point. From 1944 to the end of 1947, Sinatra worked exclusively with Stordahl on records and radio (not counting one date with Mitch Miller and several all-star and small-group collaborations). From the end of the 1948 strike onward, especially in 1949 (when Stordahl ceased conducting on Sinatra's radio shows), Sinatra worked more frequently with other musical directors. In 1950, Mitch Miller replaced Manie Sachs as CBS's head A&R man, creating a further distinction between his earlier and later years at the label.

The Stordahl association certainly represents the most fruitful or, in Sinatra's apropos phrase, "prolific" period of the singer's own career. Where Stordahl and Nelson Riddle each wrote approximately the same number of *recorded* orchestrations for Sinatra, roughly three hundred, Stordahl wrote at least that many more that weren't done on records but only played live on Sinatra's weekly shows. In terms of the total number of performances documented, there's nearly as much extant Sinatra material from the 1940s as there is from all the other decades combined, even factoring in the abundance of unauthorized concert tapes from the 1970s on. Although the actual record labels only credit "orchestra under the direction of Axel Stordahl," Stordahl seems to have been responsible for, at the very least, 90 percent of the arrangements Sinatra performed in all mediums during these years. As Paul Weston pointed out, the heavy workload required of musical directors in this period forced them occasionally to hire other arrangers, especially "when you're doing two and three record dates a week and a radio or a television show at the same time."

Stordahl's need to employ other writers, as we'll see, was also fed by his lack of faith in his own ability to score an up-tempo assignment, as well as the constant demand for new charts for all of Sinatra's recordings and radio spots. For the necessary swing charts on the *Old Gold* and *Max Factor* shows, Stordahl most regularly turned to George Siravo, but also occasionally Sy Oliver, Heinie Beau, and Billy May. (May was quick to point out that he wrote only "a couple of charts" for Sinatra to sing on *Your Hit Parade* and nothing that was ever commercially recorded by the singer in this period.) Another Dorsey vet, Richard Jones, also took care of at least one Broadway-style orchestration. But this amounted only to occasional pinch-hitting: Stordahl actually arranged the vast majority of the charts by himself, and conducted all of them. Small wonder he lost his hair so early.

One can obtain a clearer picture of Stordahl and Sinatra's symbiotic relationship at this point not only by listening to Sinatra without Stordahl, as on the *Treasury Song Parade* (which might be considered somewhat unfair to Sinatra in that most of Stordahl's work without Sinatra is also less distinguished), but also by listening to most vocal records of the period. Without question, the most interesting vocal records of the 1930s are heavily jazz-oriented, from Eddie Sauter's stylish charts for Mildred Bailey in Red Norvo's orchestra to the informal, ad-lib swing backings heard behind Lee Wiley and Billie Holiday. But most pop vocal orchestrations from the 1930s and early '40s are, to put it kindly, tedious. Few vocal records from that era by, for instance, Victor's Barry Wood, Dinah Shore, or Dick Todd are collected, listened to, or reissued today—even though these are good singers who usually did good songs, they're often defeated by lifeless accompaniments. Two of the greatest singers of the period, Bing Crosby and Connee Boswell, recorded in both jazz and straight pop settings, and it's small wonder that the greatest interest in these two artists today centers around their "hot" sessions. We listen to Crosby records exclusively for the star singer; the backgrounds on Sinatra discs, while never distracting from the singer, offer as much to listen to (if one cares to) as the foreground does. As a Crosby fan, I'm pained to admit that there's no comparison between the often merely workmanlike writing of his musical director, John Scott Trotter, and Stordahl, who became the leading exponent of the fine-tuned vocal arrangement of the 1940s.

In 1940, two hit records appeared that pointed to the future of pop vocal orchestrations. The first was the Sinatra-Dorsey "I'll Never Smile Again," arranged by Fred Stulce and Axel Stordahl. While not typical of the mature Sinatra-Stordahl sound, it certainly signified a major step in the right direction. The second was "Flamingo" by Duke Ellington's orchestra, sung by Herb Jeffries and arranged by Billy Strayhorn. Stordahl and Strayhorn here were trumpeting the news in tandem; vocal accompaniments no longer had to consist of a routine background of cycle-of-chords and choruses knocked out in cookie-cutter fashion.

"Flamingo," in particular, was the most spectacular full and through-composed score (in the classical sense) ever created for a solo voice in pop thus far. No longer were vocal charts generic and interchangeable, meant to suit any voice or any piece of material; Stordahl and Strayhorn began to tailor charts around the soloist and the selection. The orchestra could now follow the singer with passages intended expressly to complement both the musical and dramatic angles of the number, using flourishes and instrumental combinations that illustrated phrases with what Renaissance musicians called "word-painting."

As early as 1938, the trade paper *Orchestra World* noted that Stordahl's "creative work is especially evident in his construction of intros and codas, which are rich harmonically and melodically." Those openings and closings became even more important since, in his mature work, they illustrate how the accompaniment continually complements the singer, even in the moments of the work that are completely instrumental.

"Nancy (with the Laughing Face)," released in 1945, is one of the definitive Stordahl arrangements. The song originated in Sinatra's relationship with Phil Silvers and Jimmy Van Heusen, who, Sinatra recalled, "hung around my house a great deal in those days." At a party given in the spring of 1944 at lyricist Johnny Burke's house, Silvers cracked a joke that gave a case of the giggles to Burke's wife, Bessie. This prompted Silvers to characterize her as "Bessie with the Laughing Face." Van Heusen, Burke's longtime composing partner, thought that would make a good title for a song. Since Burke had resolved not to work that day, Silvers took twenty minutes and wrote the words himself. The two substituted "Nancy" for "Bessie" when Silvers got the idea of making a present of the song to Sinatra's daughter at her fourth birthday party a few weeks later.

Sinatra introduced "Nancy" on a broadcast of his *Vimms* radio series around April 1944. In July 1944 he recorded two takes of the song as part of his only completely "original" session for the V-Disc program (which usually utilized performances from his radio shows). That December, Sinatra attempted a take for Columbia, which didn't get released until fifty years later. Then, according to Silvers, everyone forgot all about it. However, when Sinatra and Silvers toured Europe for the USO in June 1945, Sinatra asked for requests, and "the first scream from two thousand men was for 'Nancy (with the Laughing Face),'" as Silvers later wrote. The GIs had fallen in love with the song via the V-Disc, which utilized a longer and slower chart than the commercial take, and when Sinatra rerecorded "Nancy" for Columbia in August, it became, as Silvers said, "one of his perennial hits."

"For the first couple of years people thought I wrote the song," Sinatra later said. "So I had to explain to them that it was Jimmy Van Heusen, and when I mentioned Phil Silvers, everybody giggled. Still, whenever I announce that I'm going to do 'Nancy,' there's a kind of a deep breath from the audience." If "White Christmas" and "Homesick, That's All" and other numbers that Sinatra also recorded in this period made servicemen nostalgic, Sinatra's song to his little girl made them think about their own wives and little girls back home.

Between the two V-Disc takes, the two issued Columbia takes, and various radio readings, there are quite a few lyric variations to the song, which are probably better diagrammed than described. Incidentally, the printed music, copyrighted 1944, naturally includes the now-familiar second set of lyrics for the last four lines, which compare "Nancy" to "Grable, Lamour, and Turner." And the printed music also includes a second libretto for the bridge ("What a wonderful treat to come home to"), which neither Sinatra nor apparently anyone else has ever recorded.

Stordahl opens and closes "Nancy" with a five-note figure—not a riff, it's played slowly, almost ad-lib, by the full string section and not intended to swing. Sinatra glides in headfirst, carrying the main melody. When backing any sort of solo, instrumental or vocal, arrangers always assign the melody to the soloist in the foreground and restrict the background to harmonic accompaniment patterns, which makes musical sense as well as focusing audience attention. (Gordon Jenkins, the most experienced of Sinatra's major collaborators, is generally given credit for this innovation, in the mid-1930s.) Stordahl rightfully showcases Sinatra's melodic capacity so completely that one can almost never tell what song is being played without the vocal up front. A Stordahl arrangement is almost like a whole "counter-song" meant to envelope and showcase the first one.

The strings, playing passages that seem to metamorphose from violins to woodwinds with no audible segue, make up the basic texture, with the brass mainly coming in for punctuation, as on the end of the second A right before the bridge. The bridge itself contrasts the diverse textures of pizzicato and arco string playing in a subtle call-and-response pattern, similar to the way most big-band arrangers contrast brass against reeds. When the lyric refers to "mission bells," the fiddlers pluck slightly agitatedly. Then, in the next line, Stordahl resolves this agitation as Sinatra returns lyrically to "Nancy" herself and the "glow" she gives you. On this line Stordahl's strings ease, legato-like, into a warm, calmer, and more relaxedly "glowing" sound.

"Axel was a *very* good string writer, and he also wrote with a very good harmonic sense," explained Weston. Stordahl was also heavily classically oriented. "Axel and I listened to Wagner and Rachmaninoff and Tchaikovsky," said Weston. And Skeets Herfurt remembered, "Debussy was one of his favorite composers. And he got a lot of ideas from Delius, too." Appropriately, on Harry Warren's "I Only Have Eyes for You," Stordahl emphasizes the coincidental melodic similarity to Debussy's *Afternoon of a Faun*. Stordahl relied on the strings and woodwinds as his main mode of expression; the rest of the orchestra, including the saxophone-centric dance band, serves mainly as a buffer for the strings. "Nelson [Riddle], for example, never really cared much about writing for strings. He would just use the strings as a pad," explained Weston, whereas "both Axel and I were more inclined to write countermelodies against the singer than a lot of the other guys." Stordahl's interest in the European classics led to what Chris Griffin characterized as the "long, lovely lines that Ax had in everything he did, including smoking his pipe." Voyle Gilmore of Capitol Records characterized the Stordahl-Sinatra sound as a "first-rustle-of-spring approach."

That classical sensibility helped Stordahl develop into the most capable conductor of all Sinatra's collaborators, as virtually all the musicians who worked under them concur (although the competition in that area is pretty meager). Stordahl went as far as hiring David Frisina, the concertmaster of the Los Angeles Philharmonic, as his own first violinist. "Axel was a good arranger for anything," says Frisina, "but with strings especially, he was really something."

Stordahl continually supported the narrative with bonus ideas that weren't in the original composition. He concocted a grand, sweeping chart on "How Deep Is the Ocean?," which was highly appropriate for a song that measures love in quantities of the infinite and on which Sinatra sings more dramatically straight than usual. To build to a climax in the outchorus, while Sinatra maintains the same tempo, the background switches from the big symphonic sounds to staccato string plucks that even someone who was not paying attention to the accompaniment would be forced to notice. In effect, Stordahl moves the background closer to the foreground to attract attention and increase tension.

Every single Sinatra-Stordahl record consists of more than a highly potent combination of a great voice and (usually) substantial material. Just about every Stordahl chart also includes what we might call a Lucky Strike Extra: a device, an angle, something additional to make the arrangement function not as just two generic choruses but as a start-to-finish through-composition.

"Tommy encouraged that," said Weston. "He liked an arrangement to have some form rather than just playing the song and letting somebody sing it—maybe an introduction that might be repeated in the middle." Weston says of Stordahl's signature intros and codas: "Axel used to have what we referred to as an 'Axel ending.' On the end of some of the ballads, like 'I Can Dream, Can't I?' [for Dorsey] and others, he would use sort of a complicated tag where he would change key a couple of times in the last four bars."

Very occasionally an idea doesn't work: in the middle of "My Romance," a choir suddenly appears from nowhere and starts singing in fast waltz time, like a gang of chaperones breaking down the door at a petting party. More often the simplest ideas work best, such as the ironic holiday chimes at the end of Sinatra's movingly melancholy "Have Yourself a Merry Little Christmas" or the rhythm section dropping out for eight bars to suspend the tempo on the bridge to "The Nearness of You" or the atmospheric tinkly saloon piano and whistling in the fade-out of "One for My Baby."

"Was it a vision," Keats asks in "Ode to a Nightingale," "or a waking dream?" Stordahl decorates "Laura," a *noir* song about a dream girl, vividly imagined but, in the lyric at least, ultimately unreal, with surreal, dreamlike motifs. Pizzicato violins suggest "footsteps that you hear down the hall," and the muffled French horns together with a flute distant enough to be several blocks away enhance the quality of the scenario. For a closer, Sinatra seems to dissolve into the ether, like a movie flashback where everybody's faces get all mushy and wavy. "Stella by Starlight" (from the Ray Milland ghost story *The Uninvited*) showcases Stordahl's ability to create the moody presence of otherworldly entities via spooky one-finger piano passages and bass lines that go bump in the night. "Laura" and "Stella" are perfect embodiments of the Sinatra-Stordahl ideal; they're depicted so vividly that you could almost swear that they were real, and not just characters in a song—characters who aren't even really there to begin with since "Stella" is a ghost and "Laura" exists only in a dream.

Sinatra's melodic descent at the end of "Autumn in New York" functions like a slow, graceful elevator ride down the Empire State Building. On "You'll Never Walk Alone" a similar keyboard figure (played by Mark McIntyre) symbolizes being alone, while the background choir represents the concept of communal solidarity. Sometimes Sinatra and Stordahl take a song far away from what the composer intended. Cole Porter's "Begin the Beguine" was first played as a rumba, yet S. and S., following loosely in the footsteps of Artie Shaw, transform it into an up-tempo swing dance piece that builds to a well-deserved climax. Contrastingly, they borrow the customary Pan-American polyrhythm of the "Beguine" and apply it to "What Makes the Sunset?," and thereby give what might have been just another love song an entirely new dimension. (In this case, that particular beat was probably written into the original tune by composer Jule Styne, since Sinatra introduced it in the locale of a Mexican restaurant in his 1945 film *Anchors Aweigh*.)

At different points in his career, Sinatra and his arrangers could be overtly irreverent, particularly, for instance, when he and Billy May would take a sentimental old song and swing it up, like "The Curse of the Aching Heart." Contrastingly, Sinatra and Stordahl were at their best when working organically and staying true to the songwriter's intentions. This was the opposite of a formula: they had to go into the musical and lyrical heart of each individual song and proceed from the inside out, starting with what the songwriters put into each song and working from there—meeting the composer more than halfway. When, on the penultimate line of "Lost in the Stars," Sinatra pauses after singing of "little stars" and then "big stars," Stordahl fills the break with accordingly little and big orchestral responses, thereby helping to put over the story that much more effectively. This distinction is present in the original cast recording of the song, but Stordahl makes the little much littler and the big even bigger. (And then, in 1963, on *The Concert Sinatra*, Nelson Riddle made the difference between the two even more dramatic.) In fact, Stordahl and Sinatra spoil us so much that when the team tackled "There's No Business Like Show Business" and came up with that rarity, a Sinatra-Stordahl chart with no extra angle, no little something special, no secret sauce, it's a distinct letdown. We're disappointed with these two when they're only as good as the next-greatest singer-arranger team.

"Axel wrote with great transparency," as his lieutenant, George Siravo, delineated. "In other words, if you look at the score, the blacker it looks on the paper, the more depressed a layperson would be. The denser it looks, the heavier it sounds." Stordahl, he expounded, knew how to avoid overcomplicating things. "You might look at his string scores and see only two or three different notes, but the results he got speak for themselves. It didn't take me long to catch on to how to do that—in my own writing."

But as important a contribution as Stordahl made to the Columbia sessions, the major musical mind at work was still Sinatra's. By 1944, Sinatra was both a master orchestrator and a supreme instrument, and the inter-ban years

(1944–47) represent his first of several artistic pinnacles. Sinatra's primary goal, like Stordahl's, was to, as they used to say, put a song over, to communicate what the words and music really mean. During Sinatra's Dorsey tenure, the leader constantly exhorted him to study Bing Crosby, especially the way Crosby made lyrics, in Mel Tormé's phrase, "ninety-nine percent" of what a singer does.

Sinatra essentially built on the natural, as initially espoused by Crosby, Fred Astaire, Benny Goodman, and Louis Armstrong, based on the idea that popular music—singing, dancing, or playing—should be an extension of conversation. He differs primarily from Crosby in that he favors the smooth, even lines of dance music from the mid-1930s, as opposed to the choppier, syncopated sound that Crosby grew up in and forever kept to some degree in his work. Sinatra was born in the same year as Billie Holiday, and both came to the same conclusions concerning how their individual musical advances could help them to put a lyric across that much more convincingly.

Like Holiday, Sinatra used longer phrases and slower tempi to achieve greater scope, a broader palette with which to communicate the dramatic underpinnings of a text. In conversationally singing the words of whatever song he was working on, Sinatra now had greater leeway to stress the words that were the most important in the context of the story. He could now emphasize key words or notes through a combination of choices related to dynamics (loud or soft) and rhythm (short versus long notes). And if the songwriters took note—especially those writing for Sinatra, like Cahn and Styne with "Time After Time"—they already made sure to attach important words to notes distinctive in terms of pitch and duration. As many a songwriter has testified, no singer was more successful in taking advantage of these musical and dramatic opportunities than Sinatra. From "If You Are but a Dream," the first Sinatra-Stordahl Columbia side, onward, it's clear that Sinatra intended to extend this idea further than anyone ever had, choosing the appropriate words, in this case "long" (meaning "want" rather than the opposite of "short"), and stretching it, well, long. He was always the quickest to look for contextually crucial words to hold: "feel" and "lonely" on "There's No You"; "alone" on "When Your Lover Has Gone"; "surrender" on "Body and Soul"; "melts away" on "All Through the Day."

The technique works in reverse, too. Sinatra can get you to pay attention to a particular word by ironically deemphasizing it for emphasis. On that most perfect Sinatra performance of "Nancy," when he arrives at the payoff at the end of the bridge (the word "hello"), he puts less stress on that crucial word than on any other one in the sentence. Here, understating the key word serves to illustrate the lovely gentleness of Nancy as well as underscoring it with a completely unaffected, wide-eyed childlike cadence; both are precisely what the song is all about.

In everything Sinatra does, he has faith in the idea that if you make telling the story—communicating—your first priority, then musical values can't help but follow. This thinking affords a naturalness to his art that defies explanation; for instance, on the phrase "lengthen in" in the 1944 *Vimms* aircheck of "I'll Remember April," he holds "in" but not "lengthen." And early in his career Sinatra apparently decided that he liked to stress the first note of the final A section, coming immediately out of the bridge, and he stresses this note in at least one out of every four songs he does. It doesn't matter that this word often turns out to be as unimportant as something like "and" in "Where or When" or "I Only Have Eyes for You," or "soon" in "If I Loved You." It just *sounds* right.

Usually, there's a musical basis for this. Jim Maher recalled a conversation with Harold Arlen in which he asked the composer, "'What songwriter would ever use a fermata on the first note of an eighth-note triplet?' Harold thought about it and said, 'No one. It wouldn't work.' I said, 'Well, you did, in "Last Night When We Were Young." And you know, Frank Sinatra is the only singer who ever picked up on that.'" But whether justified in the score or not, whatever notes Sinatra chooses to extend always sound exactly right.

Sinatra unfailingly triumphs in the development of devices that move the song forward on both the musical and dramatic planes. What we can call the "soft climax"—as opposed to the "anticlimax"—may be the most effective of these. Apart from exceptions like "Where or When" (on the first of three arrangements of the Rodgers and Hart song that Sinatra would record), "Over the Rainbow," and "All the Things You Are," the most intense moment of a Sinatra performance is rarely the last line or note. Sinatra prefers to hit the big notes in the previous rhyme or line before the end, wherever it makes the most sense to him, and then bring it home on a serenely quiet note. He often ends on a long note, but then it's almost never loud, just subtly and quietly extended. The song will just end with a feeling of "that's all she wrote—there's nothing more to be said." And this is a device that extends beyond the 1940s, and would be common throughout his great work with Nelson Riddle in successive decades.

Even when the final note is of comparatively brief duration, he generally *diminuendos* on it very slowly. On several summer 1944 radio performances of "The Song Is You" and "I'll Be Seeing You," he chooses to fade away by going up through the roof into a stratospheric falsetto note that dissolves into the ether. By the time the ban ended that fall, he seems to have decided that this device focused too much attention on the medium itself (i.e., the singer himself) and distracted from the message. He therefore switched to ending most numbers on his usual, more unobtrusive low note, which is the way he ends his 1946 commercial recording of "The Song Is You."

Even on "Time After Time," conceived by Cahn and Styne as a kind of concerto for long breaths that only Sinatra could sing properly, he ends on a contrastingly quiet note. As with many another closer, he holds it softly, so that as the orchestra swells around him you're not supposed to notice the exact point where Sinatra's voice is simply no longer there. (Although digital audio technology makes this point more discernible than 78-era shellac surface rumble.) On "You'll Never Walk Alone," Sinatra's act of fading into the ensemble (here a vocal choir as well as the orchestra) becomes part of the message of the Rodgers and Hammerstein anthem: the individual becomes one with the community; he need never walk alone.

On a certain level, Sinatra and Stordahl are offering the facade, at least, of utter naturalism; they are not seeming to tinker much with the words or music, but offering both elements as the lyricist and composer delivered them. There's certainly nothing like Mel Tormé's or Betty Carter's total reworkings of songs or Sinatra's own later transformation of ballads like "Dancing in the Dark" into hard-swing flag-wavers. Yet even a cursory listen will reveal that these gentle and easy-sounding ideas are every bit as inventive, with substituted harmonies and paraphrased melodies, as the most far-out improvisation, and are much more musically substantial than the biggest bravura, belting conclusion.

In fact, it's in the codas (and, of course, the overall approach) that Stordahl and Sinatra can upgrade B-level songs, like "This Is the Night," "So They Tell Me," and "I Want to Thank Your Folks," to the "A" class. Most often he ends quietly and post-climactically, sometimes he disappears entirely at the end, as he would on "Angel Eyes" years later. And yes, he also uses big dramatic "belt" endings where appropriate, as on "The Moon Was Yellow," "Falling in Love with Love," and, less convincingly, on "That Old Black Magic." (The latter is a song that worked better as a swinger than a dramatic ballad.) He has no single way of doing things. He lets the material determine the approach.

Thus different kinds of selections engender different tactics. Sinatra is a straight-down-the-middle pop singer, greatly influenced by pop's two next-door neighbors, academic music and jazz, although certainly more by the latter than the former. In the 1940s you will occasionally hear him adopt what could be classified as a vaguely classical stance, not only in the occasional bravura, operatic coda but also in melodies taken from European art music. During the Columbia years he went through enough of these classical adaptations to fill an album, which would have been called, obviously, *The Symphonic Sinatra*.

These included "Strange Music" and another Griegorian ditty from the Broadway show *Song of Norway*, "I Love You"; "If You Are but a Dream," which was written "after," as they say, Anton Rubinstein; "Till the End of Time," derived from Chopin (and done by Sinatra on his 1945 *Old Gold* series); that bestselling slice of Rach(maninoff)-and-roll, "Full Moon and Empty Arms"; and three Russian-inspired tunes that prove what Band of Renown leader Les Brown declared in a 1941 record, namely that "Everybody's Making Money but Tchaikovsky": "One Love," "None but the Lonely Heart," and "Moon Love" (sung live with Harry James but not recorded until 1965).

Just as the songwriters have adapted the melodies, Sinatra adopts their stylistic devices to his own needs—the long, surging notes; the high, dramatic style—purely because it suits these songs. He affords these tunes the melodic richness they deserve, and he does equally well with international folk and pop songs, such as the German-derived "Here Comes the Night" from the James era, the Neapolitan "Luna Rossa," "(On the Island of) Stromboli," and young rival Vic Damone's number-one hit, "I Have but One Heart (O Marenariello)." He rises and surges similarly on what we could call "American opera" arias, like "Where Is My Bess?" from *Porgy and Bess*, "Ol' Man River" from *Show Boat*, the "Soliloquy" from *Carousel* (particularly the ending), and occasional other collar-poppers done with far more subtlety than Mario Lanza.

The 1944 "I Dream of You" also has the feeling of a quasi-classical opus, although it is a Cahn-Styne song that may have been written for *Anchors Aweigh* (though never filmed or recorded for that production). Yet even amid the stately settings of all these numbers, Sinatra remains primarily a jazz-derived vocalist. He specializes in microscopically subtle rhythmic variations, particularly in the way he alternately accelerates and ritards the pace in the last few lines of the song, which owe far more to jazz than to opera. Likewise, the aesthetic success of "None but the Lonely Heart," the best of his Tchaikovsky pieces, has nothing to do with any classical roots that Sinatra was supposed to have. Rather, it illustrates Sinatra's continuing connection to Tommy Dorsey, who had included this adaptation in his book as a vehicle for his own trombone since 1941.

When classical melodies have already been imported to mainstream pop or when Broadway ballads borrow a soupçon of old-world grandeur, Sinatra can more than handle them. His radio work also includes some semiparodic treatments of standard operatic arias: one *Old Gold* show found him delivering a gag version of "Largo al Factotum" even funnier than Alfalfa Switzer's take on *The Barber of Seville*; on another show, he does a goofy fragment from the "Miserere" (from *Il Trovatore*) that reminds us of the Marx Brothers' monumental night at that opera. The sole notable example of him singing an aria essentially straight is "Là Ci Darem la Mano" from *Don Giovanni,* a duet with soprano Kathryn Grayson in the 1947 film *It Happened in Brooklyn.* I have played this for numerous opera singers and they all say the same thing: Sinatra isn't a proper Mozart tenor, but he expresses the point of the aria, the goal of seducing the leading lady and making her come off with him, as well as any tenor who ever sang the role.

On the other side of the musical spectrum, Sinatra is not a blues singer either, but he knows well how to sing numbers like "Blues in the Night" and "Come Rain or Come Shine," songs with hints of blues tonality and sensibility. The joint influence of Bing Crosby, the man he called the father of his career, and Louis Armstrong can be felt much more directly. In his trumpet solos, Armstrong utilized a surprising number of references to Italian opera, and in an interesting turnabout, Sinatra's occasional use of operatic mannerisms often seems directly inspired by Armstrong. The Crosby influence resounds most strongly in the 1930s and '40s pop stars who sounded the most like him (Como, Clark, Haymes), but it can also be found in stylists as distinct as Sinatra, Billy Eckstine, and Nat Cole.

The influence of Crosby is felt especially strongly in the eight standards he recorded for his first album, *The Voice of Frank Sinatra,* in 1945. And yet it also shows how Sinatra had already moved beyond his primary "inspirators" (as Louis Armstrong would say), especially in the very development of the album format itself.

The popular album, as an idea at least, had been around for about two decades before *The Voice,* and yet Sinatra was still the first major popular singer to record an all-original, to use a term that we can't totally agree on, concept album. Both *The Voice* (1945) and *Frankly Sentimental* (1947) were originally issued as 78 rpm albums, in gatefold packages that contained multiple discs. Thus, Sinatra was a step ahead of the technology; when the long-playing record was actually introduced by Columbia in 1948, he was among the first to take advantage of the new medium.

As in later Sinatra albums, the ensemble texture and resulting mood are consistently uniform. On *The Voice* especially, Sinatra and Stordahl devised a kind of chamber-group sound in order to sonically distinguish the album cuts from his regular singles. Although Stordahl had already written more traditional full-scale orchestrations of "She's Funny That Way" and "Someone to Watch Over Me" (which Sinatra had broadcast in recent months), the two then completely rethought those songs for *The Voice.* The accompaniment here derives from a classical small group, employing a core group of four strings (and occasional classical woodwinds, like the flute) and four rhythm players plus one or two horns (a format Sinatra would reprise a decade later on *Close to You*).

The emphasis on the violin as solo instrument in this "double quartet" ensemble accentuates the chamber-music feel, especially during the violin-guitar duo halfway through "Someone to Watch over Me." A solo guitar stresses the Romantic, Italianate side of the Sinatra coin, especially throughout the opening of "I Don't Know Why," which begins with guitarist George Van Eps playing an unaccompanied introductory figure. A very naked-sounding Sinatra soon joins him, and the two duet for ten bars or so before the strings slide in subtly around them. "Axel used the guitar as the prime instrument in the rhythm section," said Van Eps, who played much the same role ten years later on Sinatra's *Wee Small Hours* album. "I don't mean that it takes the place of the drums, but it adds a tonality, a sonority to the sound of the rhythm section. The rhythm is played gently, not bang-bang."

Throughout both these albums Sinatra's singing is even warmer and more tender than usual: in his hands, "Someone to Watch Over Me" becomes a moving expression of vulnerability, explaining why bobby-soxers wanted even more to mother him than to wrestle with him in the back of a DeSoto. On "These Foolish Things (Remind Me of You)" Sinatra plays two roles at once, the swain at the romantic height of an affair as well as the sadder-but-wiser ex-Romeo reflecting on the liaison from a critical distance sometime later. He takes "Spring Is Here" straighter and less jazzy than the more playful "You Go to My Head" in order to make the most of the lyricist's Hart-felt wordplay: When Sinatra sings "spring is *here*, I *hear*," he actually pronounces those two homonyms as if they were audibly different sounds. Elsewhere, on the orchestral "I Should Care," the most *Yiddishkeit* title Sinatra ever recorded, he finds several dozen different ways to phrase the three-note "hook," and each time he sings it the shading of its implications changes subtly.

He does the same on the 1947 "Always." When asked at the time of Irving Berlin's one-hundreth birthday to talk about why Berlin was such a great songwriter, Sinatra responded, "When a man writes a song and he says, 'Not for just an *hour*, not for just a *day*, not for just a *year*, but always,' that's as simple and as pure as anybody can write a piece of prose or a pop song." Sinatra makes you feel the difference between each, fully milking the value of Berlin's parallel—yet, as he stresses, deceptively simple—construction by ever so slightly varying the amount of weight given to each of those temporal increments.

"That Old Feeling," another chamber item, utilizes a Proustian trigger of emotion to set in motion a remembrance of an intrigue past. Sinatra's voice conveys quivery nervousness throughout, only relaxing into a swing feel when the words call for it, on "there'll be no new romance for me." "Fools Rush In" on *The Voice* contains a stunning Sinatraism in the way he lets the word "care" diminuendo out into the beginning of the next line, in a perfect, subdued example of emotion suggested rather than overtly expressed.

All through *The Voice* and *Frankly Sentimental,* Sinatra is resolved not just to "Try a Little Tenderness," as one of the songs is titled, but quite a lot. These may qualify as his most tender vocalizing ever. On "Why Shouldn't I?," Sinatra turns Cole Porter's wiseguy laundry-list lyric into as sincere a portrayal of passion as the Peruvian ever wrote; he does even more for the normally patronizing and patriarchal "Tenderness." After his atypical sensual humming in "Paradise," we feel we've been there.

On "Try a Little Tenderness" and "I've Got a Crush on You," Sinatra does something he rarely did: he sings the verse. Clearly, this is a further way of distinguishing the album tracks from the singles, but he also uses the verses to help set up the narratives. These songs, like "Paradise," owe a particularly strong debt to Crosby. But, as with everything else, although we can trace the lines of influence, all the songs here have been thoroughly Sinatrafied. Here and elsewhere, the concept of Crosby as both competition and inspiration directly motivates Sinatra to sound more like himself. (Around the same time, Sinatra recorded the 1873 "Home on the Range," undoubtedly inspired by Crosby's 1933 version. Abetted by Dave Barbour's graceful guitar, Sinatra actually sounds as if his home on the range, with all the goddamned deer and antelope, actually means something to him. Ironically, until 1993 this sterling sample of Americana had been issued only in England.)

On "I've Got a Crush on You" (a rare ballad arrangement by Siravo) and "Body and Soul," Sinatra is joined by the legendary jazz cornetist Bobby Hackett, whose introductions (heart-stopping cadenzas à la his idol Louis Armstrong's "West End Blues"), obbligatos, and solos immediately whisk these tracks to the pinnacle of Mount Olympus even before Sinatra's entrance. "It Never Entered My Mind" and "Crush" also signify the apogee of Sinatra's romantic style and the rarefied level of his source material, the first song laced with wry melancholia and the second with coy innocence. And both are imbued with musicality (even considering a mildly flat note in the coda of the original master of "Crush"). Alec Wilder later wrote that even with the written music in front of him, he invariably heard "Crush on You" with the variations that Sinatra worked into it. And, said Wilder, any artist who had ever heard Sinatra's record could never be tempted to return to the way Gershwin wrote it.

Wilder is surely also referring to Siravo's ingenious harmonic substitutions, as well as to Hackett's contributions. Approximately thirty years later, one of the trumpeter's own disciples, cornetist Ruby Braff, had an impromptu conversation with Sinatra about his work with Hackett. "Weren't you smart to make those great records with Bobby?" Ruby told Sinatra, in his usual caustic way. "I always wondered why you hadn't made more of them." At this point, Sinatra got a kind of faraway reflective look in his eye, and told Braff, "You know, you always think there'll be time to do all the things you want to do, but somehow there never is." (If you compare Sinatra's 1945 record of "Crush on You" with the two versions by Lee Wiley, from 1940 and 1950, you'll see the outlines of a fascinating back and forth—almost a dialogue—between the two singers.) Siravo echoed these orchestrations in a similar 1950 treatment he wrote for Sinatra of "Nevertheless" that costars trumpeter Billy Butterfield.

When *The Voice* was released in 1946, it became both a number-one selling album (in that very early, pre-LP phase of the pop album charts) and a major influence on other singers. "I was working in a record store, and Dean Martin came in every day to see me," Frank Military remembered. "And one day *The Voice* album came in, and it sold like hotcakes. I didn't know Frank, and Dean didn't know Frank, but the two of us just sat there listening to all four 78s over and over."

Sinatra learned to create a new character with each song. He shifts from attitude to attitude with every new text the way singers normally use different keys for each tune. Although he's always warm and tender and vulnerable, it's the gradations of and variations on these qualities that make him, in Wodehouse's words, "one of the godlike kind of men." "Homesick, That's All," for instance, finds Sinatra embodying the very picture of a nostalgic GI at war's end. He also perfectly captures the sense of delightfully bemused befuddlement that Al Dubin's lyric to "I Only Have Eyes for You" describes. He's glowingly wide-eyed like a young parent who is still practically a child himself on "Mighty Lak' a Rose" and "The Cradle Song" (from Brahms's "Lullaby," which he actually croons to sleeping *King* Dean Stockwell in *Anchors Aweigh*) and "The Charm of You." On both he transforms ancient warhorses into fresh, vital, and intimate experiences. On "Could'ja" and the underappreciated "Dum-Dot Song" (a swingingly swell record of an admittedly inane ditty), as well as an entire album of Christmas songs, he sings to children on their own level without talking down to them.

In contrast, he communicates rich, multilayered emotional states in "It Never Entered My Mind," one of the most subtle torch songs ever written, and "Guess I'll Hang My Tears Out to Dry." Even a "simple" Christmas song becomes a vehicle for emotional depth: he elevates "Have Yourself a Merry

Little Christmas" into an enticingly complex happy-sad ode that can stand beside Judy Garland's iconic version from *Meet Me in St. Louis*. In "Guess I'll Hang My Tears," lyricist Cahn presents us with a protagonist who is determined not to show the world his pain. He feebly attempts to distract us from it with a series of deliberately cheap-shot jokes, beginning with a title that equates love with laundry, deploying humor as a Woody Allen character might—as a defense mechanism. Does it work? The ruse only serves to magnify the intensity of his anguish. Sinatra would do better by "Tears" on the *Only the Lonely* album (with Al Viola's guitar taking the place of the harp), but even by 1946, Sinatra, at the age of thirty, is already a master.

On "Someone to Watch Over Me" and "I Don't Know Why," he sets himself up more as a forlorn, lost dog than the predatory wolf role that he would play a decade later. "I Begged Her" piles dimension on top of dimension, angle on angle: as in the film *Anchors Aweigh,* he becomes a sheep in wolf's clothing, a bashful bookworm feigning the part of a sly lothario. On "These Foolish Things," he lands halfway between the poles of the Dorsey-era virgin of "Our Love Affair" and the sagacious old stud of the 1950s, now himself increasingly qualified to stand in as a role model for younger lovers.

On some of the up-tempos of the period, usually arranged by George Siravo (about whom more later), he's brash and extroverted: "Blue Skies" marks one of Sinatra's fiercest swingers ever, with vital contributions from the soloing sidemen, including his favorite tenor of the times, Herbie Haymer. Yet on the same session in 1946, he and Stordahl also produced one of their most hauntingly introspective works, "Among My Souvenirs" (by coincidence, like "Blue Skies," written in 1927). Sinatra transforms it into an even more personal soliloquy than Rodgers and Hammerstein's "Soliloquy," in which Sinatra recites the text almost as if he were thinking out loud. Often the more conceptually spare the libretto—"Embraceable You," for one, leaves a lot to the imagination—the more Sinatra dreams up to do with it. Here, as on the slightly fuller "All Through the Day," he passes through several emotional levels within the same text.

The 1940s constitutes a far more innocent era than the 1950s or '60s, for Sinatra as well as the culture in general. On "Something Old, Something New," playing a horny young bridegroom being aroused by the contents of his blushing bride's overnight bag, he even utters, "Golly gee!" Yet Sinatra delineates the difference in the naivete of a Rodgers and Hammerstein cornfest (in the sense of trying to convey the mindset of uneducated people) and a bone-simple living Berlin text like "Always"—pure and direct for its own sake. The Voice can always pinpoint that exact shade of difference.

Even if it weren't for their rivalry (sort of) over Ava Gardner, later to become Mrs. Sinatra, it's hard to imagine Sinatra and Artie Shaw ever working together; no ship could sail smoothly under two captains. And yet the two have a lot in common in terms of their attitudes toward what made the American musical idiom into a genuine art form, and the ways in which that idiom could attain the upper brackets of true artistry. In his groundbreaking orchestra of the late 1930s, Shaw may well have been the first major musician to conceive of a standard repertory of classic American popular songs. Shaw represents the earliest exponent of a generation of musical artists who realized that there was more to pop music than this year's crop of kisses. As the bandleader put it, the idea was to take the best possible songs and orchestrate them in the best possible way; this was to become Sinatra's modus operandi as well. Up to then, no mainstream mass-market figures even acknowledged that there was any kind of song other than the latest chart-toppers on *Your Hit Parade*. The vintage show tunes that would later be regarded as classics were sung only by highly esoteric cabaret singers in obscure boîtes, or played by jazzmen in after-hours jam sessions. You didn't hear "I've Got a Crush on You" on *Lucky Strike Presents Your Hit Parade*.

Yet both Shaw and Sinatra specialized in doing new and stunning interpretations of classic songs—five or ten or more years old—by the likes of the Gershwin brothers, Rodgers and Hart, and Irving Berlin. Perhaps more than anyone else, the two men established the foundation of what today we call the Great American Songbook, and were the first to establish that America had given the world a body of music to compare with the classics of old Europe. As with many aspects of their lives, the championship of the great songs became a kind of moral imperative: Sinatra in particular announced to the rest of the jazz and pop world—and all of his fellow singers—that there was more to popular music than whatever random assortment the publisher and song-pluggers happened to be pushing that week.

Ironically, in his first starring feature film, *Higher and Higher*, Sinatra participated in a typical Hollywood demolition job of a Broadway musical with a super-sophisticated score by Rodgers and Hart. The moguls applied their "leave a little, remove a lot" treatment even more thoroughly than usual, retaining only a single and singularly undistinguished tune from the 1940 show: they kept "Disgustingly Rich" and trashed "It Never Entered My Mind." In this case they also held on to the show's rather trivial plot peg; in other words, they ate the wrapper and threw away the candy. But even if RKO had retained the whole score, within a few years the movie would probably have been forgotten anyway. Sinatra did music the greater service when he revived "It Never Entered My Mind" in 1947, along with seven other

Rodgers and Hart songs over the course of his Columbia contract* and Lord knows how many more for Capitol and Reprise.

Likewise, in countless concerts Sinatra introduced "When Your Lover Has Gone" with a sense of wonder that its composer, E. A. Swan, could come out of nowhere, write such a beautiful love song, and then disappear into oblivion. There's no doubt that Sinatra learned it from Louis Armstrong, but had it not been for the two of them, this quintessential torch song (introduced on the soundtrack of the 1931 *Blonde Crazy*, starring Jimmy Cagney) would have surely vanished as speedily as its one-shot author.

"I take great pride in the fact that I introduced Frank to a lot of the great, great songs," Sammy Cahn proclaimed. "I introduced him to songs such as 'You Are Too Beautiful.' I [would say] 'Frank, there's a song.' . . . Because he's got a good sense of music, you can lay a good song on him, [and he'll say], 'Oh, geez, that's good. Let me have that!'" In fact, a session recording exists of Stordahl and Sinatra preparing to record "I've Got a Crush on You" in which we can hear the conductor reminding the singer, "Sammy Cahn taught you this song, Frank." "That was our love, all of us," Cahn said. "We loved the great standards. How are you not going to love them? Whenever we'd be around someplace, we'd always play the great songs." Sinatra used a divining rod of talent to discover what would become the pop mainstream.

There are virtually no second-rate Sinatra-Stordahl records from the 1944–47 period. The only sides that threaten to bring down the average are a series of blues-inspired small-group novelty items done at the same time as the Stordahl sessions. That's not to say "That's How Much I Love You" and "You Can Take My Word for It, Baby" with the Page Cavanaugh Trio, and "It All Came True" with Alvy West and the Little Band, are bad; they're simply secondary items that don't measure up to the extremely high standards of the Sinatra-Stordahl material. There's not much that can compare with Gershwin and Porter. These combo sides illustrate, as we'll see, the beginnings of Sinatra developing a new up-tempo style for himself. Here he finds his initial inspiration in both the instrumental textures and jivey novelty numbers popularized by the King Cole Trio. Eventually, he would reinvent himself as a swing singer by following a different path. The repertory patterns of those two great artists would continue long beyond the 1940s: Nat Cole specialized in finding off-beat, even esoteric, airs and working wonders with them.

Sinatra's influence in determining what singers after him sang is immeasurable. By way of illustration, another artist could come along and do

---

* "Lover," "My Romance," "Spring Is Here," "You Are Too Beautiful," "Falling in Love with Love," "I Could Write a Book," "Where or When?" (along with "It Never Entered My Mind").

an album-length homage to, say, Nat King Cole (as did his own pop-star daughter) that would naturally contain Cole's best-known songs. A singer or an instrumentalist could also do an album of the songs associated with any iconic performer—Billie Holiday, Ella Fitzgerald, Tony Bennett—and it would include all the specific songs associated with that artist. Long before his death, dozens of singers were doing Sinatra tribute albums, but there's no real point to them. The songs we identify with Sinatra are "Someone to Watch Over Me," "Lost in the Stars," "You'll Never Walk Alone," "Where or When," "Ol' Man River," "Embraceable You," "I'll Be Seeing You," "Night and Day," and, most of all, "The Song Is You." In other words, songs that are so firmly embedded in our collective consciousness that one hardly requires the pretext of a Sinatra tribute to hear them. Tony Bennett told me that when he did his album *Perfectly Frank* in 1992, he wanted to include only great standards, and deliberately avoid signature themes like "My Way" and "Put Your Dreams Away."

Of all the canonical figures of twentieth-century musical culture, the artist who had the most songs directly written for him was indisputably Fred Astaire, who had all the major giants of the American songbook simultaneously penning show scores and then film scores for him. Yet how many of these classic songs would we remember if not for Sinatra? He made it a mission to prove that these classic songs were America's contribution to world musical culture—our Bach, our Mozart.

Frank Military pointed out that most of the classic songs were immediately forgotten after their initial runs were over; the shows closed, the movies were out of the theaters, the songs were almost consigned to the dustbins of history. "If you look at songs like 'Glad to Be Unhappy,'" Military noted, "they were just songs done in little cabarets by chi-chi kind of singers"—until Sinatra brought them back into the mainstream. "He even took songs out of flop shows, like [Cahn and Styne's] 'Guess I'll Hang My Tears Out to Dry' [from *Glad to See You*] and made them into important standards."

Sinatra completely transformed the way that artists approached their material—just in time for the start of the album era. That transformation even affected his own influences: prior to Sinatra, even such iconic figures as Billie Holiday, Bing Crosby, and Louis Armstrong were widely known for singing as many dog songs as classics; but after Sinatra, they spent the latter part of their careers recording great albums of classic songs.

The 1940s was Sinatra's most commercially successful years as far as big-selling singles were concerned, and by the time of the 1948 ban he had racked up sixty-three chart hits, including four number-ones. Of these *Billboard*-listed items, only five or so can be described as standard selections, yet Sinatra continued to devote at least half of his recording energies to classic tunes. He probably could have had almost twice as many hits and made twice as much money had he done nothing but new songs. One has to marvel not only at his own taste but also the unflinching support of Manie Sachs and Columbia Records in enabling him to take the high road. There was more to pop music than going for the fast buck.

"We talked things over," bandleader Les Brown said (around 1990) about his musical relationship with Sachs, which obviously paralleled Sinatra's. "I picked tunes and talked them all over with Manie. If he gave me tunes that I didn't like, I didn't do them. He was very nice about that. He wasn't a dictator. If I didn't feel it, he didn't want me to do it." It's hard to imagine anyone else having so much respect for the tastes of their artists. "Manie was one of the nicest men in this business," Brown continued, "a complete doll compared to some of them I've been around."

"Manie was the most unlikely best friend to a man like Frank Sinatra that I could think of," mused Rosemary Clooney. "He was very quiet, very correct, very soft-spoken, smart. He was close to his family and went home every weekend to Philadelphia. But Manie adored Frank from the very beginning, and I think it was mutual. I think that there was a fatherly feeling, although I don't know how much difference there was in their ages—but I think that Manie felt that way toward Frank."

Emanuel Sachs was born in Philadelphia on January 30, 1902, and he attended Pennsylvania Military College. In the early days of radio, Sachs served as head of public relations and of the "Artists Bureau" at local station WCAU. Around 1932 or 1933 he went to work for the talent agency MCA, where he stayed for the remainder of the 1930s. At some point he connected with CBS Radio magnate Bill Paley and helped him in his bid to take over the Columbia Records label from the American Recording Company. Partly as a reward, Paley appointed him head of Artists and Repertoire, a position for which he was eminently suited, despite a lack of technical knowledge about music or recording. He soon became vice president and director of the label. Sachs first met Sinatra in 1939, and the two were inseparable for nearly twenty years until Sachs's death from leukemia on February 9, 1958. Sachs's departure from the label in January 1950 proved to be one of the key factors in Sinatra's eventual downfall at Columbia.

A *Time* reporter once described Sachs as looking "so much like Sinatra that he is constantly mistaken for him." In 1944, when Sinatra's son was born, Sinatra Senior selected Sachs as Junior's godfather, to the displeasure of the priest who presided at the christening. When the padre insisted that someone more Catholic fulfill the godfather's obligations at the ceremony (Sachs was president of the Beth Israel synagogue in Philadelphia), Sinatra stormed angrily out of the church. When Sinatra married Ava Gardner in 1951, he didn't bother with a church at all, but he held the ceremony in the home of Manie's brother, Lester Sachs, in Philadelphia.

Sachs wasn't only Sinatra's rabbi, "He was everybody's rabbi," as Mitch Miller recalled. "I always used to say that if Manie were a woman, he'd always be pregnant because he couldn't say no. There are many instances. One time he was on a plane with [music publisher] Howie Richmond, and Howie says, 'Jesus, Manie, I forgot to take out insurance.' So Manie says, 'I'll give you some of mine.' And he meant it! Manie was a malaprop, too. He'd say, 'The bridges crossed a lot of water.'"

As a long-term investment, recording good music actually made money. It was the standard songs that Columbia would reissue time after time, beginning in the 78 era and continuing long into the digital age, while many of the pop hits of the era wouldn't see the light of day again until the 1993 Columbia *Complete Recordings* boxed set. Following Sinatra's example, the industry quickly adopted the idea that the standard songs would become the basic bread-and-butter of the new long-playing albums that were beginning to emerge from 1948 onward, while new songs (and potential pop hits) would continue to be heard on singles (soon in the new 45-rpm format).

The coming of the LP was only one reason Sinatra had to look forward to the future even as the union announced another disastrous musicians' ban in the fall of 1947. When the A&R men of the various labels realized that a strike was unavoidable, remembered Stan Freeman, who played piano on several sessions (usually filling in for Mark McIntyre, the singer's usual accompanist of the period) "we started doing eight or nine sessions a day just to get those things in."

The previous June, Sinatra had wound up the second and final year of the *Old Gold Songs by Sinatra* program. In contrast to *Your Hit Parade*, which he had left at the end of 1944, *Songs by Sinatra* represented perhaps the highest-minded commercial radio series in pop music: Sinatra featured songs for the ages as often as he did the best new numbers and his own hits, and even devoted whole programs to the works of Jerome Kern, Johnny Mercer, Irving Berlin, and their peers.*

His personal fortunes had risen to almost unfathomable proportions. No one ever thought that he could ever top the Columbus Day Riot of 1944

---

* Sinatra had multiple reasons for leaving *Your Hit Parade*, not least of which was that he wanted to concentrate on the new Max Factor half hour. He also explained that because he had to bear the costs of broadcasting from Hollywood, it was simply too expensive for him to do the show. The cost of the sidemen and the remote phone lines, Sinatra claimed, left him digging into his pocket well beyond his own weekly paycheck of $2,000 per show.

when he returned to the New York Paramount to an audience of thirty thousand fans.* Still, he soared higher the following year when he moved from the fading RKO to Metro-Goldwyn-Mayer. Beginning with the phenomenally successful *Anchors Aweigh,* one of the major hits of 1945 (the year the singer bought his first house in Los Angeles), Sinatra launched a string of major musicals for Metro. In 1948, the Sinatras—now four, with Frankie Jr.—relocated to even more spectacular digs in the Holmby Hills section of L.A.

No one could yet see any dark clouds on the horizon. The proof was at the Paramount. "When we played the Paramount in 1947," remembered drummer Johnny Blowers, "the stage would go up about eighteen feet, from way down at the bottom, and he'd look down [at the bobby-soxers] and go, 'Have you been here all day?' Because they'd brown-bag it; they'd bring their lunch and everything else. God almighty, we'd go on the stage at ten o'clock at night, and he'd look down and say, 'You're still here!' Because they stayed all day long!"

Sinatra was by now a multimillionaire, earning, for instance, $41,000 for a single week at the Chicago Theater in the spring of 1946. As raconteur Billy Rose wrote, "Only the Internal Revenue Service knows what this moon-kissed stripling with the bedroom in his voice nets from the records which are being passionately clutched to millions of just-budding bosoms." By 1945, Sinatra caricatures were sharing the scene with such notable figures as Daffy Duck and Li'l Abner. Even his bow ties were a national institution. Nelson Algren, in his 1949 novel *The Man with the Golden Arm,* describes his hero, "Frankie Machine," as wearing a "Sinatra"—-not even a "Sinatra tie." Pop songs like "Tabby the Cat" also contained lines like "sharp as Sinatra's tie," and bluesman T-Bone Walker sang "Bobby Sox Blues," in which he chided young girls for having their noses in a fan's scrapbook rather than a cookbook: "I ask you if you love me, you say, 'What will Frankie say?'"

Today, a faint echo of the mountainous swooning, screaming, and gnashing of teeth perpetrated in Sinatra's name remains on transcriptions of his

---

* Well before Christopher Columbus became politically incorrect, his birthday was once observed by Italian-Americans as their equivalent of Saint Patrick's Day. In 1943, Italian-Americans also used Columbus Day as an opportunity to celebrate the downfall of Mussolini and essentially the end of Italy's involvement in WWII. Sinatra's 1944 Columbus Day appearances attracted an even greater crowd; traffic was blocked all over Times Square and most of Midtown. Fully 421 patrolmen and twenty patrolwomen were required to maintain order. However, Mayor Fiorello La Guardia (in his final year in office) didn't mind—he supported the singer's campaign to educate the world (and young people in particular about what was then called "tolerance"; more about that later) and he also appreciated Sinatra's unflinching support of President Roosevelt and the Democratic Party.

radio appearances.* Now that the skinny as well as the rationalizations by noted psychoanalysts explaining the bobby-soxer phenomenon have faded, the Sinatra of the 1940s can reemerge as a major artist, to be appreciated not for the hysteria he inspired but for the music he created.

Sinatra was a true visionary, more so in these years than in any other period of his life. It was in the mid-1940s that he led his fellow singers out of the big bands and into the solo spotlight; that he became one of the first popular singers to perform in formal concert halls; that he invented the pop album with *The Voice*; and that, most important, he proved to singers that they could expand their horizons infinitely by looking beyond the hits of the moment to what we now call the Great American Songbook. In short, Sinatra looked at pop music and said what Max Bialystock says to Leo Bloom in *The Producers*: "There's more to you than *you*."

In many ways, Sinatra could envision the entire future of American music. Alas, one thing that he could not foresee in 1947–48 was the big nosedive that his own career was about to take.

---

* For a time, Sinatra attempted to bar teenagers from his live broadcasts. Both the *Your Hit Parade* and the *Songs by Sinatra* series were transcribed for distribution to servicemen via the Armed Forces Radio Network. At the time, Sinatra pointed out that the constant screaming from the peanut gallery was a turnoff to the men in uniform. "They don't like all the noise, and I don't blame them. It sounds like a Chinese hand laundry with everybody clapping." Not surprisingly, the expulsion of bobby-soxers from the studio didn't last very long, and soon enough the swooning resumed.

# 5

# ALL THE IN-BETWEEN YEARS

## *1948–1953*

*No matter how low you go, there's always an unexplored basement.*
　　　　　　　—F. Scott Fitzgerald

*For the grand destruction, one must be worthy.*
　　　　　　　—Elizabeth Hardwick

*Do not mess with Mister In-between.*
　　　　　　　—Johnny Mercer

In the late fall of 1939, Harry James lost two of his key men: not only his vocalist, Frank Sinatra, but also his drummer, Ralph Hawkins, who left James to
replace Buddy Rich in Artie Shaw's band. (Rich had left Shaw to join Tommy
Dorsey.) However, a very short time after Hawkins went to work for Shaw,
the clarinetist stormed off the bandstand, abandoning the money-making
machine it had taken him years to build up. Shaw claimed he was fed up with
the dehumanizing pressures of show business and commercial music, and
that he would never play again.

To most observers in that late-Depression year, it seemed as if Shaw was
tossing a monkey wrench in the works of the American dream: to be willing
to throw away hundreds of thousands of dollars in pursuit of what was then
an obscure concept called artistic integrity.

In later years, there would be many terms—some rather colorful—for
the spectacular fall-and-rise that Frank Sinatra experienced between roughly
1947 and 1954: the swan song, the nosedive, the year of Mondays (except
that it lasted well longer than a year), which was just as famously followed
by a resurrection so overwhelming that it virtually invented the term "come-

back." It has become a kind of morality play, which is another way of saying that it is inevitably discussed purely in terms of Sinatra's personal life. The singer's career downs-and-ups are generally rationalized away as being the inevitable product of his passionate yet tortuous romance with his second wife, movie star Ava Gardner. It would be naive to think that an artist as emotionally driven as Sinatra could participate in such a situation and have it not affect his work. Still, when we take the long view, the Gardner factor amounts to only one of many.

Ultimately, what drove the fall-and-rise was Sinatra's struggle to redefine himself as an artist and a musician and, indeed, a cultural icon, at a time when the culture all around him was changing. As we've already seen, Sinatra was already an artistic rebel cast from the same mold as Artie Shaw. He was the first entertainer in the American experience to stand for something that was bigger than he was, a campaigner for a higher level of musical discourse—and politics as well.

Reflecting on himself, Shaw tended to look at his career as being squeezed between the two extreme poles of art and commerce. In the short term, Shaw's cure was much more immediate: a few weeks after beating an angry exit from the Cafe Rouge (the ballroom at New York's Hotel Pennsylvania), he was back in the saddle again. Conversely, it took Sinatra almost five years to work through what were essentially the same problems. Yet the singer's solution was more permanent: at roughly the same time as Sinatra's "comeback," Shaw concluded that the only way to preserve his sanity was to pack up his marbles and go home for good—an irreparable loss to music.

Sinatra unknowingly took the first baby step toward disaster in September 1947, when he rejoined *Your Hit Parade*, the excessively commercial radio series that he had left less than three years earlier. During his original stint on that show in 1943 and 1944, Sinatra had been able to stay true to himself by simultaneously presenting his own series of starring shows. He did *Your Hit Parade* for the exposure and the money, but it was never a real Sinatra product—that honor went to *Broadway Bandbox*, *Vimms*, *Songs by Sinatra*, and the other shows in which he was the full-fledged star attraction. Now in 1947, when he returned to the Lucky Strike fold, the idea was that *Your Hit Parade* would take the place of his own show. For the only time in the twenty-four-year run of the program, the *Parade* would pivot around a single star singer, who would also announce most of the tunes and do many of the commercials. It was an advertising agency's dream: the combination of the top-ten format and perhaps the most popular singer on the air. But what loused it up was an element no agent could negotiate: quality, or, rather, the lack of it.

Luckily for Sinatra, his first stretch on *Your Hit Parade* coincided with the end of the golden era of American songwriting. On a single show in May 1944, for instance, Sinatra sang two well-known standards-to-be, Jerome Kern's "Long Ago (and Far Away)" and Cole Porter's "I Love You." The same episode also included two other top-drawer songs that would also remain, to a lesser degree, in the collective repertory: "I'll Be Seeing You," a 1938 number that took on new meaning at the start of World War II, and the Cuban ballad "Poinciana."

At the start of the new series in 1947 it seemed there was hope, especially since, in his first two months back on the show, *Your Hit Parade*'s second-billed singer was none other than the marvelous Doris Day herself. In fact, their duet on "There's No Business Like Show Business" was a major improvement over Sinatra's solo version on Columbia. But even though the new *Hit Parade* spotlighted Sinatra more than any other performer in the program's history, and Sinatra's own musical director, Axel Stordahl, had taken over Mark Warnow's spot as arranger-conductor, it still wasn't Sinatra's show. The man who set the tone for the program was still the imperious George Washington Hill. Thinking more in terms of radio programming rather than musical content, Hill was, as always, aiming at the lowest possible common denominator of an audience and the shortest possible attention span. Yet Sinatra, who was still very young—only thirty-one when he resumed singing on *Your Hit Parade* on September 6, 1947—was just beginning to realize that he would forever be on the other side of the fence from men like Hill.

It's not that Sinatra didn't get to sing some first-rate tunes during this second run on *Your Hit Parade* (which lasted until May 1949). (To name just a few that he never recorded for Columbia: "Haunted Heart," "Ballerina," "It's Magic," "Now Is the Hour.") And he also got to sing some first-rate standards as "Lucky Strike Extras." ("Over the Rainbow," "Great Day," "Zing! Went the Strings of My Heart," and others occasionally tiptoed in through the back door.) But the point was that Sinatra had to sing songs because they were hits; whether they were any good or not was simply not a factor.

Sinatra should have been wary when the very first song on his very first show was "Feudin', Fussin', and A-Fightin'." Now, in the vast scheme of things, this isn't a bad song; composed by two Broadway-Hollywood veterans in Burton Lane and Al Dubin, it was a huge hit on Columbia Records for Dorothy Shay, and is a perfectly entertaining narrative song for a countrified entertainer like Judy Canova, Tennessee Ernie Ford, or even Cinderella G. Stump. Yet it's singularly unsuited to Sinatra, and was probably the last thing in the world that he should have been asked to sing.

And there's the rub, bub—Sinatra could take his pick of the top ten, but was obligated to do the number-one song each week, no matter what it was. And frequently in the late 1940s, that number-one hit was a novelty of the most inane sort—the postwar years witnessed some of pop music's most trite and banal hits. In January 1948 Sinatra ventured as far afield from the path of the righteous as to treat us to the conceptually lean "Too Fat Polka"; the Arthur Godfrey hit was actually customized for Sinatra in a special-material arrangement tailored to get the most mileage out of his own distinct lack of too-fatness.

It got worse. That spring, Sinatra watched with dismay as "The Woody Woodpecker Song" flew up the charts; on the June 26 show, he can barely bring himself to introduce the vocal group's rendition—one can even hear him exclaim, "I just couldn't do it!" under the music as it starts. But on July 10, when "Woody Woodpecker" reached number one, he no longer had any choice—he *had* to do it.

In a 1948 interview with George Simon, Sinatra told the readers of *Metronome* magazine exactly "What's Wrong with Music": "About the popular songs of the day," he began, "they're so lifeless, they're bloodless. As a singer of popular songs, I've been looking for wonderful pieces of music in the popular vein, what they call Tin Pan Alley songs. Outside of show tunes, you can't find a thing." He continued, "The music business . . . must give people things that move them emotionally and make them laugh, too. But we're not doing it, and there's something wrong someplace."

"Nature Boy," which Sinatra performed frequently on *YHP* in the spring and summer of 1948, illustrates Sinatra's point. The top song of the year (along with "Buttons and Bows") and forever associated with Nat King Cole, "Nature Boy" was released more or less as a fluke, because of the second AFM ban, which, in a reprise of the situation of 1942–44, meant that musicians could not make commercial recordings for most of 1948. Cole recorded the song for Capitol in August 1947, but the label thought the piece was too weird to release; however, they consented to issue it as a B side in March 1948 because there was a shortage of acceptable Cole masters. "Nature Boy" then became what every record man dreams of: a freak hit, released at a time when all the other labels' hands were tied. Thanks to the 1948 ban, no other company could release their own orchestral version of the song that might have a chance of competing with Cole, although a few a cappella versions were tried, including those by Sarah Vaughan, Dick Haymes, and Sinatra. (Perry Como and Bing Crosby, to their credit, both demurred.)

Sinatra's musician-free recording of "Nature Boy" was his sole commercial recording during the eleven-month ban. It didn't have a chance: the sound of

Cole's voice with strings, combined with the highly original song, had made the Capitol record a blockbuster hit—one of many for King Cole. Sinatra's own singing is tender and sympathetic, but the stark choir backing gives the record as much warmth as a Gregorian chant. (On *Your Hit Parade*, Sinatra performed the song both ways, with the choir and with a more conventional string orchestra.) And even as the heavyweight crooners battled one another to steal Cole's thunder, its composer, Eden Ahbez, and a publisher of Yiddish music were crying plagiarism as they sparred over the publishing royalties. It struck no one as ironic that a song with a message of love and peace should come to symbolize how cutthroat the pop music business was becoming.

In the *Metronome* interview, Sinatra went on to complain about how most songwriters had to "prostitute" their talents if they wanted "to make a buck [because] not enough publishers are buying the better kind of music." He then elaborated on how record companies were also engaged in an unending search for the fastest buck possible. Quality songs were still being composed, he averred, but Sinatra pointed out that the mechanics of the music industry, the publishers, the A&R men, the radio deejays, would "rather take an easy song, one that's a novelty. It's a very short shot that will click right away, but that doesn't last over the years. Most publishers don't think that far ahead."

All of which was putting Sinatra himself, increasingly, on the short end of the stick. At this time, in the words of Al Capp (as well as Betty Comden and Adolph Green in *On the Town*), his troubles were multiplying like shmoos. Much of the problems can be explained in terms that were barely known, if at all, in 1948: spin-doctoring, marketing, branding. Sinatra's extra-musical image had been solidified in 1945, the year of his USO tour and of his spectacularly successful first film, *Anchors Aweigh*. He could never have made a hit with GIs had he come on like Charlie Hollywood, a smooth and polished singing star who was catnip to women and knew it. Sinatra's costar of the USO tour, the radio comic Phil "Glad to See You" Silvers (whom he would help out a few months later at the Copacabana) observed, "The soldiers had been underdogs so long, I figured they would love [Sinatra as an] underdog." The singer had already begun taking that tack on his radio shows, developing it steadily, particularly on the *Old Gold* series.

Where the initial impulse might have been to present Sinatra as a romantic Romeo (he's pretty much devoid of all personality in his first two starring roles, in 1943's *Higher and Higher* and 1944's *Step Lively*), Sinatra instead endeared himself to greater numbers by incessantly undercutting that image. He constantly cracked jokes at his own expense, usually involving his weight and his alleged puniness. On one show, to select a single example, Sinatra purports to recall exactly what his father said when he first saw him as an infant in his incubator; and then goes into "There's No You." He kept comics all over the airwaves in business, as they built up a lifetime's inventory of skinny jokes—Bob Hope in particular started a veritable cottage industry of one-liners.

Yet Sinatra could hardly convince anyone of his frailness after he flattened columnist Lee Mortimer on April 8, 1947, the first and by far the most damaging of his altercations with the fourth estate. Let it be said that virtually everyone wanted to punch Lee Mortimer, most of all his fellow newspapermen. Ed Sullivan, who almost never publicly said a bad word about anybody (even when he himself was later engaged in a feud with Sinatra), referred to his fellow columnist as a specialist in "mean needlework." "I've been accused constantly of getting in scuffles with people in the press," Sinatra claimed in a 1977 interview, "and I actually only had one physical bout in my lifetime with anybody in the press. That was Lee Mortimer, and if he [were] alive today, I'd knock him down again."

Before this incident, the papers had been inclined to go along with whatever setup the newsworthy crooner and his ingenious press agent, George Evans, had dreamed up (with the exception of the Hearst papers and other politically conservative journals that took exception to Sinatra's unflinching support of the Roosevelts). But the Mortimer incident was a game-changer; none of the reporters liked Mortimer, many considered him a disgrace to their profession, but they had to choose a side and the columnist was, in fact, one of their own. From this point on, the kid gloves were off and the honeymoon with the media was over; Sinatra would henceforth always be viewed with suspicion. This was hardly reconcilable with the Sinatra of radio and pictures who had said in one show, regarding his role in *Anchors Aweigh*, "I felt pretty much at home as Clarence Doolittle, the shy little violet from Brooklyn."

Most listeners knew that Sinatra wasn't Clarence Doolittle, they knew about his wife and growing family, but they still thought he was the boy next door—that's precisely the character he plays on the *Old Gold* and *Max Factor* shows, a charming, lovable young man who gets excited when guests like Peggy Lee and Nat King Cole come to visit, and acts like they're doing him a favor when they consent to let him sing with them.

But Clarence Doolittle wouldn't belt Lee Mortimer, nor would Clarence Doolittle be seen with Lucky Luciano. Again and again, those out-of-the-know will insist that mob support made Sinatra's career. Yet one is finally left with the impression that Sinatra's persistence in being photographed with hoodlums like Sam Giancana and Spiro Agnew only held him back. Clarence Doolittle would never leave his wife and three kiddies and thereby invoke the unspeakable D-word, a move that undoubtedly turned the public off him more than anything else. "People forget the climate in those days when Frank started running around with Ava," as Mitch Miller pointed out. "Ingrid Bergman had a child out of wedlock. Hell, everybody in Hollywood has a child out of wedlock today, and they brag about it. In those days she was banned from movies in America. When Sinatra left his wife, the priests told the kids, 'Don't buy his records.'"

Nor was Clarence Doolittle the two-fisted, high-living, skirt-chasing swinger that it was becoming clearer and clearer Sinatra was. The "hat" years differ from the late "skinny" years in that Sinatra, as the 1940s turned the corner into the 1950s, had a long way to go before he could work the high-rolling, ring-a-ding-ding image to his advantage.

Not all of Sinatra's departures from the passive, wallflower Doolittle character were negative. George Evans, who rates as at least a cocreator of the Doolittle image, threatened to provoke controversy—in a most un-Doolittle-like fashion—by encouraging Sinatra to push what was then known as a "progressive" political agenda. To the dismay of the then–predominantly conservative media, Sinatra actively campaigned for the cause of tolerance to high school assemblies and radio audience alike (and Doolittle-esque spiels such as "Get the big box of tolerance, it comes in the red, white, and blue package" did little to soften the impact). Sinatra, who went as far as to have a letter published in the liberal *New Republic*, was even branded a communist by California state senator Jack Tinney, one of an increasing number of red-baiting congressmen who were setting the stage for Joseph McCarthy.

Yet Sinatra continued to try to pass himself off as Clarence Doolittle, and it's a credit to his acting talents that he could make the character seem so believable as late as 1949's *On the Town*, especially after the tepid *Take Me Out to the Ball Game*. The Sinatra persona was growing increasingly out of sync with the Sinatra of the newspapers, and the public just wasn't buying it anymore.

*On the Town* constituted his farewell to MGM. Studio boss Louis B. Mayer was friendly enough with Sinatra to make a rare public appearance on *Songs by Sinatra* on October 8, 1946, yet Sinatra was ousted by Mayer a season or two prior to the end of the studio head's own fall from paradise. As Sinatra told the story to Sidney Zion, he had been frequently summoned to Mayer's office for father-son–style chats in which the legendary mogul would ramble on with rhetorical questions along the lines of "Why does Katharine Hepburn have to be seen in public with that goddamned communist Henry Wallace?"*

---

* Wallace, 1888–1965, had been vice president under Roosevelt and the presidential candidate of the Progressive Party in the 1948 election.

Then one day, while Sinatra and a number of other contract players were eating at the MGM commissary, one unnamed soul happened to mention that old man Mayer was in an all-body cast because of a riding accident. It seems, they said, that he fell off his horse. Up pipes Sinatra: "Nah, he fell off Ginny Simms," referring to the latest of Mayer's liaisons. A stunned silence befell the entire lunchroom. The rest of the table was shocked that he had the effrontery to actually utter such a crack within a hundred miles of the Metro lot. Sure enough, Sinatra was soon summoned once again to LBM's office and was there handed his walking papers.

But, Sinatra has acknowledged, he had seen it coming. The success of *Anchors*, among many other honors, allowed him to topple Van Johnson as *Modern Screen* magazine's most popular film personality for 1946, but not one of his post-*Anchors* efforts displayed the same box-office magic. *Till the Clouds Roll By* afforded him a guest shot, and *It Happened in Brooklyn* is today a sleeper favorite among hard-core Sinatraphiles. Then came a parade of the pathetic, starting with the truly terrible *Miracle of the Bells* (a loan to RKO), the at-least-laughably lame *Kissing Bandit,* after which, with the merely meager *Take Me Out to the Ball Game,* things were actually starting to look up a little. In fact, it's surprising that he was able to leave the studio on such a high note with *On the Town* (which, like *Brooklyn*, was modestly profitable), which finished the trilogy of pictures costarring Sinatra, Gene Kelly, and comic Jules Munshin.

Some of the nastier stuff that you can read about Sinatra goes into lurid detail on the subject of his flagrant nose-thumbing at Hollywood, his refusal to show up on time or at all, his resistance to multiple takes, and his general failure to take movie-making seriously, which runs diametrically counter to his hyperprofessional approach toward making music. In that respect, he became the opposite of Crosby, who did his best work, especially as a singer, on the soundstages and became increasingly casual about his recordings. Once Sinatra had conquered the movie medium with *Anchors Aweigh,* he seems to have given less and less of a darn about his films. They were strictly secondary—and he wasn't even particularly anxious to use his records to plug his pictures, recording only one song from *Ball Game* and none of the score to *On the Town.*

Thus, he tumbled from the priciest lot in Hollywood, making only two pictures over the next three years, *Double Dynamite* (RKO, 1951)* and *Meet Danny Wilson* (Universal, 1952), a pair of relatively low-budget projects that

---

* More accurately, *Double Dynamite* was produced in 1948 but not released until three years later, and then released with Sinatra given third billing, after Groucho Marx and Jane Russell, an obvious reflection on his declining drawing power. (Miss Russell, many commented at the time, was "double dynamite" all by herself.)

seem a million miles away from the opulence of *Anchors Aweigh*. He was also fast falling into the B-level category on radio. He left *Your Hit Parade* for another program sponsored by the Lucky Strike people, *Light-Up Time*, which began in September 1949. The show costarred Metropolitan Opera star Dorothy Kirsten, filling a function originated by Jane Powell, a semiregular in the final months of *Songs by Sinatra*.

*Light Up Time* appropriated both the time slot and the format of Lucky Strike's competitor, the *Chesterfield Supper Club*; both were on for fifteen minutes every weeknight at seven. Due to the increased demand for material, Axel Stordahl no longer had time to conduct for Sinatra on the new program. While Stordahl scrambled to keep up with the call for new arrangements, Jeff Alexander, previously known as a choral director (on Sinatra's "Nature Boy" and elsewhere), came in to conduct. After a two-year hiatus, Sinatra resumed doing movie theater tours in December 1949, occasionally using trumpet giant Ziggy Elman as his conductor. Elman also frequently stood on the podium in early 1950 on the *Light-Up Time* series. Toward the end of the series, in March 1950, Sinatra returned to New York for a nightclub engagement while Alexander remained in Hollywood to complete a film assignment. Lucky Strike then passed the baton to Skitch Henderson, who had played piano on the 1942 Bluebird session and had accompanied Sinatra at the Waldorf in 1945 and on several occasions since. One of the last big-talent, high-profile radio programs, *Light-Up Time*, Henderson explained in 1991, marked "the end of so-called rich radio."

The main problem with *Light-Up Time* was that the show ran only fifteen minutes, with barely time to squeeze in two solo spots for the star, one solo by Kirsten, and a duet in between the commercials. "We'd do thirty-two bars with the orchestra, which was a minute-thirty, and then I would do something pianistically, which we could maybe squeeze to a minute-fifteen, and then we'd do a closer with the orchestra," Henderson recalled. "So we could do a medley of three tunes—to get the song-pluggers off our backs—sometimes in as little as four minutes or four minutes and twenty seconds. What everybody forgets, and I can't even believe it when I hear the tapes, is that we had a two-minute commercial to open the show. Two minutes! Unbelievable. Extolling the virtues of Lucky Strike. Oh, it was a grind."

In a long-established radio tradition, *Light-Up Time* opened nightly with a bright fast number, almost always orchestrated by George Siravo. "It was like one chorus and a half with a couple of bars intro," said Siravo. "I think I even got [the intro] down to a bar and a half because there was a three-beat pickup vocally. Wow! That's like doing the hundred-yard dash in about a second and a half!"

Sinatra actually did the 108-bar "Begin the Beguine" on a March 1950 show and it took up practically the entire program. On the March 13 episode, Sinatra and Kirsten sing "A Fine Romance," and then Sinatra announces, "We'll buy a minute from NBC and do another chorus!" Apart from the time factor, Lucky Strike's budget did not allow for the use of a full string section every night, so the fiddles became a luxury that Sinatra was allowed to indulge in only occasionally. Between the lack of strings and the relentless pacing, the show lost the deep-focus sound, the extended, sensual romanticism that had distinguished the Sinatra-Stordahl collaboration.

By now, Sinatra was growing increasingly and understandably depressed by these turns of his personal and professional fortunes. Although it would be difficult for him to sing badly, it became harder for him to live up to his own high standards. On the December 27 show, Sinatra misses the first note on "A Man Wrote a Song"—a mediocre tune that he had no business singing to begin with—and has to start it again, and then completely fluffs the lyric on "You're the Cream in My Coffee." Henderson felt that Sinatra's heart was only really in it maybe two nights out of the five a week the show was on. "That was the beginning of Frank's problems," he said. "I think he was concerned, as anybody would be, with his life and what was going to happen. And the publicity was so negative at that time. You know, the media was pounding him."

Sinatra's personal and professional problems were leading to the parallel breakups of the two most important relationships in his life, his partnership with Axel Stordahl and his marriage to the mother of his children. Much of the blame for the downward spin in Sinatra's recording career has traditionally been pinned to Mitch Miller—not least by Blue Eyes himself, a sentiment parroted by all of his biographers. But the overall situation is much more nuanced than that, and there's the irrefutable evidence, long before Miller entered the picture, that Sinatra was well into a debilitating spiritual and artistic recession.

In December 1948, an armistice was declared between the musicians' union and the record labels; thus the second AFM ban came to an end and the gears of the increasingly enormous foundry that pop music was becoming began turning again. Yet Sinatra was unable to find his bearings throughout most of 1949. The first song that he recorded when the strike ended was, unbelievably, a country-and-western number titled "Sunflower." It wasn't bad by Nashville standards, and the melody later provided the inspiration for the title song from Jerry Herman's *Hello, Dolly!* (recorded by Sinatra in 1964), but it was hardly classic Frank. Yet even so, it shows his willingness to try something new, even if the idea didn't lead anywhere. Neither would anything else that season; other than a few new show tunes here and there (from *Where's Charley?, South Pacific, Miss Liberty, Kiss Me Kate, Gentlemen Prefer Blondes*, etc.), this is easily the driest spell of his career thus far.

Sinatra's immediate post-ban recordings are primarily notable only for their lack of distinction. The first new session with Stordahl's orchestra began with a European import called "Comme Ci, Comme Ça," whose title epitomized the blasé recordings Sinatra churned out that season. Even when given strong material, he never quite flies. In 1947, three of Sinatra's best 78s had been pairings from three new musicals; yet in 1949, he can't even get off the ground with the two big numbers from *South Pacific*. Of the two, "Some Enchanted Evening" is merely disappointing, particularly in light of what Sinatra had led us to expect with his earlier, ace renditions of Rodgers and Hammerstein's *Carousel* classics, "You'll Never Walk Alone" and "Soliloquy." In any other year Sinatra would have been able to interpret "Bali Ha'i" as the anthem of hope and distant dreams that it is; unfortunately, his sole recording of the piece finds him all but choking on poi and steel guitars.

Still, even this comparatively weak year boasted several worthwhile endeavors: a further show-tunes pairing, this one from *Miss Liberty*, yielded a yummy, "bubbly" (in Sinatra's phrase) duet with Doris Day. On "Let's Take an Old-Fashioned Walk," his partner's sunshiny attitude helps reawaken his own, while the Disneyesque "The Old Master Painter" is also cute and peppy. "Mad About You," a first-rate song by the brilliant film composer Victor Young, is the first new Sinatra-Stordahl masterpiece since 1947, replete with sweeping strings, soaring horns, and one of those precious voice-fading-into-ensemble endings.

Stordahl was not present, however, at what turned out to be Sinatra's best all-around session of the year. On July 10 in New York, the singer turned out three classics, all off the familiar ballad path but with excellently handled orchestrations by George Siravo and Sy Oliver that inspire him to new heights. "Don't Cry, Joe" is an uncharacteristically bluesy ballad, while on "It All Depends on You," Sinatra fairly brims with excitement, leaping into the fray after a catchy introductory vamp by Siravo. After a sixteen-bar instrumental break (originally written for a full chorus, half of which had to be deleted on the spot for space), Sinatra reenters, digging engagingly against the grain of the ground beat, jazzily expanding his contractions, and adding extra notes ("I can be *very* lonely"). When he shoots up to a high climax on "it all *dee-pends*" in the last line, it has the effect of a man racing up the side of a mountain.

In an interview the next day on a Long Island radio station, Sinatra told host Jack Ellsworth how pleased he was to do a new song from a forthcoming show by Jule Styne—"Bye Bye Baby" from *Gentlemen Prefer Blondes*. "He's just a wonderful songwriter," said Sinatra, who was delighted to be singing this outstandingly rhythmic show tune. He has the full support of arranger Sy Oliver and even the vocal group (which includes the arranger's wife, Lillian Oliver Clark, formerly with Tommy Dorsey). They are all very jazzed, not only by the song and the chart, but by Columbia's new recording studio, the soon-to-be legendary 30th Street facility. Less than a decade earlier, Sy Oliver was coaching Sinatra in how to swing and lay back on the beat; now in 1949, as Mrs. Oliver recalled, it was Sinatra who coached the backup singers in how to best catch the rhythmic cadences of the tune.

"Bye Bye Baby" figures in the Sinatra saga in another way. When *Gentlemen Prefer Blondes* opened on Broadway on December 8, Sinatra would be in the audience on the premiere night; it would be one of the first times he was seen in public with Ava Gardner. Likewise, another outstanding song of the season was also connected indirectly to his personal life. After "Mad About You," his best ballad of the season was "(On the Island of) Stromboli." The song itself, at the time of the recording, seemed perfectly innocent, being Sinatra's second partially Italian record and simply the theme from a forthcoming Ingrid Bergman movie. A few months later the title seemed incredibly nervy, as both the film and the actual island became synonymous with one of the most notorious scandals in Hollywood history when Bergman left her husband and family for director Roberto Rossellini. The parallels with Sinatra's situation are obvious: by the time the movie was released in February 1950, Sinatra was embroiled in a Stromboli of his own, a romantic relationship that would wreck both his home and his career.

Even without those extramusical attachments, however, "Stromboli" is a devastatingly powerful performance by Sinatra. Being faux Italian, it should have been completely bogus, yet it's far more moving than the three genuinely Neapolitan pop tunes Sinatra waxed ("I Have but One Heart" and the more overdone "Come Back to Sorrento" and "Luna Rossa"). Sinatra and Stordahl, in effect, transform "Stromboli" into what "Bali Ha'i" should have been: the island of forbidden dreams. In this case the ornaments of local color—the mandolins, zithers, and concertinas—help both singer and arranger pull it off. Stordahl's standard closing devices—fades, dissolves, and last-second modulations—have never been so captivating. Even as late as 1949, this is classic Sinatra-Stordahl—one of their last masterpieces.

If Sinatra found himself in a slump in 1949, he was by no means alone; the entire industry was changing, and all of Columbia Records seemed to be slipping. Sinatra was in a rut. Their number-two crooner, Buddy Clark, was killed in a plane crash in October, and around the same time, there was a general exodus from the CBS-Columbia camp over to the NBC–RCA Victor empire. Conductor-producer Mitchell Ayers left, as did Paley's number-one female singing star, Dinah Shore. Most surprisingly, Manie Sachs also left, ostensibly to work for NBC and devote his energies to the new medium of television.

In January 1950, when Sachs departed, the label's prospects were slim. But by the end of 1951, Columbia Records had been reborn yet again and was now, to the surprise of everyone, by far the most profitable label in the business, dominating nearly every top-ten list in *Billboard*. The transformation was due entirely to one man: Mitch Miller. "He was really the first 'record producer,'" in the modern sense of the term, said Tony Bennett. "After Mitch made it, a million other guys tried to copy his cigar and his beard."

In 1951, Miller seemed like the hero in a white hat, riding in an equally white horse to save Columbia Records from receivership. In later years, Sinatraphiles painted a picture of him that was precisely the opposite, casting him as a mustache-twirling villain. In reality, William Mitchell Miller (1911–2010) was much too complicated a character to fit into any simple stereotypical role.

Described by the *New York Times* as "the bearded connoisseur of the echo chamber," Miller was a prophet, producer, factotum, instrumentalist, conductor, A&R man, guru, TV star, mover and shaker, patriarch, and businessman, a professorial intellectual who had an uncanny knack for pleasing the man on the street. Miller had so many facets that his soul resembled one of his productions; it's almost as if all of these identities had been multitracked on top of each other. How else could he collaborate so successfully with Sinatra, Charlie Parker, Igor Stravinsky, and David Seville of Alvin and the Chipmunks fame? We can debate whether he had a positive or negative impact on popular music, but what's not debatable is that he changed it forever. To quote Tony Bennett again, "Mitch was the one who showed everybody how to be a producer."

Miller established the primacy of the producer: you could take the same elements, the same singer, the same song, and the same accompaniment, and two different producers would put them together and make two recordings that sounded completely different from each other. More than any other factor, it was now the responsibility of the man in the recording booth whether a record flew or flopped. Miller also conceived of the idea of the pop record "sound" per se: not so much an arrangement or a tune, but an aural texture (usually replete with extramusical noises, or, for lack of a better word, audio "gimmicks") that could be created in the studio and then replicated in live performance, instead of the other way around. Miller was hardly a rock 'n' roller, yet without these innovations there could never have been rock 'n' roll. "Mule Train," Miller's first major hit (for Frankie Laine) and the foundation of his career, set the pattern for virtually the entire first decade of rock. The similarities between it and, say, "Leader of the Pack," need hardly be outlined here.

Born on July 4, 1911, in Rochester, New York, Miller was a prodigy who could play Bach's two-part inventions on piano at age six. After he switched to oboe, his facility on the instrument made him, at fifteen, by far the youngest member of the Rochester School Symphony Orchestra, the Syracuse Symphony Orchestra, the Eastman Symphony Orchestra, and the Rochester Philharmonic Orchestra. Granted a scholarship to the prestigious Eastman School of Music, Miller received his diploma in 1932. At his graduation recital, Miller performed an early work written for the occasion by Alec Wilder, who became a lifelong shadow.

In light of what he became famous for, many listeners might be surprised to learn that Miller grew up a huge fan of jazz and especially the big bands. "I listened to everything. Oh, God, yes! During the Eastman days, you could get three records [for] a dollar, Blue Deccas and Bluebirds," he told me. "Hell, I was listening to Louis Armstrong, Jimmie Lunceford, Jan Savitt, and the High Hatters. I was interested in all kinds of music. I went to hear all the bands, starting with Benny Goodman, then Artie Shaw and Charlie Barnet, because each of these guys had something to say."

After graduation, he immediately established himself as one of the top double-reed players in New York. He was surprisingly modest about this—"There were never enough oboists to go around," he said—but, in reality, the Manhattan studio scene was overwhelmingly competitive. He had his pick of the most coveted oboe gigs in town, and frequently found himself playing in situations that combined classical music with pop, such as the extremely popular middlebrow orchestra led by André Kostelanetz, and two key projects conducted by George Gershwin himself: the pit orchestra for *Porgy and Bess,* as well as a touring symphony that accompanied Gershwin himself on a series of concerts.

But his bread-and-butter gig, for eleven years from 1936 to 1947, was as the principal oboist with the CBS house symphony orchestra. In these years Miller consorted with the major philosophers of jazz and pop music, most notably Wilder and John Hammond (who had met Miller through a mutual friend, Alexander Schneider of the Budapest String Quartet). Miller also played under guest conductor Stravinsky, who later described Miller as having impressed him "by his finest musicianship combined with technical perfection together with the rare human qualities of sensibility, dignity, and modesty—uncommon phenomena in our tumultuous time." And yes, it's hard to imagine that Stravinsky was actually talking about the man responsible for "Come On-a My House" and "Swamp Girl."

This was the intellectual fringe of pop music, encompassing Wilder, Hammond, and George Avakian, as well as future Columbia head (and composer) Goddard Lieberson; Sinatra was a part of this group as well (although he and Hammond had, back in the Harry James years, taken an instant and permanent dislike to one another).

Sinatra first collaborated with Miller and Wilder in a meaningful way in two groups of recordings from November and December 1945, in which their discussions on the philosophy and future of popular music left the realm of the theoretical and became concrete. Together, this was a body of music that was so far removed from the top-ten charts and *Your Hit Parade* that Columbia didn't want to release them.

"Alec [Wilder] never pushed himself," said Miller. "I would push him. Other people would push him. But Alec had a lot of feel for the offbeat." Wilder was advocating for the songwriter Willard Robison, a highly iconoclastic composer whose songs combined elements of folk and country music along with standard Tin Pan Alley elements. (His most successful song was "A Cottage for Sale," which Sinatra would record in 1959.) "Willard Robison wrote this song ["The Old School Teacher"], and it was unusual. Alec brought it to Frank and said, 'This is your type of song,' even though the subject matter was certainly different from what Sinatra had done."

Sinatra not only took the bait, he persuaded Columbia to let him record "Old School Teacher" along with a compatible new song by Wilder titled "Just an Old Stone House." They were recorded on November 15, 1945; Wilder arranged both songs and Miller conducted. Both tunes have a feeling of rural archaism, with the word "old" in their titles, which was typical for Robison, the godfather of rustic American lieder, but unusual for Wilder, resulting in one of his most beautiful works. Although the two are similar enough in theme and style to make a perfect coupling, "Old School Teacher" was only released as a V-Disc. "Just an Old Stone House" remained in the vaults until 1950 when it made an unusual B side for the more likely hit "American Beauty Rose." Apart from several star collaborations, these two lovely and introspective, if somewhat meandering and arid airs, comprise Sinatra's only orchestral date without Stordahl from the beginning of the post-Dorsey period until 1949.

But there was yet more "uncommercial" music ahead involving Miller and Wilder. Wilder (1907–1980) was one of the more curious figures in American music, a frequent writer of songs (sometimes words, sometimes music, sometimes both) as well as classical pieces. Perversely, while his so-called pop songs are often pretentious and self-consciously "arty," his chamber music works are just as often light, swinging, and downright delightful. He somehow made pop music heavy and boring but, at the same time, made classical music inviting and accessible. A quixotic figure to be sure, Wilder also served as a writer and commentator on pop music, a radio host, and the author of a controversial book on the subject titled *American Popular Song: The Great Innovators, 1900–1950*.

After the November 1945 session, Sinatra was now advocating for Wilder's instrumental music. With Miller's encouragement, Sinatra began lobbying Manie Sachs and his producers and Columbia. The problem wasn't the cost of the session—paying the musicians and technical crew—but that during the war years and immediately after, it was impossible to get the very shellac to press these records. Sachs told Sinatra, "We can't because we don't even have enough shellac to even press the stuff from our own artists." As Miller relates, "And Sinatra gave us the bad news. So I came up with an idea. I said, 'Why don't *you* conduct them? Then he can't refuse you—if your name is on it.' That's because Sinatra was so hot then. And Frank agreed, although he had never conducted. You can't fake conducting. I'm not being a bit bitter, saying Sinatra's no conductor. How can you conduct if you can't read a score, if you don't know what to tell the musicians? But, on the other hand, he had a feel for music. So I would prepare the orchestra. Sinatra was then at the Waldorf, and he would finish at one in the morning. All the top musicians were there with us at the old Liederkranz Hall on Fifty-Eighth Street. And I rehearsed all the stuff and got it ready, and Frank came in and he waved the stick. And he didn't get in the way."

Wilder later related to his friend and collaborator Jim Maher how Sinatra stared down a roomful of the hardest-boiled studio musicians in that hardest of hard towns and told them, "Listen, I don't know the first thing about conducting, but I know this music and I love it, and if you'll work with me, I think we can get it down." Said Maher, "They would have given hell to any less-than-astute so-called leader who tried to pass himself off as a conductor."

The material was released as an album titled *Frank Sinatra Conducts the Music of Alec Wilder*. The general public paid little attention—they wanted to hear Sinatra singing, not conducting—but musicians took note. The trombonist Milt Bernhart, who would work extensively with Sinatra a few years later, was one. Then a member of Stan Kenton's brass section, he remembered, "I bought myself a record player and I'd buy records. And in those days there weren't that many records to buy that were really going to be interesting to a musician. One of [the few] was *Frank Sinatra Conducts the Music of Alec*

*Wilder.* I bought that album and I wore it out." At the time, the Kenton band was playing an extended run at the New York Paramount Theatre. "I played that album backstage in a dark room, sleeping between shows. To me, that music was gorgeous."

Had "Old School Teacher" and "Old Stone House" actually been issued in 1945, they would have probably marked the first important pop record that Mitch Miller had anything to do with. He didn't begin making the transition from musician to businessman until 1947—when John Hammond became vice president of a new startup label called Keynote Records, Miller was brought in initially to run the new company's classical division. By the time Mercury Records, a somewhat more successful Chicago-based startup, bought out Keynote, Miller had taken over the company's popular output.

In 1947 and 1948, Miller filled in several times as conductor on *Your Hit Parade* with Sinatra, on occasions when Sinatra would be in New York and Stordahl and the rest of the company remained in California. Still New York's key studio oboist as late as 1950, he appeared as a sideman in a modern jazz context with Charlie Parker, Buddy Rich, and Ray Brown on Mercury's *Charlie Parker with Strings* album. He also continued to serve as Sinatra's and Stordahl's favorite oboe man, particularly on their high-minded chamber group dates.

Miller and George Siravo both remembered one session, November 5, 1947, especially keenly. At the end of one song (they don't agree which), Sinatra felt he had laid down a perfect take. The engineer reluctantly informed him that unfortunately it was several seconds too long to fit on a conventional ten-inch 78 rpm shellac disc. Sinatra felt that either of the obvious alternatives—either editing the arrangement or picking up the tempo—would, Sinatra said, "kill the feeling." While they were deliberating, a gruff, cigar-toned voice spoke up from the back of the ensemble: "We could fit the whole thing in over at Mercury!"

Sinatra looked around and spied the goateed face of Mitch Miller, who was at that time running pop A&R at the fledgling Mercury Records label, where they apparently had more up-to-date cutting equipment. Now angry, Sinatra charged into Manie Sachs's office. "When Frank told the story to Manie," Siravo recalled, "he was really hotter than a pistol. 'You mean a big fuckin' outfit like Columbia can't do what a nickel record company like Mercury do? I don't believe this shit!'" Sinatra ultimately stormed off, leaving it to Sachs and the engineers to contend with the problem of fitting the track on the disc. (Perhaps this is what inspired Columbia to invent its microgroove technology.)

"I don't think Manie had a nerve in his body. I had never once seen him get angry," Siravo continued, "but this time he was pissed! 'That fuckin' Mitch Miller! You take my word! I take an oath, this guy will never again set foot at Columbia Records as long as I'm here!'" "Manie tried to have me banned from doing any more sessions," Miller confirmed, with no hard feelings, "but arrangers would come in and say, 'I want Mitch,' so he couldn't do that." Siravo, not missing the irony of Sachs trying to bar the man who would eventually succeed him, concluded that no one would ever have thought at that time that, as he put it, "Mitch would go on to become the great white father."

It was over at Mercury that Miller produced a record that would have unpredicted, widespread ramifications for the pop music business. This was "Mule Train," which would prove a career-establishing coup for both belter Frankie Laine and producer-promoter Miller; he not only produced the record, he somehow maneuvered to prevent the other labels from doing their own versions long enough so that the Mercury disc could sell a million units in five weeks—a blockbuster hit in 1949–50.

By the time the disc hit the million mark, a fellow Eastman School graduate named Goddard Lieberson had taken over the classical division at Columbia. Lieberson advocated to Ted Wallerstein, president of Columbia Records, to consider Miller as the new head of pop singles, replacing the departing Manie Sachs. Thus, in February 1950, Miller took over the pop singles department, bringing Laine with him. (George Avakian ran the very new albums division and Lieberson was still in charge of classical.)

In a sense, Miller and Laine had ridden the mule train to the big time. Miller immediately began to put his ideas into practice. "What makes you want to dig in your pocket and buy a record? It's got to be something you want to play over and over again," said Miller. "You look for qualities to make somebody buy it. I was trying to put stuff in records that would tighten the picture for the listener."

For a few years after the big-band era was over, pop music in America had remained largely based in a swing feeling, even though most of the hits were, at the time, by singers rather than bands. Even more than his proclivity toward dramatic sound effects, Miller's first and most distinguishing move was getting away from the big-band sound—no more brass, reeds, and rhythm, no more sounding like Goodman, Basie, or Lombardo. Although he used singers with big-band backgrounds, he put harpsichords behind Clooney (famously on "Come On-a My House"), bagpipes with Dinah Shore (as she finished out her CBS contract), and French horns foursquare around Guy Mitchell, a veteran of the Carmen Cavallaro band whom he had singing manufactured folk songs and sea shanties.

At the time, most musical gatekeepers would have listed, say, Duke Ellington or Rodgers and Hammerstein as exemplars of the best in contemporary American music, role models to aspire to. But Miller marched to the beat of an entirely different drummer. Or perhaps "marched" isn't the right word. "He absolutely loved polkas," Doris Day told me shortly after Miller's death in 2010. "He would have me singing some polka or other. I would finish a take, then I'd look into the control booth, and Mitch's chair would be empty, because he'd be on his feet, dancing the polka all around the room!"

Miller's innovations pivoted around a combination of new ideas and new technology, much of it made possible mainly by the invention of recording tape: multitracking, reverberation, and overdubbing. "I think Mitch Miller set the business back thirty or forty years," opined master orchestrator Johnny Mandel, "which is inexcusable for somebody who was as great a musician as he was. He was a marvelous oboe player. But then he started hiring all these bad singers, people such as Guy Mitchell and Champ Butler—Rosemary Clooney is an exception. The singers would fuck up. And the musicians loved it because they were getting all this great overtime. Finally, the labels looked at the budgets and asked the tape companies, 'Hey, isn't there some way we can do the background, let the band go, and have the singer on his own track?'"

"Mitch had a very good commercial sense and a sophisticated sense, too," recalled Stan Freeman, keyboard soloist on two of Miller's best-remembered sides ("You're the One" by Sinatra and Clooney's "Come On-a My House"). "For instance, Cy Walter and I did two albums with Lee Wiley. I always loved Lee, she was one of my favorites, but Lee was never a big commercial success. But Mitch said we owe it to the people to record her, knowing full well it was not going to be a big seller."

It was inevitable that Sinatra and Miller, who had been friends up to now (the 1947 incident aside), would start to butt heads. Miller was being pushed by his bosses to come up with ways to make Sinatra's records start selling again. "Sinatra had to pay the IRS a big fee for back taxes," Miller elucidated. "He had gone to Manie, who got Columbia to lend him the money as an advance against royalties. Then Manie left to go to RCA. Now, I get to Columbia. Ted Wallerstein, who was then president, says, 'Mitch, we've got to make this money back.'"

The Miller-Sinatra relationship began with the best of all possible intentions and considerable optimism from both men. Wallerstein had initially instructed Miller to move Sinatra product by "getting him the best things." The producer recalled, "Of course! That was my whole point. So people [today] don't understand that. I made 'Azure-Te,' 'Why Try to Change Me

Now?,' all marvelous, fabulous records! But you couldn't give them away *at that time.*"

Thus, Sinatra and Miller, who had campaigned together for the cause of art music and Alec Wilder in 1945, became unlikely bedfellows in 1950. The new Sinatra-Miller collaboration started very fruitfully indeed with "American Beauty Rose," from their very first session together in March. Up to 1950, Miller explains, "Frank made very few rhythm songs. 'Saturday Night' was one and another one was 'It All Depends on You' and 'Five Minutes More.' I thought he should do more." The test case was "American Beauty Rose," a song by Redd Evans, a swing-oriented songwriter responsible for such jazz standards as "Let Me Off Uptown" and "No Moon at All." Miller brought it to Sinatra with the idea of doing it in a Bob Crosby vein, sort of big-band Dixieland, in a vigorous two-beat. (Some issues were subtitled, "Dixieland with a Beat.")

Sinatra and arranger Norman Leyden, who had won his wings with Glenn Miller's AAF Orchestra (and Tex Beneke's no less marvelous postwar Miller band), bounce through this irresistible swinger, which seems to be in both 2/4 and 4/4 simultaneously. Another former Glenn Millerite, multi-reed-man Jimmy Abato, blows clarinet over the top of the heterophonic ensemble, along with ex-bandleaders Billy Butterfield and Will Bradley. Sinatra joyously milks a libretto that funnily and pun-ily compares girls to flowers. "American Beauty Rose" charted, but hardly high enough to stem the tide of steadily worsening sales for Sinatra records.

With "American Beauty Rose" now a minor chart success, Sinatra and Miller elected to do an extended project predicated upon "rhythm songs." "When I [started] running Columbia," Miller elaborated, "I thought Frank should do a whole album of rhythm songs. We got Siravo to do the arrangements and conduct." The feeling among most of Sinatra's friends and observers was best expressed by Milt Bernhart, who said, "He never really was given a chance to swing, so he never really took himself seriously in that area, and at Columbia Records, they didn't, either." Only about 10 percent of Sinatra's Columbia output had been up-tempo material (although he featured faster tunes much more frequently on the radio).

The Voice's up-tempo material from the 1944–50 period reveals how Sinatra and Nat King Cole paralleled each other in terms of their ambitions to expand into each other's territories. During these same years, Cole transitioned from pianist and combo leader to pop singer with orchestra; thus in a sense, he was moving from his own idiom to that perfected by Sinatra. At the same time, while Sinatra had originally risen to fame as a balladeer, his attempts to add a swinging dimension to his vocabulary encompassed an effort to work through the King Cole Trio style. As Cole evolved into a pop singer, he learned a lot about how to tell a story songwise from Sinatra. At the same time, Sinatra was invading Cole's kingdom. He still was his own man vocally—he couldn't be anything else—but virtually all of the up-tempo recordings he made in the immediate postwar period were very much in the Cole Trio format: the bouncy, medium up-tempos, the instrumental small-group texture (usually piano, bass, and guitar), and the delightfully ephemeral material. He recorded with four groups in this fashion between 1946 and 1949: Alvy West and the Little Band, the Page Cavanaugh Trio (with whom he also worked in person), the Phil Moore Four, and the Tony Mottola Trio. With the exception of the last (Mottola's unit consisted of three of Sinatra's regular studio sidemen), all were working groups that Sinatra had heard in clubs, and almost all were heavily influenced by the King Cole Trio.

The results were generally charming—and admirable experiments—although not in the same class with the remarkable swinging he would later achieve with Riddle and May. On the one hand, these sides might have made more of a long-term impact had he sung the same kind of high-class show tunes he was recording concurrently with Axel Stordahl (almost none of these tracks, for instance, were reissued in the LP era). "I don't know who picked the songs," guitarist Tony Mottola said. "I'm sure Frank didn't pick them all. You think, why would they have him sing a dumb song like 'My Cousin Louella'?" With a few exceptions the songs selected are indeed insignificant, to say the least, for example, "It All Came True" (done with Alvy West's very bar-mitzvahy Little Band) and "You Can Take My Word for It, Baby" (written by Dinah Shore aide Ticker Freeman).

On the other hand, much of the charm that these records have may stem from the trivial nature of the tunes—which again parallels the loose and informal, seminonsensical songs being recorded at the same time by the King Cole Trio, like "Frim-Fram Sauce" and "Ooh Kickeroonie." George Avakian, who supervised the Sinatra-Page Cavanaugh date, feels that Sinatra sounds so wonderfully loose precisely because the songs didn't mean anything to him, and therefore he could just have fun with them rather than having to take them seriously.

He's marvelously off-the-cuff, particularly on the older "S'posin'" and "We Just Couldn't Say Goodbye," and shows he understands what to do with a Louis Jordan–style punch-line–oriented novelty like Eddy Arnold's "That's How Much I Love You."

The four final selections in the series, from December 1948 and January 1949, are especially Cole-ish, owing to pianist Phil Moore's reliance on block chords (a pianistic device popularized by Cole and then George Shearing, which Moore claimed to have invented). Guitarist Bob Bain claimed that the foursome, which actually included five men, among them a clarinetist (Marshall Royal) and a drummer (Lee Young), "never really sounded like the King Cole Trio because Phil wasn't a real jazz soloist like Nat. He was more of a 'comp' player, and he would just kind of tinkle around. He let Marshall play all the solos. The drums gave us a different feel in the rhythm; it was more like a Basie thing." Still, no one ever came closer to stealing the Cole Trio's thunder than Sinatra and the Moore foursome do on "If You Stub Your Toe on the Moon" (a delightful Burke and Van Heusen song written for Crosby in *A Connecticut Yankee in King Arthur's Court*), "Why Can't You Behave" (from *Kiss Me Kate*), "Kisses and Tears" (from Sinatra's film *Double Dynamite*), and in particular "Bop! Goes My Heart" (on which Sinatra hits, with difficulty, a flatted fifth).

Appropriately, when Sinatra and Mitch Miller decided to do an entire album of up-tempo dance numbers, which eventually became *Sing and Dance with Frank Sinatra* (1950), George Siravo was the choice for the role of arranger-conductor. As Sinatra said in a 1949 interview, "'It All Depends on You' is a George Siravo arrangement. He's one of the untapped arrangers, I feel. He's a very fresh style guy, he's just fine."

The very first Columbia Stordahl session (which produced "If You Are But a Dream") yielded one of Sinatra's best-remembered swing hits, the perennial "Saturday Night (Is the Loneliest Night of the Week)." While clarinetist Artie Baker and drummer Johnny Blowers add considerably to the proceedings, most of the credit for the success of "Saturday Night" (after Sinatra) should go to Siravo. The arranger cited the disc as an example of an arranger "taking liberties with the foundation of a song," implying that his substitute harmonic pattern improves upon composer Jule Styne's original. Siravo had gone on Sinatra's payroll just in time for the end of the 1942–44 AFM ban and the start of the Sinatra story on Columbia. He began writing for Sinatra on the *Vimms* show in the first week of October 1944, beginning with "Sunday" (Jule Styne's first major copyright, coincidentally). By that time, Siravo was a veteran of the reed sections of (to name just a few) Harry Reser, Glenn Miller, Jan Savitt, Gene Krupa, and Will Hudson, and would continue to write prolifically for Krupa, Shaw, and Charlie Barnet.

Siravo was born in 1916 in Staten Island, a few blocks away from the Stordahl family, but Sinatra was the one who brought him to his team. While continuing to write for Sinatra, he also worked for other singers. Sammy Cahn gave him a large share of the credit for making Doris Day's disc of "It's Magic" a hit. Returning to New York from the West Coast around 1950, Siravo eventually did singles and albums under his own name for Mercury,

Columbia, and Kapp. In his post-Sinatra period he wrote for Tony Bennett (most notably the *Who Can I Turn To?* album and hit single), Jimmy Roselli, Connee Boswell, Vic Damone, and many more.

Siravo's most memorable achievements are his orchestrations for Sinatra's two groundbreaking LPs, *Sing and Dance with Frank Sinatra* for Columbia and *Songs for Young Lovers* for Capitol. He was the first arranger to help Sinatra fully explore his swinging side. He also occasionally scored ballads for Young Blue Eyes, such as "I've Got a Crush on You," "Nevertheless," and "There's Something Missing," all of which have a jazz component in the person of a prominent horn soloist playing obbligatos behind the vocal. Siravo wrote at least a few charts every week for *Songs by Sinatra*, but Sinatra, alas, only officially recorded a few of these for Columbia.

The idea of an entire album of fast songs clearly made Sinatra nervous—now there was a technological tension on top of his other troubles, since this would be his first album in the new 33-rpm long-playing record format. What's more, there were many other pressures gnawing away on both his confidence and his voice. As reedman Sid Cooper, who played on many Sinatra sessions in these years, expressed it, "Your confidence goes, your voice goes. That's what the name of the game is."

In September 1946, Sinatra had made a surprise appearance at New York's Copacabana in support of his close friend Phil Silvers, whose partner, Rags Ragland, had died suddenly a few weeks earlier. (This was a legendary event in show business history, remembered vividly by Julie Wilson, then a semi-anonymous singer in the Copa revue and later a major nightclub headliner in her own right.) For all those years, the Copa made Sinatra repeated offers to star in his own show at this iconic nightspot, but he consistently turned them down—the Copa meant multiple shows a night, and it was harder work than, say, radio or movie theater dates. Even as late as December 1949, the Sinatra office informed *Variety* that "he [has] definitely ruled out the Copacabana, where the policy is three shows nightly."

By 1950, he couldn't afford to be so picky, and he said yes not long after that story. On March 23, 1950, he opened at the Copa for what was announced as a two-month run; at the same time, he was continuing to do the nightly *Light-Up Time* spot. He was accompanied at both venues by Skitch Henderson. A radio show combined with three live nightclub shows every evening—clearly this was a recipe for disaster, but Sinatra was determined to give it his best shot.

To that end, he was fortified by a reunion with his old friend Sammy Cahn, with whom he had been "on the outs," as Sammy put it, for about two years. Cahn recalled, "And then, when I heard he was opening at the

Copa, the phone rang: 'Sam, Frank.' 'Hey, Frank.' 'Sam,' he said, 'you got a moment? I'm opening at the Copa.' I said, 'Hey, not only did I know that you're opening at the Copa, but I've been thinking, if we were speaking, what would I have written?' 'Will you come into New York?' 'Yes, I will.'" Cahn "trained," as he said, three thousand miles coast to coast and went to work with Sinatra, writing special material and boosting his morale. "And the stuff I wrote," he emphasized, "everything worked."

The opening went well; the club was packed, Sammy was there, naturally, and so were Rosemary Clooney, a young singer who had recently graduated to the Columbia Records roster from Tony Pastor's band, and Joel Herron, a pianist and songwriter then working with Jane Froman, the nightclub headliner who was also present. Their memories were all unanimous: Sinatra sounded great, and, what's more, the room was packed for all three throat-straining sets. Sinatra began the engagement at full strength. As Herron recalled, Broadway was already rife with rumors that Sinatra was losing his voice. As soon as Sinatra burst out singing "I Am Loved," however, everybody in the joint thought, "If he can't sing anymore, then what the heck is that?" The Columbia version of the song, recorded that November, accordingly captures an ebullient Sinatra warming himself in the glow of his own aura. "Sometimes you could hear that there was just kind of a raspiness or a hoarseness," said Rosemary Clooney, who, like many others who were there, feels that reports of the death of Sinatra's voice at the Copa were greatly exaggerated. "I can't tell you he sounded bad."

Cahn was excited that the opening was a success, but it was plain to the singer's friends that he was on a self-destructive path. "After the opening, he got great reviews. I was so proud, I was so happy," he continued. "I was going back [west], and I went to the Hampshire House to say good-bye, and he was in bed. I said, 'Frank, I want to talk to you. I don't know why you're doing what you're doing. All I can tell you, if I pick up that phone right now and call a music publisher and say, 'Hey, got a song for Sinatra?'—they'll hang up on me! And Frank, you're the best. You are the best, but you're like a horse with three jockeys. Why are you doing this? I promise you, if you say to me, 'Hey, Sam, let's go, I'll stop whatever I'm doing and just stay with you, and we'll go.' He kept saying, 'I know, I know, I know.' I said, 'I'm not being a hero. You do what you can do. You'll be sensational.' So that was the low point." It was also the only point in his life when someone—even one of his best friends—could talk to Sinatra like that.

Most of the time, Skitch Henderson recalled, "the Copa was wonderful. I consider that one of the tremendous experiences of my life. And the Copa was the end-of-the-line great New York club. *Always* sold out. I mean, wall-to-wall people in that funny room and that funny, archaic [chorus] line of four girls who danced. Frank did some of the most wonderful shows I have ever known him to do at the Copa." Clooney concurred: "He was doing business. I know he was moving people left, right, and center."

Just as troubles with his throat were starting, there were also issues with the musicians. The players at the Copa were hardly what Sinatra was accustomed to at CBS Radio, said Henderson. "Nicest men in the world, but they were a terrible orchestra. We always had horrible train wrecks with them." And Henderson himself was proving to be a difficult choice. He was already famous as a radio conductor, but as a pianist he wasn't up to the task. Sinatra's drummer, Johnny Blowers, remembered it vividly: "It was the second show or the third show or something, and Frank was going to go into the medley. We did a lot of medleys. We usually opened with them, 'She's Funny That Way' and 'I've Got a Crush on You'—four or five things. You do an arpeggio, you just automatically do it, and then you go into the theme. Well, Skitch played the arpeggio in the wrong key, and not only that, but the arpeggio was, like I told you, coal falling down the steps. And he turned around and he said, 'Malcolm, take your clothes off and stop playing that piano with your knuckles. Now, give me the arpeggio.' And he called the key. I don't know why he called Skitch 'Malcolm.' But then, I understand that Skitch found him in the dressing room, and he said, 'Francis, when we finish this engagement, we won't work together again.' And I understand his answer was, 'Malcolm, when you played the arpeggio in the wrong key, you were finished.'" (They did work together again, mysteriously, at the United Nations concert of 1963.)

Jack Entratter had booked Sinatra for eight weeks—one of the longest bookings in the club's history (fully twice the norm)—and the box office seemed good enough to sustain it, but by the second month, Sinatra's chops were starting to give out. "I was doing three shows a night, five radio shows [the exhaustingly overcrowded *Light-Up Time*] a week, benefit performances, and recording at the same time," Sinatra later told Arlene Francis. And then, the last straw that broke his back—or, more accurately, his throat—was a daytime engagement at the Capitol Theatre in Times Square that began in April. "And then I opened at the Capitol Theatre toward the end of the engagement. I went out to do the third show [at the Copa] at about half-past two or quarter to three in the morning, and I went for a note, and nothing came out. Not a sound came out. And I merely said to the audience, as best I could [whispering], 'Good night.'"

This was the moment when Sinatra was biting off his first LP, which would be released as *Sing and Dance with Frank Sinatra*. "When we came to do these records, Frank's voice was in terrible shape," Miller recalled. "Frank would be in an [isolation] booth, and he'd sing a beautiful phrase, and then on the next phrase his voice would crack. But you couldn't edit! So you'd have to throw the whole thing out. I can say this now: I could have been kicked out of the musicians' union because tracking was not allowed. There were a lot of musicians involved. So what I did, to save the session, I just shut off his mic and got good background tracks. Didn't even tell him." (Columbia had used the tracking process once before with Sinatra, when he recorded his vocal on "A Fella with an Umbrella" to a prerecorded orchestral background during the middle of the 1948 AFM ban.)

"Then after it was over, I said, 'When your voice is back. . . . ' We'd come in crazy hours, in a locked building, so no union representative could come in. Then when Frank came in, say, at midnight, we would play the disc. He would put earphones on and he would sing, just the way they do now. And we would remix it. He did them very well after that, and the whole orchestra was perfect on it." Siravo and saxophonist Jerry Jerome both remembered the session slightly differently: in their collective recollection, Sinatra wasn't present at all, although they were never informed why.

A month or so before the *Sing and Dance* album was released, during Labor Day weekend of 1950, Sinatra played Atlantic City and gave an interview about the project to disc jockey Ben Heller. "We've got a lot of jazz things that I'd like you to watch for. . . . I made them with George Siravo some months ago, tunes like 'Lover' and 'Blue Heaven.' [They're] bright [and have] good jump tempos, both to listen to as a vocal and to dance to." The tracking process apparently empowered Sinatra to feel more free and loose than he might otherwise have been in trying something so new with fifteen union musicians looking at their watches. He's gloriously loose from the start, dancing in front of Siravo's muted wah-wah brass on "Should I?" (tenor sax solo by Babe Russin), offering a snappy scat sequence in place of the last line of the second bridge, and, in long-breath Sinatra style, stretching the last "I" to make it the climactic point rather than the following two notes, "love you," which taper off. He tackles "You Do Something to Me" (baritone sax break by Ernie Caceres, tenor solo by Russin) as a major-to-minor progression, again getting jazzy in the second chorus, stretching and syncopating "you" over two notes and then doubling the time in the last line, adding extra beats: "which no one else *in the world* can do!"

Throughout, as in "Lover" (piano solo by Ken Lane, trombone solo by George Arus) where he shoots for a super-high climactic note ("mine") at the end of the second bridge, Sinatra constantly takes chances and goes for broke in reaching for notes that he wasn't supposed to have been able to hit with his overworked, underconfident pipes at this low point in his career. He comes close to cracking at the end of the second chorus bridge on "My Blue Heaven," but he and Miller liked the swingingly spontaneous feel of the take and left it as it was. Siravo and Sinatra apparently conceived of the track as homage to Sy Oliver, reprising many of the telltale mannerisms of Oliver's arrangement for Jimmie Lunceford. There's the laughing, muted brass and the tremolo-dripping alto à la Willie Smith and the reprise of the interpolated repeat of the line "a nest that nestles where the roses bloom," following the example of the vocal trio on the famous 1935 Decca recording by Lunceford.

Appropriately for a song still associated with Louis Armstrong, who recorded it more than twenty years earlier, "When You're Smiling" marks Sinatra's most Satchelmouthed vocal ever, as when he pulls back at the start of the second chorus. He fox-trots back and forth with the band on the bridge to "It's Only a Paper Moon" (an update on a Siravo *Vimms* show chart from 1944) with an idiosyncratically charming sandpaper-soft note on the payoff word "love." The full-but-light beat Sinatra gets going on "The Continental" (muted trumpet solo by Billy Butterfield) perfectly suspends itself between the hard-swinging and the relaxed; it not only anticipates but very nearly equals anything on the singer's first Capitol album, *Songs for Young Lovers*, from three years later.

Alas, Sinatra the swinger was not to be accepted by the record-buying public until the Capitol era; for the world to accept a new Sinatra, he first had to die (as he would in *From Here to Eternity*) then be reborn (as he would in "Young at Heart"). Although *Sing and Dance* remains one of the seminal albums of Sinatra's entire career, it never made it to the *Billboard* LP charts. Columbia never rereleased the eight tracks (the eighth being "It All Depends on You," a Siravo chart from July 1949) together on a twelve-inch LP, and Sinatra himself obscured *Sing and Dance* by rerecording six of the eight on his 1959 Capitol album *Sinatra's Swingin' Session!!!* The original *Sing and Dance* didn't enjoy a proper reissue until the 1996 CD, in which it was slightly retitled *Swing and Dance with Frank Sinatra*.

In retrospect, the album was a crucial step in Sinatra's evolution, a major leap in the direction of the mature Sinatra sound of the mid-1950s, particularly the classic jazz albums *Songs for Swingin' Lovers!* and *A Swingin' Affair!* But in 1950, no one was listening.

Mitch Miller was right about one thing at least—the "tracking" process saved the *Sing and Dance* project. But there was no chance for overdubbing at the Copa. Sinatra made the front page of the May 3 issue of *Variety* when he canceled the rest of his engagement and spent the next few months in the company of Jimmy Van Heusen, resting and tending to other business in Florida, the Mediterranean, Paris, England, and home in Los Angeles. He also made his first TV appearance on May 27, *The Star-Spangled Revue*, hosted by Bob Hope; he sounds glorious on "Come Rain or Come Shine," an arrangement that reuses part of the introductory material from his chart on "Don't Cry, Joe." By the end of June, he was ready to record again.

The only question was what.

Miller, naturally, had his own answer. The *Sing and Dance* album had been a true collaboration between producer and artist, both Miller and Sinatra approved of everything that went on the finished release, and it reflected equally the tastes of both men. The musicians themselves rarely had "problems with Mitch," bassist Herman "Trigger" Alpert recalled. "Although working with him was never as musical as working with Frank, let's face it." But since Columbia wasn't selling any records doing it Sinatra's way, Miller felt the need to step in and take over. From this point on, Sinatra's Columbia releases were increasingly Mitch Miller productions that happened to utilize Sinatra's voice.

In the Sachs era, Sinatra and Stordahl generally operated as their own producers, in the modern sense of the term. This is evident on several existing sets of session recordings taken from Columbia "safeties" (sixteen-inch 33⅓ backup recordings of entire sessions, from start to finish), in which the singer and the arranger are heard making sure the sound of everything is exactly right, and, say, instructing a trombonist to move a fraction of an inch closer to the mic and the bassist (usually Trigger Alpert) to play a little louder in the bridge of the first chorus.

Now with Miller taking over as a hands-on producer, there was bound to be tension. "Frank never [had to run things himself] with me," Miller insisted, "because how could he complain? The sound was [perfect with] Percy [Faith] and me [in the control booth]." Not surprisingly, there were times when things got hairy. Blowers recalled that once Sinatra instructed Miller, "'You don't tell the band what to do from the control room. Tell me or tell Axel, and we will tell the guys.' Now, I don't guess Mitch heard him very well because Mitch would forget about that, and the next thing you know, he was telling the band to do this and do that, and this was annoying Frank no end. Then we would sit down and listen to a take.

"With Frank and Axel, you corrected mistakes. You made your own dynamics. Frank didn't want [anyone else] turning dials; leave the damn dials alone. But Mitch did. I guess it was a couple or three times or something. But then all of a sudden one day I guess Frank had as much as he could stand, and finally, quietly, he just looked at the control room and said, 'Mitch, out'— and Frank always pointed his finger—and he said, 'Don't you ever come in.

Don't you *ever* come into the studio when I'm recording again.'" Blowers remembered that "Mitch never came again. Frank wouldn't permit it, because he knew what he wanted." Perhaps this incident occurred at one of the very last Columbia dates; Miller certainly seems to have been present at nearly all of Sinatra's later Columbia sessions. And well before *Sing and Dance* failed to become the salvation of The Voice's career, Miller had already proceeded along to plan B.

For the remaining two and a half years of his Columbia tenure, Sinatra's recorded output is stupefyingly schizophrenic, alternating between pinnacles such as "Hello, Young Lovers" and "I'm a Fool to Want You" and nadirs such as "One-Finger Melody" and "Tennessee Newsboy." As trumpeter Chris Griffin explained, "Frank was kind of mixed-up at that time." Clearly the classic Sinatra-Stordahl sound was no longer selling like it had five years earlier; both Miller and Sinatra were keen to explore new areas as it became increasingly clear that people "weren't buying the great records." *Sing and Dance* is notable as perhaps the only new direction that the two of them could agree on.

The first Sinatra record that shows a distinct Mitch Miller influence is "Goodnight, Irene" (backed with "Dear Little Boy of Mine"), which was recorded immediately after the *Sing and Dance* dates. This is not a song that Sinatra would have sung under any other circumstances. It reflects the better angels of Miller's nature: it's a fresh arrangement for singer and choir, and far from a straight-out "cover," or "knockoff," of the Weavers' huge hit; it also illustrates the producer's prescient early belief in the commercial possibilities of folk and country music. While not true Sinatra, neither side is actually bad. The idea of Sinatra singing Leadbelly may sound a bit off the wall, but the two sides are surprisingly palatable. Sinatra sings them straight, with the same sort of depth and purity that he would later invest in the Kingston Trio's "It Was a Very Good Year." Miller also plays it straight, for once disavowing hooks and gimmicks for a simple, effective arrangement that smoothly combines his choir with a chiming organ. "Irene," which is billed as by "Frank Sinatra with the Mitch Miller Singers," reached number five on the charts in early August, giving Sinatra his biggest hit of the entire "nosedive" period.

That this song scored a hit for Sinatra seems to have chagrined the singer as much as it pleased him. When he played Atlantic City that August, he brought with him his standard rhythm section of the period (Graham Forbes, piano; Matty Golizio, guitar; Frank Carroll, bass; and Johnny Blowers, drums). Blowers recalled that the very substantial crowds ("It was a madhouse") kept demanding "Irene." "I don't think Frank liked it too much, but it was a big hit for him. I used to think to myself, 'How in the world did they ever get Frank to do this?' That Mitch Miller, what a cornball! But anyway, Frank did it—and it was big. It went over."

In Sinatra's Atlantic City interview with Ben Heller, which took place backstage at that same theater, the following dialogue transpires:

> SINATRA: We've got a new one that's moving pretty good called, you'll excuse the expression, "Goodnight, Irene."
> HELLER: Hey, that's a nice tune.
> SINATRA: You wanna bet? (pauses) Naw, it's really cute.
> HELLER: You oughta do a lotta songs like that.
> SINATRA: Don't hold your breath!

Miller didn't hold his breath: he planned to follow up the success of "Irene" with two similarly faux-folkie pieces that were good to go for Sinatra by November, "My Heart Cries for You" and "The Roving Kind." Sinatra was to record them in a session set up in a brief window of opportunity during a layover in New York while traveling from Los Angeles to Africa (on the trail of Ava Gardner). "We came to the studio right away, and I played these two songs for them," Miller remembered. "He looked at Sanicola, he looked at Benny Barton, then he said to me, 'I'm not going to do any of that crap.' I had musicians hired, I had the chorus hired. The session was supposed to be that night because he was going away the next morning." When, at the last minute, Sinatra refused to do them, Miller quickly replaced Sinatra with a young singer named Al Cernick, who had recently been touring with society-piano bandleader Carmen Cavallaro. The two tracks that Sinatra had turned down would now launch the career of the recently signed singer, who was now known as Guy Mitchell.

Miller finished the story: "I dare say if Sinatra had done them at that time, I don't think they would have been hits. If he did them perfectly. Because the prejudice against him personally at that time, wrongly, was outrageous." But every time Miller landed a hit, he grew stronger and harder to refuse.

"One-Finger Melody" typifies the kind of Miller-style inanity on which Sinatra was willing to waste his talent. It seems probable that Miller brought Sinatra the song and offered him the publishing rights (which went to Sinatra's firm, Barton Music) as a further inducement to sing it. It's one of the dopiest discs he ever did, replete with a "Chopsticks"-like piano part. It's obvious which "one finger" this number suggests.

Dog songs of this pedigree were increasingly the rule. Yet at the same time, in direct defiance of the economic climate of this phase in the singer's career, the Sinatra-Stordahl combination continued to turn out some of its finest work deep into the Miller era, and the trilogy of songs from the recently opened Rodgers and Hammerstein milestone *The King and I* represents the collaboration at its Olympian zenith: "Hello, Young Lovers," "We Kiss in a Shadow," and "I Whistle a Happy Tune."(A decade later, Sinatra would add a fourth tune from the show to his repertory, "I Have Dreamed" on the *Concert Sinatra* album.)

To give "Hello Young Lovers" a slyly Eastern atmosphere, Stordahl had drummer Blowers obtain a set of miniature cymbals from the Zildjian percussion firm. This proved to be only the first stumbling block in trying to get that particular tune down on wax. "We made twenty-two takes on 'Hello Young Lovers,' [after which] we hated that song!" said Blowers. "Next door to [Columbia's studio on] Thirtieth Street was a bar. And we wanted to get out of that studio so fast, we beat each other to the bar to see who got his drink the fastest. That was a long date, but it had to be done."

"Hello Young Lovers" opens with a minor-key, vaguely dissonant string passage playing under Blowers's chinking oriental bells. Sinatra sings slowly and deliberately, as if every word were a two-ton boulder and he was Sisyphus pushing them up to the mountain. He imbues the bridge with even more gravitas, in spite of Hammerstein's vivid imagery of flying down the street with wings on one's heels. Then, in the final A, he extends the irony by extolling his young-lover listeners not to cry while he is on the very verge of tears. The piece moves gradually from East to West, from Asian percussion to European strings. But as Sinatra reaches the dramatically defiant conclusion, the oriental motif returns behind him, then quickly swells up as if to envelop him, as singer and orchestra dissolve together in a cinematic fadeout.

On "We Kiss in a Shadow," Stordahl is like a theatrical director as much as an arranger, and he builds the scene to suggest lovers meeting illicitly in a Siamese garden. The air is filled with delicately fluttering songbirds, as depicted via a five-note theme that flits about between various flutes and woodwinds. To help the words paint a picture of the lovers set free into the world outside, in the final part of the song we no longer hear the caged birds because they have been freed to fly. But "Shadow" ends with the songbird motif returning, signifying that this episode of liberty was only a pipe dream. We end with the songbird motif, now a symbol of confinement, grounding us back in reality. The figure, now established as an audio symbol of gilded cage repression, is repeated on one, two, three woodwinds (the last a bassoon) capped by Blowers's chimes. Sinatra knows well why the caged bird sings.

"I Whistle a Happy Tune" may have been the most immediately significant of the three since it suggests that Miller's ingratiating use of extra-musical noises can actually make a valid contribution to a Sinatra record.

The unidentified whistler who puckers throughout the record is a charming touch, helping the singer to assume the correct little-boy naivete, especially in contrast to the melancholy, sagacious narrator of "Hello Young Lovers." The song is another triumph of acting as well as singing; Sinatra further conveys a fittingly wide-eyed gaze by singing squarely on the beat and syllabifying big words like "de-cep-tion" as if he had just learned them. When, at the windup, Sinatra wants to convince us that he has conquered fear itself by whistling the happy tune, he relaxes his grip on the beat and starts to sound more like himself.

*The King and I* was a huge hit on Broadway, and this was, after all, Frank Sinatra at his apogee. Yet these three sides were barely noticed at the time. Between classic show tunes, swing numbers, and pseudo folk songs, Sinatra in 1950 had found the most success with the latter. Miller's motto was, then and always, "Try something!" In this period the singer and producer found yet another avenue to explore: big-voiced ballads of the sort that were doing boffo business for other singing Romeos of the era—Mario Lanza, Frankie Laine, Tony Martin, and the very young Tony Bennett. Throughout the likes of such heavy-sounding (and often classically derived) songs-for-corseted-crooners as "Take My Love," "You're the One," "Come Back to Sorrento," and "Luna Rossa," Sinatra is trying to come up with something suitable for this increasingly bombastic period of pop music. Even "I Hear a Rhapsody," which he had broadcast as a sensual Latinate dance piece with Tommy Dorsey a decade earlier, is reborn as a big melodramatic number with the lightness of an anvil.

Even most of Sinatra's up-tempo numbers from his last two years on Columbia have a top-heavy, overdone feeling to them, particularly "Birth of the Blues" and "Bim! Bam! Baby!" Unlike the best of his work with Riddle (or even Siravo), they're not light and swinging but big and heavy, though their rhythmic momentum is undeniable—like a freight train coming right at you. Yet Sinatra continues to try to come up with something congruous with his own artistic persona. "There's nothing more pathetic," as author Vicki Baum observes of her destitute aristocrat in *Grand Hotel*, "than a nobleman who cannot help but remain noble."

These heavy-handed pieces led to an all-time Sinatra masterpiece, "I'm a Fool to Want You." The song originated largely by accident. Joel Herron, a Sinatra fan since the Dorsey era and a friend since both were employed at the Riobamba in early 1943, was musical director at the Copacabana in the mid-1940s and, not long after, accompanist to Jane Froman. He had been using Brahms's Third Symphony as a theme song, and a lyricist friend of his, Jack Wolf, got the idea of using the andantino from the symphony as the basis for a love song. Herron adapted the Brahms theme and wrote an eight-bar bridge for it, and Wolf titled it "Take My Love." Wolf then brought it to Barton Music, knowing that if Ben Barton liked it they would not only have a publisher but an important artist to record it in Barton's partner, Sinatra.

Sinatra recorded "Take My Love" in November 1950 and also featured it on his CBS television show (which premiered on September 19); but, like most of his records of the time, it went nowhere. Later, Herron recalled, "Take My Love" "was used in an MGM film called *Undercurrent* with Katharine Hepburn and Robert Taylor. That season Herron was conducting for a radio series called *The MGM Theatre of the Air*, which opted to do an adaptation of *Undercurrent*. "But then we couldn't use 'Take My Love' because of some sort of cross-licensing problem," Herron said, "so they asked me to write something else. . . . Trying to compose something similar, I came up with the melody that later became 'I'm a Fool to Want You.'"

Upon realizing that "Fool to Want You" was a better, not to mention more original, song than the number that had inspired it, Wolf brought the new number to Barton, and Sinatra recorded it. "When they played us the side, I freaked out when I heard it," remembered Herron. "He changed part of the lyric. When the session was over, we were with Ben Barton and Hank Sanicola, and Jack and I went off by ourselves and said, 'He's gotta be on this song!' We invited him in as a cowriter."

Stordahl, who based his orchestration closely on the original song demo scored by Herron and arranger Joe Gordon, made it even more somber by adding a choir in the final half-chorus. According to legend, Sinatra filtered the song through his faltering relationship with Ava Gardner, which was at once breaking his heart and cremating his career. Reaching the bridge, Sinatra really socks it to us, and when he utters the phrase "time and time again" twice, he skillfully extracts totally different meanings each time, musically and dramatically, following the melody optimistically up on the first and depressingly down on the second. At the end of the release, Stordahl amplifies the singer's angst with a solo "crying" violin.

After packing an opera's worth of pathos into a single thirty-two–bar chorus, Sinatra is said to have become so overcome with grief that he bolted from the studio in tears. Yet "I'm a Fool to Want You" is more than an aural manifestation of the Frank and Ava soap opera. "That's bullshit!" said Miller. "Because what he's drawing is the emotion from *your* personal life. He's saying it for *you*."

Herron described his own involvement with "Fool" as a "historical accident," meaning that the success of this particular record, one of the classics of Sinatra's career, reflects more on the singer than on the songwriter. That success came almost entirely in the future. Initially, "Fool" reached only number fourteen in the *Billboard* charts and sold thirty-five thousand copies, which, Herron said, "was nothing for a Sinatra record [except in those lean years]. We thought we were done for." Undoubtedly, a competing recording by Billy Eckstine, which ironically reached the market first, cut into Sinatra's sales.

What's really amazing about the Miller-era work is that so much of it sounds so good even though Sinatra was having serious problems with his chops at the time. "He was under a lot of pressure," Chris Griffin recalled. "That's the only time I ever saw him tight on a few record dates." "We would be on a record session, and we just couldn't get a take in. [His voice] would just crack up," trumpeter Zeke Zarchy confirmed. "We'd take a break for fifteen to twenty minutes. [On one session] we went three hours overtime at double pay. On one of the breaks they sent out for hot tea, and then we waited around for forty-five minutes, and we never completed it. They finally called the session to a halt because his voice wouldn't hold up. These things could happen to anybody. Stress, overwork, it all ties in. It wasn't all of a sudden. He had a very tough schedule—all stars do—and it all just broke down."

These difficulties are testified to only by the memories of his associates. They are not borne out by the recordings. Even on the tracks that weren't issued for forty years, it's rare to find a bad note. The Voice sounds slightly thin on "Faithful" and a few other sides, but you can't find a single example of out-and-out bad singing. It's even harder to find an instance where Sinatra doesn't put all he has into every song, from the stunning "I Could Write a Book" to the inane "Tennessee Newsboy."

This period actually abounds with great little-known Sinatra sides, like the jaunty "Walking in the Sunshine," an exceptionally fine number performed as an industrial-strength swinger arranged by Siravo. On "My Girl," a merely serviceable ballad, Sinatra bends notes in a manner that anticipates his Capitol sound, using microscopic diminuendos and interesting stresses; the line *"when* the *night* is cold"* could be on any song on *Young Lovers.*

Yet when one thinks of the Frank Sinatra–Mitch Miller collaboration, it's the abominations that first come to mind. In the listener's eye, Sinatra can be visualized as the hero of a children's cartoon. On one side, Mitch Miller materializes as a bearded devil in a puff of cigar smoke, prompting the singer with his pitchfork to compromise his standards with the motto "Make millions with mediocrities." Sinatra's high-minded halo-wearing artistic conscience perches on the other side, telling him to harken instead to the angel on his shoulder and to stick with the caliber of material he did best: great songs, great arrangements, greatness.

Miller, who died in 2010, had almost sixty years to resent the contempt in which Sinatra and his fans held him. "Sinatra [later] said that I brought him all these shit songs, I forced him to do shit songs. You cannot force anyone to do a song. People don't understand this." In the most literal sense, Miller was right. He never had to force Sinatra or anybody else to do anything they didn't want to do. His track record did most of the forcing for him. If Miller went to artist A with a song and he turned it down, and then the song became a hit for artist B, "then the next time you bring a song to him, he's going to listen."

With other artists, Miller wasn't always quite so diplomatic; when Rosemary Clooney was dubious about "Come On-a My House," he threatened to terminate her contract. But, she told me, that was extreme behavior for Miller; normally he was much more "kind and sensitive" than that. Miller and Tony Bennett both admitted that he practically had to pin Bennett's arms behind his back to get him to do most of the numbers that established his career.

"Mitch kept giving Frank this terrible crap to record," says Paul Weston. Weston feels that Miller was so insistent and persistent, and such a good *convincer*, that he was impossible to fluff off, and that Sinatra, who was already terribly in debt to Columbia and not feeling very sure of his own better judgment, was particularly vulnerable to Miller's demands. "Frank was so disgusted and teed off at having to do that, it was ridiculous." Weston pointed out something that Miller never denied, that the novelty songs were an even bigger crapshoot (in several senses of the word) than the ballads—that a stupid comedy song had no better chance of striking it rich than a great love song. "You can't believe the crap that he had Jo [Stafford] record, tunes like 'Underneath the Overpass' and 'Chow, Willy,' stuff that just died."

In both Clooney's and Bennett's cases, all parties concerned would probably agree that the fact the songs became hits rendered the opinion of the artists rather irrelevant. Sinatra probably wouldn't have been thrilled if any of his Miller-produced novelties had been hits (such as "Goodnight, Irene"), but it made him all the more miserable that they flopped. It's enough to make you agree with Milt Bernhart's contention concerning the later Columbia work: "If the things were up-tempo, they were stupid. Those Mitch Miller things were all wrong for him."

In 1951 and '52, Sinatra was trying to move ahead into new directions, but also to return to his roots. He was moving into new media like television, and also experimenting with different kinds of radio formats, as on his show *Meet Frank Sinatra*, and, at the same time, he played several engagements at the New York Paramount Theatre over these two seasons. During one such run in 1952, the *New York World-Telegram* indulged in what must be one of the most extreme examples of a newspaper kicking a celebrity when he was down, with a headline trumpeting that crowds were "Gone on Frankie in '42" but simply "gone in 1952," delighting in announcing to the whole world that the theater was largely empty during these runs. (Sinatra could perhaps later take satisfaction in that his career would last considerably longer than the *New York World-Telegram*, which published its last issue in 1966.)

It was the Paramount Theatre that provided the genesis of Sinatra's most infamous record, that dog tune to end all dog tunes, "Mama Will Bark." Both at the Paramount and on the CBS-TV series, Sinatra would share the stage with the towering entity known as Dagmar, who, in twenty-first–century parlance would be known as a performance artist. A statuesque blonde—made even taller by a mountainous flaxen "do"—Dagmar seemed to be the result of some genetic cloning experiment gone awry, resulting in a hybrid of Steve Reeves and Jayne Mansfield. Born Virginia Ruth Egnor, she was a regular on Jerry Lester's early television show *Broadway Open House* who soon eclipsed the star in popularity. She was famous for revealing more cleavage than anyone had previously dared to display on television—it was Dagmar who christened the new medium as "the Boob Tube"—but she took the "dumb blonde" character to new and extreme heights and, in surviving footage, is genuinely funny—as in spoonerisms like addressing Axel Stordahl as "Mr. Strudel." (When the band wolf-whistles her, at the mention of her twisting around with all her might in "Ballin' the Jack," she responds, in a total deadpan, "Please gentlemen, your union isn't *that* strong.")

Dagmar first appeared with Sinatra at the Paramount Theatre in January 1951, and she would make numerous appearances on his television show that year. She's heard on a fascinating document that only recently surfaced, a live shortwave broadcast from the Paramount for French radio. The twenty-minute program is a rather amazing microcosm of what actually happened at Sinatra's movie-theater stage shows. After starting with an introductory band number, the remaining six songs balance swingers ("When You're Smiling" and "My Blue Heaven") with classic ballads, like "Hello, Young Lovers," and "April in Paris," which he introduces as a "great Axel Stordahl arrangement." (Joe Bushkin was officially leading the band for Sinatra during this engagement.)

The Paramount-Paris broadcast also contains the first Sinatra duet with Dagmar, on the 1949 rhythm-and-blues hit "Rag Mop," with goofy new lyrics apparently by Sammy Cahn. ("You're an exquisite flower / Built like the Eiffel Tower / Prettier by the hour / Better turn off your power / You'd frighten Eisenhower!") As Eileen Barton, a longtime Sinatra costar (who worked with him frequently in these years) put it, Dagmar "was just a big buxom Southern gal, that's all." Her name and ancestry may have been Swedish, but her accent divulged her West Virginia upbringing.

Mitch Miller was immediately struck by the chemistry between Sinatra and Dagmar, which is apparent on the Paramount Theatre broadcast and the surviving television episodes, explaining why she became a semiregular on the series. "In that show he had this dumb blonde, Dagmar, and they did a bit on the stage," Miller said. "So this song came in—you know, that 'Mama Will Bark' thing. And I thought, '[Let's] try this novelty.' Now, first remember," Miller added, "nobody brings Sinatra in the studio [to do something] that he doesn't want to do. I don't care who it is. Then, he had the right to approve the release—or not. So he could have bombed it all the way."

Miller continued, "I even put 'I'm a Fool to Want You' on the other side to ensure [the sales of] it." Furthermore, Dick Manning, composer of "Bark" (who would later have a success with "Fascination"), had previously landed a big hit with a similar animalistic aria entitled "The Pussy Cat Song (Nyow! Nyot Nyow!)." So there were many reasons why "Bark" might have scored a hit, but as Miller also said, "With novelties you never know. We made this record as a shot in the dark."

The two major misconceptions concerning "Bark" are that it was a total flop ("The only good it did me," Sinatra famously said, "was with dogs") and that it was the worst record of Sinatra's entire career. Truth to tell, if "Bark" had just died, no one would ever have heard of it and it wouldn't have kept coming back to haunt Miller and Sinatra. It did get on the charts (only to number twenty-one), which didn't make it a real hit, but did mean that a lot more people bought it than *Sing and Dance with Frank Sinatra.*

"Mama Will Bark" is certainly no dumber than "Come On-a My House." (Can you imagine if Sinatra had to reprise it at every concert, the way Clooney was obliged to keep singing "My House"?) "Frank probably thought Mitch was kidding when he brought that thing in," said Chris Griffin, who played trumpet on the date, "but that's the kind of song Mitch thought was really great!" The song's most salient features are a vaguely Latin American rhythm (tango? Rumba? *Pasodoble?*), a lyrical reference to Joyce Kilmer (whose poem "Trees" was a favorite of furry, four-legged friends everywhere), and Sinatra's convincingly canine impression of Jimmy Durante. As we hear him conga-ing about with this tone-deaf doggy diva, the very air abounds in dog howls (supplied by one Donald Bain) and we become increasingly convinced that, just as the lyric tells us, this is the "doggone-dest thing" we've ever heard.

Throughout 1951, he persevered with the CBS-TV series and the multiple runs at the Paramount. Skitch Henderson recalled, "[Columnist] Earl

Wilson, God rest his soul, really pounded the town for two days to get all of Frank's [old friends] to go down to the Paramount to see him. It was really a sad night because nothing was working. You're embarrassed for somebody that you love when things don't work. It happens to all of us at one time or another." Sinatra appreciated the support but probably would have preferred not to be seen by old chums at this particular time. Mel Tormé and Milton Berle went to see him together during this period, and Tormé told me, "I thought he couldn't sink any lower than that. That was the fall that preceded the rise."

In spite of his career doldrums, Sinatra was all over the airwaves in the early 1950s—which wasn't so much an indication of his popularity as a testament to CBS's ongoing faith in him—in spite of the fact that Manie Sachs was now long gone. As he cracks rhymiingly on one program, "This is Paley's bad guess on CBS." On October 7, 1950, Sinatra launched his first TV program, and despite his faltering popularity and obvious unease in the new medium, the sixty-minute show made it through two seasons. For conductor Stordahl the benefits were more personal: on the January 27, 1951, telecast, Sinatra announced the marriage of the arranger to June Hutton, lead singer with the Pied Pipers and featured femme vocalist on the program. (She was also the sister of the celebrated female bandleader Ina Ray Hutton.)

While the comedy sketches on the *Frank Sinatra Show* seem embarrassingly primitive today—this is truly 78 rpm television—most of the music on these CBS outings is much better than you'd expect. Sinatra commissioned new charts from his regular writers, particularly Stordahl and Siravo, and at least one new one, Neal Hefti, who arranged a fascinating, minor key treatment of "Get Happy." Besides that, and apart from being the last extended project Sinatra and Stordahl would work on together, the show produced little of professional significance. Sid Cooper, who subbed occasionally in the orchestra, recalled that from the band's perspective "it seemed like a big mixed-up situation at that time."

Sinatra had initially negotiated, in the summer of 1949, with the Mutual Broadcasting System to do a celebrity disc jockey radio show, which apparently never got off the ground. Around 1950–51, he did make it back to radio with *Meet Frank Sinatra* on CBS. Heard today, the show seems like an unwieldy combination of *Songs by Sinatra* and *Oprah*. In addition to singing with a rhythm section, Sinatra gave members of his studio audience the mic and exchanged snappy *You Bet Your Life*–style dialogue with them as well as with occasional guests such as Billy Eckstine, Richard "Junco Partner" Hayes, and Jule Styne. The show made so little impact that even hardcore Sinatra aficionados have barely heard of it. Musically speaking, the series, which ran through the spring of 1951, deserves some attention. His subtly swung versions of "'S' Wonderful," "One for My Baby," "The Moon Was Yellow" (all from the January 3, 1951, show), recorded with a hip rhythm section only, anticipate Sinatra's "Swingin' Lovers" era of half a decade later.

By 1952 it was all winding down: the movies, the TV and radio shows, the recording career, the nightclubs, the theater appearances, everything. His final MGM picture, *On the Town*, had been a huge success, but since then he had only made two features, both decidedly in the B category, *Double Dynamite* (1951) and *Meet Danny Wilson*, which at the time looked as if it would be his last: it quickly opened and closed in March 1952. In that year, he was gradually dropped by everybody: his agency (MCA), his network, his record company, and the entire movie industry. Many years later he was able to discuss the period with some objectivity: "In my mid-thirties I began to see things from a different angle, and I found that I became more tolerant of people," he said in 1977, "maybe because I had been knocked around a little bit. Nancy and I had a separation, and that hurt a great deal. Those things happen, unfortunately. Nobody likes it. I hadn't seen the children for a while, and I was kind of faltering a little bit in my work. I think I began to take stock."

After the humiliating debacle of "Mama Will Bark," relations between Sinatra and Miller disintegrated even further. In November 1951, Sinatra married Ava Gardner; Dick Jones played piano, Axel Stordahl was the best man, and Manie Sachs let them use his brother's house for the occasion. Yet like loving Ava Gardner, hating Mitch Miller became one of the emotional centerpieces of Sinatra's life.

Rosemary Clooney remembered working in Vegas at the same time as Sinatra during this period and how he slammed Miller and, in particular, "Come On-a My House" with the same vituperativeness he reserved for columnists. "He was knocking Mitch, not me," Clooney said. "But nevertheless, a little of the fallout got dropped on me." Shortly after, Sinatra's "second," Hank Sanicola, sent a note of apology to Rosemary.

Also in November 1951, Sinatra informed *Billboard* that he was not planning to renew with Columbia when his contract ran out in December the following year. He further reported that he was negotiating with both RCA Victor and Capitol Records as possible future homes. "Chief beef hinges on Sinatra's claim he isn't getting a fair shake on song material," the story said. "Sinatra has waged a long-smoldering feud with Mitch Miller." That was putting it mildly.

It all came to a head on June 3, 1952, a date that encapsulates all the highs and lows of Sinatra's in-between years in a single session. Although it marked the first of several thousand dates with his favorite drummer, Alvin Stoller (and only the second with pianist Bill Miller), this penultimate Columbia session proved the very apex of Mitch Miller's dream and Frank Sinatra's nightmare. Axel Stordahl was supposedly the musical director, and Paul Weston was officially the producer and A&R man. Mitch Miller, however, making one of his rare in-person appearances on the Coast, was dominating the proceedings and calling the shots. It's doubtful that Sinatra had any input whatever, but it is commendable that although he was supposed to have completely lost his chops by now, he nonetheless managed to squeak out no less than five very acceptable commercial masters in a single session.

"Frank was going through a very tough time with his voice," Weston recalled, "and it was very difficult for him to even get through a three-minute vocal. Frank was disgusted. It wasn't *his* fault, you know." As for the material itself, whether Miller-inspired or not, soft ballads were out. Sinatra first trots out "Luna Rossa," a big, dramatic, semiclassical table pounder with a chiming choir, and gets nowhere with it. Then comes Heinie Beau's brash but beautiful arrangement of "Birth of the Blues," a chart so down and dirty it could accompany Blaze Starr. Although certainly entertaining and often ranked a Sinatra classic, both this piece and "Bim! Bam! Baby!" (arranged by either Beau or Siravo) demonstrate how absolutely essential Nelson Riddle would become in devising a brassy and swinging yet subtle sound that finally worked for Sinatra. Here, even more than on the three 1951 Harry James numbers, Sinatra goes for an aggressively nasty sound (anticipating his 1966 "That's Life") that is at once invigorating and a little disturbing.*

In trying to sing the blues, Sinatra does better with "Paris Blues" (the subtitle for "Azure-Te") than he does with "The Birth of the Blues." "Azure-Te" (orchestrated, again, either by Siravo or Beau) consciously touches on that same abrasive sound as one of several textures that it juxtaposes to act out a narrative. The piece plays the concepts of "Paris" and "blues" off each other by alternating between taxicab horns that agitatedly beep a phrase from Gershwin's *An American in Paris* against the blaring brass characteristic of American swing. More baguette than beguine, its atmosphere suggests a Louis Jourdan movie, although "Azure-Te" was in fact introduced by Louis Jordan, whose pianist, Wild Bill Davis, had written it (and would later arrange "April in Paris" for Count Basie).

---

* In a 1959 TV appearance, Sinatra gives credit for the idea of him doing "Birth of the Blues" to Manie Sachs, adding that this song is the one that started to turn his career around again. The first statement is quite possibly true, the second almost certainly isn't. (This is on the memorial program *Some of Manie's Friends* on NBC March 3, 1959.)

"Tennessee Newsboy" rates as perhaps the single most extreme Miller concoction ever, on a par with "Mama Will Bark." Written by Percy Faith and "Bark" author Dick Manning, it serves as an unofficial sequel to "Chattanoogie Shoe Shine Boy," a 1950 Red Foley hit, successfully covered by Crosby and less so by Sinatra. "Mitch wanted to do some horrible song," said Weston, "and he brought in [Wesley] 'Speedy' West, a [country] guitar player who was famous for making his guitar sound like a chicken. So Frank sang the vocal, and Mitch rushed out into the studio, and everybody thought he was going to congratulate Frank for getting through—because he did it well. He rushed right back past Frank, and instead hugged Speedy West, because he'd made a good chicken noise on the guitar." Although Ted Nash takes a surprisingly good tenor sax solo here, Sinatra mainly remembered this tune as the one where Mitch Miller brought in Joe Siracusa, best known as one of Spike Jones's percussionists, to play the washboard. Weston heard Sinatra say, "Mitch, really? A washboard?"

At the end of 1952, Sinatra must have felt as if he were staring at a musical dead end. Jim Conkling, a former top man at Capitol Records, had recently taken over at Columbia, and his first assignment was to let Sinatra go. As Conkling's friend Milt Bernhart pointed out, this "was not a slap in the face or a hardship for Sinatra; he didn't want to be at Columbia anymore." But to where? Sachs was at RCA, but RCA Victor wasn't interested; yes, Manie said, he could force the issue, but wasn't Frank better off at a label where he was actually wanted? And there was also Capitol Records, where Conkling may well have advised Sinatra to get in touch with his replacement, one Alan Livingston.

The final two Columbia sessions took place in June and September 1952. Bill Miller recalled that not long after the September date he "heard him on the phone telling someone, 'Hey, I just fired Columbia!'" Sinatra would record only one more tune for the label, on a split session with the long-forgotten Mindy Carson. It's often been printed that Columbia only gave Sinatra a split session as a way of brushing him off. Actually, having two vocalists share a date was a fairly common practice. Tony Bennett did many of his sessions that way at that time.

In December 1944, when Sinatra quit *Your Hit Parade* for the first time, the last song he performed on the program was "Don't Fence Me In," which could be taken as a comment on the restrictive nature of that show's format. In his final months at Columbia, Sinatra recorded a number of tunes with allegedly autobiographical titles: "The Birth of the Blues," "There's Something Missing," and "Don't Ever Be Afraid to Go Home," an odd choice for a man whose sleeping quarters were open to doubt—having broken up permanently with one wife and constantly breaking up with another. And then there's the one about the idol who had "Feet of Clay."

Sinatra's parting shot to Miller was "Why Try to Change Me Now?" The last Sinatra Columbia side, it was the first song of note by the twenty-three-year-old composer Cy Coleman. Coleman reported that on the date Sinatra slightly altered the melody of the original opening interval. "I listened to the record and it sounded so natural, the way Frank did it, that I thought to myself, 'He's right!' So I left it that way. I changed the music! That's the first and only time I've ever done that."

Miraculously tender and sensitive even by Sinatra standards, the song allows him to convey an unapologetic humility rarely heard from him before or since. "Why Try to Change Me Now?" makes for a far more moving piece of self-analysis and, ultimately, affirmation than the comparatively shallow "My Way." Much more so than the Paul Anka text, it brings us close to a reasonable approximation of the real Frank, whatever that might be. The song also receives a beautiful arrangement credited to Percy Faith, in the best Stordahl flute-and-celesta tradition. Stordahl, as it happened, had recently signed an exclusive contract with Capitol Records and now could have done a date with Sinatra only with that label's permission.

The Sinatra-Stordahl sound had by now run its course; Sinatra was working with other writers and Stordahl with other singers. Stordahl would conduct for Sinatra on The Voice's first date for Capitol in 1953, and then the collaboration ended abruptly. Milt Bernhart recalled a story, perhaps apocryphal, that began circulating around the time the "comeback" was getting into gear. "Frank got a call to play a theater in New York, so he called up Axel, who by that time, on the strength of his Frank Sinatra reputation, had started getting shows here in Hollywood. . . . So Frank called him and said, 'We're leaving Sunday for New York.' And Axel said, 'God, Frank, I just began this show with Eddie Fisher.' And Frank said, 'Apparently you didn't hear what I said. We're leaving Sunday for New York, and we're going to be at the Capitol Theatre.' And Axel said, 'I can't do that, Frank. I've got a contract.' Frank said, 'Good-bye,' and hung up—and that's the last time they saw each other until that Capitol date ten years later [the 1961 album, *Point of No Return*]. Period."

Other, closer friends of both men dispute this account. According to Billy May, "Sinatra's career was kind of taking a nosedive then. He was looking for a change of scene. . . . I can't see how it could be a personality conflict, knowing both those people." And Paul Weston, who was close to Stordahl all of his life, recalled that Stordahl never had anything negative to say about Sinatra. "There wasn't any rift or anything like that as far as I knew."

Talking about his "Year of Mondays" with Sidney Zion, Sinatra would say, "I lost a great deal of faith in human nature because a lot of friends I had in those days disappeared. I don't say it begrudgingly because I [learned] something about human nature after that. I found out, or at least I think I understood, that some people don't know how to help. They want to, but they don't quite know how to do it. They're either shy or afraid they'll louse it up and make it worse than it is. Because later on, when things got better for me, I just came back and kept working. I did lay down for a while and had some large bar bills for about a year, I think. But after that I said, 'Holiday's over, Charlie, let's go back to work.'

"And then I began to meet these people who disappeared from my life—almost all of them, except for one or two dear, dear friends. I saw them and I said, 'How are you? How've you been?' And they were astounded, they were absolutely stunned that I even spoke to them. That's when I became aware of the fact that perhaps they didn't know how to handle it, they didn't know how to come to me and say, 'I haven't got much money, but I can lend you X amount of dollars.' Which I didn't want anyway because I was picking up a little job here and there. But at least out of that I learned something about human nature. Even if I fell on my butt, I learned a great deal about that."

This was Sinatra's *Don Giovanni* moment: he announces to the world that he has to be himself, even if it means that he's going to be dragged down to hell at the end of the opera. The next few years revealed that though he couldn't change who he was, he could re-create himself as a better version of who he is. At the end of the short film *The House I Live In*, Sinatra's Oscar-winning attack on racial intolerance, the singer admonishes his juvenile congregation, "Don't let 'em make suckers out of you." He wasn't going to let anybody make a sucker out of him, either. Rather, he was about to be redeemed, as T. S. Eliot wrote in *Four Quartets*, "from fire by fire."

So don't count him out yet. The ballet ain't over till the swan dies.

Postscript: I interviewed Mitch Miller many times, about Sinatra as well as other aspects of his career. But there was only one instance when I ever spent "quality" time with him on a social occasion (rather than a formal interview). This occurred a day or so after Sinatra died on May 14, 1998. It was a party for the author Joan Peyser, whose rather Kitty Kelley–like biography of George Gershwin had just been published in paperback. We had lots of mutual friends there, including James Maher (Alec Wilder's collaborator on his famous book *American Popular Song*), avant-garde composer Milton Babbitt, and Frank Driggs, the jazz historian, archivist, and producer, who was also Joan's boyfriend.

It was a complete coincidence that we happened to be "hanging" with Mitch right after Sinatra had passed and the news media was entering the climax of the grieve-athon that would continue for what seemed like weeks. This was still well before Sinatra's funeral on May 20. Mitch had been watching the news channels and he was astonished at the reaction; you could tell that it irritated him that the man who had caused him so much aggravation was now receiving so much adulation. "All this attention for Sinatra?" he grumbled. "The whole time I knew him, he gave me nothing but trouble." Mitch seemed stuck on that phrase, and he repeated it a few times for effect, "Frank was nothing but trouble to me. That's all he was, just a lot of trouble."

Jim and I glared back at him. Now it was our turn to be incredulous. "But Mitch," Jim asked, "wasn't he worth it?"

Unexpectedly, Mitch paused in his tracks. It was the only time I ever saw him looking introspective and reflective, as if we had just taken the piss out of him, as the British say. It was as if, fifty years after the fact, he finally realized the long-term value of what Sinatra had brought unto the world, and how important his own role in the Sinatra saga had been.

Mitch got a wistful look in his eye, and he finally answered us. "You know, I guess he was."

# THE HAT YEARS

■—■—■—■—■—■—■—■—■—■

*"The Afternoon of a Faun"*

# 6

# WITH NELSON RIDDLE

## *1953–1979*

*Grant me Paradise in this world; I'm not so sure I'll reach it in the next.*

—TINTORETTO
(aka Jacopo Comin, aka Jacopo Robusti, 1518–1594)

Was there ever a more perfect, more powerful, or goose-bump–raising record than Frank Sinatra and Nelson Riddle's "I've Got You Under My Skin"? Creating and releasing enough tension for any six Alfred Hitchcock movies, Sinatra and Riddle build from tender whispers in a lover's ear to primal, orgasmic screams. And that use of contrast turns out to be one of the team's central strategies, as gradually becomes clear while the arranger lays down the foundation for the track: a basically Count Basie–esque beat, well-defined and highly danceable. Like the majority of Sinatra's mature recordings, the track is in three sections: an opening chorus by the singer (occasionally—well, make that rarely—preceded by a verse), an instrumental break of some kind, followed by a concluding chorus (or half chorus) by Sinatra. His first chorus here is already both swinging and passionate—more so than any singer had attempted previously. Then, in the instrumental break, Riddle keeps the swinging beat going but introduces some very "daring" modern harmonies on top of it. He gets even farther out by presenting a section of trombones that sound like warring rhinoceri, and the winner of the melee is trombonist Milt Bernhart, who comes screaming out of the ensemble in a jarringly dissonant solo.

Bernhart is only briefly Sinatra's alter ego, his black swan; then the singer returns for an "outchorus" (the second half of the song, from "I would sacrifice anything" onward). Sinatra starts the outchorus precisely where Bernhart leaves off; the trombonist's highest note, both emotionally and musically, becomes his lowest, in a climax that extracts full meaning from both Cole Porter's lyrics and melody, at once sophisticated and primitive, intellectual and physical, rapturously romantic and yet understated. Sinatra is simultaneously a poet and a caveman, a creature of pure id but also pure super-ego, capable of grabbing even the most Frank-resistant listener way down at the bottom of the soul.

In the 1940s, Sinatra's romantic ballads made little girls keel over in their bobby socks. More recently, Sinatra had graduated from simply being the object of amorous attention to an inspiration. The lyrics of "Hello, Young Lovers," which he recorded in 1951, purport to offer advice to the lovelorn, but Sinatra is more accurately lending his formidable powers of seduction to millions of budding romances. "Skin" shows the more aggressive Sinatra that men like, the warrior with a conscience who speaks more directly to them than Monday-night football or locker-room boasts of backseat conquests.

But it's not only his perfection of faster tempos that separates the man from the boy when comparing 1950s to '40s Sinatra. In ballads, too, the Chairman of the Board reflects a significant advance over the Voice That Is Thrilling Millions. "I've Got You Under My Skin" is merely one of sixteen remarkable performances recorded in October 1955 and January 1956 for *Songs for Swingin' Lovers!*, Sinatra's definitive (certainly) and best (probably) collection of up-tempo standards. As a parallel, the 1958 album *Frank Sinatra Sings for Only the Lonely* resounds as his most moving gathering of downer love songs. His most iconic "saloon song," in the singer's own phrase, is "One for My Baby (and One More for the Road)," but my candidate for the number that best reflects his growth as a balladeer is a comparatively lesser-known number, namely "It's a Lonesome Old Town." This may be the unkindest cut of all thirteen songs originally earmarked for that classic album.

There's irony in everything about it. Written in 1930, "Lonesome Old Town" had served its whole life thus far as the theme song of bandleader Ben Bernie, known even at the birth of radio as "The Old Maestro." When people heard the six notes that defined its tune, they had been conditioned to expect a band as corny as Guy Lombardo's combined with ancient vaudeville spieling as schmaltzy as that of Ted Lewis. Sinatra and Riddle could have treated "Lonesome Old Town" as a takeoff on Bernie, as Spike Jones or Dean Martin might have done. To induce audiences into accepting the song on a serious level, however, the singer-arranger team had first to strip "Lonesome" of its sentimental excesses and then reconstruct it as a bona fide exercise in musical drama.

By coincidence, both "Skin" and "Lonesome" utilize Riddle's own instrument as a musician himself, the trombone, as a second voice, accompanying and abetting Sinatra. Both also reflect the direct inspiration of Bill Russo, an arranger and composer who is generally regarded as the best of the "serious" writers (as opposed to the more swinging writers, like Bill Holman) of the band book for Stan Kenton and His Orchestra. Where the Riddle-Sinatra "I've Got You Under My Skin" alludes to the polyrhythms of the Kenton-Russo "23 Degrees North, 82 Degrees West," "Lonesome" hints at the twinkling-stars background effect Russo devised for Kenton's "Improvisation" and "Over the Rainbow."

Riddle's use of trombone soloists is particularly telling: "Skin" is firmly grounded in the big-band swing of Count Basie and Jimmie Lunceford, and here the trombone soloist is the very modern Milt Bernhart, best known at the time for his long tenure with Kenton. Paradoxically, Riddle's background behind Sinatra on "Lonesome Old Town" is amazingly modern, using contemporary classical touches that almost suggest one of the better scores for 1950s science fiction movie. Here, instead of a modern trombonist, Riddle recruits the more traditionally-oriented player Ray Sims (best known for his work with Les Brown's Band of Renown, as well as for being the older brother of sax star Zoot Sims), whose playing has a warmer tone and a distinctly old-fashioned vibrato; again, Riddle's primary weapon is contrast.

Riddle's musically progressive textures appropriately expand the context of the song's lyric: Sinatra is no longer singing simply about a town that's grown lonesome and old; our protagonist now confronts an entire universe of despair. The two voices, Sinatra and his shadow, Sims, wander about this god-forsaken landscape aimlessly in search of love but finding only an interstellar abyss of emptiness. The warmth of the two "voices" only serves to underscore the unending vacuum that is creation. All human effort and emotion amount to nothingness. There is no protection from the pain, no safe place. We are all merely Lucky Strike Extras in the vast *Hit Parade* of existence.

The rapture of *Songs for Swingin' Lovers!* and the nihilism of *Only the Lonely* represent Riddle's personal two favorite albums of the twenty-one that he collaborated upon with Sinatra. They can also be safely described as the high points of their relationship and the zeniths of the careers of both men, individually and as a team. Still, they are hardly singular pinnacles. We could point to *A Swingin' Affair!*, *Swingin' Lovers'* sequel, as perhaps an even more thrilling ode to sensual syncopation, while *In the Wee Small Hours* and *Close to You*, prequels to *Only the Lonely*, are in many ways no less disturbing juxtapositions of eroticism and anguish.

In truth, virtually all the Sinatra-Riddle albums can be easily described as masterpieces; their collaboration was sainted from the first downbeat counted off at the first session onward. The seven essential works of their association were made for Capitol Records between 1953 and 1958: *Songs for Young Lovers* (recorded in 1953, although not entirely a completely true Sinatra-Riddle product, as we shall see), *Swing Easy!* (1954), *In the Wee Small Hours* (1955), *Songs for Swingin' Lovers!* (1955–56), *Close to You* (1956), *A Swingin' Affair!* (1956), and *Only the Lonely* (1958).

These seven projects are buffeted by only slightly lesser efforts, including five anthologies of independently recorded single cuts, *This Is Sinatra!* (1953–55), *This Is Sinatra Volume Two* (1954–57), *Look to Your Heart* (1953–55), *All the Way* (1957–60), and *Sinatra Sings of Love and Things* (1957–62). Further, there are two subsequent "real" albums diminished only slightly by extramusical circumstances, *Nice 'n' Easy* (1960) and *Sinatra's Swingin' Session!!!* (1960). Riddle and Sinatra also collaborated on two soundtrack souvenir sets, *Pal Joey* (1957) and *Can-Can* (1960). Lastly, five no-less-noteworthy postscripts: *The Concert Sinatra* (1963), *Sinatra's Sinatra* (1963), *Sinatra Sings Days of Wine and Roses, Moon River, and Other Academy Award Winners* (1963–64), *Strangers in the Night* (1966), and *Moonlight Sinatra* (1965), all produced for Sinatra's own label, Reprise Records, in the 1960s.

Neither jazz nor American popular music in general ever got any better than this.

One of F. Scott Fitzgerald's final literary creations was Pat Hobby, a has-been hack screenwriter antihero character who stood for the down-on-their-luck movie industry hangers-on, those not-always-sympathetic conmen who represented the author's worst fears about himself. (Fitzgerald writing about Pat Hobby was a bit like Sammy Davis Jr. singing about "Mr. Bojangles.") Hobby's views on the subject of war are in direct contrast with those of Jake Barnes, the far more admirable hero of Ernest Hemingway's *The Sun Also Rises*. Whereas Barnes returns from war "half a man," Hobby views war as an opportunity for growth. Hobby's heroes and heroines come marching home with their batteries recharged, their spirit strengthened, their scope expanded. The Chinese— or is it the Hindus? (or maybe it's the Orthodox Jews)—have a belief that one should never pray for growth or strength, because the only way to achieve such growth is by going through extremely difficult and trying times.

In 1953, Sinatra began to "come back" from the depths of his own private Armageddon, a personal cataclysm that had centered around the woman who later personified Papa Ernie's own Lady Brett. Using a war movie— *From Here to Eternity*—as the vehicle with which to announce his second coming, Sinatra's artistic abilities had indeed undergone a remarkable renewal and growth. "You have to scrape bottom," he told a friend at the time, "to appreciate life and start living again."

When pianist Bill Miller first went to work for Sinatra in 1952, he joined the singer at his all-time lowest point. In the first few months of their association, Miller witnessed The Voice's career slide from bad to worse: Sinatra's split from Columbia Records and the failure of his television series, not to mention his stalemated movie career, all in the context of his tumultuous relationship with his second wife. Sinatra in 1953 was like Japan in 1946; there was no other option but to rebuild everything from the ground up. No longer tied to either coast for broadcasting or picture work, he took to the road for several months and gradually added a new dimension to his work beyond the familiar sound of the Sinatra-Stordahl collaboration. He played the Chase Hotel in St. Louis (October, shortly after the final Columbia date), then two weeks at the French Casino in New York, a nightclub constructed out of what had been the Earl (around Thanksgiving). He was up to some interesting doings in Boston, in January: he played the Latin Quarter in the evening, but for two days he accepted a spot job as a guest disc jockey on Boston station WORL, doing two four-hour shows, playing some of his own recordings and others as well.*

It's important to note that Sinatra was well on the path to something new even before either Nelson Riddle or Capitol Records entered his life—even though it's obvious that the full-scale "comeback" wouldn't have happened without them. Obviously, during this period he still sang some of his 1940s ballad hits, the romantic songs for which he was still best known, but the new focus of his attention was a new book of smaller-scale up-tempo arrangements that he had commissioned from George Siravo. This was the one point that he and Mitch Miller had agreed on: that he should be doing more swing numbers, and that Siravo was the ideal man to arrange them. Sinatra continued to follow this path even after the 1950 album *Sing and Dance with Frank Sinatra* failed to become the hit that he needed.

Frank Military, who went to work for Sinatra's publishing company around 1952—and thus became part of his entourage—put it this way: "I think what happened was that Sinatra kept growing, and he outgrew [what he had been doing in the 1940s]. That's basically what it comes down to. He knew he needed something more, and he got it. I think that's very important to say, that Frank kept moving when everyone else stood still." These new Siravo charts were clearly a stepping stone to the "something new" that Sinatra was looking for; unfortunately, as 1952 ended and 1953 began, he was, for

---

* These dates are listed in the Giuseppe Marcucci discography/chronology *Where or When*. And wouldn't it be fascinating if an aircheck turned up, so we could hear what Sinatra was playing as well as his thoughts on music in January 1953, the very eve of the big comeback.

the first time in his fifteen-year-career, now without a recording contract and the means to put this new music down on wax.

The first sign that things were about to change for Sinatra occurred when he shifted his management to the venerable William Morris Agency, and came under the personal attention of Abe Lastfogel and Sam Weisbord, two of the WMA's top men. The agency represented more actors than it did singers, but it seems like their first priority was to get Sinatra recording again, rather than finding him work in a picture. Apparently, the agency cold-called the various labels that hadn't turned Sinatra down already, and were genuinely surprised when one label executive actually expressed interest. He was Alan Livingston, and he had recently taken over as vice president in charge of A&R and sales at Capitol Records (replacing Jim Conkling, who had left Capitol for Columbia).

"Sinatra had hit bottom, and I mean bottom," recalled Livingston. "It's hard to imagine now, he was so down-and-out. He had been under contract to Columbia Records, and nothing was happening. When his contract was up, Mitch Miller let him go, and he could not get a record deal. He could not get a job in a nightclub, and his buddies couldn't help him—even with his old friend Jilly [Rizzo] in Atlantic City. Manie Sachs, his closest buddy, couldn't give him a job. Manie was at RCA and wanted to sign him, but the A&R department there said, 'Forget it.'

"So I was sitting in my office one day, and the president of the William Morris Agency called me, a man named Sam Weisbord, whom I knew well," Livingston continued. 'And he said, Alan, we've just taken on representation of Sinatra. Would you consider signing him?' And without hesitation, I said 'Yes.' He said, obviously surprised, 'You would?' That's how bad it was. So Sam brought Sinatra in to meet me. I had never met him before. He was meek, a pussycat, humble. He had been through terrible times. He was broke, he was in debt, Ava Gardner had left him. I was told he had tried to kill himself on occasion. He was at the lowest ebb of his life, which I'm sure Frank would acknowledge to you—it's no great secret. Everybody knew it.

"Frank and I talked, and I signed him to a seven-year contract, one year with six options, which is as long as you can sign anybody. I gave him a standard royalty of 5 percent and gave him a scale advance. He was glad to have a place to make records. And that's how I signed Sinatra." The signing took place on March 14, 1953, at Lucy's Restaurant in Hollywood, with Sinatra aides Hank Sanicola and Frank Military present.*

---

* This was Livingston's own account, as he related to Chuck Granata and me on June 14, 1992. Other people tell different versions; for his part, Dave Dexter also claimed to have instigated the signing entirely on his own. Sinatra could have also easily found his way to Capitol via either Axel Stordahl or Jim Conkling.

The ink was barely dry when Livingston spoke at the company's annual national convention. "We had every salesman in our distributing company there, every branch manager; every district manager; every promotion man. There must have been a couple of hundred people. And I got up at these meetings and talked about future artists and recordings, and I announced that we had just signed Frank Sinatra," said Livingston. The collective staff of Capitol Records, Inc., was so overwhelmingly underwhelmed that they groaned en masse. "My answer to them was, 'Look, I can only judge on talent. I can't judge what people did in the past. I only know talent, and Frank is the best singer in the world. There's nobody who can touch him.' And I feel that way still."

Only two Capital A&R men were even vaguely supportive, Voyle Gilmore and Dave Dexter. Dexter was quite enthusiastic and Gilmore a bit less so, but Sinatra didn't want to work with Dexter (the producer and writer later claimed that this was because he had panned one of Sinatra's Columbia discs in *Down Beat* years earlier), so Livingston appointed Gilmore as Sinatra's producer. "I knew Frank would pick his songs," said the VP, "and that he knew what he wanted to do."

Choosing a musical director for Sinatra would prove more problematic. "Frank came in and said he wanted to work with Axel Stordahl, whom he'd been working with the better part of his career," said Livingston. Stordahl was under contract to Capitol, but Livingston had a better idea. "I said, 'Do me one favor and yourself a favor. Work with Nelson Riddle.' We were very high on Nelson. He was marvelous. Nelson knew how to back up artists and make them sound great without interfering with their singing. He knew where to bring the orchestra in, where not to. He was just a marvelous underscorer for a vocalist. So I wanted Frank to have the benefit of that."

Was this the first time that Sinatra had heard that name, Nelson Riddle? He would have been very familiar with the hits that Riddle had already orchestrated for Nat King Cole (even though Riddle's name actually wasn't on most of them), especially "Mona Lisa" and "Unforgettable." Sinatra knew that he needed something new, but just the same, Stordahl represented a kind of comfort zone. He was about to break new ground, but nonetheless his initial impulse was to recruit an old friend, someone he knew that he could rely on, to help him through this process. There was no way this could work, it would be like trying to climb a mountain while still keeping one foot on the ground. Axel Stordahl had been the most important man in Sinatra's world right up to this very moment. As he told Livingston, "I've worked with Axel Stordahl for practically [my whole career]. I can't leave Axel. I've got to work with him."

Livingston worked out a compromise with Sinatra whereby they agreed to try a new Sinatra-Stordahl session on Capitol. If the records sold, so be it, but if they didn't, Sinatra would try a date with whoever Livingston and Gilmore picked, meaning Riddle. "So we put out the first records with Axel— including 'Don't Make a Beggar of Me' and 'I'm Walking Behind You'—and nothing happened," Livingston continued. "I was determined to get Frank with Nelson Riddle."

"Frank had to be sold Nelson Riddle," said Bill Miller. "It was Capitol's idea to utilize Nelson, and after the first couple of sessions, he thought, 'Well, that's it.' Then when Frank tried Nelson on ballads, he said, 'Whew, we gotta be careful with him,' because Nelson had these harmonics—he used these polytones, G over A, A over G, all that. I said, 'Hey, Frank, it's different. It's working.'"

At thirty-two, Riddle had already established himself as a young musical director to watch out for, even though circumstances had thus far kept his name from circulating beyond the inner recesses of the industry. In 1953, Riddle was a burgeoning major talent seeking a style he could call his own, while Sinatra was desperately in search of a new sound powerful and fresh enough to reestablish him as pop music's most significant force. It was kismet that they should be forced together, almost against their will.

The most celebrated vocal arranger and musical director in history, Nelson Smock Riddle Jr., was born on June 1, 1921, in Oradell, New Jersey, a few towns away from the Sinatra home in Hoboken. "Smock is a Dutch family name," his son Christopher pointed out, "and it probably should have been allowed to go the way of a lot of unfortunate names, but it was carried on with my father." Riddle never liked the middle name, but with characteristic causticness he passed it on to his firstborn, Nelson Smock Riddle III.

Nelson Smock Riddle Sr. was one of those musical amateurs who George Bernard Shaw said would probably wind up in heck. Like Irving Berlin, he could pick out a tune on the black keys of the piano, which wasn't so bad if you didn't mind hearing everything in F-sharp (or if you had the ability to write "White Christmas"). "My father owned a trombone, which was mine for the reaching for," Riddle recalled not long before he died, "and he accompanied me in such hit tunes of the day as 'Harbor Lights' and 'Red Sails in the Sunset,' which made my toes curl because they were so boring."*

"Nelson was a very bright kid," said Bill Finegan, one of Riddle's earliest professional associates. "He was sardonic in his youth, and on the grim side.

---

* Almost all of the quotes from Nelson Riddle here are taken from the radio interview and profile conducted and produced by Robert Windeler of KCRW in Santa Monica (1984–85). (And to a lesser extent, one by Jonathan Schwartz of WNEW in New York, May 29, 1983.)

He had a sense of humor and we had a lot of laughs together, but he could be very grim." Many of Riddle's friends have described him as having a caustic, self-deprecating sense of humor, which in reminiscing about his family and his boyhood in New Jersey was often turned on his father—but even more often on himself.

"We didn't feel the Depression at all," Riddle said, because "my father made his own Depression. It was all the same to us because we were already in a depressed state by the time the Depression got there." By way of example, Riddle recalled that after eight weekly lessons on the trombone, his teacher told him to go home and not come back because "your father hasn't paid me for the first lesson, let alone the eighth one." The lessons were a dollar each, and the Riddles didn't have the money. Then, turning the screws on himself, he continued, "Anybody worth his salt would have gone out and sold some papers. I don't know why that didn't occur to me. I guess I was a spoiled brat."

"Nelson played trombone, and he wanted to learn about jazz. He claimed he didn't know anything about it," Bill Finegan recalled. "Somebody told him about me." At the time, Finegan, who was only four years older than Riddle and lived just a few towns away, had recently sold his first arrangement to a name band (Tommy Dorsey's "Lonesome Road"). "So he came, and I started writing out jazz choruses for him on the trombone," Finegan said. "I noticed he was talented, and one thing led to another and I said he ought to be a writer and got him started writing."

Riddle wrote his first arrangement in 1938; the tune was Arthur Schwartz's "I See Your Face Before Me."* "When I studied arranging with Bill Finegan, inflation had taken over; lessons were now two dollars," Riddle recalled. "Bill came to me one afternoon quietly and diplomatically, and he showed me a piece of paper and said, 'This is a check your father wrote me. It bounced.'" However, Finegan cautioned, "I don't know if that story is true. Nelson liked to tell things like that."

In early 1939, Finegan joined the writing staff of the rapidly rising Glenn Miller Orchestra. Not long after, the eighteen-year-old Riddle landed his first break with a national band in a new outfit led by Tommy Reynolds, a clarinetist who not only played like but also happened to look like Artie Shaw. Primarily a section trombonist, Riddle also wrote some arrangements for the band and went on studying closely with Finegan. Riddle had already moved on by the time Reynolds first recorded in December, but it is conceivable that

---

* Riddle recounted this in his 1983 interview with the composer's son Jonathan; he and Sinatra would, famously, put their definitive stamp on "I See Your Face Before Me" on their 1955 masterpiece album *In the Wee Small Hours.*

some of the thirty-three titles Reynolds recorded for Vocalion and then Okeh in 1939 and 1940 include arrangements by Nelson Riddle.

"I helped him put some charts together for Reynolds and some other bands, too," some of which he might have also played in, recalled Finegan, who continued to serve as Riddle's mentor until the younger man moved to Los Angeles after the war. "Bill Finegan got me started in the business," Riddle said later, "and some of the sounds you heard [in my work] early on might have emanated from him because I idolized him in those days. I still do, because I think he was one of the front-runners of fine arranging." "Nelson was a protege of Bill Finegan, and he had a lot of talent," remembered Larry Elgart, who worked with them both when all three worked with Elgart's brother Les's first band in 1945. "A lot of Nelson's choices of fourth chords and harmonies and things like that come straight from Bill."

Riddle made his first impact with Charlie Spivak's orchestra, the highly respected trumpeter's second attempt at bandleading. Reed player Harry Klee, who would become Riddle's lifelong friend and coworker, had joined Spivak's band a few months before Spivak himself did, back when the group worked in a roadhouse called the Nightingale on the highway to Richmond, Virginia, under the direction of a local leader with the unfortunate name Bill Downer. Although Spivak had been a much-respected soloist and lead player with half a dozen major bands, he was unsure of what he wanted in his first band, which stayed together only a few months at the beginning of 1940. By April or May, "somebody recommended that Spivak come and hear [Downer's] band," said Klee. "Spivak came through, and he offered to pick up the whole band. He made Bill a manager, and we went on the road with him."

"They used to call him cheery, chubby Charlie Spivak," said Riddle, describing his first important boss. "He was very pleasant and an excellent trumpet player. Charlie's control of the instrument and his tone, and so on, were magnificent. He had the control and breathing apparatus on the trumpet that Tommy Dorsey had on the trombone. Tommy became one of the great legends of all time. Charlie didn't." Where Riddle had begun writing arrangements for Reynolds almost immediately, according to Finegan, Spivak was considerably slower to recognize Riddle's abilities in that area; one sideman remembered that "Nelson was not Charlie's idea of a great arranger."

"I think the first arrangement that Nelson wrote for Spivak was 'White Christmas,'" said Harry Klee. "That was a pretty big seller for Spivak." Riddle also recalled scoring Josef Myrow's "Autumn Nocturne," recorded by Spivak several months earlier. "White Christmas" may have made a bigger noise commercially, being the top-selling band version of the biggest tune of all time, but the arranger was more proud of "Nocturne," because even though

"Claude Thornhill had a great record out on that," said Riddle, "Myrow [said he] liked our arrangement very much."

"When we had a rehearsal of the band," Klee recollected, "Nelson would pass out little slips of paper with, oh, maybe six, eight, or ten bars of music on them, where he was trying a new kind of voicing—you know, for new sounds. And he did this all the time back then, cataloging what he thought was good and discarding what wasn't." Said Riddle, "I learned quite a bit in that band."

In 1943, at age twenty-two, Riddle was a prime candidate for Uncle Sam, an involuntary career readjustment that he didn't especially relish. "My dad wasn't particularly patriotic," said Chris Riddle, "and regarded the entire war as a personal inconvenience." Riddle had been told that the Merchant Marines needed musicians for its band and that by serving with that branch for a year he could avoid being drafted in the regular army. He entered a Merchant Marines band stationed at Sheepshead Bay, Brooklyn, and later fondly remembered this service hitch: "It helped me no end, and I learned I loved to write for strings."

After his discharge, Riddle was thrilled to work for eleven months with Tommy Dorsey because, as he put it, "Tommy had even more strings than they did in the Merchant Marines." The band's guitarist, Bob Bain, recollects that "the first time I played one of Nelson's arrangements was with Tommy, a song called 'Havana.' Nelson wrote only ballads, Tommy didn't give him any jazz things. Nelson loved it because [it meant that] he could write for strings. Bill Finegan and Sy Oliver were writing a lot of the great jazz things."

After concentrating so hard on writing for a string section, Riddle next had to learn how not to rely too heavily on one. Dorsey instructed him, "You're making the strings too important. One day I might want to dump the whole string section—basically it's a tax deduction. I want to have that flexibility. When I get rid of them, I want to have an [arrangement] I can still play." Riddle "was crushed. I felt really badly about that. But I revised my plans so he could use them without strings. Actually, it wasn't bad training to be able to write both ways."

In his year with TD, beginning around June 1944, the orchestra's most lucrative venue was the *All-Time Hit Parade* radio series, which teamed the band with a different big-name guest star every week. On the September 17 show the celebrity was Frank Sinatra, although it's unlikely Riddle and FS actually shook hands at this time.

Eventually, Riddle reached a traumatic career crossroads with Dorsey. A few years afterward, when clarinetist Willie Schwartz first mentioned Riddle to Mahlon Clark, Clark asked, "Is he a good arranger?" Schwartz answered

"*Great* arranger. Half-assed trombone player, but he's an excellent arranger." While Riddle was with Dorsey, it was Finegan who "talked him out of playing the trombone. Nelson got to the point where he was a good writer," whereas on the trombone "he could [solo a little]. He just was nothing special. I told Nelson, 'When you play in the band and write, the leader treats your writing like it's a hobby. He'll play the stuff, but you won't get paid much for it,' which was true in those days. So he spent a couple of days with me, and I kept talking to him. And after much agonizing, he finally agreed to give it up."

Around that time, an accident occurred that ensured that Riddle would never play the trombone professionally again. He had hoped that his hitch with the Merchant Marines would keep him out of the "real" war, but the military changed its rules, and in April 1945 he was drafted. He stayed in the regular army until June 1946, leading a band for the officers' club in Fort Knox, Kentucky. During that time, he was injured in an accident in which a garage door somehow came down on his head and knocked out his front teeth. Because one high-ranking officer had liked his band, he arranged for the officers' dentist (rather than that of the enlisted men) to work on Riddle's teeth. "For the rest of his life he had pivots for front teeth. You couldn't tell," said Chris Riddle, "but he didn't play after that."

Riddle's new bride, Doreen Moran, whom he had married in South Carolina in October 1945, supported him in his resolve to arrange full time. Immediately after the war, he wrote for Tommy Dorsey and Spivak (including Spivak's hit "Laura"), and he and Finegan both arranged for a new orchestra led by trumpeter Larry Elgart. Although Elgart never claimed to be a swinging soloist himself, he leaned toward the new progressive jazz sounds that bands like Gillespie's, Herman's, and Kenton's were beginning to explore. Not surprisingly, the first Elgart band went bankrupt, and when the trumpeter-leader struck gold eight years later, it would be strictly with a businessman's bounce band that had no pretensions to anything else.

After Elgart's early band folded, Riddle went to the Coast, and he and Finegan rarely saw each other, unofficially ending their mentor-protege relationship. "The difference between Bill and Nelson," as the trumpeter's brother and later co-leader, Les Elgart, conjectured, and the reason "Nelson attained a lot more success than Bill is that although Bill was still a genius, Nelson wrote with a lot more abandon. Nelson wrote more freely."

Riddle himself acknowledged as much. Speaking of the Eddie Sauter–Bill Finegan Orchestra, Riddle said, "I thought it was magnificent. They had some sounds there that were incredible. [But], and this isn't negative . . . it was so intellectual that perhaps some of the emotion was not present. Both Sauter and Finegan were internal people, and neither was outgoing or gregarious at all. They were quiet, studious people, and I think some of their work shows that. It shows in the clockwork precision and intricacy of their work, but it also might occasionally show in the lack of fire and drive."

Riddle's activities are harder to trace in his freelance period, although we do know that it was Bob Crosby who brought him out to the West Coast not long after he was mustered out of the service.* Crosby later claimed that he first met Riddle by accident in a dentist's waiting room; however, a former fellow Dorseyite, guitarist Bob Bain, then in Crosby's rhythm section, actually introduced Riddle to Crosby. "He was looking for an arranger," said Riddle, "and I sort of foisted myself on him." Riddle wrote a few pieces for Crosby (including "I'll Never Be the Same" and "Night and Day," which he remembered fondly), but the singing bandleader's promise of work was negated by a situation with the IRS, which made it economically impossible for Crosby to put a group together at that time.

Although Riddle later described himself in this period as being "stuck in a strange town with no union card and back to basics again," he immediately fit into Los Angeles's busy studio recording scene, writing for records and radio. Around 1947 he impressed NBC's West Coast musical director Henry Russell enough to receive frequent assignments, and Bob Bain also remembers Riddle writing for accordionist Ernie Felice. "He was doing anything just to make a few bucks," said Bain. "He would write for anybody in those days. It was just work, for $100 to $150 an arrangement." In these years he also studied string orchestration formally with the Italian composer and teacher Mario Castelnuovo-Tedesco. "That was on the GI Bill, incidentally," he said in 1983, "so by the time I hit Capitol in 1950, I knew my way around the orchestra fairly well."

The first commercial recording outfit to give Riddle a shot at arranging for pop singers was not Capitol, however, but Decca, where Sonny Burke, who had worked with Riddle in Spivak's band, ran the show. Riddle is believed to have written as many as twenty-five arrangements for Bing Crosby in these years, as well as for other singers at Decca. He also gained his first opportunity to conduct at a record session on a Crosby date. "I remember the date because I had to call his wife," Bain explained. "I had promised Doreen that I would call to let her know that everything went okay."

Around 1949 or 1950, Riddle also started receiving some hand-me-down work from Sinatra's rhythm specialist, George Siravo. They had first met in

---

* One manifestation of how prolific he was can be easily documented: he and Doreen had six surviving children: Nelson Smock Riddle III (1947), Rosemary (1948), Christopher (1950), Bettina (1954), Cecily Jean (1962), and Maureen Alicia (1962). A seventh child, Lenora Celeste, was born in 1957 but lived only six months.

the middle of a session at Columbia's Hollywood facility. "The first time I ever laid eyes on Nelson, he was on crutches and was so bandaged, he looked like a mummy. He looked like somebody in a war hospital scene. He told me he was driving while he was bombed, and he hit a tree while going through Beverly Hills. He had been laid up in the hospital. He said, 'If you're overladen with work, if you have any crumbs, if you could throw me a bone, I would greatly appreciate it.' That's how he got a foothold at Columbia."

Exactly how much or how little Riddle wrote at this time is unknown, since he never received credit. Riddle didn't begin to emerge from anonymity until 1950, when an accident led to "Mona Lisa," the first hit record he would be associated with. Sonny Burke, who in addition to his Decca duties had directed some sessions for Mel Tormé and other Capitol Records artists, apparently brought Riddle to the attention of the label. At the time, Nat King Cole had reached the halfway point in his transition from pianist and leader of the King Cole Trio to a mainstream pop singer with orchestra, and in his dates for Capitol he alternated between a full big band and his world-famous combo.

Producer Lee Gillette wanted to try another format for Cole, a big gospel-style choir to back the singer on a pseudoreligious excursion called "The Greatest Inventor (of Them All)," obviously inspired by Sinatra's "The Old Master Painter." Since the number was primarily choral, Gillette appointed Les Baxter, a former vocal group singer and contractor, to direct the session, and Baxter subcontracted Riddle to write at least one of the strictly orchestral, non-choral tunes on the date.

That song was "Mona Lisa," which became Cole's biggest hit to date. It established the pianist as one of the strongest-selling singers in the industry and also launched the career of Baxter, first as a musical director for singers and later as an early guru of what became known as "easy listening" and "space-age bachelor pad" music. About the only one "Mona Lisa" didn't affect immediately was its ghostwriter. Baxter did at least two more sessions with Cole, generally also written by Riddle, the second of which produced another blockbuster in "Too Young." As Riddle recalled, however, Cole soon learned who Riddle was and liked his work "very much, and that was my wedge."

Riddle's long-awaited chance to get his name on a record and begin a relationship with a major singer came through a magnanimous gesture from fellow arranger Pete Rugolo. Although Rugolo had briefly been Cole's first regular arranger-conductor, he nonetheless pointed out to Cole's manager, Carlos Gastel, that "Mona Lisa" and "Too Young" were actually Riddle's work. "I told Carlos that Nelson should be given a chance because he was so good," said Rugolo. Riddle soon graduated from ghostwriter to full-time musical director for Cole—for approximately ten years and well over 250 songs. "I was never as commercial as Nelson," Rugolo said. "Once Nat started with Nelson, that's when he really hit. So he just kept Nelson with him."

In August 1951, Riddle began conducting his own arrangements for Cole, and receiving credit for same. Within a few months he was writing for as many singers as he could make time for on Capitol, including Mel Tormé, Kate Smith, Jerry Lewis, and, thanks to friend Billy May, Ella Mae Morse (a novelty blues singer for whom he concocted the hits "Oakie Boogie" and "The Blacksmith Blues"). By 1952 he was writing for singers across the whole spectrum of labels, most spectacularly Billy Eckstine on MGM, for whom he crafted two stunning ten-inch songbook albums, one of Rodgers and Hammerstein songs, the other of Duke Ellington.

Yet at thirty-one, Riddle was still considered a newcomer when Livingston and Gilmore brought him to the attention of Frank Sinatra in 1953. According to several musicians and other observers at the first Sinatra-Riddle session, virtually everyone present had been told that the charts Riddle was about to conduct had been written by Billy May, who was already a known quantity to the singer in 1953. Sinatra was still reluctant to consider a new musical director but was not averse to doing a guest-star team-up with a name band, as he had already done with Xavier Cugat and Harry James, and would do again many times. In 1953, Billy May was a name bandleader. Having landed several hit records for Capitol with his "nonworking" studio orchestra, he decided, with the label's encouragement, to actually take a band on the road.

As it happened, the very period May was out doing one-nighters occurred at the precise moment when it was decided to combine the name value and sounds of Frank Sinatra and Billy May. At his very first Capitol date (conducted by Stordahl), Sinatra had already experimented with a Billy May–style background on one tune: May's own composition, the upwardly modulating, blues-tinged "Lean Baby" (the title signifying a description, not an instruction). "Lean Baby" had been arranged by Heinie Beau, who was at that time both May's and Stordahl's (not to mention Paul Weston's) premiere deputy, closely following May's original instrumental hit.

"Lean Baby" charted, if not spectacularly, and from there Sinatra and Gilmore decided to do a follow-up Sinatra-May session. Capitol asked May to arrange and conduct, but May, out somewhere in the boondocks, was on the road and had his hands full. Gilmore saw this situation as a potential opportunity for Nelson Riddle. May recalled, "They said, 'Would you mind if we got Nelson Riddle to do them in your style?' They would use the same studio guys that I had used. I said, 'No, go ahead.' And we worked out a deal for a royalty."

Riddle was probably not thrilled at the prospect of anonymously aping the distinctive style of another writer, even that of a close comrade whose work he admired; at this point it must have seemed like he was always a ghostwriter, and never a bride. But, as trombonist Milt Bernhart remembered, "he did it for the reason that he wanted to be there." In other words, to get a shot at working with Frank Sinatra. Said May, "It came out where I got all the credit, but Nelson did the work."*

"So I went in," said Riddle, remembering the date, "and did two sides like Billy May would do them—'South of the Border' and one other ['I Love You']—and two sides as I would do them, 'World on a String' and 'Don't Worry 'Bout Me.'" All the musicians at the date were told that the charts were by May, and the records were released as "Frank Sinatra with Billy May and His Orchestra." Bernhart remembered, "Those people who were on the date—Si Zentner, Tommy Peters, Conrad Gozzo, Pete Candoli, and the rest—had worked quite a bit with Billy May. They were definitely fooled and were convinced it was Billy's writing!"

It's conceivable that even Sinatra himself was taken in. It was likely that he had gone over what he wanted in the carts with Gilmore well beforehand; both tunes were certainly his choices: he had been singing "South of the Border" at least since the song was new in 1940 (not only with Dorsey, but with Spike Jones, who was only slightly more outrageous and slightly less musically hip than May, in 1944). Sinatra had probably learned "I Love You" (not the Cole Porter classic, but a 1923 show tune from *Little Jessie James* by Harlan Thompson and Harry Archer) from the great 1939 Jimmie Lunceford–Sy Oliver recording; it pops up occasionally on his 1950–51 broadcasts. He had also been doing "World on a String" at a number of 1952 engagements, even using it as an opener at the Chez Paree in Chicago.

Alan Dell, then a Capitol employee (and later more famous as the guru of all good pop music at the BBC), remembered that Sinatra had walked into the studio on April 30, 1953, expecting to see the full frame of Billy May on the dais. "When Frank came in, he saw a strange man on the podium and said, 'Who's this?' I said, 'He's just conducting the band. We've got the Billy May arrangements.' So he sang 'South of the Border' and 'I Love You' and said, 'Great. What happens next?' I said, 'Try this one,' and they went into

---

* May, who also had been forced to labor anonymously for too many years, promised he'd return the favor; and he did, several years later when he ghosted for Riddle on a television assignment. "Oh, I helped him on a lot of things like that," May continued. "We worked back and forth. We were good friends."

'World on a String.' Then he said, 'Hey, who wrote that?' I said, 'This guy, Nelson Riddle.' He said, 'Beautiful!' And from that the partnership started."*

The partnership did not get under way immediately after that first date, however. According to Milt Bernhart and several other musicians, the second Sinatra-Riddle session, which was to have been the first non-"ghost" date, occurred soon after the April 30, 1953, session. Bernhart recalled that this session began with "Wrap Your Troubles in Dreams" (which Sinatra and Riddle would remake a year later on their second album). Riddle called the downbeat, but before singer and orchestra even got the first take down, Sinatra stopped everything cold. "The band stopped, and Frank said to Nelson, 'Call a break.' So the contractor said, 'Take ten.' Sinatra crooked his finger at Nelson, and the two of them walked out of the studio…don't know why, but I followed them. They went out into the hallway and into a smaller studio."

This was *it*, the all-crucial "aha!" moment: the single instant that would define the miraculous collaboration of Frank Sinatra and Nelson Riddle. The two men stood behind the soundproof glass and talked—or rather, Sinatra talked while Riddle listened. While the rest of the sidemen broke out a deck of cards, Bernhart positioned himself where he could watch them unobserved. He couldn't hear what Sinatra was saying, but, as he told the story, he didn't have to.

"Nelson was standing frozen, and Frank was doing all the talking. His hands were moving. He wasn't angry, but he was obviously telling him something of importance. I was positive I knew what Frank was saying to him. I could tell by the arrangement. It was very 'busy.' *Very* busy. There were all kinds of things going on behind the vocal. Frank undoubtedly told him that 'When you're writing, write a fill for me when I'm through singing but don't write a concerto behind me.'

"Nelson had a lot of technique as an arranger, he had been studying around town with very legitimate teachers like Castelnuovo-Tedesco. But some people have to be told to take it easy when they're writing for a singer.

"When we came back, the date was over. Sinatra could have dumped him. Other singers would have said, 'Well, get another guy,' if they were as important as Frank Sinatra. But he didn't. Which means that he recognized something in Nelson that a lot of people wouldn't."

---

* Dell's memory was slightly askew: the two pure-Nelson numbers, "I've Got the World on a String" and "Don't Worry 'Bout Me," were actually taped prior to the pseudo-May pieces, "I Love You" and "South of the Border." This concurs with Bill Miller's memory of the session: "We did the first two tunes with Nelson, then he made an announcement. He said, 'Now we have to make like Billy May' because Billy obviously couldn't be there. So Nelson was asked to write à la Billy May, which he did pretty well."

If the *Billboard* charts are to be believed, Sinatra's first few Capitol sessions were no more successful than his final year or so at Columbia. The new label's A&R crew, particularly Livingston and Gilmore, were excited by the sound of the second and third dates, which got him away from the "out-of-tempo, rustle of spring" sound of the Sinatra-Stordahl era. The May-styled "South of the Border" has Sinatra swinging harder and more convincingly than anything he had done at any time previously (even singing the best of Siravo's charts), and "World on a String," with its magnificent decrescendo opening, presented a newer, more confident Sinatra.

The next date, in May, produced "From Here to Eternity," which offered concrete evidence of the long-awaited career turnaround that everyone was praying for. "From Here to Eternity" had been a line from Rudyard Kipling's classic poem, "Gentlemen-Rankers" (a text that had already been softened into "The Whiffenpoof Song") that James Jones had used as the title of his bestselling novel of 1951. He sold the movie rights to Columbia Pictures, and then, when Columbia's Fred Karger and lyricist Bob Wells went to work on a title song, demanded a piece of the action in terms of both credit and royalties. (Jones's name is on the song, even though he didn't write any of it, which didn't endear him any to Karger and Wells.)

The song itself was no better or worse than dozens of movie themes (usually with lyrics by Sammy Cahn) that Sinatra would later tackle with Riddle. Prior to the date, Sinatra had asked the songwriters to "add a little tag": the first chorus ends with "this love that you left with me will live from here to eternity" but the second chorus has three extra words, "this love that you left with me—*this endless desire*—will live from here to eternity." The extra "tag" was Sinatra's idea. Wells came to the recording session and, as he put it, "Frank was down and out before that movie, and he was so insecure at the end of the date he said [humbly], 'Was that alright, Bob?' and I said, 'That was great, Frank.'" The payoff to the story came only six weeks later, when Wells happened to see Sinatra at NBC, by which time he was back to being his usual exuberant and highly confident self. "I said, 'Hello Frank' and he says, 'Hi kid!'

Sinatra had already been shooting the picture *From Here to Eternity* for two months at this point. Sinatra knew the film, his first in two years, could potentially have considerable ramifications for his career, and thus he had gone to almost ridiculous extremes with Columbia Pictures majordomo Harry Cohn to land the role. Milt Bernhart gives Sinatra credit for having the instinct to realize how important *From Here to Eternity* would be: "If you had just read the book, why would that change a person's whole life? Why would that have mattered? Frank knew that it would. He knew where he was going."

Suffice it to say that *Eternity* put Sinatra back on the top of the movie trade and all of showbiz. It wasn't just because it was a major film, his first "serious" role and his only Oscar as an actor, or because it was the major box-office hit of the year. There was considerable symbolic value to his portrayal of Angelo Maggio—the most remarkable of Sinatra's cinematic underdogs—a skinny little private who runs afoul of a bullying sergeant (played with formidable menace by Ernest Borgnine) and, miraculously, refuses to back down; he sticks to his guns, even though it means dying because of it. No less an impartial judge of Sinatra's career than Mitch Miller observed, "By getting stomped to death in that movie, [it was like] he did a public penance for all [the wrongs he had done]. You can chart it. From the day that movie came out, his records began to sell." The message of *Eternity* was clear: the old Sinatra is dead! Long live the new Sinatra.

Miller was fundamentally right, but the process was gradual. Sinatra stayed out of the studio until the end of the year, but he continued to "woodshed," as jazz musicians say, on the road long into the fall. He made his first peacetime tour of continental Europe in the summer, which turned out to be an unqualified disaster, inspiring such *Billboard* headlines as SINATRA LAYS EGG IN NAPLES, NEEDS COP AID and MR. SINATRA, GO HOME! He did a bit better in Britain that July: two BBC appearances on a program called *Show Band Show* find him in surprisingly good voice. But unfortunately, apart from a stunning "Don't Worry 'Bout Me" (much better than the record, and including the verse), The Voice was in a disappointingly disagreeable mood in his concert at the Opera House in Blackpool.

But from the day that *Eternity* was released, August 17, 1953, Sinatra was touched with that old "comeback" magic. At the end of that month he did a week at the 500 Club in Atlantic City to what *Variety* labeled a "standing-room-only" crowd. Moving north, he began one of the truly charmed engagements of his career, at the Riviera in Fort Lee, New Jersey. (One night both Harold Arlen and Manie Sachs were in the house.) The trade papers were close to ecstatic, and the mainstream press was also falling in line. He was also gathering momentum via appearances on *The Buick-Berle Show* with Milton Berle, *The Colgate Comedy Hour* with Ethel Merman, and at the Sands in Las Vegas in October.

Sinatra had previously played the Riviera exactly a year earlier. During that 1952 engagement, Frank Military recalled, he had already had something of his "Capitol" sound (this was before "Why Try to Change Me Now?") but had yet to be rediscovered by his audience. "Before *Eternity*, nobody showed up. Nobody even came to the dressing room [to congratulate him]. I said, 'Where are all the people?' He said, 'These people only come out for stars, and I'm through with them!' The following year *Eternity* comes out. We go back to the Riviera, and you can't get into the dressing room! I said, 'Frank, you said you were never talking to these people.' He said, 'There are no other kind of people!'"

One "location recording" of the Riviera engagement does exist, but it has circulated only among collectors and is in horrible sound (the band is all but inaudible). Fortunately, Sinatra wanted to capitalize on the exuberance of this immediate post-*Eternity* mood, and decided to document these "road" arrangements on what would be his first Capitol album, *Songs for Young Lovers*. Sinatra, it is said, then sold Gilmore on Siravo's work by bringing him to hear the band book in action at his October gig at the Sands in Las Vegas.

The Siravo orchestrations Sinatra used at the 500 Club, the Riviera, and the Sands (among other venues) used eight musicians, although they may have been written for a slightly larger ensemble. When Sinatra and Gilmore decided to record these charts in Los Angeles (Sinatra avoided recording in New York during the entire Capitol era), they again recruited Riddle to conduct. For the album, Sinatra used eleven men, indicating that the orchestrations had either been trimmed for live appearances or perhaps beefed up for recording. In any case, the sound quality on the Riviera tape is just good enough to confirm that the *Young Lovers* charts are practically identical to the ones Sinatra was using on personal appearances at this time.

"This is something new as far as I'm concerned," Sinatra announced at the Riviera. "We usually have eighteen brass and guys with [all kinds of] saxophones and Freddie Martin–style stuff, but we decided to try something different this time." As clarinetist Mahlon Clark recalled the *Young Lovers* sessions: "Frank used the arrangements he was using on the road then, written for a small band," of two reeds, four strings, guitar, piano (or celesta on "Little Girl Blue"), bass, drums, and harp. "I remember that they were tattered and worn," said Clark, and unlike most arrangements that studio men were called upon to play, "they were not new. Nelson brought in only one new chart of his own, written for that combination, and it was 'Like Someone in Love.'"\*

For Riddle, it was yet another ghosting job, even though this time it was he who was getting his name on the album and not Siravo. (The sole credit on the album reads, "accompanied by Nelson Riddle," which probably annoyed Riddle and Siravo equally.)† Still, assuming that this date took place

---

\* Frankophile Jonathan Schwartz, who has seen the arrangement of "Violets for Your Furs," reports that it is credited to Dick Jones, an orchestrator who turns up at multiple points in Sinatra's career, usually always pinch-hitting for someone else.

† Siravo occasionally came into the King Karol record shop in New York where Sinatra fan Bob Sherrick was then working and would gripe that he had been gypped out of his credit

after the aborted session that Bernhart described—in which Sinatra deemed the charts "too busy" and called the whole thing off—this turned out to be a learning opportunity for the young arranger. Here was precisely what Sinatra was looking for in terms of orchestrations that swung, provided a colorful background, and supported him without getting in the way. He would learn those lessons well; within a short time Riddle was doing a better job of that than Siravo, or indeed, any other musical director, but in 1953 he still had to catch up to the older man.

*Songs for Young Lovers* is a remarkable album; it doesn't sound anything like Riddle's work, and not much like *Sing and Dance with Frank Sinatra*, arranged by Siravo three years earlier. But it does resemble Siravo's own later albums of chamber jazz with strings, such as *Polite Jazz* (a twelve-inch album from circa 1955 on the Kapp label), enough that it's a wonder anyone could have mistaken the charts for Riddle's.

Both Siravo and Riddle often include original introductions and counter-melodies, but Siravo almost constantly riffs unobtrusively behind the main vocal line in a way that seems much more firmly anchored to the swing era. For instance, Siravo relies heavily on a rhythm guitar (Allan Reuss or Al Hendrickson) playing a solid four, often in unison with Mahlon Clark's clarinet, in a fashion highly reminiscent of the Benny Goodman–Charlie Christian small groups. This comes through on the riff underpinning "I Get a Kick Out of You" and "They Can't Take That Away from Me," both of which effectively cannibalize the bridge as an ad-lib verse introduction. The charts are light, airy, and swinging—unobtrusive as Sinatra demanded—but the rhythmic language is more big band than bebop; there's none of the contemporary classical influence that's all over Riddle's work, none of those Riddle-style polytones that Bill Miller talked about. There are echoes of Count Basie's 1950 octet and Artie Shaw's Gramercy Five, not Ravel and Debussy.

For his part, Sinatra has never sounded more amiably energetic than on his premier Capitol album and, indeed, on the whole first year of sessions for the label. "My Funny Valentine" in particular would become an iconic Sinatra classic, a chart that he would continue to sing as late as *Duets* forty years later. The outline of the piece seems very much like Sinatra's own idea, particularly the coda, which changes time signatures back and forth from 4/4 to 3/4 and also briefly alludes to "Bess, You Is My Woman Now." (Sinatra also deserves credit for rescuing this song—which had barely been heard or

on *Young Lovers*—and nobody believed him. Many years later, Tony Bennett happened to be speaking with Riddle and mentioned that he would soon be seeing Siravo. Riddle then told Bennett to pass along to Siravo his apologies—even though he was hardly responsible for Siravo being cheated out of his credit on the album.

recorded since being introduced in the 1937 show *Babes in Arms*—to begin with.)

The singer is so rhythmically astute in "A Foggy Day" that he transforms three syllables from an Ira Gershwin line into a stop-time break: "lost its charm" could be "Oh, play that thing" in "Sugar Foot Stomp." And on the same song, when he repeats "shining" four times—just because it sounds so good—"shining" is exactly what he's doing. Although Bill Miller (who plays superlative accompaniment behind Sinatra in the ad-lib verse) dismissed "I Get a Kick Out of You" as "too square," it became the most-heard Siravo arrangement to remain in Sinatra's working "book," and he continued to perform it virtually every time he found himself in a small-group context. (It must be said that Miller was so overwhelmingly pro-Nelson that he tended to dismiss most other arrangers.)

"Like Someone in Love" is immediately identifiable as Riddle's work, not only because it spotlights one of his soon-to-be signature sounds, the flute, but it also employs the quasi-impressionistic harmonies that Riddle would gradually perfect. Riddle plays two reed sounds against each other, Mahlon Clark's clarinet and Skeets Herfurt's flute. "Skeets had some beautiful alto solos, but I remember he was having a hell of a time with the flute part!" said Clark. "He was struggling, I was sitting there thinking, 'Thank God it's him, not me,' because I didn't play flute at all." But even though the majority of *Young Lovers* wasn't Riddle's writing, it was an auspicious debut album for the new partnership, and "Like Someone in Love" in particular pointed the way to the future.

With "Young at Heart," recorded two sessions later, Sinatra at last landed a major record hit to complement the cinematic sensation of *From Here to Eternity*. "Young at Heart" is a hymn to recharged batteries. If in *Eternity* Sinatra had done the requisite penance—the proper number of prayers and Hail Marys to kiss off his previous life, how better to begin his next one than with a text about starting over? Although soon connected to a rather dour and melodramatic flick (his only vehicle, alas, with the superlative Doris Day), the song "Young at Heart" is entirely believable sweetness and light throughout. Riddle douses Sinatra in a large field of strings that never become heavy; the arranger makes sure of this by trimming the tops of their sonic range with a flock of even higher and lighter flutes. Riddle's orchestra shines brightly but never more brilliantly than Sinatra himself. The comeback was now complete.

"Young at Heart" also symbolizes the vocal arrangement Sinatra was looking for when he beckoned Riddle aside a few sessions previously for some on-the-job instruction. As late as the Riviera gig (September 1953), when

Sinatra introduces his arrangers, the singer mentions Riddle but also refers to "the head man, Axel Stordahl." "Young at Heart" is the disc that finally "consummates" his musical marriage to Riddle. Sinatra had never been completely off the charts (even "Mama Will Bark" made it to number twenty), but "Young at Heart" marked the first time since 1947 that he topped them. Although he and Riddle each collaborated with others in this period, by and large the professional marriage remained intact. For the next and most remarkable phase of both of their lives, they would be a team.

Sinatra and Riddle remained essential to each other because each man pushed the other to heights neither could achieve individually. It remained for Riddle to develop both the ballad side and the swinging side of Sinatra, or rather to extend the legacies of Axel Stordahl and George Siravo (and before him, Sy Oliver). And the Sinatra-Riddle sound has since become what we think of when we think of Sinatra; their work together was so definitive that Sinatra's entire pre-Riddle period can be dismissed as a prelude, the post-Riddle era to an afterthought.

Theirs was often a tense but amazingly symbiotic relationship. For Riddle, the collateral benefit from his association with Sinatra was a career boost of the kind that could have never happened without him. "[Sinatra] was very good to me," he explained. "He opened some doors which, without his intervention, would have remained forever closed to me because the music world in this town was a tight, scared, greedy crew. It was even in those days when work was a lot more plentiful; there were [still] eighty musicians for every job." As Billy May put it, "Frank was good for Nelson. Christ! You make a record with Sinatra, boy, you start getting calls. I started hearing from MGM to do pictures and things like that, just suddenly, out of the blue. And Nelson got that, too."

Riddle made Sinatra's comeback and the so-called second phase of his career possible, but Sinatra not only enabled Riddle's career as a professional musician, but empowered him as an artist as well. The first ten years or so of Riddle arrangements, from the few we know of from his big-band tenures to the early Cole charts, reveal an orchestrator of obvious talent but little recognizable style. Even more than Cole, who was never as involved with his big-band accompaniments as Sinatra, working with Sinatra was the catalyst that inspired what would soon be instantly identifiable as the Nelson Riddle sound.

Lightness shines as the primary ingredient of the Riddle style. Whether he has ten brass swinging heavily or an acre of strings, Riddle always manages to make everything sound light; that way, the weightiest ballad doesn't become oversentimental or insincere, and the fastest swinger never sounds forced. Like his predecessor, Axel Stordahl, Riddle started with early–twentieth-century impressionists like Debussy and Ravel, particularly the second and third pieces in the latter's *Le tombeau de Couperin* suite (orchestrated in 1926). "Sometimes Riddle will throw on a nice dissonant chord at the end of a ballad," composer Joel Herron observed. "It's like holding up a sign saying, 'Speak to Ravel.'"

At the end of "It Never Entered My Mind," the intro and coda of "Gone with the Wind," and throughout "I'll Never Be the Same," Riddle employs a faux Oriental "wind chimes" figure. He once said this motif derived "from my obvious admiration of the French impressionists. They were fascinated by the characteristics of the music of another land, and it was nothing at all to them to bridge the gap and use those characteristics for their own purposes. In the *Mother Goose Suite* [*Ma mère l'Oye*], there's the 'Empress of the Pagodas,' which is a distinctly Oriental scene seen through the eyes or heard through the ears of a French impressionist."

"I loved how Nelson used Ravel's approach to polytonality," said Quincy Jones. "Nelson was smart because he put the electricity up above Frank. He put it way upstairs and gave Frank the room downstairs for his voice to shine, rather than building big lush parts that were in the same register as his voice. Nelson wrote some of the greatest arrangements for vocalists that I've ever heard."

But it would be wrong to overstate Riddle's debt to classical music; like Billy May and other composer-arrangers who graduated from the ranks of swing bands, Riddle learned just as much from Ellington and Strayhorn and the great writers of the swing era as from the Europeans. "Nelson Riddle's role model was Duke Ellington," said Bernhart. The jazz influence is apparent on the surface; the classical leanings can be detected primarily in the deep background.

As with Ellington, the instruments and the specific instrumentalists that Riddle composed for were crucial to his emerging style, and even more so were the idiosyncratic sounds of the musicians themselves, especially Sinatra. Both men were products of a big-band background, and Riddle reinforced Sinatra's conviction that the musicians best equipped to support him were not the conservatory-trained studio staff players of earlier generations, but guys who had cut their teeth as teenagers in the touring swing bands. Riddle leaned strongly toward veterans of the "progressive-minded" Woody Herman and Stan Kenton organizations. "When Nelson started to work at Capitol, he was looking for fresh blood," said Bernhart. "Before Nelson, the studio people were convinced we couldn't read or wouldn't show up. There was a bad reputation." Trumpeter Harry "Sweets" Edison, tenor sax Ted Nash, clarinetist Mahlon Clark, and flute specialist Harry Klee (like trombonist Juan Tizol, Klee was featured as a solo voice for texture and color but rarely as an improvisor) are probably the regulars Riddle featured most extensively as soloists.

Bass trombonist George Roberts was among the closest to Riddle personally and one of the most essential to him musically. Riddle also used Roberts as a sounding board. "He said he needed identification." Riddle had experimented earlier with a variation of the famous George Shearing Quintet sound, using a tightly harmonized blend of piano and vibes for the memorable introduction to Nat Cole's "Unforgettable." The arrangement proved a success and was a hit not only in 1951 but in 1991 for Natalie Cole (well after the deaths of both Riddle and her father) and Riddle worked variations of that intro into Cole's "It Happens to Be Me" and "If Love Is Good to Me." Still, he realized that this kind of gimmick could grow stale if used further—a conclusion eventually arrived at by Shearing himself.

In working and talking with Roberts and his other musicians, Riddle gradually developed a combination of Roberts's bass trombone, flute, muted trumpet, and strings as key ingredients of his signature sound. Roberts had first played professionally in the navy and attended a Los Angeles conservatory after the war. He eventually worked with Gene Krupa, where he first modulated from the traditional tenor trombone to its big brother, the bass instrument. After a stint in Las Vegas with a sweet band (Ray Herbeck and His Music with Romance), Roberts toured for two and a half years with Stan Kenton, where he was first widely heard. Kenton once introduced a Roberts feature number (the unrecorded "Yesterdays") by claiming that here was the first bass trombonist who used the instrument for more than "blowing roots and tonics at the bottom of big chords." Urbie Green told Roberts, "You're the only guy who plays that thing like a trombone."

On the "Young at Heart" date, Riddle dropped the trumpets and had the trombones, abetted by two French horns, assume most of that section's responsibility (in addition to their own). Roberts would be Riddle's most employed instrumentalist over the years, prominent on, to name just a few, "Makin' Whoopee" on *Swingin' Lovers*, "How Deep Is the Ocean" on *Nice 'n' Easy*, and throughout the 1964 *Academy Award Winners*. Roberts trails Sinatra like Philip Marlowe on "In the Cool, Cool, Cool of the Evening"; and while Ol' Blue Eyes extols the glories of "Swinging on a Star," Roberts grunts gleefully, as if to answer that he'd rather be a pig.

Pianist Stan Freeman, who worked with Riddle and Sinatra separately, points out that "although all the arrangers were good, Riddle was the best of them all. His use of everything in the orchestra I thought was just wonderful, and really complemented Sinatra's singing more than the others. He had an identifiable style—you knew a Nelson Riddle arrangement when you heard it." Not only is a Riddle arrangement immediately distinguishable from a chart by any other writer, but you can instantly tell a score in *Songs for Swingin' Lovers!* from one in *Sinatra's Swingin' Session!!!*, and one in *Nice 'n' Easy* from one in *Moonlight Sinatra*. Although they all share common elements, no other arranger could create so many different universes, each with its own stylistic glossary and set of rules, for Sinatra to inhabit.

That style is still a work in progress on Sinatra's second Capitol LP, *Swing Easy!*, which, like *Songs for Young Lovers*, was a ten-inch album containing eight songs; it was taped in April 1954 and released in August. Unlike *Young Lovers*, *Swing Easy!* was arranged entirely by Riddle; the one possible exception is "All of Me," possibly based on a chart that Siravo wrote for Sinatra at Bill Miller's Riviera in 1953, though liberally rewritten by Riddle.

As we've seen, the evolution of the classic Sinatra "concept album" form had a technological imperative. First, there was the advent of microgroove recording, which made slower-spinning and hence longer-playing "phonodiscs" possible. Even more important, the perfection of the process of recording on tape and the development of high-fidelity microphones now made it possible to capture the most delicate nuances. One could now explore enough minute details from track to track to fill an entire album of eight to twelve or even sixteen songs in a similar mood. The fuller frequency range made Riddle's entire sound—and therefore his career—workable, dependent as it was on contrasting the strings above with the trombones below. Riddle, whose best work could never have been captured on coarse-grooved 78-rpm singles circa 1945, utilized the new technology to the fullest, making every chart explode in a rainbow of orchestral color.

Not surprisingly, the first theme Sinatra tackles in this brave new era is fast and swinging, up-tempos having been one trail he rarely traveled in the Columbia era. "Sinatra in the 1940s was the crooner with the bow tie," said guitarist Al Viola, who worked with Sinatra in both eras. "With the Page Cavanaugh Trio [who accompanied Sinatra frequently between 1945 and 1949], we hardly did any up-tempo things. When he came back in the '50s, I noticed right away that he was still a crooner with the teenagers and all that, but now he was also *the* swinger. He had a real strong baritone, and he was more into the swinging things, like 'Lady Is a Tramp.'" Soon Sinatra would be declaring "Oh! Look at Me Now" to all who doubted, tellingly reusing that first important fast tune he ever recorded (with Dorsey in 1941) as the climax of *A Swingin' Affair!* And when Sinatra sings "I'm in the groove again" near the end of "Taking a Chance on Love" on *Swing Easy!*, he isn't just whistling "Dixie."

Although not as purely jazz styled as his later collaborations with Red Norvo and Count Basie, *Swing Easy!* finds Sinatra constantly altering the melodies and reimagining them with far more abandon than anything he dared attempt in the previous decade. On "Just One of Those Things," the tender kiss-off piece that opens *Swing Easy!*, Sinatra fashions his equivalent of a twelve-bar blues chorus out of the words "good-bye and amen." Likewise, on "Get Happy" Sinatra repeats the opening line over and over beneath a fade-out coda, like a lick being stated and echoed by a trumpet or saxophone.

*Swing Easy!* also marks the first appearance in Sinatra's world of trumpeter Harry "Sweets" Edison. Born two months before Sinatra, like the Old Man himself he stayed on the road as long as possible, up until shortly before his death in 1999. Edison originally came to glory with Count Basie's breakthrough band, where he was possibly the most celebrated member of the brass section from 1937 to 1950, and an internationally acclaimed master of the art of the trumpet obbligato. In the early 1950s, he served as musical director for the expatriate star Josephine Baker in her homecoming tour, but he would always be better known as a soloist than a bandleader. Edison is best remembered as a studio player, one of Sinatra and Riddle's most important star players, but he told me that he never particularly liked studio work and always preferred to play in front of live audiences. Edison blamed—if that's the right word—his Hollywood studio years on a particularly status-conscious wife. From roughly 1952 to 1965, he played on thousands of dates, funneling the funds into his Hollywood lifestyle. She "had" to own a house in Hollywood "and go every Saturday to the beauty parlor. I don't know why she had to get her hair done so often," said Edison, adding, "The only happy marriages I ever had were when I was broke."

Lester Young christened Edison "Sweets," and for over sixty years the nickname served as a perfect description of Edison's playing. Rarely as direct a player as, say, Roy Eldridge or Harry James, Edison shared with his frequent costar Benny Carter a unique capacity for playing at you from around the comer. He constructs pithy, angular, yet always swinging phrases that approach the melody from odd angles and he often seems to be playing obbligatos even when he's flat-out soloing (as in "Jeepers Creepers" on *Swing Easy!*). Edison's skill as a master melodist allows Riddle to play with perceptions of foreground and background; the instrumental section of "We'll Be Together Again" on *Swingin' Lovers* consists of the main ensemble playing a variation on the melody, which is phrased quickly to allow Edison plenty of room for his interline statements. With Edison and Riddle, the heckling from the sidelines often becomes more important than the show on center stage—not while Sinatra (or Fitzgerald or Garland or Clooney or whoever) is singing, as he had to learn the hard way, but during the instrumental breaks. In Riddle's work, those breaks are just as fascinating as whatever the star singer is doing.

Edison in particular was a past master at saying an awful lot in a very few notes, and most of his parts on Sinatra records consist of merely an extremely well-placed handful of beeps. Sinatra and Riddle came to value Edison's beeps so highly that he was rarely expected to play with the regular trumpet section. Rather, he would be positioned to the side of the ensemble, wearing headphones and playing into his own mic, waiting for precisely the right moment to inject his tasty trumpet remarks into the foreground action. He was treated more like a second singer, a duet partner, than a mere sideman.

Edison, the only musician to figure prominently in the careers of both Frank Sinatra and Billie Holiday, one of Sinatra's major inspirations, said that it wasn't a question of knowing *what* to play behind a singer so much as *when*. "You have to wait for them to breathe or something," he said. Or, as Riddle put it, "I think the muted trumpet can make a comment and yet not get in the way of the singer." Edison reported that although he disliked Hollywood and the studio scene, he nonetheless considered working with Sinatra and Riddle a highlight of his career, even as he did working with Lady Day.

Riddle said of Edison's playing in general that whatever the situation, "he certainly caught the mood." Adding that Edison was responsible for most of the whimsy on his records, particularly *Swing Easy!*, *Swingin' Lovers!*, and *Swingin' Affair!*, Riddle continued, "The humor is in Harry's head. You show him what you want, you delineate the area that he's going to play in, and he's the one who actually makes the humor of the comment. You just show him where. He can be on my team anytime."

Edison was also celebrated as the studio fraternity's resident "character"; according to one story, Sinatra once stopped an entire session—thirty men waited around on Capitol's time—so that he and Edison, both rabid baseball fans, could catch a few innings on television. Riddle recalled an instance when "Harry Edison showed up at a Sinatra date with a policeman on each arm. I think he'd run several red lights, and the cops nailed him. He said, 'I'm on my way to work with Sinatra,' and they said, 'Sure, you are!' He said, 'right, come on with me, and I'll show you.' So they marched him into the recording session, and there was Frank and everybody. They released him and laughed and walked away."

On *Swing Easy!*, Sinatra sought the sound of the orchestra led by vibraphonist Red Norvo in the late 1930s, which costarred singer and his wife, Mildred Bailey (a key influence on Sinatra, Tony Bennett, Rosemary Clooney, and many others); the pair were billed as "Mr. and Mrs. Swing Band." While Riddle never goes so far as to mimic Eddie Sauter (Norvo's musical director and later the professional partner of his own mentor, Bill Finegan), he does emphasize Norvo's instrument, the vibes, here played by studio percussion virtuoso Frank Flynn. Flynn later recalled that both Sinatra and Riddle were delighted with the way the vibes were used in *Swing Easy!* and added that he considered the album the best thing he ever did. (With the possible exception, he told me, of his solo on Riddle's and Ella Fitzgerald's "Midnight Sun.") It worked wonderfully, yet Sinatra and Riddle never opted to use the vibes that particular way again. (However, the celesta more or less assumes that role in *Songs for Swingin' Lovers!*, particularly on "You're Getting to Be a Habit with Me," "Pennies from Heaven," and "Swingin' Down the Lane," and throughout *In the Wee Small Hours*.)

Flynn may have been close to the truth when he said that the charts reminded him more of Ellington than Sauter. The trombones do engage in a hocket passage (playing individual lines that overlap in a disjointed hiccup-like fashion) in "Jeepers Creepers," much the way Ellington had his "pep section" do in the 1938 "Braggin' in Brass." "Wrap Your Troubles in Dreams," with its clean, streamlined swing that must be the diametric opposite of the original, overbusy chart of a year earlier (the one that Bernhart spoke of), sports a very hot chase chorus between two outstanding soloists, clarinetist Eddie Miller (of Bob Crosby fame) and trombonist Ray Sims. Sinatra's own vocals have never come closer in jazz feeling to early 1940s Billie Holiday. In using a more-or-less standard fourteen-piece dance band instrumentation, making this one of Sinatra's only sets without strings, Sinatra and Riddle more likely sought to refer to the swing era in general rather than to any specific band or artist.

Still, Sinatra doesn't quite take it all the way. *Swing Easy!* is a major step forward from the Siravo albums, *Sing and Dance with Frank Sinatra* and *Songs for Young Lovers*, but it is a starting point, not a final destination, on the road to the Riddle-Sinatra swing masterpieces, *Swingin' Lovers* and *Swingin' Affair*.

Around the same time as *Swing Easy!*, Sinatra and Riddle were also developing Sinatra's swinging side in a series of singles; even as the two were perfecting the concept of the popular album, they were continuing to do some of their very best work in the 45 rpm format. Whereas the songs for the albums were almost always selected by Sinatra, producer Voyle Gilmore had the job of sifting through new songs to find suitable material for the singer. Everything Gilmore brought to Sinatra was subject to his approval, and at the same time he was generating a significant number of songs himself, not least through his side activities as the owner of the publishing firm Barton Music.

With his very first album, *The Voice*, back in 1945, Sinatra had established that albums were the medium for songs that had already proven their worth as classics and that singles were to be used for new songs that were potential hits, for deejays and jukeboxes as well as consumers. "We came to that decision and it was a very definitive conclusion, that for albums we wanted standard product," as Alan Livingston confirmed. "Now, that's not true today. But at that time, that's all we would do on an album, standard product. You might slip in a new song, but unlikely. Whereas a single, you try to make a hit out of it. Then if it were a hit, you could put it in an album, or name the album after it. That was a general concept, not just with Frank, but with Nat and everybody else." This was the way Sinatra had operated on his Columbia albums and, indeed, largely for the rest of his career.

The songs he was doing on Capitol singles were generally not on the level of the crème de la crème of the American songbook, the Cole Porter, Rodgers and Hart, and Gershwin Brothers songs that were the backbone of the albums (although there is a lovely reading of "Someone to Watch Over Me" from 1954 that sounds like it belongs on an album). Sinatra did help introduce a few songs in this medium that became standards, most successfully "The Man That Got Away." It was introduced by Judy Garland in her own "comeback" vehicle, *A Star Is Born* (and forever part of her canon), but Sinatra's version (with appropriate pronouns) was no less impressive. The song was even more moving as he grew older, and he reintroduced it into his concert repertoire in the 1970s and '80s. But by and large Sinatra utilized the singles medium to transform otherwise unknown songs into minor gems, like "Take a Chance," "Ya Better Stop" (with its ingenious parody of a "fadeaway record" ending), and "Why Should I Cry Over You?"

The early Capitol years were also particularly rewarding in terms of his relationship with Sammy Cahn and Jimmy Van Heusen, two songwriters who had never previously worked together; he helped forge them into a partnership whose primary responsibility was providing him with material when he needed it, and they became effectively his "in-house" scribes. Their works for Sinatra, in these years, first separately and then together, include the irresistibly bouncy "Same Old Saturday Night" (discussed in the introduction to this book), "You'll Get Yours" (one of the most violent of all Sinatra songs), "I Could Have Told You" (one of several songs Van Heusen published under a pseudonym in these years), "Three Coins in the Fountain" (the most visible example of Sinatra singing the main title theme of a movie in which he doesn't otherwise appear), and "Hey! Jealous Lover" (a quasi–rock 'n' roll number* written by a pair of neophyte songwriters that Cahn apparently

---

* Sinatra also made a more elaborate attempt at addressing the nascent kiddie-pop market in 1955, with a highly doo-woppy disc of "Two Hearts, Two Kisses" and "From the Bottom to the Top," backed by a quartet named the Nuggets. This was so early in the game that Elvis Presley was still under contract to Sun Records.

spruced up to make Frankworthy). Another movie theme, Van Heusen's "Not as a Stranger," is a particularly flamboyant use of Riddle's signature polytonal approach; the shower of shimmering harmonies that surrounds the singer, while similar to what the arranger sprinkled on Nat Cole on "I Am in Love" and on Billy Eckstine on "Seabreeze," is positively resplendent.

The first two notable hits of the Cahn–Van Heusen/Sinatra/Riddle four-some were both connected to film and television (and, indirectly, theater), and both were closely intertwined with dating and mating rituals of the age of anxiety. "Love and Marriage" was the key song in the team's highly thoughtful, Broadway-style musical adaptation of Thornton Wilder's classic *Our Town,* while "The Tender Trap" was derived from the 1954 film version of a 1954 play by Max Shulman (of *Dobie Gillis* fame). "The Tender Trap" was, like "Young at Heart," a key signifier of the new age of Frank; as film scholar Tom Santopietro has pointed out, the opening sequence, in which Sinatra walks toward us from the horizon, singing this song and leading into the main titles, is clearly a symbolic means for the singer to announce, "Look out baby, I'm back—with a vengeance!"

Sinatra's most successful single of the 1950s was "Learnin' the Blues," a song that also captured his character and the era remarkably well, especially as it was the work of an inexperienced tunesmith. Sinatra later recalled that of all the song submissions he received over the years, there was "only one that was sent to me that ever had any—to use a strange word—*professionality.* It was called 'Learnin' the Blues,' and it was written by a girl named [Dolores Vicki] Silver from Philadelphia. . . . She never wrote another one that I know of." The song had been a local hit single in Philadelphia for singer Joe Valino, then known as the Sinatra of the City of Brotherly Love. With its infectious riffs (a whole trumpet section beeping like Edison) and vibraphonic backgrounds, "Learnin' the Blues" was one of the biggest sellers Sinatra ever had. Yet though it has been sung frequently by contemporary singers in tribute to Sinatra, he almost never reprised it in concert.

The singles that Sinatra made for Capitol, especially from 1953 to 1956, contain very nearly as much great music as those first two ten-inch albums, *Songs for Young Lovers* and *Swing Easy!* Sinatra would continue to make out-standing singles for the rest of his career, but his most consistently great work in the 45 rpm medium comes from the early Capitol Records years. In 1955, he would make his first twelve-inch album, *In the Wee Small Hours*; now was the time for making masterpieces.

Between 1955 and 1958, Sinatra and Nelson Riddle recorded the five works that mark the highpoint of their collaboration—and, indeed, of either career—*In the Wee Small Hours, Songs for Swingin' Lovers!, Close to You, A*

*Swingin' Affair!*, and *Only the Lonely*. That accomplishment looms even larger when we realize that this quintet of masterpieces was merely a fraction of the total output of either man: beginning in 1957, Sinatra made other albums with Billy May and Gordon Jenkins (in addition to maintaining a full schedule of movies and television shows, as well as occasional personal appearances) and Riddle continued to work with Nat King Cole as well as Garland, Fitzgerald, Clooney, and many film and video assignments of his own.

It's become common currency for us to differentiate these as "ballad" albums vs. "swinging" albums, but in the Sinatraverse things are rarely if ever that black-and-white. *Songs for Swingin' Lovers!* and *A Swingin' Affair!* represent truth in advertising—both albums are as "swingin'" as the titles promise—but *In the Wee Small Hours* is perhaps an even greater and more purely jazz album than either of the two *Swingin'* records. While *Only the Lonely* might be classifiable as a more classically styled ballad album, it also has its fair share of bluesy torch songs, and *Close to You* is an album of consistent tempos but mixed moods, many humorous, combining elements of chamber music from both the jazz and classical side of the fence. (*Wee Small Hours* represents the Billie Holiday side of Sinatra, *Only the Lonely* is Stravinsky meets Raymond Chandler, while *Close to You* is equal parts Budapest String Quartet and Rodney Dangerfield.)

In the initial years of the comeback, it became clear the reborn Sinatra was now as great a swinger as he had always been a balladeer, but his singing of sad love songs had grown proportionately as well. While the swing sessions brought a bold new dimension to his canon, his ballads were still his forte. Perhaps it was only because he had established his strength and masculinity by swinging with so much ferocity that Sinatra garnered the fortitude to walk around with his heart on display and his inner feelings as exposed as he does on *Wee Small Hours, Close to You*, and *Only the Lonely*.

Sinatra, the ballad-singer of 1955 and onward, was a significant improvement over that of 1945 and also that of 1950, for reasons that surely include his personal experiences. He understood love and loss at forty better than at thirty or thirty-five; but conversely, his renewed faith in his abilities to sing any kind of a song at any tempo gave him the confidence to dig deeper into his own most personal, most intimate feelings—it gave him the inner strength, as it were, to be vulnerable. It wasn't merely a matter of experience; it was a matter of having the craft to turn that experience into a broader, deeper, more expressive kind of music.

On his first Capitol session, he proved that the time-tested Sinatra-Stordahl ballad style no longer made magic—or money. Sinatra sounds breathless and thin on several patches of "I'm Walking Behind You," while

"Don't Make a Beggar of Me" turns out to be a listless waltz—a time signature that never really excited The Voice to begin with. Both seem a million miles away from mid-1940s masterpieces like "Laura" and "Nancy."

One disappointment of the early Capitol years is a 1954 date with trumpeter Ray Anthony's band, with charts by former trombonist Dick Reynolds (author of "If I Ever Love Again," which Sinatra recorded in 1949); it provides another example of how badly he needed Riddle. "I'm Gonna Live till I Die," is a generic opener, the kind that every flamboyant Vegas entertainer would do on *The Ed Sullivan Show*; in and of itself, it's a better song than many of the numbers he recorded on Capitol singles in these years, but it's a decidedly inferior Sinatra record. The flip side is "Melody of Love," a lugubrious waltz (which dates back to 1903) that overtaxes the singer's pipes, as if The Voice were trying to cover too much harmonic ground—the range is just too wide for him, and the emotional content too narrow. It almost seems as if Sinatra is experimenting by making a track without any kind of dramatic content or even a climactic moment.

Almost as if to immediately prove his worth to Sinatra, Riddle rewrote an arrangement of "Day in, Day Out" (which Sinatra had first sung in 1939 with Harry James) that Stordahl had done for Sinatra on their 1953 Capitol date. Comparing the 1953 Stordahl and 1954 Riddle treatments of "Day In" further illuminates the sharp degree to which Sinatra outlined his arrangements beforehand and how two different arrangers translated that outline into a finished chart—the same tempo, the same one-chorus format, the same basic construction. The 1953 chart is classic Stordahl, with a somewhat grandiose pounding pattern ignited by Sinatra on the word "pounding." On the 1954 chart, Riddle very subtly softens this device in a way that renders both structure and song more relevant to the Sinatra of the Capitol era. (As it turned out, neither treatment made it onto commercial vinyl in its day. Sinatra decided he preferred "Day in, Day Out" as a swinger and waited until 1958 for Billy May to provide him with such an arrangement.)

"Sinatra's voice went through range changes," as Sammy Cahn observed. "His sound changed. He went from the violin with Axel, that pure violin sound, to the sound underneath, the viola, with Nelson." Along with the deepening range, Sinatra also widened his rhythmic vocabulary and gained a more vivid emotional palette. But these gifts had a price tag: along with his innocence he lost a chunk of his chops. He no longer possessed the intonation that was so consistently accurate during the Stordahl years. Sinatra never sang flat in the 1940s, but occasionally, in the classic Capitol period, The Voice was a little under pitch. At times he was doing this for emotional effect, but it may be overgenerous to claim that it was always deliberate. Superprecise intonation was simply no longer the point: Sinatra and Riddle were creating a way of moving audiences that depended less on always hitting the right notes and sounding sweet. The emotional-musical vocabulary had grown so large that Sinatra had transformed himself into perhaps the sole vocal artist capable of sustaining a single mood for sixteen songs, exploring every variation, every gradation. In terms of Sinatra's own attitude, there's more variation as well: in the 1940s, Sinatra sounds consistently vulnerable on virtually every song, even the up-tempos. In the 1950s and beyond, Sinatra only sounds vulnerable on the slower love songs and ballads, whereas on the swinging numbers he sounds supremely confident.

Despite remarkable consistency, he is never exactly what his album covers claim. The image that graces *In the Wee Small Hours* could easily have fronted a mid-1950s paperback of a hard-boiled crime novel or a film noir movie poster. The cover seems like a response to *Songs for Young Lovers*; in the 1953 album, Sinatra is revealed standing under a lamppost, one hand in his jacket pocket and the other holding a cigarette, gazing approvingly at happy couples, the sweethearts on parade, as they walk by, arm in arm. Hello young lovers, he seems to be thinking, I've had a love of my own. *In the Wee Small Hours* was released only fifteen months later, but what a difference: same Sinatra, same suit and same fedora, same cigarette, and the same lamppost, but this time Sinatra is alone, instead of looking at others, his eyes are half-closed and looking vaguely downward. He's not seeing the street scene at all; this time, the gaze is strictly internal.

The cover was just one indicator; in its outer manifestations, this third Sinatra-Riddle Capitol album was the most ambitious, starting with its size—sixteen tracks—or fully as long as the two previous albums put together. As noted, it was his first in the new twelve-inch LP format, and it even tested the limits of that new technology (Capitol also released it as two ten-inch discs for those listeners who hadn't upgraded to twelve-inch turntables). *Wee Small Hours* also inaugurated Sinatra's tradition of using a title song to set the mood, something he continued doing off and on for the rest of his career. Often he would commission a new song from his "in-house" tunesmiths, Cahn and Van Heusen (most famously "Come Fly with Me," "Come Dance with Me," "Only the Lonely," and "The September of My Years"), but for *Wee Small Hours* he used a tune brought to him by an old friend.

David Mann had been a studio pianist (he plays the lovely, Claude Thornhill–like intro to Sinatra's 1944 record of "I Begged Her") who had since transitioned to becoming a successful songwriter ("No Moon at All," "There! I've Said It Again"). He and his lyricist, Bob Hilliard, characteristically worked in the middle of the night, and it was during one such nocturnal songwriting session that they came up with the idea of a tune about the night itself. The next morning, they were taking the song to a publisher when they saw Sinatra and Nelson Riddle (the latter on a rare visit to New York) stepping out of a cab. Shortly thereafter, the writers were demonstrating the new song; by then they had been joined by Bill Miller, who remembered that the second that Sinatra heard "In the Wee Small Hours of the Morning" he realized that this was going to be an important song for him. "He loved it instantly," as Mann recollected. "He said, 'Fellas, that's my kind of song. We'll do it.'"

On the previous albums, Sinatra and Riddle kept the instrumentation very consistent from track to track; that was one of the elements that made an album an album. On *Wee Small Hours*, they experimented with varying the accompaniments while still maintaining a uniform mood. The ensembles vary in size between a five-piece rhythm section by itself and one abetted by a full string orchestra. At the core of it all is Bill Miller, in his customary spot at the piano, George Van Eps playing rhythm guitar, bassist Phil Stephens, drummer Al Stoller, and a second keyboardist, Paul Smith, on celeste. In general, the instrumentation is either rhythm or rhythm plus strings; the familiar cast of horn players is not present. The major exception is Sweets Edison, who plays two outstanding solos on the numbers with the strongest jazz associations: Duke Ellington's "Mood Indigo," on which he lays down a figure that Riddle would later expand into the background riff for "Witchcraft," and Harold Arlen's "Ill Wind." The latter contains one of Sweets's longer solos in Sinatraland: he stretches a mere eight bars into thirty gloriously erotic seconds.

"Ill Wind" also has a haunting Benny Carter–like alto obbligato by Skeets Herfurt (Skeets and Sweets, together again), while Mahlon Clark's clarinet effectively frames "What Is This Thing Called Love?" with a fetching original lick. (An alternate take reveals Sinatra had originally planned a substantially longer arrangement of the Cole Porter classic, with a full second chorus, that opened with sixteen bars of Clark playing against the strings.) The title/opening track sets the pace, with the two textures—rhythm and strings—playing off each other in a perfectly invisible arrangement. One isn't conscious of the accompaniment or, for that matter, even Sinatra's voice, just the emotion emanating from the speakers—it seems to transmit itself in a pure, ethereal form, using The Voice as a conduit.

Indeed, in all contexts and all degrees of either agony or ecstasy, even if Sinatra falls slightly short of the occasional note tonally, he always hits precisely the right tone emotionally. Listening to "Deep in a Dream" on *Wee Small Hours* and "The End of a Love Affair" on *Close to You* makes you think that if Sinatra put the tiniest bit more emotion in his singing he might sound hysterical, and yet if he were to pull the most minuscule bit back, he would come off sounding detached. As he approaches his fortieth birthday, he has become a master at finding the perfect balance between too much and too little.

In playing the strads and rhythm off each other in *Wee Small Hours,* the two keyboards afford the rhythm crew greater presence, although neither Miller nor guest celestaist Paul Smith can be described as a heavy-handed player. Sinatra began using the five-piece format independently of Riddle, on his final regular radio series, *To Be Perfectly Frank.* This charmingly modest program had launched in the immediate wake of *Eternity,* in November 1953, and continued for a year as a twice-weekly fifteen-minute sustaining program before a shampoo corporation picked up the tab and rechristened it *The Bobbi Show.** A refinement of the anarchic *Meet Frank Sinatra,* Sinatra was reincarnated as a singing disc jockey, spinning his own platters as well as those of other artists, and also usually singing one original number per show (which were probably prerecorded at sessions of four tunes or more).

Sinatra was at his all-time jazziest on these shows, done in the same time period and frame of mind as *Swing Easy!* He generally taped the new performances for the series with Bill Miller leading a five-piece group of clarinet and four rhythm players (sometimes including pianist Graham Forbes, his most frequent accompanist of the immediate pre-Miller period), referred to on the air as "The Sinatra Symphonette." On at least a few shows, the band included a piano-celesta front line, with Paul Smith to play the smaller, more tinkly keyboard. The spirit of the program spilled over into the rhythm-oriented *Swing Easy!,* as you'd expect, but also into *Wee Small Hours,* where Miller and Smith again make like a hip Ferrante and Teicher.

On *Wee Small,* Riddle augments the five rhythm players with fiddles on three sessions, one of which also uses one trumpet and four reeds. On a fourth date, departing from established Sinatra tradition, the singer recorded four songs using just the five-man unit. Sinatra set up and sequenced "Glad to Be Unhappy," "Can't We Be Friends?," "I'll Be Around" (on which a celesta riff spins a punningly circular pattern), and "Dancing on the Ceiling" so seamlessly amid the twelve-string tracks that few listeners even notice the absence of an orchestra. (Along with two tracks on *French Horn Jazz,* a 1953 album by horn soloist John Graas, these amount to a very rare example of Riddle writing for a small jazz group.)

---

\* Luckily, the series was also partially transcribed by the AFRTS, ensuring that a number of episodes survive today. A few sample songs were issued on the 2015 CD package *A Voice on Air.*

Sinatra and Riddle rely on Bill Miller even more than usual on *Wee Small Hours*, counting on the pianist to exploit his background in jazz and conduct the date, and also help to chart the tunes for the rhythm section from Sinatra's verbal sketches. "Frank said, 'I want to pretend you just sat down and you're going to fake a tune behind me,'" Miller recalled, "and I said, 'You want it to sound strictly right now, off the cuff?' He said, 'I want some of the tunes to sound unrehearsed.' I agreed with him, but I still took the liberty of writing out the parts for the bass player and Paul Smith and everybody so that we all played the right chord changes." Miller's presence is keenly felt on the orchestral tracks as well—his keyboard intro to the title track is one of the definitive instrumental moments in the Sinatra canon.

"Last Night When We Were Young" was recorded a year before the other fifteen tracks; Sinatra may not have known what the final destination of the track would be when he and Riddle laid it down on March 1, 1954. It fits in with the rest of the album, but is unique just the same, and overall may rate as the most powerful performance in the set. Perhaps the most dramatic operetta-style work by the normally blues-oriented Harold Arlen, the piece could be one of the better "heavy" ballads by Jerome Kern (à la "Yesterdays") or Sigmund Romberg ("Lover, Come Back to Me").* Sinatra does not resort to trying to sing it with a "big" belting voice, the way he might have a few years earlier. Instead, with its classical resonance, this track anticipates *Only the Lonely* in terms of Riddle's deep, dark colors and the way Sinatra makes even nihilism an intimate experience.

*In the Wee Small Hours* is rarely listed as one of Sinatra's extreme-downer "suicide albums," those very aptly described by his son as the kind that should be sold "by prescription only," the most extreme examples of which have to be *Only the Lonely* (1958) and *No One Cares* (1959). The dark moods of *Wee Small Hours* are leavened by injections of both jazz and black humor, yet the indirect result is that it makes the album more three-dimensional and therefore more believable, and therefore perhaps even more disturbing.

Nelson Riddle had long since passed his audition with Sinatra, but with this album a new high point had been reached. It was *Wee Small Hours* that fully ensured the future of the collaboration. "That's what I think hit Sinatra," said Miller. "That's what gave him the inspiration to say, 'Hey, let's do more of that.'"

---

* The song had been written for the popular operatic baritone Lawrence Tibbett to sing in the 1935 movie *Metropolitan*; although he recorded it, the song didn't make it to the final cut of the film. New York deejay Jonathan Schwartz reported that when someone played the Sinatra record for Tibbett, he responded by saying, "I see," meaning, "Oh so *that's* how it should be sung."

Much of Sinatra's art in the mid-1950s is concerned with death and rebirth: he dies in *From Here to Eternity* but trumpets his rebirth in the famous opening sequence of *The Tender Trap*. Along the way, he reinvents the Private Angelo Maggio character of *From Here to Eternity* as Nathan Detroit, the lovable loser of *Guys and Dolls*. (Despite the artist's opinion on the subject, as he announced from the stage in many concerts, he would not have made a good Sky Masterson in 1955.) Then there's *The Man with the Golden Arm*, in which protagonist Frankie Machine figuratively goes to hell and back. The apotheosis may be *The Joker Is Wild*, in which he gives a harrowing performance as the real-life Joe E. Lewis, an entertainer who is literally murdered by gangsters yet somehow comes back, like Lazarus from his cave; as Joe E., he ultimately triumphs, but at considerable personal cost. (Sinatra's character in his immediately preceding film, *Pal Joey*, was also inspired by Lewis; but then it seems clear that "Joey Evans" was likely based to a degree on Joe E. Lewis in the original stories by John O'Hara to begin with.)

Musically speaking, *In the Wee Small Hours* was about closure, saying goodbye, farewell, and amen to the dire nosedive period of the early 1950s. Sinatra had already announced the start of his renaissance, as we have seen, with "Young at Heart," but the real, full-length statement of rebirth came in 1955 with the album that he titled *Songs for Swingin' Lovers!* It's no accident that the album begins with the ultimate song about fresh beginnings, with bells to be rung and songs to be sung, which makes that point even better than "Young at Heart." (Which may explain why "You Make Me Feel So Young" became an all-time Sinatra concert perennial, and why he rarely sung "Young at Heart" again, even though the latter was a bona fide hit single.)

As the title suggests, *Songs for Swingin' Lovers!* was a logical step forward from *Songs for Young Lovers* and *Swing Easy!*, as well as from *Wee Small Hours*. And swing is the thing, a key element of the way Sinatra sustained his career from 1953 onward, well into the ages of Elvis and Aquarius. In 1946, the big bands were essentially put out of business by an ill-advised federal tax on dance venues, and with big government having essentially fired all the big bands, there wasn't much music for kids to dance to by the early 1950s: you had Perry Como on one side and Dizzy Gillespie on the other, neither of whom aspired to do for dancers what Harry James or Count Basie had done.

The rise of rock 'n' roll a few years later was doubtlessly facilitated more than anything by its strong dance beat. And yet this too was a key reason that Sinatra could keep going at a time when Dick Haymes and Bob Eberly were out of the running and even a superior balladeer like Johnny Hartman had to struggle. Even then, deep thinkers who wrote for *Down Beat* and *Metro-*

*nome* were wasting time and ink arguing over who was a jazz singer and who wasn't, but what mattered at the cash box was who created dance music and who didn't. There's a reason that the cover of *A Swingin' Affair!* depicts Sinatra in front of a dance floor crammed with happy fox-trotting couples. This was party music.

As early as 1950's *Sing and Dance with Frank Sinatra*, the singer was striving toward the creation of the perfect mixture of "vocals that dance." And while Siravo had been brilliant, Riddle was even more so. The ideal of dance music was perfected both in the rhythm—the most significant inspiration was not only Ellington and Basie but the very danceable, modish two-beat approach of Jimmie Lunceford and Sy Oliver—and in an orchestral style that could support the singer even while dancing all by itself. Sinatra and Riddle referred to this as the "heartbeat" tempo, and it was the product of their joint apprenticeship in the big bands. To the uninitiated, "swing" inevitably means a fast tempo, but Sinatra and Riddle knew better.

It's often considered a compliment that a superior orchestrator can make a group sound larger than it actually is, so it's to Riddle's credit that he never hits you over the head with the idea that thirty men are actually playing at once. The depth of the larger ensemble is there whenever Sinatra needs it for emotional enhancement, but most of the time Blue Eyes and the band swing economically, not to mention mightily.

The up-tempo albums, especially the two *Swingin'* ones, could be listened to by music fans, but were more specifically designed to be played at parties. Like other aspects of technology, Sinatra used the sheer length of the LP to his advantage; you could now get over twenty minutes of dancing in without have to flip the platter from side A to side B. For each of the two albums, Sinatra recorded sixteen songs, one of which was dropped: "Memories of You" on *Swingin' Lovers* and "The Lady Is a Tramp" on *Swingin' Affair*. (In a really weird coincidence, he ended three albums almost in a row with a remake of a classic from the Dorsey era: "This Love of Mine" on *Wee Small Hours*, "How About You?" on *Lovers* and "Oh! Look at Me Now" on *Affair*.)

Sinatra's own "phrasing," to use the singer's preferred term, may be less frisky and jazzy on *Lovers* and *Affair* than on *Swing Easy!*, yet it's here that he begins to cultivate the more abrasive sound that we associate with his work in the mid-1960s, as on the Basie albums for instance. In the great jazz tradition—a conceit that we associate with Ethel Waters and then Louis Armstrong—Sinatra usually sings the opening chorus comparatively straight, but gets increasingly playful on the second chorus of nearly all of these tracks. Every one of the numbers on these three albums consists of either two full choruses or a chorus and a half.

Many have instrumental breaks of eight or sixteen bars, and Riddle fills most of the blank space, either between lines or choruses, with the most suitably fitting filigrees: Sweets Edison beeping; George Roberts grunting; Harry Klee's lithe, birdlike flute; or Mahlon Clark's clarinet. On "Swingin' Down the Lane" Riddle brilliantly contrasts two trumpets against each other, Conrad Gozzo playing open bell with a Harry James–like swagger and vibrato, against Sweets buzzing around him like a mosquito. (Riddle's intro here was later borrowed by a British arranger who reused it for Matt Monro's "My Kind of Girl"—in the same key, no less.) The instrumental break in "Too Marvelous for Words" pays homage to Duke Ellington—there's an interchange between the band and bassist Joe Comfort, in a rare solo, that comes directly from such Ducal classics as "Ko-Ko" and "In a Mellow Tone." Far from cluttering up the landscape, Riddle's additional bits of business enhance the vocals and the main melodic line; with Edison as a role model, all of the key Riddle sidemen could, in Bernhart's words, "make history in three and a half beats."

With each of his initial three "swing" albums with Riddle, Sinatra gets progressively deeper into a feeling of abandon with the lyrics. Always a rhythmic master, the balladeer Sinatra specializes in long legato phrases and the swinging Sinatra delivers a song in short, staccato bursts. He doesn't just chew a song up into short phrases here: he often twists them and playfully slaps them around, like a Harlem Globetrotter rolling the ball across his shoulders. This is a rhythmic and dramatic exercise, the musical specifics of which derive from Sinatra's association with Buddy Rich and his love for Louis Armstrong and Tommy Dorsey.

It's especially effective when he contrasts the two approaches, as on the steadily modulating "From This Moment On" on *Affair,* in which he extends the main phrase but still emphasizes key syllables such as "hoop-de-do songs" by delivering them in brief percussive barrages. Likewise, on "Memories of You" he seamlessly integrates a staccato-like stress on syllables in the middle of a long legato line ("*your* face beams *in* my dreams").

Sinatra likes to kid a lyric—to have fun with it—which he often does, Armstrong-style, by interjecting slight, spontaneous alterations; "but he's so willing" becomes "this cat's so willing" in "Makin' Whoopee" (*Lovers*), while "I Won't Dance" (*Affair*) contains the first documented appearance of the Sinatra catchphrase "Ring-a-Ding-Ding," which was born as a nonsensical signifier and eventually grew into a Cahn and Van Heusen song (and an album title in 1960). These phrases are generally authentically ad hoc, as illustrated by the few alternate takes that have been heard. There are three such alternates of "Stars Fell on Alabama" (*Affair*), apparently taped the week before the final master, and they document the singer gradually working out his modifications, such as "stars fractured 'Bama."* These ad-libs help Sinatra to bounce the text like a toy balloon, but without popping or deflating the intent of the lyric. He makes it bend without breaking.

In his inventive use of ingenious introductions, codas, and countermelodies, Riddle seems like a direct upgrade of Axel Stordahl, just as the Sinatra of 1955 is an improvement over that of 1945. That they have so much in common shows us how Sinatra sought out this quality in his collaborators, and, having found it, nurtured it and encouraged it. Riddle places a descending, flutey phrase at the start of "Stars Fell on Alabama" (which Sinatra doubtless learned from Jack Teagarden) that depicts falling stars, similar to one that he would expand into the extended, dramatic opener to "Lost in the Stars" almost ten years later in *The Concert Sinatra*. Other Riddle "extras" are not nearly as programmatic: rather than alluding to gospel sounds, the mock-spiritual "Lonesome Road" (which Sinatra learned from Armstrong) opens with Bill Miller plunking out a distinctive vamp in the bass range, followed by a Latin rhythm pattern played on a shaker.

As with so many other Sinatra albums, work on *Swingin' Lovers* started with a tentative, experimental session (on June 30, 1955) that he quickly discarded. That date commenced with a Riddle run-through of "I Thought About You," an unusual number both in its ABAB pattern and because it marked one of the rare works composed by Van Heusen with a text by Johnny Mercer. Not that this June 1955 attempt was "too busy"; it was just different. This original orchestration starts with a big ensemble intro, then Edison playing behind Sinatra for his first sixteen bars, and next features Juan Tizol for most of the sixteen-bar instrumental section. The final arrangement, recorded in January 1956, opens very quietly, with a Klee flute introduction; the woodwind passage then continues behind Sinatra for the first eight bars of the refrain. Sinatra and Riddle divide the second chorus in a most ingenious manner: Riddle plays the first A with prominent Edison; then Sinatra sings the first B; then Sweets and the ensemble again play the second A instrumentally; and Sinatra takes it out with the final eight bars, the band capping it with a variation on a Basie tag. He doesn't get as hot and exciting as "I've Got You Under My Skin" or "The Lady Is a Tramp," but gives the effect of starting the song as a ballad and finishing as a flag-waver.

From the moment he started planning it, the *Swingin' Lovers* project had "hit" written all over it. As we've seen, the opening track, "You Make Me

---

* Considering that librettist Mitchell Parish already took considerable liberties when he described "'Bama" as a fairyland—few of us who have lived there would think of it as such—Sinatra's goosing up of this particular text doesn't seem quite so impertinent.

Feel So Young," amounts to "Young at Heart" in swingtime. Sinatra captures that same brand of childlike exuberant innocence, making the most of lyricist Mack Gordon's charming schoolkid-awkward syllabification of the word "in-div-id-u-al" (as on 1951's "Whistle a Happy Tune"). *Swingin' Lovers* was such a success that the sequel, *A Swingin' Affair!,* arrived before the year was out. A still-brassier, harder-hitting set than *Lovers, Affair* may be an even more exciting affair all around. However, in comparing the two albums, *Lovers* has one unfair advantage: "I've Got You Under My Skin," which resonates as Sinatra's coup de grace of up-tempo masterpieces.

At the very last minute he decided to include "Skin" on the session of January 12, 1956, which meant, Riddle recalled, that "it was a work of pressure because I had to stay up quite late one night and finish it." Riddle wrote, as usual, according to Frank's specifications. "He said, 'I want a long crescendo.' Long crescendi, like other dynamics in music, whether they be long crescendi or long diminuendi, are another color; without them music can become unpalatable, tasteless, and uninteresting." The arranger added, "I don't think he was aware of the way I was going to achieve that crescendo, but he wanted an instrumental interlude that would be exciting and carry the orchestra up and then come on down where he would finish out the arrangement vocally."

One of the first things Riddle thought of was Ravel's *Boléro*, which he described as having "the most calculatingly orchestrated crescendo" and an "absolutely tantalizing slow addition of instruments to this long, long crescendo, which is really the message of *Boléro*, and it is excruciating in its deliberately slow addition of pressure. Now that's sex in a piece of music." For the arranger, like Sinatra, sex and music were interchangeable. "I remember [once when] my mother and father were having a screaming match," said Chris Riddle, "and she said to him, 'All you ever think about is music and sex!' I was about sixteen, and the next day I asked him about it. He looked at me with a twinkle in his eye and said, 'After all, what else is there?' Music and sex! I mean, he really saw things that way. That was like a window into his insides."

However, Riddle was stuck for an idea for this particular patch of color. "I was sitting home one day when Nelson called me up and said, 'Frank wants a long crescendo in the middle of "I've Got You Under My Skin,"'" recalled George Roberts. "Nelson said, 'Do you know any Afro-Cuban rhythmic patterns and things like that?' I said, 'Well, why don't you steal the pattern out of Kenton's "23 Degrees North, 82 Degrees West" [from 1952]?' He said, 'How did it go?' I gave him the beginning trombone lines for that Afro-Cuban thing, and he expanded that for the long crescendo that Frank wanted." "I remembered a Stan Kenton record," Riddle corroborated, "and that trombone back-and-forth thing. I was always fascinated by it. I tried to find an equivalent to use behind singers, and that was my version." Riddle swiped from Bill Russo only conceptually; he does lay several Latin rhythm patterns over each other, but it's hardly the exact same polyrhythm that Russo employed in designating the coordinates of Cuba.

Like Russo, Riddle uses the passage to lead into a trombone solo, played by Milt Bernhart. The former Kentonite recalled that both Sinatra and Riddle seemed to know that this would be a special track and they were resigned to keep doing take after take until they had it exactly right. Bernhart had conditioned himself to Sinatra's more customary way of working: if you can't get it in four or five takes, tops, drop it and possibly try again later. For that reason he put everything he had into the first few takes of the number and feels he was spent by the time they got to the take Sinatra wound up using.

"Toward the tenth take," Bernhart recalled, "somebody said in the booth, 'Could we get the trombone nearer to a microphone?' I mean, what had they been doing? So they said, 'There's a mic there for the brass.' It was on a very high riser. The engineer asked, 'Can you get up to that one?' And I said, 'Well, no, I'm not that tall.' Somebody said, 'Why don't we get a box?' So they were looking for a box. I don't know why there wasn't a grip, but Frank Sinatra himself went and got a box and brought it over for me to stand on. It was funny."

Bernhart felt silly standing on the box, and while he has claimed he ran "out of gas" at least a dozen takes before the one that got used, his performance has become one of the most widely heard trombone solos ever recorded. Bernhart later reported that he didn't realize at the time that Riddle had based this whole instrumental sequence on the chords to the bridge to "Skin."* But it's this very atavistic, off-the-chord energy of the solo that burns it into your brain with such sizzling force. And yet as passionate as Bernhart gets in his twelve bars or so, he pales beside Sinatra, who returns to ram the lyric home with nothing short of orgiastic fury.

Said Riddle, "I remember bringing [the chart] to the recording, and everybody was very impressed." It marked one of the few times the musicians on a Sinatra date actually stood up and applauded the principals: star, writer-director, and supporting player. "I know the evening that we did it," Riddle recalled, "he expressed considerable enthusiasm for the arrangement, and I guess later on, when he took the tape home and played it, he was even

---

* Bernhart remembered well reading over the manuscript page at the session. "If I had known it was the bridge, I would have used that as a guide. I didn't know exactly what this was supposed to be because it had chords, but it was only really one chord. He just put down all these flats, and it was a flat chord. It's not easy to do on the trombone. The more flats, the harder. So that threw me a curve. What am I supposed to do in those few little beats? Something hysterical, something historical."

more enthusiastic. As it turned out, it was sort of a cornerstone recording for both him and me.”

*Swingin' Affair!,* as issued, doesn't have one individual cut that stands out as much as “Skin” does on *Lovers,* but the set as a whole packs even more wallop. *Affair* is leaner and meaner: there are far fewer filigrees, less of the highly ornamental filling of every space that we find on *Lovers.* On one of the four dates, Sinatra downplayed the string section to accentuate more of a big-band sound, emphasizing *swingin'* over *lovers.* On the same date Sinatra and Riddle recruited drummer Irv Cottler. Cottler wasn't as flexible a stylist as their usual first choice, Alvin Stoller (who was much more comfortable with tempo changes, for instance), but he was a powerhouse pounder who solidified the straight-ahead feeling.

Cottler, who first recorded with Sinatra on the “Skin” session, became his regular “road” percussionist on and off for thirty-three years. “Nelson has a beautiful approach to building a chart,” was how Cottler described such archetypical works as “Skin” and “The Lady Is a Tramp.” “He starts with a foundation and builds up to the roof. Other writers start from the roof and go down, but where can you go from the roof?”

*Lovers* included several slower pieces; “We'll Be Together Again” is actually one of Sinatra's most moving ballads ever. *Affair,* however, is practically all variations on “Skin”; crescendi and bolero patterns abound. Almost every track is directly or indirectly patterned after that chart, starting slow and gradually mounting in dynamics, speed, and intensity. Sinatra had sequenced “Skin” at the start of the second side of *Lovers* for easy spotting with the tonearm, and *Affair* swings further by opening with the strongest “Skin” follow-up, “Night and Day.” In redoing the best-remembered song from his premier session as a soloist, Sinatra was again declaring, Oh! Look at me now (which is how he ends the album).

Like “Skin,” “Night and Day” is a Cole Porter classic that Riddle redecorates with a polyrhythm and builds to a trombone feature, this time the valved brother of the instrument as handled by its leading exponent, Juan Tizol. A twenty-year veteran of the Duke Ellington orchestra, Tizol became Riddle's resident Ellingtonian; he is also heard prominently on “From This Moment On” and “I Got It Bad (and That Ain't Good)” (as well as on Nat Cole's “A Blossom Fell” and many other Riddle tracks). Said Riddle, Tizol “had, to me, a very exotic sound on that valve trombone.” Tizol's solo is less orgiastic than Bernhart's, but he creates a whole different kind of tension to set up Sinatra's outchorus.

Sinatra had planned one additional number for *Affair* that would rival and possibly even exceed “Skin” for excitement, namely Rodgers and Hart's

"The Lady Is a Tramp." Sinatra already knew that "Tramp" would be a crucial number in his forthcoming film *Pal Joey,* so he decided to save that cut for that picture's souvenir soundtrack album. In its place, Sinatra inserted "No One Ever Tells You," a new song by British composer Carroll Coates, which is the only non-standard on the two *Swingin'* albums. Recorded some months earlier, "No One Ever Tells You," which takes Sinatra through some blues territory, nonetheless fits perfectly into the album.

Viewed more properly as part of *Swingin' Affair,* "Lady Is a Tramp" also slowly increases in force as the piece progresses, Sinatra starting with Bill Miller's ever-perfect piano accompaniment, and Riddle adding other elements one at a time—violins, horns, and the now-expected (but hardly predictable) fills from Edison and Klee (on flute). It's almost as if Sinatra and Riddle wanted to summarize—in a single track—everything they had accomplished on the three swing albums, starting with the economical playfulness of *Easy* (Riddle reconceiving the main melody as a groovy riff), moving to the dances-with-strings of *Lovers,* and ending in the hardcore, ecstatic euphoria of *Affair.* Sinatra had developed a favorite device of singing one phrase (especially the last few words of a bridge) a cappella for both dramatic and rhythmic emphasis, as on "Foggy Day." It never worked more effectively than here, where the ensemble drops out long enough for Sinatra to utter two and then three syllables: the brass crashes and then rests as Sinatra sings, "She's broke." The brass erupts again and immediately pauses once more as Sinatra goes into "but it's oke!"

No less than "Skin," "Tramp" would be a Sinatra classic, performed thousands of times over succeeding decades. "[Frank] seemed to take a particular delight in [Tramp]," said Riddle. "He always sang that song with a certain amount of salaciousness. He savored it. He had some cute tricks with the lyric, which made it especially his." Many of the live versions, not surprisingly, gather and disperse even more ecstatic energy than the Capitol reading. Sinatra performed what might be the single most exciting version on the *Bob Hope Chevy Show* of April 8, 1957 (also part of the ramp-up to the *Pal Joey* movie). Here, instead of intoning the three words "but it's oke" (Lorenz Hart's slangy shorthand for "okay") Sinatra merely pauses for three beats, along with the band, shrugging his shoulders and silently registering an expression that's "oke" as "oke" can be.

What kind of influence did *Songs for Swingin' Lovers!* and *A Swingin' Affair!* have on the larger world of popular music? "It was as if you went to Vegas and hit five jackpots in a row," arranger-composer Neal Hefti stated. Indeed, with both *Swingin' Lovers* and *Swingin' Affair* released within fifteen months of each other, Sinatra and Riddle were more than on a roll. "As far as I'm concerned, no one has even come close to what Nelson achieved with Sinatra," said Hefti. "This isn't taking anything away from any of the other people. It's just that the moon and the stars were in the right position at the same time, with Frank and Nelson, *plus* Capitol Records, *plus* Frank being so exuberant because he had won the Academy Award. It was all of these things. God! That enthusiasm just keeps going on and on and on! It's just like the Richter scale: each new thing makes the last number ten times higher. It was just unbelievable."

With the two *Swingin'* albums, Sinatra and Riddle had changed the whole paradigm of pop. Before 1955, a love song was a love song and a rhythm number was generally something quasi-nonsensical; it's the difference between "Love Is Here to Stay" and "I Got Rhythm," both by the Gershwins. Louis Armstrong had already led the way in taking a pop song and making a jazz number out of it, but Sinatra proved that you didn't have to lose the romantic angle in the process, that a song could be a swinging jazz number and still be full of passion and eroticism, that these factors could work together instead of cancelling each other out. When he talked about "swinging lovers," he wasn't just coming up with a clever album title or marketing phrase (nor was he referring to polygamy), he really meant it.

As Hefti indicated, the impact was tremendous; just at the very moment rock 'n' roll was coming in, Sinatra reinvigorated "traditional" pop with so much new energy and ideas that it ensured that what we call the Great American Songbook would always be with us—as indeed, it still is, more than sixty years later. It's safe to say that Sinatra launched an entire industry with *Songs for Swingin' Lovers!* Male singers who were multiple generations younger than Sinatra were particularly keen to pick up on it: Steve Lawrence, Jack Jones, and especially Bobby Darin, who can be said to have more or less based his whole career on *Swingin' Lovers.*

*Swingin' Lovers* inspired not just a cottage industry, but an entire supermarket chain—it was the Whole Foods of inspired, adult pop music, in direct contrast to the Walmart culture that was springing up all around it. In contrast, *Close to You* (1957), the album sandwiched in between *Swingin' Lovers* and *Swingin' Affair,* influenced almost no one and to this day is generally prized only by Sinatra aficionados. Yet that doesn't make it any less of a masterpiece. Even the cover of *Close to You* is different: it's virtually the only classic Sinatra set to show The Voice/the Chairman in the actual act of singing, with mic in hand and eyes closed. This is by far the least conventional of the Capitol series and the only one not in print continuously from its original release to the end of the LP era.

*Close to You* was Sinatra's way of bringing closure to a project that, in a sense, he had launched ten years earlier, with his first album, *The Voice of Frank Sinatra* (released in 1946). As we have seen, Sinatra mastered the spanking new art of the pop album partly by recording these eight songs in a musical setting that was very different from the pop singles that he was concurrently making. This was the start of The Voice's "chamber sessions," which he continued to do in other dates in 1947. Rather than their customary full-scale orchestra with strings, for these dates Sinatra and Axel Stordahl combined a four-piece swing-band-style rhythm section (piano, guitar, bass, drums) with a classical string quartet (two violins, viola, cello). And for extra oomph on some of the 1947 titles, they upped the ante by adding horn soloists; on "I've Got a Crush on You," it's the legendary cornetist Bobby Hackett.

Over the next decade, Sinatra formulated the idea of returning to that format—four rhythm players plus four strings—and this time building the project around the Hollywood String Quartet. Thus, *Close to You* also sprang forth from Sinatra's long-standing personal and professional relationship with the quartet's founders, the first violin and cello, Felix and Eleanor Slatkin. The Slatkins had founded the quartet around 1940, not long after they were married, at which time Slatkin was serving as concertmaster at Twentieth Century Fox pictures and Eleanor was playing for Warner Bros. All four members of the quartet were primarily employed by movie studios, and the group was formed with the ambition of playing both the traditional string quartet repertoire as well as commissioning new works. The HSQ suspended operations during Slatkin's war service but after 1946 reconvened with his assistant at Fox, Paul Shure, as second violin and Paul Robyn on viola. During the 1950s, Slatkin conducted the Hollywood Bowl Symphony Orchestra, which became one of Capitol's major classical music attractions, and the HSQ served as that orchestra's little-brother chamber group. (Felix and Eleanor Slatkin, as successful as they were, never achieved quite the renown of their son, Leonard Slatkin, the celebrated conductor of the Saint Louis Symphony Orchestra.)

Felix Slatkin first appeared on a Sinatra session in 1946; Eleanor initially turns up in the following year. The most intense period of their working together began with the Riddle-Capitol era in 1953 and ended with Felix's death in 1963. During that decade, Sinatra and Riddle insisted on using Slatkin not only as their regular concertmaster but as a backup conductor to support both Sinatra and Riddle in their baton work.

"We became very, very close friends and saw a lot of him between the recordings in those days, and spent many weekends with Frank at his home in Palm Springs," remembered Eleanor Slatkin. "Frank, as you know, has a tremendous collection of classical records, and he fell in love with the quartet.

So he said, 'You know, I think it would be a terrific idea to do an album with a string quartet.'" The potential problem was that the quartet by itself might not be enough to support a popular vocalist—even one who exceeded many operatic tenors and baritones in terms of technique, artistry, and execution. Elaborating on "I've Got a Crush on You" and the other 1940s chamber tracks, as Paul Shure recalled, "Nelson decided to use a string quartet and [four rhythm], and each tune would have another instrument. He'd have string quartet and French horn [Vince DeRosa], string quartet and flute [Harry Klee or James Williamson], string quartet and trumpet [Sweets Edison], string quartet and solo violin [Slatkin]. It was all a core of string quartet writing with different instruments added."

Actually, the string quartet more than dominates the instrumental proceedings almost all the time, with the additional instruments heard only occasionally; even though they're present most of the time, they're generally consigned to the deep background. Clarinetist Mahlon Clark plays on just "I Couldn't Sleep a Wink Last Night" and the originally deleted "If It's the Last Thing I Do"; while Edison shows up only once, to telling effect on "The End of a Love Affair," where he leads our hero through the purgatory of a romance gone sour like a trumpet-toting Virgil. (Sinatra learned the tune from one of his most significant mentors, the godmother of cabaret songstresses, Mabel Mercer.) Vince DeRosa's French horn assumes the role and register normally filled by George Roberts, grunting low in the background. DeRosa also plays on "Don't Like Goodbyes," "It Could Happen to You," and "I've Had My Moments," but here Riddle uses him more for coloration than as a featured improvisor. In effect, DeRosa solos *so low* that we're barely conscious of him.

On the first date, Sinatra attempted only one tune, and that he rejected it without trying any further numbers that day indicates he felt that he and Riddle had not yet come up with the perfect sound for this unusual "double" ensemble. It took longer to record *Close to You* than any other Sinatra album before *Trilogy*: five sessions stretched over eight months, from March to November 1956.

Even a cursory listen will reveal that it was well worth the effort: it's hard to disagree with Shure's assertion that, "musically speaking, I think it's the greatest album that Sinatra ever did," even considering Shure's understandable bias. This is surely Sinatra's most intimate and delicate singing ever, and he imbues every track with an attention to nuance remarkable even for him. On the *Swing* series as well as the "suicide" albums, such as *Only the Lonely* and *No One Cares,* the singer paints with broadly upbeat or tragic strokes; contrastingly, *Close to You* could have been rendered with an eyebrow pencil.

It's the difference between grand opera and chamber music, the Mozart of the Haydn Quartets versus that of *Die Zauberflöte*.

As Riddle mentioned, he usually counted on Edison and, to a lesser extent, his other regulars for the humor content of his albums, especially the *Swing* sets. *Close to You,* however, jettisons most of the two- and three-beat knickknacks Riddle typically employs to fill Sinatra's empty spaces (excepting the "guitars" and "trumpets" sound referenced in the lyrics to "I've Had My Moments" and "End of a Love Affair"; apparently such literalism was too much for him to resist) for a sound that's dramatically starker yet emotionally more expansive.

Yet *Close to You* has more of a comic quotient than any other Sinatra-Riddle project, because Sinatra's singing extracts so much irony from the songs themselves. As both programmer and singer, Sinatra has compiled a perfect selection of tunes to fit the requirements of the context, being at once deeply moving and darkly comic. On "P.S. I Love You" and "Everything Happens to Me," Sinatra is careful not to jump too hard on the obvious gag lines—like Bob Hope, he deliberately understates his punch lines—while on the more sullen "It's Easy to Remember" and "Blame It on My Youth," he furrows out the few optimistic angles buried deep in the texts.

As always, one must marvel at Sinatra's capacity to find the most appropriate song. Anyone else who sat through the 1934 *Hollywood Party* could only snicker at the effrontery of a film that missed the boat on the standard "Blue Moon" and cast Jimmy Durante as Tarzan (more accurately, "Schnarzan"). Certainly no one but Sinatra would have discovered that this box-office disaster contained such a tellingly ironic libretto as Walter Donaldson's "I've Had My Moments." (The 1934 song anticipates the 1937 "A Foggy Day" in its opening half-step movement, foreshadowing to Gershwin's minor third, as well as its Gershwinesque repetitive rhythmic patterns.) Sinatra conceives of "Moments" as a beautifully schizophrenic battle of inner moods, one overt braggadocio, the other acutely self-conscious humility. It's a perfect song to go on the same collection as "Everything Happens to Me," in which romance and self-deprecation are intermingled in perfect balance, each making the other more believable.

With an irony most appropriate to the *Close to You* collection, Sinatra claimed that "There's a Flaw in My Flue," the single funniest item of the sessions, was not actually intended for the finished LP. During World War II, Bing Crosby, in a special soldiers-only broadcast, introduced a music and comedy routine he called "Your All-Time Flop Parade" (itself a parody of Sinatra's first important show, *Lucky Strike Presents Your Hit Parade,* and its brother, the *All-Time Hit Parade*). With songs by fellow funsters Johnny

Burke and Jimmy Van Heusen, Crosby and guests like Judy Garland and Ethel Merman offered up such deliberately amateurish airs as "Yachting," "Hammacher-Schlemmer, I Love You," "Silver-Coated Moon," and others that foreshadowed the marvelously mediocre music of Jonathan and Darlene Edwards. "There's a Flaw in My Flue" had been introduced by Crosby and Merman on Der Bingle's *Philco Radio Time* show of March 23, 1949.

Nancy Sinatra, among others, later reported that her father recorded "Flaw in My Flue" as a gag to rib Capitol's A&R department: how long would it take before Voyle Gilmore realized that this tale of fireside pipe dreaming, with lines like "smoke gets in my nose," was a rather elaborate joke, a well-calculated pulling of somebody's hairy leg? If such was indeed the case, then Sinatra outsmarted himself. The lyric was not much sillier than the next most laughable (unphotographable) song on the album, and Sinatra sang it with such sincerity and so little camp that it obviously belonged on *Close to You.* It might have made it, too, had Sinatra not wised them up to his gag at the eleventh hour. There were two further songs, Sammy Cahn's "If It's the Last Thing I Do" and Rodgers and Hart's "Wait till You See Her," perhaps *Close to You*'s best track, which did not make it onto the album at the time because the basic twelve tracks already totaled more than forty-five minutes, or roughly as long as the sixteen on *Wee Small* and *Swingin' Affair!* (Fortunately, all three were included in the CD edition in 1987.)

"Nelson was a master at what, I guess, you'd call 'counterpoint,'" Mahlon Clark observed. "He wrote wonderfully for strings and had a knack for writing things 'fat' so they sounded large." Riddle had found a perfect middle ground between the classical (as in Mozart) and the jazz (as in Benny Goodman) tradition of the chamber group. "Everything Happens to Me" seems to be all fiddles, the other instruments barely noticeable, while "It's Easy to Remember" relies mainly on vibes and flute that update the keyboard textures of the Cole-Riddle "Unforgettable," as the quartet stays in the background. Throughout, the strings sound harmonically rich in the European sense, but the rhythm section keeps things moving, without the static beat that usually prevents anything vaguely classical from working in a jazz or pop context. It sounds neither too longhair nor too jivey. Considering how full the vocals and the orchestrations are, it's amazing how each track comes off as a marvel of understatement.

*Wee Small Hours* was hardly all gloom and doom, apart from "Last Night When We Were Young" (and even that bears a pregnant-with-hope pause); it suggests a dark point that we hope will be followed by the dawn. *Close to You* depicts that sunrise, with Sinatra's protagonist refusing to wallow in self-pity but rather taking a self-deprecatingly bittersweet look at his own romantic foibles. The singer then proceeded to record what many consider to be his greatest ballad collection, *Frank Sinatra Sings for Only the Lonely*. This he painted in colors so pitch-black that no light could possibly escape.

On the afternoon of May 29, 1958, Al Viola, his guitar still in its case, strolled into the Capitol Records Tower for what he had been told would be a recording session with Sinatra and Riddle. Indeed, that's what it was, but what he saw when he opened the door gave him pause. "We had so many musicians," Viola recalled thirty-five years later, "that when I got to the first date, I thought it was a union meeting! I thought a whole bunch of guys had gotten together to talk about an election or something. But no, all these musicians were actually there to work."

There were almost fifty musicians in the studio that day, the first session for *Only the Lonely*, and the ensemble on that album parallels a symphony orchestra in other aspects even beyond its size. Most of the previous Riddle albums used something more like a traditional 1940s swing band with a full string section attached—you could hear the roots in Ellington, Basie, and Lunceford—but the 1958 album was conceived from the foundation up as a more classically oriented project. That first session (which was actually one of two dates done on the same day, at 2:00 PM and 8:00 PM), for instance, involved ten classical woodwinds (two flutes, two clarinets, two bass clarinets, two oboes, and two bassoons), three French horns, and then twenty-one strings (twelve violins, four violas and four cellos, plus harp). There was also a soupçon of jazz brass, one trumpet (Pete Candoli), and three trombones (as usual, very prominent in Riddle's writing). But the real proof of Sinatra's intentions was in the rhythm section, which was fully doubled, with a jazz and a classical player in each of the chairs, Bill Miller and Harry Sukman on piano, bassists Joe Comfort and Mike Rubin, and percussionists Frank Flynn and Bill Richmond. Overall, the writing sounds like a classical album with occasional overtones of jazz or blues, rather than the other way around.

What makes it more classical than any other element, however, is the use of rhythm. For many of the twelve tracks—especially the title song, as well as "Angel Eyes," "Willow Weep for Me," "Guess I'll Hang My Tears Out to Dry," and elsewhere—Sinatra also specified the use of a far less clearly defined tempo than in anything he had sung up to that time. And here, Sinatra and Riddle reached an impasse; Riddle's formidable skills as a creator of music (an arranger who was more creative and original than most composers) had far surpassed his rather limited abilities as a conductor. While shading, dynamics, and other elements are vitally important in the art of directing a symphony, the biggest part of what a conductor does is tempo. For dance bands, conducting is—as distinct from the symphony—mostly a secondary consideration. A Duke Ellington or Count Basie can count off the tempo and then sit back at the piano for the rest of the tune; it's when the orchestra has to either change tempos or play rubato, or without a clear-cut tempo, that the great classical conductors, the Toscaninis and the Bernsteins, are distinguished from the dance band directors, like Les Brown or Glenn Miller.

Milt Bernhart, who played on all the sessions of *Only the Lonely*, pointed out, "Nelson never pretended to be a conductor. Conducting is an art unto itself. None of the jazz arrangers had any conducting experience when they began to write. He had never, ever considered himself in line to be a conductor. Suddenly, there he was. Nelson took some lessons, studied with a few people, such as Felix Slatkin, so that he could do better. On motion picture calls, it was all you could do to follow him." "He made it tough on the musicians in that he wasn't that correct about what he did with his motions," added reedman Ted Nash. "But fortunately, most of his stuff was in tempo, except the endings and things. But he just sort of waved his arms around and kept everybody together informally like that." The musicians got through it because, Skeets Herfurt concluded, "we were used to all sorts of conductors."

On *Only the Lonely*, Riddle would certainly have gotten lost in the ad-lib sections of his own arrangements. Most musicians agree that Sinatra, who conducted three albums for Capitol more than a decade after his Alec Wilder instrumental sessions of 1945, wielded the baton at least as skillfully as Riddle, if not more so. But because he never cared to do what Mel Tormé later successfully pulled off (and later than that, Frank Sinatra Jr.) in terms of singing and conducting at the same time, this didn't help him any while planning *Only the Lonely*.

Sinatra had originally conceived the 1958 *Only the Lonely* as a project for himself and Gordon Jenkins, a follow-up to their 1956 *Where Are You?* Not surprisingly, when Sinatra wanted to do a grandiose, semisymphonic album, his first thought was Jenkins. However, the composer-conductor was busy in Las Vegas, and Sinatra realized that Nelson had the chops to write full-scale "concert music" even better than Gordon. With Jenkins, the point of reference would have been something more like Tchaikovsky; Riddle's work is more in the arena of Stravinsky (the oboe intro to "Goodbye" suggests *Le Sacre du printemps*).

The project started on May 5, 1958, with Riddle himself conducting. It was not a notable success; three songs were attempted, but nothing was usable. A few other changes were made—for one thing, a different kind of guitar sound was used on the intro to "Guess I'll Hang My Tears Out to Dry." (George Van Eps had played on the May 5 take, presumably using his self-developed seven-string instrument, whereas Al Viola plays on the issued version (on a more conventional gut-string guitar). Sinatra also wanted to get as much of the album done before leaving for Europe; while there in June 1958 he would shoot the movie *Kings Go Forth* and also give a famous concert in Monte Carlo (conducted by Quincy Jones and introduced by Noel Coward). It also seems feasible that Sinatra, being sensitive to Riddle's feelings, deliberately wanted to reschedule the date for a moment when Riddle was going to be out of town. "I was booked to do a tour of Canada with Nat Cole that summer," Riddle recalled.

Making *Only the Lonely* a direct extension of *Close to You*, Sinatra gave the call to the best classical conductor who was in his immediate circle, Felix Slatkin. "Felix was always available for Frank," said Eleanor Slatkin, and in May 1958, Sinatra "just called and said, 'I want you to do an album with me.' And of course, Felix was thrilled." Viola added that "Felix was top-notch. I mean, that was really conducting because this wasn't in dance tempo. This was almost like a mini-symphony, the way Nelson wrote it." Said Riddle, "I wrote all the arrangements, but Felix Slatkin, a fine violinist and fine conductor, did the session, [while] I was up in Edmondton, Alberta, or one of those places."

When Riddle later cited *Only the Lonely* as "the best vocal album I've ever done," he explained to Alan Dell, with his usual caustic sense of humor, that this was "because I had time to work on the arrangements—a week!" Elsewhere, Riddle stated that he could typically write three or four arrangements in a single day; therefore, to do twelve in a week was an unexpected luxury. It's also indicative of Riddle's sense of irony that his "favorite" album should be the one most linked in his mind to the most extreme personal tragedy. He wrote the orchestrations "at a time when my mother was in Sinai Hospital with terminal cancer. I think the somber circumstances of [my] mother dying contributed to the darker colors of the album." She died a few weeks before the sessions began. Riddle added, "And I had also lost a daughter three months earlier"—referring to Lenora, who was six months old when she died of a respiratory problem—"so if one can attach events like that to music, perhaps *Only the Lonely* was the result."

Riddle also implied that it was merely a quirk of fate that Slatkin happened to conduct one of the dates for the album. However, Sinatra chose to tackle the charts with the most difficult out-of-tempo passages on the Slatkin session, which suggests that he was being very specific as to the skill levels of his possible conductors. Furthermore, he made May 29 a double session; first from 2:00 PM to 5:00 PM, then reconvening from 8:30 PM to 11:30 PM. Apparently, he wanted to commit as many of the more difficult numbers as possible to tape while he still had a tactful excuse to use a conductor other than Riddle; the Slatkin session did indeed take care of all the tougher, tempoless tunes. Over a long and demanding day, Sinatra and Slatkin ran down eight songs: six that were used on *Only the Lonely*, as well as "Monique," the Elmer Bernstein theme (lyric by Cahn, arrangement credited to Slatkin) from *Kings Go Forth*; lastly, there was one unissued track: "Lush Life." *

The exquisite Riddle arrangement of "Guess I'll Hang My Tears Out to Dry" (first recorded by The Voice in 1946) suspends much of the rhythm during the voice-and-guitar-only verse and all of it during the bridge. Viola explains that "one of the notes [on the verse] was very difficult, so I did a classical tuning for that special note. That way I didn't have to worry about the fingering. It also was a pedal point note, and at that time we were at the key of F-sharp. That's why it came off so good and rang out so clear and sharp."

The 1946 "Angel Eyes" was first sung by its composer, Matt Dennis, a major pianist-singer as well as songwriter, and popularized by him in the 1953 film *Jennifer;* the first notable recordings were by Herb Jeffries (on Exclusive Records in 1946), Ella Fitzgerald (who once named it as her favorite song), and Nat King Cole. But with the release of *Only the Lonely,* it immediately became inseparable from Sinatra. (The only thing the Sinatra version lacks is the verse, which Dennis and lyricist Earl Brent didn't actually write until twenty years later.) Here the mood is extremely minor and noir (this song sounds like the cover of *In the Wee Small Hours* looks); Riddle's arrangement closely parallels Brent's libretto in that the piece gradually falls increasingly out of meter, thereby underscoring the protagonist's sense of confusion and the overarching sense of impending doom.

The arrangement of "Ebb Tide" (the work of composer Robert Maxwell, whose work drew upon aspects of both popular and classical music) follows the same trajectory, only in reverse, using the rising and falling of the orchestra, following the suggestion of Debussy in *La Mer*, to depict the motion of the ocean. Sinatra floats rhythmically as if on a life raft, although for much of the piece he is deliberately out of sync with the aquatic/orchestral undertow. He seems to be fighting the current, resisting its pull by rowing in the opposite direction, until the conclusion of the text, when the protagonist and the world, represented by the elemental force of the water, are at last at peace.

---

* Luiz Carlos do Nascimento Silva, in his 2000 *Put Your Dreams Away: A Frank Sinatra Discography* (a masterful work that, unfortunately for me, had not yet been published at the time I was writing the original edition of this book) states that Sinatra attempted "Lush Life" as Capitol master E 19257. Later, after three takes, that matrix number was reassigned in the union report to "Sleep Warm," a single that was then recorded on September 11, 1958.

The subject matter may be romantic defeat, but *Only the Lonely* is a triumphant album in every other aspect. The only misstep was Billy Strayhorn's "Lush Life," which Sinatra had the good sense to realize was not right for him or the album. (We'll talk about it more later, when we discuss Sinatra's complicated relationship with Duke Ellington and Strayhorn.) It's very clear in listening to the uncompleted takes that "Lush Life" doesn't fit in with the likes of "Willow Weep for Me." This very dark 1932 torch song finds Sinatra in a grimly expressive mood, stressing and stretching the word "weep" so much that he seems on the very precipice of falling out of tune. Trumpeter Pete Candoli takes the Edison role here, and does so well that in a later interview Riddle remembered the trumpeter as being Sweets himself. (Then again, as we've seen, Riddle wasn't present on this date.) Though not written in a conventional minor key, "Willow" is nonetheless filled with minor and augmented chords. Riddle described it as "sort of a shady, mysterious, sad sound that occurs to me anytime I see a willow tree."

Part of the strength of the album is the highly original way Riddle and Sinatra combine elements of contemporary classical music with those of the blues; the very complex and the very basic. As we've seen, the somewhat Kentonesque arrangement of the 1930 torch song "It's a Lonesome Old Town" suggests a barroom ballad of the twenty-first century; a ballad for broken hearts in outer space.

The most classical piece is, famously, the title song, commissioned and published by Sinatra, which pushed everyone to the limits of their abilities, the arranger (Riddle), the conductor (Slatkin), the composer (Cahn), the lyricist (Van Heusen), and a classical pianist: Harry Sukman was brought in to play the Chopinesque passages heard throughout. It's a singularly unique piece of songwriting from Van Heusen, employing highly avant-garde modal-style harmonies some months before Miles Davis recorded his breakthrough modal jazz album *Kind of Blue* (in which a deliberately minimal melody gets repeated over and over in different registers and varying degrees of musical-emotional intensity). As he does with most of the album, Sinatra delivers "Only the Lonely" (later sung, surprisingly although memorably, by Aretha Franklin), which lays out in a highly unusual pattern (A A' A A' B A A"), in a single devastating chorus.

The Riddle-directed numbers from the remaining two sessions for *Only the Lonely* use more conventional jazz-pop tempi and are no less effective for it. "What's New," which is full of entrances that take so long for Sinatra to come in that you're pulling your hair out in suspense, again casts Ray Sims as trombone-playing company for Sinatra's misery. Paradoxically, the two most old-fashioned pieces, "Blues in the Night" and "Lonesome Old Town," become the furthest out and most Stravinskian; Riddle's treatment of the Arlen tune also evokes *Le Sacre.*

"Goodbye," composed by Gordon Jenkins and adapted by Benny Goodman as a closing theme, concludes the A side of the original album. The song itself features a one-measure, six-note instrumental "response" to the central melody line that seems typical of the "moaning" passages in Jenkins's arrangements, originally expressed as G G F, G G F, but also repeated, with the tension heightened, as G G F#, G G F#.* Riddle first states the figure in more of a Jenkins style, arco on the deep double basses, but then transforms the phrase into something deeper than the composer could ever have conceived. "The idea of that [phrase] being a mandatory thing bothered me, although I'm crazy about the song, I always have been," Riddle recalled. "You just find another way to do something that might add a little touch of freshness." Riddle has the two-part lick echo throughout the orchestra on all kinds of instrumental textures—as if all of creation were conspiring against the thwarted lover with a resounding, ineffable "goodbye."

In terms of its durability in the Sinatra canon, the most successful song on the album is Arlen and Mercer's "One for My Baby" (first recorded by Sinatra in 1947), which was a staple at nearly every Sinatra concert going forward. In talking about the arrangement for "One for My Baby," Sinatra once said, "There are times, if I want to do something that has a lonely effect, we go back to the [solo] piano or an alto saxophone as part of the orchestration." ("Baby" has both.) When Sinatra and Riddle were both back in Los Angeles at the end of June, they taped the remainder of the album together. At the end of the June 24 session, he laid down "One for My Baby" with just Bill Miller (the remaining musicians had, apparently, convened to a nearby public establishment, having one for the road), a track that was finally issued in 1990.

"One for My Baby" is a direct extension of "Angel Eyes"; both are the ultimate examples of what Sinatra once called a "saloon song." As we've seen, even in the earliest days of his career, Sinatra never sang professionally in anything like a saloon or a low-class dive of the sort that the protagonist of "Angel Eyes" and "One for My Baby" stumbles into. But Sinatra wasn't talking about himself singing these songs *in* saloons, rather he meant that they are songs *about* saloons; all the action takes place in that twilight world

---

* It was a long-standing tradition among ex-Goodman employees that whenever they heard this theme, no matter where they happened to be, they were compelled to sing the following words over the famous six-note filler riff: "Go to hell, go to hell." Billy May, irrepressible wiseguy that he is, once concocted a mambo version of "Goodbye" in which the band chants "Cha, cha, cha-cha, cha, cha" atop this famous figure.

where the sunlight never permeates. (The same is true of "Lush Life," which probably explains why he wrongfully thought it was worth a try.)

As mentioned, Sinatra sang this song in thousands of concerts, and in many of them he offers a spoken introduction that elaborates on how the character in the narrative is frequenting the saloons not just to quench his thirst and anaesthetize his pain with alcohol, but to find someone to talk to him. The whole performance is deeply influenced by Humphrey Bogart in *Casablanca*, coming from an age when men, whether acting or singing (and whether in real life or in a musical/theatrical performance), were considered sissies (and generally had their lights punched out) if they showed almost any kind of emotion, especially vulnerability; Bogart was a touchstone of inspiration. In the iconic "As Time Goes By" sequence, Bogart's Rick shows that even tough guys could get their hearts broken. The dynamics between Rick and Sam are cleverly replicated: Rick is talking and spilling his guts out, Sam is just playing a song in the background, pretending that he doesn't hear what Rick is saying, trying to help his friend feel better by not acknowledging his heartache and not playing the song that will set him off. Miller plays behind Sinatra but at the same time he makes it sound like Sam, riffing in the background, and not following Rick the way an accompanist usually does. Mercer's text has the hero talking to a silent bartender, but in Sinatra's reading, inspired by Bogart, he has conflated the bartender and piano player into a single figure.

Sinatra had been trying to create the archetypal reading of a saloon song for some time by 1958; he hints at the idea in his 1947 Columbia recording of "One for My Baby." The classic Sinatra-Miller version had been perfected by 1954 when he sang it in his film *Young at Heart*, and it's also heard in June 1957, in his great concert in Seattle; both of these readings are nearly identical to the June 24 studio version. That track is clearly a blueprint for Riddle, who the next night added a very light, unobtrusive sheen of strings as well as an alto sax obbligato by Gus Bivona. "We did it in one take," Miller said of the issued version. "We were in the key of E, which puts the alto in C sharp or D flat. A dumb key, but it worked."

Of the two takes, the piano-only version (June 24) is stunning, and well-deserved of our attention, but it's easy to see why Sinatra preferred the second treatment (June 25). The shimmering violins, which are felt more than heard, make the emotional content of the performance sound even starker and more desperate. "One for My Baby" is the finest piece of musical acting Sinatra has ever turned in. He has never sounded closer to the end of his rope, and he makes the lyric come alive, word by painful word, in an intimate reality that's as frightening as it is believable.

*Only the Lonely* was a transitional project for Sinatra and Riddle. It was their only album together in between the end of 1956 and the middle of 1960. Sinatra was already diversifying his portfolio, so to speak, by creating other albums with other collaborators (specifically Jenkins and Billy May), which doubtlessly helped to extend the long-term success of his career. But the cost of this was that Sinatra and Riddle would never be as close, musically, as they were in the 1953–55 ramp-up period and even more so in the years of their five masterpiece albums, 1955 to 1958. The rest of the collaboration over the next twenty years would include some classic albums, but they would never surpass the landmarks of 1955–58.

*Frank Sinatra Sings for Only the Lonely*, as it was more fully titled, was thus a singular pinnacle, a high point that he would never surpass. But then again, neither would anyone else.

Even as Sinatra's collaboration with Riddle was transitioning at the end of the 1950s, so too was the singer reconsidering where he stood with Capitol Records—and beyond that, the larger music industry. He switched producers, from Voyle Gilmore to Dave Cavanaugh, which couldn't help impacting the way he worked with Riddle. Gilmore doesn't seem to have done anything in particular to have incurred Sinatra's displeasure; he just, in the words of Billy May (who was also personally closer to Cavanaugh), somehow got on "Frank's shit list." Both Bill Miller and Alan Livingston feel that Gilmore "deserves more credit than he got." Miller said, "I wasn't sure of [Gilmore] in the beginning, but occasionally he'd have an idea of his own, like [how to] cut up an arrangement, and some of those things worked." Riddle has recalled that although "Sinatra picked his own things," Gilmore nonetheless "presided as a benign face and presence in the proceedings. Voyle was very easygoing and a very pleasant man."

Frank Military, then officially working for Sinatra's publishing company, described the most remunerative example of Gilmore's ability to pick songs for Sinatra. During the filming of *Pal Joey* in 1957, Capitol got hungry for a new Sinatra single, but the singer had even more on his plate than usual at this particular time. When Sinatra, Sanicola, and Military arrived at the famous Capitol Tower studio, "Voyle came in with a pile of records maybe a foot high. So Frank said, 'What's that?' Voyle said, 'Songs we're gonna play to see what we're gonna pick.' Frank said, 'No, pick *one* song. That's it.' So Voyle picked one disc, put it on the turntable, put the needle on, and it was a song called 'Witchcraft.' We all sat and listened. As he played it and it finished, Frank looked at us and we looked at him, and Hank shook his head no. And Frank said to Voyle, 'Play it again,' so he put it on again, we went through it again, and he looked at us and Hank again. Then he said, 'This is the song *I* want to record. You guys put whatever songs you like on the rest of the session, but this song I like.' So he had great taste. It was a fabulous song. We went in and recorded it. It took him two and a half hours to get that one song down, but he got it down right."

Introduced by a descending riff (similar to that which Riddle had suggested in "Mood Indigo") and laid out over a pattern vaguely like Ravel's *Boléro*, "Witchcraft" became another touchstone in the Sinatra canon. Composer Cy Coleman was justifiably proud of that disc, citing it as an example of a "good marriage" in which "the words belong to the melody. That's when the lyric and music are good, too. . . . You can't pull them apart." The song originated with lyricist Carolyn Leigh, who had written "Young at Heart" (with jazz arranger Johnny Richards); she came up with the key phrase "It's witchcraft," and Coleman had originally devised another, more "exotic" melody to fit it. However, when poking around at the piano, he came up with another melodic line that they both instantly realized was better suited to the title.

The ongoing success of the Sinatra-Riddle singles, as well as the albums, only contributed to the confusion that Riddle felt as his working relationship with Sinatra was becoming increasingly less monogamous. "Sinatra took good care of Nelson," Alan Livingston explained, and up to that point he "would not work with anybody else. Riddle was his man. And Frank was very protective of him: he took Nelson on the road with him and did everything he could for him. And Nelson was delighted because he emerged far bigger than he had been before that. I mean, [before Frank,] Nelson was not really that well-known. Sinatra took him with him, really. Sinatra appreciated him, so it was a good relationship."

"And was that way for a while," Milt Bernhart elaborated. "Almost [like] a marriage. It was day and night. Picture calls, television, records, everything you can think of. Day and night. He wasn't home enough. His wife became jealous of [the time he spent with] Frank." As Sinatra put it, "Nels is the greatest arranger in the world, a very clever musician, and I have the greatest respect for him."

Riddle would continue to helm the majority of Sinatra's projects, including virtually all of his TV shows and movies. But in 1956 Sinatra began experimenting with other collaborators. Without intending any slight to Riddle, he had at least two good reasons for turning to Billy May and Gordon Jenkins. First, he didn't want to be "married" to any one particular arranger's sound; he feared that ten years earlier he had relied too heavily on Stordahl and thus been chained to one approach when his audiences tired of the Sinatra-Stordahl style. Like Nat King Cole, who wisely switched from a small combo to solo microphone when his trio was at the very height of its popularity, Sinatra knew that the time to try something new was well before what he was currently doing had worn out its welcome. Second, as early as 1956 Sinatra had begun to think about not only controlling but also owning his recorded performances outright. Whether he could achieve that in conjunction with Capitol or if he needed to go elsewhere, he seems to have anticipated wanting a brand-new sound to distinguish the new venture. Riddle, who would arrange five final albums for Sinatra on Reprise between 1963 and 1966, was still his most frequent partner, but his was no longer the only name on Sinatra's dance card.

"Right at the point that Nelson felt he was Sinatra's boy, just when he had gotten used to the idea, Frank started to look around and try other people," remembered Bernhart, "for no reason in particular, not as a slur, not as a slap in the face—but Nelson took it that way." Riddle, whose ego was but a fraction of those of the Hollywood hotshot arrangers who got rich imitating him, was incapable of taking Sinatra's decision as anything but a slight. "Frank used Nelson for many albums until one day he decided on Gordon Jenkins," recalled Frank Military. "I remember Nelson calling me and saying, 'What did I do? What's the matter?' I said, 'Frank just wants a different sound.' But Nelson was really upset about it. However, Frank knew what he wanted; he needed a change, he needed to get something fresh happening."

Riddle seems to have little reason to be upset that Sinatra was having an occasional fling with other orchestrators since he himself was working with so many singers—even Sinatra's two closest rivals of the early 1950s, Cole and Billy Eckstine. Out of necessity, Riddle would write for anyone who would pay him roughly one hundred dollars a score. The fee was officially five dollars a page, and arrangers did not begin to receive additional royalties for sales of their work until long after the role of orchestrator, as it existed in Riddle's era, had faded from popular music. "It wasn't right. It wasn't fair," said Livingston, "but we obviously weren't going to change the industry." In struggling to support six children, two wives (eventually), and a house in Bel Air, Riddle worked himself into an early grave.

The record business's treatment of the orchestrators who were its life blood may seem a little cold-blooded in retrospect, but nobody besides the bandleader or star whose name was top-billed on the label received royalties at that point, and often not even him or her. Billy May was sent statements for the steadily selling series of instrumental albums and singles under his own name (not as an accompanist); Gordon Jenkins raked in considerably more loot as a composer than he did as an orchestrator, even though he had only a handful of hit songs to his credit. But despite the best intentions of

Capitol, neither would happen for Riddle. "The company really tried to give Nelson an opportunity to be an artist in his own right and in his own name," Livingston pointed out. "What we were trying to do was give Nelson something of his own that he could make a royalty on."

Riddle made instrumental singles as well as albums of dance and then easy-listening music (the two best are the 1957 *Hey . . . Let Yourself Go* and the 1958 *C'mon . . . Get Happy*) and penetrated the charts on several occasions, with "Brother John" and "Lisbon Antigua." According to Livingston, these "were done as a gesture to Nelson," although they "were of some value" to Riddle. Still, his solo career "never really happened to any extent. He was never *the* record star. He was the accompanist." Riddle also proved his worth as a composer of what, for lack of a better term, we might call "vernacular concert music" with his 1958 *Cross Country Suite*, an excellent work—a triumph of American concert music in fact—but not exactly a bestseller.

What's especially ironic about Riddle's life is his decades-long envy of Henry Mancini, an approximate contemporary in age and experience who succeeded where Riddle—and almost everyone else—failed in terms of establishing himself as a brand-name composer, conductor, and movie maestro. As Bill Finegan pointed out, "Nelson was a better [orchestrator] than Mancini ever could hope to be." However, it wasn't Mancini's skill as an arranger that Riddle coveted, but the younger man's aptitude for creating his own lucky breaks. The Midas-touch Mancini, along with the other major hitmakers of the 1960s, was blessed with a remarkable flair for crafting memorable melodies that stood him in good stead with both the counting house and the Oscar and Grammy committees. "Nelson said to me once that he would have traded all those arrangements, for which he was paid a flat fee, for one song of Mancini's. Just one song!" Bernhart continued, "But Nelson wasn't a songwriter, he was an arranger. For which you don't get riches—not like Hank!" Livingston concurred: "Everybody envies Hank Mancini."

What Riddle earned, however, was the near-worship of his colleagues. "I always loved doing things of Nelson's," said Mahlon Clark. "I told him once. After a date we went over to a bar and were having a drink. I said, 'Every time I do a date with you, I come out feeling like I've accomplished something. With so many other leaders, it's just making noise, getting it over with and getting the hell out.'" "It's doubtful Riddle ever felt the same way," said Livingston. "I think he never really appreciated his own talents."

"Nelson was really a genius," claimed Bernhart, "a quiet genius and a troubled one. He really was a big success, but you'd never know it to talk to him. He was a man who figured that he had missed the boat somehow." "Nelson was a very warm, sensitive guy," Livingston recalled. "We used to sit at lunch, and he'd just bare his heart to me. I mean, tell me how miserably unhappy he was and that he didn't know what to do with his life." "Nelson was best at telling stories about his life, which were so tragic they were funny," says fellow trombonist and arranger Billy Byers. Television producer-director Bob Scheerer added, "Whenever he got a new assignment he would say, 'Here's another telephone pole in the desert of life!'"

When Sinatra went to May or Jenkins, he wanted to draw on what they had achieved on their instrumental recordings and with other singers. With Riddle, however, Sinatra exercised far greater control. He seems to have been more demanding of Riddle than of May or Jenkins, and Riddle internalized this to the degree that he lived in mortal terror of Sinatra's rejecting one of his arrangements. They had to be perfect so that Sinatra could not possibly find anything that had to be changed. Riddle would stay up all night if necessary to make his charts just so, ignoring his wife and family in the process.

Other well-known Hollywood arrangers delegated work to assistants and pinch hitters without shame when their workloads were too heavy; Stordahl, May, and Paul Weston all relied heavily on Heinie Beau, for instance. Riddle's ego and his financial situation prevented him from taking that route very frequently. "I could always tell" when Riddle was presenting the work of another writer, said Rosemary Clooney. "I never questioned it because I knew if he needed to, he needed to. It meant he was really swamped. It happened, but only rarely.

"God knows he was a workaholic. That's all he did," said Clooney. "He got along with very little sleep and smoked too much." Billy May explained, "He got a divorce, and he had a big settlement to pay. Then he got another wife, and she was expensive—and it was a big hassle. So he was always writing. He had to write. He couldn't say no to anything. You would think that after a while it would get to be garbage, but it was *all* quality stuff. With all that trouble and everything, when he sat down to write, he really turned out a good-quality product, whether it was jazz or a ballad or whatever the hell it was. I admire him very much."

Other arrangers agree. "We were angry with Nelson because he was so great and he worked so cheap," adds Billy Byers. "When somebody that great is giving it away because of lack of self-worth, or whatever, it made us angry. I wasn't envious, but I wish he could've had more, because he deserved it."

Money wasn't his only problem. According to Chris Riddle, "My father unfortunately had a penchant for being swept off his feet by young lady singers. Then he'd feel guilty and come to my mother, and get on his knees and confess—which was the wrong thing because she lacked self-confidence, and that tore her to pieces, to know that he was doing this. She's the last person he should have told." While these were mostly brief encounters, Riddle also experienced a full-fledged affair with Rosemary Clooney (also married, but hardly happily) that lasted at least six or seven years.

"Music is not only a profession and an art to me," Riddle once said. "Through the years, particularly in trying times, it has been, and still is, a protective wall." Riddle made a perfect partner for Sinatra because of his corresponding capacity for sadness and elation. "Nelson naturally sort of breezed through everything. Nothing upset him," said Ted Nash. "He was more somber than Axel or Billy. Nelson never had much of a personality with the guys. He liked working with us and all that, but he didn't give you a feeling of any warmth." Mahlon Clark remembered that Riddle "hardly ever laughed."

Anyone who has heard "Makin' Whoopee" on *Songs for Swingin' Lovers!* knows that he is in the presence of an ironic sense of humor of the highest order. Those close to him, like Clooney, knew that "Nelson had a big streak of bitterness. But I could usually kid him out of it. Because he liked to laugh. He was very funny. Very dry, but very funny." Occasionally Riddle even used his characteristic deadpan puss as a tool for playing practical jokes: Riddle once told Bing Crosby that a certain guitarist had a drinking problem, and Joe Bushkin then spent months trying to convince Crosby that the austere Mr. Riddle had actually been pulling his leg.

With all of his personal problems, it's no surprise that Riddle was greatly troubled when it became clear that he was no longer the go-to guy for Sinatra, the one man who had made most of his career possible. By 1960, having only done one album with the singer in four years, he seems to have resigned himself to the privilege of being The Voice's most frequent collaborator, though no longer his only one. In that year, it became apparent that the collaboration, and possibly even Sinatra's entire recording career, was doomed to become a casualty of his rapidly deteriorating relationship with Capitol Records. By April, after much negotiation, Capitol heads Glenn Wallichs and Alan Livingston agreed to release Sinatra from his long-term contract (renewed for another seven years in 1958), leaving him free to concentrate on his own newly founded label, Reprise Records, once he had completed an agreed-upon number of releases for Capitol.

Sinatra began planning his first projects for Reprise Records while he still had four albums left to do on his Capitol contract. Even knowing he would be forced to compete with himself, Sinatra never had it in him to turn out less than his best. Unable to compromise his music, Sinatra also agreed not to rerecord any songs he had done on Capitol for Reprise for a certain period. Sinatra then decided to focus on what he had already been leaning toward in his albums with Gordon Jenkins: producing definitive versions of tunes he had previously waxed in his Columbia tenure. (This was a period when many veteran recording stars were remaking their earlier hits and classics in hi-fi and stereo.) Thus, when Sinatra sings "I've Heard That Song Before" on *Come Swing with Me!,* he really means it.

The two remaining Capitol albums with Riddle contain very few songs that are completely new to Sinatra's world, primarily the somewhat out-of-place title track on *Nice 'n' Easy* and three tunes on *Sinatra's Swingin' Session!* Sinatra wasn't about to let that prevent these from being essential sets, however; *Nice 'n' Easy,* in particular, can hold its own against any other Sinatra album. An exquisite collection of ballads that doesn't sound the depths of despair as had previous sets, Sinatra and Riddle painted *Nice 'n' Easy* in stunningly vibrant yet subdued pastel colors.

The two men recorded twelve glowingly warm standard love songs over three sessions in March 1960. Nobody remembers what the original title for the project was, although it may well have been *The Nearness of You.* Both the song and the use of it as a title were dropped when Sinatra decided to replace it with "Nice 'n' Easy" as the lead-off track. Although the team of composer Lew Spence and Alan and Marilyn Bergman had already written a number of successful singles for Sinatra (such as "Sleep Warm," "Half as Lovely (Twice as True)," and "So Long, My Love"), the singer rejected "Nice 'n' Easy" in a flamboyant manner the first time that he heard it.

Then again, Spence himself hadn't thought much of the central melody of the song the first time it occurred to him; he discarded it immediately, and only because he and the Bergmans happened to finish another song early did he bother to demonstrate the unfinished fragment for them. Alan Bergman instantly thought of the title "Nice 'n' Easy," and with that much to work with, the rest of the melody and lyric came quickly. Shortly afterward, Spence demonstrated the song to Sinatra during a break from the filming of *Ocean's 11,* but the singer's initial reaction was to pick up the music with the tips of his fingernails and let it fall to the ground like so much garbage.

Fortunately, Hank Sanicola realized the song's value and over the next few weeks kept playing it whenever Sinatra was within earshot. Sinatra finally asked, "What is that cute little thing you keep playing?" And, as Spence recalled, "Hank told him it was my song and that he was recording it in a couple of weeks. Frank said, 'Well, I better get Nelson and give him a key. I don't remember giving him a key on that one.' Frank not only recorded it but decided that he would make it the title of an album." Sinatra devised his classic coda, which reprises the tag and false ending, from Count Basie's "April in Paris" ("like the man says, one more time," which itself plays off the last line, "nice and easy does it every time") on the actual date.

With its finger snaps and gentle swing, "Nice 'n' Easy" has little in common with the rest of the album. Riddle coated the set with a soft sheen of brilliantly arranged strings and the most prominently displayed coterie of sidemen he had ever used, spotlighting a different sideman on almost every track—but not making a point of it. Thus we hear Plas Johnson's tenor on "That Old Feeling" and "Nevertheless," George Roberts turning in one of his fullest statements ever on "How Deep Is the Ocean?," Harry Klee on "Fools Rush In," trumpeter Carroll Lewis making like Bobby Hackett on "Nevertheless" and "She's Funny That Way," two stunning Felix Slatkin solos on "Try a Little Tenderness" and "Mam'selle," and a classic coda delivered by Bill Miller on "I've Got a Crush on You." (On CD, the album sounds even better with "The Nearness of You" restored. Deleted from the original release, the track was issued initially on the hodgepodge collection *Sinatra Sings . . . of Love and Things.*) For his part, Sinatra has never sounded more convincingly blue and pensive; this is make-out music that is no less pleasurable than the activity it's designed to accompany.

As an album of vaguely upbeat ballads—no noir or suicide songs here— *Nice 'n' Easy* might be described as a genial update of Sinatra's 1940s sound. (The mood is also reminiscent of several albums by Nat King Cole, for whom love wasn't always a suicidal thing, either.) The final Sinatra-Riddle project for Capitol is *Sinatra's Swingin' Session!!!* (recorded in 1960, released in 1961), which can similarly be characterized as a virtual remake of Sinatra's first long-playing album, *Sing and Dance with Frank Sinatra. Swingin' Session* reprises six out of the eight songs on that 1950 set (while a seventh, "Lover," appears anew on *Come Swing with Me!*).

Riddle had all the arrangements ready to go for *Swingin' Session*, but as he later recalled, when Sinatra arrived at the date the singer surprised him by announcing that he wanted to do all the tunes at tempos twice as fast as he had previously planned. Riddle hadn't written any four- or five-minute epics to begin with, so Sinatra's decision left them with a whole bunch of tracks that were short enough to fit on an answering machine message and a twenty-five-minute album—not that much longer than the original ten-inch *Sing and Dance* disc. (Sinatra later performed Riddle's "My Blue Heaven" in the original slower tempo live at an Australian concert in 1961.)

This was by no means typical of the four contractual obligation albums: "You Go to My Head" on *Nice 'n' Easy* and "That Old Black Magic" on *Come Swing with Me!* both clock in at four minutes or more, as do three tracks on *Point of No Return*. One is left to wonder if it's mere coincidence that the longest tunes on *Swingin' Session* happen to be the three nonremakes. "Blue Moon," for instance, finds Sinatra improvising all sorts of imaginative harmony lines around the melody. That tune, incidentally, marks one of the only items in the Sinatra discography suggested by Bill Miller. The pianist recalled, "He said, 'Pick a tune for me. What would you play if you were going to sit down at the piano right now?' I said, 'Oh, maybe "Blue Moon."'" He said, 'Okay. Call Nelson and tell him to make 'Blue Moon.'"

Woody Herman once went to hear his friend Glenn Miller playing at a dance, and to his surprise, the famously cool-handed bandleader was playing everything about twice as fast as usual. When Herman asked why, Miller said, "I don't want those *mother-fathers* [not the actual word] to dance, I want them to listen!"* Sinatra had come to the same conclusion, and doubled the metronomic count in order that the *Swingin' Session* album should justify its extravagant title. The increased speed gives the charts a euphoric, extra-punchy feeling, so that on "Should I" both Sinatra and tenorist Buddy Collette (visible on the cover), who shares the reed solos with Plas Johnson, move so fast they almost sound as if they're hyperventilating. At one point on "My Blue Heaven," Sinatra even eliminates the first syllables of each A section to keep everything moving.

So it's darn the torpedoes, full speed ahead. The frenzied pace enforces the frantic feeling of fun, making this Sinatra's most trimly swinging set—less like Lunceford and Oliver and more like Basie or Goodman. Riddle even uses the strings in a rhythmic fashion, which is to say barely at all most of the time, and has them plunk away pizzicato in swing time on his treatment of "Always," de-waltzed from 3/4 into 4/4. For all the relentless energy that Sinatra and Riddle displace, they remain true to the spirit of the songs— and themselves. "September in the Rain," with its booming bass coda by Joe Comfort, "Always," and "I Can't Believe That You're in Love with Me" have well-conceived closers combining original lyric and musical variations that Sinatra all but throws directly into the audience, as if in a 3-D movie. Far from being too fast, "When You're Smiling" (the opener) even gives Sinatra time to detour through an unanticipated Louis Prima impression.

The two contractual obligation albums with Riddle are both extremely strong—they only suffer in comparison to the masterpieces of 1955–58. By Sinatra's standards—in terms of his attitude toward Capitol Records in 1960–61—they are much better than they need to be, or even than Sinatra probably wanted them to be.

On June 1, 1962, Sinatra and Riddle played London—but not together. Riddle was in the UK to work with Shirley Bassey, and Sinatra was nearing the

---

* Story courtesy Gary Giddins.

final leg of his famous World Tour (he was accompanied by a sextet, without a conductor of any kind). A BBC-TV interviewer catches Riddle on the red carpet and asks him, "Have you a feeling that perhaps you'd like to be conducting again out front here for Mr. Sinatra this evening?" Riddle does not look happy to be there and even less so with the question. "I've had enough for tonight, thank you," he says, taciturnly. This is in marked contrast with the interviews with Bassey and Matt Monro, who can barely contain their enthusiasm for seeing Sinatra.

It was around this time, 1960–62, that, with Reprise Records a reality, Sinatra redoubled his efforts to move in new directions. It further exacerbated the widening gap between them that Riddle was under contract to Capitol and could only work for other labels with difficulty. (It was only with Capitol's permission, for instance, that Riddle was permitted to work on the masterpiece *Ella Fitzgerald Sings the George and Ira Gershwin Songbook* for Verve Records in 1959.) As a result, the two collaborated on a mere two singles between 1960 and 1963. Riddle had accepted that Sinatra would seek new sounds from such past masters as May and Jenkins, and later Johnny Mandel and Sy Oliver; but Sinatra's turning to a relatively unknown quantity named Don Costa rankled him. "When Don Costa showed up and got into the picture, Nelson was very hurt," said Milt Bernhart. "And those around town knew that."

By 1963, Sinatra had sowed enough oats with other writers and the contractual matters had resolved themselves, so he and Riddle could renew their partnership in earnest. Over the next five years they would collaborate frequently, turning out five entire albums. Riddle would also arrange a number of individual Sinatra tracks for various other Reprise projects as well.

These five Reprise albums are hardly the Sinatra-Riddle equivalent of the post–L. Frank Baum *Oz* books, meaning a familiar cast of characters achieving a significantly lesser level of magic. Nothing quite reaches the twin peaks of *Swingin' Lovers* and *Only the Lonely*, but these five mid-1960s albums are less concerned with climbing back to familiar heights than they are with marking out new territory. Sinatra and Riddle work with new instruments, such as a prominent guitar background on "Moon River," Brazilian percussion and bossa nova patterns on "I Wished on the Moon," and a Hammond organ throughout the whole *Strangers in the Night* set. Sinatra finds new ways to put over very oversized, dramatic ballads in *The Concert Sinatra* (1963) and new ways to swing on *Strangers in the Night* (1966). He also explores alternate methods of organizing songs via not only emotional but thematic juxtapositions.

Only *Sinatra's Sinatra* (1963), the least-regarded of the Sinatra-Riddle Reprise albums, attempts to rekindle the old fire with the original pair of sticks. Here's an album inspired by economic rather than artistic necessity, in which Sinatra attempts to compete in record stores with earlier hits still controlled by Columbia and Capitol, this time with a greater profit participation for himself. Still, *Sinatra's Sinatra* remains true to its concept of presenting new versions of Sinatra's personal favorite songs and not merely regurgitating the twelve titles that happened to sell the most. The two newest charts, fresh Riddle scores for songs originally recorded with Stordahl, fare the worst: "Nancy" has lost the bloom of her youth and Sinatra can't summon the same spark he had infused her with in 1945. Likewise, the singer has simply outgrown the rather naive "Oh, What It Seemed to Be." Riddle's rerecordings of his own charts vary in practice, although all the instrumental backings sound more spectacular in the new stereo setting.

"I've Got You Under My Skin" finds trombonist Dick Nash sitting in for Bernhart, who had a film call he couldn't get out of, mixing his own licks in with quotes from Bernhart's classic 1956 solo. "Of course, everyone has to end that solo with the phrase that Milt used," said Nash, "which is Milt's trademark. I felt you *had* to use that, it fits the tune so well." Sinatra gets "damn well" animatedly aggressive here and on "Witchcraft" and elsewhere, and on "Young at Heart" he sounds a little more knowing for having been around the block a few times in the intervening years. "In the Wee Small Hours" marks perhaps the most successful remake, deliberately substituting a nicer 'n' easier lightness for the noir drama of the 1955 original.

On the whole, it's too bad that the 1963 Sinatra doesn't work as hard at wooing these tunes away from his younger self as he does on *Academy Award Winners* at winning "Cool, Cool, Cool of the Evening" and "Swinging on a Star" away from Bing Crosby and "The Continental" and "The Way You Look Tonight" from Fred Astaire. *Sinatra's Sinatra's* greatest benefactions are the three Cahn and Van Heusen classics that defy the concept of remaking earlier hits, particularly this second-time-around version of "The Second Time Around," which Sinatra had initially recorded in 1960 as the first Reprise single. "Call Me Irresponsible" finds Sinatra riding in like the cavalry to save a swell song from an epic barker of a clambake called *Papa's Delicate Condition*. (Cahn was proud of the way he built the lyric around rhythm rather than rhyme, ending each line with a five-syllable word. "Not bad," he frequently said, "for a guy from a one-syllable neighborhood.") As for "Pocketful of Miracles," that seems to be "High Hopes" spelled sideways, a spoonful of Frank Capra-corn swallowed with a wordless kiddie choir. Both tunes could be anagrams for "Swinging on a Star" and signify rare instances of the great Sammy Cahn working in the shadow of Van Heusen's former lyricist, the great Irish blarney salesman, Johnny Burke. For a "least" album by the team, *Sinatra's Sinatra* is still pretty damn good.

As for the remaining 1960s sets, *The Concert Sinatra* (1963) derives just as much from Sinatra's career-long quest for extended song forms as it does from his partnership with Riddle. Likewise, *Strangers in the Night* (1966) comes out of his ambition to be contemporary with the psychedelic '60s. The two efforts signify the widest extremes of the collaboration: *Strangers* works on the most minimal and accessible level to digest tunes of both the classic and contemporary pop traditions; *Concert* goes for the most highbrowed works they can transform into ambitious, quasisymphonic arrangements. *Concert* also represents the closest Sinatra would come to a composer "songbook" album. Celebrating the twin titans of the integrated story musical, all but one (Kurt Weill's "Lost in the Stars") of its eight extended selections derive from Richard Rodgers and/or Oscar Hammerstein.

Where the 1956 *Close to You* represented Sinatra and Riddle at their most intimate, *The Concert Sinatra* finds them at their most epic. Where *Close* utilizes a chamber group, *Concert* deploys a complete philharmonic contingent. Riddle's orchestrations are particularly adept at humanizing the largest backup group any pop star would ever sing in front of. The arranger commences the first track, "I Have Dreamed," with the miraculously light sound of his familiar flutes and has his enormous contingent of string players enter so slowly, almost imperceptibly, as if to suggest an engineer gradually turning up the volume.

Tragically, Riddle had been deprived of one of his most crucial voices not long before the album: Felix Slatkin had died immediately prior to the session, and, as Eleanor Slatkin recalled, Sinatra insisted that she participate as a kind of work therapy to keep her from being overcome with grief. "Unless she agrees to play," Sinatra said, "I won't do the album." In spite of the absence of Felix's familiar violin sound, by the outchorous of "I Have Dreamed" the excitement has snowballed to the point where, although Sinatra never sounds as if he's straining, he has taken his chops to the very outer limits of where they can go.

Riddle is virtually invisible on "Soliloquy" and "Ol' Man River," two songs that don't leave much room for, say, moving the bridge to where the verse is supposed to be. The arranger does insert a characteristic Riddleism on "My Heart Stood Still" (which Sinatra had performed on a 1960 TV appearance in a lighter Riddle chart, but not recorded). As Sinatra begins a modulation from the verse to the chorus, at the very moment when the lyric mentions castles that "rise in Spain," Riddle dangles a few castanets to distract attention from the key change. Likewise, the pronunciation of the words "my heart's do-main," is classic Frankish phrasing.

In contrast, "Lost in the Stars" is a showcase as much for the arranger as the singer; a chart with an original and strikingly Stravinskian forty-five-second intro. Riddle depicts heavenly bodies skittering about the cosmos before our aural "eyes" focus on one lonely being on one little star. This is perhaps the most striking example of Riddle's spectacularly vivid polytonal approach, which we have heard on Sinatra records as far back as "Three Coins in the Fountain" from ten years earlier. (That same arrangement would be rerecorded the next year by Sinatra and Riddle on the *Academy Award Winners* album.)

"Lost in the Stars" nihilistically illustrates that man has been abandoned by God and is thus ultimately alone in the universe; it's a philosophical antecedent to both *Angels in America* and *Watchmen*. "You'll Never Walk Alone," conversely, argues that the solidarity of humankind counts for more than the existence of any suprahuman being. On this track and throughout *Concert Sinatra*, Riddle's charts are especially supportive of the swelling and surging that Sinatra is aiming for—his more "concert-style" singing (which is very different from, say, what he does with Count Basie) and that he accomplishes here even more effectively than with Stordahl. The single-note–style piano solo on this quasi-spiritual, used so effectively by Stordahl, sounds even better in Riddle's big, big, big-band orchestration. And for all the big-voiced singing that goes on in this *Concert* setting, the two still get in some tenderly sensitive balladeering before the very big ending of "Bewitched."

It's also somewhat ironic that for the twenty-five years of his career so far, by 1963 Sinatra's most frequent partners in the quest for long forms were Axel Stordahl and, as we shall see, Gordon Jenkins. Yet Sinatra's most ambitious and perfect achievement in the field of formal concert music was achieved not with either one of those supremely qualified collaborators but, surprisingly, with Nelson Riddle, the same arranger more normally charged with what Billy May referred to as Sinatra's "bread-and-butter" music.

*Days of Wine and Roses: Academy Award Winners* (1964) and *Moonlight Sinatra* (1965) amount to the only actual Sinatra-Riddle "theme" albums. That means, in this case, that the individual songs of each are united by related conceptual material. In the first, it's the supremely irrelevant fact that each song happened to win an Oscar for best song introduced in a motion picture; the second contains ten out of the approximately ten thousand great popular songs that refer to the Earth's satellite in their titles and lyrics. (Sinatra was obligated to do the most well-known Academy Award–winning songs, even "Secret Love," about which he says in one of the recording sessions, "I'm not too thrilled with the song, I might add, before we go on record.") The nine classic Sinatra-Riddle sets for Capitol are more musically linked by similarities of tempo and mood, but Riddle keeps the colors no less delightfully consistent on *Academy Award Winners* and *Moonlight,* and this in spite of how both sets intermix upbeat swingers alongside heart-wrenching love songs.

The Oscarcentric set opens with the two money songs by Johnny Mercer and Henry Mancini, both of which are featured in the album's title, sort of—officially, the full title is *Frank Sinatra Sings Days of Wine and Roses, Moon River, and Other Academy Award Winners*. From what we know about Riddle, the arranger was doubtless gnashing his teeth over being importuned to arrange the million-dollar melodies of the man whose success he so coveted. However, as an entrepreneur Sinatra sensed correctly that the record-buying public wanted to hear him doing these songs, and as a singer, he relished sinking his own teeth into Mercer's vividly gnomic and abstract texts. While it doubtlessly peeved Riddle to invest so much energy into making Henry Mancini's melodies sound better than ever, Sinatra obviously relished the chance to show what he could do with two of Johnny Mercer's finest latter-day lyrics.

He was hardly alone in this—the two songs seem to have been performed by virtually every singer over thirty in the period. Still, Sinatra and Riddle infuse these two very familiar songs with a pervasive feeling of freshness, thanks to an original approach so strikingly fresh that it's almost perverse. "Wine and Roses" originated with a film about a couple struggling with alcoholism; before that it had been a television play (on the prestigious *Playhouse 90*), but both playwright JP Miller and lyricist Johnny Mercer were inspired for their title by a phrase from "Vitae Summa Brevis," an 1896 poem by Ernest Dowson. As written and as interpreted by most singers, "Days of Wine and Roses" is a definite downer, in contrast to "Moon River," in which Mercer is no less poetic but considerably more vaguely optimistic.

Yet Sinatra and Riddle completely invert the paradigm, turning "Wine and Roses" into a medium-bounce swinger, with George Roberts grunting all over the place. Contrastingly, Vince DeRosa's French horn moans low on "Moon River," expressing a Tom Sawyer–like yearning for faraway places with strange-sounding names. In the foreground, Sinatra and Riddle's melancholy mood negates the huckleberry friendliness of the text. "Wine and Roses" is now a comparatively happy song, while "Moon River" is bittersweet and melancholy. In *Breakfast at Tiffany's*, Audrey Hepburn sings it like a wide-eyed child or a young adult with big dreams; Sinatra takes the deeper approach of singing like an older man reflecting on the hopes and dreams of his youth—some realized, others not so much. Sinatra's "Moon River" is rather like the way Judy Garland sang "Over the Rainbow" in her forties, like a woman who had already been over the rainbow, to Oz, and back.

Several of the musicians who played on the sessions for the album remembered distinctly that it was put together, recorded, packaged, and shipped even more quickly than usual—it had to be taped in January 1964 and released in plenty of time for Oscar Night in April. In order to keep up the pace, some of the charts, it's been claimed, may be the work of one of Riddle's deputies, such as Gil Grau. Yet it can't be said that any of this haste made waste of any of the finished product. The ballads in *Academy Awards* include the only reading of "Secret Love" that makes the song work, again with a mature attitude rather than the younger-than-springtime idealism Doris Day originally bagged the Oscar with. Similarly, Sinatra's "It Might as Well Be Spring" brings a more relaxed, second-time-around sensibility to a piece previously associated with Dick Haymes's more virginally anxious treatment, in which he sounded more literally as "busy as a spider spinning daydreams." The closest thing to a disappointment is "Love Is a Many-Splendored Thing"; the team would have done well to rethink it, the same way they had the Mercer-Mancini songs, or maybe even swung it. As it stands, this barrel of corn is too heavy for even the mighty Sinatra-Riddle weightlifting tag team to hoist off the ground.

As Sinatra ramped up for the 1964 Academy Awards (he had actually hosted the ceremony the previous year), clearly the emphasis was on the two Mancini-Mercer songs that had won, consecutively, in 1961 and '62. But what would have surprised Sinatra is that the most played track in the 1964 album is "The Way You Look Tonight"—he opened the sessions with it, using the Jerome Kern–Dorothy Fields classic as a kind of warm-up. Like "My Heart Stood Still" on *Concert Sinatra*, Sinatra had dabbled with "The Way You Look Tonight" over the previous twenty years, singing it occasionally on the air (and on a V-Disc) but never a commercial recording. It's more like filler on the album, not exactly a throwaway, but clearly he never realized it would be the money song.

The arrangement is an archetypical Sinatra-Riddle swinger, in the same class as the Kern-Fields "I Won't Dance" (on *Swingin' Affair*). As trumpeter Zeke Zarchy said (quoted earlier in this volume), "I defy any instrumentalist to swing like [Frank] does with his voice on that record." "The Way You Look Tonight" (from the 1936 *Swing Time*) was relatively under the radar until 1991,* when Sinatra acolyte Steve Tyrell sang it in the comedy *Father of the Bride*; since then, Kern's melody has become the ultimate wedding song, and reflected glory has been shined on Sinatra. It's become one of his most popular tracks in the post-CD era of streams and downloads, which is kind of amazing as it was just a one-shot for the singer, who never sang it again. Anticipating Tyrell, there is an unmistakably paternal warmth to Sinatra's rendition; he sounds more like he's singing it to Nancy Jr. rather than Nancy

---

* Although it had been, Sinatra researcher Ken Hutchins points out, "the song Budweiser used for TV commercials that featured both FS and Jr. during the Ultimate Event tour in 1988."

Sr.—he's not the suitor here, he's the father of the bride. In that sense, this addresses the paternal Sinatra that we have recently encountered in "Soliloquy," only here he's in tempo; this could be part of an album titled *Songs for Swingin' Fathers*.

Sinatra and Riddle do especially well by Kern's interstitial "humming" phrase (those four wordless notes that express even more than Field's brilliant lyrics ever could). Every time the arrangement reaches that phrase (at the end of each A section), the strings play it in a slightly different key. At that point, Sinatra, who has rarely exuded so much energy, warmth, and vitality, splits the phrase with the ensemble as if they were breaking open a bottle of Chianti Classico together. Even when they were only going for a filler, Sinatra and Riddle couldn't help but create a classic.

Reflecting artist George Bartell's cover illustration, singer and arranger render *Moonlight Sinatra* in a marvelously expressive palette of blue and purple tints. *Wee Small Hours* and *Only the Lonely* take place in a night without stars, but the nocturnal setting of *Moonlight* is almost as bright as day. This is the difference that C. S. Lewis articulated between mere empty "space" and the magnificent richness of "the heavens," particularly on "Moon Song." An album for snuggling rather than wrist-slashing, the *Moonlight* moods range here from the flag-wavingly up "Oh, You Crazy Moon" to the grandly Tchaikovskian "Moon Love." "I Wished on the Moon" (Dorothy Parker this time, not Fields) constitutes a study in contrasts all by itself, opening with a somber, heavy, out-of-tempo verse, itself one of Parker's most poignant pieces of poetry, then moving to a gently Brazilian-flavored refrain. All of these moonlight moods are depicted in their blue hues as deep purple dreams.

Repertory-wise, *Moonlight* also amounts to Sinatra's most ambitious homage to his original inspiration, Bing Crosby. Fully half the album's tunes had been introduced on the screen or on wax by Der Bingle: "Moonlight Becomes You," "I Wished on the Moon," "The Moon Got in My Eyes," and "The Moon Was Yellow." Though never sung by Crosby, "Reaching for the Moon" had served as the title song of his first solo feature-film appearance in 1931.

Papa Bing had originally introduced "The Moon Was Yellow" in 1934, and Sinatra had first addressed it in 1945 in a heavily dramatic reading that edged toward the more traditional leading-man style of Allan Jones and Tony Martin. Returning to the tune in 1958 (originally issued as a single), Sinatra and Riddle restructured it along the basis of the previous year's "April in Paris" with Billy May, reemploying the bridge as a sort of in-tempo verse. (This treatment of the song was convincingly scaled down for a sextet during Sinatra's 1962 world tour.) Sinatra's third "Moon Was Yellow," for the *Moonlight* album, keeps a glimmer of the original's lightly Latin feeling, opening with a flute and guitar and shadowing the singer with maracas. But it's a much mellower south-of-the-border groove than the roses-in-the-teeth of his earlier renditions, relaxing from a torrid tango into a gentler bossa beat. And what of the bridge-as-verse device? Sinatra has found a more copasetic home for it, using the idea to open the entire album at the intro of track one, "Moonlight Becomes You."

In his 1948 interview with George Simon, Sinatra, talking about his favorite kinds of music, referred to "all the great Glenn Miller things"; several Miller sidemen later worked extensively with Sinatra, including Zeke Zarchy, Trigger Alpert, Willie Schwartz, and Billy May. Miller, whose theme song was his own "Moonlight Serenade," was inclined to include as much moony material in his band book as he could. In 1965, Sinatra used Miller as his secondary source for lunar laments, among them "Moonlight Mood," "Moon Love," and "Oh, You Crazy Moon" (also recorded by Tommy Dorsey), in addition to "Moonlight Serenade."

"Moonlight Mood" opens with a particularly successful reading, accompanied only by Bill Miller's piano, of a little-known verse to a very-little-known Peter DeRose song. (A lovely tune that suffered in the wake of the 1942–44 recording ban, though it was waxed in the day by Glenn Miller and the Casa Loma Orchestra, and by Sinatra on a war-era transcription.) "Moon Love," based on the *Andante cantabile* (second movement) of Tchaikovsky's Fifth Symphony, proceeds at a stately yet down-to-earth tempo and becomes especially convincing at the conclusion, where Sinatra diminuendos out, disappearing in the style of "Angel Eyes" on the word "disappear." The only number on the disc not derived from Crosby or Miller was "Moon Song," which had been introduced by the stalwart Kate Smith, who had considerable experience with hauling her moon-shaped self over numerous mountains.

Riddle's careful use of the strings affords *Moonlight* its particular shade of starriness, and he brings them down in order to accentuate the rhythm section on "Oh, You Crazy Moon," along with a swaggering trumpet obbligato, probably Conrad Gozzo or Pete Candoli. "Oh, You Crazy Moon," an early work by Sinatra sidekick and role model Jimmy Van Heusen, is the most Basie-like piece on the album; you could almost swear you're hearing that unmistakable Marshall Royal–led reed section.

In many ways, the most moving song on *Moonlight Sinatra* is also the simplest. At least three separate sets of lyrics were written for "Moonlight Serenade." Glenn Miller employed his own melody strictly instrumentally and generally only as an opening and closing theme. Sinatra infuses it with a double shot of romance while keeping it no less danceable than when under its composer's baton. But the triumphs are more than rhythmic; "Moonlight Serenade" has a rather generic lyric by Mitchell Parish—a "serenade" in the "moonlight," how novel! But Sinatra makes the very basic quality of the text work to his advantage. The words describe a young swain standing at his childhood sweetheart's gate and gazing up at the moon; Sinatra's reading, recorded two weeks before his fiftieth birthday, seems to reflect the perspective of a middle-aged man reflecting nostalgically at his romantic and callow youth, even as he dreams about one more walk around the garden.

In this profoundly melancholy reading, Parish's rather cookie-cutter text now seems as moving as the best of Lord Byron: "So, we'll go no more a-roving / So late into the night, / Though the heart be still as loving, / And the moon be still as bright."

It may not be a coincidence that "Oh, You Crazy Moon" has overtones of Count Basie. In 1967 Sinatra would mastermind a three-way parlay—himself, Billy May, and Duke Ellington's orchestra. A rumor has long circulated that in the same period Sinatra was also considering a triumvirate teaming of himself, one of his heavy-duty writers, and a legendary American orchestra; this time the other two sides of the triangle were to be Nelson Riddle and Count Basie. He never did get around to a Sinatra-Basie-Riddle ménage because, it seems, he channeled that same energy into the 1966 album that became *Strangers in the Night.*

In 1964, when "Softly, as I Leave You," Sinatra's cover of a British hit by Matt Monro (long billed as the Blue Eyes of Britain, although the song itself was actually Italian), began climbing the *Billboard* charts, Reprise assembled an instant album around it with miscellaneous singles. In 1966 Sinatra landed another surprise smash success with a song about which he has been especially vocal in expressing his dislike, "Strangers in the Night," by the German producer-composer Bert Kaempfert. This time, however, Sinatra and producer Sonny Burke decided to take the high road in using "Strangers in the Night" for an album of material that immediately overshadowed its title track.

Even though the album is subtitled "Sinatra Sings for Moderns," not every song here can be described as "modern"; rather, the tune stack is a highly copasetic mix of the very new (like the title song) and the very vintage, as in a pair of Walter Donaldson songs that Sinatra evidently remembered fondly from his boyhood. There are two songs written by British songwriter Tony Hatch for Petula Clark, and Sinatra makes them work in two very different ways: "Call Me" is a genuine and first class sultry swinger in a vaguely Basie or Lunceford mold, whereas he plays "Downtown" for laughs by making fun of it and with it. The song has a rather rigid go-go beat to it, and Sinatra reconciles himself to this by throwing in an extra syllable to adjust his phrasing to the beat, so he repeatedly sings "*oh* downtown" every time he comes to the title phrase. By the end of the track, the "Oh" has morphed into a verbal grimace à la Jackie Gleason.

Playing up the Basie relevance, the *Strangers* collection is the only Sinatra-Riddle project to utilize Hammond organ as played by studio keyboardist Artie Kane. The use of the organ was obviously inspired by the way Basie played it and worked it into his big- and small-band settings. "You're Driving Me Crazy" had been a Basie perennial, using both the original title and head melody as well as a famous variation on its chord changes titled "Moten Swing." Sinatra and Riddle had almost certainly heard *Let's Face the Music!*, a 1961 Nat King Cole album in which Cole himself played several organ solos within a *Swingin' Lovers*–type framework, arranged by Billy May.

Tenor sax star Jimmy Forrest, who certainly knew from electric organs, once told Joe Goldberg that as accompaniment the instrument "gives you more scope. You feel as if you have a big band behind you." Riddle and Sinatra use the organ as if it were a whole other orchestra; most often the instrument and the orchestra don't play at the same time but trade phrases back and forth like two warring big bands in a Savoy Ballroom battle. The string section, present but playing a far less prominent role on these two sessions, also functions as yet another band; appropriately, only two of the three "orchestras" present can be sensed in the same sentence. Whenever the Hammond is heard behind the band, Kane was instructed to play softly so that the electronic strains can take the place of the strings; when the fiddles appear, the organist sits out that chorus or part of a chorus.

The organ is also the sound of sacred music, from the pipe organ of Bach's time to the electric organs of the African American church; thus there's considerable spillover between gospel music and the blues. Although the straight-up twelve-bar blues are hardly Sinatra's forte, both the organ and the vaguely Basieish feeling give Sinatra the support he needs to make this one of his bluesier excursions. Riddle's lean arrangements suggest a bridge between the patented idiosyncratic swing of the Sinatra-Riddle tradition and the more mainstream swing that Basie used to back Joe Williams. Comfortable with neither the blues nor rock, Sinatra here brings the blues-rock "Call Me" into his own idiom by meeting it halfway.

In fact, the nine Riddle tracks on *Strangers in the Night* are quite possibly Sinatra's overall most successful attempt at coming to grips with the changes in popular music that he could no longer ignore by the mid-to-late 1960s. For this album, he and Riddle conceived a brilliant new version of his earliest hit, "All or Nothing at All," in which the contemporary pop trappings are entirely consistent with the traditional Sinatra-Riddle sound. Here there's not only a suggestion of the rampaging trombones we associate with "I've Got You Under My Skin," but Kane's organ solo is also a major part of the ferocious instrumental interlude at the center. This was at least the fourth arrangement of the Jack Lawrence–Arthur Altman song that Sinatra had performed, but it would be the one that he would continue to sing in his concert appearances for the rest of his life.

The Count's influence also helps bring a touch of the blues to three jazz-age goodies by Walter Donaldson: "My Baby Just Cares for Me," in which Sinatra is bulwarked by more grunting Roberts; "Yes, Sir, That's My Baby," where he lets the ensemble "sing" the first two notes for him; and "You're Driving Me Crazy." On "My Baby Just Cares for Me" Sinatra had kidded his New York–area roots by choosing to pronounce the word "choices" as "*cherces*." On "Crazy" he sounds like it's his "*cherce*" to pronounce the line "would hurt me" as "would *hoit* me"; instead he changes his mind at the last second, and then reiterates the last two words correctly. Yet the momentum he achieves on this particular take (number three) so pleased Sinatra that he chose it over another take in which he got the three notes right the first time but didn't swing as hard.

*Moonlight Sinatra* and *Strangers in the Night* both contain a waltz, and that waltz offers a microcosm for the rest of the album. *Moonlight* is warm and nostalgic, but deceptively modern, with up-to-date harmonies and contemporary rhythms, and its waltz, Irving Berlin's "Reaching for the Moon" is a perfect fusion of past and future. Rodgers and Hart's "The Most Beautiful Girl in the World" (from the 1935 *Jumbo*), however, has been changed so much that it's no longer in 3/4 but in a very hard-swinging four. It's a furious two and a half minutes of sheer excitement, with Riddle tossing not only all sorts of countermelodies and polyrhythms, but in addition to the big band and organ there's even a bongo player, giving the piece something of a Latin clave feel (similar to Riddle's iconic arrangement of "Come Rain or Come Shine" for Judy Garland). They rev it up from the romantic to the rhythmic, overloading the chart with so many flying organ licks and bongo beatings that it explodes, zooming on a roller-coaster ride fast enough to give the old girl heart palpitations.

The most Basielike track is not one of the standards, it is the new show tune, "On a Clear Day (You Can See Forever)"; during the session, Sinatra instructed the orchestra, "Let it lay back now. Don't push any phrases, let 'em linger." "Clear Day" uses some of Riddle's familiar textures, along with structural and temporal devices associated with Basie's stylists, such as Thad

Jones, Ernie Wilkins, and Neal Hefti. Riddle is particularly keen to pick up on the great Basie tradition of stop time and rests, having the whole megillah simply pause before Sinatra's entrances for both dynamic and rhythmic effect and then having the ensemble surge in at twice the volume. The coda, too, in which Sinatra repeats "on a clear day" over and over, steadily building in excitement, pays such successful tribute to Wild Bill Davis's iconic arrangement of "April in Paris" that one fully expects to hear the Count's stentorian tones piping out, "One more time" and "One more once!"

However, there would be no "one more time" for the Sinatra-Riddle partnership, not really. The collaboration, as we'll see, would reach its last pinnacle with "Summer Wind," a song, appropriately, about the end of a relationship. The nine Riddle charts on the *Strangers in the Night* album would represent the last fully realized, top-drawer examples of the Sinatra-Riddle collaboration.

"Toward the end, Nelson didn't particularly like Frank," said Bill Miller. "He felt as if he was being fluffed off." The relationship had started to go south long before the five albums of the Sinatra-Riddle renaissance (1963–66), and continued to decline into the 1970s. In the years immediately before and after his retirement (1971–73), easily the least interesting of his career, Sinatra would rely heavily on Don Costa to try to translate top-forty hits into the Sinatra idiom, with mixed results. Between 1967 and 1977, Sinatra called Riddle only on a handful of occasions: for several television shows and concerts, one minor album (*The Sinatra Family Wish You a Merry Christmas*, 1968), and two singles ("Blue Lace" and "Star!" from 1968). There's also "Evergreen," a song not really worthy of either man, or even of co-composer Paul Williams (though I confess, if I have to listen to this song, I'd rather hear it by Sinatra than anyone else).

It shouldn't be inferred that Riddle and his two wives and five surviving children were going hungry during these years. Although the adult pop-record business was very slowly drying up, Riddle found more lucrative work writing television and then film scores, an avenue opened to him by Nat Cole and Sinatra; his first full-length scores were for their films *St. Louis Blues* and *Johnny Concho*, both in 1956. Although he won an Oscar for his work on *The Great Gatsby* in 1974, neither his film music nor his own recordings made him a household name—he would never be a name above the title, like Hank Mancini, or, for that matter, Sinatra or Cole. Worse, as Chris Riddle pointed out, the Oscar somehow became the "kiss of death" for Riddle's career; potential clients perhaps feared that the award would put him out of their price range. He was also no further along in the happiness department, divorcing

Doreen to marry his longtime secretary, the former Naomi Tenenholtz, a marriage that all who spoke to me described as a disaster.

A potential rekindling of the greatest collaboration in popular music was underway in 1976 and '77. Sinatra and Riddle began work on a true "concept album," a thematic collection (as *Academy Award Winners* and *Moonlight Sinatra* had been), a set of songs based on women's names. Sinatra had gotten married again in July 1976, and a few months later he recorded "Evergreen" and "I Love My Wife," both of which are filled with strong matrimonial sentiment, even though the latter (the title of Cy Coleman's latest show) is a considerably better vehicle for those feelings.

Then, in March 1977 Sinatra and Riddle laid down six completed tracks and Riddle recorded orchestral parts on at least another four. These include a remake of "Nancy" considerably warmer than the 1963 reading; a swinging treatment of Buddy Clark's hit "Linda" that annexes an electric piano to the mix; and a fine performance of a disappointingly subpar Van Heusen–Cahn song dedicated to "Barbara," the new (the fourth and final) Mrs. Sinatra. All the tracks that have been officially released (three came out on *The Reprise Collection* in 1990) and privately circulated make one wonder why Sinatra decided not to complete the project, exalting the glories of the fair sex and using the wonderful "I Love My Wife" as the topper. *Here's to the Ladies*, as the album was to be called, might be called the album that got away; it's the best Sinatra album that never was.

We don't know what put the kibosh on *Ladies*, but we do have some insights into why the next planned Sinatra-Riddle project was aborted. By the end of 1977, Sinatra was planning his massive *Trilogy* project, ultimately released in 1980—with only one arrangement by Riddle, George Harrison's "Something." Although the title referred to the past, the present, and the future, its underlying meaning, to Sinatra fans at least, implied the three arrangers most closely associated with the mature Sinatra: Riddle, May, and Jenkins. Unfortunately, that wasn't what Sinatra and Sonny Burke had in mind; Sinatra long since had operated under the impression that Don Costa would be his Riddle (or his Stordahl) of the soft-rock era, and nobody but Costa would be considered for the "Present" portion of the album. Anyone who has heard Riddle's treatments of contemporary ditties on *Strangers in the Night* or, for that matter, "Something" on *Trilogy* must acknowledge that Riddle leaves Costa in the dust (with no disrespect to the younger arranger) even on this godforsaken continent. "Something," discussed in chapter ten, is quite possibly the single greatest track on all of the epic *Trilogy* project.

Sinatra had initially intended Riddle to handle the "Past" section of *Trilogy*, but by the time recording began, the two men had already passed the point of no return. Billy May recalled that around the time the set was being planned, he was having dinner with Riddle and a German record producer for whom both were making albums. "So in the course of the conversation, the German guy started asking Nelson about Sinatra, and Nelson got very angry. I'd never heard him talk that way before. He got very vehement about how he didn't like Sinatra anymore and how he felt that he had been taken advantage of." Milt Bernhart, who was closer to Riddle on a personal basis at this time, recalls that a testimonial dinner, a fundraiser, was to be given in Riddle's honor at the Century Plaza Hotel in Spring 1978. "So they figured they ought to try to get Frank Sinatra. Nelson said, 'Sure, you can try. I don't know him. I haven't worked with him for a while. But go ahead and try.' They got hold of Frank somehow, and his office said okay. On that basis they sold out the house at a thousand dollars a plate."

All would have been fine except that, as conductor Vincent Falcone remembers, Sinatra's business manager, for whatever reason, went ahead and booked the singer on that same date. "So they called Nelson and asked him to postpone the date, which he did. It was an incredible feat, to postpone this date with all these celebrities, and so forth. I mean, who could imagine a tribute to Nelson Riddle without Frank Sinatra? They rescheduled it, and I think the same thing happened again. And I don't know why Sinatra didn't overrule him. I just don't have any idea. I never discussed it with Frank. It was a touchy spot."*

Bernhart remembers that on the day of the dinner "Nelson almost died then and there. They had to find somebody else." Gregory Peck stepped in (according to Peter Levinson), and "that was a far cry from Frank Sinatra. And the audience, I'm afraid, wasn't thrilled. So Nelson went around mumbling about that for several years: 'He let me down.' It was a big blow." Most of his friends simply chalked it up to Riddle's paranoia and poor self-image. "I'm sure Sinatra has his side of the story," said Billy May. "I think it's basically just a misunderstanding that got out of hand. But it's too bad because they worked together so well."

Sinatra was already working on *Trilogy* at this point, and was hoping that Riddle would be part of it. Bill Miller felt that both parties acted childishly:

---

* The late Peter Levinson has more details on the dinner in his 2001 book *September in the Rain: The Life of Nelson Riddle*, some from the late Frank Sinatra Jr.: Initially Sinatra agreed to present the award to Riddle in Los Angeles on March 13, even though he was scheduled for a week of concerts in Fort Lauderdale at that time. (Apparently he would have flown up and back just for the ceremony.) But then he became ill and had to postpone, and he also had to make up for concerts that had been cancelled because of the illness. Levinson believed it was Sinatra lawyer Mickey Rudin who somehow talked Sinatra out of attending the dinner in order to fulfill those concert obligations in Florida.

"I think Nelson got an assignment from Frank, and he turned it down. So Frank [grumbled], 'Who needs you?'" Falcone added, "One time Frank and I were in the dressing room in the suite at Caesar's Palace. We were talking about Nelson, and I was shouting his praises. Frank turned to me and said, 'Call Nelson on the phone and ask him if he'll write a chart for me.' And I said, 'Wow, man. I'm going to be a part of history here.' I was a casual friend of Nelson's, so I picked up the phone and I called him. 'Nelson, Mr. Sinatra asked me to call you. He would like to know if you would write an arrangement on . . .' whatever the song was. I don't remember. And there was just dead silence on the other end of the phone for a good ten, fifteen seconds, and Nelson said, 'Tell him I'm busy.' And he hung up."

When *Trilogy* became a reality, the "Past" part of the project went to May instead of Riddle. "I saw Nelson around that time," said May, "and he said, 'Did they call you to do the *Trilogy* album?' I said, 'Yeah, I'm going to do it.' He said, 'Good, because that's what I was supposed to do. You're getting it on account of me.' I said, 'Well, then, I owe you one.' But we had been doing that for a long time, you know."

Chris Riddle has his own theory as to why his father turned down *Trilogy*: because he wanted to do all three sections himself—in other words, all or nothing at all.

Riddle's mother had died of liver cancer, and when he himself underwent an operation in 1980, most of his friends were surprised to learn his liver was shot. "I like a glass of vodka, but I never drank so that I was inebriated," he said. "I had a weak liver, and I suppose I was one of those guys who should never have anything to drink." Chris Riddle added, "At that time the doctors told me that 95 percent of these operations were successful and that people who undergo this procedure normally have at least five more years. Well, that's exactly what Dad had, five years."

In those last five years the orchestrator caught the first glimpse of the Riddle renaissance when he was approached by pop star Linda Ronstadt. Born in 1946, Ronstadt is a highly respected singer of pop, country and western, traditional Mexican songs, and, in one famous case, operetta. Ronstadt had first been exposed to Riddle's work and what was by then known as the Great American Songbook by journalist Pete Hamill, and she was then encouraged to work with Riddle by both Hamill and the arranger's former lover and lifetime friend, Rosemary Clooney. When the idea presented itself, as Ronstadt remembered, "I didn't know if he was still alive or if he was like seventy or something."

Ultimately Ronstadt and Riddle would make three albums together, which amounted to a blessing—albeit a mixed one—for the veteran arranger as well as for music in general. *What's New* (1983), *Lush Life* (1984), and *For Sentimental Reasons* (1986) were all widely successful, and Ronstadt was especially generous with both credit and compensation. The sales of the three LPs helped bring Riddle closer to true celebrity than he had ever been. (Two of the three were nominated for Grammy Awards.) At the time of his death, in October 1985 (a full year before the third album was released—and with his picture next to hers on the cover) he was a considerably more recognizable name than he had been five years earlier.

Ronstadt had been a major name in other kinds of music, and it was her voice and personality that made pop perennials out of "Blue Bayou" and "Desperado." Yet she lacked the combination of interpretative skill and musical know-how necessary to interpret jazz and standards, and her albums of these don't sound any better today than they did thirty years ago. Rosemary Clooney did what she could to coach the younger singer and even recorded tracks for her to study, but Ronstadt continually falls short when she tries to sing anything with a traditional pop or American songbook sensibility.

Ultimately, the albums accentuate the generation gap rather than bridge it. Discussing the difference between the 1950s and the '80s, Riddle observed, "We were in there editing the tapes from the things we'd done, and she was doing a few bars here and there. She asked, 'Nelson, how did they do those thirty years ago?' I said, 'We did 'em in one piece. We did four sides in three hours. Try that!' It takes her a whole goddamned week to do four sides, and she thinks she's going fast!"

"For once, Nelson made a sweet deal on those Ronstadt things," Billy Byers reported. "The record company didn't want to pay for the arrangements, so Nelson took a percentage. And he made a killing!" Ronstadt's talent was hardly inspirational—she hadn't the faintest idea what to do with the lyrics or tunes that she was attempting—and Riddle's writing for her represented the soggiest and least inspired of his forty-plus years of writing.

Rosemary Clooney defended the Ronstadt-Riddle albums up to the time of her own death in 2002. "What Linda did for Nelson was courageous and beautiful," and, she says between the lines, it brought him a little closer to "happy" even if he would never express that feeling in public. "Some friend of mine ran into Nelson in a supermarket," remembered Byers. "He said, 'Nobody likes my stuff anymore and I'm getting phased out of the business.' But this was *after* the Ronstadt records came out!"

But the oddest event of Riddle's final months was his "absolution" of Frank Sinatra. In January 1985, Sinatra, a former liberal turned Grand Old Party animal, asked Riddle to accompany him to a dinner given in celebration of the reelection of Ronald Reagan. "Frank spent the whole evening hanging out with my dad," Chris Riddle recalled, "even when Barbara [Mrs. Sinatra] brought this or that Republican bigwig to shake his hand. Frank fluffed them off so he could give all his attention to Dad. When we got home, I asked him what they were talking about all that time, and Dad said, 'We were talking about old times. Frank wants to make some more albums. He wants to record all the great songs that he missed over the years.'" The younger Riddle added, "I could tell that the fence was mended."

A few days after Nelson Riddle died at sixty-four on October 6, 1985, his daughter Rosemary entered his office to pick up a couple of pictures of her father and family. She noticed an unfinished chart on the piano, and though she didn't take note of what song it was, she saw that it was from the proposed Sinatra-Riddle album. With an irony that would have amused the arranger himself, Riddle—unlike Billy May (*Trilogy: The Past*), Gordon Jenkins (*She Shot Me Down*), and Axel Stordahl (*Point of No Return*)—would never have his "last hurrah."

"Nelson, from what I understood from him, was not crazy about the Linda Rondstadt project," said one associate who wishes to remain unidentified. "He did it, but from my standpoint it wasn't his greatest writing. . . . There was a generation gap. But were he to have done one more album for Frank, I'm sure it would have been the absolute pinnacle of his career. And I think the world has lost something because of that."

Not long before his death, Riddle told Robert Windeler on KCRW radio in Los Angeles, "There is no particular story, and if there is one, I don't know it. [Sinatra] is not inhibited by any particular loyalty. He did not feel that that was an application of loyalty, and perhaps he was right. He had to think of Frank. I was hurt by it, I felt bad, but I think I was dimly aware that nothing is forever. A different wave of music had come in, and I was closely associated with him in a certain [other] type of music. He would have been putting added weights around his neck to try to pry me loose from that identity which we shared. So he moved into other areas. It's almost like one changes one's clothes. I saw him do it with Axel Stordahl, my favorite; I should have realized that it would be my turn. He just moved on."

"All the good things that happened just didn't matter as much as they should have," Bernhart observed, poignantly. Reiterating that Sinatra's desire to add the colors of other writers to his tonal palette was never intended as an affront to Riddle, Bernhart concluded, "Mr. Sinatra needs new worlds to conquer. That's a true artist."

In his lifetime, Riddle so completely represented the definitive sound of great American pop that he was taken for granted. All of his classic albums with Sinatra and Nat King Cole were routinely ignored by the Grammy people, for instance, who preferred to wait until the Ronstadt projects before honoring our greatest vocal arranger. Gary Giddins reported that he failed to take Riddle seriously until jazz tenor champ and arranger Al Cohn pointed out to him how highly musicians and other writers regarded Riddle. Riddle died at the very dawn of the digital era, but in the last thirty years virtually all of his important music has been widely available, from the groundbreaking albums with Sinatra to his other vital collaborations (Cole, Fitzgerald, Clooney, Garland, Keely Smith) and his own albums (including his rather remarkable concert work, the 1958 *Cross Country Suite*).

"He was a good musician all the way around," as Billy May said a few years after Riddle's death. "Since he's gone, I've heard a lot more stuff that I had no idea he did. Things are coming out now of his that I was completely unaware of. And every once in a while I'll hear something that just knocks me right off my feet. It makes me think about what a good musician he was."

"Summer Wind," which comes immediately after the title track on the 1966 *Strangers in the Night* (the team's final completed, full-length album), represents the last masterpiece collaboration of Sinatra and Riddle. The song reached only number twenty-five on the pop singles chart (and number one on the easy-listening chart), but it undoubtedly rates as the most keenly appreciated "inside" favorite of many regular Sinatra customers. Like "Fly Me to the Moon," it's been called a "turntable hit," meaning that although it only reached number twenty-five (as opposed to "That's Life" from the same year, which charted at number four) everybody seems to know it. The grassroots popularity of "Summer Wind" is confirmed by its placement in films like *The Pope of Greenwich Village* (1984), its constant demand on jukeboxes (and now, streaming services), and its status as a perennial request of Sinatra fans at his shows during his two-decade concert period.

Usually the only name mentioned in connection with the writing of "Summer Wind" is Johnny Mercer's—who does deserve considerable credit for one of his best-ever lyrics. The song actually originated in Germany, with a melody by Henry Mayer (otherwise known in the States for "My Melody of Love," also recorded by Sinatra), and was successfully recorded by Danish vocalist Grethe Ingmann. Mercer's English-language text was introduced in the States in 1965 by Bobby Vinton and Perry Como. Both the Ingmann and Como versions are highly countrified, with piano passages rendered in the "slip note" style of Floyd Cramer. (Como's otherwise deadly dull recording also includes the very rare second verse, unsung by Sinatra.)

Despite the origins of "Summer Wind," the phenomenon described is more Italian than German in nature. In southern Italy, the *sirocco* breeze arrives every year from northern Africa, signifying the end of summer. Its coming and going, like that of the "Ebb Tide" on *Only the Lonely,* can be used as a dipstick to compare romantic and personal happiness with the passing of seasons. It's one of Mercer's most familiar and brilliant ploys to use nature as a symbol: birds carrying a message from one lover to another, a river as a carrier of far-flung hopes and dreams, falling leaves or a wind to symbolize the coming of autumn and end of love. No wonder Sinatra famously described Mercer's lyrics as containing "all the love you ever lost and all the wit you wish you had."

Sinatra's definitive reading of "Summer Wind" cast himself, as usual, as the jilted lover, while the *Strangers* album's two orchestras—the Hammond organ (played by Artie Kane) and the big band—share the role of the wind itself. Riddle has constructed a remarkably catchy leitmotif to represent the breeze, which makes one question his oft-confessed inability to compose melodies. This figure is first stated on the organ and then reiterated by various voices in the band—the high reeds, the low reeds, the baritone sax in solo— and then becomes a countermelody and background riff to Sinatra's exposition of the central melody. The summer wind, as depicted by this figure, is a symbol of loss, a point of comparison between what has been and what is. At first the breeze blows in gently, illustrating to the protagonist the difference between what has been and what is. As Sinatra's emotions mount, the wind and the music waft upward into a crescendo of hurricane-like intensity with the help of two modulations (starting in D-flat, then going to E-flat and, finally, F). Like a tornado, it reduces the hero's happiness to rubble and then softly drifts away, as tenderly and as cruelly as it entered.

Even if the Sinatra-Riddle relationship was about to blow away in the same fashion, they had already completed an uncountable number of classic singles tracks, television shows, motion pictures, and miraculous albums. Together, they transmuted a technological breakthrough into an artistic triumph, creating a new art form and producing its greatest works. When Théophile Gautier made his observation about great art that "the work comes out more beautiful from a material that resists the process, verse, marble, onyx, or enamel," he could have added twelve-inch vinyl pancakes to the list.

Working together, Sinatra and Riddle had already ineffably altered the course of musical culture, showing that there were more possibilities in the American songbook than are dreamt of in anyone's philosophy—that there was more depth, more possibilities for a wider range of interpretations, than anyone had imagined. They raised the bar and threw down the gauntlet for anyone and everyone who has come since; it's hardly surprising that younger singers, as we've mentioned (like Steve Lawrence, Bobby Darin, and Jack

Jones), would respond to the challenge, but so to would the singer's contemporaries (like Ella Fitzgerald, Jo Stafford, Dick Haymes). Perhaps even more remarkably, even Sinatra's own inspirations, the titans who came before him, like Bing Crosby, Louis Armstrong, and Billie Holiday, were all moved to make albums that were deliberately patterned on the model of Sinatra and Riddle. It's not too much to suggest that what Sinatra and Riddle achieved with this kind of music was so overwhelming that to create something new, something that wouldn't use Sinatra and Riddle as a starting point, the next big bang in American music would come from an entirely different kind of pop—cue Elvis Presley.

Woody Allen famously said that he wanted to achieve immortality by "not dying." Sinatra and Riddle achieved it by creating, in fourteen albums and dozens of singles, perhaps the greatest body of work in all of popular music.

# 7

# WITH BILLY MAY

## *1953–1979*

*I too am not a bit tamed, I too am untranslatable.*
—WALT WHITMAN
"Song of Myself"

*Spare me from drunkards and soldiers in love.*
—RUMER GODDEN
*Enchantment*

"Billy May is always driving," Frank Sinatra once said, and then he elaborated: "Recording with Billy is like having a bucket of cold water thrown in your face." Billy May's life and music are nothing short of Rabelaisian in their tendency toward outrageous extremes. The mottos of Gargantua, "I drink for the thirst to come" and "Appetite comes with eating," could be lyrics to a Billy May instrumental. May, who spent several years as arranger-composer for Daffy Duck and Tweety and Sylvester, could be portrayed more accurately in a Tex Avery cartoon than in a print profile.

There's a classic, cartoonlike story that, though it may not be entirely accurate, certainly illustrates the animated antics of Edward William "Billy" May (1916–2004). I heard it from several musicians during the writing of this book, one of whom was Rosemary Clooney, who, even though she too suffered from addiction issues (no less than May himself) and even though she wasn't present when the alleged incident occurred, was a notably reliable source of information.

The tale starts with a certain Hollywood arranger, who shall be nameless here, but who was notoriously unoriginal. As Rosemary told me in 1992 "Billy didn't like this guy and said that he copied everything. He would even go to the point that he'd hire the same musicians that Nelson Riddle had worked with and say, 'How would Nelson phrase this?'" The last straw broke May's back when he learned that this arranger, then an executive at Verve Records, had the ego to order a director's chair with his name on the back on a brass plaque, the kind that you might see Alfred Hitchcock sitting in on a movie set. The chair was stored in the Capitol Records Tower, whose recording facilities Verve often rented.

"Billy got drunk and started yelling, 'I built this building,' and then went roaring into Capitol," Clooney continued. "He was looking for that chair. And he was going from floor to floor. . . . The security guards were after him. They said, 'Please, Billy, you can't.' . . . He said, 'I want the chair.' He was like a bull, you know? When he finally found the chair, he just threw it right out a window!" May eventually learned to restrict his awesome intake with the assistance of Alcoholics Anonymous; fortunately, he never attempted to curtail the brilliant audacity of his music.*

This was the kind of Paul Bunyanesque tall tale that musicians loved to tell about May, in large part because Billy had become a kind of a folk hero for them but also because such outrageousness is eminently characteristic of May's music. May's primary weapon is contrast: each sound that comes must be radically different from the sound that preceded it; a high string passage that's already a stalactite more chilling than you'd expect must be followed by a reed ensemble that oozes enough slurping vibrato to outreverberate an entire section of Ben Websters.

Like Sinatra himself, May became a hero to the members of the Los Angeles Musicians Union Local 47, not only for his supreme musicality but for his warmth and clown prince personality. "I always felt that most people who wanted to be musicians probably got stuck working in a garage or something," May explained, "so those of us who were lucky enough to do what we loved should at least have some fun with it."

"Billy was about my favorite guy to work with," said saxist Ted Nash, "because everything was so loose, and his stuff was so playable. Everything

---

* As mentioned, I had heard this story from numerous musicians, although only one of them was actually an eyewitness, and that was May himself. Billy objected to this story and insisted that it never happened this way; that it was just a minor incident that got blown out of proportion. In his own account, he simply sat on the chair in question, and accidentally broke it. After twenty years, I find that it's still prudent not to name the other arranger (who died in 2017) directly, though, Lord knows, his identity would be easy enough to find out through Google or any rudimentary internet search. The "other" arranger himself told a version of the story that's closer to Clooney's account than May's: "Billy May, when sauced, was awful to me. [He said] 'How the hell does a kid like that get to work with Ella? He knows shit about music!' . . . In a drunken rage, Billy May picked up my chair and threw it against the wall, breaking it in pieces."

was right, and he appreciated the guys so much. It was a very exciting kick to do all that stuff with him, like the *Sorta-May* album and the Sinatra sessions. We really looked forward to going to work on those nights when we knew what we were going to be in for."

Like most of the so-called "conductors" on the pop music scene at the time (who, unlike the classical conductors, did not have the benefit of a formal musical education), May was not a particularly skilled conductor in the sense of a Toscanini or a Stokowski; in fact, Bill Miller identified May as the worst stick-wielder he and Sinatra worked with, "with all due respect to his musicianship." As Dick Nash described it, "Billy's beat was a big sweep. He would start up by his ear and come down by his hip with his right arm, and then he'd go back up to his ear again, down to his hip, one-two-three-four, and the four was at the ear again." However, Nash added, "But then, Stravinsky wasn't a great conductor, either."

"He would give a cutoff, and it would look like he was chopping down a tree," said Harry Klee, "but everybody knew that they had to cut off with that." His skill level was roughly comparable to that of his colleague Nelson Riddle; but, as many musicians felt, May was able to inspire a greater performance from his sidemen through the sheer force of his personality. As Eleanor Slatkin put it, "Billy was certainly not what one would call a conductor. But somehow he inspired you in a way that Nelson couldn't."

Skeets Herfurt offered a somewhat more basic depiction of May's conduct as a conductor: "Billy used to stick his finger up his nose and then point it at somebody, and then flip it—and that would be our downbeat! That's pretty raw, but he always did it that way."

Percussionist Emil Richards recalled still another novel method that May employed to count off a tempo. "In his drinking days he would [be holding] a fifth of one-hundred-proof vodka, and he'd go, 'One, two,' and then on three and four he'd chugalug maybe the whole fifth! Meanwhile, he was beating out three and four with his hand, the red lights were on, and the band was to come in after four—and we were all trying not to laugh. All the while Frank was going, 'I don't believe this guy. I just don't believe this guy!'" During his days of wine and roses, alcohol was a key part of May's musical identity; another typical stunt that Herfurt remembered was to announce sternly at the beginning of a date, "There'll be no drinking *off* the job!"

Conversely, May was also universally regarded as the fastest and most efficient orchestrator to work in Hollywood. When May was doing an album with George Shearing, the pianist, who was blind and therefore didn't use written music, dictated a tune to the arranger. Richards remembered, "George told Billy, 'I want to play you this tune that I'd like to do, and then I'll go back and tell you where I want the strings and everything else.' Shearing played the melody once through and then announced, 'Okay, now we'll go back to the beginning, and I'll show you where the brass should be.' And Billy said, 'Well, take it from after the bridge because I've got that much orchestrated already.'"

While continuing to utilize Nelson Riddle as the main dish on his musical menu, Sinatra turned to Gordon Jenkins and then Billy May—with whom he already shared quite a history—when he was hungry for other flavors. Sinatra also conceived of his "concept" albums with May along different lines. The Sinatra-May partnership began in earnest with *Come Fly with Me* (1957), which also marked Sinatra's first "topic" album that linked songs together through similarities in their titles and texts rather than their music. On *Come Dance with Me!* (1959), Sinatra sustained the highest energy and the most uniform set of tempos he would ever attempt. *Come Swing with Me!* (1961) serves as Sinatra's unsentimental paean to the swing era by reprising familiar favorites of the 1940s in a spectacularly unconventional orchestral setting. The three major Sinatra-May albums of the Reprise period, *Swing Along with Me* (1961), *Francis A. & Edward K.* (1967), and *Trilogy: The Past* (1979), also have singularly individual approaches.

Sinatra and May first met in 1939 when the singer was with Tommy Dorsey and the budding arranger was playing trumpet and writing for Charlie Barnet (whose band also included Sinatra's future pianist, Bill Miller). Barnet was not exactly famous for keeping his sidemen well disciplined; his own high-living, hard-drinking, skirt-chasing lifestyle set an example for the rest of the band.

May had been already writing arrangements and playing trumpet and other horns with Pittsburgh's leading dance orchestra and was somewhat more sophisticated than the legends portray him. Born on November 10, 1916, he took up the tuba in high school and learned how to write a band arrangement because, he said, of his ego: "I got to be such a good tuba player that the tuba parts were pretty dull. I sat in the rear of the stand and thought, 'The world's never gonna hear me sitting in the back of this band playing *woomph, woomph.*' So I started looking at the other instruments and tried to figure out how they worked. I didn't realize it at the time, but I was intrigued with becoming an arranger and an orchestrator." He had switched to trombone by age seventeen, the year he began working professionally with Gene Olsen's Polish-American Orchestra.

By 1938, May had worked his way up from Olsen through the bands of Al Howard and Lee River, and finally landed a spot with Baron Elliott, who led what was essentially a local-level clone of Guy Lombardo's orchestra. Although it was considered, in May's recollection, "the most successful band in Pittsburgh," the group's innate lack of musicality threatened to drive May nuts, and he taught himself to play trumpet essentially to relieve his boredom. He gradually worked himself up to becoming the band's first trumpeter; the section's original leader had more technique and more of a traditional sweet-band trumpet tone, but May, in his own parlance, had more "balls" in his playing—which, fortuitously, suited the vaudeville shows that the Elliott band frequently accompanied.

One night in June or July of that year, "Barnet came into town and I heard his band on the radio. Boy! I went out and asked him if I could make an arrangement for him. And he said, 'Yeah, we're gonna rehearse tomorrow.' So I stayed up all night and wrote a chart, and I went into the business with Barnet." Remaining in Pittsburgh, May wrote half a dozen or so charts for Barnet, but their relationship was interrupted by the leader's sudden decision to spend a few months in Bermuda with the latest in a long succession of Mrs. Barnets.

When Barnet re-formed around late 1938–early 1939, he invited May to join him in New York, initially as a writer. When one of the band's trumpeters fell ill, "we pressed Billy into service at the last minute," Barnet recollected. "He did such a tremendous job that from then on he became part of our trumpet section as well as our writer."

Barnet and May were off to a flaming start with "Cherokee," a classic of the big-band era that May had consolidated from ideas that originated when playing the Indian-inspired tune impromptu on the stand. "Cherokee" had previously been recorded by composer Ray Noble as part of a suite of Native American–inspired melodies and by Count Basie as a jam session vehicle. Nonetheless, the hit went to May and Barnet's brilliantly swinging arrangement, the leader citing "Cherokee" as "the biggest hit of my career." The team followed it with a number of harmonically daring sequels, including Noble's "Comanche War Dance," the themeless "Redskin Rhumba," and "Pow-Wow." May and Barnet, who would remain close friends for the next fifty years (until the leader's death in 1991), reunited in 1954 for a twelve-inch LP of Indian love calls, which included the other movements of Noble's original Native American suite.

In the summer of 1939, Barnet, following Basie's lead, decided to add a fourth trumpeter; he thus commissioned May to rewrite the entire book to accommodate the extra brassman. Barnet also encouraged May to write as many jazz instrumentals as he liked, including "Lumby" (named after the barrel-chested, lumberjack-like individuals who comprised the band's trumpet section) and the masterpiece soprano-trumpet battle "Pompton Turnpike" (a few years later, that trumpet solo would be played by another Sinatra associate, the young Neal Hefti), as well as pop tunes that ran the gamut from Rodgers and Hart to "He's a Latin from Staten Island."

Like Jimmie Lunceford's band, the Barnet crew combined rock-hard swing with a sense of humor. They paid homages to the bands they liked in titles such as "The Duke's Idea" and "The Count's Idea" while taking potshots at the Mickey Mouse units they abhorred: "The Wrong Idea," May's most notable effort as a vocalist (not to mention trumpeter, arranger, and composer) savaged the hell out of Kay Kyser, Sammy Kaye, and Guy Lombardo in one fell swoop.

On October 4, 1939, while the band played at the Palomar in Los Angeles (a day after they had done a remote broadcast from that venue), the ballroom burned to the ground, along with the band's entire library and instruments. (In October 1979, a pickled Charlie Barnet called up Billy May and asked, "Do you realize it was forty years ago tonight that we burned the Palomar down?") May and Barnet humorously commemorated the disaster with an original novelty called "Oh What You Said (Are We Burnt Up!)," in which the band chants "Oh Palomar!" Still, no one was laughing when May and the Barnet crew were forced to re-create the book from their collective memory.

"I was with Charlie for two years, and it was quite an experience—quite an education to work in that band," said May. "Glenn Miller was aware that Barnet was getting popular, and he found out that I was doing most of the charts. Miller was kind of power-hungry, so he offered me a job." May joined the Miller band at the Cafe Rouge at the Hotel Pennsylvania (as in "Pennsylvania 6-5000"), New York, on the night that Roosevelt won his third presidential term in 1940. His main incentive at the time was financial: the base pay was $150 a week, nearly twice what Barnet was paying. With additional checks for playing broadcasts, recordings, and films, as well as his arrangements, May was bringing home $300 a week, a stupendous sum in the early post-Depression era and one that eventually subsidized his first home in California. May compared the switch from Barnet to Miller as "like moving from going to work in an amusement park to working in a factory," but he eventually conceded that his Glenn Miller experience "helped me immensely. I learned a lot from Glenn. He was a good musician and an excellent arranger."

Unlike Billy and Charlie, Miller and May were hardly fast friends or drinking buddies. May had little appetite for Miller's military-style taskmastering as well as the somewhat monostylistic nature of the band and characterized the leader as "a mountain of resentments." For his part, Miller didn't appreciate May's refusal to place his tunes with Miller's publishing company or his reluctance to use the patented Miller clarinet-led–reeds sound in every one his charts. Miller also had two full-time arrangers in Bill Finegan and

Sinatra described Harry James, with whom he toured for six months in 1939, as "a dear friend and a great teacher." As the great trumpeter's wife, Louise Tobin, has confirmed, "In six months with Harry, Frank learned more about music than he'd ever known in his life up to that point." A master of the blisteringly hot as well as the swaggeringly sentimental, "The Horn" provided his young singer with the best possible model of how to pack an emotional wallop. On the bandstand in the early years (*above*), with Margie Carroll in tow. (Charles L. Granata Collection) A late 1960s reunion (*below*) in the rehearsal studio. (Wayne Knight Collection)

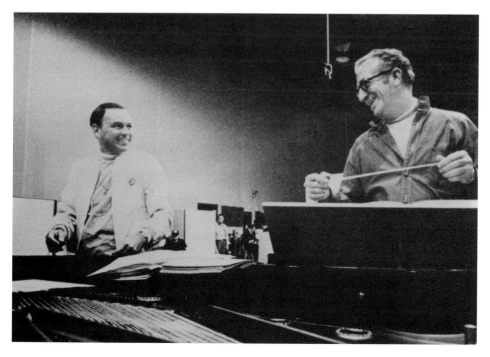

The Voice, around the time of his 1944 *Vimms* radio show, with two of his favorite performers—Judy Garland (*right*), an occasional broadcasting costar deep into the television era, and Bing Crosby (*below*). (CHARLES L. GRANATA COLLECTION) Often identified by Sinatra as "the father" of his career, Crosby's lyric-driven yet supremely musical approach was indeed a major influence on Sinatra as well as every other vocalist of the 1930s onward. In this crooner summit, Der Bingle is for once the comparatively conservative dresser. (WAYNE KNIGHT COLLECTION)

At Columbia Records in the mid-1940s, Sinatra preferred the exquisitely romantic sound that had already propelled him to national celebrity. He combined the legato, deep breath-based sense of rhythm he had gleaned from Tommy Dorsey with the tenderest and most emotionally vulnerable exposition of a love lyric that any singer had ever mastered. Then he wrapped the whole concoction in the impressionistic string textures (and gently swinging pulse) of longtime orchestrator Axel Stordahl. In the studio in 1944 with Stordahl (*top*) and the control booth at the 1946 *Metronone* All-Stars date with, left to right, George T. Simon (the *Metronome* writer who produced the date), Columbia Records executive Mitchell Ayres, drummer Buddy Rich, and occasional artistic conscience Alec Wilder. One of the final Columbia dates, February 6, 1952 (*left*). (Charles L. Granata Collection)

Two more unusual shots from "The Voice" era of the mid-1940s: at a theater date with Charlie Spivak (*right*), the bandleader who gave Nelson Riddle his first national exposure. The cast of Old Gold's *Songs By Sinatra* radio show (*below*), spring 1945, including Sinatra, Skitch Henderson, June Hutton (who married Axel Stordahl in 1951) and the Pied Pipers, plus fellow traveler Sid Caesar. (WAYNE KNIGHT COLLECTION)

The passing of the torch. The last date with Axel Stordahl as his regular music director, and the very first session for Capitol Records (*above*), April 2, 1953. A mid-1950s Capitol date with Stordahl's successor, Nelson Riddle (*below*). Although the singer had actually been singing uptempo since his Harry James tenure, the Sinatra of the '50s is more strongly associated with with hard-swinging material than The Voice of an earlier era. More than simply singing fast, what Sinatra achieved with Nelson Riddle on Capitol Records was a renaissance of the great swing band tradition, as refitted with the harmonic sophistication of contemporary classical style. On a series of classic albums that ranged from 1953 to 1966, Riddle was the only orchestrator Sinatra completely trusted in terms of expressing "sadness as well as elation." (CHARLES L. GRANATA COLLECTION)

Capitol days, continued. An emotionally charged moment at a record date (*above*), capturing the intensity that has always been Sinatra's unique province. Sinatra with Voyle Gilmore (*below left*), his producer (or, more accurately, coproducer) from 1953 to 1958. This session marked the first date to be held in Capitol's newly erected "stack-of-records" shaped tower, February 1956, as well as Sinatra's most auspicious performance as a non-singing orchestral conductor. Sinatra's work as a baton-wielder, it should be noted, was no superstar's indulgence. Most of the musicians who played on this and other dates under Sinatra's direction acknowledged that he was a more than competent conductor on pop material, at least as good as most of the arrangers who normally held the stick on Sinatra sessions. Sinatra directing the orchestra at a Capitol session, circa 1955 (*below right*) (Charles L. Granata Collection)

In the 1960s (*left*), Sinatra, now working for his own self-owned label, Reprise Records, expanded his horizons while maintaining his long-established turf of ballads and swingers. (WAYNE KNIGHT COLLECTION) Collaborating with over a dozen brand new arrangers, Sinatra's projects ranged from sets as bold and brassy as *Ring-A-Ding Ding!* with Johnny Mandel, and *Sinatra and Swingin' Brass* and *Sinatra-Basie* (notice the rare shot, *below*, of Mr. Basie *not* at the piano) with Neal Hefti, to projects as soft and intimate as the two *Francis Albert Sinatra and Antonio Carlos Jobim* albums. (CHARLES L. GRANATA COLLECTION) Sinatra seemed to be marshaling all the resources of the hip—adult pop and jazz, from Basie and Ellington to Bossa Nova—to take a stand against the forces of squareness that were surrounding Reprise's lonely island of musical sanity.

Twentieth-century icons: Sinatra in front of an audience, late 1940s (*left*) and early '60s (*below*). (CHARLES L. GRANATA COLLECTION) When a singer brings a lyric to life, we typically call the process "interpretation." Sinatra elevates interpretation into his own personal three-minute slice of reality the same kind of reality that Jimmy Cagney spoke of when he defined the art of acting as being able to "stand on the balls of your feet and tell the truth." Whether Sinatra is enacting "One for My Baby" so vividly true to the lyrics that you actually see the bartender with the bent ears wiping down glasses, or "throwing away" the lyric to some 1920s bauble reinvented as a rhythm song Sinatra is never less than eminently believable.

Jerry Gray, so although May served with Miller for two years, he arranged only about twenty charts for that band in that time—a fraction of what he had done for Barnet. May pointed out that he was not responsible for any of the band's signature hits, but he did write the beautiful left-field introduction to Finegan's "Serenade in Blue." Further, Miller only bothered to record about half of what May wrote for him.*

Their differences were such that by the spring of 1942 Miller and May wanted to call it quits. May had run into pianist Buddy Cole, who was then playing for his brother-in-law, steel guitarist and bandleader Alvino Rey (both men were married to members of Rey's main attraction, the King Sisters), and Cole extended an invitation to May to arrange whatever he wanted for the Rey outfit. When Miller found out, he at first threatened to fire May but instead asked him to stay a few months longer because Miller was planning to fold his civilian band as soon as he landed a commission to form a Glenn Miller Army orchestra. But Rey couldn't offer May a permanent spot, because the war situation was gradually forcing him to disband. While working for Rey, May decided to move to Los Angeles, the band's home base and also the home of his first wife, Arletta; he knew she could move in with her parents in the event that his number came up in the draft (which, fortunately, didn't happen).

In later years, it became commonplace to deprecate May's prowess as a brassman. In a 1979 concert, Frank Sinatra described him as being "of the days of the dance bands, when he was a third trumpet player, a very bad third trumpet player. He had an embouchure like a guy sucking a Popsicle! But he became a brilliant arranger, and he still is, and always will be." Sinatra is exaggerating for comic purposes; Miller thought enough of May's playing to feature him as a soloist on at least as many records as Bobby Hackett—and that's really saying something.

Even so, by the end of his Miller tenure May realized that his future lay more in writing. "He was never that great [as a player]," says Dick Nash. "He would admit to you himself that he was never a real soloist. And that's why he got into writing." Shortly after going out on his own, May participated in his one major session as a jazz trumpeter with a small group. This was with Jack Teagarden and the Capitol Jazzmen; May later claimed he was only called

---

* May and all the other Miller men were later surprised to learn that with the ongoing interest in the band in the 1950s, even their minor numbers were restored to print by RCA, along with many charts that Miller had performed only on airchecks. As part of a divorce suit in 1954, May let his ex-wife keep the royalties for his tunes and then learned afterward that Universal Pictures was about to make *The Glenn Miller Story* with Jimmy Stewart. As a result, his ex's first royalty check amounted to about $12,000.

because their first-choice trumpeter, Big T's kid brother Charlie Teagarden, never showed up.

More important for his career, May gained a toehold as a trumpeter, arranger, and composer in the ever-burgeoning broadcasting industry. A brief gig with Bob Crosby led to steady work for five years with the bandleader's brother Bing, and his musical director, John Scott Trotter (arranging "On the Atchison, Topeka, and the Sante Fe," among other numbers, for the older Crosby). Similarly, a stint with the Ozzie Nelson band developed into his first position as a leader when he replaced Nelson as the in-house bandleader on *The Red Skelton Show*.

While continuing to work for Skelton and Crosby, May also played and occasionally wrote for the Hollywood *Your Hit Parade* orchestra, conducted by Axel Stordahl to back Frank Sinatra. "When Axel got stuck and needed some help, I did a couple of things for Sinatra," said May. In later years, May was only able to recall one of the tunes he arranged for Sinatra on the radio, Cole Porter's "Don't Fence Me In." (They probably all were up-tempos, a chore he shared with George Siravo and Heinie Beau, and none were recorded commercially.)

Around 1945 or 1946, May began to ghostwrite occasionally for Paul Weston, then musical director for Capitol Records. He gained another ally at the fledgling label when he encouraged an old friend, Jim Conkling (who was married to still another King sister), to take a staff position there. Conkling went on to become president of Capitol and, later, two other major labels as well, Columbia and Warner Bros. Capitol eventually began using May as a second-string house director for the assignments Weston didn't have time to take, including such B-level singers as tenor Clark Dennis and jazz yodeler Ella Mae Morse.

His star rose again when a newcomer to the A&R department, Alan Livingston, began to develop a line of children's records. May, who by then had considerable experience underscoring the cartoonish capers of Red Skelton's Mean Widdle Kid on the radio, was a natural to do the music. Beginning with "Sparky's Magic Piano" and "Bozo the Clown" and moving on to the familiar Warner Bros., Walt Disney, and Walter Lantz characters, May and Livingston soon dominated the newborn market. "Jesus, every grandparent in the world bought those things," remembered May, who recorded approximately sixty kiddie albums for the label and landed his biggest hit as a composer with "I Taut I Taw a Puddy Tat." With their storybook packages, the Capitol kiddie records cornered the market on children's audiovisual entertainment until, as May recollected, "TV came in and knocked the bottom right out." Fortunately, by that time both Livingston and May had used their success in the juvenile music field as a springboard out of it: Livingston would become president of Capitol when Conkling and Weston moved to Columbia.

Until the early 1950s, May was still working at hand-me-down projects for Capitol, such as *Join the Band*, an early album produced for amateur and student musicians ("Sit in with these big band backgrounds") and an excellent series of Latin American dance records released under the pseudonym "the Rico Mambo Orchestra." May graduated from the B list to the A list completely by accident in 1952: he had made an album of dance music, and although it was done in his own style, May's name was overshadowed by that of Arthur Murray, the well-known baron of ballrooms and bouncing businessmen. However, said May, the label "liked those sides so well, they put them out as singles," including "All of Me" and "Charmaine"; they were then astonished to learn that they had a string of hits on their hands. As May put it, "That's what put me in the band business." Around the same time, May started backing the label's more prestigious artists in a "guest star" capacity, most notably its number-one singer, Nat King Cole.

May, who had criticized Glenn Miller for sticking to an immediately identifiable formula ten years earlier, at once became Hollywood's most talked-about arranger-bandleader because he had created a reed-and-brass sound that no one could forget. "That's when I started writing the 'slurping saxophones,'" he said. "It was a sound that had been around a long time, a lot of guys had done it. A lot of saxophone players were doing it individually, and I thought it would be interesting to have the whole section do it." Skeets Herfurt recalled, "One time Billy asked me, 'Skeets, can we do that just like Willie Smith does in the Lunceford band? Can we do that with a sax section, with all those smears and those big glissandos?' I said, 'Sure, why not?'"

Herfurt elaborated: "He always voiced the reed section in thirds, and then he would double the two: he would have an alto and a tenor and an alto and a tenor. They would be playing in thirds, and we had lots of slurs and things, and that's the way he got that sound." Eventually, Willie Smith, who with Duke Ellington's Johnny Hodges and Ben Webster had inspired the "slurping" sound to begin with, joined the ranks of Hollywood studio musicians and became May's first choice on alto. When Smith was on the road with Ellington (as Hodges's replacement) or Harry James, May employed the more-than-capable Herfurt as lead slurper. "It was an easy enough sound. Pretty soon everybody started doing it, and it lost its distinctiveness," May said. "But I had it first. I made some money on it." If May had originally conjured up the slurping sound as a gimmick to attract attention, it nevertheless became a very musical device in his capable hands.

As Larry Clinton had done fifteen years earlier, after the success of a series of recordings with an all-star studio orchestra, May decided, with Capitol's encouragement, to launch an actual working and touring dance band. "Billy had a rush of blood to the head that he wanted to have a band, and he certainly had the talent," Nelson Riddle recalled. "And he had what at least passed for a new sound, which was the hardest thing of all, those slurping saxophones." It was every musician's dream to be presented as a star leading his own orchestra, and even though May couldn't get the top-echelon players he used in the studios to leave their families for the road life, he was especially proud of the mainly younger men he did use, including future studio star Dick Nash and ex-Miller trumpeter Johnny Best.

"Billy would just come out and beat the band off and do his thing," Nash remembered. "He'd talk, maybe introduce somebody, the singer or whatever, but he wasn't a big, flamboyant kind of flag-waver as a bandleader. He just wasn't the Sammy Kaye type. And though he played trumpet well, he wasn't a Doc Severinsen, who would get out there and flash it up." May added, "I never have enjoyed being a bandleader in the sense of a Ray Anthony–type person. When someone would come up to me and say, 'Would you please play happy birthday to Myrtle?' I was just as apt to tell him what Myrtle could do with her birthday. If you're gonna be in that position, you gotta be like Lawrence Welk."

In addition, May insisted on playing his trumpet solos on standard tunes in weird keys, such as "Embraceable You" in B-natural (commonly regarded as a hillbilly key). Nash continued, "So I asked him one time, 'Why do you do that?' He said, 'Oh, just to keep my mind from going stale.' He'd have to think about what note came next—to keep from going nuts at having to play the same tunes the same way night after night."

"So," May concluded, "I sold the Billy May band's personal appearance rights to Ray Anthony," who appointed once and future leader Sam Donahue its conductor. "I preferred to be an arranger and to live in California, doing the work that I had been doing prior to that. So after a year and a half on the road, I came back."

It was during that year and a half that Sinatra showed up on the doorstep of Capitol Records, suitcase in hand (metaphorically speaking), ready to restart his career with a fresh, new sound. In his first sessions for the label, Sinatra tackled a "cover" of Billy May's bluesy original "Lean Baby," and a deliberately May-styled hit single of "South of the Border" and "I Love You," arranged à la May by Nelson Riddle. May, at that time, was shouting "ah-one and ah-two" for dancers somewhere south of Savannah. Milt Bernhart, who played on the pseudo-May date, has speculated that "Billy was on the road with a band that was breaking his bank account—which is very funny, sadly funny. But if he had been in town instead of on the road, who knows what history would have produced? If Billy had been here, then Nelson would not have had the opportunity. Not a chance."

May and Sinatra next crossed paths when the singer commissioned the arranger to compose and orchestrate an original concert work for *Tone Poems of Color,* a semi-symphonic instrumental album Sinatra conducted in 1956. Billy May's "Purple" comes right after Gordon Jenkins's string-heavy "Green" and starts out somberly, although not as overtly sentimentally as its predecessor. As befitting one of the gayer colors, "Purple" also has lighter episodes in which the tempo changes drastically with the aid of a Latin percussion section—hardly standard equipment for a symphony. "Some of the pieces got more complicated than others," May recalled. "Some changed tempos and things like that and some of them got a little over Sinatra's head as a conductor. So Felix Slatkin, who was playing first violin, stepped in and helped him."

In the fall of 1957, a few months after completing his first two albums with Jenkins, Sinatra at last decided on the perfect project for May's skill set: *Come Fly with Me.* Up until 1957, Sinatra had always shown considerable humor in his music, particularly when he sang those Joe E. Lewis–inspired bon mots or Nelson Riddle's witty orchestrations. But only with Billy May did Sinatra feel completely comfortable injecting an overtly comedic note into the proceedings. With Stordahl and Riddle, Sinatra has no reason to sing a song other than that he thinks it's good or, in a few cases, when one of the coproducers thought it was good. With Billy May, however, Sinatra began recording numbers that hadn't much value in and of themselves ("Isle of Capri," for instance) but that the team could just plain have fun with.

With May, Sinatra explores his latent fascination for songs that represent the antithesis of the top-drawer Broadway standards he typically favored. For every "Embraceable You" written in the 1920s there were ten songs like "Give Me My Mammy" or "My Little Bimbo Down on the Bamboo Isle." May and Sinatra developed a knack for parodying these songs at the same time they were performing them. Only with May, for instance, does Sinatra really delve into the realm of exotica. These cheap and potent songs of the 1920s and '30s generally depict affairs between American (read: Caucasian) men and the variously colored women of faraway places with strange-sounding names, romances that invariably end not with benefit of clergy but with tomorrows that never come. In other words: "Let's go 'south of the border' and get laid."

Up to now, Sinatra had generally avoided this genre, except for "On a Little Street in Singapore" with Harry James and "Pale Moon" and "Neiani" with Dorsey. He had actually been singing "South of the Border" since at least early 1940, but didn't make the decision to actually record the song until he realized it was possible to work with Billy May. Here was a collaborator with whom he could make exceptional and expressive music without necessarily taking the song that he was singing seriously; this was sort of a hard-swinging approach to what might be called "camp" in other circles.

May had first alluded to non-Western lifestyles in the "Cherokee" Indian cycle with Barnet back in 1938. He told me that he was reattracted to exotic effects by his favorite postwar big band, the Eddie Sauter–Bill Finegan Orchestra. "They had outstanding musicianship and a wild combination, and they carried the dance band business to a wonderful extreme, the way I would have liked to have seen it go. In the '50s, when hi-fi and stereo first started coming around, Eddie and Bill started monkeying around with all those exotic percussion sounds. Before that, you really couldn't get a decent sound on the orchestra bells or the glockenspiel, the big tam-tam, the big gong, and things like that. They were pioneers in that." For his own part, May said, "I just followed up on it."*

As fascinating as their music was, Sauter and Finegan lacked the belly-laughing humor and driving danceability of Billy May. In his whimsical voyages south, east, and west of the border, May kept finding himself "In a Persian Market," playing either "The Desert Song" or a "Song of India." By 1956, May was already, in pianist Paul Smith's words, "the guru of arrangers—the daddy of 'em all!" That Sinatra should appoint May as his fellow traveler on an album revolving around the theme of international schlepping, with the first side climaxing in "On the Road to Mandalay," was a foregone conclusion. (In fact, it was after *Come Fly with Me* flew to number one on the *Billboard* pop album charts that the master learned a thing or two from the pupil when Bing Crosby reanointed May as a jazz-pop singer's number-one travel partner by installing him at the helm of not one but two world trip packages of duets with Rosemary Clooney, *Fancy Meeting You Here* for RCA and *That Travelin' Two Beat* for Capitol.)

In programming this latest "concept album," Sinatra went even further than he had gone in his thematic sets with Riddle. For four concept albums in a row from 1957 to 1959, Sinatra started by commissioning (and then publishing) original title songs by Sammy Cahn and Jimmy Van Heusen. In the case of the first two Sinatra-May albums, the team wrote closing as well as opening songs. When Cahn submitted the original lyric to Sinatra on the title

---

* "Brassmen's Holiday," the opening track of his highly successful 1958 album *Billy May's Big Fat Brass*, is the May arrangement that sounds most like Sauter-Finegan.

track, "Come Fly with Me," one line originally went, "If you could use / some exotic *views* / there's a bar in far Bombay." According to Cahn, Sinatra originally recorded it as such. Then, at the end of the date, Cahn informed Sinatra that he had additionally written a slightly racier alternative lyric. Cahn considered that text—which substituted "booze" for "views"—suitable for Vegas but not for a family-oriented Capitol Records release. Upon learning this, Sinatra immediately re-corralled the musicians, who were then heading off for some exotic booze of their own, and rerecorded the song with this somewhat more colorful line.

The classic Sinatra-Riddle albums up to that point had managed to work their magic by working in both a very specific musical and emotional range. *Come Fly with Me*, however, makes use of a considerably wider palette, alternating between rock-hard swingers and lovely and lush romantic interludes, all tied together by the idea of sighing for exotic lands. Sinatra may not be quite so schizophrenic as he seems, however: the four loveliest love songs (with the most similar titles)—"Autumn in New York," "April in Paris," "Moonlight in Vermont," and "London by Night"—were all done at the same session.

The three wackiest rhythm numbers—"Isle of Capri," "Let's Get Away from It All" (not an expansion of a Sinatra-Dorsey classic, like Riddle's "How About You?," but a concisely effective cut-down), and "Mandalay"—none of which required strings, also rated a date all to themselves. ("Blue Hawaii," the only comparatively indistinct chart on the set, might have been better served if May only had indulged in some raucous mock-island effects.)

For one who got "in the band business" with brash up-tempos, May turned out to be a surprisingly sensitive—but never sentimental—writer of romance. He led Sinatra through the singer's most effective straight-ahead waltz ever, "Around the World." (Sinatra was one of many movie stars who made a cameo appearance in Mike Todd's smash 1956 film of Jules Verne's *Around the World in 80 Days*.) May later described this as "the best ballad in the album. Victor Young won an Academy Award for that [film's score]. That's a beautiful tune, and Frank sang the shit out of it, too. Boy! He's really a good singer."

No one but Sinatra and May could so seamlessly juxtapose "Isle of Capri," which they treat as a send-up of Tin Pan Alley conventions, with such a wistfully nostalgic treatment of the rhyme- and cliché-free "Moonlight in Vermont." In "Autumn in New York," May finds nuances of almost dire melancholia undreamed of even by the great Axel Stordahl. "Moonlight in Vermont" would probably go on to become May's best-known ballad arrangement; Sinatra would sing it at a million concerts over the years, including, memorably, on a 1958 television duet with Ella Fitzgerald.

"Billy is so diversified," is how pianist Lou Levy put it. "He's probably the greatest all around in terms of humor as well as seriousness, and different modes like the Mexican Mel Tormé album (*¡Olé Tormé!*), which is another great album." As Peggy Lee said, "If I had to pick someone for a desert island arranger, it would be Billy because he can write every style for brass or strings or for large or for small, and he writes with such humor as well as beauty."

May is most frequently applauded for his explosive sense of dynamics, color, and humor. "Brazil" uses a marimba (although otherwise the chart explores the song's longtime big-band association rather than its South American roots), while "Isle of Capri," which double-times into a pasodoble, brings a mandolin into the picture in its instrumental break. The latter tune (frequently sung by wags as "'Twas on a pile of debris that I found her") also marks the return of May's trademark slurping saxes. The arranger had largely abandoned these grandiose glissandi by 1957, omitting the reeds altogether for his Grammy-winning *Big Fat Brass* album of 1958. In fact, Nelson Riddle usurped the slurps on "South of the Border" (included on the CD issue of *Come Fly with Me*). One suspects May revived the sound partly in response to its effectiveness on "Border," because "Isle of Capri" is in every way a follow-up to that 1953 single.

*Come Fly with Me*'s masterpiece, an adaptation of Rudyard Kipling's "Mandalay," resounds as Sinatra's and May's most outrageous piece of persuasive percussion. The track was likely inspired by a highly swinging arrangement of the Kipling poem by Jan Savitt and his Top Hatters from 1939, featuring the band's supremely hip vocalist, George "Bon-Bon" Tunnell, who sings "Come you back you swingin' soldier"; Sinatra eventually amended this to "Come you back, you mother soldier." For decades, English Sinatraphiles regarded the track as a rarity because it was initially dropped from UK pressings due to Rudyard Kipling's un-Kiplingly stodgy estate (this being only twenty years after the poet's passing). "Kipling's daughter had the nerve to ban that in England. How dare she?" Sinatra sarcastically complained at his June 1958 concert in Monte Carlo. "Of course, she drinks a little bit, so we'll forgive her!"*

---

* Sinatra took special delight performing "Mandalay" before an audience of mostly British descent in Melbourne, Australia, in 1959: "This particular song was written from the poem by Rudyard Kipling. Now it seems that we have done a rather different version of 'Road to Mandalay,' so that his family has objected, and anywhere in the British Empire it's not to be played on the record. So they took it off the long-playing record of *Come Fly with Me* and replaced it with 'Chicago.' But this is an unusual version of 'Road to Mandalay,' it's comedic, but it swings, it jumps. I think that Rudyard Kipling's sister [*sic*] was chicken not to let us put it on the record."

After the success of the film *From Here to Eternity*, with its Kipling-in-spired title, Sinatra seems to have nurtured a spiritual kinship with Kipling's recurring hero, the warrior with a social conscience. In 1962, he made a film called *Sergeants 3*, which borrowed the title of the *Soldiers Three* story collection and, in a bizarre cowboy transmutation, the plot of "Gunga Din" (They're all fightin' Indians!). Accordingly, *Sergeants 3* marked the first of several Sinatra films to be scored by Billy May.* Sinatra also skirted the edges of "If," the most popular work of the poet's lifetime; "Pick Yourself Up," which Sinatra recorded in 1962, alludes to "If" at the end of its bridge ("you'll be a man, my son"), and on Sinatra's 1951 televison series he sang a 1934 British pop offering called "If" (then a hit for Perry Como) that amounted to a somewhat less witty swipe from the composer's countryman. (In 1974, he recorded a different song titled "If," a contemporary-rock–era ballad by David Gates of the band Bread.)

Kipling published "Mandalay" (along with "Gunga Din") as part of his 1892 collection *Barrack-Room Ballads*. The poem was set to music in 1907 by Oley Speaks, and it became a staple of the standard British baritone's art-song repertoire; in the 1920s, several dance bands began playing the tune instrumentally and in fox-trot tempo. The May arrangement begins by trimming the libretto into song form, omitting entire sections (including one that includes the line "I've a neater, sweeter maiden in a cleaner, greener land"). The singer swings the famous opening lines on top of an undulating bass vamp in order to thoroughly Sinatrafy Kipling's old "Burma broad." While Sinatra sasses her with his ring-a-ding-ding attitude (throwing in "come you back, you mother soldier!" at Monte Carlo), May does the same with percussive bumps and beeps aplenty. When the piece threatens to go into a march in

---

* The strangest result of Sinatra's fascination with Kipling and "Gunga Din" is a 1966 spoken-word recording that he made at his home in Palm Springs. In 1962, ABC-Paramount had released a very bizarre 45 rpm single, "The Last Blast of the Blasted Bugler," credited as a Phil Cammarata production. It sounds like someone conceived of this as a spoken word/ dramatic reading record, but the label decided to release it as a novelty/comedy record. We hear the narrator (one Sonny Gianotta) briefly describing the climactic scene of "Gunga Din," in which a bugler warns his patrol of impending attack but is himself killed by the enemy—and the bulk of the three-minute record is the sounds of a battle (depicted in old-time radio fashion, with sound effects representing horses, guns, etc.) and a bugler being butchered. For reasons that have been lost to history, Sinatra rerecorded this single (on June 10, 1966), adding his own voice to the brief introductory narration and using the sound effects from the 1962 single. Was Sinatra considering some sort of dramatic or spoken-word series for Reprise? We'll probably never know. (The track has only been issued on two very rare semiprivate, collectors-only CDs, *Frankly Different* and *Sinatra Unreleased*. Mind you, this is not a performance that merits wide release.)

the instrumental, like a British (not French) foreign legion of Bengal Lancers, May quickly dragoons it back into swing time.*

But the pièce de résistance is the delightfully baffling ending—or lack of same—which never ceases to surprise listeners no matter how many times they've heard it. "Billy had the arrangement written," recalled percussionist Frank Flynn, so that "Frank sings, 'And the dawn comes up like thunder,' and I had this thirty-two-inch gong which really 'spoke' when I hit it, and then the arrangement went on for another half chorus." "We had a very difficult ending on the thing, and finally we made one take, and there was a pause there after the gong," Skeets Herfurt said. "However, when we got to the gong, Billy just kind of waved his hands to signal 'Don't say anything.' And instead of going on, Frank put on his hat and threw his coat over his shoulder, like he does, and walked out of the studio!" Herfert continued, "We all laughed like mad. We said, 'What's happening? Is Frank going to come back and do it again?' No, that was the way they put it out." May much preferred Sinatra's spontaneous ending, using it as if to acknowledge, "You're a better man than I am, Francis A." Sinatra memorably sang the arrangement on a May 1958 episode of his ABC-TV series, and on this occasion, guest Ella Fitzgerald took it upon herself to sing the last line of the song, "out of China, 'cross the bay."

Drummer Alvin Stoller offered another explanation—not corroborated by others at the session—as to why "Mandalay" ends so abruptly, namely that May might not have actually had time to finish the ending. "I tended to procrastinate," May told me, in a characteristic understatement. Paul Weston once joked that May was a very conscientious worker; he would always be sure to *start* working on his arrangements at least three hours before every session. "Then he'd take whatever he had to the session and start recording, start the band, and continue to score from the podium. Meanwhile, these little people would be scrambling up the stairs to the copyist with two score pages at a time. But he always finished, and the arrangements were always great." (Both May and Weston might have cut him a little slack; it's not like May was goofing off, rather he was constantly writing and trying to keep up with his enormous workload. For all the major orchestrators of the era, work was a constant case of triage.)

---

* In the May 1, 1958, issue of *Down Beat*, columnist "George Crater" (a nom de plume for Ed Sherman) opined, "I note with some amusement that the Rudyard Kipling estate has forbidden [the] British release of Frank Sinatra's 'On the Road to Mandalay'; Capitol is substituting another track for it. How about 'Yankee Doodle'?"

"If the session was at eight," Alan Livingston elaborated, "a few minutes after eight, Billy would come in with a copyist behind him, still copying, literally, at the session. If we had four sides to do, as usual, the first three would be done, but the copyist was still doing the last one." Sinatra amplified, "With Billy, you don't get the copies of the next number until you've finished the one before." Ted Nash added, "We'd get through one tune and bring out the next one. It wouldn't be finished, but we had to get it down. So he'd have to half-arrange the thing out of his head. He'd start assigning notes. 'All right, third alto take this note and go up half a tone.' And he'd assign notes to all the guys in the band. And sure enough, he'd get the date done somehow, but it got pretty hairy!"

As if recording so much weren't enough, at the time of *Come Fly with Me,* May was also handling the "cues and bridges" every week for the last great original radio comedy series, *The Stan Freberg Show.* "Billy May's the only man I ever knew who could conduct a full orchestra and chorus while he was stone drunk," claimed Freberg collaborator (and cartoon voice artist) Daws Butler. "He could hardly stand up, but he never missed a beat." Said Frank Flynn, "I remember one afternoon when we were rehearsing with Stan and we were going to work with Frank that night." Recalling the circumstances under which May arranged the title track, "Come Fly with Me," with its remarkable taxiing-down-the-runway intro, Flynn continued, "I can remember Billy saying, 'Geez, I still have to write two arrangements for the date tonight!' This was at four in the afternoon, and we were going to work at eight that night."

But tall tales of May's larger-than-life antics should not detract from his musicianship; it's to his credit that he could behave so extravagantly and still be regarded as a consummate professional. "Billy May was the most *meticulous* of arrangers," stressed Eleanor Slatkin. "When you looked at his manuscripts, it was as if they were *printed,* they were so gorgeous. He might have acted sort of, well, carefree, but when it came to the music, he was a perfectionist."

Nelson Riddle remained Sinatra's "point man" for bread-and-butter projects, like the bulk of his Capitol singles, but by the mid-1950s Billy May had already developed a reputation as the go-to guy for duets: Nat King Cole and Dean Martin; Bobby Darin and Johnny Mercer; Crosby with Clooney or with Louis Armstrong; and Sinatra with Keely Smith, on a pair of Cahn–Van Heusen titles, "Nothing in Common" and "How Are Ya' Fixed for Love?," in 1958. (May would later reprise the role of duets master on some key projects in 1962 and 1963, about which later.)

By the end of 1958, Sinatra and May were back at the Capitol studio, working on a follow-up to *Come Fly with Me.* "That first album was so successful, we did a second one," said May. Returning to Sinatra's metaphor of the Billy May style as the equivalent of a faceful of ice water, *Come Dance with Me!* resounds as their splashiest effort ever. Whereas *Come Fly with Me* is somewhat frivolous, what with all the comic mock-exotica, *Come Dance with Me!* is leaner and meaner; this is Sinatra's most straight-ahead collection of, as the back-cover copy promises, "vocals that dance." The first completely stringless Sinatra set since *Swing Easy!*, *Come Dance* is so intense in its devotion to hardcore super-swing that it practically becomes ascetic. This is a set in which the swinging beat is everything, and it's to Sinatra's credit that he can tell a rather complicated narrative, as on "Dancing in the Dark" (which even includes the verse, which he doubtlessly learned from Bing Crosby) and still keep the beat going.

As with *Come Fly with Me* and *Only the Lonely*, Sinatra came up with the concept for the album as well as the title, then commissioned Sammy and Jimmy to write the title song. The title songs, as Cahn told me, practically wrote themselves. "'Come Fly with Me,' easy. 'It's Nice to Go Trav'ling' [the closer on *Come Fly*], easy. 'Come Dance with Me,' easy. We get to the closing song of *Come Dance with Me!*, and Van Heusen and I couldn't think of a song about dancing that Irving Berlin hadn't already thought of! He covered all the bases of dancing, has he not? 'Cheek to Cheek' [also in *Come Dance with Me!*], 'Change Partners,' 'Let's Face the Music and Dance.'" (The bulk of these had derived from Berlin's long association with Fred Astaire; Sinatra had already recorded Berlin's Astaire number "It Only Happens When I Dance with You" in 1948.)

Thus, Sammy and Jimmy were stuck for an idea. "Sinatra is used to me coming back the next day with whatever song he asks for. When he doesn't hear from us, he's on the phone: 'Hey, where's that last song?' I remember; I turned to Van Heusen and said, 'Hey, let me ask you a question. Has there ever been a "Last Dance"?' Van Heusen says, 'Gee, I don't know.' We call ASCAP. There's a 'Save the Last Dance for Me' [a 1931 waltz and later a 1960 R&B hit by the Drifters] but no 'Last Dance.' Well, we wrote that song as fast as you can speak."

Cahn also recalled that at the date he suggested a memorable Sinatraism, encouraging the singer to stress "when *will* we leave / but *till* we leave" in the last chorus. It marks one of those occasional cases when Sinatra accentuates a syllable that doesn't necessarily mean anything to the lyric but does wonders for the melody, and thereby further sparks the whole piece.

At once taut with tension and swingingly relaxed, *Come Dance with Me!* includes other notable dance-directed ditties, such as Arthur Schwartz's masterful "Dancing in the Dark" (Sinatra even swings the verse) and "I Could

Have Danced All Night." The nineteen-piece orchestra suggests any one of the powerhouse big bands, that, as Vachel Lindsay might have put it, bellowed and gored in the WWII era, with May's sidemen focusing all their energies on spotlighting the singer. Sinatra strikes a perfect balance between his kinder, gentler approach of the 1940s and his more hostile, antisocial sound of the '60s onward. As any credible big-band musician or actor knows, making your entrance properly is half the battle. Sinatra is never more exhilarating than when he returns for his outchorus, especially on "Too Close for Comfort" and "Baubles, Bangles, and [Cool, Cool] Beads" where he reenters during a rest just a microbeat before the orchestra.

When Billy May blasted the unnamed conductor who pissed him off, one of the charges he levelled was that this "kid" had never been with a band. A legitimate criticism. Both May and Sinatra had, and the experience shows. More than any other album, *Come Dance with Me!* springs from Sinatra's ambition to reinvent the swing era in his own image and improve it, doing what big bands were supposed to do—providing a swinging beat for dancers—and with a romantic aspect as well. Sinatra is revisiting what he achieved with James and Dorsey (and May with Barnet and Miller) and moving beyond it—this is what big bands would sound like in some alternate reality where they had never been taxed out of existence by the government and then usurped by rock 'n' roll.

As with *Songs for Swingin' Lovers!* and *A Swingin' Affair!*, the idea was that the swinging elements and the sentimental ones would not cancel each other out. As Cahn's lyric rightfully inquires, "For what is dancing, but making love, set to music playing?" The spirit of Count Basie hovers over the proceedings: in Sinatra's second chorus, he opens in an impish Frankish manner by singing "Come on Cutes / Put on your Basie boots / And come dance with me." A few months later, when Oscar Peterson recorded his homage to the Chairman, *A Jazz Portrait of Frank Sinatra*, he opened his version of this song by annexing Basie's familiar introduction to his theme, "One O'Clock Jump."

Basie also resonates throughout "Baubles, Bangles, and Beads," the latest in a long line of transformations for that tune. It had begun life in Saint Petersburg, Russia, in 1881 as part of the String Quartet No. 2 (second theme of the second movement) by Alexander Borodin. Robert Wright and George Forrest adapted this waltz theme into "Baubles, Bangles, and Beads," one of the major love songs of their 1953 hit Broadway musical *Kismet*. The most radical reinvention came five years later when Sinatra and May reconfigured the melody from 3/4 to 4/4 swing time; Sinatra swings it with an especially playful sense of abandon, as in the second chorus when he interjects, "*you're gonna* make somebody dream so"—but especially so in the coda, wherein he and May take what is essentially the famous three-note Basie ending tag and outfit it with the words, "Cool—cool—beads!"

As if to prove that there's more to jazz than soloing, the only notable individual excursion in all twelves songs is a brief break for Bill Miller in "Day In, Day Out" (Sinatra's third recording of the tune for Capitol). The one musician whose presence can be heard and felt day in and day out throughout the album is Alvin Stoller, who enjoyed the distinction of being not only Sinatra's and May's preferred percussionist but the most in-demand drummer of the great years of the Hollywood pop and jazz recording boom. Born in 1925, Stoller pounded tubs for at least a dozen major bands in the late swing era, earning his early rep with Benny Goodman and Charlie Spivak (where he first worked with Nelson Riddle). One of Buddy Rich's closest friends and disciples, Stoller proved himself a contender in 1945 when he credibly stepped into Rich's unfillable shoes in Tommy Dorsey's orchestra.

Leaving TD in 1947, Stoller freelanced around New York with big bands at the city's movie and vaudeville theaters and with dozens of variously sized units on Fifty-Second Street. He first played for Sinatra (as well as for the supporting act, the Will Mastin Trio with Sammy Davis Jr.) at the Capitol Theatre, circa 1948, and first recorded with him at the infamous penultimate Columbia date of June 1952. By that time Stoller had moved to Los Angeles, where he found more work than he could handle in the studios. Initially, both Sinatra and jazz producer Norman Granz seem to have cast Stoller in the same role that Dorsey assigned him—as a more available and less pugnacious Buddy Rich. "Alvin even looked like Buddy for a while," affirmed Mel Tormé. In fact, when Rich himself was in need of a drummer to play behind him on his album *Buddy Rich Just Sings*, Stoller was the one who got the call.

Within a short time, however, Stoller had amply proved he had a style of his own, a way of propelling a big band with terrific power yet with a beat that was always flexible and loose. Considering himself more of a studio player than a jazz musician, Stoller practically lived in the studios for several decades, playing for everyone from Billie Holiday and Bing Crosby to the soundtrack for *West Side Story*. Stoller was inevitably the first drummer Sinatra, May, and Riddle called when they had a date coming; May in particular all but refused to record if Stoller wasn't available. Early on, May also cast Stoller as an anemic "vocalist" on "The Dixieland Band" and "Fat Man Boogie" (where he sarcastically squeaks, "Eddie Condon?") for his Billy May Orchestra. In 1957, May paid tribute to Stoller by writing an orchestral showcase for the drummer (somewhat inspired by "The Hawk Talks" by Duke Ellington and Louis Bellson), titled "Brushed Off."

Unfortunately for Sinatra, Stoller was too comfortable in the studios to take the road. When Stoller was called back East to attend his father's funeral during the *Swingin' Lovers* sessions, he recommended Irv Cottler as his substitute. May and Riddle also used Cottler when Stoller was unavailable. "Irv was a fine time drummer, but he really had no technique," Bill Miller explained. "He could do a two-bar fill great, maybe four. Beyond that, forget about it. He just didn't have the chops. Not like Alvin. That's why Frank used Al on almost all of the albums."

In *Come Dance with Me!*, Stoller decorates Sinatra's and May's work with brilliant splashes of rhythmic color throughout and no end of rimshots on precisely apropos afterbeats (as on the triple repeat of "Something's Gotta Give"). The drummer rated both May and Riddle as masters of writing for percussion. He gave Riddle props for being smart enough to write "just a very passive type of drum part," because he trusted Stoller to come up with something better than anything he could think of. "Billy was just the opposite," fully annotating a percussion part with every last little figure he wanted, all of which were flawless. "Billy has in his head what he wants on paper, and you just play that," Richards elaborated. "In fact, Billy would start yelling, 'That's not in there! What're you doing?' I learned real early not to mess with Billy's music."

*Come Dance with Me!* never had the traction of its predecessor, *Come Fly with Me*. In later years, Sinatra would continually reprise many of the charts from *Come Fly*, including the title number, and interestingly enough, many of the ballads, like the ones about New York, Paris, and especially, Vermont. Contrastingly, he seems to have rarely ever sung anything from *Come Dance* again, but just the same it's a very moving album—in multiple senses of the word. It achieves its goal of "vocals that dance" more successfully than any other project.

Alvin Stoller shines particularly brightly on "Saturday Night (Is the Loneliest Night of the Week)" (on *Come Dance*), a tune that offered Sinatra a chance to improve on his 1944 hit; in the process the singer switched arrangers from one Stordahl deputy, George Siravo, to another, Henry "Heinie" Beau (1911–1987). By 1958, Beau had become May's and Paul Weston's most reliable aide-de-camp, writing three of the charts on *Come Dance*. Unlike nearly all of Sinatra's regular orchestrators, Beau was as capable an instrumentalist as he was an arranger, and he typically exploited both skills by including spots for his solo clarinet in many a Sinatra chart of the 1940s. Beau is probably the only arranger to work continually with Sinatra from the Dorsey days through the Reprise era. "Whenever Paul or I would get stuck, Heinie would help us out," said May. "Heinie Beau was a very gifted man—and fast," recalled trumpeter Zeke Zarchy. "You needed something done quick, and he'd have it." May added that "Heinie worked for both Paul and myself, so he could imitate either one of us. He wrote like me because that's what I wanted."

Beau was also responsible for much of Sinatra's final two Capitol albums, both from 1961: *Come Swing with Me!* (conducted by Billy May), on which he wrote seven of the twelve charts, and *Point of No Return* (conducted by Axel Stordahl), for which he wrote three. These were the two albums that the singer made to fulfill his contractual obligation to Capitol Records, and Beau's services were required because the idea was, more than ever, to get them finished as quickly as possible. May was especially busy in 1961: in that year, he worked on Ella Fitzgerald's *Harold Arlen Songbook*, *Stan Freberg Presents the United States of America*, *Polynesian Fantasy* by the Out-Islanders, *Shall We Swing?* by Glen Gray and the Casa Loma Orchestra, *Horn A-Plenty* with Al Hirt, *The Invitations* (a Liberty album by a group that May described as "three mandolin players who couldn't read!"), Ethel Merman's *Merman . . . Her Greatest!* (for Reprise), Nat King Cole's classic *Let's Face the Music!*, and Vic Damone's *Strange Enchantment*—and that's in addition to scoring numerous television series (*Naked City, Acapulco*) and movies, such as Sinatra's *Sergeants 3*—as well as two albums with Sinatra.

The last of the three Sinatra-May albums for Capitol, *Come Swing with Me!* relaxes from the almost tyrannically tight tempi of *Come Dance*, giving May a chance to draw on his roots in the Sy Oliver–Jimmie Lunceford tradition. Sinatra and May not only include Oliver's original "Yes, Indeed!" but directly quote from Oliver's iconic treatment of "On the Sunny Side of the Street" for Tommy Dorsey. (Coincidentally, on the very same days that Sinatra was recording *Come Swing* for Capitol, he was also taping *I Remember Tommy* for Reprise with Oliver himself.)

*Come Swing with Me!* had its roots in May's very successful Capitol album of 1958, *Billy May's Big Fat Brass*. This recording was a brilliant example of technological and musical innovation inspiring each other. May devised a strikingly original ensemble of six trumpets, four trombones, five French horns, and two tubas, plus an expanded rhythm section with piano, guitar, bass, drums and two additional percussionists, plus harp. The idea was that there were no saxophones or strings, but rather that they divided the brass ensemble into two distinct halves, i.e., so many trumpets, trombones, horns, and tuba on each side, and had them play against each other in a way that showed off the capabilities of the new stereo recording process, in titles like "Ping Pong." (The album also included "Solving the Riddle," May's homage to his colleague, Nelson.) Even the cover was ingenious: a cartoon depicting the corpulent conductor carrying two big armfuls of brass implements.

"Frank heard the *Brass* album and mentioned that he'd like to do an album using that sound," said Billy. Sinatra wanted to produce this album for his new label, Reprise Records, but Capitol, who had released the original *Big Fat Brass*, claimed it was rightfully theirs; since Sinatra still owed them an album, he agreed to let them have this one. The idea was to reuse the same double–brass band technique and also employ the stereo effects to the max. Said May, "That's one of the things that Frank and Capitol agreed on."

Sinatra and the label agreed on very little at this time. Where Sinatra had initially been very keen to make this album, he was less than pleased that the now-despised Capitol would receive the fruits of his labor. Thus he decided that the tune stack of the project would consist primarily of tunes that he had previously recorded in the 1940s for Columbia Records; of the twelve songs on the album, only five were Sinatra "virgins."

"We went through [the repertory] together, and Frank said, 'These bastards want me to do these standards.'" May reported, "He said, 'I don't know what to do with "Sunny Side of the Street." I don't know how to make it.' He realized that I had the same problems he did, and he was right. What are you going to do with 'Black Magic'? Frank had been singing that son-of-a-bitch for twenty years. What more could we do with it? That was the attitude he and I both had with that album."

May contended that the album was also not helped by Sinatra's determination to get everything done as quickly as possible. "He just wanted to get the sides in," said May. "He didn't spend any extra time on them, but we just ran everything down and got them in as fast as we could. He sang everything at least twice, and there were no deliberate problems one way or the other. I mean, we were aware that he was pissed off at Capitol, and everybody in the studio was trying to be nice to him."

On one level, this was an ambitious undertaking—May's *Big Fat Brass* format was too unconventional to ever become overused or trite—for instance, there's a harp break on "Day by Day" right where we least expect it, and "American Beauty Rose" gleefully but artfully contrasts the tubas, the lowest instrument in the orchestra, with the highest, the tinkly-tinkly plinks of the celeste. But at the same time, even without May's testimony, one can tell that this is a casual effort for Sinatra, and here it works to everyone's advantage. In spite of himself, and in spite of his feelings toward Capitol Records, he's actually having a good time—and thus the listener does as well. Far from being the angst-ridden product of precarious artist-label relations, *Come Swing with Me!* amounts to one of the happiest productions of the entire Sinatra canon. On the gospel-infused, "Yes Indeed!," Sinatra fairly brims with joy and enthusiasm—more so than on most of *I Remember Tommy*, thank you very much.

As an arranger, May limits himself to two textures, brass and rhythm, and, naturally, two channels, left and right, but he beefs up both sections, using no less than nine trumpets (including such brass athletes as Mannie Klein, Conrad Gozzo, Johnny Best, and Zeke Zarchy), seven trombones, and a quartet of French horns. This latter foursome is usually in the deep background but is audibly prominent as a section on "American Beauty Rose."

"Those albums became a kind of a tour de force among brass players," French hornist John Cave recalled, referring to *Big Fat Brass* and *Come Swing with Me!* "Considering the type of music and the way it was aimed for the ceiling, it was amazing that you could get four horn players who could play it! And do it in unison. I don't think the horns missed a thing in the whole album, and that's very unusual, too." Turning to the rhythm section, May throws in a harp, used strictly as a big guitar for timekeeping purposes, as well as three members of the vibe family and a harpsichord for a one-bar break on "American Beauty Rose." In addition to using the reliable Joe Comfort's string bass, May employs a tuba as a brass bass, so even the rhythmic functions of each orchestration seem to brag in brass.

May was not necessarily interested in dividing his sounds by section for the stereo separation, although the trumpets and trombones do battle beautifully in the Sy Oliver–inspired intro to "On the Sunny Side of the Street." More often, he breaks the trumpets all by themselves into high and low subsections and has those two teams challenge each other, as in "Paper Doll." Although his distinctive saxes, slurping or otherwise, were not invited to the party, his patented device of punctuating brass bleats with xylophone plinks has rarely been more effective. "Having the vibes play the lead with the brass section really put the cutting, percussive edge on the brass," said Emil Richards. In addition to making the brass sound brassier, "it also punctuates the staccatoness of the rhythm and brings out the top line of everything much better. Billy utilized that a lot, and I used to love it because it gave me nice lines to play with the brass." This is heavy metal for real.

Sinatra continues to use his signature vocal devices beautifully, as well as inventing new ones. There's the pause between the dehyphenated "you" and "are the lover" on this definitive four-minute "That Old Black Magic," and his unexpected swoop downward on "I would die" in "Lover," as well as that song's amazingly easy sounding final three notes. *Come Swing with Me!* is one of the few Sinatra albums on which Cole Porter is not represented, but we might describe it as a breathtaking display of, to borrow a phrase from his *Silk Stockings,* "glorious Technicolor and stereophonic sound."

Although Sinatra couldn't land the May brass project for his own label, he decided to split the difference into two subsequent albums for Reprise: an all-new May set, taped only two months later, in May 1961; and *Sinatra and Swingin' Brass* with Neal Hefti in 1962. Thus there were two Sinatra-May albums recorded in 1961, the Capitol album in March and the Reprise album only two months later in May; and when the Capitol album was set for release in July, Sinatra made sure that his Reprise album would also be released in that same month.

The Sinatra-May Reprise album—actually only the second Sinatra LP for the new company—bears a photo on its cover of the blue-eyed one popping through a pair of double doors, which suggests swinging both as in saloon doors and as in Billy May. Even the album's title is as baffling as the ending of Mandalay. Originally issued as *Swing Along with Me* (Reprise FS-1002), that title was first bannered on the front and the back covers (next to a shot of Sinatra making like Arnold Palmer—yet another kind of swinging). Then Capitol complained to a judge that this title came too close for comfort to their own release, *Come Swing with Me!*; as a result, on later pressings of FS-1002, the title was changed to *Sinatra Swings*. (The 1990 CD edition is identified as *Swing Along with Me* on the front and *Sinatra Swings* on the back, both spines, and disc label.)

This fourth Sinatra-May meeting is also their last "classic" album together—their future team-ups would be on projects (the Ellington album and the *Trilogy* project) with a definite agenda. Whatever we choose to call Sinatra-May number four, the album belongs to the same mindset as the three 1956–61 Capitol collaborations. The tune stack ranges from songs that Sinatra would have heard in his youth—songs that he might have yelped atop his father's bar as a toddler (including the turn-of-the-century "The Curse of an Aching Heart," which he had sung with the Hoboken Four in 1935)—to a few souvenirs of the swing era and the 1940s (the latest being the 1949 "Don't Cry, Joe" by Chicago clarinet master Joe Marsala).

The highpoints of the album are many, ranging from exotica that is even better than anything on *Come Fly with Me* ("Granada" and "Moonlight on the Ganges") to lean-and-mean swingers à la *Come Dance with Me!* To clarify, everything on the disc swings just as much as both titles promise, whether the tempo is medium ("Have You Met Miss Jones?") or up ("I Never Knew"). The most danceable item may be the swing era favorite "It's a Wonderful World," from the band book of Jan Savitt; although that Philadelphia-based unit was famous for a very rigid "shuffle rhythm," May's interpretation (he had previously arranged the same number for Barnet in 1939) is in a more loosely-swinging 4/4.

Another swing standard, Benny Goodman's "Don't Be That Way" ends surprisingly abruptly, an apparent twist on the un-ending of "Mandalay." There are also two tunes that might be defined as camp classics, "The Curse of an Aching Heart" and "Please Don't Talk About Me When I'm Gone." While these had already been saved, as Bing Crosby would say, from "tired tenors at tea parties" by Fats Waller and Billie Holiday, respectively, Sinatra and May swing them even more righteously and rhythmically than ever before. The singer is especially playful in the second chorus of "Please Don't Talk About Me When I'm Gone," swimming against the rhythmic currents and jumping on and off the beat with uncommon vigor.

The saxophones are back on all twelve tunes, and for the final session, the strings—not heard on a Sinatra-May date since 1956—return. In many ways, this is the most remarkable session of the three: we get one exceptionally bluesy ballad, his superior remake of the 1949 "Don't Cry, Joe" (officially titled "Don't Cry, Joe (Let Her Go, Let Her Go, Let Her Go)" and those two new "travel" pieces, "Ganges" and "Granada," both of which amount to Sinatra spectaculars: "Granada" is the latest *Cucaracha* conquest, in the tradition of "South of the Border," and "Moonlight on the Ganges" takes him back to the pagoda of "Mandalay."

"Moonlight on the Ganges" is a slice of Tin Pan Alley exotica from 1926 that jazz musicians adopted and raised as their own, including Glenn Miller in 1935, Benny Goodman and Eddie Sauter in 1940, and Tommy Dorsey and Sy Oliver in 1942, where Sinatra most likely first encountered it. Like "South of the Border," this is still another tale of loving and leaving a non-Western babe, identified in the text as "my little Hindu." Like an occident guide in pith helmet and jodhpurs, Sinatra guides us through an extravaganza of Far Eastern percussion.

As Sinatra observed (in a 1981 interview), "Billy May almost always uses the extra percussion, like vibraphones, xylophones, bells, and chimes and all that jazz." For "Ganges" (which is highly inspired by the 1952 Sauter-Finegan version), contractor Bill Miller must have put the call out to every tub-thumper in the L.A. union to recruit an entire section of gongs, chimes, vibes, xylophones, kettle drums, woodblocks, and fine Oriental bric-a-brac. May makes the brass and strings dance around these various tchotchkes with a seven-veiled sense of mystery and intrigue: Marlene Dietrich in a gorilla suit. Never has Sinatra's technique of soaring over the ground beat of his accompaniment taken him so far aloft—nor has it ever before seemed so necessary for him to stay in the sky above rather than the polyrhythmic Persian market below.

Both pieces are as much showcases for Sinatra's still-evolving vocal techniques as well as May's bag of tricks. Sinatra is surrounded with Latin percussion on "Granada," as once again the hard-swinging and frivolously exotic components of the performance alternately complement and compete with one another, even as the soft strings chase around the blaring trumpets and clamoring castanets. Written in 1932, this piece by Agustín Lara (author of the somewhat less dramatic "You Belong to My Heart") served as a vehicle for everyone from Deanna Durbin to Bing Crosby but was mainly identified with quasioperatic Latin belters like Carlos Ramírez. Frankie Laine delivered a particularly dramatic rendition, in which he vehemently snarled out his consonants as if he were whipping a galley slave; later, in the 1960s, "Granada" became, courtesy of Bill Holman, an exhibition piece for big-band orchestral fireworks for Stan Kenton.

Only Sinatra and May realized that only by treating "Granada" with an arch sense of humor did more extreme aspects become palatable. (Two different edits of the track have been issued: the longer cut, at 3:38, is even more fun than the shorter edit, at 2:45.) Sinatra enters theatrically; then, by the end of the bridge, just when the pot of chili threatens to explode, May releases a little steam heat with smooth and swinging string passages: from toreador to cuspidor. Sinatra puts just the right extra emphasis on the "d" sound in "snow-clad" so that it resonates warmly in our ear, and then lightly and musically syncopates the musical term habanera with a gentle, Crosbyesque trill. May had cha-cha-chas on his brain thanks to a recent Capitol album he had done of big-band themes played in mock-mambo style. So to spin a fresh variation on the climactic choir in "South of the Border," May closes "Granada" with the sidemen cha-cha-chanting that phrase. (A slightly less urgent unissued alternate take has Sinatra capping the chart with an "*Olé!*" He performed a quite possibly even stronger one-chorus version as part of his 1966 TV special, *A Man and his Music, Part II*, which he concludes by chanting his "cha-cha-cha!")

*Swing Along with Me* reaches a boil with "You're Nobody till Somebody Loves You." Although from the string session, this number, written and introduced by sweet bandleader Russ Morgan in 1944 and thoroughly convincingly put over by the King Cole Trio the following year, strikes the listener—almost literally—as the hardest-hitting tune on the set. "You're Nobody" starts excitingly, with a left-field string introduction and Sinatra delivering a straight, swinging chorus, loping almost tenderly behind the beat and backed by a light string shimmer. Bill Miller eases into the turnaround (change of choruses) with gentle, Basie-style tinkling.

The second thirty-two bars get louder, forsaking the fiddles, although where the traditional second chorus of a number like *Swing Along*'s "I Never Knew" is wilder and jazzier, pregnant with unexpected pauses, here the second time around is sharper and more clearly focused. Sinatra concludes this chorus by repeating the penultimate phrase twice, as if he were going to end it here, but surprises us by swinging into, lo and behold, a full third chorus. He reaches for a long note in the last "A" section ("*above*") and then winds up and throws as if he were Dizzy Dean, the strings adding to the intensity by jumping back in a reaffirming choir in the last few bars. This is what one Sinatra sideman meant when he compared The Voice's voice and attack to "a big, strong swinging horn."

*Swing Along with Me/Sinatra Swings* worked out so well that it outfoxed itself: it was so good, that there was no topping it, and satisfied whatever need there was for a classic Sinatra-May album in the Reprise catalog. In the first few years of the new operation, Sinatra concentrated on new collaborators, such as Johnny Mandel, Neal Hefti, Robert Farnon, and others. (Reprise Records, however, kept May busy with, among other things, an album with Ethel Merman.) Between 1961 and 1967, Sinatra and May's paths occasionally intercepted; he would rerecord May's classic chart on "Come Fly with Me" several times (for his musical autobiography, the 1965 *A Man and His Music* set; live at the Sands with Count Basie; and again in 1993 for *Duets II*) and he would continue to sing "Moonlight in Vermont" for the rest of his life; it was one of his favorite ballads.

In the early days of Reprise—which coincide closely with the Kennedy administration—May was unofficially anointed as the official musical director for the Rat Pack, even as Sammy Cahn and Jimmy Van Heusen were the group's official scribes and in-house songwriters. This was primarily due to May's gift scoring duos and trios (as Bing Crosby, among many others, had already taken advantage of) but also, one suspects, because May was very much the fun-loving and heck-raising type (more so than the stone-faced Nelson), even, as Sinatra acknowledged, "when he was sober."

In the early Reprise era there were a few oddball Sinatra-May singles, generally with a film connection. In March 1962 (at the same date as his final Capitol track, "I Gotta Right to Sing the Blues," arranged by Skip Martin), he attempted two May/Cahn/Van Heusen pieces, "The Boys' Night Out" and "Cathy"; the latter only got as far as an orchestral track. "Pass Me By," which actually was completed and issued on a 1964 Reprise single, was a May chart from a singles session in 1964, in which the other two tunes were arranged by Riddle. "Pass Me By" is an oddity, a Cy Coleman–Carolyn Leigh song from the film *Father Goose* (the 1964 comedy starred Cary Grant and Leslie Caron) written as a virtual paraphrase of their jaunty Broadway march "Hey, Look Me Over" (from 1960's *Wildcat*) with cockneyisms borrowed from "I've Got a Lovely Bunch of Coconuts." This circus parade piece, complete with Disneyland-style mixed chorus, is as corny as Kansas in August, and highly agreeably so. (An outtake survives in which the singer chants, "If you don't drink my whiskey, pass me by!" Peggy Lee was able to get more of a swinging beat in her Capitol recording, although that was also done as a parade march.)

Alas, it's a shame that "Boys' Night Out" was never heard at all until the 1995 *Complete Reprise* "suitcase." (Patti Page wound up singing it over the titles of said movie, the 1962 sex comedy *Boys' Night Out.*) Sinatra's vocal is spirited, to say the least, and May's characteristically audacious arrangement includes such irreverent asides as a police whistle and brief quotes from "Entrance of the Gladiators" (the original circus parade march) and Stan Kenton's *Artistry in Rhythm.* In lines like "Hey there mister / Build a fence around your sister / It's the boys' night out," Cahn's lyrics captured the ethos of the Rat Pack better than anyone: three middle-aged frat boys who'd never gone beyond high school but who were showing the whole world how to have grown-up fun.

May and Cahn were at the heart of the Rat Pack's most iconic single, a 1962 pairing of two sides starring Sammy Davis Jr.: "Me and My Shadow" by Davis and Sinatra, and "Sam's Song" by Davis and Dean Martin, both of which were considerably buttressed by amiably Vegas-style special-materials lyrics by Cahn. "Shadow" was a particularly incisive song choice for the era of Kennedy and King: the 1927 song exemplified a very specific racist vaudeville trope, in which a white entertainer would sing and dance a melancholy soft-shoe while being "shadowed" by a mute black dancer. This was precisely what Ralph Ellison was talking about in *Invisible Man*: the idea that the humanity of the African American people is never seen. In this old vaudeville bit, black people are, very literally, shadows. While Judy Garland had recorded the definitive ballad interpretation (courtesy Gordon Jenkins, on her 1957 album *Alone*), Sinatra and Davis (abetted by May and Cahn) turn the stereotypes around on their ear. Rather than being about a lonely Caucasian and his black shadow, in this version the two men are equals—they hit the town and do all the night spots together, proud and unashamed, even as Sinatra continued his one-man campaign of desegregation among clubs and hotels in New York or Vegas or wherever he happened to be. This is a boys' night out with a vengeance, as well as with a larger social purpose.

The "Shadow" and "Sam's Song" singles belong to the age of the Reprise Repertory Theater, a four-album series from 1963 in which May and Riddle shined equally as arranger-conductors. May was responsible for the two most exciting trio performances in all of Rat Packery: "We Open in Venice" from *Kiss Me Kate,* with Sinatra, Martin, and Davis; and "The Oldest Established" from *Guys and Dolls,* with Sinatra, Martin, and Bing Crosby. May also arranged the single best-remembered number in the whole project, Sinatra's solo take on "Luck Be a Lady."

Years later, during his concertizing period, Sinatra said often enough that when producer Sam Goldwyn cast him for the 1955 technicolor adaptation of *Guys and Dolls*, he assumed that he would play the high-rolling, high-glam gambler Sky Masterson. Even so, Sinatra did a brilliant job as Nathan Detroit, playing him as a variation on Angelo Maggio, the lovable loser who won him the Academy Award in *From Here to Eternity*. Still, the notion that he was cast as a schlemiel rather than a romantic leading man continued to rankle him, and in 1963 he settled that old score in two ways: first by grabbing off Sky Masterson's best songs for himself in a cast-album production of *Guys and Dolls*; and second by spearheading his own *Guys and Dolls* cinematic variation titled *Robin and the 7 Hoods*, with the Rat Pack as singing gangsters and Sammy and Jimmy handling the score.

The May-Sinatra "Luck Be a Lady" may be the single most celebrated product of their collaboration, one that Sinatra continued to sing for the remaining thirty years of his career, on virtually every concert going forward. (As with "Granada," there's a particularly compelling television performance on the 1966 *A Man and his Music Part II* special.) Sinatra and May fit together perfectly here, in terms of both music and attitude—Sinatra's swaggeringly jocular embodiment of a gambler's flamboyance and the tight, even swing of May's streamlined aggregation. May had originally arranged the piece at a pace closer to the breakneck speed that Robert Alda and Marlon Brando carried off in the Broadway and Hollywood productions, but Sinatra suggested that they take it a bit more leisurely. Their reading of "Luck Be a Lady" has since become so definitive that all the original-cast versions now seem ridiculously fast. Frank Loesser wrote the piece to depict smarmy Forty-Second–Streeters bereft of necks shooting craps in a sewer; Sinatra and May transform these Damon Runyan types into smooth-groove Vegas high rollers, complete with glitzy, brightness-at-midnight lighting and gold Visa cards.

And yet for all of his swagger, there's an impassioned, vulnerable side to Sinatra here—May signals this quite literally when he brings in the strings. Confident as he may be, there's no guarantee that luck, in Loesser's brilliant metaphor, will actually treat him like a lady. God knows, plenty of women have walked out on him (Sinatra, or Sky, and Nathan as well). So the piece becomes more like a plea, or even a prayer. Loesser wisely doesn't resolve the question within the number itself: we are not shown the outcome of that all-important roll of the dice until the next scene. Sinatra knew all about luck, what it was like to have it, as well as what it was like to be deserted by this particular lady. Thus, the song ends with the ambiguity that has become

Sinatra's stock in trade: we leave our hero without learning whether luck will play nice with him or if, as is so often the case, she'll be the lady that got away.

In the fall of 1967, either Bill Miller or producer Sonny Burke notified May that Reprise wanted him to serve as musical director for an album that would combine Sinatra with the legendary American composer-bandleader Duke Ellington, which would eventually be released as *Francis A. & Edward K.* May was selected not only for his familiarity with the idiosyncratic voices of both halves of the proposed equation but because of his reputation as a musical mimic. "Billy May can write any way, like anyone," explained trumpeter Zeke Zarchy. "If you say you want a Duke Ellington arrangement or a *this-guy* arrangement, Billy can write like that. But he also can write like himself." (May had previously re-created the sounds of Jimmie Lunceford and Kay Kyser for Capitol and would later rerecord virtually the entire swing era in stereo for Time Life Records.)

The idea of May writing for Ellington was as much a surprise for Sinatra as it was for May. On some level he had been considering a collaboration with Ellington for at least twenty years, and when he began planning the Ellington album in earnest in the early Reprise years, he assumed that Billy Strayhorn, Ellington's composing and arranging partner of twenty-eight years, would handle the orchestrations. But after years of illness, Strayhorn, who was only a month older than Sinatra, died after a long illness on May 31, 1967. (It's been said that Sinatra paid part of his medical expenses.) Plans for the album continued, however, and Sinatra and Burke switched from one Billy to another. Far from resenting being second choice, May remembered, "I felt very flattered that they asked me after Billy died."

May's relationship with Strayhorn, who had also grown up in Pittsburgh, went back even before Strayhorn went to work with Ellington. "I started my professional career at a little place on Station Street in Pittsburgh called Charlie Ray's," Strayhorn once reminisced. "They had a little place upstairs, and the bandstand was about a flight and a half up. Billy May used to come to this place and play trumpet and trombone. He would come up and sit with us in our little nest. We were up above the room in a little bandstand, above the steps. They used to throw people down the steps every night, unruly people."

When May went to work for Charlie Barnet at the end of 1938, he discovered that the leader was such an obsessive Ellington devotee—the most dedicated Ellingtonian that ever was—he could not have learned more about Ellington's music had he apprenticed with the Duke himself. In his two years with Barnet, he scored a number of Ellington items, including "In a Mizz," "Rockin' in Rhythm," "The Sergeant Was Shy," "Ring Dem Bells," and "Merry-Go-Round," that were faithful both to their sources and Barnet's burgeoning style. While with Glenn Miller, May conceived of a brilliantly Millerized treatment of "Take the 'A' Train" that wrapped Strayhorn's melody in Miller's patented clarinet-led reeds.*

"Duke was a big influence on me since the days I was with Barnet," said May. "He was such a pioneer, you know. He really did amazing things. I have records of Duke's from the '30s, and God! They're doing things that some of these modern bop guys are just doing now." In the early 1950s, when he launched the Billy May Orchestra, first in the studios and then on the road, May's primary inspirations were Ellington and the two-beat sound of the then-defunct Jimmie Lunceford band, as masterminded for Lunceford by future Dorsey-Sinatra arranger Sy Oliver. When May later related to Oliver how influential he had been, "Sy told me that Duke was a big influence on him and that he actually got that [Lunceford] sound from Duke. There are some two-beat things that Duke did, and he just didn't follow up on it. But Sy told me that's where he got the idea." The two-beat "All I Need Is the Girl" on *Francis A. & Edward K.* illustrates the myriad connections between the sounds of Ellington, Oliver, and May.

Sinatra first met Ellington in about the spring or summer of 1942. "He was with Tommy Dorsey," Ellington later wrote. "They all came down to the College Inn at the Sherman Hotel in Chicago where we were playing, and I think it was just about the time he was ready to split the Dorsey gig. I could tell that by the way Tommy said goodnight to him!" Always one for fancy handles, Ellington seems to have perpetually referred to the singer as "Francis." Sinatra had also already become close with the blind baritone Al Hibbler, who in May 1943 became the major male vocalist of the Ellington band.

In the fall of 1942, Sinatra and Ellington crossed paths again when the singer, by that time playing as a single, shared a movie theater bill with the Ellington band at the State in Hartford, Connecticut. "I played three days at a theater in Hartford when Ellington was there," Sinatra later recalled, "and believe me, it was one of the biggest kicks of my life." Both were to enjoy major triumphs within a few months, Sinatra at his breakthrough New York Paramount booking that December and Ellington at his premier Carnegie Hall concert a few weeks later.

Ellington and Sinatra probably didn't spend much time together offstage during the Hartford engagement because the composer was furiously strug-

---

* May's arrangement of Irving Berlin's "Say It Isn't So" on the album *Billy May Plays For Fancy Dancin'* detours unexpectedly through the piano solo and countermelody of "'A' Train"; the same album also contains a thoughtful recasting of the Ducal classic "Azure."

gling between shows to finish the forty-five-minute *Black, Brown, and Beige* in time for Carnegie Hall. The film was the horror classic *Cat People,* and Ellington later quipped to aide Stanley Dance that he wasn't sure which had the greater impact on his muse while he wrote this pivotal piece—Sinatra or *Cat People.* When Ellington guested on Sinatra's *Broadway Bandbox* program later in 1943, *BB&B* was a subject of their banter. However, Sinatra and Ellington possibly did work together informally later that year: as Billy Strayhorn remembered (in 1962), Sinatra would occasionally sit in with the Ducal aggregation during their stay at New York's Hurricane Club.

Sinatra's love for Ellington's music was well known, although he rarely attempted to combine the Duke's ideas with his own. Sinatra recorded far fewer songs by Ellington than he did by, say, Walter Donaldson. Only two Ellington tunes appear on the classic Sinatra Capitol albums, "Mood Indigo" on *In the Wee Small Hours* and "I Got It Bad" on *A Swingin' Affair!* In the Reprise period, only "I'm Beginning to See the Light" (like Duke's "I Didn't Know About You," done on an aircheck in the mid-1940s) turns up, on the 1962 *Sinatra and Swingin' Brass.* In 1955, Sinatra and Nelson Riddle also recorded a Capitol single of "How Could You Do a Thing Like That to Me?," a pop tune by Ellingtonian Tyree Glenn based on the melody of the 1947 "Sultry Serenade," which the trombonist had written and performed with Ellington. (On a 1966 television show with Sammy Davis Jr., the two performed a medley that included snatches of "Don't Get Around Much Anymore" and "Take the 'A' Train.")

Alas, Sinatra would never record a Billy Strayhorn song—even though "Something to Live For" or even "'A' Train," as a swinger, would have suited him perfectly. Sinatra did attempt to sing the composer's best-known vocal ballad, "Lush Life," which proved a rare example of Sinatra's reach exceeding his grasp. His plan was, as in so many Sinatra projects, to take it all the way— to include the song in his epic semiclassical ballad album *Only the Lonely* with a masterful arrangement by Riddle.

But then everything went south. This date was already overlong, and Sinatra, always pressing his limits, had a lot of difficult arrangements to learn. Bill Miller, who played a key piano part on the Riddle arrangement of "Lush Life," recalled that "Frank didn't take the trouble to learn it properly." It's worth noting that of all the times we interviewed Bill, and all the songs we asked him about, this was the only time Miller ever accused Sinatra of not being prepared. But there's more to it than that: Riddle conceived of a masterful chart that juxtaposed Miller's deliberately out-of-tune, tinkly piano part against a Coplandesque string section. But heard in the fragment that survives from the session, it just doesn't work for the song—this is a tune in which the simplest treatment, usually just voice and piano, is inevitably the most appropriate.

"It's a rather complicated song, and I think Frank would have been momentarily put off by all the changes that had to go on," said Riddle. "Not that he couldn't have sung it with ease and beautifully had he tried a couple more times." Well, maybe. Strayhorn's words-and-music opus is not a classic Sinatra saloon song the way that "Angel Eyes" and "One for My Baby" are; unlike in the Matt Dennis and Arlen-Mercer laments, the protagonist of "Lush Life" feels sorry for himself in a particularly erudite way. Nat King Cole made a classic record of "Lush Life" (Strayhorn hated the orchestral accompaniment) and Sinatra acolyte Johnny Hartman recorded the version that most people know (with John Coltrane); but every time I listen to the Sinatra fragment, I never feel like this is a lost masterpiece.

On the sole circulating partial take of the three allegedly recorded, Sinatra gets through the out-of-tempo "verse" section but breaks down in the refrain. Clearly, the song isn't working for him, nor he for it. It isn't just the tempo or lack of it, or all the "clydes" (tricky notes) in the piece (the melody is full of the most complicated accidentals in popular music, double sharps and the like); it is simply, as Cole Porter would say, the wrong song in the wrong style. After several attempts to get through it, he knows he's licked. And he makes a joke out of it, going into an imitation of the Kingfish, a figure of fun (so to speak) from the popular radio program *Amos 'n' Andy*. In the Kingfish voice, he announces his resolution to "put that one aside for about a year." Sinatra later told Miller that he had decided to "leave that one for Nat Cole."

Ten years earlier, at his Columbia Records session of November 9, 1947, Sinatra was making small talk with producer George Avakian. Avakian informed Sinatra that Ellington would be recording in the same studio two days later. Sinatra then said something to the effect of "You know, I've always wanted to make a record with Duke." Avakian, a keen fan of both men, summarily brought Sinatra's idea to Manie Sachs, but the A&R chief wasn't particularly interested. "As great as Duke was, he wasn't selling a lot of records for us at that time," said Avakian. "Manie realized that Ellington was important and that he should be on the label, but he didn't give him a lot of attention."

Cut to November 1962. Sinatra is in Northbrook, Illinois, working with Sammy Davis Jr. and Dean Martin (known to posterity as the Rat Pack, even though they were never officially billed by that name) at the Villa Venice. At the same time, the Ellington band, on its never-ending tour, is playing one-nighters in the Midwest. The two converged in Chicago on November 28 at the Ambassador West Hotel; Sinatra and Reprise Records announce the signing of Duke Ellington, whose long-term contract with Columbia Records had expired a few months previously. Not only would Ellington now record exclusively for Reprise, but he would be given license to create an "Ellington Jazz Wing," in which he could sign and produce artists whose work he liked outside of the Ellington fold.

According to most accounts, this was strictly a handshake agreement, and it lasted until mid-1965, when Sinatra's own interest in being a music industry mogul was starting to wane. Yet in that comparatively brief span of time, Ellington himself made nine "Ellington" albums for the company, in addition to those he produced by other artists (famously Bud Powell, Alice Babs, and Dollar Brand aka Abdullah Ibrahim, all recorded in Europe). The day after the press conference, November 29, Ellington launched into a busy season of sixteen studio sessions for Reprise, which continued until February 1963. But the one question that fans of both Ellington and Sinatra wanted to know was when, exactly, would they make an album together? One was announced as early as 1964.

Sinatra had already recorded with a number of Ellingtonians, including Juan Tizol, Willie Smith, and Al Sears. Three of Duke's men appear with Sinatra on the 1946 Metronome All-Stars date: Johnny Hodges, Lawrence Brown, and Harry Carney. One of the first albums to be released on Reprise was *The Warm Moods* (Reprise R2001) by the most iconic of Ellington tenor saxophonists, Ben Webster, who also played on the 1962 *Sinatra and Swingin' Brass,* on which he solos lustfully on "I'm Beginning to See the Light."

The output of Sinatra and Ellington ran along parallel lines when *The Concert Sinatra* and *The Symphonic Ellington* were recorded on two different continents in February 1963. Commercial considerations equally affected both artists, as could be witnessed on releases such as *Sinatra '65* and *Ellington '65,* and on occasions when both were importuned to record Beatles songs. In 1966, Sinatra arranged for Ellington to write the score to his film *Assault on a Queen*—perhaps the only notable aspect of that forgettable thriller.

Sinatra also had a long-standing agenda to work with Billy Strayhorn that extended well before and after the "Lush Life" debacle. According to the composer's biographer, David Hajdu, one of Strayhorn's personal partners remembers numerous calls going back and forth between the two of them during this period. However, Ellington himself was always overly protective of his most crucial collaborator, sometimes in ways that could be construed as furthering his own interests. He soon got wind of Sinatra's offer and squelched it, not by ordering Strayhorn to turn it down, but by overloading him with so much work at this particular point that he could never even begin to consider outside offers.

For Sinatra, there was another route to Strayhorn: his old buddy, singer Al Hibbler, who had left the Ellington organization in 1951 for a successful solo career (and who would become a profound influence on singers as disparate as Della Reese, Ray Charles, Lou Rawls, and even Tony Bennett). After several hit singles and a series of excellent albums for Decca, Hibbler's career was gradually running out of steam by 1960, thanks partially to his breaking from his former manager and partially to his involvement with the civil rights movement. However, Sinatra realized that a new Hibbler album, with state-of-the-art production and ace arrangements (by Gerald Wilson), could have financial as well as musical merit, and personally called Hibbler to suggest such a project in 1961.

And he still wanted Strayhorn. Hibbler remembers, "When I went with Sinatra to Reprise, Frank asked me, 'Can you get Strayhorn?' I said, 'I doubt it, man.' I asked Strayhorn, and Strayhorn went and told Duke." Hibbler continued, "Duke came to me and said, 'Man, I don't appreciate you trying to take my arranger! You took what you could get from me, and now you're tryin' to break up my band!' I said, 'No, I wouldn't do that.'" Still, it was a beautiful album (featuring most of Sinatra's own rhythm section, including Bill Miller, Al Viola, and Joe Comfort), *Al Hibbler Sings the Blues: Monday Every Day*, perhaps the last great recording of his long career. (It includes, along with several Hibbler-Ellington favorites, a harrowing reading of Sinatra's epic torch song, "I'm a Fool to Want You.")

This might have been the incident that provoked Ellington into leaving Reprise in 1965. "They weren't too close, because Duke always accused Frank of trying to take Billy Strayhorn from him," Hibbler told me, "and he accused me of trying to help him." For the remaining nine years of his life, Ellington became a free agent contractually, producing his own sessions (as in effect he always had), and selling the masters to whatever outfit was interested. He would record only one more album for Reprise, and that was *Francis A. & Edward K.*

All this was in the background when Billy May began working on the arrangements for the album in 1967. The process began, as always, by setting the keys with Bill Miller for the eight tunes already selected by Sinatra and producer Sonny Burke. Ellington had a long history of working with worthy star vocalists, famously Bing Crosby in 1932 and in two groundbreaking albums with Rosemary Clooney and Ella Fitzgerald. Both the Clooney and Fitzgerald projects had been songbook albums of all Ellington-Strayhorn compositions, and Ellington had more recently made a glorious, if little known, songbook album with the brilliant Swedish soprano Alice Babs, recorded with Duke himself in Paris in 1963 for Reprise.

In 1967, Sinatra wanted May to provide a bridge between the Ellington universe and his own; thus he chose a mixture of old and new (and largely non-Ellington) songs that belonged in the middle ground. Sinatra rarely chose to duplicate what other singers had done before him and wasn't a great believer in the songbook concept to begin with. (His closest thing to a song-book at that point was the 1967 collaboration with Antônio Carlos Jobim, and even that wasn't all-Jobim.) Among the selections was all of one contemporary hit, Bobby Hebb's "Sunny," and that too is graced lovingly by Harry Carney's endlessly resonant baritone sax lines. Sinatra restricted the tune stack to eight extra-long tracks, leaving plenty of room for the imaginations of both May and the soloists—Johnny Hodges, Cootie Williams, Paul Gonsalves, Lawrence Brown, and the rest—to stretch out.

In late fall 1967, the band was playing through the Pacific Northwest and opened a weeklong engagement at a club called DJs in Seattle on December 1. May and Miller flew in to try out the charts in a rehearsal without Sinatra. "We rehearsed them all afternoon and, Jesus, the rehearsal was terrible," said May. "They were all terrible sight readers in that band. The drummer, Sam Woodyard, couldn't read music at all. But they had a trick where he had to watch one of the saxophone player's feet for when he'd stop playing and when he'd start. So the second time through, the saxophone player would mark his part, and he'd move his foot or something, and that would be the cue for the drummer. It was all shit like that."

Most of the studio men whom Sinatra, May, and Riddle generally worked with had apprenticed in the touring swing bands. Still, in the studios it was just as important to be able to read a piece of music as if it were a newspaper as it was to be able to play with a strong swing feeling, for a Sinatra sideman anyway. However, Ellington's sidemen didn't learn Ellington's music by read-ing it, said May: "They got it by playing every night, and when they got it, it was fine." Many of the finest improvisers couldn't have made the studio grade, reading-wise. Harry Edison was an exception, and he told me that when he first went to work in the studios that in the beginning Riddle was especially generous in coaching him with his sight reading. (Still others were different: Louis Armstrong was highly musically literate, and took great pride in his sight-reading ability.)

"We went through the whole album, we rehearsed it all," May contin-ued. "Duke made a big issue out of saying to me, 'Oh, get the music ready and we'll rehearse it. We'll play these on the job. I'll play Frank's vocal part on the piano.'" May and Miller attended the band's performance that night, and when Ellington began calling May's charts, they assumed he was going to keep his word. "Well, they have two weeks before the session," May recalled thinking as he and Miller flew back to Los Angeles that night. "If they keep playing them every night like that, they're bound to nail 'em, and everything'll be alright."

However, the Ellington organization was not only the greatest conglomeration of pure talent that the jazz world has ever known, it was also a band of prima donnas who could only be held together by the biggest ego of them all. Each of Ellington's major players had the talent, the star power, and the reputation to be a leader in his own right. Cootie Williams and Johnny Hodges had been leading groups of their own for years, and many must have felt that it was only the color of their skins that was keeping them sidemen, virtually anonymous outside of hardcore jazz fans. As Mel Tormé had learned in a disastrous tandem billing at New York's Basin Street East, the Duke and his men typically invested energy only in playing Ellington and Strayhorn's own music. Tormé's and May's accounts agree that the band just didn't care to put any effort into the work of outside arrangers. As May put it, "The older Duke got, the more full of [himself] he became."

Rather than just go into the studio cold, someone had the forethought to schedule a rehearsal—something rarely done in those days—with May and the band on December 8, at the Western Recorders studio, where the album would be taped three days later. It's not known if Sinatra was present, but May was at the podium and Ellington was at the piano. From the first downbeat on, May realized that "they [had] never touched the charts again! They never even looked at 'em after that day." In a 1982 interview with Stanley Dance, May added, "the trumpet section wasn't making it on the session, but it wasn't my place to say so. 'Let's try it again' was all I could keep saying."

The solution was to add trumpeter Al Porcino to the section, a veteran of the big-band era and a master studio player and sight reader. (May added, "It helped a lot when Al Porcino came in and sat back there." May also said that Jimmy Jones, an expert pianist and accompanist known for his long years of touring with both Sarah Vaughan and Ella Fitzgerald, filled in for Duke on much of the album. It seems unlikely that Sinatra would have wanted another pianist besides Bill Miller, but certainly not impossible.)

The two actual sessions were held on December 11 and 12. "I guess it was kind of in doubt as to whether all of the band would show up," engineer Lee Herschberg recalled. "The guys would have been playing the night before, and maybe having a few drinks, or whatever. So the first day was kind of up in the air as to whether we would get anything done or not. I don't think the guys in the band started arriving until about forty-five minutes after the session started."

As it happened, there was an objective observer (and nonparticipant) in the form of Milt Bernhart, who happened to be playing a date in the adjoining studio. "You never saw such completely disconnected people in your life," observed the trombonist. "There was Johnny Hodges and Paul Gonsalves, and they were thinking about what they were going to have for dinner that night—everything else but this. It had reached Frank, too. He wasn't really thrilled. At that point somebody wheeled in his birthday cake. It turned out it was his birthday."

Part of the problem was also Sinatra himself. He was not in his best voice that week and sounds too thin in some spots and overly heavy in others, and he occasionally comes up short in the pitch department (like the somewhat whining last note on "Come Back to Me"). Sinatra doubtless realized he wasn't operating up to his usual technical standards, and if this had been any other occasion, he probably would have postponed the dates. But realizing the impossible logistics of getting both himself and the Ellington band in the same studio at the same time, he decided to go through with it.

He also had the option of recording orchestral tracks for himself to overdub vocals at a later date, but he might have been aware that both the Clooney and Fitzgerald albums with Ellington had been overdubbed, and realized that they suffered because of it. Even though the voice is thin, what is good about the album is the on-the-spot, in-person empathy between Sinatra and the Ellingtonians, in a way that could have been captured only with them all in the same room at the same time. Once the sessions began in earnest, Sinatra, May, Ellington, and Ellington's handful of prima donnas—now with two of the dominant personalities guiding them (three if you count Billy May) put their egos aside and got down to work. It finally didn't matter that their collective sight-reading skills weren't up to snuff. As Herschberg stated, "They were just such an incredible band, it was like they were joined at the base of the skull by some invisible thing. They just locked into everything. It was an amazing session, really."

"The best big band that Duke ever had, in my estimation, was about 1940, when he had just added the fifth saxophone and got Ben Webster, to 1942." Said May, "that's what I tried to write for, to go for that sound. But by 1967 it was completely gone, they had started to go to pot although they still had that distinctive sound." This was one point where I disagreed with Billy: fifty years after Ellington's death in 1974, most scholars regard the mid-1960s band as one of the Duke's all-time greatest, as is borne out by two of his all-time masterpiece albums, *The Far East Suite* (1967) and . . . *And His Mother Called Him Bill* (1968). To May's credit, the music on the Sinatra sessions sounds exactly like the great Ellington band of its era.

"That was a hard album, and there's some disastrous shit in there," as May put it, "but some of it's awful good." The disc starts with "Follow Me," from *Camelot,* the musical fable that titled a political era in which Sinatra had played no small part. The relationship of Sinatra and the John F. Kennedy campaign and administration has been documented in spectacular detail (most readably in James Kaplan's *Sinatra: The Chairman*), although with regards to his music it's worth noting that Sinatra and librettist Sammy Cahn had transformed their hit "High Hopes" into a JFK jingle in 1960. (And he also sang "That Old *Jack* Magic" around the same time that he and May rerecorded Johnny Mercer's original text for *Come Swing with Me!*). It's anyone's guess if Sinatra might have been thinking of his on-again, off-again friend—murdered four years earlier—when he sang "Follow Me"; but listening to Sinatra, it's hard not to think about *Camelot's* depiction of "the wisest, most heroic, most splendid king who ever sat on any throne." A few months later, the assassinations of Bobby Kennedy and Martin Luther King in 1968 announced the final curtain of that "fleeting wisp of glory known as Camelot," and Sinatra and Ellington anticipated that too with "Follow Me" (which was actually recorded last at the second session); in their melancholy interpretation, it's a song more about endings than beginnings. (In a further connection, Kennedy and *Camelot* lyricist Alan Jay Lerner had been in the same class together at Harvard.)

That chart's languid pace and bluish mood set the tone for the album. The Clooney and Fitzgerald sets had proffered a mixture of fast and slow numbers, but Sinatra, who prefers a more consistent tone, decided to concentrate on torpid tempi. The tempos are comparatively slow, but, unlike *Only the Lonely* or *No One Cares*, the mood is more sensual than suicidal; the overall feeling is close to Ellington's most famously romantic album, *Ellington Indigos.* Nothing is ad-lib, rather, it's a perfect inspiration for really close slow dancing. Yet at this hardly horse-race speed, as May put it, "'Follow Me' swings like hell!"

*Francis A.* contains some of Sinatra's most concentrated singing. Whether it was the newness of the setting or because he was afraid of missing notes, Sinatra bears down with an extreme intensity. Instead of sounding unrelaxed—in fact, he's quite loose on "All I Need Is the Girl" (his first of only a few recordings of a Stephen Sondheim lyric)—he sounds more keenly centered than ever. For the first time since the 1940s he abstains from familiar Frankisms such as "baby" and "jack" and avoids the expected ad-hoc lyric alterations.

There's only one Ellington original out of the eight, and that's far from his best-known song. "I Like the Sunrise" had been written for Al Hibbler to sing at the start of the composer's 1947 *Liberian Suite,* written in celebration of the hundredth anniversary of the first African republic founded by freed slaves. The song, which features the composer's own lyrics, has a distinctly spiritual quality, it sounds like a true forerunner of Ellington's famous *Sacred Concerts* of twenty years later; Sinatra sounds amazingly humble as he sings, even miraculously penitent. Like "Follow Me," "I Like the Sunrise" (with its references to black history) was an appropriate aria for a fading Camelot and the civil rights era, and Sinatra sings it with reverential majesty. Still, he supposedly phoned Hibbler after the session and told him, "You're the only guy in the world who can sing that goddamned thing!"

There are two "travel" pieces: "Yellow Days," which was by the celebrated Mexican composer Álvaro Carrillo and originally titled "Se te olvida"; and "Poor Butterfly," an American pop song inspired by an Italian opera depiction of a Japanese noblewoman. "Yellow Days" shows that May was one of the few arrangers ever completely capable of capturing the Ducal sound, what Strayhorn labeled "the Ellington Effect." Following a stunning Johnny Hodges solo, the band takes off on a tangent in the spirit of those extra sections of melody that Ellington added in many of his compositions ("Cotton Tail," for one) that go beyond the standard form of the popular song—though if you listen carefully, this "extra" section is actually based on the original Carrillo tune. "Butterfly" belongs with "South of the Border," as a classic and now-familiar tale of an American Pinkerton loving and leaving a femme foreigner. (Professor Henry Higgins to the contrary, by and large we are not a marvelous sex.) "Poor Butterfly," the 1916 song, boasts a second chorus from Sinatra that's at once powerful and contemplative.

"Indian Summer" also originated in the WWI era: it was first published as a piano instrumental in 1919 by American operetta master Victor Herbert; the piece was transformed into a pop song when Al Dubin added the lyrics twenty years later. By common consent, this is the most beloved song on the album. May himself admitted that it was "just outstanding" and Riddle cited it as the single greatest arrangement ever written for Sinatra, the only one penned by another orchestrator that he wished he had written. The beauty of the piece is its simplicity; it never attracts attention to itself or the ensemble but functions as a velvety background for Sinatra and Johnny Hodges, who contributes one of the most sensual solos of his life. Milt Bernhart describes it as "the only thing really good that happened" on the date: "Hodges played that alto solo in the middle, and it's really quintessential Johnny Hodges."

Bernhart has explained that Sinatra and his musicians usually had an unspoken empathy, preferring not to blow their cool; only if a soloist played something really extraordinary would Sinatra offer more than one or two complimentary words. The most enthusiastic Bernhart ever saw Sinatra get was after the playback of "Indian Summer": "He said, 'My God! That's unbelievable, John.'" Hodges, as usual, said nothing.

Sinatra bookends *Francis A.* with two key songs from consecutive Alan Jay Lerner shows, concluding with the set's one out-and-out up-tempo, "Come Back to Me" (he had already recorded "On a Clear Day" from the same score on *Strangers in the Night*). For this hard and fast number, May turned for inspiration to Ellington's famous "Diminuendo and Crescendo in Blue," first written and recorded in 1937 and spectacularly revived at the 1956 Newport Jazz Festival. May himself insisted that he liked "the old version better because there's some really nice clarinet things." May features tenor saxophonist Paul Gonsalves extensively here, as he was on the 1956 "Diminuendo"; he remembered the tenor saxophonist, who drove the crowd wild at Newport with twenty-seven spontaneous choruses, as "an exciting player." To say the least.

Apart from Gonsalves's soaring statement, "Come Back to Me" has Sinatra and the band racing and roaring and rocking in rhythm, the muted trumpets wa-wa-ing in double time and the brass skyrocketing into dissonances that vaguely suggest Stan Kenton. May concludes with a stuttering stop-and-start finish reminiscent of Ellingtonian train portraits like "Daybreak Express" and "Happy Go Lucky Local," thus ending a generally blue-tinged album on an upbeat note. By the time the train winds to a halt, you know you've been on a breathtaking ride, and you walk away convinced that, for all the *mishegoss* that went into it, you've just listened to a great album.

The overall experience clearly was not a magical one for either Ellington or Sinatra; neither, to the best of my knowledge, ever cited it as a career highlight. In his 1973 book of reminiscences, *Music Is My Mistress*, Ellington praised Sinatra for his 1940s campaign against racial intolerance and also for rallying to his support once in the 1950s when several of his bandsmen were caught in a gambling raid that the papers threatened to blow into a big scandal. He also mentioned a "recent" occasion on which he had again surprised Sinatra on his birthday by showing up at his party and bringing his band with him. But he didn't mention *Francis A. & Edward K.* Pity.

In 1967, Sinatra had called on May to arrange an album following the death of Billy Strayhorn. Twelve years later, May was again his second choice, and once more he didn't mind at all. (In the interim, they had done a single together, "The Best I Ever Had" from 1976.) As we've seen, Sinatra initially asked Nelson Riddle to orchestrate *The Past*, the first disc of *Trilogy*. It may have worked out for the best; Sinatra wanted to evoke the big-band era, the years of his young adulthood in the 1930s and 1940s, and May was much more firmly grounded in that tradition between them. "I felt badly Nelson and Frank had had a little difficulty between them," said May, "but I was very happy that I got the assignment."

This project marked a rare occasion when the arranger was consulted in the choice of repertory. Not only did May and Sinatra convene at the singer's compound in Palm Springs, along with Sonny Burke, general publishing factotum "Sarge" Weiss, and longtime crony Jimmy Van Heusen, but Gordon Jenkins, who was involved in an entirely other part of the album, also came along to offer his two cents' worth. May had a distinct memory that no pianist was present, so Jenkins, whom May tactfully described as "not the world's greatest piano player," was impelled to serve in that capacity. (I wish I had thought to ask Billy why Van Heusen wasn't playing; he had been a highly capable keyboardist in his day, although he might have been in a state of physical decline by 1978–79.)

The text on the finished package of *Trilogy* describes the criteria for *The Past* as "songs generally written before the rock era," and nine out of the ten come from the big-band years or earlier. "The approach for *The Past* was that they went by composer," May recalled. "They had a stack of songs, all kinds of 'em, that Frank was considering. What were Irving Berlin's big hits in this period? What were Richard Rodgers's? Sarge had complete catalogues of their songs!" May also remembered that many of Van Heusen's earlier songs were discussed, including the possibility of a remake of "Deep in a Dream" from the *Wee Small Hours* album (none made it onto the finished disc).

Sinatra and May also discussed the possibility of paying tribute to various band sounds of "The Past" by orchestrating various numbers in the style of, say, Benny Goodman or Woody Herman. Again, they decided against it. "The minute you start fooling around and start trying to use the Glenn Miller sound, for instance," explained May, "you realize that's an instrumental sound; it doesn't work in the background behind a vocal. Frank was smart enough to know that after he brought it up. So it was more a matter of just getting a feeling of that era rather than being specific about any particular band."

Since *The Past*, like several Sinatra sets before it, referred in part to the singer's own, he decided to limit the tributes to the two bandleaders who had sired him, Harry James and Tommy Dorsey. Neither homage, however, would be a remake of a number he had sung with those bands. "I Had the Craziest Dream," with a vocal by the Queen of the Canaries, Helen Forrest, had been one of James's biggest hits in 1943. "In fact, Frank was talking about bringing Harry in on the session," said May, "and then he said, 'Aw, God knows what kind of a record deal he's got, and we'll have to get clearance from some son of a bitch. Fuck it. Charlie'll play the shit out of it anyway.'" Charlie

Turner, at this time Sinatra's lead and solo trumpeter, indeed captures James's soaring brilliance and bravura; nonetheless, one feels that James himself, who was still playing magnificently at this time (I heard him at the Bottom Line) could have done better.

Dorsey had never recorded "But Not for Me," but Sinatra and May conceived their treatment along the lines of "Tommy Dorsey and his Sentimentalists," very much in the manner of "I'll Never Smile Again" and "Stardust." A vocal quartet makes like the Pied Pipers, phrasing very slowly in super-close harmony, The Voice rising at first only from the vocal ensemble for key lines and the entire bridge, accompanied by a celesta. As in "Smile Again," the two vocal choruses are divided by an instrumental bridge consisting of a strictly-from-Dorsey trombone solo, played by Dick Nash. "I didn't have any idea what we were going to do until I bumped into Billy on the way into the studio," recalled Nash. "He said, 'Oh good, Frank told me that he wanted you to do your Tommy Dorsey shit.'"

"It was a lucky coincidence that the tune of 'But Not for Me' happened to perfectly fit that category," said May, "so Frank said we could do it that way." While May also wrote a reed section passage behind Nash that could have been written by Sy Oliver in 1942, he brings in the strings in a deliberately un–Axel Stordahllike way. Further, Sinatra sings the verse—not completely unheard of in the big-band era, but hardly common—divided into two sections, the first backed by strings, the second, effectively, by a spare solo piano. Here they sing the verse in the middle, a structure perfected by Bing Crosby in the 1930s.

"Street of Dreams" is Sinatra's third commercial version of the Victor Young opus (and one of four repeats in *Trilogy*); it was inspired by a Sinatra-May precedent. "Frank likes the arrangement I made for him of 'You're Nobody till Somebody Loves You' [from *Swing Along with Me/Sinatra Swings*], and this was the same idea. I wrote a counter-line that swings pretty good," May elaborated. "So he said, 'Do it the same way.' But unfortunately I had to call him in New York and tell him, 'Hey, man, "Street of Dreams" is only sixteen bars, and we're gonna have a short record.'" Sinatra suggested using the song's verse, which he wasn't familiar with, so May sang it to him in Young's original march tempo. While the refrain itself can be construed as surreal and even upbeat, the very dramatic verse, performed convincingly by Bing Crosby (1932) and Tony Bennett (1959), anchors the text to a despondent tale of drug addiction. "Oh, fuck it," Sinatra responded. "We'll just make a short record."

They expanded "Street of Dreams" after the fashion of "You're Nobody till Somebody Loves You" by adding a juicy intro, a full third chorus, and, unexpectedly, a super-long *outro*: an instrumental of forty seconds that continues long after The Voice has stopped singing. "He liked the way the thing was swinging on the end there," May explained, "so that's why we extended the ending so long, to a fade." Sinatra had originally intended to use "Street of Dreams," with its three key changes, as his concert closer; the long coda would provide him with plenty of time to take a bow and beat it. (It also sounds like it could underscore the end titles of a movie.) But after *Trilogy* was released and "New York, New York" became the Sinatra super hit of the era, there was no way he could end his concerts with anything other than that ode to the Big Apple. Shortly thereafter May prepared a more concise and conclusive closer for "Street of Dreams."

Sinatra and May recorded nine of the ten songs (all of them except "All of You") over three sessions in July 1979. "Then by September, Frank said his chops were in better shape and he could sing higher," said May. "It was a pretty complete overhaul." Some tracks were taken, unaltered, from the original July dates ("It Had to Be You" and "Craziest Dream"), and some were strictly retakes using the same charts ("More Than You Know"). But for others, May raised the key half a step ("They All Laughed" and "My Shining Hour"), added or removed the verse, and generally revised or rewrote most of the orchestrations.

One tune from July, "The Surrey with the Fringe on Top"—which would have been the only Richard Rodgers piece on the set—was discarded entirely because Sinatra and May decided, "it was a buncha shit! I don't know why he picked it. He didn't like what he did on it vocally, although he did like the arrangement." A rehearsal take released in 2015 (on a centennial package titled *Ultimate Sinatra*), shows that, like the 1958 "Lush Life," it's the wrong song in the wrong style. Sinatra was again inspired by Nat King Cole and his hard-swinging version of "Surrey," but it's way too fast and too patter-y, and this run-through shows him struggling to keep up. (It's also notably inferior to the charming live radio version from 1945 that was issued by Columbia on the CD *Sinatra Sings Rodgers and Hammerstein*.) Next!

They replaced it with Cole Porter's "All of You," from the 1954 *Silk Stockings* and by far the most recent tune in *The Past*. Though Sinatra uses the more family-friendly lyric ("sweet and pure of you" as opposed to "take a tour of you") in this fast and snappy run-through (two thirty-two-bar choruses in less than a minute and a half), there's no shortage of characteristically Frankish virility.

In *Come Fly with Me*, Sinatra and May were visiting other continents; in *The Past*, the collaborators are visiting another era, although occasionally retracing their own footsteps backward. As with *Come Fly*, the moods are mixed, from swinging to romantic, though never dire or melancholy. Sinatra is marvelously wistful and forlorn in "Craziest Dream" and close to his all-time tenderest in "More Than You Know" and "My Shining Hour," even if some of the notes seem beyond the range of his sixty-three-year-old chops—as the orchestra and strings swell behind him like Hulk Hogan flexing his muscles. Conversely, he's agreeably aggressive on "Let's Face the Music and Dance," all but snarling—"*Har! Har! Har!*"—as he lets the past laugh on "They All Laughed," and he gets more animated with each consecutively punchier chorus of "All of You" and "Street of Dreams."

May's style is overall lush, romantic, and relaxed, full of splendidly simple and effective charts, like "It Had to Be You," that leave little to suggest the work of the Technicolorful whimsy of "Granada" or "Mandalay." Only the first track, "The Song Is You," and the last, "They All Laughed," betray May's distinctive earmarks; "More Than You Know" concludes with a string figure that suggests May paying homage to Riddle. "Laughed" and "Street of Dreams" at times suggest May's always-welcome post-Lunceford two-beat, the first in particular wobbling warmly. Even the large vocal chorus, something Sinatra rarely used since the Stordahl days (it generally spells sudden death in a non-Muzak context), generally fits the mood and only occasionally comes off as pasty. Further evoking the 1940s, Sinatra and May chose a big-band texture that never conceals the imperfections in Blue Eyes' equipment, making him sound more vulnerable and therefore more believable, as opposed to "You and Me (We Wanted It All)" on *The Present*, on which Don Costa protects The (thinning) Voice with more cover-ups than even Nixon ever dreamed of.

May was particularly impressed with Sinatra's outline of "My Shining Hour." It builds to a shining moment (more famously heard in "Ol' Man River") where Sinatra athletically connects the last note of one section to the first of the next. Said May, "He knows what he wants. He said, 'When we get to the bridge there, I'm gonna pull the long breath bit.' That was the Tommy Dorsey thing in which you take a lot of breath in, and when everybody thinks you're gonna have to stop and breathe, you fox 'em and carry over the phrase. He's a master at that. He deliberately made sure that I knew he was gonna do that, so I enhanced it by making the fucking band come up there. I put some chromatic harmony under it, and it really paid off. I have to say that it wouldn't work with every singer. Frank really knows what he's doing."

The team's familiar irreverent attitude dominates the conclusion of both "They All Laughed" and "Let's Face the Music." At Sinatra's suggestion, the first concludes with the entire ensemble collapsing in a round of guffaws. In a manner particularly befitting a tune about paying the fiddlers, May winds up "Face the Music," following the coda, with a very brief Latin brass fanfare. "All the mariachi bands in Los Angeles used that as their sign-off at the end of the set, and Frank was aware of that," May pointed out. "Vern Yocum [Sinatra's copyist and brother of Pied Piper Clark Yocum] made Frank a very complete part with lyrics and a little sketch about what was happening. It was written in three-quarter time, and Frank looked at it and said, 'What the fuck is that on the end there?' I said, 'Ah, you'll see. You'll like it.' And he did." The unexpected tag takes its place alongside "Ay! Ay! Ay!" in "South of the Border" and "Cha! Cha! Cha!" in "Granada"—it sounds like gladiators announcing to a coliseum full of ancient Romans that "We who are about to get plastered salute you!" (It's similar to the way that May gets all mariachi on our ass at the end of his classic instrumental of "It Happened in Monterey" on the 1956 album *Billy May Plays for Fancy Dancin'*.)

"Billy did an incredible job," in the opinion of pianist Vincent Falcone, who played on the album. "I mean, he did *The Past* as well as it could be done. He captured everything." And no one disagrees. When *Trilogy* was finally released, *The Past* was resoundingly hailed by critics and collectors alike as more than just the best of the three discs but justification enough for purchasing the entire package.

"I did mine first," he said, modestly ascribing his success to factors other than his own talent. "And everybody tells me that mine is the best of the three—only because they know the songs better, although Don Costa did a wonderful job on his." *Trilogy* would have been an even better buy had it consisted of three entire discs of Sinatra and May working on worthwhile material, as even the chicks and ducks and geese scurrying from the "Surrey with the Fringe" suit Sinatra a lot better than the nauseating "That's What God Looks Like to Me." Those who expected *The Past* to be nostalgic or sentimental soon learned that it was much less so than either *The Present* or *The Future*.

"And that," said May, "was the last really major thing I did for Frank, other than a couple of odds and ends." Some of these various bits and pieces saw the light of day in 1995 on the *Complete Reprise Studio Recordings* suitcase. In 1982 and again in 1983, Sinatra and May made several attempts at recording a new tune by Sammy Cahn and Jule Styne called "Love Makes Us Whatever We Want to Be." October 1986 found Sinatra and May taping "Only One to a Customer" by Styne and Carolyn Leigh, an affably snappy number that he also performed in concert a few weeks earlier. (The singer announces it as his first attempt at the tune, and tells us that it was "arranged by Billy May—when he was sober.") From the same session, "The Girls I've Never Kissed" is the only song Sinatra ever recorded by Jerry Leiber and Mike Stoller, two of the most successful songwriters of the second half of the twentieth century. It's a reflective aria, tailor-made for Sinatra; Sinatra sang it at the Golden Nugget (on New Year's Eve 1986), describing it as being reminiscent of "September Song." (It will also remind longtime Mike and Jerry listeners of their "Some Cats Know" for Peggy Lee, and, even more directly, of Gordon Jenkins's "This Is All I Ask.")

In June 1988, Sinatra called a session with May where they attempted two standards: "My Foolish Heart," which was also issued in the *Complete Reprise* suitcase, and "Cry Me a River." They never got as far as an actual take on the second, but someone surreptitiously made a tape of Sinatra singing with his vocal mic turned off; you can just about get an idea of what it would have sounded like, another potential Frank-and-Billy classic. Too bad. However, "My Foolish Heart" is darn good, it would have fit easily as a bonus track on *The Past*; even though the vocal isn't perfect, it's full of expression, he absolutely nails the lyric and fully captures the mood of the song and of May's expert chart. "My Foolish Heart" is everything that we want and expect the seventy-two-year-old Sinatra to be. (After all, who do you think he is, Tony Bennett?)

Billy May was the only one of Sinatra's big four collaborators (Stordahl, Riddle, Jenkins) who outlived the Old Man—by six years, checking out at the age of eighty-seven on January 22, 2004.

We talked many times during the writing of this book; he was very patient with my questions, not to mention very frank. Around 1991, a Japanese film producer opened negotiations with the Sinatra office to try and get the Old Man to sing the main title theme of a forthcoming film. The music was by Maurice Jarre. Sinatra said he would consider it, but only if Sammy worked on the lyrics and Billy did the orchestration. Jarre had won much-deserved Academy Awards for *Lawrence of Arabia* and *Doctor Zhivago*, but this particular theme was so minimal that May felt that there was virtually nothing to arrange. May told Cahn, "Look, I'll make the arrangement, but I'm not into the business of changing other people's songs." According to May, the producers had gone as far as commissioning the chart from May, hiring all the necessary musicians and booking studio time, before they even had a firm commitment from Sinatra. When the singer finally decided not to go through with it, the filmmakers next considered contacting Ella Fitzgerald—but that never happened either. But I'll never forget a conversation that we had on the subject:

Me: "Maurice Jarre—would you say that he's a classical-type composer?"
Billy: "No, he's a *Godzilla Eats the Steel Pier*–type of composer!"

What were his final thoughts on Sinatra? "I used to have a house in Palm Springs, and I'd see Frank socially once in a while. We had a lot of fun down there, but I never got that close to him. We'd have a ball some night, and then maybe I didn't see him for a couple of years." May felt that their professional relationship has lasted so long because neither was ever dependent on or beholden to the other. They just happened to work together on some very happy occasions when a particular project had Billy May's name written all over it. Comparing his Sinatra experience to that of his close friend Nelson Riddle, May remarked, "Nelson felt that Sinatra uses people and things like that, and for all I know maybe he does. But, see, some people allow themselves to be used. That's why I say I like it the way it is."

Tenor sax player Ted Nash felt they worked together so well "because Billy never was in awe of Sinatra. He was just another singer, and he'd come on the date. 'Okay, how's it going, Frank? Here we go, let's make a tune.' Where the other guys sometimes would be uptight, knowing Sinatra's reputation. Because he could come on pretty strong if he didn't like something. So they were always concerned that something would happen. But Billy didn't care. If you didn't like what he did, he'd change it to suit you. What's the difference?"

Sinatra never expected May to be subservient to him. "Sinatra treated him differently" than he did, say, Don Costa, said Vince Falcone. "He respected his time, he respected Billy's right to say no. If Don ever said no to the Old Man, the Old Man wouldn't speak to him for two weeks. But Billy was different because Billy kept his distance." Nash added, "Frank sometimes has uptight people around him, but Billy was so loose. He would go, 'Let's go, Frank. Let's make one of these turkeys.' And Frank would break up, because he dug Billy's style with that type of thing."

As Sinatra himself told Robin Douglas-Home, "Billy handles the band quite differently from Gordon or Nelson. With Nelson, for instance, if someone plays a wrong note, he'll hold up his hand and say quietly, 'Now in bar sixteen, you'll see that it says the brass comes in half a note after the woodwinds' or something like that. But Billy—there he'll be in his old pants and sweatshirt, and he'll stop them and say, 'Cats, this bar sixteen, you gotta go *oomp-de-da-da-che-ow*! Okay? Let's go then, cats!' And the band will go."

Emulating one of his own role models, Axel Stordahl, May didn't let much get to him. "I know what I like, I know what I like to write, and I know what has influenced me and what's successful. I know where I can steal money, and I know where I can make it. If you're in any kind of business, you know that sometime you're going to have to do something that's junk, and you do it anyway. But I know if I'm gonna do an album with Frank, then it's gonna be an important album, and I'm gonna try harder."

We should be grateful for any attitude that kept these two masters working together so productively and for so long. No other collaborator so decisively helped him sound his great barbaric yawp over the rooftops of the world.

# 8

# GORDON JENKINS AND THE SEARCH FOR LONG FORMS

## *1956–1981*

*As long as a whore's dream.*
> —BEN HECHT
> (on *Gone with the Wind*)

*All us tough guys are hopeless sentimentalists at heart.*
> —RAYMOND CHANDLER

A simple man stands out on the edge of a cliff, peering into the heavens, trying to fathom the ways of God and the universe.

In earlier and more naive—that is to say more racist—generations, dramatists often colored this man black. Even such forward-thinking sages as Oscar Hammerstein considered this to be perfectly natural casting, and Paul Robeson had no reservations about playing such a character. Hammerstein and Jerome Kern wrote "Ol' Man River" for Robeson to sing in the original production of *Show Boat* in 1927, and it became the original Broadway ode to the mysteries of both human existence and intolerance. The great man once described the text as "a song sung by a character who is a rugged and untutored philosopher. It is a song of resignation with a protest implied."

By the standards of the era, it was considered "progressive" to call attention to man's inhumanity to man—and the inequality of the races—although the language in which songwriters did so was frequently in terms that are regarded as condescending today. At least "Ol' Man River" was sung by an actual African American; another song that made pretty much the same point was "That's Why Darkies Were Born" (by Lew Brown and Ray Henderson), which was introduced by the operatic baritone Everett Marshall, wearing blackface, in the 1931 edition of *George White's Scandals*.

The song's choice of language was unfortunate, needless to say; but then, too, the first word of one verse of "River" in the original, unexpurgated libretto (and as recorded by Al Jolson) had been the dreaded N-bomb. And Robeson made a powerful and moving recording of "Darkies." Both songs implied that there was injustice in the world, and stated plainly that one race of people was treated poorly at the hands of another; however, both were resigned to the idea that the best that anyone could do about it was wait for their reward in the afterlife. Like many Tin Pan Alley anthems written by Jewish songwriters (though Hammerstein was actually less Jewish than most), these songs present African Americans in the same light as Hebrews in the Old Testament, not only "to pick the cotton" and "plant the corn" but that "to stoke the train that would bring God's children to green pastures." Evidently, to take up the black man's burden meant to shoulder both the suffering and the spiritual obligations of the rest of the world.

In the next generation, another big song addressed the same big issues, this time implying that injustice and inhumanity could be blamed on an absentee deity. Kurt Weill and Maxwell Anderson originally wrote "Lost in the Stars" for one show, which was ultimately unproduced, but then later it became the title of a completely different one. In both cases, the song was ultimately about racial inequality, and how it invariably leads to tragic consequences. The song was first conceived for *Ulysses Africanus*, an aborted work that was intended as a vehicle for Paul Robeson (not coincidentally) about a newly emancipated slave in the aftermath of the Civil War. Then it famously served as the centerpiece of Weill and Anderson's masterpiece "musical tragedy" *Lost in the Stars* in 1949. The implication of the song is clear: we can look to God for guidance, but we can't depend on Him to protect us from each other; as Cassius tells us, "the fault, dear Brutus, is not in our stars but in ourselves."

From the very start of his career, Frank Sinatra was consistently searching for bigger songs that dealt with bigger issues. Like Kern, Hammerstein, and Weill, he was motivated by a crusader's need to sing a song that could uplift the entire world. If Sinatra's renditions of "Ol' Man River" and "Lost in the Stars" help those texts to transcend the time in which they were first staged, it's partly because he has divorced them from the specific racial angles they were originally written to comment on. Sinatra's "Ol' Man River" is no longer about levee workers on a Mississippi riverboat, and his "Lost in the Stars" is no longer about the wretched of the earth suffering in the mines and prisons of apartheid; they are now about the entire human condition. Sinatra makes them into something universal, something relevant to all mankind.

"He was always looking ahead," as Zeke Zarchy, who in 1946 was the lead trumpeter with the Sinatra radio orchestra on the West Coast, recalled. "I remember once I was at his house for dinner. There were half a dozen people there, and we all walked into his den where he had his hi-fi set up. He played us some things from *Carousel*, which had just come out. We heard the big 'Soliloquy' that the main character sings, and we were all impressed with it. Frank said, 'These are the kinds of things that I want to do.' At that time he was just doing his regular ballad stuff. And sure enough, he went into that field."

Sinatra's career-long quest for big texts and big issues runs parallel to and eventually joins a similar search by composer and orchestrator Gordon Jenkins. The two men would first unite to extend Sinatra's series of saloon-song sets. Gradually, they would join forces in a crusade for the ultimate musical depiction of the plight of mankind; for a time, the two would be like Don Quixote and Sancho Panza, riding off, tilting at windmills (they might be giants, you know?), in search of the Impossible Song.

Like so many other threads of the Sinatra legacy, the singer's earliest attempts at addressing larger issues in expanded song forms were made in his big-band "apprenticeship" period. Tommy Dorsey gave what would be known as the "concert" treatment (a leftover from the legacy of his onetime employer, Paul Whiteman) to several standards, and the major concert number involving Sinatra would be their 1941 treatment of "Without a Song." Although Sy Oliver fashioned a very full six-minute treatment of the piece, he nonetheless treated Vincent Youmans's melody simply and eloquently. The leader himself opens "Without a Song" with a full first chorus of trombone— this at a time when he rarely played more than sixteen bars on a typical opening. Sinatra then sings the full refrain, backed by celeste accompaniment from Joe Bushkin, the overall sound being very similar to "I'll Never Smile Again."

"Without a Song," originally written by Vincent Youmans and Edward Eliscu (and co-credited to Billy Rose) for *Great Day*, a short-lived Afrocentric show from 1929 (one of many unsuccessful follow-ups to the 1922 blockbuster *Shuffle Along* by Flournoy Miller and Aubrey Lyles), is another Broadway spiritual about the relationship between man and God, once again focusing on the Negro race. It's another attempt by white show tunesmiths to write from a black perspective: "A darkie's born, but he's no good nohow, without a song." One can only imagine how Sy Oliver felt about that line, but Sinatra got rid of it as soon as possible. The Sinatra-Dorsey-Oliver "Without a Song" was the singer's first epic, it filled up one twelve-inch side, a whole minute longer than a standard ten-inch 78 rpm single. (There's an even longer six-minute version, extant from an aircheck, that adds a full chorus of tenor from Don Lodice and a more elaborate, Luncefordesque closing cadenza by Oliver.)

By 1943, "Ol' Man River" had become a part of The Voice's permanent repertoire. *Show Boat* had doubtless formed a part of his musical background; all of its songs were much-heard hits during Sinatra's formative early teens. When the show was new, in 1927, Bing Crosby, then still in the midst of his own big-band apprenticeship (with Paul Whiteman), recorded the first jazzy, up-tempo version of "Ol' Man River." Taking his cue from the Young Groaner, the Old Man remained primarily in swingtime for a long time; Hammerstein and especially Kern must have cringed with every new recording they heard.

Sinatra originally addressed "Ol' Man River" during his first concert tour, in the summer of 1943, in which he sang it at the Hollywood Bowl and New York's Lewisohn Stadium, among other lofty venues. He began singing it regularly on his various radio shows shortly thereafter. Sinatra's idea was to restore the song's dramatic tempo as well as its philosophical implications, which seemed even more relevant in the era of the war against fascism. The piece had been written for Robeson but was actually introduced on Broadway by the African American baritone Jules Bledsoe; yet Sinatra didn't have to sing like Bledsoe (you can tell the world I said so). While not sacrificing any of the piece's power, he raises the level of the tune from a blustering basso to his own lighter and more beautiful baritone, making the message of the piece more believable and true. In the early to mid-1940s, the singer gradually grew into the song, restricted by the constraints of commercial radio, which tended to favor short numbers. Sinatra's earliest known broadcast of "River" trims the verse and limits him to a single two-minutes chorus. By May 1944, he felt secure enough to reattach the rest; and in October, Sinatra sang "Ol' Man River" in the company of that master of pop concert music, Paul Whiteman. Finally, with the end of the musicians strike, in December 1944 he at last makes a commercial Columbia recording of the now-classic Sinatra–Axel Stordahl version of the Kern anthem.

That treatment is so staggeringly definitive, it makes all the previous versions—Robeson, Jolson, even the swing and fox-trot versions—seem severely dated by comparison. Even Hammerstein's jazz age Ebonics—his faux "colored" slang—doesn't get in Sinatra's way. He actually seems to "bend" and "bow" with his voice when he comes to those words in the verse. The rendition offers two stunning early examples of The Voice's high-wire acts: first, there's the Dorsey-style long-breath joining of the last note of the bridge to the first note of the final A section. Stordahl supports this with underlying harmony that's both chromatic and dramatic. In contrast, the accompanist turns up the tension on Sinatra's second vocal super feat, the agonizingly long note at the climactic "*a-long*" by suspending both the orchestra and the beat entirely. (This, for once, is a musical theater–style belt ending, more like Judy Garland than typical Sinatra, who generally favored more intimate endings.)

He kept singing "Ol' Man River" regularly for the remainder of the era. On the occasion of an August 1945 tribute to Kern (then still with us) at the Hollywood Bowl, he extended it to four and a half minutes; MGM made it the climax of their 1946 Kern biopic *Till the Clouds Roll By.* "My idea with that song," composer Kern once commented to the crooner, "was to have a rabbity little fellow do it—somebody who made you believe he was tired of livin' and scared of dyin'. That's how you do it, Frankie." Still, the composer would have had to admit that an aura of majesty permeates the many Sinatra readings, even the visually overdecorated MGM version. The studio tried like blazes to muffle the message of the song: first, they cut the verse, then they draped Young Blue Eyes in what appears be one of Liberace's cast-off white tuxedos, and finally perched him atop a white Roman column out of an Andy Warhol nightmare. (Nobody works on the Mississippi around here, boss.) Still, even Louis B. Mayer himself failed to prevent the pure power of the song—and its plea for a more just God—from resonating through.

In search of something to fit on the flip side of "River," which required a twelve-inch 78, Sinatra and Stordahl came up with a fascinating miscalculation. It's hard to label "Stormy Weather" a flop, since both the singing and the orchestration are so beautiful in themselves, even if they don't quite suit the song. Sinatra would perform this chart only once more, on a V-Disc issued in 1947. On that occasion he would introduce "Stormy Weather" as "a song that tells of the blues." Yet the Sinatra-Stordahl treatment, with its upbeat sound and optimistic attitude, thoroughly nullifies the blues base of the tune, a defeat unfortunately underscored by the presence of an especially pallid vocal group. Harold Arlen had written the melody in a major key, and this is one of the major-est interpretations, especially in the way that Stordahl re-harmonizes the title phrase—this treatment could be called "Sunny Weather." Only the growling trumpeter Yank Lawson effectively catches the blue mood, his muted solo capturing the voice-like cadences of a blues singer. Sinatra's 1959 interpretation, with Gordon Jenkins, finds him probing more convincingly darker colors.

"Stormy Weather" also amounts to one of the rare standards that Sinatra and Stordahl recorded for Columbia without "auditioning" it first on the radio. Their next "big song" would be Cole Porter's "Begin the Beguine," which was ambitious in terms of its structure (108 bars) rather than its social implications. The team had worked on it extensively before they deemed it ready to commit to shellac. It had first been premiered in the 1935 musical *Jubilee*, and neither the song nor the show was a huge hit in that season; in fact, no one much paid any attention to it until Artie Shaw's breakthrough 1938 swing version. Although Fred Astaire and Eleanor Powell danced to "Beguine" very memorably in *Broadway Melody of 1940*, "Beguine" remained the property of the swing groups (somewhat ironically, since it was originally conceived as a Pan-American dance number). It was even a jazz hit all over again in 1944 thanks to pianist Eddie Heywood.

The song's imposing length could scare off many an aspiring (and perspiring) vocalist—even Astaire never attempted to sing it. Sinatra was trying to bite it off as early as late 1943, on the radio, and tried a four-and-a-half-minute arrangement that drags slightly and doesn't quite sustain its extended length. There's Stordahlesque string figures and Dorsey-style celeste, and of all things, a Hawaiian guitar plucking out an annoying arpeggio in the coda. But by summer of 1944, he was singing a perfect treatment, one that was romantic and swinging at the same time, with no shortage of both dramatic and rhythmic moments. Alas, the 1946 Columbia version isn't quite this good; the label didn't want to go to the trouble of releasing another twelve-inch disc, so Stordahl and Sinatra had to speed up the tempo just for it to fit on a standard ten-inch 78. The Columbia recording doesn't quite reach the heights of the 1944 radio performances, but it made the charts for him and briefly became a signature, a song that he continued to sing frequently throughout his radio years.

During this period, when radio sponsors choked on their Chesterfields at the thought of a number that ran over two minutes, Sinatra was frequently turning in three-and-a-half- or four-minute epics on the air, even on the highly reactionary *Your Hit Parade*. Inevitably, he also turned to standard works of heavy musical, if not political, stature, such as "Dancing in the Dark" and "Long Ago (and Far Away)."

And then there was "The House I Live In," Sinatra's heaviest number, both ideologically and otherwise; he sang it on the air, for Columbia, and in an Oscar-winning movie short. *The House I Live In* resulted from the labors of three writers long associated with humanist concerns: lyricist Lewis Allen (a pseudonym of Abel Meeropol, best known for Billie Holiday's iconic "Strange Fruit"), composer Earl Robinson (author of the once-famous *Ballad for Americans*, an extended cantata for solo baritone voice and chorus), and screenwriter Albert Maltz, who would suffer the dubious distinction of being one of the original Hollywood Ten—the most infamous victims of the Red Scare and the blacklist.

The song was first heard in a wartime revue titled *Let Freedom Sing*, which ran for a week in October 1942 (and featured Sinatra's future MGM costar Betty Garrett). When Sinatra decided to sing it, in early 1945, the war was reaching its conclusion; so the first thing that the singer decided to do was to drop the second verse, much of which is highly specific to the wartime era. Sinatra realized that "House" was perfectly in keeping with the enlightened politics of the Roosevelt administration as well as the World War that was, at least temporarily, serving to make bigotry unpopular.

In 1945, Sinatra was actively conducting a one-man campaign against what was then called "racial intolerance" that was encouraged by his press agent and close friend George Evans. "George was very political and so was Frank, and in that period he was very liberal in his politics," Evans's assistant Budd Granoff told me. "George was always trying to create the image that Frank was more than just a pop singer, and he had a friend who was a principal at a high school in the Bronx. It was George's idea to get Frank to go and address this high school auditorium and talk to the kids about juvenile delinquency. But Frank said he didn't feel qualified, he didn't feel he could handle it. But George pressured him and pressured him and pressured him, and finally Frank did it, and it wound up on the front page of the *Daily News*.

"It was a big front-page story with a picture of Frank talking to these kids. Well, Frank saw the response this brought, so they embarked on a nationwide tour. Frank started to address groups of kids in different cities. I think he did about ten cities, and this got a whirlwind of publicity and sort of changed the image of Frank from being an ordinary record star into a public figure of some importance. In those days performers weren't political activists, but he was one of the first ones."

In April 1946, Sinatra guest-hosted reporter and radio commentator Drew Pearson's radio show; it was probably the most direct and overtly political speech of his entire career. Just to include a few excerpts: "We let the people fight for the peace, but we won't let them own it. . . . The very intolerance we fought so bitterly in Germany goes unchecked here at home. . . . In a country that not one full year ago fought for four freedoms—freedom of speech, freedom from want, freedom from fear, and freedom of worship— Negro men are being lynched by carefully-organized mobs . . . their wives are being shot, and violence, such as beatings to death, is being exerted on the Negro race." He goes on to attack the Ku Klux Klan as "an organization in which every member stands for everything the United States Constitution will not stand for. . . . The only way the KKK and other organizations can be beaten is through education. Bigotry is a form of adult delinquency." Doubtless the speech was written by Evans, but Sinatra reads it as sentiments that he agrees with and is willing to put his career on the line for.

As Granoff acknowledged, yes, there was a career benefit to these activities, but also a considerable risk, and there were other, less potentially dangerous and controversial things Sinatra could have done if he were primarily interested in receiving media coverage. In those days a large part of the press was controlled by ultraconservative barons of industry, such as William "Rosebud" Hearst, and Sinatra left himself wide open to attack from all manner of pro-Republican, anti-Roosevelt columnists. As columnist Billy Rose observed in 1947, "Taking potshots at Sinatra in print is a good way [for newspapermen] to butter up the publisher who's paying [their] salary." For any entertainer to take a stand on a matter outside of show business was unfathomable in 1945; this was another of Sinatra's moves that took the rest of the world twenty years to catch up with him.

In 1945, the National Conference of Christians and Jews, the Bureau for Intercultural Education, and other such organizations bestowed commendations on Sinatra for his work against prejudice. By now "The House I Live In" was the musical cornerstone for this multimedia crusade. When producer Frank Ross suggested making a film out of one of these tolerance speeches, along with a song to the same effect, the singer phoned the prestigious director Mervyn LeRoy, whom he had met by chance on a train trip several months earlier. They recorded and shot the film in two days in May 1945. Then in August, over the course of several special broadcasts aired to celebrate the Allied victory in Europe, Sinatra found the perfect occasion to introduce the song in public; he recorded it later in the month for Columbia.

Sinatra featured the song many times on his *Old Gold* show, particularly between the autumns of 1945 and 1947; in the Academy Awards ceremony of March 1946, both Sinatra and LeRoy received special Oscars for the film—the first for both men. Seen today, the film is charmingly optimistic, especially when seventy years later we don't seem to have learned anything, but Sinatra's performance is as powerful and moving as ever. It isn't so much the speech that Sinatra gives that's so effective but rather the fact of his giving it. The ideas Maltz touched upon in his screenplay, echoing the lyrics, anticipate Edward R. Murrow's famous report on Senator Joseph McCarthy in 1954: "We cannot defend freedom abroad by deserting it at home." (Sinatra later told Murrow in a CBS-TV interview that his Oscar for *The House I Live In* meant even more to him than the one he subsequently won for *From Here to Eternity*.)

By the time the "150 years" mentioned in the lyric had grown to "200 years," Sinatra had returned to "House" on numerous occasions, including a reenactment of the short-subject script on his CBS-TV series in November 1951. Sinatra was never officially blacklisted, even though he was famously liberal and a "progressive" in terms of taking a leadership role in the area of civil rights and racial equality. The same can't be said for the songwriters, Meerpole and Robinson, who, as the latter told me, depended largely on revenue from Sinatra's record and film performance to get through the dark years of the blacklist.

In 1960, Sinatra famously tried to break the blacklist by announcing the production of a new film that would give full on-screen credit to a blacklisted writer—the same Albert Maltz; he only dropped the project under pressure from the Kennedys. Just the same, he commissioned a new arrangement from Nelson Riddle, which he performed on his ABC-TV series at Thanksgiving. It was that arrangement that he sang, famously, at the pre-inaugural gala for President John F. Kennedy on January 19, 1961, right after "You Make Me Feel So Young," a song about starting over followed by a song about the larger meaning of America. A few weeks after the assassination of the thirty-fifth president, Sinatra recorded the Riddle arrangement (now incorporating a large chorus, Fred Waring's Pennsylvanians) for a multi-artist Reprise album titled *America, I Hear You Singing*. He kept doing the song well beyond the American bicentennial in 1976 and the one-hundredth birthday of the Statue of Liberty in 1986; there are especially moving renditions from several of his best latter-day shows, such as the Main Event from Madison Square Garden in 1974 and the Concert for the Americas in the Dominican Republic in 1982.

In many ways, the original 1945 Stordahl version of "The House I Live In," as documented by Columbia and RKO, is the most powerful. It is a model of drama and timing, with Sinatra intimately involved with the big things and the small, the laughter and the tears; even the pauses carry precisely the proper increments of weight and wait. The piece ends, fittingly, with a suggestion of "America the Beautiful" in the coda and remains an ardent entreaty for ethnic and religious equality. It's hardly surprising that the "House" expanded along with the country and Sinatra's concert career; but while the latter versions are more grandiose, when played today they are no less moving. The song continues to exemplify that brief shining moment in our history, at the end of the war and immediately afterward, when good music and good politics were but two sides of the same coin.

During the same period when he was frequently singing "The House I Live In," Sinatra recorded "Lost in the Stars," another poetic comment on man's inhumanity to man, in August 1946. The explanation as to how Sinatra came upon the song has itself been lost—if not in the stars, then somewhere. We know that Kurt Weill and Maxwell Anderson apparently wrote it as early as 1939 for the unproduced *Ulysses Africanus*, but that still doesn't explain how Sinatra got hold of it three full years before *Lost in the Stars* opened on Broadway. Tony Bennett (who famously sang it at his Carnegie Hall concert in 1962) succinctly describes the show as a story about apartheid in South Africa, as indeed the 1949 "musical tragedy" is; but that policy of apartheid was not introduced in South Africa until 1948, and the novel that inspired the show, *Cry, the Beloved Country*, wasn't published until the end of that year.

However Sinatra happened upon the tune, "Stars" immediately became another cornerstone of his platform of progressive social and musical ideology. Drawing on metaphors alluding to African folklore, Anderson's text amounts to a prayer to a God who is less omnipotent than impotent. Musically it amounts to a most unassuming concert piece: it clocks in safely at 3:13 (although an AFRS radio version from three months later adds another twenty-five seconds), and Sinatra's vocal, which follows a fourteen-second intro, is altogether gentle (belt-free) and even danceable. Sinatra's vocal is tender and compassionate, more a lullaby to Little Nancy and Frankie Junior than a cautionary tale.

The 1963 version, heard on *The Concert Sinatra*, has considerably more teeth to it—the underlying message seems to be that the problems we thought we could solve right after the war have gotten worse rather than better; that Sinatra has been singing this message for almost twenty years and people still refuse to listen—"Lost in the Stars"—seems like Sinatra anticipating the grand feeling of disillusionment that the rest of the country would experience a few months later with the president's assassination.*

Sinatra seems much more agitated and less forgiving in his 1963 "House" than in 1946, and Nelson Riddle's "concert" orchestration retains all the strengths of Stordahl's original while at the same time improving on them. The extended introduction (the famous Riddle "polytones") seems to depict a vast starscape, in which the bed of strings represents the blackness of the heavens while the chirping woodwinds become the twinkling stars. The climactic moment arrives when the singer speaks of "little stars," and then, "big stars,"

---

* As is well known, Sinatra was already disillusioned with the Kennedys after what he perceived as a slight, when the president stayed at Bing Crosby's house rather than Sinatra's during a trip to Palm Springs a year earlier in March 1962. Less known is that the Kennedys likely dropped him because of his efforts in 1960 to break the Hollywood blacklist and produce a film written by Albert Maltz, who had done the scenario for *The House I Live In* in 1945.

depicted first by a small cluster of flutes that's then contrasted by a massive tumult of strings; the two men keenly make us feel the difference between little and big. The song depicts inhumanity and injustice in another place in order to show that it can happen here. The text may refer to the mythological vocabulary of another continent even as the music uses interstellar imagery, but the shock value of "Lost in the Stars" hits us right at home. Here is truly a song of resignation, with a protest implied.

Which brings us to the granddaddy of all Sinatra "concert" works, the famous "Soliloquy" from *Carousel*. As the story goes, the number was written late in the rehearsal stage of the show; it took Oscar Hammerstein two weeks to perfect the "poem," which was summarily set to music by Richard Rodgers within two hours. In 1989 Sinatra said of the piece, "I just [wish] more performers would do it. If they [only] had the guts, they've got the talent [and] big voices, but nobody does that." Sinatra had the guts.

Manie Sachs indulged The Voice in giving him two sessions in April and May 1946 to attempt the eight-minute work, which they broke into two halves for the A and B sides of a twelve-inch 78; the break arrives after the line, "My kid ain't even been born yet!" The two dates resulted in two complete, issuable masters of "Soliloquy." At the risk of getting too deep into discographical ephemera, the April take was issued on V-Disc and, fifty years later, on the Sony CD *Frank Sinatra Sings Rodgers and Hammerstein*; the May take, which was originally issued on 78 as part of Columbia's green-label Masterworks series (usually reserved for classical music), is now on Sony's complete *Columbia Years* boxed set. (For what it's worth, the take originally heard by soldiers hews more closely to the stronger language heard in the actual show, whereas the May take softens and sanitizes it, i.e., he sings, "I'll try, by *God* I'll try" at the conclusion of the first take and "I'll try, by *gosh* I'll try" at the end of the second.)

As everyone knows, "Soliloquy" ranks as the ultimate hymn to fatherhood and paternal responsibility, although listening to lines like "You can have fun with a son / But you've got to be a father to a girl," one is keenly aware that Hammerstein is inside the head of this one particular character rather than trumpeting a truism to all mankind. The work also exemplifies an aspect of Sinatra reveled in by his legions of followers if not as openly celebrated: after we've gotten off on Sinatra the carouser and Sinatra the tender romantic, we also want to see his serious and stoic side. No matter how many babes he beds or bottles he belts down, we tell ourselves that he's still thinking about his kids and family.

The notion of personal growth and change are at the root of all drama, but "Soliloquy" may signify the first instance in musical theater where that evolution actually occurs in the middle of a song. And Sinatra and Stordahl take full advantage of Rodgers's brilliant device for illustrating this idea: at the very moment where our hero postulates, "What if he . . . is a girl?" (saying the word "girl" as if it were "drug addict")—at that point, how strange is the change from major to minor? All the musical and textual ideas of the first half are thereupon echoed, coming back in a distorted form as if to haunt us, a device we know from opera and more contemporaneously in film scores (or, for that matter, by Duke Ellington in his extended instrumental "Reminiscing in Tempo"). On the 1946 record, the second half also extends the antihero's premature reverie on the subject of his girl child by adding a passage ("when I have a daughter") that appears on the original cast album and on Sinatra versions early and late; he omitted it from the otherwise definitive *Concert Sinatra* version in 1963.

In 1955, Sinatra was cast as the lead (Billy Bigelow) in the movie version of *Carousel.* That much is clear; however, over the last sixty years, there has been a veritable cottage industry devoted to arguing why Sinatra didn't appear in the film; the sheer quantity and diversity of possible reasons challenges Kennedy assassination theories. But in retrospect, it seems clear that Rodgers and Hammerstein wanted a big strapping brute, like John Raitt in 1945 or Gordon MacRae in 1955; and in this period, most of Sinatra's movie characters were essentially variations on Angelo Maggio and Nathan Detroit. Even more so, my personal theory is Rodgers and Hammerstein simply considered Sinatra too hip for the room to play one of their heroes (or even antiheroes); they wanted someone with a basic musical comedy squareness.

All of which is a pity—Sinatra could have made an awesome Billy Bigelow. A wonderful but incomplete reading of the 1955 "Soliloquy" has been issued on the Rhino boxed *Frank Sinatra in Hollywood 1940–1964.* This version is arranged and conducted by Richard Jones, a former Dorsey arranger who wrote occasional charts for Sinatra throughout the 1940s and had since become head of classical A&R (and producer-arranger for Jackie Gleason) for Capitol. "Frank wanted to give him a job," said Bill Miller, "and he [let Jones arrange] 'Soliloquy.'" Rather than biting it off in big four-minute chunks, Sinatra used modern tape techniques to tackle the piece in segments, to be spliced and edited together, movie-style. He wasn't able to finish it in one session, and before he could return to the thing, the movie deal fell through, losing him his interest in the piece at the time. Miller didn't feel it was a great loss—and he described Jones's chart as merely a "stock arrangement"; but Sinatra is singing exceptionally well on the incomplete version that has been issued.

"Finally," Miller concluded, "Nelson did the right one." This new "Soliloquy" on *The Concert Sinatra* is slower (clocking in at about the same time but with one segment of lyrics deleted), stronger, more majestic, and, as Miller says, definitive. This is indeed the right one. The 1963 version is about balances: Sinatra striking the right mix of aggressiveness and tenderness, Riddle finding the border between Broadway bravura and his own, less earthbound imagination. Although the piece has been attempted by Mel Tormé, Sammy Davis Jr. (in a surprisingly touching rendition for Decca), and Jack Nicholson (in the film *Heartburn*), Sinatra's "Soliloquy" remains the only time the work has been completely successful outside of the show that spawned it.

And he continued to bring it back from time to time; there are several outstanding readings extant from the 1980s (including one from December 1988 that was issued on the CD *Sinatra 80th: Live in Concert*) in which he takes in at an even slower tempo. This late-in-life reading is both magisterial and grandfatherly, with the seventy-two- (or possibly seventy-three-) year-old Sinatra keenly feeling every word, every emotion, every change of Billy Bigelow's mind as he attempts to process the idea of fatherhood. And, at eleven minutes long, it could be called *From Here to Paternity.*

A few months after the *Carousel* movie debacle—or whatever it was—Sinatra went to work on an extremely ambitious project of a very different nature. This was his instrumental album *Tone Poems of Color.* Inspired by the poetry of Norman Sickel, a radio writer who had worked on the *Perfectly Frank* series, Sinatra commissioned original works for full orchestra from a talent pool that began with his Capitol cronies Nelson Riddle and Billy May. He also invited old friend Alec Wilder and three movie orchestrators he had worked with (or would, soon enough), Jeff Alexander, André Previn, and Elmer Bernstein. (The only major Sinatra collaborator conspicuous by his absence was Axel Stordahl.) This work was true multimedia, or at least, as much as could be done in 1955: each track on the album represented a color, a poetic text by Sickel, and an original piece of music by the eight different composers, played by a sixty-piece orchestra.

Sinatra had recorded this symphonic, if not strictly classical, program as a rather auspicious way of breaking ground and officially cutting the ribbon on Capitol's own recording studios in their new pancake-shaped skyscraper on Hollywood's Vine Street in February and March 1956. This was an auspicious occasion: Sinatra's first session at the Capitol Records Tower, and only his second project as a conductor. (He hadn't conducted on a date since the 1945 Alec Wilder instrumental sessions ten years earlier.) The musicians who participated on the 1955 dates all agreed that Sinatra wielded the baton at least as skillfully as most of his arrangers, if not more so.

"One thing that I really enjoyed was when Sinatra conducted," reminisced reedman Ted Nash. "He was so serious about that. It wasn't a throwaway thing. Everybody wants to be something they're not. A singer wants to be an arranger, and a comedian wants to be a singer, and Sinatra really wanted to do a good job conducting on that. He was just real serious and wanted that thing to turn out great." Sometime later, Sinatra admitted "Do you know what I really am? A frustrated conductor!" (He said at that time that he was about to commission Nelson Riddle to compose "a complete concerto for Spanish guitar" for himself to conduct, but that idea apparently evolved into his 1962 album *Frank Sinatra Conducts Music from Pictures and Plays*.)

Eleanor Slatkin remembers that on two of the four sessions for *Tone Poems*, concertmaster Felix Slatkin "was damn near conducting [the strings] from his chair, but Frank was so gifted musically that he could bring it all off. Felix kept his group in shape very well." Nash added, "In the woodwinds, we were really concentrating with Frank and working hard to get everything just right." Said Harry Klee, "Frank was a wonderful conductor. That's the first I ever knew that he could conduct." "He surprised everybody," added Bill Miller. "We knew he couldn't read, but he knows when the notes go up or down. He knows about 'pianissimo,' 'piano-F,' he knows what all that means. He's pretty fearless. He did all right!"

Most of the writers, particularly the swing-oriented Riddle and May, stepped outside of their characteristic styles to tackle their *Tone Poems* colors. However, the somber strings and heavy mood of "Green" automatically announced the presence of Gordon Jenkins. If you were listening to the track randomly on the radio, you would have no trouble identifying the style of Jenkins, on any kind of blindfold test. Even the one-finger piano solo that opens the piece—actually played by Miller—simulates Jenkins's own distinctively minimal, individual-note keyboard style. Although Sinatra had previously sung several of the arranger-composer's pop song hits, such as "San Fernando Valley," on the *Vimms* show, the romantic, Tchaikovsky-eseque "Green" represented a milestone: this would be the very first time that Frank Sinatra worked directly with Gordon Jenkins.

"Billy May is driving, while Nelson has depth," Sinatra once said, "and with Gordon Jenkins, it's all so beautiful and simple that to me it's like being back in the womb." Sinatra had a place in his toolbox for all three, as Billy May humbly elaborated: "Frank would more or less pick Gordon Jenkins if he wanted to do something sentimental with strings, and then he would get either myself or Nelson—mostly Nelson—to do just the nuts and bolts stuff."

Although all three of them had established themselves with Nat King Cole before starting to work with Ol' Blue Eyes, each took a different route to attracting his attention. Riddle would spend a lifetime making other artists look good, Billy May proved himself a hit-making bandleader in his own name, and Gordon Jenkins was that rara avis, an equally successful songwriter and arranger, and in another guise, a businessman and impresario. Sinatra had first met Jenkins during one of his early visits to the West Coast with Tommy Dorsey; in 1946, he heard six sides that Jenkins had scored for Judy Garland, and from that point onward, he said, "I always dreamed about him doing some work for me."

When Sinatra collaborated with Nelson Riddle, the two men worked together to create a new sound; Riddle, as I've said elsewhere, was a blank page upon which Sinatra could write, and as much as Riddle helped pull the singer out of his Ava-era doldrums, Sinatra too was largely responsible for much of Riddle's career. It's impossible to imagine the lives of either man had they not worked together. With May and Jenkins, Sinatra was collaborating with two established musical auteurs whose sonic signatures were already known commodities in the pop music world. May was known for a bright, swinging sound and a belly-laugh sense of humor, but he could also arrange beautiful ballads like "Moonlight in Vermont." Jenkins's signature sound, by comparison, was dark, heavy, somber—sober, even—and grandly gothic.

If May was, at one point, in essence a ghostwriter for Duke Ellington, Jenkins could be a ghostwriter for Tchaikovsky. In his most characteristic work, he doesn't fit most definitions of a jazz arranger (you wouldn't confuse him with Neal Hefti or Bill Holman), yet he made an invaluable contribution to many classic jazz recordings by Louis Armstrong, Billie Holiday, Peggy Lee, Ella Fitzgerald, and others. (He also wrote theme songs for two of the greatest swing bands of all time, Benny Goodman and Woody Herman.)

Jenkins's key strength was in the area of what we now refer to as "narrative." Here, he more than earned his place among the big four of the Sinatra canon (the first being Stordahl, who set the stage for all of them).

Gordon Hill Jenkins was born in Webster Groves, Missouri, a small town near Saint Louis, on May 12, 1910, the son of a church organist who also played piano for local movie theaters, and the younger brother of a local bandleader. A Decca sleeve note later claimed that Jenkins became "a master of orchestration" because "he had learned to play practically every instrument." In 1925, Jenkins won an amateur contest in Saint Louis playing his ukulele, a competition hosted and judged by no less than the all-time *ukemeister*, Cliff "Ukulele Ike" Edwards himself. Still in his teens, Jenkins played banjo in his brother's band at a nearby summer resort; twenty years later, on a radio show, he surprised his musicians by playing vibraphone with a small Dixieland band.*

---

* This was on *The Bob Burns Show*, starring the then-famous countrified, bazooka-blowing comedian, and the band was called the Suitcase Six. Jenkins was eventually replaced in this by the more practiced Frank Flynn, who remembered, "Hell, anybody's going to sound better because Gordon was hardly a vibes player."

By several accounts, Jenkins was an excellent conventional piano player—using all ten fingers—but became famous for a very unconventional style in which he outlined a tune by playing one note of the melody at a time, which was accentuated by a close-miking technique. Jenkins never took credit for the sound, which was anticipated in various earlier recordings by the British bandleader-songwriter Ray Noble, but he used it to generate a series of chart hits for himself in the 1940s and it became a kind of trademark for him.

He played professionally from the age of ten, gigging around Webster Groves in various small-time saloons, and shocked the conservative (albeit hard-drinking) Midwesterners around him when he dropped out of high school to play piano in a local speakeasy.* He also played with a local band-leader named Joe Gill who was ensconced at the Hotel Chase in Saint Louis, and he worked his way up to a spot at local radio station KMOX.

He left Missouri for the first time in 1930, with another local band, this one directed by Henry Santry (known to have been leading an early jazz band in Cleveland a decade earlier). "It didn't work out," Jenkins said later. "He didn't like me and I didn't like him, so we called it off. I was pretty close to New York, so I decided to go there. Out of seven million people I knew just one, and he didn't seem to be able to get me a job." The composer would later reflect on this first New York experience in his 1945 composition *Manhattan Tower*. When Jenkins came down with influenza, he returned home to Missouri. There the young man took a job at the local Fox Theatre, accompanying vaudeville acts, often with original music. He married his high school sweetheart, Nancy Harkey, in 1931.

The following year Jenkins landed a major break when he got the chance to fill in for Isham Jones's ailing pianist while the famed bandleader was playing the Coronado Hotel in Saint Louis. A legendary arranger and pioneer of the modern dance band format, Jones was a milestone man in serious popular music and a worthy role model not only for Jenkins but for proteges as diverse as the great jazz bandleader Woody Herman and the songwriter and film score composer Victor Young. Jones himself was a fantastically successful songwriter; Sinatra would record at least three of his songs: "Swingin' Down the Lane" (on *Swingin' Lovers*), "It Had to Be You" (on *Trilogy: The Past*), and "The One I Love Belongs to Somebody Else" in the company of Gordon Jenkins (as well as with Dorsey and Sy Oliver). Among other things, Jenkins

---

* For this edition of this book, I'm incorporating information from the 2005 *Goodbye: In Search of Gordon Jenkins*, a biography of the maestro by his son, journalist and sportswriter Bruce Jenkins.

supplied Jones with a brilliant dance band reimagining of Sergei Rachmaninoff's Prelude in C-Sharp Minor, played as a swinging fox-trot.

In later years, Jenkins gave major credit to both Jones and Young, who was already directing his own series of dance band recordings by 1930–31, as his primary inspirations. "I was fortunate enough to meet Victor when I was twenty-two years old," he recalled, explaining that Young "heard something" in one of the younger man's orchestrations "that attracted him. . . . He asked me if I would take a walk with him, so we went for a three-hour walk in Lincoln Park in Chicago, and he talked to me about music and what a chance I had to be a success—and some of the things I'd done wrong on the record date, some of the things I'd done right. He'd never seen me before, and he took three hours to teach me things that you don't know when you're twenty-two: when to let the singer sing, when to fill in, and so forth. I think I learned more in that afternoon than you could learn at college about practical writing. Something like that keeps you going a long time. When I got home, I was ten feet off the ground."

Jones also helped Jenkins launch his career as a songwriter, and recorded his first notable tune, "Blue Prelude," in 1933. This rather dark ode, which later became Woody Herman's theme song, was composed by tuba player and arranger Joe Bishop, and Jenkins supplied the lyrics. By 1934, Jenkins had landed two more hits and standards the other way around: "P.S. I Love You" and "When a Woman Loves a Man" were Jenkins's melodies with lyrics by Johnny Mercer. Still, Jenkins was capable of writing both: the 1956 "Married I Can Always Get" is a show-tune–like composition in which the words are in a class with Jerry Herman or Sammy Cahn. He wrote both words and music for his most famous song, 1935's "Goodbye," which Benny Goodman selected for his ending theme. (Bruce Jenkins revealed that "Goodbye" was inspired by a girlfriend of the composer who died in childbirth, while carrying his stillborn baby.)

By 1936, Jones was ready to retire and disband (temporarily, it turned out), and Jenkins, to his surprise, was hired to orchestrate and conduct a Broadway revue titled *The Show Is On*, which ran for six months at the Winter Garden in 1936–37. The stars onstage were Bert Lahr and Beatrice Lillie, but the biggest names were in the songwriter credits—the Shubert Brothers somehow enticed no less than Vernon Duke, George and Ira Gershwin, Richard Rodgers and Lorenz Hart, Arthur Schwartz and Howard Dietz, Harold Arlen and Yip Harburg, Hoagy Carmichael (who rarely if ever wrote for Broadway), and even Herman "Dodo" Hupfeld all to contribute songs to the score. And the production was conceived, staged, and designed by Vincente Minnelli. It was during rehearsals for this show that Jenkins made a major breakthrough in the art of pop music orchestration: up until this time, when an orchestra accompanied a singer, they typically played the melody under the vocal. Jenkins rightfully concluded that the accompaniment and the star were getting in the way of each other, so he arranged to have the ensemble play just a harmonic background while the singer sang. Even *Variety* took notice: "As a result of Jenkins's handling, the fiddles do not play the melody with the vocalist and drown out her voice in the process. Jenkins's idea is to accompany the singer, letting her voice carry easily and naturally through the music."

The twenty-six-year-old Jenkins grew restless with having to conduct the exact same music the exact same way for eight shows a week ("I even offered to rearrange the music free of charge") and jumped at the chance to join the music staff at Paramount Pictures. However, after anonymously scoring *The Big Broadcast of 1937, Artists and Models, Blossoms on Broadway* ("which I've been living down for several years"), *College Swing,* and others, he gradually realized that Hollywood appealed to him even less than Broadway. "There are always five relatives doing a job [that] one could do," he complained, "and you have to please a bunch of guys who don't know *Madame Butterfly* from 'Chopsticks.'" After an altercation with an ego-tripping mogul, Jenkins left both Paramount Pictures and the larger studio system in general.

The mediums that best captured his imagination were radio and then recordings. Gogo DeLys, a singer he had worked with in New York, married one of the heads of NBC's West Coast operation and recommended Jenkins. Within a short while he was in charge of all musical direction on all Los Angeles broadcasts, where he was in a position to give the very young Lyle "Skitch" Henderson his first spot as a conductor. In the early 1940s, Jenkins began regularly writing arrangements for Decca Records; on Martha Tilton's 1942 Decca disc of Cole Porter's "The Wedding Cake Walk," Jenkins's accompaniment could be easily mistaken for John Scott Trotter or Vic Schoen. He freelanced for various labels until 1945, when he went under contract to Decca as conductor and musical director.

In the immediate postwar era, Jenkins came into his own. Up to now, we've been comparing him with his colleagues in Sinatra's world: Stordahl, Riddle, and May. But a more apt comparison might be with such later music makers as Henry Mancini, Burt Bacharach, Michel Legrand, and Antônio Carlos Jobim; all of these composers were songwriters, conductors, performers, and headliners in their own right as well as orchestrators who worked with pop stars—they were all, to use a twenty-first-century term, brand names, much more so in their own time than, say, Nelson Riddle (who yearned to achieve that status but never quite did).

Jenkins made a name for himself with the larger public as musical director for the extremely popular crooner and Sinatra rival Dick Haymes. In his Decca years, he became the only conductor to work with Haymes, Billie Holiday, Ella Fitzgerald, Louis Armstrong, Al Jolson, the Andrews Sisters, Peggy Lee, and Judy Garland (not all in the same session). He was equally busy working on radio and recordings, doing his own sessions, and arranging for headliners. At one point in the late 1940s, between his songs, his work with star singers, and releases under his own name, no fewer than five of the top ten singles were his productions, including the blockbuster hits "Maybe You'll Be There" and "Don't Cry, Joe."

Although neither of these songs was Jenkins's own, he was no less prolific in these years as a composer, and scored highly with two works of Americana that caught the nostalgic mood of the country during the late war years, "San Fernando Valley" (inspired by the area where he and his wife had settled to raise their three children) and "Homesick, That's All"; both were sung by Sinatra (both on the radio, the second also on a Columbia record). Over the years, Sinatra would sing at least five other Jenkins songs (not including *The Future*), both with and without the writer on the podium: "P.S. I Love You," "Goodbye," "This Is All I Ask," "How Old Am I?," and "I Loved Her."

Bruce Jenkins's book paints a picture of a warm, familiar, down-to-earth, and often hard-drinking guy. That was mostly around the musicians and coworkers with whom he felt the most comfortable. In interviewing dozens of musicians who worked with Sinatra, I generally found that usually the younger the age, the more distant they found Jenkins (and, proportionately, the more critical they tended to be of his work). Most Sinatra sidemen remembered Jenkins as being at least a little bit uptight, although engineer Lee Herschberg, who saw a different side of Jenkins from his seat in the engineering booth, felt that this was because Jenkins, even after all those years and all those hits, tended to get "a little bit nervous about being in the studio. . . . But he was a really incredible guy. I mean, just an amazing guy!" Skeets Herfurt, closer to Jenkins's generation, described him as being "not at all outgoing. He was a very quiet man, but very talented."

Jenkins may well have developed the mask he wore in public—serious, sophisticated, and slightly dour—as a way of covering his homespun Midwest background. Joel Herron, composer of "I'm a Fool to Want You," which Sinatra remade with Jenkins, said that the conductor was about as merry as "Oxford dons walking around in England, with caps and gowns" and long faces. Even Skitch Henderson, who was both a fan and a friend of Jenkins, characterized him with one single word, "dour," adding, "I was always apprehensive of him," adding for emphasis, "Always. Always!" The nicest compliment that most musicians emphatically paid Jenkins was that he was, as Frank Flynn put it, "a real gentleman."

Yet there were other circumstances in which Jenkins's coworkers saw quite a different side of him. "I always saw Gordie as like a small-town kid," recalled dancer Dante DiPaolo, referring to Jenkins's zeal for his hobbies, such as carpentry and photography. "He had those kinds of qualities." DiPaolo (who later married Rosemary Clooney) worked with Jenkins extensively in Las Vegas, where Jenkins composed and conducted the music for a series of big casino nightclub revues, most notably at the Tropicana (Sin City's answer to the Copacabana; their shows were staged by the same producer, Monte Proser). DiPaolo added, "I knew him as a very fun guy. He just wanted to hang out with the younger people and have fun."*

And Vegas wasn't the only place where Jenkins let his hair down. Although much of his work seemed highly influenced by nineteenth-century Russian classical music, Jenkins was a tireless devotee of traditional jazz (even to the point where he worked a Dixieland blues into *The Letter*, his rather bombastic musical-drama concept album for Judy Garland). He made a point to use the best traditional jazz and swing drummers he could get for his sessions on both coasts, Nick Fatool in Los Angeles and Johnny Blowers in New York. "Gordon was a real jazz-crazy guy. He insisted on using jazz guys on all his dates," said Blowers. For years, the prize that Jenkins had his eyes on was Louis Armstrong, and in 1952 he and longtime colleague, Decca producer Milt Gabler, conceived the idea of presenting Armstrong like a mainstream pop singer, complete with full orchestra and choir. "Gordon stood up on his little podium," as Gabler described the session, "so that all the performers could see him conduct. But before he gave a downbeat, Gordon made a speech about how much he loved Louis and how this was the greatest moment in his life." Gabler added, "And then he cried."

And yet that love of Dixieland and early jazz styles hardly endeared him to many of the Sinatra sidemen, who were mainly of the bebop generation—this being a time when the traditionalists (led by Armstrong) and the modernists (led by Dizzy Gillespie) were widely portrayed in the music press and elsewhere as being at war with each other. Jenkins even encouraged Arm-

---

* Jenkins also let his hair down, so to speak, as a songwriter in Vegas, as opposed to his more high-minded musical dramas. The Capitol album *Gordon Jenkins Conducts Monte Proser's Tropicana Holiday* boasts a bevy of busty backstage babes on its cover, while the disc itself collates high points of three such revues. Jenkins's original tunes include "Sex" and "I Feel Like a New Man," which features the lines, "With his head on my shoulder / He can leer at my brassiere."

strong to denounce the modernists by crafting for him a special parody of the famous Yale anthem, "The Whiiffenpoof Song," which they retitled "The Boppenpoof Song." Today it seems like a rather sour-grapes point of view; it didn't win any converts for the Dixieland cause at the time.

These demurrals are just a few of the opinions of Sinatra's players, most of whom tended to be younger. Bill Miller, the oldest in this group, named Jenkins his least favorite arranger: "I didn't like his writing at all; his stuff was so dull and boring. The piano parts were so simple that they were terrible!" "He was a little more old-fashioned" than Riddle and May, Dick Nash explained. "He didn't have the knowledge of the newer harmonies that would work and fit, like the flat ninths and raised ninths, and flat fives, and so forth. He didn't utilize a lot of the new technology, so therefore it was kind of old hat and boring." Milt Bernhart elaborated: "I'm not a big fan of Gordon Jenkins, and everybody who ever wrote an arrangement felt the same way. Nelson wouldn't bum-rap him, and neither would Billy May, but if they were pressed, they would say, 'Well, Gordon doesn't really know an awful lot about harmonies and orchestration'—and he didn't. When he took somebody else's song, the harmony was right out of the lead sheet. He couldn't expand on it; he couldn't alter changes to make them prettier. Axel took everything and made it into a better piece of music! And Nelson could also do that, and so could Don Costa."

Much as I hate to disagree with Milt, who was a major source of both information and wisdom to Chuck Granata and me, but May actually had many positive things to say about Jenkins; and if there's one thing Billy May never was, it was diplomatic—if he felt a certain way, he wasn't shy about telling you. (And so did Johnny Mandel, an arranger even younger and more connected to the modern jazz world than May.) Riddle and May were especially effusive regarding Jenkins as a songwriter. Billy told me, "He was a good friend of mine and a great guy. He was a good songwriter and wrote some beautiful songs, especially 'This Is All I Ask.' I've been a fan of Gordon's for a long time. I was admiring him in the days when I was just starting out, when he was writing for Isham Jones." Riddle said he was "crazy about" the song "Goodbye," which he orchestrated for Sinatra when the composer was unavailable, and he added that he "admired Gordon so much for having written it." Composer Joel Herron, although he professed to be critical of the Sinatra-Jenkins albums, also said, "I think the most important thing that he wrote was 'Goodbye.' I played it at my wife's funeral, and better than that I can't say."

Miller was Jenkins's severest critic, with the exception of the New York deejay Jonathan Schwartz, who has embarked on a relentless and often absurd anti-Jenkins vendetta for nearly fifty years. The pianist found what he judged to be Jenkins's technical inadequacies extremely frustrating. "He would want, for example, a D-minor-seventh, but he would have an F chord written or play an F triad and put a D in the bass. Why not just write 'D-minor-seventh'? He would never just voice it the way it's supposed to be voiced. And some of his voicings in the reeds were militaristic sometimes, with oboe and bassoon. Why? They just didn't mesh."

But here's the larger truth: music and art aren't always necessarily about D-minor-sevenths. Musicians themselves are not always the best judge of music, any more than actors would be the best reviewers of movies; they can't help but have their own agenda, their own set of considerations and criteria—particularly in the modern era, when the harmonies were growing ever more complex, with possibly too much focus on chord changes rather than connecting with an audience, and jazz was, not surprisingly, losing much of its fan base. Jenkins, to his credit, kept his focus on the narrative, rather than the musicological minutia. None of Sinatra's other collaborators could have created a song as moving as "This Is All I Ask" or the album *September of My Years*, in which the orchestrator wove thirteen songs by disparate authors into what amounts to a remarkable suite or song cycle and delivered the precise balance between grandiosity and simplicity, the universal and the personal, that the collection called for.

As a conductor, Jenkins was highly unusual in that he was left-handed (in Jenkins's libretto for *The Future*, Sinatra refers to him as "Lefty"). "He was very hard to follow," said violinist Paul Shure, "because he wasn't a lefty who beat [time] the correct way—he beat backwards! So if you were on the wrong side of him and you weren't prepared for it, it was very hard to follow." Perhaps the most remarkable document of this is a film made by the CBS News crew in 1965, when they were following Sinatra around, and he allowed them, for the first and virtually only time, to set up cameras in one of his recording sessions. Oddly, they seem to have stuck one camera directly under the conductor's right armpit, and from that angle he seems to be flailing away with both arms—it almost looks like he's chopping wood. He doesn't just give the tempo and send the band on its way, he conducts very exactly—and extremely dramatically—leading the ensemble through every single little beat.

Lee Herschberg felt that Jenkins's musical acuity more than compensated for his southpaw status. He could "always conduct. I've never seen anybody command as much respect on a podium as Gordon did. He had an incredible sense of pitch. He could sit there with an orchestra of thirty or forty people and look at someone and say, 'You're out of tune. You better tune up.' He was amazing that way." Nick Fatool agrees: when asked if Jenkins was difficult to follow, the drummer answered, "No, I never found that. Not for me. But maybe the violins or somebody [would feel differently], but hell, [I thought] Gordon was a great conductor." Vincent Falcone added, "[Frank] told me that even though Gordon conducted with his left hand, he always said, 'Pay attention to this guy!'"

What Miller and some of the other musicians criticized as technical shortcomings were, ultimately, beside the point; they were too busy being trees to get a proper perspective on the forest. What attracted both Sinatra and the public at large to Jenkins was his songwriter's sense of both melody and drama. Certainly Jenkins wasn't as versatile as May or Riddle, who could do lots of different things in lots of different styles; but the surfaces he did create, for Sinatra especially, are inevitably precisely pertinent to what the vocalist is singing over them—and often quite beautiful in themselves.

Sinatra valued Jenkins just as highly as his other major collaborators; as Nick Fatool and others have testified, "Frank sure loved Gordon." When pressed to explain why Sinatra seemed to think so highly of Jenkins, even Bill Miller finally admitted, "There's a certain squareness about Frank; I say that affectionately. He has an old-fashioned side, and Gordon Jenkins represents that. As a singer he doesn't hear the harmonies the way we would. He hears those high singing strings—that was Gordon's gimmick." Indeed, Jenkins depends so heavily on the strings that his orchestrations sound like nothing without them—as Sinatra learned when he misguidedly attempted "September of My Years" and, even worse, "It Was a Very Good Year" live with the Basie band—and nary a fiddle in sight—in *Sinatra at the Sands* in 1966.

Paradoxically, Jenkins's biggest booster is the youngest musician ever to be admitted into Sinatra's inner circle, pianist and conductor Vinnie Falcone. Another piano player, Lou Levy, said Jenkins's style "was emotional more than it was harmonic," and in response Falcone added, "and isn't that what it's about?" He elaborated: "Gordon attacked the strings differently from the way many arrangers do in that he would double certain voices and stack them. So when he did one of those sweeping things, you had several octaves of the same sound coming down.

"It's always been a dream for me to develop a style so that no matter what you do, it's always identifiable," Falcone continued. "And I have to say that Gordon achieved that. When you hear George Shearing, you know it's George Shearing; it's the same for Art Tatum or Miles Davis. You can't say that for everybody, only for very, very, very few people. You really can't say that unequivocally for Don Costa, who was one of the greatest that ever lived. Not that this diminishes Don's talent, but it certainly is a credit to Gordon that he developed those little signature things so that when you hear his arrangements, you just know it's Gordon Jenkins."

As we shall see, Sinatra's work with Jenkins runs to two opposite extremes, both of which are contingent on the skills of "Lefty" as a songwriter as well as an arranger/conductor. On one level, Sinatra saw in Jenkins a potential partner in highbrow experiments, not only in a lofty Europeanization of barroom ballads but eventually in extended structures that transcend conventional song forms. On another level, Jenkins could take material from folk and even rock sources and render it relevant to Sinatra. In the immediate pre- and postretirement periods, when Sinatra was most concerned with appealing to a generation that thought Irving Berlin was a city with a wall through it, he turned to Jenkins especially frequently. "No one could deny," as even Bernhart confessed, "that Jenkins had a knack for getting to the heart of a certain kind of a song, especially 'It Was a Very Good Year.'"

Old-fashionedness was exactly what Sinatra and Voyle Gilmore had in mind when they assigned Jenkins the task of orchestrating *A Jolly Christmas from Frank Sinatra*. The twelve tracks on this seasonal set fairly hang from the chimney with simplicity and seasonal high spirits. That's because Jenkins has chosen to build suspense—to wait before letting his cat of high, moaning strings out of his Santa sack. "I'll Be Home for Christmas" contains the sole discernible glimmer of Jenkins's signature string section sound, and even there it's prominent only for a brief instrumental passage.

On this particular set, Jenkins employs a choir (the Ralph Brewster Singers), in place of his more customary string figures, as the basic element of the background behind Sinatra. This is unusual for Jenkins: he favored choral groups on his own "name" records, but usually left them out of his vocal accompaniments for star singers. This would suggest that Jenkins favored what was essentially a simple combination of two primary elements, either solo voice and strings or choir and strings; or here, solo voice and choir. To use all three elements—star voice, choir, and strings—Jenkins seems to feel, would be too much.

Intriguingly, the most distinctive chart is the least typically Jenkinsian of them all: the opening "Jingle Bells" commences with the chorus cooing a jivey version of the nineteenth-century tune, in a framework inspired by the 1950 pop-R&B hit "Rag Mop"; when Sinatra enters, he is immediately sympathetic to the proceedings and swings lightly and politely over them. On "The Christmas Song," "Mistletoe and Holly," "The First Noel," and others, Sinatra sounds vocally much like he did ten years earlier on his first Christmas album, *Christmas Songs by Sinatra*. On the more "serious" and traditional religious songs such as "Hark the Herald Angels Sing," and "Adeste Fideles," he sounds like the deeper, more mature Sinatra of the 1950s, and majestically so.

Throughout, Sinatra is never less than convincing, whether jingling bells or hanging a shining star upon the highest bough in "Have Yourself a Merry Little Christmas." Christmas music, fairly scarce in the swing era, came into its own in the 1950s, the era of albums and television (Christmas was a much bigger deal on TV than it had ever been on radio or even in the movies), a period when all the major pop singers eventually got around to doing sets of holiday songs. Many had their own signature Christmas songs: Bing Crosby's "White Christmas," Nat King Cole's "The Christmas Song," and "It's Beginning to Look a Lot Like Christmas" by Perry Como. The two such songs most closely associated with Sinatra are both done definitively here: "Mistletoe and Holly," one of the few songs written by Sinatra himself, along with two pallies from his Barton Music enterprise, Doc Stanford and longtime associate Hank Sanicola, and "The Christmas Waltz" by Sammy Cahn and Jule Styne. The latter is a singularly beautiful song that Sinatra would have been proud to be connected with. He ends on a note of utter charm, simply and directly intoning the two words, "Merry Christmas."

Sinatra kept the Christmas spirit going; at the end of the third and last session, in the Capitol Records Tower in July 1957 (in what was likely a sweltering summer), he threw a full-scale party for the musicians, singers, engineers, Capitol Records staff, and assorted onlookers, thereby trading in his usual "ring-a-ding-ding" for a "ho! ho! ho!"

Jenkins later recalled that there was some trepidation about whether or not the atmosphere would be quite so jovial. The conductor was a taskmaster who liked to have things go his way. As Nick Fatool put it, "All he wanted you to do was just play what he wrote, and don't add anything to it." And the singer was well known for not liking to be bossed around, to put it mildly.

According to Eleanor Slatkin, there was some conflict over the choice of concertmaster (for the string section). Jenkins and Sinatra both had their own favorites: for Jenkins it was usually David Frisina (who also worked extensively with Sinatra), while for Sinatra at this point, the first violin and cello were almost always Mr. and Mrs. Slatkin. Jenkins went along with that, but Eleanor said, "He was told he *had* to use me, and he didn't like it at all." (Also, according to Mrs. Slatkin, the older conductors, like Stordahl and Jenkins, were reluctant to work with female musicians.)

But that, somewhat to the surprise of the conductor, turned out to be their first and last disagreement. "The first time we worked together, a hundred people showed up because they thought it was going to be a free-for-all,"

Jenkins reminisced.* "He had a reputation of being tough to work with, and I also have a reputation for not holding back. So the studio was just jammed [with people] waiting for the fight to start. And we never did have any fight, not ever. We have never had a cross word."

If Jenkins, no less than Sinatra, toned down his sonic trademarks on *A Jolly Christmas,* they appear in spades on *Where Are You?* (released around the same time as the Christmas set, although actually recorded several months previously), and even more promisingly on the 1959 *No One Cares.* "Just Friends" contains Jenkins's famous spiraling strings motif, which aurally suggests a carpet being rolled open *up* a flight of stairs. The device is well known to anyone familiar with either of Sinatra and Jenkins's two 1965 meetings, the *September of My Years* album and Jenkins's segment of the *Man and His Music* television special.

On all four of his classic downbeat ballad albums from 1955 to 1959 (not counting the more optimistic *Close to You*), Sinatra included one blues-tinged song: "Mood Indigo" on *Wee Small Hours,* "Blues in the Night" on *Only the Lonely,* "Baby, Won't You Please Come Home?" on *Where Are You?,* and "Stormy Weather" on *No One Cares.* On each of the Jenkins Capitol sets he also made a point of doing at least one classically derived number: "I Think of You" (via Rachmaninoff) on *Where Are You?* and "None but the Lonely Heart" (after Tchaikovsky) on *No One Cares.* (And, as we've seen, the traditional sacred carols on *A Jolly Christmas.*)

*Where Are You?* and *No One Cares* contain a total of twenty-four tracks. (One of these, on the latter album, Isham Jones's "The One I Love Belongs to Somebody Else," was originally dropped from early stereo editions because of the shorter playing time of that format, but restored for the 1991 CD edition.) Sinatra loved to contrast the simple with the grandiose: the two albums contain two arty songs by Alec Wilder (both four-word question titles beginning with "Where?"), "Where Is the One?" and the incredibly dirge-y "Where Do You Go?"; a legitimately semiclassical Leonard Bernstein show tune, "Lonely Town" (from *On the Town*); and "Autumn Leaves," the famous Hungarian-French chanson describing dead plants.

All of which underscores how Sinatra regarded Jenkins as the perfect partner with whom to reexamine the European string textures of his work with Axel Stordahl; at least half of the songs on these two sets are remakes from the Columbia period. "If you're going to make comparisons, which are

---

* Most of the quotes from Gordon Jenkins in this chapter are from a radio interview with deejay (and game show host) Wink Martindale, probably done in the late 1970s.

always dangerous, you could compare Gordon to Axel," Skitch Henderson observed. "Because it was that kind of wonderfully romantic style of writing which fitted Frank's voice, I felt, a great deal." The depressing "Where Do You Go?" immediately moves beyond the romantic and into the funereal; a hymn for the spiritually bankrupt, it would make a perfect soundtrack for a public-service film designed to document the plight of the homeless.

This was a fairly spectacular season for Jenkins: he was working on three of his all-time greatest collaborations, Nat King Cole's *Love Is the Thing* and Judy Garland's *Alone* (along with Sinatra's *Where Are You?*). *Love Is the Thing* has Jenkins wrapping Cole's silvery baritone in a heavy, warm blanket of violins in a program of love songs that are upbeat in mood though decidedly not so in tempo. Recorded in December 1956 in the new stereo process, *Love Is the Thing* zoomed to number one on the pop album charts, becoming Cole's biggest selling LP in his lifetime.

Several key Jenkins ideas appear throughout his work in this period: on "Paradise" (on the second Cole-Jenkins album, 1958's *The Very Thought of You*), the strings "sing" certain key phrases that are normally hummed by the singer. Jenkins employs a similar gambit on Sinatra's "I Don't Stand a Ghost of a Chance with You," in which the strings almost literally verbalize the words "I know I must," before Sinatra finishes the line with, "I'm dreaming." "Don't Wait Too Long" on *September of My Years* similarly contains a chorus in which a single-note piano solo takes the words out of Sinatra's mouth. The opening title track, "Where Are You?," boasts Sinatra's purest and most relaxed Cole-style singing ever.

But if Sinatra wanted Jenkins's sumptuous strings for his first foray into stereo, the resemblances to the Cole albums end there. Sinatra-Jenkins was automatically a deeper and darker experience than Cole-Jenkins, Sinatra insisting on offering more than love songs; these were ballads with a grabbing angle and a story to them. (Cole paid attention; his third and final album with Jenkins, 1962's *Where Did Everyone Go?*, was also much darker than its two predecessors.)

The high, moaning strings are heard throughout; one is almost never conscious of brass, except for three low-blowing French horns (heard to great effect on "There's No You"), a handful of woodwinds, and a barely audible rhythm section (with Fatool usually playing brushes). "Jenkins did do some good writing for woodwinds," said reedman Harry Klee, "but he actually just used the woodwinds as a cushion under the strings."

Jenkins almost never does anything to deliberately attract attention to his arrangements. The French horns that function as foghorns at the start of "I Cover the Waterfront" and the countermelody behind The Voice on "Where

Is the One?" are exceptions. David Frisina, concertmaster for the Los Angeles Philharmonic and Jenkins's preferred first violinist for many years, said of the arranger, "Gordon wrote beautifully for strings. He wrote very simply, and he couldn't get complicated. He liked to have a lot of violins playing the melody, and when he did, I tell you, it sounded oh so beautiful."

Jenkins brings out some of Sinatra's most compassionate performances ever, both on the slightly more varied *Where Are You?* and the all-downer *No One Cares,* both of which use Billie Holiday–influenced crawl tempos. Sinatra continues to sing very tightly behind the beat, temporarily relaxing his grip on it as he comes out of the bridge on "Waterfront" as if to convey even greater resignation.

On "Laura," he employs a much fuller, juicier voice that fills both stereo channels. Many of the other twenty-three tracks on these two sets find him utilizing a much thinner, more emotionally charged vocal palette, signifying extremes he could not have reached in the Stordahl era—he deliberately wants to sound desperate, like he's reached the end of his rope and even gone beyond it. Never before could he have made the shadows steal across a lonely room so vividly, as he does in "I Think of You" and throughout much of *No One Cares*; on "A Cottage for Sale," in particular, Sinatra seems to be on the verge of real tears.

Even Jenkins's detractors are forced to admit that the two albums have undeniable highlights. "I Can't Get Started" and the remake of "Why Try to Change Me Now?" make for perfect Sinatra anthems (considerably more so than "My Way," for instance), especially the former, with its theme of brash bravura chopped down to size; Sinatra was the only singer truly capable of singing (from the 1936 original) "All the papers, where I led the news / With my capers" and speaking the literal truth. "Started" also anticipates the 1981 Jenkins-Sinatra "Thanks for the Memory" with its new set of lyrics, supposedly by Ira Gershwin himself.

Both collaborators seem to have considered Leonard Bernstein's "Lonely Town" the high point of *Where Are You?* By 1956, Sinatra had wanted to do the song ever since he first heard it in *On the Town,* the groundbreaking Broadway musical from 1944. In fact, that was how Metro-Goldwyn-Mayer was able to entice him (along with Gene Kelly) back into sailor suits for the 1949 film version of the musical. According to Betty Comden (who wrote the lyrics, the book, and the screenplay with her longtime partner Adolph Green), there was little chance of Sinatra's character, Chip, getting to do "Lonely Town," which had been written for Kelly's character, Gabey, since there was no appropriate way to work in the Chip character doing such a heavy, moving ballad—by far the most powerful in the score. "The last day of shooting came, and they said, 'That's a wrap!' He said, 'Well, where's my song? When do I do "Lonely Town"?' And they just said to him, 'It's out. You're not doing it.' And he was very, very angry."

The *Where Are You?* reading more than makes up for the injustices done to both Sinatra and Bernstein by MGM (namely, denying one the chance to sing the other). Most of "Lonely Town" uses especially minimal backing to deliberately call attention to Sinatra's nervous tremolo, making him sound all the more devastatingly lonely, as well as underscoring the emptiness of all existence—until the fitting phrase "unless there's love," at which the full string section enters to emphasize the message that love is the answer to loneliness. Asked to name his favorite Sinatra performance, Jenkins responded, "For many years, [Frank's] and my favorite were the same. He thought that 'Lonely Town' was the best record he ever made, and I did, too. Now I think it would be a toss-up for me between 'Lonely Town,' 'Laura,' and 'Send in the Clowns.' 'Lonely Town' has such a feel to it: the orchestration, the way he sings it . . . so well!"

One of the key components of this particular chart, its distinctive French horn introduction (probably played by Vince DeRosa), had been suggested by Sinatra himself. That intro is a nest of overlapping allusions: "Lonely Town" famously begins with a reference to "New York, New York," the showstopper that more or less opens Act I of *On the Town*. "I had a recording of a piece of symphonic music, I can't think of the name of it," he told Sid Mark in 1984, which started him thinking about "the beginning of 'Lonely Town,'" the singer said, "and Gordon liked [the idea], obviously, and used it, and it worked out very well, too." The Maestro enthusiastically endorsed Sinatra's idea for the opening, not least because, as French hornist John Cave recalled, "Gordon Jenkins was a horn maniac. He just loved horn! He had [us] wall to wall all the time. He always used it almost like a solo instrument—he always had lots of solos."

Other elements of the Sinatra-Jenkins "Lonely Town" derive from the arranger's own machinations. As he put it, "I got carried away and put in a few free bars of 'Never Leave Me' from his extended work *Manhattan Tower* at the end." While Jenkins speaks of inserting a royalty-free excerpt from this tune in "Lonely Town," the quote is heard for less than two seconds here. "Never Leave Me" turns up much more prominently in Jenkins's arrangement of "Chloe" for Louis Armstrong; it's so intrinsically similar to his basic, much-used major-minor "moaning" motif that we can say it's used extensively in the *September of My Years* and *She Shot Me Down* albums.

"I'll Never Smile Again" is Sinatra's sole version of his earliest major hit not to use the 1940-style close harmony vocal–group-and-celesta treatment;

in one passage, it goes very high.* "Cottage for Sale," conversely, builds down to a beautifully conceived un-climax of Jolsonesque basement-low pedal notes. This is a minority opinion, not shared by fellow Frankophiles or the song's composer, but Sinatra turns in a much more moving "I'm a Fool to Want You" (originally recorded six years earlier) the second time around, dropping the melodramatic choir and adding more real drama with an especially poignant extra outchorus. It's worth noting that Sinatra recorded the song twice, once in the year that he and Ava Gardner were married, then again in the year when they were officially divorced.

Finally, *Where Are You?* ends brilliantly with "Baby, Won't You Please Come Home?"; Sinatra also sang this Clarence Williams blues ballad in the company of Bing Crosby on *The Edsel Show* (CBS-TV, October 13, 1957). In both performances, he almost seems to be stepping outside of himself, as if observing his own performance from someone else's perspective and basking in the warmth of his own radiance. Sinatra has weighed the disparate elements—the earthy, blues-based melody on one side of the scale and the epic, larger-than-life string passages on the other—and places himself squarely in the middle. It's a perfect way to end a Sinatra album.

Sinatra had added May and Jenkins to his sonic palette partly because he was reluctant to be too closely associated with any one collaborator, the way he had been during the late Stordahl era. This also led him to feel, as Frank Military recalled, that "something was happening to his voice. So we did the sessions for *Where Are You?* and they were magnificent. When we finished the last cut on the album, Frank said, 'Let's get a copy, we'll take it up to the house.' So we went up to his place and played the acetate. It was absolutely fabulous. We listened to the whole thing. He turned to me and said, 'I thought for a minute I was losing my voice.' I said, 'God, there's no indication of that here. It's the most magnificent album I've heard for a long time.'"

Sinatra was also delighted with the sales of *Where Are You?*, which reached number three in *Billboard,* not far behind Cole's *Love Is the Thing,* and began planning an even heavier and sadder downer set as a follow-up, which even-

---

* According to Bill Miller, "Smile Again" nearly became a major train wreck at the *No One Cares* sessions. One passage "goes from B-flat to D," he recalls. "But Gord went right up to an F-seventh, real high. It was terrible! It had to be a D chord in there. It had to be. I played it down. I asked Frank what to do, and he said, 'Well, shit, have Nelson change it.' I called Nelson, and he rewrote the four bars. And of course he didn't sound like Gordon Jenkins. When you hear that arrangement, when it comes to going up to the D chord, you can tell it's Nelson, that it was an insert. I remember that vividly." (I have to admit that I've listened to this track many times and can't find anything that sounds like Riddle—to me, at least.)

tually became the 1958 *Only the Lonely*. Even after Jenkins informed Sinatra that he was too busy in Las Vegas to undertake the project, Sinatra retained Jenkins's most celebrated composition, "Goodbye." In 1959, Sinatra and Jenkins reteamed for the above-discussed *No One Cares*; then in January 1962, Sinatra had a whole other idea in mind when he planned his first set with Jenkins on Reprise.

In analyzing Sinatra's career in hindsight, like a team of Monday morning quarterbacks, we can fairly accurately reconstruct his decision to do certain records. The Billy May albums, *I Remember Tommy*, and the Basie series, for instance, all seem like natural and obvious ideas that Sinatra almost could not have helped thinking of—they practically sprang to life fully grown, as if from the head of Zeus. In a million years, however, we'll never be able to figure out how he conceived of the *Come Waltz with Me* album, which was released as *All Alone*, a set of archaic ballads, primarily from the teens and twenties, rendered in 3/4 time.

*Come Fly with Me* and *Swing Along with Me/Sinatra Swings* contain the kind of loopy exotica that appealed to Sinatra's senses of both rhythm and humor. Likewise, one senses that *All Alone* gave both Sinatra and Jenkins a chance to address the stoic sides of their natures through a genre of music that had been a crucial part of each man's early artistic evolution—that "old-fashioned" side of Sinatra. *Where Are You?* and *No One Cares* pay lip service to such eclectic highbrows as Bernstein, Wilder, and Duke (Vernon, not Ellington). It's key, then, that none of the nine antiquities on *All Alone* were written by the intelligentsia of Tin Pan Alley who were writing waltzes at the time: no Kern, no Youmans, no Rodgers. Rather, Sinatra and Jenkins have chosen to confront a more basic, even atavistic kind of ur-pop tune—such as "Are You Lonesome Tonight?," which, although it provided Elvis Presley with his most memorable ballad in 1960, is actually so old it was originally published as "Are You Lonesome To-night?" The set also includes no fewer than five numbers from that master of playing (and composing) a simple melody, Irving Berlin, including "What'll I Do?," "When I Lost You," and "Remember."

As mentioned above, the original title for this 1962 album was *Come Waltz with Me*, and Sinatra went so far as to go to the trouble of commissioning a new title track from Cahn and Van Heusen. Given the circumstances behind *Swing Along with Me*, it would make sense that the fear of a similar legal brouhaha with Capitol Records would have impelled Sinatra to use a title that was anything other than "Come *Something* with Me." But it turned out for the best, in any case: the song that the team came up with, "Come Waltz with Me," was hardly their finest work, nor one of Jenkins's top arrangements. And with its comparatively bright intro and slightly faster tempo, the song just didn't fit in with the rest of the album. Sinatra also may have felt that using the word "waltz" in the title gives away the whole show, whereas the less musically specific "All Alone" affords more of an air of mystery and romance to the interconnecting factor among these (now) eleven songs.

Far from being stillborn, the song "Come Waltz with Me" (the only time Sinatra actually deleted a specially written title track) was eventually introduced by Steve Lawrence. "[Arranger] Sid Feller and I were doing an album of waltzes at the time," said Lawrence, "and Sid evidently met with Sammy [Cahn]. . . . So Sammy said, 'I got a great song.'" Taking the cue, Lawrence and Feller wisely titled their album *Come Waltz with Me* (which, like Jo Stafford's *Do I Hear a Waltz?*, isn't nearly as magisterial as the Sinatra-Jenkins album). When the 1992 CD of *All Alone* at last restored the missing track (wisely as a bonus track, rather than the opener), Sinatra's decision to omit it now seemed even smarter. Although we're glad to hear the song, it just doesn't fit: the original album begins superbly with "All Alone" and concludes even more so with "The Song Is Ended (but the Melody Lingers On)"; even had Sinatra commissioned Irving Berlin directly, no one could have written a better closer.

Another appropriate title might have been *Ruminations at Dusk*, for all of the songs are painted in the reds and yellows of a midwestern sunset. You feel as though you're rifling through faded song sheets in an old-time small-town music shop at closing time. Further, each of the nine "oldies" tunes concerns itself with an absence, so that even apart from the fact of their age, each song has a built-in factor of nostalgia and longing for a happier past. To make this concept even more real on "All Alone" and "The Song Is Ended," the deceptively uncomplicated Berlin ballads Sinatra uses to begin and end the set, Jenkins conjures up an ethereal "air" voice. Portrayed vocally by Loulie Jean Norman, Hollywood's number-one "vapor girl," this incorporeal entity serves to illustrate the fantasized presence of a departed other.

All of which explains why the comparatively recent songs on *All Alone* don't quite fit. Sinatra had included them perhaps to show that the waltz lives on, yet the more optimistic "The Girl Next Door," from 1943, cheerfully looks forward to a love affair; while Cahn and Van Heusen's disappointingly minimal movie theme "Indiscreet," from 1958, describes one in progress. (Paradoxically, it could be the Sinatra of *All Alone* is internalizing the words to "The Girl Next Door" as if in a flashback, like an old stud reminiscing about his first love. However, that concept may be too *meta*, even for me.)

Still, for all the unrestrained emotion of Jenkins's "sobbing and throbbing" strings, we can't approach his work without sensing the kind of decorum that goes with buttoned shoes—a sort of starched-collar correctness, a formalness. Sinatra has no such reservations, however, and on many levels the central drama of the album emerges from the tension between the singer's impassioned pleading and the quaint parlor setting of the backgrounds. The third key element, the waltz factor, affects the other two, making the backdrops seem more formal and the singing even more fervent. The time signature speaks to Sinatra's sense of rhythm and brings out the most in him, no less than any of the swing albums. He responds to the 1-2-3, 1-2-3 time signature by remaining even further behind the beat than usual; this, combined with the heaviest-sounding voice he had yet brought to a recording session, results in some of his most powerfully passionate singing.

The set illustrates an observation that Jenkins once shared with Nick Fatool: "We were drinking after a record date, and Gordon said, 'Frank puts himself in the mood to sing a [particular] song.'" The drummer felt that Sinatra did an especially good job of putting himself in the mood to do these prehistoric waltzes, particularly "Are You Lonesome Tonight?" PR man Peter Levinson, who attended the sessions for *All Alone*, recalls that "'Frank looked like hell when he came in. It was as if he'd just been to nine orgies. Nobody could believe that he sang as beautifully as he did on that album."

One imagines that Sinatra considered *All Alone*, like the later *Francis A. & Edward K.*, at once a personal triumph and a professional disappointment. Both were great albums that racked up his smallest sales of their periods, consisting as they did of especially idiosyncratic song choices and arrangements that he almost never sang again in either concerts or television appearances. *Where Are You?* and *No One Cares* charted at numbers three and two, respectively (and even they probably didn't sell as much as the two Cole-Jenkins albums of the 1950s), but *All Alone* made it only to twenty-five. Apparently, it was not the serious, old-fashioned side of Sinatra that moved product in record stores or garnered airplay.

When Sinatra returned to his comparatively more traditional "big song," as in "Ol' Man River" and "Soliloquy," a year later on *The Concert Sinatra*, the quality of the music and the quantity of the sales figures were more in check. Although Jenkins had the greater reputation for dealing with extended song structures, Riddle was the superior choice to handle the *Concert* set. He characteristically plays off Sinatra's gift for economy and intimacy, in contrast to Jenkins, who elaborates on Sinatra's sense of spectacle. Works like "Lost in the Stars" and "I Have Dreamed" are already big enough, and the last thing they need is for Jenkins to inflate them further with his emblematic grandiosity. It's typical of Sinatra to do big grandiose versions of simple songs (like "Baby, Won't You Please Come Home?" or "All Alone") and, conversely, relatively simple treatments of epic concert pieces.

Jenkins and Sinatra take a simple song like "Remember" and elevate it to a concert work; Riddle and Sinatra start with an epic like "Ol' Man River" and make it intimate. The *Concert Sinatra* album succeeded as forty minutes of relatively light, albeit emotionally deep, orchestrations of very heavy songs; meanwhile, the Sinatra-Jenkins collaboration continued on its course of weighty treatments of increasingly more rudimentary material. Riddle could take a complex song, like "Lost in the Stars" or "Soliloquy," and bring it down to earth, but Jenkins could take a bare bones Tin Pan Alley item like "All Alone" or "Remember" and inflate it into something larger than life.

From there it seemed like a natural progression for Sinatra to take advantage of Jenkins's natural empathy for folk music. Unshaven, unwashed folk singers in blue jeans, banging away on guitars, may seem completely inapposite to Jenkin's legions of violinists in tailcoats, but he had a surprisingly keen appreciation for this genre of music. As A&R man for Decca Records, Jenkins was perhaps the first mainstream producer, even before Mitch Miller, to realize the mass-market possibilities of folk music; during these years, this music meant more to readers of the *Daily Worker* than they did to those of *Variety*. When Jenkins wanted to bring the Weavers to Decca in 1949 and the top brass turned him down, he so believed in their commercial potential that he signed them to a personal contract; in other words, if the group's records didn't sell, he would have to pay them out of his own "San Fernando Valley" money. That the Weavers-Jenkins "Goodnight, Irene" sold so well that an artist as unlikely as Frank Sinatra was importuned to cover it, offers evidence enough of what an astute judge of the market Jenkins was.

That idea finds full expression in the 1965 *September of My Years*. While *Where are You?*, *No One Cares*, and especially *All Alone* are classics, *September of My Years* is a true milestone in the canons of both men. No, Sinatra didn't trade in his tux for a pair of overalls and a banjo; but the centerpiece of the album is a true modern folk song—"It Was a Very Good Year"—and most of the songs here have a similarly atavistic, ur-natural feeling. This is not an album where Cole Porter or Rodgers and Hart would have fit in; our hero is not down in the depths on the ninetieth floor, nor is he sipping orange juice for one before dashing off to a matinee, and he is decidedly not jetting off for a weekend in Paris to ease the bite of it. Rather, he is thinking about the number of springtimes that he has already enjoyed over the course of a lifetime, as well as the remaining Septembers that he has left before him. He is entreating beautiful girls to walk a little slower so that he may recall the conquests of his youth (as well as the ones who said no and the gals who got away), and he is entreating his children and grandchildren to include him in their fantasy worlds. He is remembering a time when the wind was green, like a living thing, even though sometimes his sacroiliac isn't what it used to be. And although sometimes it gets lonely early (doesn't it?), he doesn't mind, because he's had a love of his own. This is the warm, sweet September of his years.

In 1965, Sinatra was about to turn fifty. From a certain perspective, this hardly seems like the September of anyone's years. (It didn't to me when I wrote this book, in my early thirties, and nor does it now that I've reached my mid-fifties.) It was barely twenty-five years since he had left Harry James, and he would remain on the road for another three decades at this point. But from the point of view of Sinatra himself in his forty-ninth year, fifty was a milestone to be surmounted; by a weird coincidence, nearly half a dozen of the most essential men in Sinatra's life, mentors and father figures, all perished in their fifties: Tommy Dorsey, Axel Stordahl, Manie Sachs, Felix Slatkin, George Evans (his first and most important public relations guru), and, later, Don Costa. (And in jazz, and music in general, there were plenty of greats who never made it even to middle age.)

Thus, in Isaac Asimov's moving phrase, in memory yet green and in joy still felt, the scenes of his life rose sharply into view. Even if forty-nine seems a tad too young to contemplate going gently into that good night, we should be grateful that Sinatra had the foresight to assemble this musical "last will and testament," while he was still young enough to be of sound mind and voice. "The songs all had a thing about age and growing older," said Jenkins, "and I was exactly the right age to do it, as he was. We were talking about it on the date, that neither one of us could have made that album at any other time in our lives."

By any standards, *September of My Years* was a staggeringly ambitious album, one in which Sinatra and Jenkins took the so-called concept album format to an entirely new level. (And these are the two men who, perhaps more than any other, can be said to have originated the pop concept album, between *The Voice* and *Manhattan Tower*, both recorded in 1945.) *September* consisted of thirteen songs that took a long-term view of life, for which Jenkins provided orchestrations that are sufficiently sober and yet, in the best tradition of his work for Nat King Cole, evidence a hard-won optimism. For the 1956 *Come Fly with Me*, Billy May devised big-band arrangements that reflected the sense of whimsy inherent in goofy old travel songs like "Isle of Capri," and in the 1966 *Moonlight Sinatra*, Nelson Riddle scored orchestrations that reflect the vast richness and profound depth of the heavens. For this album, Jenkins and Sinatra came up with a profound collection of songs around the "September" theme, but for the only time in his career, only three of the songs ("September Song," "Last Night When We Were Young," and

"Hello, Young Lovers") were standards; the other ten were either relatively recent or specifically commissioned for this project.

All three of the standards are songs that Sinatra had previously recorded; this is actually his third version of "September Song" (following a Columbia single in 1946 and Stordahl's chart for *Point of No Return* in 1961). Back in the day, it seemed more relevant to compare the various versions, but now that seems beside the point; Sinatra was in a different place in 1965 than he had been in 1954, at age thirty-eight, when he recorded the version of "Last Night When We Were Young" that eventually became part of *In the Wee Small Hours*. That interpretation, like everything else, seemed to be all about Ava, but this one is about life in general, perhaps even about everything Sinatra had ever done in his life that he ever regretted or wished that he could change. (Another song be darned, he had more than a few regrets in his life.) In Jenkins's outsized orchestra, more than Riddle's more intimate one, Sinatra seems to be contemplating everyone else's "sighs and kisses" as well as his own. Likewise, on the 1951 "Hello, Young Lovers," Sinatra is clearly thinking of the loves of his own, whereas in 1965, he seems to be genuinely addressing all young lovers everywhere, perhaps starting with his own children.

Of the thirteen songs, not one is a conventional love song sung by the protagonist to his object of desire; instead, each is a meditation intoned inwardly (and therefore to the entire universe as a whole) by an old stud to himself. Even "September Song," originally written to be sung by the hero of *Knickerbocker Holiday* to his young leading lady, has had a few pronouns altered so that Sinatra can direct it internally. Compared to the previous "September Songs," in this one, Sinatra sings like he has all the time in the world.

Still, the standards are overall less notable than the other tracks, which include songs directly written for the album. Sammy Cahn and Jimmy Van Heusen contributed two songs for the project, which turned out to be two of their all-time best. Both numbers, "It Gets Lonely Early" and the outstanding title track, "The September of My Years," show that they clearly understood whom they were writing for. "It Gets Lonely Early" sounds like it was written with a Jenkins orchestration in mind; it's hard to guess who thought of the opening gambit—the chimes of a clock, striking to show the passing of time—Van Heusen or Jenkins. If you didn't know, you could easily assume the words and music for this one were by Jenkins himself.

"The September of My Years" is a superior ballad by the team best known for supplying Sinatra with his lightest, most swinging, and ring-a-ding-ding-ing moments. Cahn said, famously, "Sinatra spends his days with me and his nights with Van Heusen," and the proximity to the singer pays off here: they capture both the night and day of Sinatra, having him describe himself "as a man who has always had the wandering ways" but now is feeling increasingly sentimental and oriented toward family and long-term relationships as he grows older. Boom. They totally nailed it.

When Sinatra was profiled in *Life* magazine on the occasion of the impending fiftieth birthday, it was then that he uttered what Gary Giddins has described as "his famous encomium" regarding Tony Bennett (without quoting it too much, "the best singer in the business, the best exponent of a song"). It may not be a coincidence that he was thinking about Bennett at this particular moment. No fewer than three songs on *September of My Years* seem to have been learned from Bennett: "Once Upon a Time" had come from Charles Strouse and Lee Adams's flop show, *All American*, but Sinatra likely first heard it as the flipside of Bennett's blockbuster, "I Left My Heart in San Francisco"; Jenkins's own "This Is All I Ask" had also been initially popularized by Bennett, although he was much too young—thirty-three at the time—to sing it; and "Don't Wait Too Long" by Sunny Skylar (a character of the big-band era, songwriter, and occasional novelty vocalist) had been sung by Bennett in 1964's *The Many Moods of Tony* (and revived by him on his 2014 album with Lady Gaga). Wonderful as Bennett's interpretations are, all three songs all so gloriously animated by Sinatra and Jenkins that it's hard to imagine that they could have been written for any other purpose.

Jenkins's own "How Old Am I?" is certainly good enough to earn a place on the album, if hardly in a class with "This Is All I Ask." Jenkins also apparently was responsible for bringing in "When the Wind Was Green," a beautiful song by Henry Stinson that completely fits the mood of the album; Jenkins had first recorded it with Dick Haymes in 1949. There's also one song by Alec Wilder (lyric by William Engvick), "I See It Now," which, truth to tell, is perhaps the only comparatively weak composition in the set; it seems thin and redundant compared to the other songs on the set, which say the same things but with greater clarity and originality.

Wilder served a more vital role as being the conduit to Bart Howard, who would contribute the thoughtful "Man in the Looking Glass," a song that originates with Sinatra's admiration for cabaret diva supreme Mabel Mercer. "One day the phone rang, and it was Alec [Wilder]," Howard told us in 1992. "He said that he was helping Frank get an album together about his turning fifty years old. And Frank had remembered that I had done a song for Mabel Mercer, called 'It Was Worth It.'" This was a pioneering song, an ode of reflection and self-celebration from fully a generation before Edith Piaf and Sammy Davis Jr. opened the floodgates of self-aggrandizing anthems in the 1960s. The first idea was to adapt "It Was Worth It" into a masculine aria, but this proved futile. Howard said, "It simply was a woman's idea. Everything, every joke, and everything in it that was a good line, would had to, had to be sung by a woman"; by this he means like "When down in the dumps, / I can put on me pumps / and dance again." (It also was in ¾ time, a signature more in Mercer's wheelhouse than Sinatra's.)

So "It Was Worth It" wouldn't work for Sinatra, but Howard now had the Chairman's attention (especially since Sinatra had successfully recorded Howard's "Fly Me to The Moon" a year earlier). Howard then submitted song after song to Sinatra, all of which were rejected as being "not Frank Sinatra material." "So I said to Alec, 'It just kind of seems so hopeless, I don't think he's ever going to use any song of mine.' And so he said, 'Well, just a minute.' And he got Frank on the phone, and I was able to thank him for his record of 'Fly Me to the Moon.'" Howard's persistence paid off and he scored heavily with "Man in the Looking Glass," in which he had the brilliant idea of writing a lyric that was reflective in multiple senses of the word, being about a mirror. It's another key example of a master lyricist, as Cahn did, writing specifically for the Sinatra persona. It turned out to be one of the key songs on the album and one of the absolute best in the Bart Howard songbook.

But there can be no doubt that the album's masterpiece was Ervin Drake's "It Was a Very Good Year." Ervin Drake (1919–2015) was, for most of his career, a competent and frequently inspired songwriter who had written numerous hits, such as "I Believe"; "Tico-Tico"; "Perdido"; "A Room Without Windows" from his show *What Makes Sammy Run*; "Castle Rock," which Sinatra had recorded with Harry James; and one all-time jazz standard, the Billie Holiday classic "Good Morning Heartache." For several years he had the notion to build a song around the conceit of wine vintages, the way that sommeliers will talk about some years being better than others (and actually claim to be able to taste the difference). Drake wrote the song in 1961, when music publisher Arthur Mogul gave him the hot tip that Bob Shane of the Kingston Trio, perhaps the most popular group of the entire folk music boom, was coming to the office the next morning and if Ervin could submit anything appropriate by then, they'd consider it. He wrote "the whole bloody thing," he said, in fifteen minutes—which meant, since he already had such a strong idea, and had twenty years of songwriting experience behind him, that the song practically wrote itself.

The trio accepted it and it appears on their 1961 album *Goin' Places*. Heard today, the original Kingston Trio version, built around a solo vocal by Shane, sounds amazingly minimal; to Sinatra's ears, it would have seemed more like a songwriter's demo rather than a finished commercial recording. Sinatra heard the track on the radio, he stopped at the nearest gas station, put a nickel in the pay phone, and immediately made a call to Jenkins. "Frank told me that he instructed Gordon to get a copy of the song 'It Was a Very Good Year' and make an arrangement for him, and to make it schmaltzy. Frank was taking a big risk, because everything Gordon did was already *schmaltzy*. You know, Frank famously said that the way Gordon wrote for strings, if he had been Jewish, it would be unbearable." Thus we have a folk song by a Jewish songwriter, written to sound like a traditional Anglo or American air, that has been schmaltzed up (in glorious D-minor) by a Missouri WASP and a Hoboken Italian.

Drake was on vacation in London with his first wife and family when the publisher tracked him down to his hotel to congratulate him on the Sinatra recording. That was the first time that Drake knew about it, so the publisher played him the entire four-and-a-half-minute track over the phone. Drake was, needless to say, completely overwhelmed, *verklempt*. His first thought was to send Jenkins a very gracious telegram, the gist of which was "I am amazed by your beautiful orchestration. You made my song sound as wonderful as one of your own marvelous songs." And that is indeed what Drake and Jenkins had achieved: between Drake's music and lyrics and Jenkins's orchestration, they had come up with the perfect Jenkins song for Sinatra.

Famously, the song uses the repetitious pattern of a folk song (such as Pete Seeger's "Where Have All the Flowers Gone?," also a hit for the Kingston Trio), in which each of the four verses seems like a variation on the previous, maintaining as much of the previous verbiage as possible. Now the old stud is in his wine cellar, sampling memories of his storied past, and choosing between them as if they were wines from different years. A tall blonde from 1956 becomes as a Petrus '82. Our hero describes his passing years more in terms of the women in his life, from "small-town girls" at seventeen, to "city girls" at twenty-one, and "blue-blooded girls" at thirty-five; presumably his own circumstances are rising in parallel to theirs. In the last verse, he more heavily reinforces the central metaphor of the wine vintages, describing his life as coming "from fine old kegs / From the brim to the dregs / It poured sweet and clear."

Each verse becomes an episode in a man's life, and between each of them Jenkins inserts a wailing string-and-oboe passage that grows increasingly severe with each segment until, by the end, the whole section sobs and throbs to the Nth power. This is also a quintessential example of Jenkins's "wailing, moaning strings." As Bill Miller said, "He had that little thing where we used to kid, when he'd go from minor to major or major to minor. And right after the record date we'd all walk out singing, *'Gor*-don *Jen*-kins.'" Another pianist, Lou Levy, added, "Gordon had his identity and his sound. Everything was sort of a wail and a moan. He had a way of getting that kind of sound. I could take only so much of it, but with Sinatra, it worked. And I know Frank liked it. How can you knock an arrangement like 'Very Good Year'? That's really sort of a masterpiece."

Sinatra and Jenkins recorded "Very Good Year" on April 22, 1965. (Ten minutes of session material, alternate and breakdown takes, are known to exist, and, miraculously, a CBS News camera crew was present.) The song was instantly proclaimed as the most successful and satisfying track from an altogether successful and satisfying album. The session footage was included in the CBS profile of Sinatra, shown on November 16, and the song itself became one of the centerpieces of Sinatra's groundbreaking NBC special, *Frank Sinatra: A Man and His Music*, on November 24. The *Man and His Music* version is especially moving, as the singer and arranger use it for a framework around a medley of relevant songs, starting with a new Jenkins chart on "Young at Heart"; two from the *September* album, "Last Night When We Were Young" and "Hello, Young Lovers"; and "The Girl Next Door" from *All Alone*. The segment is surely a highlight of the Sinatra-Jenkins collaboration. (A year later, Sinatra and Jenkins devised an equally moving ballad medley segment for the 1966 special *A Man and His Music, Part II*. The 1966 medley used a new Jenkins treatment of "Just One of Those Things" to frame "My Heart Stood Still," "But Beautiful," and "When Your Lover Has Gone.")

Sinatra also sang "Very Good Year," less successfully, in his 1966 album *At the Sands* with Count Basie's Orchestra (but, alas, no strings). But the song quickly became a major concert staple for him—something that his audiences adored hearing him sing live—that he would continue to perform regularly for the rest of his life—thankfully, with strings. As he grew older, and the September of his years became October and then November and December, the song grew ever more poignant. My favorite performance, however, comes from the mid-1980s, in which he starts the song as usual with "When I was seventeen" and after a long pause, he finishes the line, "I was a pain the ass!" He then interjects to the audience, "isn't everybody at seventeen?"

And thus it came to pass that Sinatra and Jenkins moved in a direction that, if graphed visually, would resemble the printed music to one of the arranger's sweeping descending phrases. The team gradually moved from highbrow to middlebrow Tin Pan Alley, and then swooped another step downward to quasifolk music and then to quasirock, each level going for a simpler order of composition. The climactic full-length Sinatra-Jenkins project would be released in 1980, the epic *Future* disc of *Trilogy*. But in the fifteen or so years between *September* and *The Future*, Jenkins worked on many odds and ends, singles, and portions of albums.

The first of these arrived in 1967, when three tracks on the album *The World We Knew* were Jenkins's work: "This Is My Love" (which Sinatra had cut eight years earlier as "This Was My Love") and two movie themes, "Born Free" (which was reborn free a decade later as the title theme to *Star Wars*) and "You Are There," from Sinatra's own film *The Naked Runner*. All three of these fairly meager melodies benefit immensely from Jenkins's inflationary tactics. Whether or not these songs were any good to begin with, Sinatra and Jenkins make them into something seriously better than they were before. Up to now, Sinatra had commissioned Jenkins exclusively to work on grand old songs with him (excepting the "special material" on *September*); these three tracks represent the first more-or-less-new, bread-and-butter songs that they would do together.

But hardly the last. Jenkins made important contributions to Sinatra's two immediate postretirement albums, *Ol' Blue Eyes Is Back* and *Some Nice Things I've Missed*, in which the charts are divided between him and Don Costa. The best one can say about many of these tracks is that Jenkins makes them better than they would have been without him. The songwriter who best represents what Sinatra was going for in this period is Joe Raposo (1937–1989). "Noah," alas, is easily the young composer's nadir, being an uneasy mix of childishness and overbearing pretension, rather like the worst of Andrew Lloyd Webber. At least his "You Will Be My Music" has a metaphor Sinatra can sink his teeth into, and succeeds on that level, but Jenkins is somewhat sabotaged by the inclusion of a rock-pop rhythm section. (The personnel lists two guitars, two keyboards, and three bassists, clearly indicating a mix of electric and acoustic instruments.) Kris Kristofferson's "Nobody Wins" achieves exactly what Sinatra hoped it would: between Jenkins being Jenkins and Sinatra being Sinatra, they have transformed a good country song into respectable Sinatra material.

There are two Jenkins arrangements from this period, "Send in the Clowns" on *Ol' Blue Eyes* and "Empty Tables" (issued as a single), that Sinatra used for a while in the mid-1970s; he then decided that he preferred them both without any orchestrations and continued to sing them with only Bill Miller's piano accompaniment. "That arrangement of 'Send in the Clowns' was easy to play," said Milt Bernhart, "but it didn't do much for the song." That actually describes the way I feel about "Empty Tables"; although the music is first-rate Jimmy Van Heusen and the words are first-rate Johnny Mercer, the chart is not one of Jenkins's best. In fact, there are touches that don't even sound like Jenkins: an alto sax obbligato following Sinatra here that's totally inapposite to any other Jenkins-Sinatra collaboration. However, the Jenkins "Send in the Clowns" is, in my estimation, an underappreciated gem. Stephen Sondheim wrote it as a waltz for his 1973 show *A Little Night*

*Music*, a story set in Sweden at the turn of the twentith century. While many versions follow the folkified treatment of Judy Collins's hit single, Jenkins restores more than a hint of old European formality to the song, giving it a kind of Grand Guignol quality, that flavor of epic tragedy that we love so much about Jenkins—or at least, that I do. (Jenkins himself described it as "the best song [written] in the last twenty-five years.") Don't let me be misunderstood; the Sinatra-Miller piano-only version of "Clowns" is quite wonderful, but I maintain that the Sinatra-Jenkins treatment (which he sang at Carnegie Hall in 1974) is also, to use Sinatra's favorite adjective of praise, quite marvelous.

More Sinatra-Jenkins gems are scattered hither and yon, like buried treasure, throughout the sessions of the mid-1970s. In September 1974, Sinatra had Tommy Dorsey on his mind, and he and "Lefty" turned in two superlative updates of vintage 1941–42 ballads, "Everything Happens to Me" and "Just as Though You Were Here." Although these tracks were orphaned until the *Complete Reprise Studio Recordings* suitcase, they are absolute gems. Jenkins's charts could have easily been written for *All Alone* or even *Where are You?* Sinatra thoroughly reexamines both texts, making them live and breathe anew, this time from the perspective of the October of his years. It illustrates what a bass-ackwards period this was, when junk like "Noah" was immediately released and gems like these two Dorsey updates went unheard.

The Dorsey-era tunes were put aside in these years while Sinatra pinned his hopes on the works of younger songwriters like Joe Raposo. This, it seemed to Sinatra, was the wagon to hitch his star to in terms of attracting the younger generation; in fact, the generation that Raposo had already conquered was the youngest of them all, in terms of his extremely successful songs for *Sesame Street*. Sinatra would record six of Raposo's songs in this approximate period, which is far more than anyone else, even his old standbys Sammy and Jimmy. (For the record, they are "Bein' Green" on *Sinatra & Company*; "Noah"; "You Will Be My Music," which Sinatra introduced as his "protest song" in contemporaneous concerts; "Winners" and "There Used to Be a Ballpark" on *Ol' Blue Eyes*; and the orphan track "The Hurt Doesn't Go Away.")

In his short lifetime and since, Raposo is still best remembered for his children's songs, including his excellent score for the 1977 animated feature *Raggedy Ann and Andy*. But his single best work is also his most mature, "There Used to Be a Ballpark"—and it's also probably Sinatra's most memorable recording of the immediate postretirement period. The song was inspired by the Ebbets Field stadium, where for five decades the Brooklyn Dodgers—and the rest of the borough—hung their hopes and dreams. There's something iconic and even mythic about baseball that just isn't true for other sports; a song about ice hockey or women's lacrosse just wouldn't have the same cache.

(Having said that, it must be admitted that Sinatra makes "Monday Morning Quarterback" into something powerful and moving.)

For both Raposo and Sinatra, the song came out of left field. (Raposo was from Fall River, Massachusetts, so it's hard to imagine that he had any direct attachment to Ebbets Field; but the Dodgers were well known to be Sinatra's favorite team, even after both he and they relocated to Los Angeles.) It starts like an old codger reminiscing about the legendary ballpark, long since demolished to make way for a housing development; Raposo astutely begins the lyric with the word "and" ("And there used to be a ballpark"), which makes it sounds like we're opening on the speaker already in mid-ramble. Within a few lines it becomes clear that Sinatra is talking about something much broader than baseball or sports. As with the movie *Field of Dreams,* singer and songwriter use the game as a symbol for bigger issues, and lines like "The old team just isn't playing / And the new team hardly tries" make this as stinging an indictment of the decline of American culture as anyone has ever expressed using the medium of popular song.

"I think people didn't understand the significance of it, the idea about the Dodgers and the ballpark," said Lou Levy, who served as Sinatra's pianist on various occasions when he sang the number. "It's great if you know what it means, but a lot of people just sat and wondered what the song was all about. Likewise, I know kids who go to see the *JFK* movie who have no idea what the Bay of Pigs was. Lots of times nobody knew what the song was talking about, and it just didn't come across." Still, one hopes that even people who only know Leo Durocher for his urbane, Noel Coward-like bon mots would react like the thousands of Brooklyn boys in the 1960s and '70s who looked at the housing tract erected on Ebbets Field and wondered what it all meant. "There Used to Be a Ballpark" has an air of mystery and mystique that speaks to millions who never so much as threw a pop bottle at an umpire.

With "Ballpark," we know immediately that we are in the company of three great storytellers, Raposo, Sinatra, and Jenkins. It makes me think about someone's description of watching Laurence Olivier on-screen as King Henry the Fifth: the viewer said he was neither an Englishman nor a patriot, but that in watching Olivier he became all these things. That's the effect that "Ballpark" has on me—it actually makes me think that baseball might be something important, something worth caring about. (Anyone who knows how apathetic I am toward professional sports knows that this is no small accomplishment.) "Ballpark," is, in fact, the next Sinatra-Jenkins masterpiece after "It Was a Very Good Year."

"Gordon's whole thing was the story," Dick Nash pointed out. "I mean, that was his forte." *Trilogy: The Future,* the next and most ambitious phase of the

Sinatra-Jenkins team-up, sprang more from recurring motifs in each of their individual careers than from anything they had achieved jointly thus far. As we have seen, Sinatra had a predilection for "big songs" of the "Ol' Man River" and "Soliloquy" variety, which he had developed steadily from the Dorsey era up to *The Concert Sinatra*. Jenkins, too, had a yen to speak to big topics, not just with big tunes but with big bunches of songs, joined together in a format that amounted to a pop song cycle in the Schubertian sense of the term.

Jenkins began developing ways to use music as a form of extended audio drama when he was a staff conductor for NBC in the early 1940s. He had worked with, among others, Arch Oboler, a suspense-oriented dramatist who was to radio more or less what Rod Serling later was to television. As musical director for Dick Haymes's Autolite-sponsored show in the mid-1940s, Jenkins crafted a series of what they called "Autolite Operas"—ten-minute musical sketches spotlighting Haymes, frequent costar Helen Forrest, and other guests as well as the NBC orchestra and chorus. The "operas" amounted to a combination of protracted medleys of familiar songs with new lyrics as well as original material, constructed in the form of a musical narrative with connecting dialogue.

*The Dick Haymes Show*, like most radio shows built around movie stars, was based in Hollywood; but for a period around the time of the end of the war, the whole company came east to do a few shows in New York. This was Jenkins's first extended visit back east since he had left the city almost a decade earlier; then he was a struggling arranger and composer, now he was a musical director on one of the top programs on the air and a successful songwriter. He started reflecting back on his younger years there, his lifelong love affair with New York, and his fascination with the city as a young man from Missouri.

At the end of 1945, he put that fascination into tangible form with *Manhattan Tower*. There's no standard musical term to describe it; the closest thing might be a "song cycle" or a musical fantasia, a combination of various forms, solo songs, works for chorus, instrumental interludes, all held together by text delivered by a non-singing narrator (Elliott Lewis). The only way to describe it is with a term from a later era, a "concept album," from the same time as Sinatra's *The Voice* (1945), although even more ambitious in that it consisted entirely of original material.

It took a while for *Manhattan Tower* to catch on, but it gradually became one of the major successes of the early album era. The 1945 recording was originally released in four parts, as two twelve-inch 78s in an album; and then as an early ten-inch LP. Decca later claimed that it sold over half a million units, a remarkable statistic considering that it contained no well-known songs and no big-name stars or Broadway or Hollywood tie-ins.

For Jenkins, *Manhattan Tower* was the gift that kept on giving: he would perform the work as a stage show in New York (at the Capitol Theatre in 1949) and Las Vegas (at the Thunderbird in 1953), as well as on *The Ed Sullivan Show* (then titled *Toast of the Town*, in 1950). In 1956, when Jenkins shifted from Decca to Capitol Records, the new label contracted him to rerecord and enlarge *Manhattan Tower* as a full twelve-inch LP in high fidelity. Around the same time, it also served as the basis for a television special on NBC's *Saturday Spectacular* series. And there would be even more full-length recordings of *Manhattan Tower*, by Patti Page and Robert Goulet (with Jenkins conducting). Jenkins added "Married I Can Always Get" to the score for the expanded edition, but the most performed song from the work was invariably "New York's My Home," thanks mainly to classic recordings by Sammy Davis Jr. and Ray Charles.

Less successful were Jenkins's attempts to create a follow-up to *Manhattan Tower*. Some of these, like *Seven Dreams*, had their moments (*Seven Dreams* contains the melody that Johnny Cash borrowed for "Folsom Prison Blues"), but in general, none of them can be considered a success. There was *California*, with a libretto by a professional lyricist, Tom Adair, that was vastly inferior to Jenkins's own in *Manhattan Tower*; and the infamously awful *The Letter*, written for Judy Garland (but which also included an excellent "breakout" song, "That's All There Is, There Isn't Any More"). Later, he tried again with *What It Was, Was Love* for Steve Lawrence and Eydie Gormé, an "AlbuMusical," i.e., a combination LP and television special. On the whole, in this area Jenkins might be compared to Meredith Wilson: he had one great work in him—as with Wilson and *The Music Man*—but that was all. *Manhattan Tower* was sui generis; with the possible exception of Mel Tormé's brilliant *California Suite*, no one else ever even attempted anything like it.

Jenkins was slowing down by the 1960s—or rather, the traditional pop music business, as he knew it, was slowing down around him. Although he had done scores for a few films (Arch Oboler's 1945 *Strange Holiday* and *Bwana Devil*, the breakthrough three-dimensional feature, in 1953), he had never gone into that area as fully as such younger arranger-composer-conductors as May, Riddle, and Johnny Mandel. Jenkins may have felt the crunch as the emphasis of pop music shifted away from his kind to another kind, even though, ironically, albums like *Pet Sounds* and *Sgt. Pepper's Lonely Hearts Club Band* had been deeply inspired by *Manhattan Tower*, even if the Beach Boys and the Beatles probably weren't aware of it. In his sixties, Jenkins worked with Sinatra on the postretirement albums and other sessions, as well as the 1980 feature *The First Deadly Sin*. He also arranged and conducted on Harry

Nilsson's *A Little Touch of Schmilsson in the Night* (1973), one of the best-remembered albums of the era and one of the first in which a contemporary pop-rock star sang a collection of songbook standards (and, on the whole, one that holds up much better than the Ronstadt-Riddle albums of a decade later, as excellent as Riddle's work on those may be).

Bruce Jenkins has found a letter where his father proposes an extended musical portrait of Sinatra as far back as 1959. The idea began to become concrete around 1977, when Jenkins and producer-bandleader-composer Sonny Burke paid a call on Frank Sinatra. "I was working in Vegas when Gordon came up with Sonny," as Sinatra recollected in 1984, "and they said, 'We want to talk to you about a piece of material that Gordon is thinking about.' And he told me about it, and I said, 'Boy! That's a lot of music. That's a lot of work.' He said, 'Yeah, I know, but I think I could do it. I think I know exactly what I want to do.' Then, at the next visit to Vegas two or three months later, they came up again and brought up a reel-to-reel tape. We put it on the machine, and I tell you, it put me away the first time I heard it. It really knocked me out."

*The Future* was the third and final part of *Trilogy* to be taped as well as in the album sequence. "I worked on it for many months before we did it because I wanted to be sure it was all right," Sinatra said. "It was all brand new. Everything was brand new." Vincent Falcone elaborated, "We spent weeks [going over it], and not only on the road. I spent a great deal of time with him up at the house in Beverly Hills. We used to go down to the projection room where the piano was. It was a separate building down by the pool, and we spent hours down there! I had to teach him all of that material because it was all original."

The project required even more personnel than *The Concert Sinatra*. Not only was there a full symphony orchestra, but vocal contractor Marlene VerPlanck hired a full chorus of backup singers—nearly a hundred performers in all. As recording engineer Lee Herschberg told us, no studio in Los Angeles was big enough to hold that many people, so he and producer Burke had to set up a remote recording operation at Hollywood's Shrine Auditorium.

"Sure it was difficult," Falcone continued. "It was difficult [even] for me to learn it! I had to remember it all, too. Because when we went to the recording session, backstage at the Shrine, there was a lot of stuff where there was no piano part written. And it was my job to make sure that [Sinatra] toed the line, so to speak. And I used to go to him after several takes and tell him, 'You'd better do that over again' or 'You'd better listen to this because you're not going to be happy with it.' I would do things that other people were afraid to do."

In the long run, there's no apologizing for *The Future*. Talk about trying to predict the future; no one who's ever heard Sinatra's lowbrow misfires—from "Mama Will Bark" to "Noah"—could have guessed that he would undertake the most spectacular disaster of his recording career in trying to take the high road. Up to now, he had stumbled only in his rare, uncharacteristic attempts to talk down to his audiences—those moments when he underestimated their taste—but *The Future* blew it by addressing ideas that were at once too grandiloquent and too stupid.

This third disc of *Trilogy* almost resists description. This is an extended work of six movements, three of which are distinctly titled "The Future," originally issued as two sides of the third disc of *Trilogy*. (The three-LP package is more formally known as *Trilogy: Past Present Future*.) You get a sense of Jenkins's overwhelming ambition in the opening section, "What Time Does the Next Miracle Leave?" He's trying to do multiple things at once: after we hear an orchestra tuning up, the singer introduces himself by his full name; he sings "My name is Francis Albert . . ." at which point the choir interjects, rather like a Greek chorus, "Francis Albert Sinatra."

From there, he tells us that he intends to enjoy the future as much as he's enjoyed those "very good years" of his checkered past (with a quote from the Ervin Drake song). This leads into a guided tour of the solar system, in which interplanetary rockets travel from one heavenly body to another in a manner very much like a train; and as in the days when trains were the primary mode of travel, there's an announcer calling out the planetary stations as if they were Anaheim, Azusa, and Cucamonga. Jenkins is trying to be whimsical, with a libretto like a children's science-fiction picture book from the pre–Apollo spaceflight era, more Buck Rogers than Luke Skywalker. Beautiful women (the kind that won't leave in the morning) greet him on Venus, while apparently Jupiter and Saturn are a galactic agricultural belt, and Pluto is "Hades," a prison planet where the more dangerous souls are confined. If that isn't enough, Jenkins is trying to interweave Sinatra's own personal mythology throughout; here, the Old Man sings of being met on Uranus by a welcoming committee bearing cheese pizza and vino, while, rather scandalously, he tells us that on Pluto, "It's pure hell, when your journey ends there, / But you can bet your ass, I'll meet a lot of friends there."

This is a work that conforms to George Bernard Shaw's description of Wagner's music—full of brilliant moments and excruciating half hours. "World War None!" uses militaristic music, including snare drums and a march tempo, to rail against mankind's unstoppable need to destroy itself. The next three cuts on the disc actually make up *The Future* per se, described on the jacket as "A Musical Fantasy in Three Tenses for Frank Sinatra, Philharmonic Symphony Orchestra and Mixed Chorus." The selections, or "tenses," are titled "The Future," "The Future (Continued) 'I've Been There!'," and "The Future (Conclusion) 'Song Without Words'."

While the notion of a three-part suite-within-a-suite sounds confusingly complex, Jenkins frames it with the simplest music he could come up with, a basic blues sung by his wife, Beverly Mahr, a studio vocalist and soloist with an affinity for the blues (and a voice similar to the great jazz singer Lee Wiley). The twelve-bar melody seems a close relative of "Crescent City Blues" from *Seven Dreams*, also sung by Mahr. The two had met while working on the Haymes show in the mid-1940s; at that time, Mahr was the "Miss" in that show's vocal group, Six Hits and a Miss. An accomplished studio singer on *Manhattan Tower* (she was the original soloist on "New York's My Home") and featured on *California* well before she became the second Mrs. Jenkins, Mahr participated in almost all of Jenkins's dates that required a chorus. (The two also collaborated on a full-length album together, the 1964 *Gordon Jenkins Presents My Wife the Blues Singer* on Impulse! Records.)

Among the more copacetic moments are two "sub-songs" that could easily stand on their own, "I've Been There!" and "Song Without Words." The first is a lovely song all around, if a bit derivative of Jenkins's own "This Is All I Ask," except that if he was paternal in 1965 he's grown more grandfatherly by 1979; and what's more, he's glad he's not young anymore. The title "Song Without Words" isn't entirely accurate: it isn't a song but a six-minute work that incorporates several songs, ending with another chorus of Miss Mahr's blues (about hiring a gypsy to help predict the future). But there is a long wordless section, mostly instrumental, with the choir occasionally singing wordlessly; a better title might be "Song Without Frank." In addition to Mahr's blues, it also includes some lines, sung by soprano Loulie Jean Norman, about building a "little house on a star." Norman was the most famous "vapor voice" or "air girl" in postwar Hollywood, and supplied many an ethereal voice on pop records and soundtracks. (She's prominent on "Remember" on *All Alone* but is best known to popular culture as the wordless soprano over the titles of the original series of *Star Trek*.)

After the three movements of *The Future* (that is to say, the three-part *The Future* per se), the disc concludes with "Before the Music Ends." Again, signs of Jenkins's overarching ambition are everywhere; much of the format is a musical soliloquy clearly inspired by Rodgers and Hammerstein, although the content is more like one of Sinatra's rambling Vegas monologues set to music, complete with insider references to Dino, "Sarge" (Sinatra lieutenant Irving Weiss), "Chester" (aka Jimmy Van Heusen), and "Lefty" (the southpaw maestro from Missouri himself)—and that's not to mention Schubert,

Beethoven, Verdi, and Puccini. "Frank sort of liked that type of thing because he felt it gave him a wider scope," said Loulie Jean Norman, "But I couldn't make heads or tails of it."

In all my experience around Frank fans, I've only encountered two individuals who tried to defend *The Future*: one is the young film historian and journalist Karina Longworth (born in 1980, the year *Trilogy* was released), who devoted an entire episode of her podcast *You Must Remember This* to what she called "Frank Sinatra in Outer Space." She points out that traditional Frank fans (like myself, Bill Boggs, and Chuck Granata) are inclined to dismiss *The Future*, but she insists that there is much to enjoy for fans new to the Sinatra idiom, who approach it without any baggage or preconceived notions.

The other is Sinatra's conductor at the time, Vinnie Falcone. "I cannot understand anybody criticizing that work," he told us in the early 1990s. "The criticisms were that it was too much ego from Sinatra, but they missed the whole point entirely! The point was the past, the present, and the future! *Trilogy* was conceived as the culmination of an incredible career. Yet he wasn't old enough to hang it up, so there was a future. And the future, as Gordon saw it, meant saying thank you to his friends and reminiscing while he was still in the business. It's a retirement without being retired"—sort of like a testimonial. "It may not have been classic Sinatra, but it wasn't intended to be." As Billy May put it, "You gotta look at it this way. If Frank liked it and Frank commissioned it, then Gordon did a good job. I was down there when they recorded it, and, Jesus, it was sensational!"

It's easy to be critical of the *Future* from the perspective of the future (it doesn't sound any better in 2017 than it did in 1980), but at the time it also made sense that *The Future* would dovetail perfectly with Billy May's *Past* and Don Costa's *Present*. Still, even in hindsight I can't help but wish they had approached the future the way they had with *September of My Years*. Following a disc of vintage songs and then a second of contemporary songs, it would have made the most sense to put together a collection of philosophical songs about life, love, and the future by going to Sinatra's "stock company" of great songwriters: "Chester" Van Heusen and Sammy Cahn were still writing (Van Heusen was actively involved in the album), as were Alec Wilder, Bart Howard, Ervin Drake, Joe Raposo, and especially Lefty himself. They might have expanded the purview to include such top contemporary writers as Michel Legrand, Marilyn and Alan Bergman, or even musical theater composers like Stephen Sondheim, Jerry Herman, or Cy Coleman and sympathetic pop writers like Burt Bacharach, Henry Mancini, or Jimmy Webb. The results might have been a little hokey, but they were bound to be better than *The*

*Future*, which, again from the same perspective of hindsight, seems like one of the great missed opportunities of Sinatra's career.

Sinatra defended *Trilogy: The Future* by claiming that the critics and others who rapped it "just didn't understand it at all." Nevertheless, with the next and last project that he worked on with Jenkins, Sinatra made a point of returning to their roots: saloon songs. "Gordon was getting old and sick, and Frank wanted to do one last album with him before he died," said Falcone. "He wanted it to be Gordy's last stand, if you will. And I think a lot of that came from the fact that Gordon received such criticism for the *Trilogy* album."

*She Shot Me Down* (1981) was the album that got away, arriving all but unnoticed between the overall, highly acclaimed *Trilogy* and the more heavily hyped *L.A. Is My Lady*. *She Shot Me Down* is the (almost) all-new album that *The Future* should have been; its nine tracks include two standards, two "found" pieces, and five items essentially written with Sinatra in mind.

Like much of *Trilogy: The Present*, *She Shot Me Down* would be taped in New York, where Sinatra had the benefit of recording with the same supertight orchestra he had long been touring with. Even though Jenkins had never worked with this particular reed section, he quickly came to appreciate its facility. When he counted off the first tune, lead alto player Sid Cooper, who solos on "South—to a Warmer Place," reported, "There were little touchy things [in the chart], and he wasn't used to the saxophone section. And after we played the first tune—and we played it very well—he called [contractor] Joe Malin over and whispered in his ear: 'Whatever we do in this album, give Sid Cooper double scale.' And when Joe came over and told me that, well, I was really flabbergasted. And I mean, I did nothing for it except what I always did, which was to make everything the best I could under the circumstances." (Cooper also reported that the band was still teasing Lefty by moaning "*Gord*-on *Jenk*-ins" atop one of his major-minor moaning motifs.)

The meat of the album, you might say, is seven charts by Jenkins, although the bread, you might also say, are the two by others that open and close the nine-song collection; Stephen Sondheim's "Good Thing Going," arranged by Don Costa (who replaced Sonny Burke, who had died in May 1980, as the set's overall producer) and Nelson Riddle's medley of two classic torch songs, "The Gal That Got Away" and "It Never Entered My Mind," clearly an act that nothing could follow, to close.

In the thirty-five years since *She Shot Me Down* was released, the album has grown in stature; it's not a stretch to label it as, overall, the single most satisfying work of Sinatra's entire postretirement period. The album is mostly comprised of newish songs, using that term to distinguish them, roughly, from standards. Apart from Riddle's saloon song collage, the only song that would have been familiar to listeners at the time was "Thanks for the Memory"; and even then, most everyone only knew it as a vehicle for Bob Hope's jocularity, rather than the bittersweet torch song that they heard here. Truth to tell, most of the seven other songs haven't been heard from again,* but that actually works in their favor: because we're not overly familiar with these songs, most of which are excellent, they still have the power to surprise us.

One of the bigger surprises is the opener, "Good Thing Going" (from Sondheim's *Merrily We Roll Along*). Compared to what follows, the arrangement is fairly lightweight; this is the Don Costa of *Some Nice Things I've Missed*, unfortunately, not the Costa of *Sinatra & Strings*. It's a song of love and loss, but hardly grandly tragically so; a saloon song where the protagonist is drinking lite beer. The second track, "Hey Look, No Crying" (by Jule Styne and a new lyricist named Susan Birkenhead) has a hero telling us he's not going to cry over the woman who's leaving him; he makes like he was expecting the worst all along. For a relatively young lyricist, it's a very astute tactic: having Sinatra sing about not crying automatically makes this just about the saddest thing we've ever heard. By track number three, "Thanks for the Memory," we are fully plunged into the deep end of the pool; this is full-throttle Sinatra-Jenkins at their most epic, abetted by a new text from the song's original lyricist, Leo Robin (about eighty at the time). It was to the credit of both Sinatra and Jenkins (as well as Robin) that they could take a song that for multiple generations had served as a lighthearted closer for America's number-one comedian and make it into one of the darkest and most somber moments in pop music. And thank you so much.

*She Shot Me Down* was not only Gordy's last stand, it also amounted to the last hurrah of another longtime Sinatra associate, composer, intellectual, and all around general crank, Alec Wilder, who died in 1980. Said Falcone, "The only disappointment to me on that album was the fact that, although Alec Wilder was a great writer, he was on his way out also. [Frank] wanted to do those songs of Alec's, 'A Long Night' and 'South—To a Warmer Place.' They were written for him. Again, they weren't exactly classic Sinatra, but he got the right arranger because they were right up Gordon's alley."

As we've seen, Wilder spent nearly fifty years trying to get people to take the American Popular Song (the title of his famous book) more seriously by

---

* However, a few of the more astute contemporary singers working the clubs out there, like Eric Comstock, have picked up on Leo Robin's new lyrics for "Thanks for the Memory" that Sinatra sings here.

writing deadly serious popular songs; he seems to have been on a lifelong quest to take the fun out of pop music. There are two songs here by the team of Wilder and Loonis McGlohon, a North Carolina–based pianist, songwriter, musical connoisseur, and radio host. "South—To a Warmer Place" is the closest the album comes to a truly light moment, yet the song is so minimal that it strains under the weight of the titanic arrangement; in fact, the song and the arrangement don't get along nohow. (If only the song had been written in 1948, Sinatra could have done it with the Phil Moore Four or Alvy West and the Little Band at the Hotel Edison.)

"South—To a Warmer Place" has Wilder attempting the kind of humor that was hardly his forte, and ultimately it's far more grim than cheerful. Yet "A Long Night" is precisely perfect for the triumvirate of Wilder, Jenkins, and Sinatra. As mentioned at the start of this volume, the song had been written by Wilder for Johnny Hartman, and only went to Sinatra when Hartman couldn't be coerced into doing it. It's a singular piece in the Sinatra canon—the closest thing to it is a completely obscure number he performed on his radio show in 1953 titled "The Most Blues."* Both pieces are more like poetry recitations set to music, with Sinatra espousing in what seems like free verse, the text sounding like a mashup of Jack Kerouac and Mickey Spillane. This piece actually fits the cover of *In the Wee Small Hours* more than anything on that 1955 album does (the song is more about empty street corners than saloons full of despondent drunks).

There's one song each by Jenkins ("I Loved Her") and Costa, though Costa's song, "Monday Morning Quarterback," is arranged by Jenkins rather than the composer. They're both about looking back at a busted-up relationship through the lens of twenty-twenty hindsight, and also about second chances, or more accurately, the lack of same. The first especially reminds me of Dante's depiction of fortune-tellers in the afterlife, doomed to spend eternity looking backward for daring to have the effrontery to think that anybody besides God could see into the future.

"I Loved Her" was, according to Bruce Jenkins, inspired by a magazine panel cartoon that Frank sent to Gordon, in which a woman is breaking up with a man by telling him, "It'll never work, Virgil, I'm herbal tea and yogurt, and you're cola and Twinkies." Sinatra had the insight to realize that the idea would make a great basis for a song, and Jenkins had the craft to actually turn it into one, originally titled "But I Loved Her." It's a song in shorthand:

---

* "The Most Blues" amounts to one of the minor mysteries of the Sinatra canon; he sang it, if that's the word, on the 1953 radio series *To Be Perfectly Frank*; and, to be perfectly frank, I have no idea who wrote it or how it got to Sinatra, or even why he chose to sing it, but it's truly one of the most unusual and inexplicable pieces in all the Sinatraverse.

"She was polo / I was racetrack," or "She was afternoon tea / I was saloon." As heard on the album, Sinatra sings one full chorus, followed by an instrumental break (with a Jenkins-style melody-note piano solo apparently played by Falcone), and then a half chorus of new lyrics, which seems like something Sinatra would have requested; the twist ending (which I'm not going to spoil for you. You're welcome) is pure Lefty.

This time Sinatra placed the central track, the album's bid for immortality, at the end of side A. "Bang Bang (My Baby Shot Me Down)" began its existence in the most ignominious of circumstances, a song by pop poseur Sonny Bono, an undernourished talent if ever there was one. (Bono did many things in his life, but wasn't as good as he should have been in any of them: a songwriter, a singer, or, later in life, a politician—not to mention a skier.) It was originally sung by his wife Cher in a horrendous upbeat single that, in the bridge especially, sounds like a ghastly Gypsy wedding. Frank Sinatra might have never noticed the piece, and no one could blame him, had it not been for Nancy Sinatra, who sang it on her 1966 album *How Does That Grab You?* Although her treatment (which she also sang on her father's 1966 TV special, *A Man and His Music Part II*) also has excessive pop touches, like an overbearing psychedelic guitar that wails away throughout, at least she makes it sound something like a torch song, or even a saloon song. Sinatra taped a perfectly acceptable version of the Jenkins chart in 1973 (in the middle of the *Ol' Blue Eyes* sessions, though not issued until the *Complete Reprise* suitcase), but opted to rerecord it in 1981.

But nothing can prepare us for the magnitude of the Sinatra-Jenkins adaptation, which is like "It Was a Very Good Year" to the Nth power. Again they've taken a ludicrously simple melody and made an orchestral spectacular out of it; again they maximize the dramatic value of the text's repetitive parallel construction. Here the contrast between the minimal nature of the material and the high Gothic drama of the vocal and the arrangement almost sounds like a punch line in and of itself, as if Wagner were composing an opera based on "The Itsy Bitsy Spider." The central metaphor of Bono's lyric is thinner than Sinatra himself ever was, riffing on a children's game, kids running on "horses made of sticks," using their fingers as pretend-pistols, pointing at each other and shouting "bang bang." The narrative progresses, and as the two kids grow up she's still shooting him down, now over a background of what sounds for all the world like Bach's Toccata and Fugue in D Minor. If it it's not quite up to the level of "A Very Good Year" or "There Used to Be a Ballpark," it isn't for lack of trying, and it was a worthy note upon which to conclude the collaboration.

Reminiscing about his years of working with Frank Sinatra, Jenkins felt that a kind of magic took place between the two of them. "It's as close as you're gonna get without being [of the] opposite sex. Because I like to have him right in front of me, and I just never take my eyes off him. It's kind of a hard thing to describe, but [there's] a definite mental connection between the two of us when it's going down well. He lets it loose. He's all over the place when he's going. He doesn't hold anything back.

"But the excitement with [Frank] is following him, because he likes to wander around. He doesn't necessarily do a song the way he rehearsed it. So you have to never take your eyes off him. I wouldn't dare. You have to just never let up or relax for a minute. He'll leave you; he'll stop in the middle of a bar and talk to somebody [ringside]. Then you've got to figure where he's gonna start again or whether he's gonna start at the beginning. He might give you a little hint, but he might not, and he assumes you'll be there.

"Frank is withdrawn. He's the charmer of all time when he feels like being charming. Nobody comes close to him. But when he quits laughing, you're not any closer to him than you were before. You talk about high standards—he's the inventor! The things that he's gotten into, scrapes and bad publicity, in my opinion are only because he expected more of people than they ever delivered. If he hires you to do something, he expects it to be the absolute world's best, whether it's cutting the grass or playing the piano. He never questions how much money—he pays whatever you want, really—but he expects it to be absolutely perfect. And it depresses him when it isn't.

"Also, I stay away from him as much as I can when we're not working. It's a temptation to hang around him because he has so much to offer, but I figure that we've gotten along fine by not being buddies. So when we get through at night, if he goes out the left door I go out the right door. I think it's worked out fine."

Sinatra eulogized Jenkins [to Sid Mark] simply and eloquently as "one of the modern geniuses of good pop music." *She Shot Me Down* would be Jenkins's last triumph, and it would also be Sinatra's—his last unequivocally great record. Jenkins died of a disease named after another left-handed legend, Lou Gehrig, at seventy-three on May 1, 1984.

"There was something about Gordon that Frank liked," said Loulie Jean Norman. "I know Gordon just adored Frank Sinatra. It was a real love affair, musically, between those two." Certainly no other singer-arranger team had so completely mastered the art of emotional exhibitionism—the art of hanging one's tears out to dry.

# THE TUX YEARS

■ ■ ■ ■ ■ ■ ■ ■ ■ ■

*"The Lion in Winter"*

# 9

# LOOKING FOR THE HOOK

*1960–1971*

*Go on being uncommercial. There's a lot of money in it.*
—JEROME KERN

In 1967, Frank Sinatra recorded "The World We Knew (Over and Over)," a German song written in the general style of what a later generation would describe as a "power ballad." It wasn't what we would think of as a rocker or a tune for dancing, but it was unquestionably in the style of the contemporary era, an oversized, unsubtle "belt number"—an anthemic song from an anthemic era. Written by the German producer and composer Bert Kaempfert, "The World We Knew" was an attempt to follow up on the huge success of the previous season's "Strangers in the Night." This clearly isn't Sinatra's type of song, but he gamely goes along with the general conceit. With Sinatra, we expect a thoughtful, contemplative "big number" like "Ol' Man River" (or the other songs on *The Concert Sinatra*), or perhaps a self-reflective number like those on "September of My Years." But even so, he injects genuine feeling into "The World We Knew."

One can only conjecture that he's literally thinking of the world he once knew—which is quite likely something very different from what Carl Sigman, who wrote the English lyrics, probably meant. The world Sinatra knew is a world where a song by Cole Porter or Richard Rodgers could be a big hit, and the most popular band in the land wasn't the Beatles but Tommy Dorsey. The pain and the anguish in Sinatra's voice indicate clearly that he realizes that the world he once knew is now gone with the wind.

Exactly what had changed? And how? About ten years later, a conversation transpired between two singer-songwriters, Joni Mitchell and Jimmy Webb, that illuminates the sea changes that had divided the world Sinatra knew from the world in which they were currently living, in the 1970s. As

Mitchell observed to Webb, "These days I'm expected to write the music, write the lyrics, do the arrangement, play the guitar, sing the melody, maybe even overdub the backup vocals—even produce the whole album." She then paused and added, "You know, I'm pretty much just doing a half-assed version of what it would have taken ten different guys to do just a few years ago." * One of Sinatra's contemporaries, the legendary Billy Eckstine, put it another way. "It's not enough to be a great singer anymore," he said to David Hajdu, "now you have to write the fuckin' songs."

The central conflict in the history of popular culture in America is not, as many assume, a question of art versus commerce. In fact, the career of Frank Sinatra—like that of Ella Fitzgerald, Tony Bennett, Nat King Cole, Duke Ellington, Miles Davis, and many others—teaches us that art and commerce can work together rather spectacularly. Rather, it's a fight on two fronts: popular artists gradually wresting control of their work and at the same time trying to convince the public that the word "artist" is as relevant to them as "popular."

Sinatra had spent the first twenty years or so of his career gradually building up to the point where he could claim that he both controlled and owned what he produced. Control was comparatively easy: after leaving Dorsey, Sinatra always had the willpower to go with his own judgement (except in one notable instance, as we have seen, during the early 1950s). Still, only the first five years or so of the existence of Reprise Records were nirvana to Sinatra; by the end of the 1960s, circumstances had once again compelled the singer to work with material outside his own personal taste.

Throughout the 1960s, the music and the industry attached to it were constantly growing. Sinatra himself was a key mover in all of these changes, some of which he directly advocated for, but others completely horrified him. In his youth, the music business operated along lines that ran parallel to the Hollywood studio system: singers were like actors under contract to Warner Bros. or RKO; they had no say in what they sang or how they sang it. The bandleaders were the equivalent of moguls, and even they were under the thumb of publishers, radio sponsors, and advertising agencies. Even as powerful and astute a figure as Bing Crosby, Sinatra's original role model, was content to leave the matter of selecting songs up to his producers, most notably the sagacious Jack Kapp (who, it must be said, rarely steered him wrong). In the big-band era, singers like Doris Day and Rosemary Clooney never thought to question the judgement of bandleaders and A&R men; a

---

* I'm paraphrasing, but this is the overall gist of the conversation, as reported to me by Jimmy Webb in an interview circa 2010.

few years later, in their solo careers, they simply showed up at the studio and sang whatever producers like Mitch Miller told them to.

Sinatra provided inspiration for various key followers—Tony Bennett, Peggy Lee, Mel Tormé—to follow in the trails he blazed. Even in the "Mama Will Bark" era, Sinatra was the rare singer to whom the record execs offered the courtesy of approval; the next step was to make such control a God-given right, rather than a courtesy, and after that, to claim a greater share of the rewards. Sinatra couldn't have known he was helping to open a Pandora's box—or even letting loose a Trojan horse. Within his lifetime, the industry would completely reverse itself, into the business model that Joni Mitchell described, where pop artists were considered inauthentic (i.e., phonies) if they didn't do everything—especially write their own songs—and the single musical ideal that Sinatra had done more than anyone to perfect and popularize—the notion of interpretation—would be completely irrelevant.

Still, it was a long way between *Tone Poems of Color* (1956), Sinatra's first "officially" self-produced album, and *Ol' Blue Eyes Is Back* (1973), the release that heralded the end of Sinatra's retirement. At the start of 1953, Sinatra was at the absolute nadir of his career; by that spring, he was well on the way to the "comeback" (with "Young at Heart" and *From Here to Eternity*). By 1956, he was ready to make moves toward where no singer had gone before, in the general direction of both control and ownership of his own product. As suggested, parallel steps were being taken, especially in the television era: while radio and movies had been controlled strictly by power brokers, television was opening doors for performers to establish themselves as moguls: Sheldon Leonard, Danny Thomas, Desi Arnaz, and Lucille Ball.

In many ways, it was a propitious moment for such a sea change: the music business had been growing in profits and power since the Depression; even as late as 1939, the American Recording Corporation, the vestige of the old Columbia Records, was only able to stay intact with the aid of CBS Radio. By the 1950s, with the two-pronged popularity of the new album format (generally for grown-ups) and the ever-expanding market for pop singles increasingly aimed at youngsters (who weren't yet being called "baby boomers"), the record industry was now a very high-profit enterprise. When Sinatra was a teenager, he listened to the big bands on, among other labels, Decca Records, a firm that clawed itself into some market share by selling well-known artists for a highly competitive thirty-five cents. In 1954, Decca had grown so far in power and resources that they were able to take over Universal Pictures; twenty years earlier, it would have been the other way around. Around the same time, Capitol Records, which was in the middle of being acquired (and thus empowered) by the British conglomerate EMI, erected one of the most auspicious landmarks on all of the West Coast, the famous Capitol Records Tower.

Around this time, Sinatra formed both Bristol Productions and Essex Productions, the former to handle his film work and the latter for recordings. (When Sinatra signed the contracts to star in *The Joker Is Wild,* the film was produced by Bristol and the soundtrack album—never released—was to have been produced by Essex.) *Tone Poems* was both the first Sinatra release with the Essex name and the first to be taped at Capitol's new pancake stack–shaped office building and studio.

For his part, Sinatra's own "stock" was also on the rise, and some months before his first Capitol contract was scheduled to run out in 1957, he negotiated a new seven-year pact for considerably more dough. "When we took him on two-and-a-half years ago, Frank couldn't get a record [deal]," Alan Livingston of Capitol told *Down Beat* in 1956. "Now, every company in the business is after him, and it would be silly to deny that he has had generous offers from every quarter." Livingston was referring specifically to Victor Records, which was making a bid for Sinatra when dealings with Capitol stalled. To finance his own ventures, Sinatra raised capital from Capitol, so to speak, in the form of a sizable advance against future royalties.

Sinatra wanted to give the impression that Essex was now producing and owning all Frank Sinatra recordings. He informed the trade press that Essex was a "full-fledged independent record company" and that he himself remained "only nominally a Capitol artist," and tried to give the impression that all Sinatra product was merely distributed by Capitol. Essex was even interested in signing other artists and announced it was negotiating with the Beachcombers with Natalie (a group that in December 1956 had opened for Ol' Blue Eyes at the Sands, an establishment in which Sinatra also had a piece of the action). Alan Livingston told us, however, that Frank wasn't fooling anyone, least of all the Capitol brass, who still held all the rights and the purse strings. No matter what Sinatra put in the trade papers, the Essex arrangement was "purely a paper deal for tax purposes. We still owned every Sinatra record made at Capitol, and in perpetuity." The main advantage of the Essex arrangement was to give the singer capital and gain status with the IRS, so that his royalties would go into a corporation rather than be taxed as personal income.

Sinatra was growing increasingly ambitious and decreasingly satisfied with this arrangement and went so far as to claim that it affected the quality of his work. "Some of my [later] work for Capitol lacked the spark that it might have had," he told Robin Douglas-Home. "You can't give your best when you're not happy with the people you're [working] for. I wasn't happy with Capitol, and I'm afraid some of those later albums show it."

The first manifestation of Sinatra's discontent was his switching producers, from Voyle Gilmore to Dave Cavanaugh. Billy May felt that this was a change for the better. "Dave was a musician's musician. He was a good arranger and everything, plus he had been a saxophone player and Frank knew that. And, to put it subtly, Cavanaugh wasn't on Frank's shit list."

Throughout 1958 and 1959, Sinatra repeatedly insisted to Capitol chairman Glenn Wallichs that Essex had to become what the singer was telling *Variety* it was: a genuine subsidiary label, owned by his office but reaping the benefits of the distribution system Capitol had built up over fifteen years. Wallichs flatly turned him down. "It isn't that the deal Frank proposed was so terrible," said Livingston. "It was just totally contrary to everything going on in the record business then. And Glenn said, 'If I give it to you, Frank, I've got to give it to Nat Cole. I've got to give it to so-and-so and so-and-so. You're disrupting our whole business.' But Frank went off in a huff and said, 'Screw you. I won't record anymore. You can't make me sing.'"

Sinatra himself continued: "I said I wanted to quit Capitol even if it meant not recording at all for two years until the contract ran out." Indeed, starting a one-man recording ban was the only bargaining leverage Sinatra had. Between finishing *No One Cares* in May 1959 and starting *Nice 'n' Easy* in March 1960, Sinatra didn't record so much as a single. (He broke his strike only to participate in five tracks for the *Can-Can* soundtrack album; clearly he had a vested interest in promoting his film.)

Even as Sinatra's proposal to create a subsidiary "imprint" within the Capitol aegis was being rejected, he set about acquiring a label of his own. Around this time he came into contact with Norman Granz, owner and operator of Verve Records, and began negotiating to take over that rapidly growing concern. Sinatra and Granz supposedly had gotten as far as agreeing on a sale price of two million. That arrangement did not go through, and Verve was summarily acquired by MGM Records.

At least two stories have been told as to why the deal failed. According to the first, when MGM heard what was happening, they instantly offered Granz an additional half million over what Sinatra was proposing on the condition that Granz sell immediately—in other words, not take the offer back to Sinatra for a counterbid. Sure enough, the first thing Sinatra said when he calmed down was that he would have gladly matched Metro's offer.* The

---

\* It's been said that Sinatra and Granz held a long grudge against each other, which explains why Sinatra never got to make the album of his dreams with Ella Fitzgerald. (Granz was not only her producer, he was also her manager, a position that some have viewed as a conflict of interest.) However, Sinatra made three classic television appearances with Fitzgerald, in 1958, 1960, and 1967, so Granz was willing to cooperate with Sinatra at least to a certain point.

other story is that someone in Sinatra's office loused up the deal—perhaps deliberately. He continually postponed appointments to sign the papers and kept asking to examine and reexamine the company's books; when MGM entered the picture, Granz was relieved to go with them. Why would the adviser not want Sinatra to buy Verve? Purchasing a corporation would have provided Sinatra with certain income tax advantages, but perhaps he could have done even better by starting a label of his own.

Which is where Sinatra was by 1959: trying to build his own company and simultaneously extricate himself from his Capitol contract. The sole benefit of the Verve fiasco had been Sinatra's coming into contact with Morris Ostin, the company's young controller and secretary. Known to all simply as "Mo," he soon became Sinatra's aide-de-camp in this new project of organizing a record company. "I helped build that," Sinatra told Ostin one day as he pointed to the Capitol Records Tower. "Now let's build one of my own."

Around the fall of 1960, Bill Miller, in his role as orchestral contractor, began notifying Sinatra's regular sidemen that they could soon expect to receive paychecks from a new client. "We're going to be doing a lot of dates in the near future," he told percussionist Emil Richards. "Don't let it out yet, but Frank's starting his own label." In December 1960, Sinatra and Ostin officially announced to the trade that the new company's name would be "Reprise." (Alan Livingston insisted that Sinatra always pronounced it "re-PRIZE" rather than the more common "re-PREEZE," although others have disputed this.) The name held a double meaning: the first part indicated the company's slogan, "Records you'll want to play again and again," and the second was that Sinatra intended to give his artists the benefit of his experiences at Columbia and Capitol in that the rights to masters would eventually revert back to the performer, who was then free to "reprise" them in whatever fashion he or she wished.

Ostin, the firm's original vice president and general manager, remained top dog until he stepped down at the end of 1994. The first "artist and repertoire man" named in the early announcements is longtime Sinatra colleague, violinist and conductor Felix Slatkin, but he didn't stay very long in that capacity. (He seems to have been working for Liberty Records from 1960 to his death in 1963.) In October 1959, the Sinatra office announced that the "operations head" of the new concern would be Morty Palitz, who had been one of Sinatra's producers at Columbia and was concurrently A&R chief of Jubilee Records. This deal also never went through, and Sinatra instead hired arranger and producer Sonny Burke. A onetime bandleader best known for his work with Jimmy Dorsey and Charlie Spivak, as well as for the songs he wrote with Peggy Lee (the *Lady and the Tramp* score) and Lionel Hampton ("Midnight Sun"), Burke had headed up Decca Records' West Coast recording activities. He had become available thanks to a stroke of misfortune that seemed anything but fortuitous at the time. "When Decca was about to be sold to MCA, the company eliminated all contracts with executives, including Sonny's and mine," Milt Gabler told me. "But then Frank grabbed Sonny right away." Joining Reprise in 1960, he became Sinatra's personal producer until his death in 1980.

The first Reprise album to be released was, surprisingly, not by Sinatra— it was *The Warm Moods* by saxophone colossus Ben Webster with strings, which had been, in all probability, produced and recorded independently, in January 1960, and the masters then sold to Reprise. Best known for his remarkable tenure with the Duke Ellington Orchestra, Webster was also the reigning monarch of boudoir tenor, and had already recorded several successful albums of "make-out music" with a string section. *The Warm Moods* was beautifully arranged and conducted by Johnny Richards, composer of "Young at Heart," who likely had been the conduit to Sinatra.

Reprise would attempt to build a full jazz wing (with Duke Ellington himself at the epicenter) as well as a comedy department (their biggest star was one of Sinatra's key spiritual inspirations, the legendary song-and-joke man Joe E. Lewis, whom Sinatra had portrayed in his 1957 film *The Joker is Wild*). But in the long run, Reprise was known as the label for the Rat Pack—Sammy Davis Jr. and Dean Martin, in addition to the Chairman of the Board himself—and for swinging lovers like Rosemary Clooney, Jo Stafford, Keely Smith, and other top song stylists of Sinatra's approximate genre and generation. All were enticed to leave their current recording concerns and join Sinatra for unprecedented artistic freedom and profit participation.

Before Sinatra himself could record for his own label, there was still the matter of his Capitol commitment. Wallichs and Livingston had come to realize that there was no stopping Sinatra now that he wanted out, and their primary concern was to get as much product out of him as they could. They reached the compromise for four "contractual obligation" albums described earlier, three of which were finished within a year: *Nice 'n' Easy* (March 1960), *Sinatra's Swingin' Session!!!* (August 1960), and *Come Swing with Me!* (March 1961).

Although the music itself does not bear out Sinatra's not-exactly-unbiased opinion that his later Capitol recordings suffered, these sides were not produced any too easily. On several of these dates, musicians witnessed a rare glimpse of the famous Sinatra temper that the newspapers were so keen to write about but that he had almost never brought into a recording studio.

Billy May has recalled attending a date circa 1960 (otherwise undocumented) when Nelson Riddle conducted and Sweets Edison sat in his familiar solo trumpet chair. "In those days Frank was deliberately being his petulant worst because he was pissed off and didn't want to be there," said May. To express his annoyance, Sinatra constantly complained about the microphone setup and kept demanding take after take, finding fault both real and imagined with each run-through.

"They'd get to, like, take twenty-eight, and Frank gets to the end of it. Nelson cuts the band off, and Frank starts looking around trying to figure out what he's going to get mad at this time. Sweets had a high, squeaky kind of voice, and just as the echo [of the take] was dying away, before Frank can think of anything, Sweets says, 'Shit, baby, you can't do it no better than that!' It broke Frank up so bad, he just fell right on the floor. That's become one of the great stories of our industry. We use it all the time. Someone says, 'Are you happy with the record?' And everybody says, 'In the immortal words of Sweets Edison. . . . .'"

Sinatra had spent most of the 1940s working closely with Axel Stordahl, with occasional side projects involving other collaborators; then in the 1950s, the great bulk of his musical direction was handled by Nelson Riddle, with the exception of some extracurricular albums by May and Jenkins. Now, in the 1960s, Sinatra was seeing the wisdom of Bing Crosby's philosophy that it was wise for a popular singer to work with "a lot of different arrangers." Crosby wrote in his autobiography, "Whenever a good arranger or a good band was free and without previous contractual obligations [as head of his own label company, Sinatra could even work around those], we grabbed them for a few dates."

"He wasn't missing anything, he just felt that he needed a change," explained Frank Military. "He just wanted to get a different sound, which he did." Between 1960 and 1967, Sinatra recorded an exceptional series of nine "one-shot" albums with that many different arrangers and bands: *Ring-a-Ding-Ding!* with Johnny Mandel (1960), *I Remember Tommy* with Sy Oliver, *Point of No Return* with Axel Stordahl, *Sinatra & Strings* with Don Costa (all 1961), *Sinatra and Swingin' Brass* with Neal Hefti, *Sinatra Sings Great Songs from Great Britain* with Robert Farnon, *Sinatra-Basie* arranged by Neal Hefti (all 1962), *It Might As Well Be Swing* with Count Basie's Orchestra and arrangements by Quincy Jones (1963), and *Francis Albert Sinatra & Antônio Carlos Jobim* with arrangements by Claus Ogerman (1967).

Remember also that these were done in addition to the classic sets Sinatra continued to turn out in the 1960s with his three long-standing collaborators from the Capitol era, Nelson Riddle (five new albums for Reprise, recorded between 1963 and 1966), Billy May (two, in 1961 and 1967–68), and Gordon Jenkins (two albums, 1962 and 1965). All these writers succeeded in helping Sinatra expand his musical palette while remaining true to his own heritage, to go forward by building on what he had already achieved.

In December 1960, Sinatra finally taped his first album for Reprise, *Ring-a-Ding-Ding!* arranged and conducted by Johnny Mandel. Sinatra had decided that with the new venture he wanted to get even further away from the classic Sinatra-Riddle sound that he had "come back" with about seven and a half years (which doesn't mean a helluva lot) earlier. The collaborator he chose was Johnny Mandel. Born in New York in 1925, Mandel had played trumpet with Joe Venuti and other bands before coming into his own as a modernist orchestrator and composer with Boyd Raeburn's progressive jazz aggregate in the late 1940s.*

Sinatra would have come across Mandel's name several times in other contexts: when he played bass trumpet in Count Basie's brass section in 1953 and also when he orchestrated *Hoagy Sings Carmichael* (the "Stardust" composer's most successful venture as a vocalist) in 1956. Mandel had also done excellent orchestrations for three outstanding baritones in Sinatra's approximate wheelhouse, Dick Haymes, the Haymes-influenced David Allyn, and Vic Damone. (Allyn and Sinatra had been friends since 1939, when the former toured with Jack Teagarden's orchestra.)

Thus, if Sinatra had heard of Mandel before 1960 it was as a writer of either progressive jazz or straight ballads. (Then too, he might have been familiar with Mandel's groundbreaking jazz score to the 1958 film *I Want to Live!*) "I didn't get to make many records at that time," said Mandel, "because even though I'd been in the business for quite a while, I hadn't gotten enough of a name that they'd use me on records. So I wrote a lot of club acts, and one of them was for Vic Damone. Vic used to play the Sands, and we had a real dynamite act at the time. I'd written a lot of hard-swinging things. And Sinatra came in and heard it, and he came up to Vic and asked him, 'Who did those?' And Vic told him. So I think that's where he got the idea for the swinging things."

Having decided to do a disc with Mandel, Sinatra arranged to get together with the arranger and Bill Miller. Mandel said, "I'd known Bill for quite a long time, so [Sinatra] had Bill bring me out to the Columbia ranch where he was shooting *The Devil at 4 O'Clock*. And he started telling me about how

---

* In 1948, Sinatra had said of Raeburn, "I don't understand his stuff. Maybe it's a little too far ahead for me. I don't think, though, that as a national liking it has much of a future."

he was finished with Capitol and was starting this new company. Everything was going to be different, he was even going to press the records in different colored vinyl, and all that sort of thing. He had a lot of ideas.

"I remember just watching his eyes as he was talking about the company, and they were sparkling. You know, he had the most striking kind of blue eyes. Man! They drill right through you! I mean, when he looks at you, he really looks. And when he's telling you something, you see this great animation and conviction there. I think they probably ran into some snags in manufacturing, because the records did come out looking pretty much like other records, although they had his picture on the label. But he made sure they had very good quality vinyl. You could tell he was very, very proud of this thing."

"Ring-a-ding-ding" had long been one of Sinatra's personal pet expressions, appearing most famously as a throwaway substitute for the original lyrics of "I Won't Dance" in *Swingin' Affair*. (It's also heard in "C'est Magnifique" in *Can-Can* and in the special-material lyrics to the Sinatra–Sammy Davis duo "Me and My Shadow.") In various television variety show comedy routines from the Rat Pack period, Sinatra would use the phrase as the replacement punch line of a joke, the actual meaning of which, he implied, was too risque for television. Sinatra apparently brought the phrase to Sammy Cahn and Jimmy Van Heusen with the idea of making it into the title song of what would be his first Reprise album, and the songwriters started with the template of their own enormously successful "The Tender Trap" from 1955. In the late 1950s and early 1960s, "The Tender Trap" was a virtual mantra for the courtship rituals of an entire generation, and songwriters for movie titles and pop singles were cloning it left and right (one of the better ones being Bobby Darin's "That's the Way Love Is").

As a song, "Ring-a-Ding-Ding!" is slightly more complex, structurally, than "The Tender Trap"; the central melodic section is six lines and three rhymes, as opposed to four. The general trajectory of the narrative parallels "Trap" very closely, describing the collision of two pre–sexual revolution archetypes, the swinging bachelor and the no-less predatory husband-hunting female; by the end of the bridge, our hero is already hating himself for being single. The final A section rhapsodizes over the wedding and the happy-ever-after.*

The "Ring-a-Ding-Ding!" title and its repeated references to bells suggested appropriate carillon effects to Sinatra, who asked Mandel to "put some

---

* One phrase requires explanation: "presto, you do a skull." This is archaic vaudeville slang for a "double take," an expression of extreme surprise, wherein one's face comes to resemble a skull. Mitzi Gaynor talks about "doing a skull" in Sinatra's 1957 film *The Joker Is Wild*.

bell sounds in there." This led to a field day for percussionist Emil Richards and his celebrated collection of unusual chimes and bells (much as Billy May's chart on "Moonlight on the Ganges" gave Richards the chance to use his exotic percussion implements). "We all loved Mandel," said Richards. "The thing about Johnny is that normally when you pick up a chart to play, you want to change a couple of the chords to make it sound a little more interesting. But with Johnny's music, all you have to do is play what's on the paper, and he does all the substitutions for you. Everything is already there; there's nothing you have to fill in."

Mandel and Richards use tubular bells for orchestral color in several spots, and they contrast these deeper chimes with tiny plinks from triangles and xylophones, most notably in the very elaborate introduction to "Ring-a-Ding-Ding!" Those bell effects appear throughout the album, as in the title song, wherein church bells underscore the line in the reprise of the chorus, "the village bell will sound in the steeple"; and in the intro to "A Foggy Day" where Richards's bells, in a sense, play the role of London's famous Big Ben. In the climax of "In the Still of the Night," Sinatra heightens the drama by slowing down and stretching it out, while Richards suggests the passage of time with appropriate bell sounds.

Mandel was—and remains—a proud admirer of May and Riddle. In the title song and elsewhere, he makes the brass sound brassier by having the trumpets phrase in unison with the staccato plinks of the xylophone. Both "In the Still of the Night" and "You'd Be So Easy to Love" are hard-swinging arrangements of Cole Porter ballads that fit the profile of such classic Sinatra-Riddle-Porter masterpieces as "I've Got You Under My Skin" and "Night and Day." Here, the more modern West Coast trumpeter Don Fagerquist essays the role of Sweets Edison, and trombonist Frank Rosolino (like Milt Bernhart, a former Kentonite) takes the central solo à la "Skin."

At times, Mandel seems to have studied Riddle and May and is making a conscious effort to emulate the best of both (the minor key intro of "Easy to Love" shows that he has clearly solved the swinging Riddle). But though the tempos on *Ring-a-Ding-Ding!* move at roughly the same speed as Sinatra's earlier "swingin'" albums, here the singer and arranger gradually achieve an entirely new kind of swinging feeling. "A Fine Romance" is an especially brilliant example of Sinatra swinging like crazy while using his impeccable diction to add detail to his musical character. Most people associate the act of swinging with mangling the pronunciations (sometimes in a very clever and colorful way, as in the best of Sinatra's hero, Louis Armstrong)—dropping "g"'s and the like—but here Sinatra very properly pronounces the words "tom-ah-toe" and "po-tah-toe," in a way that would do Fred Astaire proud.

This track, more than the others, is an aural parallel to the cover painting, which depicts Ol' Blue Eyes suavely adjusting his bow tie, his blue eyes (exactly as Mandel described them) blazing and his pinky sticking out, as if he were precisely in the middle of inviting his sugar to tea—so to speak.

"Nelson had a lot more of Tommy Dorsey in him, and Dorsey had Sy Oliver writing for him," said Mandel. "Sy had created the Lunceford sound, of course, which used more of a two-four concept than four-four. But Billy always thought more in four. He came out of the Charlie Barnet band, which had more of an Ellington influence. Whereas I came out of the Count Basie band. And that's where I was thinking, and that's the way I wrote in terms of a rhythmic approach. It's not a question of saying one is better than the other."

In *Ring-a-Ding-Ding!*, the first of Sinatra's series of "one-shot" pairings, the singer achieves, in both the rhythm and the overall orchestral textures, the perfect balance of sounds we expect from both the singer and the accompanying orchestra. "Frank always insisted that you use his rhythm section," said Mandel, adding that Mel Lewis probably would have been his own drummer of choice. But the home team rhythm section, especially Bill Miller's elegant comping (the chordal accompaniment that pianists are expected to provide for singers and other soloists) and Irv Cottler's rich (as in Buddy) percussion foundation, lets you know this is going to be a Sinatra production even as the curtain is still going up. It's in the horn solos that we most clearly hear Mandel's work; he was free to use more modern-oriented players, such as Bud Shank on alto, Fagerquist, and Rosolino. Mandel also makes his presence felt in the voicings of the brass and reeds, the latter led by the sax giant Joe Maini. "I used him on everything," Mandel explained. "He was probably the best lead saxophone player I've ever known. Listen to the way the saxes sound on that album—they don't sound like that on anything else Frank ever did."

*Ring* opens with the two strongest tracks in the set, the title and Harold Arlen's "Let's Fall in Love." As Lorenz Hart famously opined, listeners "like to recognize the tune" (and "savvy what the band is playing"),* and when they hear a melody that they're familiar with, they generally start applauding. Realizing that this moment of recognition constitutes a dramatic epiphany, Sinatra developed the tactic of delaying that recognition in order to increase the suspense: sometimes he would use the unfamiliar verse of a familiar melody for that purpose, and at other times (famously on "The Moon was Yellow") he would take the bridge of a song and repurpose it as a verse. "Let's

---

* These lines are the opening of a 1939 song by Rodgers and Hart, "I Like to Recognize the Tune," from the Broadway musical *Too Many Girls*. The song was recorded brilliantly by Mel Tormé but, alas, never by Sinatra.

Fall in Love" is the most notable example of Sinatra delaying recognition for as long as humanly possible by doing both.

He starts with the bridge, which is well known enough that listeners will find it vaguely familiar, yet strange enough that it won't tip everybody off. He then moves on to the verse, which had barely been sung at all since Harold Arlen himself recorded it in 1934. We then arrive at the one significant alteration of a chart made by Sinatra on the date itself: both singer and ensemble rest for an entire measure before leaping into the refrain. "He stuck an empty bar in there," said Mandel, "which was a very good change." It heightens the tension, "because nobody's ever heard this verse before, and it makes you wonder what's coming next. What made him think of it, I'll never know, because I wouldn't have thought of it. But then after you hear that you say, 'Well, of course!'" ("Be Careful, It's My Heart" uses rhythm in a similarly dramatic fashion, with Sinatra similarly rushing the initial phrases of each A section so that he can luxuriate in comparably pregnant pauses.)

Mandel characterizes himself as a slow worker, especially compared to Riddle, a thirteen-carat workaholic who was determined to do as many jobs as possible. Where Riddle could turn out an album's worth of charts in a week, Mandel said that he still requires at least a month to do his best work. "If somebody has to have a club arrangement overnight, I can do that," he said, "but it's going to sound as if I wrote it too fast." Sinatra originally assigned Mandel fourteen charts, which he did not have enough time to do (among other things, the orchestrator began taping a full-length album with Mel Tormé a week before *Ring-a-Ding-Ding!*).

Time forced Mandel to farm out one entire arrangement and sections of two others. He wrote the intros, codas, and instrumental portions of "When I Take My Sugar to Tea" and "Easy to Love," while Dick Reynolds (who had arranged the Sinatra–Ray Anthony session of 1954) wrote the actual backgrounds behind the vocal. Even so, an impartial lay listener would have to disagree with Mandel's contention that the Skip Martin–ghosted chart on "Be Careful, It's My Heart" "doesn't even sound like me," especially since the sonic signature of trumpets enhanced by xylophones (May à la Mandel) is also heard on this Irving Berlin classic.

Thus it must have been frustrating for Mandel that he did finish two whole arrangements by himself that never made it to the album: "Have You Met Miss Jones?" because it was too slow, and "Zing! Went the Strings of My Heart" because it was, if not exactly too fast, somewhat awkward rhythmically. Actually, neither goes too far, but they're not exactly danceable and therefore not exactly right for the terpsichorean mood of the album. They don't succeed in the way that "Let's Face the Music and Dance" does, in building in intensity while maintaining the dancing beat. And unlike the aptly named "I've Got My Love to Keep Me Warm," they fail to generate the proper amount of emotional-musical heat.

Coincidentally, both of the deleted songs start with their infrequently heard verses, although neither works anywhere near as well as "Let's Fall in Love." "Zing" commences comparatively sluggishly in the verse and rather clumsily shifts tempos for the refrain. "I guess for some reason he wanted to do the verse slow," said Mandel, who hadn't heard "Zing" at all until 1990. Sinatra had initially informed Mandel that he wanted to use "Miss Jones" as the one near-ballad on *Ring* but when he heard the chart on the session, he exclaimed, "This sounds like a different album" and then added (off-mic), "This doesn't belong on an album called *Ring-a-Ding-Ding!*" After a complete run-through and a half, the decision was made to shelve the tune. Sinatra revived the Rodgers and Hart number as a straight-ahead swinger with Billy May in 1962.

It's easy to see why "The Coffee Song" (which Sinatra had first heard at the Copacabana in 1946 and recorded shortly thereafter) would have taken Mandel so much time to orchestrate: the chart has more things going on than there are coffee beans in Brazil. Working with two completely different choruses' worth of lyrics (albeit with the same bridge), Sinatra and Mandel wend their way through a relentlessly rhythmic rumba pattern, the arranger's very adroit use of the string section (on the bridges), a series of countermelodies (including one that ascends chromatically, behind "a politician's daughter"), and several unexpected modulations.

Sinatra did not choose to include the verse on "You and the Night and the Music"; but even so, it's a brilliant and compelling minor-key swinger, originally written as more of a dramatic, torchy ballad by Arthur Schwartz and Howard Dietz, reminiscent of Cole Porter at his best. There's an absolutely ingenious intro by Mandel, one that he described as his favorite. At the end of the second chorus, Sinatra again heightens the drama—and brilliantly drives home the authors' original intention—by singing the key words on the line "*if* we could *live* for the moment" a fourth higher. "In the Still of the Night," which Mandel names as his overall favorite item from the set, also rises gradually in pitch and increases in power.

Mandel added, "I would have loved to have done a ballad album with Sinatra." The two talked about reuniting in the early 1980s, during a season when Mandel unfortunately was already all booked up. Sinatra also got around to recording two of Mandel's superlative movie theme songs, "Emily" and "The Shadow of Your Smile" (the latter with Mandel's former leader, Count Basie). So, for better or worse, *Ring-a-Ding-Ding!* remains a superlative once-in-a-lifetime collaboration. It's hard to imagine how they could have topped it.

In February 1961, the first release package from the new Reprise Records hit the stores: Sinatra's *Ring-a-Ding Ding!*, Ben Webster's *The Warm Moods*, Sammy Davis Jr.'s *The Wham of Sam*, *Mavis* (by singer Mavis Rivers), and *It Is Now Post Time* by Joe E. Lewis. Both sales and reviews were as strong as Sinatra had hoped. When advance orders on *I Remember Tommy* from later in 1961 totaled 200,000 units, Sinatra said (to Robin Douglas-Home), "The order was something of a record figure in my experience. It makes me laugh when I think back to when we started Reprise. The buyers all thought it was a joke, you know—the boys getting together for a laugh. They treated us pretty carefully at first, but now we're well underway." Before 1960 had ended, Sinatra had recorded three singles arranged by Riddle and conducted by Slatkin, and in March he started work on another album with another arranger.

In 1961 or early 1962, Sinatra hired arranger, trumpeter, and former bandleader Neal Hefti to come on staff at Reprise, initially as a producer. Like Mandel and most of the other younger writers Sinatra worked with in the Reprise period, Hefti had long been a fan of Sinatra and his arrangers, particularly Riddle and May. "Tommy Dorsey had one of my favorite bands when I was in high school," Hefti pointed out, "because he had Axel to write the ballads and Sy Oliver for the swing tunes. That combination has yet to be equaled." Hefti added that while Ax and Sy divided the responsibilities of supplying Sinatra with arrangements in different moods, "Nelson did both—and he was the best."

No one would disagree with that—Riddle was indeed the greatest of all of Sinatra's collaborators, and Sinatra knew it. However, in the early years of Reprise, Riddle was not available to Sinatra. Riddle was still under contract to Capitol Records, and now that Sinatra and Capitol were on different sides of the fence, Capitol was not about to let them work together for the time being. However, it's revealing in light of Hefti's observations that Sinatra's first move was to harken back to Riddle's two major predecessors, Sy Oliver and Axel Stordahl. While *Ring-a-Ding-Ding!* and the albums with Hefti and Count Basie take a more forward-looking stance, *I Remember Tommy* with Oliver and *Point of No Return* with Stordahl show that Sinatra wisely intended to keep the past as part of his future. (Can it be coincidence that he rerecorded "I'll Be Seeing You," one of the most notable ballads from his Dorsey days, in two completely different new arrangements, with both Oliver and Stordahl, within a few months of each other?)

After winding up the *Tommy* project and the two albums with May, Sinatra finally got around to the project he had long been putting off: the final contractual obligation album for Capitol. "Just before Sinatra finished at Capitol, he did an album called *Point of No Return* with Axel Stordahl," recalled guitarist Al Viola. "It was a little heartbreaking to make because Axel was suffering from cancer."

"I'm sure his lawyers had to do a lot of talking to get him to do it," Milt Bernhart suggested. "I have a feeling he said, 'Let them sue me.' But Mickey Rudin [Sinatra's main attorney] must have said, 'Frank, don't be a fool. What do you need being sued? Do the album!'"

Either Capitol producer Dave Cavanaugh or Sinatra himself remembered that Axel Stordahl had directed Sinatra's first Capitol session eight years earlier, and from there came the idea of using him for the date that everyone now knew would be Sinatra's final session for Capitol Records. Viola recalls that Mrs. Stordahl, former Pied Piper June Hutton, had gone to Cavanaugh to lobby on her husband's behalf. "She knew that Frank was leaving Capitol, and she also knew that Axel wanted to get in one last album with Frank because he might not be around much longer," said Viola. Because the project was put together so quickly, Stordahl was importuned to recruit the services of ghostwriter Heinie Beau for three tunes (the arranger-reedman had just served in the same role on the Sinatra–Billy May *Come Swing with Me!*).

Sinatra was conflicted, and remained so throughout the taping. On some level he continued to be indifferent. "Frank didn't care," Milt Bernhart felt. "It didn't mean a thing to him. Somebody from Capitol must have said, 'Would Axel Stordahl be okay?' and he probably said, 'I don't care who you get!'" At the same time, Sinatra somewhat welcomed the opportunity to say goodbye, good luck, and amen to the man who had played such an important role in his success story from 1940 to 1953. "Frank couldn't wait to leave, but he decided to do the album as a favor for Axel," Al Viola clarified. "If it wasn't for Axel, he wouldn't have done that album." Bill Miller felt that Frank wanted Axel there as a parting gesture—"You know, 'my old buddy.'"

"I got a call to do the two sessions, and I was really thrilled," recalled Bernhart, who said that for nearly twenty years he and his wife had referred to the 1942 Sinatra-Stordahl record of "The Night We Called It a Day" as "their song." "I couldn't believe I was going to be there, because this was a reunion of those two people. When we went in to do those dates, Frank didn't show up right away, so we had time to rehearse and run the charts through with Axel.

"When Frank came in, he walked right to the microphone and said, 'What's up?' There were quite a few people there [in the "audience"] and a big orchestra. There was electricity in the air for everybody but Sinatra. So he took the first tune and said, 'Okay.' I'm not even sure we ran it through because pretty soon we were doing one take on everything, and that's the way it went. After an hour he was through with six numbers, and he said goodbye and was out the door—and he did that two nights in a row. We got no more than one or, tops, two takes on everything. On several, Cavanaugh came out of the booth and said, 'Frank, we had a little trouble with the bass on that last take,' but by that time Frank had torn up the sheet. 'I'm sorry,' was the way he put it. 'Next number.' You had to be there to see it."

The most notorious instance of Sinatra's indifference would have to be "These Foolish Things." On the master take, the last note was somehow unsatisfactory, so on the issued version, before we hear the final "you" we are subjected to a rather brutal tape splice, reminiscent of those on Charles Mingus's masterpiece, *Tijuana Moods*. "I don't think he gave them a second chance," Bernhart speculated. "They might even have had to bring in another singer. It's conceivable that he may not even be singing on that." More likely, Cavanaugh had his engineer splice in the concluding "you" from the first chorus or possibly from the previous take—if there was one—and the vocal tone changes completely between the "of" and the "you."

While *Point of No Return* doesn't boast an original title song (what Sammy and Jimmy could have done with that one), it still has a lot going for it. With another arranger Sinatra might have done more remakes of Columbia Records sides, but he could see little point in asking Stordahl to redo his own charts. They therefore settled on an almost all-new program, remaking only "I'll Be Seeing You" from their Dorsey days plus "September Song" (the least but not the last of his three commercial versions) and "These Foolish Things" from the Columbia period.

Since his previous session with Sinatra eight years earlier, Stordahl had written virtually nothing of interest; yet *Point of No Return* shows that he could still make mincemeat out of most arrangers working in 1962, and even give Riddle, May, and Jenkins a run for their money. Sinatra, for his part, couldn't force himself to sing badly: he may sound a trifle detached on "It's a Blue World" and "These Foolish Things" (as we know from the testimonies of the participating musicians, he was clearly not feeling it) but compensates with "I'll See You Again," which uses one of his favorite structural devices, the bridge-as-verse. "I still think the album is one of the best things I ever heard," said Bernhart. "If you listen to 'I'll See You Again,' it's hard to believe that it was done in a single take. But it was." Bill Miller added, "I remember even throwing some Nelson Riddle–style polytones in there."

Stordahl's string writing is as formidable as ever, while his work with brass and reeds has actually improved—especially the horn crescendi on "I'll Be

Seeing You" and "Memories of You." Said Bernhart, "You talk about classics, to me, 'When the World Was Young' is a classic." Throughout, Stordahl also makes prominent use of the rhythm section, which seemed almost superfluous on many 1940s dates; now the bass and drums really have something to do.

We can be grateful for *Point of No Return* at the very least because it gave Sinatra the opportunity to record "There Will Never Be Another You," as well as "I'll Remember April" and "As Time Goes By." "Somewhere Along the Way" is a beautiful nod to his old friend, Jimmy Van Heusen, who composed this gem under the nom de publication Kurt Adams. Stordahl and Beau also achieve superlative results with the reed section: Beau's "Memories of You" contains a beautiful coda built on give-and-take between Sinatra and Ted Nash on soprano sax.

More than any of his other albums, *Point of No Return* documents a great artist in transition: the orchestrations feel like earlier Frank, but the voice itself is his early-1960s sound—hear how he stretches the word "sweet" for several measures on "I'll See You Again." Personally speaking, the most bittersweet tracks are "It's a Blue World" and "A Million Dreams Ago," two songs, not exactly standards, from the big-band era. "Blue World" was associated with Ray Eberle and Glenn Miller, and "Million Dreams" with Eddy Howard and Dick Jurgens's orchestra. Like so much of the album, they are both songs of goodbye.

And that's the feeling that Sinatra tapped into on *Point of No Return*, on multiple levels. "I remember after we did the first tune," said Viola, "I went over to June, and she had tears in her eyes. She said, 'You have no idea what this means to Axel. He so wanted to do this album with Frank, he wanted to have this last hurrah.'"

That's also why "It's a Blue World" and "A Million Dreams Ago" are so important. These are both rank-and-file, bread-and-butter songs of the dance band era, the kind that were mass-produced by the thousands in those years by the publishers who could still collectively be called Tin Pan Alley. And they were identified with grade-B vocalists; no one ever thought Eberle or Howard was anything like a rival to Sinatra, Perry Como, or Dick Haymes. Sinatra is digging deep into the minutiae of the era that spawned him, tapping into their very ordinariness and transforming it into something unspeakably profound.

Both "Blue World" (Beau's arrangement) and "Million Dreams" are in something closer to dance tempo and feature prominent saxophones, just like they would have in 1942. Stordahl's chart on "A Million Dreams Ago" stands out especially; more than any other piece here, it is truly in dance tempo and transports us back to the dawn of Sinatra's career. It's in stark contrast to the rest of the album: even "I'll See You Again," which was written as a waltz (and is how it's heard here) is in more of a concert tempo, but "A Million Dreams Ago" is, amazingly, a slow and very romantic dance. Sinatra even harmonizes closely with the reed section; the tenor and alto saxophones become the final incarnation of the Pied Pipers or the Sentimentalists.

Thus Sinatra was not only saying goodbye to Capitol Records—which by now was, in millennial slang, his "frenemy"—and to Stordahl, but to much more: to the entire big-band era, to his years on the bus, to his youth, to the days when he figured out how to sleep in his tuxedo without creasing it and could hit the bandstand in his own actual God-given hair. (Again, it cannot be a coincidence that he chose 1961 to say goodbye to both Stordahl and Sy Oliver.) When Sinatra sang the words "Goodbye, good luck, old friend," he must have been staring straight into the eyes of Axel, who would be dead of cancer within two years at age fifty. That was the only way the two men could communicate their love for each other; Sinatra had a proclivity toward friendly insults as his means of expressing affection, and Stordahl, as Miller put it, "said about two words per session, whether he needed to or not."

Stordahl's work underscores the feeling that Sinatra is both at the end of one great period in his life and the beginning of another; a perfect midway point between the best of what he had done in his youth and the most amazing things he would accomplish in maturity. And then, as a means of tying it all up with a bow, like one of his signature neckties of the WWII era, Sinatra titled the album *Point of No Return*.

"I am a symmetrical man," Sinatra once said, "almost to a fault."* Sinatra had yet one more album to make in 1961, which spoke to his inner sense of symmetry. His career in this period was marked by quantity, quality, and, yes, symmetry: during the first twelve months of Reprise's official existence, he had done two full-length sets with Billy May, as well as two albums with collaborators so old that they were brand-spanking new. There was also an up-tempo set with a younger arranger with whom he'd never worked before; and now, to balance the scales, the only gap left to fill was to do the same with a ballad album. This would be *Sinatra & Strings*, his first of many projects with Don Costa, a fast-rising and extremely talented orchestrator and producer. *Sinatra & Strings* is a brilliant album, one of Sinatra's all-time best, but, alas, something of a false spring. Although the two would go on to make lots

---

* The quote is from the 1965 profile of Sinatra in *Look* magazine, so we can be reasonably sure that he actually said this. This is in direct contrast to his 1962 "interview" in *Playboy*, which was, famously, ghostwritten by Reprise staffer Mike Shore.

of music together, some of it very excellent indeed, nothing else would ever be as good as this, their first collaboration.

Just as *Ring-a-Ding-Ding!* sounds viscerally different from Riddle and May, *Strings* builds upon Sinatra's accomplishments with Stordahl, Jenkins, and Riddle again. As with *Ring-a-Ding-Ding!*, Sinatra wasn't necessarily looking for a new tailor, but a new suit of clothes, a new sound, a new kind of feeling in terms of his work with ballads and string sections; he wanted to create something new, but that would build on his work up until then. Something of the present that would be grounded in the past.

This is precisely what he achieves with *Sinatra & Strings** beginning with the opener "I Hadn't Anyone till You," with its combination of high drama and relaxed sensuality. In fact, *Strings* owes even less to previous Sinatra ballad albums than *Ring-a-Ding-Ding!* owes to preceding swing sets. Everything on *Strings* tells us we are in the presence of a new and worthy stringwriter. This is not a set of saloon songs; while the performances are always moody and occasionally bluesy—particularly "Come Rain or Come Shine"—they're never torchy like those on *Only the Lonely* or *No One Cares,* or darkly comic like *Close to You,* or overtly pensive and squirmy like *Where Are You?* Neither euphoric nor despondent, Sinatra herein occupies what is, for him, a unique emotional space.

"Do you know who Don Costa really was all the time to Frank?" Sammy Cahn asked. "Don Costa was Axel all over again, with those deeper, fuller strings." *Sinatra & Strings* makes a perfect follow-up to *Point of No Return* in that Costa, as Cahn observed, taps into the legacy of Stordahl, the romantic sound the duo had perfected in the 1940s, as opposed to the shadowy, sharply nihilistic edge of *Only the Lonely* and *No One Cares.* Like Stordahl's, Costa's ocean of fiddles seems at once ethereal and somber, perfectly suiting Sinatra's mood, which is neither sanguine nor melancholy. Even when Costa dips his paintbrush of strings into the relatively darker hues, drummer John Markham's brushes keep the proceedings from becoming maudlin.

Sinatra's singing is even more larger-than-life than usual as he uncharacteristically and surprisingly makes use of big endings, a device not normally found in his toolkit. And yet "All or Nothing at All," his bravura, big-note number from the Harry James years, becomes withdrawn and almost shy, emphasizing the "nothing at all" rather than the "all"; when Sinatra sings of "the kiss in your eyes" and "the touch in your hand" in the bridge, he really makes you *feel* it.

---

* Most sources give the album's title as *Sinatra and Strings*, with the conjunction "and" spelled out. However, the album's cover clearly shows the title with the word "and" represented by an ampersand, so that is how it shall be referred to in these pages.

Sinatra intones "That's All" with equal tenderness, treating the first eight measures (A) as if they were a verse, yet he doesn't take them rubato—not exactly. Rather, by restricting the background to just Miller's piano, he deemphasizes the rhythm, and when the orchestra enters on the second eight bars (A1), Sinatra never actually changes tempo but simply brings the beat front and center. This also affords the opening section the feeling of a nursery rhyme, perfectly underscoring the innocence and vulnerability of the character Sinatra portrays in the lyric. The bridge, relying heavily on octave leaps, has a much more mature attitude, and Sinatra gets the most out of this, too.

"That's All" was written by Bob Haymes, a former band singer and B-movie actor turned songwriter. *Strings* also includes a tip of the fedora to the composer's crooner brother, Dick Haymes, forever associated with "It Might as Well Be Spring" (which Sinatra would record again three years later on *Academy Award Winners*). Whereas this song is normally the epitome of Rodgers and Hammerstein's middle-American piety, Sinatra here makes it one of the darker items on the disc, particularly when he slows down on "feel" and then rushes to compensate on "in a melancholy way." When he gets to the phrase "spinning daydreams," he repeats it, not for emphasis, but to make it seem like more of an internal mantra, singing to no one but himself—which is, he makes clear, precisely what a daydream is.

While *Strings* includes Sinatra's fourth and probably all-time smoothest "Night and Day," most of the album's repertoire consists of first-time attempts at standards that he had somehow missed the first time around. These include an extremely heartfelt "Misty" and "Prisoner of Love," the latter being the theme song of the original Italo-American singing heartthrob, Russ Columbo, as well as a huge 1946 hit for another *paisano,* Perry Como.

*Strings* also contains Sinatra's sole mature attempt at the song most frequently cited as the quintessential American popular song, Hoagy Carmichael's "Stardust." He had sung it with James (on an aircheck) and Dorsey ("Smile Again"–style, ensconced within the Pied Pipers vocal group). "Stardust" plays on the idea of delaying the instant of recognition, which you might think he had already taken to its furthest extreme in "Let's Fall in Love" (on *Ring-a-Ding-Ding!*). Here he puts it off for so long that the record's over even before we reach this epiphanous moment—which is a fancy way of saying that Sinatra's "Stardust" contains only the verse, an artistic decision that supposedly teed off Hoagy Carmichael no end. ("I wrote a whole song, not just a verse!" he allegedly exclaimed on hearing the track.*) Sinatra was not

---

* It strikes everyone—including, doubtless, Costa himself—as weird that Sinatra only recorded the verse; but yes, this is how he planned it—it's not like he recorded the whole song and then cut the chorus for time reasons, or anything like that.

only trying to find a new approach to this most recorded of all pop classics but also was telling us that the verse is unduly neglected. It's a very stately opener for a song originally conceived as a jazz instrumental, and no sixteen bars of music had been treated so rhapsodically since Nat King Cole's "Nature Boy."

To beef it up, Costa penned an elaborate introduction, proving he wasn't averse to writing what amounted to a verse for The Voice. This intro was a key reason why Sinatra guitarist Tony Mottola cited "Stardust" as his favorite Sinatra performance. "Don sets it up like almost a tone poem in the beginning," he said, "and it could stand by itself as a classical piece. Then Frank just sings this lovely verse, and then Don ends it, as he does in the beginning. Whoever thought of that idea—whether it was Frank or Don or whoever— it's completely original and absolutely beautiful." He's right about that, yet few listeners would agree with Mottola and cite it as their favorite. The act of removing the chorus makes it seem more like a laboratory experiment than a heartfelt piece of pop music, like a tale without a dog. Beautiful as it is, this "Stardust" is ultimately not what we would call satisfying.

"Yesterdays" contains a similarly celestial intro, suggesting that the singer is reflecting on his "happy, sweet sequestered days" from a vantage point beyond time and space. Sinatra's point of departure is clearly Billie Holiday's dark, bittersweet interpretation from 1939—in fact, he seems to be deliberately twisting the word "then" in a nod to Lady Day. The darker attitude would seem to be a deliberate attempt to make the somewhat florid language of lyricist Otto Harbach seem more believable, especially giggle-producing expressions like "forsooth" and, especially, "gay youth."

Sinatra and Costa follow "Stardust," appropriately, with another song in which love is reflected in the stratosphere, "Come Rain or Come Shine." Harold Arlen's harmonies are similar to Carmichael's "Georgia on My Mind," in the first few lines especially; here Costa's chart seems informed by Ray Charles's treatments of both "Georgia on My Mind" and "Come Rain or Come Shine" (both the work of Ralph Burns). As elsewhere, Arlen's melodies appeal to the bluesier aspects of Sinatra's singing. Like those master blues singers Big Joe Turner or Jimmy Rushing, Sinatra makes us believe that he's got all these reservoirs of feeling stored up inside of him; thus when he sings, he's releasing that emotion in small, carefully controlled doses, not like a faucet but rather like molasses leaking slowly out of a barrel. "Come Rain or Come Shine" may be the album's masterpiece; it's certainly the best-remembered tune on the set, effectively combining the high drama of grand opera (as suggested by the strings) with the pure power of the blues, as reined into song form by Arlen and Johnny Mercer.

*Sinatra & Strings,* as originally released, consisted exclusively of standards—ten to be precise—but two lesser-known titles were recorded for the set but not widely issued until the CD era. There would have been nothing wrong with a couple of new faces in this roomful of old friends; yet the bonus tracks, "As You Desire Me" and "Don't Take Your Love from Me" (which Sinatra had recorded earlier that year with Billy May), don't work on the same level as the rest of the disc. "As You Desire Me" is in the same vein as "Gone with the Wind" on *Only the Lonely,* being another song by Allie Wrubel that bears the name of a movie in which it was not heard. The song's slight melody buckles under the weight of Costa's atypically portentous chart, particularly in a Chopinesque piano part that, fortunately, lightens up shortly into the piece. "Don't Take Your Love from Me," by Swing Era/Tin Pan Alley character Henry "The Neem" Nemo, fares better, being an homage to one of Sinatra's key inspirations, the brilliant Mildred Bailey. Both bonus tracks benefit from prominent and sensitive rhythm guitar work by Al Viola.

Sammy Cahn, who was not represented on this album (most of the songs heard here are from before 1940), expressed the opinion that "Don Costa was a *genius.*" If everything Sinatra and Costa had done together had been on the same level as *Sinatra & Strings,* then Sammy Cahn's compliment would have been something considerably more than mere songwriter's hyperbole.

It would be difficult to imagine that the output of any artist in any period could be any more charmed than Sinatra's was in the first full year of Reprise's existence, especially when one factors in the remaining contractual obligations for Capitol. These concluded, much to Sinatra's pleasure, with "I've Gotta Right to Sing the Blues," a single arranged by veteran writer Skip Martin. Most famous for arranging Les Brown's "I've Got My Love to Keep Me Warm" and the stunning orchestration of "A Shine on Your Shoes" that Fred Astaire sings in *The Band Wagon,* Martin occasionally pinch-hit for Sinatra around this time on dates conducted by Johnny Mandel (*Ring-a-Ding-Ding!*) and Neal Hefti (the Reprise single "Nothing but the Best"). Sinatra recorded "Right to Sing the Blues" at his own expense at the Reprise session of March 6, 1962, on which he also attempted the wacky Billy May chart of "Boys' Night Out." Charmed is indeed the word.

In 1962, Frank Sinatra would release no fewer than five albums (*Sinatra & Strings, Sinatra and Swingin' Brass, All Alone, Great Songs from Great Britain,* and *Sinatra-Basie: An Historic Musical First*), in addition to starring in three theatrical feature films (the all-time classic *The Manchurian Candidate,* and the less-than-classic *Sergeants 3* and *4 For Texas,* not to mention a cameo appearance in *The Road to Hong Kong*). He also maintained his usual full schedule of television appearances (of which the greatest, by far, was an earth-shattering team-up with Judy Garland on the great enter-tainer's CBS-TV special in February). Sinatra's output in this year is all the more impressive considering that he spent fully three months on the road, away from Hollywood and the recording studios, engaged in a venture that remains unique in his career.

This was the World Tour. It was barely mentioned in the press at the time, as Sinatra wanted it, and, although the entire tour was copiously doc-umented by live recordings, none of these concert tapes were legally issued until roughly three decades after the fact. Yet it remains one of the most remarkable events in the Chairman's professional and personal lives.

Buddy Rich, Sinatra's onetime sparring partner in the Dorsey band, was one of the first to talk openly about the world tour, as he did on a *Merv Griffin* show in the early 1970s: "He took [six] of the best musicians in Los Angeles," said the drummer. "He chartered an airplane, went to Japan, went to London [to raise money] for the orphanages. He paid the transportation of the entire technical crew, plus the musicians, plus the entertainers. He gave every musician a set price plus their expenses for hotels and food. And nobody ever knew about it. He just went over and did this out of the good-ness of his heart. You gotta be some kind of a beautiful man to do this."

Sinatra's motives were, indeed, entirely philanthropic. Describing him-self as an "overprivileged adult," he set out to raise money and goodwill on behalf of the world's underprivileged children. There has been some specula-tion as to where the original concept of the tour came from: biographer James Kaplan suggests that one of Sinatra's press agents (yes, he had them) came up with the idea, which is entirely possible, even though it was hardly a publicity stunt. A few cynical types have postulated that Sinatra wanted to get as far away from the USA as possible following a moment when he had been rather ignominiously dumped by the Kennedys (for the singer, this was a painful turn of events, considering the extent to which he had gone to bat for JFK; his support had been crucial in the 1960 election).

However, Emil Richards, who played vibraphone on the tour, remem-bered specifically that the suggestion came from Mr. President himself. "Jack Kennedy asked Frank to do this world tour to help needy children of the free world," recalled Richards, "Kennedy asked him to do it under the auspices of the State Department. But Frank had recently bought his own jet, and he said, 'No, I'd like to do it on my own—I'd like to sponsor it.'"*

---

* Considering the dates, it seems unlikely that the decision to undertake the World Tour had anything to do with the Kennedy snub. The central event that ended the Kennedy-Sinatra friendship occurred when the president elected to stay at Bing Crosby's house—rather than Sinatra's, as he'd anticipated—during a visit to Palm Springs March 22–24, 1962. Sinatra

Another sideman on the tour, Sinatra's longtime guitarist Al Viola, remembered that Sinatra had other, more personal motivations for wanting to hit the road: the Chairman had just gone through a very public romance, engagement, and then breakup with dancer Juliet Prowse—he needed to "get his mind off what happened." In wanting to put that relationship behind him, he also had a hankering to spend a little quality time with the love of his life, the "ex" from whom he never could quite exit, Ava Gardner, then living in Madrid.

Still, his motives were clearly more philanthropic than personal or professional. All of these (whether avoiding the Kennedys, or running away from one relationship and toward another) indicate reasons why Sinatra would have enjoyed spending time away from the States; but none of them explains why he would invest so much time and effort in a charitable venture. If he merely wanted to get out of the country, why not just spend a month sunning himself on the French Riviera? It would have been a lot cheaper and easier.

The tour, on which Sinatra and six musicians wound steadily westward (from Mexico to Japan to Europe), had its origin in a series of concerts that Sinatra had given in Australia three years earlier. In 1959, he toured down under with vibraphonist Red Norvo's quintet (another occasion in which he found the means to enjoy a tête-à-tête with the ex–Mrs. Sinatra, who was then on location for the picture *On the Beach*). "The higher up you get in this business," Sinatra said at one of the 1959 concerts, "the more opportunity you have to work with the people you want." Introducing Norvo to the crowd, he continued, "This is a man I have tremendous respect for, musically and personally. I've always wanted to work with his band." The music for the 1959 and 1962 tours grew out of Sinatra's long-standing admiration for the small groups of Norvo and Benny Goodman, particularly the many occasions when the vibraphonist and the clarinetist worked together.

Norvo and Sinatra had been friendly since 1939, when the pioneering percussionist tried to hire him as a second singer for his orchestra. It was his wife and musical partner Mildred Bailey who had first alerted Norvo to the young crooner's obvious talent. Although Sinatra had recently committed himself to Harry James and never regretted it, his admiration for Norvo's great band of the late 1930s knew no bounds. And he wasn't alone: Dinah Shore,

---

had been informed of this change of plans about two weeks earlier (as reported by Jim Kaplan), say about March 10, and the World Tour began on April 15, when he played the first concert in Mexico City. The rehearsals and planning of the tour, not to mention Sinatra clearing all of his busy schedule, would have taken much more than a month or even five weeks of preparation. All of which indicates that he had to have been planning the tour well before the Kennedy incident.

Mel Tormé, Tony Bennett, and many other singers named that group—billed as "Mr. and Mrs. Swing"—as one of their favorites. As Norvo acknowledged, "The arrangements that Eddie [Sauter] made for Mildred were just perfect vocal arrangements. I mean, absolutely perfect. I'm sure Frank realized that."

Then Red added, without a note of egotism, "That band had a lot of character that 'stage' [music industry] people at the time appreciated. But it was a soft band, and it was much too early. It might have been a big commercial success ten years later. I felt that it was way ahead of its time." Not coincidentally, Sinatra latched onto at least three of Norvo's sidemen as regulars in his musical stock company: pianist Bill Miller, drummer Irv Cottler, and saxist Herbie Haymer (until he was killed in a 1949 auto accident).

At around the time of the vibes-heavy *Swing Easy!* in 1954, Sinatra was hearing quite a bit of Norvo and his trio, as were Bing Crosby and the other denizens of Palm Springs who frequented the Desert Inn. Said Norvo, "It was actually the only jazz you could hear in Palm Springs." The first times Sinatra and Norvo actually worked together were on film projects, starting with the uncompleted animated production of *Finian's Rainbow* in 1954. (Norvo was part of an all-star group, also including Oscar Peterson, that played an extended jazz instrumental passage on "Old Devil Moon.") Sinatra arranged for Norvo and group to be seen in a cameo in his 1958 war movie *Kings Go Forth* as well as a memorable on-screen sequence in cahoots with Dean Martin in the 1960 Vegas caper epic *Ocean's 11*, in which they jointly introduce the Cahn and Van Heusen standard "Ain't That a Kick in the Head?"

Norvo was already a presence in Las Vegas, playing with his trio (with bassist Red Wooten and guitarist Jimmy Wyble) at the Tropicana until Sinatra hired him away to work at the Sands, where he opened in the lounge at Easter 1958. Norvo considered the move an upgrade, and thus was empowered to expand to a quintet. He added a drummer (by the time of the Australian concerts, it was Johnny Markham) and a remarkable young multireed player from San Francisco named Jerry Dodgion, who had been recommended by Norvo's brother-in-law, the famous trumpeter Shorty Rogers. Norvo was hired for a six-week stint at the Sands, but the quintet wound up playing there for six months. "Frank liked the band. He listened to jazz all the time," Norvo reported. "And that's the kind of music he wanted in the lounge."

While listening to Norvo in Las Vegas, Sinatra hatched the idea of employing the group in the same fashion that he'd employed the Page Cavanaugh Trio for several seasons a decade earlier. In some cases, especially in far-flung locales, the group would serve as a core rhythm section for the "house" orchestra and a supplement for regular accompanist Bill Miller. When Sinatra played a benefit or a charity event and there was no budget for a full orchestra, the quintet would be the whole show behind Sinatra.

Around February 1959, Norvo and his four sidemen, joined by Miller, spent a week learning the singer's repertory and working out small-group arrangements. The rehearsals took place at Sinatra's house, but the star joined them only occasionally; after all, he already knew the charts. The six men performed together for the first time at a benefit for cancer research in late February at Los Angeles's Shrine Auditorium, and then the combination did their first "paying" engagement at the Fontainebleau in Miami. "From now on," Sinatra announced to the capacity crowd at the Shrine, "in our personal appearances we're going to work together."

After the Shrine (and after Sinatra taped the *No One Cares* album that same month), the Sinatra-Norvo combination flew to Australia for two concerts in Sydney and Melbourne. Fortunately, someone in the sound booth turned on a tape recorder each night, and these two concerts (March 31 and April 1), which were finally released (combined into a single sequence) in 1997, are by far the most important live recording of Sinatra from the Capitol era.*

To use Sinatra's own lingo, he swings like a *mother* (technically, that's only half a word) on the April 1 (Melbourne) concert. As loose and unfettered as he was throughout the 1950s, Sinatra offers a more aggressive brand of jazz singing here that points to his Basie albums of the 1960s. He's never sounded more inspired and animated, generating so much happy energy it's a wonder that the continent could contain him. "The smaller group did give him more freedom," explained Jerry Dodgion, elaborating that the informal format also encouraged Sinatra to vary the program and the arrangements from show to show whenever he toured with a small band. "He could be different every night, which is more in keeping with a jazz group."

The ballads are felt more keenly than ever, particularly "Angel Eyes" and "One for My Baby" by Sinatra and Miller, with the rest of the ensemble taking five. The swingers are even swingier than usual, especially "The Lady Is a Tramp" and "At Long Last Love." Sinatra seems to have been particularly pleased to sing the Riddle *Swing Easy!* treatment of "All of Me" with the man who inspired that album. When, in the opening bars of "I've Got You Under My Skin," he gleefully exhorts, "Get your hand off that broad!" his inspiration is clearly Fats Waller. And it's particularly thrilling here and on the other

---

* The opening act, comedian Stan Freberg, a long-standing favorite of Sinatra's, was, alas, not recorded. However, he had already made a memorable guest appearance on Sinatra's ABC-TV show the previous year. Sinatra would also make a surprise, unbilled cameo appearance on Freberg's own ABC-TV special in February 1962.

two final numbers, "Mandalay" and "Night and Day," when a local Aussie orchestra joins the quintet.

"I don't think he ever sang any better in his life than on that tape," said Norvo. "I loved the way he sang with the small band. It was very free, and he was right on top of everything we were doing. He just melted into it, I thought. He took responsibility, he beat off the group and everything, he did his own thing. And the band played great for him, they loved working with him." Norvo felt that Sinatra came off so well because in these shows he never presented himself as a star in front of a backup band but was one of the musicians, down in the trenches with the rest of the unit. Norvo added, "He gave us the feeling he was part of the group."

Sinatra remained "part of the group" for some months to come. He and Norvo spent the last two weeks of April treating the paying customers at the Sands to the same program of hard-driving jazz that they'd done down under. On another occasion, the quintet served as a last-minute substitute at the Sands for Dean Martin when that entertainer was apparently too deep in his cups (even by his own capacious standards) to appear. From July 25 to August 1, Sinatra and Norvo did an eight-day, eighteen-show stand at the 500 Club in Atlantic City. This time the singer broke the house attendance record that he'd set three years previously, bringing an estimated ten thousand people into the nightclub and $150,000 into the happy hands of owner Skinny D'Amato. The Norvo unit also played for Sinatra at the opening of his own little place in the sun, the Cal-Neva Lodge, at about this time.

As they had been in Atlantic City, the Norvo Quintet (with the addition of Miller, now a sextet) was an ideal accompaniment for occasions when there was neither budget nor space for a full orchestra, such as a short series of political rallies for Senator Kennedy leading up to the November 1960 presidential election. There were at least two shows at the Sands in October, one of which featured Eleanor Roosevelt as a speaker. But Jerry Dodgion vividly remembered a rally hosted by a group called "Key Women for Kennedy" and held in September 1960 at the Hollywood home of Sinatra's friends Tony Curtis and Janet Leigh. According to Dodgion, just as Sinatra was about to go on, a reporter materialized from nowhere and tried to corner the singer into giving an interview right then and there. The altercation that resulted, thankfully, was merely verbal and not physical. "Frank started getting salty with the guy. . . . 'I'm not going to go on the stage now until you leave. Do you want to explain to the four hundred women who are out there why I'm not going on?' And the guy got out of there really quick. It was terrific!"

For those of us who weren't around to watch this brief victory over the fourth estate, the most exciting document of the Sinatra-Norvo collaboration after Australia is the singer's December 1959 ABC-TV special, *An Afternoon with Frank Sinatra*, in which he turns in a sizzling interpretation of "Too Marvelous for Words" and a miraculously intimate "Here's That Rainy Day" backed by Norvo and company.

This was a heady time for Norvo: other longtime fans and friends were also incorporating him into their music; he toured with Benny Goodman, who, like Sinatra, used Norvo's quintet as the core of his own band; recorded with Dinah Shore on a charming Capitol album titled *Dinah Sings Some Blues with Red*; and appeared with both Sinatra and Shore on television. Sinatra himself wanted to sing his own blues with Red, but his antagonistic relationship with Capitol Records at this time prevented him from bringing such an exciting new idea to the people he now considered his adversaries.

Sinatra wanted to employ Norvo's group in the same fashion for his summer dates in 1960, but the vibraphonist was on the road with the King of Swing. So for the first time, Sinatra and Bill Miller assembled what the pianist called the "Red Norvo idea," sans Norvo. They hired the ace vibraharpist Emil Richards, only recently returned from the road with George Shearing, as the harmonic-rhythmic nexus of the unit, to fill the Norvo role. Miller also called in rising reed doubler Paul Horn, drummer Sol Gubin, and representatives of two small classic 1940s groups who had since become Sinatra mainstays: Page Cavanaugh's guitarist, Al Viola, and the King Cole Trio's former bassist, Joe Comfort. (Even as late as 1960, it was a risky proposition for a white singer and band to tour with an African American bassist. The group was not legally allowed to perform in many parts of the country, including New Orleans and the rest of Louisiana.) Frank Sinatra and the Bill Miller Sextet, as the combination was billed, opened at the 500 Club in July 1960.

Sinatra gave Norvo the first call for the World Tour early in 1962, but plans for the reunion again fell through. "I think we were working at the Wagon Wheel up in Lake Tahoe," recalled Norvo, "when I got a call from Frank's attorney, Mickey Rudin, and he said, 'You wanna go?' There was some mix-up there. I don't know what it was. I understood that they just wanted me not the band, and I couldn't just disregard my whole band." Sinatra and Miller reassembled the Bill Miller Sextet; this time the bassist was the talented Mexican-American Ralph Peña and the reed man was Harry Klee, principally for his skills on flute, along with Miller, Richards, Viola, and Cottler.

Again, the six men rehearsed extensively at Sinatra's own house, with the singer occasionally joining them. This time several of the arrangers who had written the full orchestrations of Sinatra's current repertoire actively participated in scaling them down to sextet size. Neal Hefti wrote some sketches based on his own arrangements (including "Goody Goody"), as did Johnny

Mandel ("In the Still of the Night") and Billy May ("You're Nobody till Somebody Loves You"). Miller took care of the rest himself: "I just kind of condensed everything down to size from the original charts, so that was really no problem. They were sketches more than full arrangements." Despite using only six men, the voicings are thick and rich. "So we basically sounded like the big bands in all of his recordings," said Klee.

Leaving the States on April 15, 1962, the entourage gave its first concert at Mexico City's International Theatre and then played two televised shows in Tokyo. After appearances in Hong Kong and Korea, they spent the longest part of the trip in Israel: seven concerts, six cities, nine days total. Following several days off in the middle of May (at which time Sinatra paid a call on the former Mrs. Sinatra in Spain), the party hit Athens. Then in Italy they performed in three different theaters as well as a TV studio where they filmed six songs for local television. Following three shows in London, Sinatra and company gave what has become the best-known performance of the tour, at the Lido in Paris. Only two shows followed, at the Olympia theater (also in Paris) and at a gala benefit hosted by Princess Grace at the Monte-Carlo Sporting club in Monaco.

The general trajectory of the tour was westward ho; alas, simultaneously, Sinatra's voice slowly went steadily south. The highly concentrated amount of work, plus the constant touring (never an easy undertaking, even in the dawning of the jet age) and the philanthropic aspect of the tour, the visiting of orphanages and hospitals, was bound to take its toll on his chops; so too did Sinatra's customary rounds of socializing and partying. As for Sinatra's spirits, first they soared, and then they plummeted. The musicians on the trip remembered that Sinatra beamed like a schoolboy with a crush on the girl next door, dreaming about all the wonderful times he would have with Ava as soon as they reached Spain. In "I Get a Kick Out of You," when he reached the line "Some like the perfume in Spain" he would interject a lusty "Yeah!" No one was surprised, however, when the reunion failed to go as planned, and went south as well, just like all of Frank's other reunions with Ava. Eventually the visit disintegrated into another nasty spat. From that point onward in the tour, when Sinatra got to the same line about "perfume from Spain" in the Cole Porter song, he would cry "Blecch!" (as indeed he does on the recording of the London concert from June 1).*

---

\* The entire matter of "perfume from Spain" is "objectionable." As scribe Robert Kimball explains in *The Complete Lyrics of Cole Porter*, the line, as written for the 1934 show *Anything Goes*, is, correctly, "Some get a kick from cocaine." The bit about Spanish perfume is merely some publisher's squeamish and misguided attempt to sanitize Porter's narcotics reference. For that matter, other than in this song, does Spain have any kind of international reputation whatsoever as a center of olfactory arts? Sinatra himself sang it in at least three different

Although a movie camera and sound crew were present for at least part of the tour, the only documents officially produced at the time were two twenty-minute film featurettes, *Frank Sinatra and All God's Children* and *Sinatra in Israel*, neither of which was ever shown theatrically or on television. Considering how great Sinatra is on some of these concerts, it's truly shocking how few have been officially sanctioned for release by Sinatra Enterprises. In 1994, one of the Paris concerts was released as *Sinatra & Sextet: Live in Paris*, and twenty years later, a rather beautifully filmed video of the June 1 London concert was included in the boxed set *Sinatra: London*.*

The most famous concert in the series is, alas, easily the worst, in terms of Sinatra's actual performance. The Paris show features a road-weary Sinatra at the very end of the tour; it was obviously selected for the sound quality of the recording, rather than the shape of Sinatra's voice. While Sinatra is giving it his all, at this very late stage in an exhausting voyage, he had very little to give. This was long before pop stars were able to junket from country to country in luxury, and the strain of the concerts as well as the impromptu appearances Sinatra made almost every day in local orphanages and hospitals were taking their toll on him. While *Melody Maker*'s Ray Coleman, in reviewing the Gaumont Palace concert in Hammersmith, London (June 3), described Sinatra as evincing the "height of professionalism," even he felt obliged to add, "At times he sounded coarse, even nasal, and he certainly found it tough to sustain the note on certain occasions—notably on 'My Funny Valentine.'"

"Near the end there his voice was getting pretty roughed up," confirmed Al Viola—and this was virtually the only time I ever heard Al utter a criticism of Sinatra, whether musically or personally. "In fact, Monte Carlo [June 9] was pretty rough." By the time they reached Paris (June 5 and 6), Sinatra had little voice left. When he recorded in London a week later (June 12–14), he had next to nothing that he could sing with. Discussing the complete itinerary at the Jerusalem show, Sinatra told the audience, "When I arrive home, I'm going to check into a hospital!"

---

ways: in the classic 1953 *Songs for Young Lovers*, Sinatra came as close as he ever would to the actual Porter line ("Some, they may go for cocaine"), and for most of the 1962 World Tour, he sang about "perfume from Spain." But, later that year, on the *Swingin' Brass* album, he changed the line to "Some like the bop-type refrain"—also not authentic Porter. (Later, as in 1974 in Australia, Sinatra sings about "cocaine from Spain," which seems to be splitting the difference between the two.)

* As this new edition was being prepared, a new boxed set was released, titled *World on a String*. The package on the whole is highly recommended, especially the DVD, which contains the Hibiya Park, Tokyo Concert of April 21, 1962, as well as the two documentaries *Frank Sinatra and All God's Children* and *Sinatra in Israel*, and some remarkable television commercials for Perugina chocolate that Sinatra filmed during his stay in Italy in May.

Which is the state that he was in at the Paris concert. Tapes of earlier shows in the tour have long circulated among collectors, and these reveal a much stronger Sinatra, in full command of all of his considerable powers. The concerts from Italy (from the last week of May, thus far heard only in inferior sound) and Japan (April 20 and 21) are so wonderful as to rival the excitement of the 1959 Norvo concerts. We had to wait fifty years to get the June 1 Royal Festival Hall concert, wherein an ebullient Chairman overflows with the energy that's completely gone by the Paris concert of a few nights later. The tape tells the tale: in London he sang twenty-nine songs and stayed on stage for over an hour and a half; in Paris, he did twenty-three songs in about seventy minutes, much of which he successfully killed with a long, rambling monologue.

"Frank worked especially well with the small group," said Viola. "If you listen to those tapes, you'll hear that he was kickin' our [collective] ass! I mean, he was loose! He would turn around to us as if to say, 'Hey you guys come on. This is a concert!' He didn't want us to sound like we were hanging out at some bar." Or, as Sinatra chastises his band in Melbourne in 1959, "Nobody sleeps in this act, Freddie!"

Apart from the hard swingers, which naturally proliferated throughout the tour, some of the most remarkable performances Sinatra created at this time are a series of extremely intimate, low-key duets with Viola's guitar. While "I Concentrate on You" and "Try a Little Tenderness" do not seem to have been recorded on any of the taped concerts, "Night and Day" is far and away the highlight for the Paris show, at which, despite his obvious weariness at this point, Sinatra turns out an overpoweringly sensitive reading of the Porter classic.

The 1962 World Tour was a remarkable event in which Sinatra continuously pushed himself to swingier, jazzier heights. The thirty concerts given in ten weeks amount to the World Series of Sinatra. The only disappointment, apart from the unfortunate fact that as late as 2016, most of the best performances from the tour (other than London and Tokyo) have yet to be legally released, is that Sinatra never followed up on what he had achieved in this extraordinary musical pilgrimage. The group was remarkably together after two and a half months on the road, and given a week or two of rest, Sinatra's chops were doubtless back to peak form. It remains a mystery why he never recorded a fresh album with the sextet in the Los Angeles studios. At the precise moment in his artistic evolution when he was looking for new sounds and new challenges, he had found one, and, for once, did not take it all the way.

"I got the feeling," said Richards, "that [this jazz sextet] was going to be the kind of bag Frank was going to stay in, and in a sense he did, because he tried to keep as much of the group together as possible. The group worked with Sinatra at the Cal-Neva not long after coming back to the States, according to Viola, and they also returned to the 500 Club. At the Athens concert, Sinatra announced that he intended to do a similar World Tour every year from then on. But it was an anomaly that those six top studio men had ever left the lucrative Los Angeles locale to begin with; and while Miller, Cottler, and Viola would devote their careers to Sinatra, Peña, Richards, and Klee once again renounced the road. There continued to be talk of recording a studio album for a few years, but in 1964 the sextet's band library of written music was irrevocably lost when Bill Miller's house was destroyed in a Los Angeles mudslide (which, more unfortunately, also claimed the life of his wife, Aimee).

Although the Sinatra-and-sextet idea would never be heard from again, there were two immediate ramifications of the 1962 tour: first, it rekindled the jazz side of Sinatra, which found its greatest expression in a series of meetings with Count Basie beginning later that year. But the tour also touched off Sinatra's interest in the musical cultures of other lands, which resulted in a flawed but remarkable studio album, also unique in the Chairman's career. During the Paris concert, Sinatra announces that he's going to sing a song about his favorite city. After a wisecrack about Helsinki, he goes into the Mandel arrangement of George and Ira Gershwin's "A Foggy Day." However, the *Great Songs from Great Britain* album would concentrate on songs actually written in the British Isles rather than simply being about them, as written by Americans.

The lyrics to "A Garden in the Rain" refer to "a touch of color 'neath skies of gray." The finished *Great Songs from Great Britain* is an album of similarly conflicting textures: the unending pastoral richness of Robert Farnon's orchestral backgrounds contrasts sharply with the startling thinness of Sinatra's voice. Had Farnon been aware in advance that he would be dealing with a Sinatra with only a fraction of his powers, he might have come up with arrangements that could more artfully conceal the singer's vocal shortcomings; instead, all of those blemishes come directly to the fore; the settings expose them rather than cover them up. All the tempos are extremely slow, so this set of romantic ballads leaves Sinatra with no place to hide.

Sinatra knew how he was sounding and perhaps would have canceled the three dates had forty-two musicians and at least that many of his English associates not set their hearts on attending. Trumpeter Stan Roderick, who described the sessions as "the biggest record date of the year," had given up other, better-paying work just to be there, explaining, "I turned it down for the honor of playing with such a singer." Sinatra was also loath to cancel sessions that had been set up so far in advance. As early as 1959, the British

*Melody Maker* magazine reported that Sinatra had "big disc plans" for recording in London, and in December 1961 he began to assemble the repertory. Around Christmas, Alan Freeman, a producer at Reprise's Great Britain affiliate, Pye Records, received an assignment from boss Louis Benjamin with the warning that "if you take it, you're raving mad." Freeman was soon in touch with Mo Ostin regarding a set of Sinatra songs *from* Great Britain and recorded *in* Great Britain. (To make it even more British, an offer was extended to Sir Winston Churchill, a very serious avocational painter, to provide a picture for the album cover, but the former prime minister respectfully declined. More's the pity.)

"Oh, I was thrilled to pieces!" said Freeman. He immediately gathered the music for nearly seventy homegrown songs that he considered "suitable." Sinatra sifted through these and eventually boiled them down to the eleven that he ultimately recorded; of these, at least two had been selected by Sinatra before he even received Freeman's package. Coincidentally, these were the only two to stretch the boundaries of the concept: "Now Is the Hour," also known as "Maori Farewell Song," came from New Zealand, and "Garden in the Rain," whose author, Carroll Gibbons, had been born in America but made his reputation as leader of the house band at London's Savoy Hotel.

Eventually, Sinatra narrowed it down to one song apiece from each of the major English songwriters, including "We'll Gather Lilacs" by Ivor Novello and Ray Noble's "The Very Thought of You." (Sinatra had done Noble's "Love Locked Out" on the *Close to You* album and "The Very Thought of You" on several 1940s broadcasts.) "I'll Follow My Secret Heart" marked the second Noel Coward tune Sinatra had recorded in nine months (the other being "I'll See You Again" on *Point of No Return*). Sir Noel himself would have attended the dates had he not been in France at the time.

The selection process led to Sinatra's third studio recording of "If I Had You" (which originated in England but was primarily the work of the American Ted Shapiro, a prolific composer who was also Sophie Tucker's musical director) and of "London by Night" by Carroll Coates (who had also written "No One Ever Tells You" on *A Swingin' Affair!*). "London by Night," which Sinatra had first heard sung by Julie London circa 1951, when he and Ava were visiting London, had also been published by Sinatra's firm, Barton Music, in the United States.

From Sinatra's perspective, the single best-known British love song—one that most listeners assumed was American—was doubtless Eric Maschwitz's "These Foolish Things (Remind Me of You)." He had already recorded that classic twice (in 1945 and 1961) and chose in its place the same composer's more thematically appropriate "A Nightingale Sang in Berkeley Square."

According to Freeman, "When the story got out that this session was going to happen, Eric called me up and nearly drove me mad. 'For God's sake, make sure this song gets in. It would be the crowning of my career to have Sinatra record one of my songs!' [Freeman's anecdote fails to mention that Maschwitz's "These Foolish Things" was already on both 1945's *The Voice* and 1961's *Point of No Return*.] I told him, 'Obviously I'll send it over, and I think it would stand a great chance.' And personally, I think that's the one that came out best on the album."

From the beginning, there was no question as to whom the musical director would be. Robert Farnon and Sinatra had first met casually back in the Dorsey era when the former played trumpet for conductor Percy Faith, a friend of the Sentimental Gentleman. "I thought he was marvelous, absolutely wonderful," Farnon told us. "Up to that point I was a Crosby fan, but not anymore. There wasn't anyone else, really. I became one of Frank's biggest fans and admirers."

Sinatra and Farnon didn't cross paths again for another twenty years. In the meantime, fellow Canadians Faith and Farnon achieved international reputations by heading in different directions, but each eventually worked with Sinatra. Farnon settled in London during the war and quickly established himself as England's most imaginative auteur of what was then called "light music." In the 1950s, Sinatra became friendly with the arranger's brother, Brian, who worked as a conductor in Las Vegas. "When Sinatra went through there, Brian used to play some arrangements of mine for him," Farnon recalled. "Don Costa also was a champion of mine with Sinatra. I think it was Don more than anyone who suggested my name when Frank mentioned that he wanted to do an album of British material."

If there's any previous Sinatra album that *Great Songs* reminds us of, it's *Sinatra & Strings,* with Costa. "Here's a guy who is very influenced by Farnon," explained Tony Bennett. "You hear a lot of Farnon in Don Costa. In fact, so many orchestrators borrow from Farnon, it's what I call 'sweet thievery.' If you want to write string arrangements, only the best of them come up to Farnon. Every orchestra leader in the world knows his name. He writes for 109 men, and it's like silk, it sounds so effortless." Bill Miller can remember the first time Sinatra mentioned the project to him. "As long as we're over there, let's do an album with Farnon," he informed the pianist. "After all, he's one of the best."

Farnon provided a string sound for Sinatra that's as well suited to the singer as those of Stordahl, Jenkins, and Costa. "That was another reason I listened to all of Frank's records," said Farnon. "Being an arranger, I enjoyed the scores that Axel and also Gordon Jenkins provided for him. Both those arrangers were my cup of tea, as it were. They had a style that I just enjoyed so much." Milt Bernhart independently arrived at the same comparison. Citing Stordahl as a masterful arranger for strings, the trombonist added, "Robert Farnon may be the only writer-arranger who's a little bit ahead of Axel."

After Sinatra narrowed down the repertory to eleven selections, he and Miller set the keys with some input from Nelson Riddle. At this point, Freeman, in London, began coordinating with Sinatra in Los Angeles and Farnon, who lived on the isle of Guernsey. The first hitch came when Farnon discovered that the key to "If I Had You" was way off—a full fourth away from where Sinatra could sing it comfortably. Freeman checked over his paperwork and concluded that the cable operator was responsible for the error. "I knew what the key should be because I knew his range," said Farnon. "And so I just took it from there. Frank was very pleased when I told him that I had figured out what key he should actually sing it in. It just happened to be right."

The song list and the keys were virtually the only instructions Sinatra gave to Farnon. "They gave me carte blanche and just told me to go ahead and write—which I did," the arranger recalled. "It was a delight to work that way. That was one of the things that was so nice about him. It was lovely to have that freedom." Sinatra and Farnon met again at the time of the Royal Festival Hall concert (on June 1) to go over the charts with Miller and make sure the keys and tempos were suitable. The day before the session, Freeman had flown in Bill Putnam, Sinatra's favorite engineer, not so much to supervise the recording but to make sure all was as the Chairman liked it. On the evening of June 12, Sinatra arrived at the CTS Studios in London's Bayswater district in a Rolls-Royce lent to him by Douglas Fairbanks Jr., and said to Farnon, "Let's see how it fits, huh?"

Four trumpeters, four trombonists, eight saxophonists and woodwind players, five rhythm men (including both Bill Miller and a local pianist, as per union rules), twenty assorted strings, and an uncountable horde of well-wishers (several dozen in the control room alone) had already arrived. "There were so many people there who had nothing to do with the recording," said Farnon. "There were people all around us, sitting on my podium, under the piano, on the piano. . . . The studio was absolutely crammed with people, and Frank loved it. He didn't mind at all."

The listening crowd held their breath and Sinatra kept his cool when the first number, "If I Had You," turned out to be a double disaster. First, he had difficulty making his initial entrance after Farnon's elaborate, though subtle, twenty-five-second introduction, largely taken by the trombones. Then, once that had been worked out, the concert grand piano that Miller was playing became inexplicably incapacitated. Freeman said that he had a piano tuner "tune it and retune" it all day but that the instrument somehow broke in the middle of Miller's solo. Miller's recollection is that "somebody forgot to tune the goddamn thing, which was unheard of." Freeman somehow had neither a repairman nor a backup piano on the premises, but it occurred to Sinatra to ask if a celeste might be handy. When one hears the finished "If I Had You," it's difficult to imagine that Farnon had ever intended to use anything but a celeste. Luckily, this was the only number to include a keyboard solo. "I don't use too much piano with orchestra because we have the guitar," said Farnon. "Both are essentially playing the same thing, and one interferes with the other" (hence the guitar coda of "Garden in the Rain"). Miller thereafter retired to the sidelines while the local man took over the remaining ten tunes.

One should be glad that they persevered, because "If I Had You" may well be the most-aired track on the set, perhaps because of Farnon's unintentionally Riddle-esque references in his use of the bass trombone and an Edisonian trumpet obbligato (probably played by Stan Roderick). The somewhat brisk tempo allows Sinatra to sound stronger than on the very slow numbers, while both Sinatra and Farnon make myriad uses of the song's simple melody. Sinatra plays with the rhythm by adding extra syllables in the second chorus ("I could climb the *very* highest mountain" and *"also* cross the burning desert") to aid him in getting around long, sustained notes. When the singer reaches those hot sands, Farnon conjures up a steamy phrase—you can literally feel the heat rising from the dunes—that could have been heard in England's major cultural achievement of 1962, the film *Lawrence of Arabia.*

Long before "If I Had You" was in the can, Farnon and Freeman realized that their star runner was hopping on one leg. "He was finding it difficult to sing," said Farnon. "His voice was tired, and it was breaking a lot. He was very angry with himself." The orchestra members were duly sympathetic and supportive. "You're often disappointed when you hear a live session by someone who has only been a name on record," said trumpeter Ray Premru. "With Sinatra, I wasn't." Baritone saxophonist Ronnie Ross added, "Sinatra impressed me enormously. It was a change to hear a good session by a singer who really knew what was up." Farnon recalled an instance when Sinatra "was having great difficulty with 'Roses of Picardy,' and he stopped the orchestra and just looked up at the ceiling, and cried, 'Don't just stand up there. Come down and help me!' And that broke up everybody. Oh, it was a lovely moment."

And so it went.* After finishing four tunes in three hours with great difficulty, Sinatra summarily "disappeared" without so much as a "'scuse me." Most likely, he felt he had let everyone down and couldn't bear to face the dis-

---

* The *London* boxed set also includes a number of outtakes. Additionally, two hours of studio session material are included in a privately-issued double-CD set called *Inside Great Songs from Great Britain*, part of a series of collector's issues that cover most of the early- and mid-1960s Reprise albums.

appointed mob. Over the next two nights, thirty-eight musicians (the trumpets were no longer needed), the crowd, and a substandard Sinatra returned, nailing down another four and then three more tracks. On the third night, Nelson Riddle, in London on unrelated business, also put in an appearance. (Both Freeman and Riddle questioned some of Sinatra's phrasing on "The Gypsy," recorded the previous night, and coincidentally, Farnon's least favorite of the eleven tunes. Sinatra listened dutifully to their suggestions, but maintained that his was the way to go.)

After more than fifty-five years, the debate regarding *Great Songs from Great Britain* continues. Do Farnon's lush orchestrations and Sinatra's trying so hard compensate for the thinness of his voice? One particularly feels disappointed at "We'll Gather Lilacs." At face value, Sinatra would hardly seem the lilac-gathering type, but for most of the track the singer is expert enough to convince us that he actually does give a hang about sniffing those bloomin' blossoms. When he reaches the end, however, the vocal line thins out inappropriately exactly at the point where the arrangement calls for him to surge confidently. Likewise, he is unable to animate "We'll Meet Again," an overly stoic "no emotions, please, we're British" kind of love song that perhaps had no business being revived after the Blitz.

We also come across moments where the singer's fatigue contributes to the melancholia of the material, as in "Now Is the Hour" and the ironically dour "Garden in the Rain." His cracking on both utterances of the phrase "somebody else" on "The Gypsy" (also recorded by Charlie Parker during an epiphany of emotional exhaustion) could be chalked up to part of the interpretation.

But the album's strong moments are very strong. Apart from "If I Had You," Sinatra sounds completely convincing on "A Nightingale Sang in Berkeley Square," aided by Riddlelike flutes (portraying the ornithological entity referred to in the title) and a sumptuous trombone solo from Ted Heath veteran Harry Roche. During the date Sinatra also seemed delighted that the bearded trombonist hit a clinker, informing him, "I'm afraid you got a little bit of whisker in there, mate," and then hanging over the engineer's shoulder as the nervous techie spliced out the bum notes right then and there. Sinatra also succeeds in phrasing the line "there was/is magic abroad in the air," which appears in both "Nightingale" and "London by Night," in two such different ways that one almost doesn't notice the coincidence.

It's unlikely that Freeman thought "Roses of Picardy" had any chance at all of making it to the final cut (and originally it didn't, only surfacing as a CD bonus track). How could anyone have envisioned this World War I artifact as potential Sinatra material? Paradoxically, it's this oldest and most archaic flower in the bouquet that comes off as the hippest. On its own, "Roses" is what might be considered a dated piece of "concert" material, composed by "Danny Boy" author Frederic Weatherly and first popularized by Irish tenor John McCormack. In the half century since "Roses" had first sprouted, the number was remembered only dimly in its native country as a rather prissy vehicle for a semiclassical exhibition by saxophone virtuoso Freddy Gardner.

"Roses" grows around a rather simple metaphor, namely that love blossoms like a flower, but soon, also like a flower, love dies. That's not much to work with, but Sinatra and Farnon empower this paper-thin dramatic hook with as much depth as a mystery by Dashiell Hammett. It even starts ominously, with an out-of-tempo verse in a minor key, Sinatra being intriguingly introduced by a subtone clarinet. The lyrics to the verse are tantalizingly vague, the rose simile not becoming clear until the refrain, by which point Sinatra has us hooked. As with his "Where or When," from here the tune builds to a captivating climax in a single powerful chorus. (It's more like a Judy Garland belt number or a Tony Bennett showstopper.) One only notices vocal problems by listening carefully to the last few lines (and, indeed, in the session outtakes that have circulated among Frankophiles), and it's easy to forgive these in the light of how hard Sinatra is trying and how profound his level of feeling is throughout this moving number.

Freeman, who listened to the complete session tapes again in the 1970s, speculated that Sinatra already decided to junk "Roses" even while he was recording it, much as he did "Miss Jones" during *Ring-a-Ding-Ding!* The producer recalls that Sinatra was kidding around and clowning with a vengeance during the recording of "Roses," giving the impression that he didn't take it seriously in the least—which is precisely the opposite of the idea one gets from listening to the cut on the finished disc.

In retrospect, "Roses" blooms as the most radiant flower of the album. Of the eleven tunes, Sinatra had the most trouble with this song, and for that reason he left if off the original release. At the end of the final session, he and Freeman uncorked another bottle of Jack Daniel's and proceeded to listen to playbacks of all three nights' work. The singer then instructed the producer, "Scrub 'Roses of Picardy.' I don't like it." Freeman argued to have the song remain, but Sinatra remained insistent. "He wasn't holding his notes well," said the producer. "There were notes that should have been held, and he was cutting them off, and it wouldn't have sounded right even [if we had covered up the weak spots] with echo." However, Freeman added, "I still think it's a great pity he decided to scrap it because he had so much emotion. It was the most beautiful Bob Farnon arrangement. And he sang it so beautifully, with tremendous *feel*. There was so much feeling in that."

The entire album nearly suffered the same fate as those dying "Roses of Picardy." Sinatra could have rerecorded his vocal parts over the orchestral track at any time he wished, yet instead he elected to make the ten remaining *Great Songs* his only important work never to be released stateside until the CD era. Over the next thirty years the original British LP became a highly sought-after collector's item, and it was issued in various permutations (both legal and otherwise) in Italy, Germany, Japan, and elsewhere. The long-awaited American CD issue parroted the Japanese release (including a libretto with obvious gaffs, i.e., "down by tennis lights" instead of "Down by the Thames / Lights that sparkle like gems"). But on the whole, the final album was worth all the tribulations, and, for Americans, worth the wait. For all of its faults, *Great Songs from Great Britain* remains one of Sinatra's most compelling musical voyages. As in "A Garden in the Rain," surely here is charm beyond compare.

Most of the early Reprise sets used artists' renderings rather than photographs for their covers. The cover of *Sinatra and Swingin' Brass,* recorded four days before the World Tour got under way (and preceded by another set of Sinatra and strings, *All Alone,* with Gordon Jenkins) depicted Blue Eyes in fittingly bright, "brassy" colors. The album inside does not precisely mirror the packaging, however; while the jacket promises no-holds-barred swinging on the level of *Swingin' Affair* or the Billy May albums, *Swingin' Brass* turns out to be a far more controlled, yet no less delightful, forty minutes of rhythmic romping. Not that it doesn't have its freewheeling moments. The first seven songs accelerate in energy, from the comparatively restrained "Goody Goody" (which opened nearly all the World Tour concerts), which Sinatra phrases sure-footedly on the beat, to the cacophonous "Tangerine," which commences with a dissonant brass crash. (Although Sinatra sings two complete choruses of "Tangerine," he unfortunately repeats the main lyric rather than going for Johnny Mercer's witty second chorus, as associated with Helen O'Connell.)

But "Swing" is indeed the crucial term. Much of the repertoire consists of songs fashioned from band instrumentals ("Don'cha Go 'Way Mad" was originally a hit for Illinois Jacquet as "Black Velvet"), written by jazz composers (Ellington's "I'm Beginning to See the Light"), associated with swing bands (Benny Goodman's "Goody Goody," Glenn Miller's "Serenade in Blue"), or favorites of swing musicians ("Love Is Just Around the Corner" and "Tangerine"). And when Sinatra and arranger Neal Hefti intersperse songs by Cole Porter ("I Love You," "At Long Last Love," and "I Get a Kick Out of You"), Gershwin ("They Can't Take That Away from Me"), and Kern ("Pick Yourself

Up"), they make these classic show tunes and standards sound as if they had originally been conceived as swing-era rhythm novelties.*

As we have seen, Sinatra had initially hired Hefti both as a general producer for Reprise and as an arranger on such releases as Dean Martin's *French Style*, *Alice Faye Sings Her Famous Movie Hits*, and *Themes from TV's Top 12: A Neal Hefti Spectacular Featuring 40 Guitars and 8 Pianos*. "Somebody from Reprise called [not Sinatra himself in this case] and asked me if I wanted to be a producer," Hefti recalled. "I had never done that before, so I said yes. That was my last exclusive contract. I couldn't work for anybody else but Reprise for about a year."

In retrospect, Neal Paul Hefti (1922–2008) is best known, by far, for his extensive work in movie and, especially, television soundtracks; even people who have never heard "Night and Day" can hum the opening themes to *Batman* and *The Odd Couple*. But, like virtually all of Sinatra's collaborators, he began his career in the big bands, first with Woody Herman's remarkable original "Thundering Herd" during WWII and then, a decade later, as one of the major forces of Count Basie's "New Testament" orchestra. *Swingin' Brass* was a natural idea to bring to Hefti, who, like Billy May, had originally been a trumpeter—and actually a very good one, his most famous moment as an instrumentalist being his two-horn "duel" with Charlie Barnet's soprano sax on the Barnet classic "Pompton Turnpike."

Hefti wrote dozens of his own swing classics, first for Herman ("Blowin' Up a Storm," "The Good Earth," "Wild Root," and especially "Caldonia") and even more so for Basie ("Splanky," "Cute," and those two little darlings, "Li'l Darlin'" and "Little Pony"). Basie even paid Hefti the ultimate compliment of recording entire albums of his work. As Frank Foster, the Count's lieutenant and eventual successor, recalled, "Even before I joined the band I heard Neal's 'Plymouth Rock,' and I just fell in love with that tune. When I first started writing, Neal and Ernie Wilcox were my two principal influences. The bulk of his stuff was really, really good. I still love to play 'Splanky.'"

Hefti also recorded prodigiously as a house musical director for Coral and Epic (and was responsible for the last hits of both Tommy and Jimmy

---

* The one major rhythm writer whom the set overlooks, alas, is Hefti himself. Many original instrumentals that Hefti had written for the band books of Woody Herman and Count Basie had become widely accepted as big-band classics, and several eventually attained acceptable lyrics. "Softly with Feeling" and "Plymouth Rock" became, thanks to Steve Allen, "Oh, What a Night for Love" and "Cool Blue," while Bart Howard made "Li'l Darlin'" into "Don't Dream of Anybody but Me." "Girl Talk" became a Tony Bennett staple not least because of Bobby Troup's lyrics. Jon Hendricks supplied lyrics to "Little Pony," "Two for the Blues" (the latter also recorded by the arranger's wife, the excellent band vocalist Frances Wayne Hefti), and "Li'l Darlin'" (a different set of words from the lyrics by Bart Howard).

Dorsey), accompanying singers (including his wife, fellow Herd vet Frances Wayne) and jazz soloists (including Coleman Hawkins and Georgie Auld). At the same time, he made albums as a bandleader under his own banner, ranging from jazz (*Hefti Hot 'n' Hearty, The Band with Young Ideas*) to easy listening that refused to insult its listeners' intelligence (*Singing Instrumentals, Pardon My Doo-Wah*). And, like Billy May, Hefti actually took his own orchestra out on the road for several brave seasons during the band-resistant 1950s.

He first worked for Sinatra around 1951. "I did a couple of charts for Frank that Axel didn't have time to do," Hefti recalled. "I was a friend of Axel's, and once in a while he'd call me up and say, 'Can you help me out, I'm really in a jam!' He asked me for a chart on 'Get Happy' [telecasts on February 17 and March 17, 1951], and I had a sort of gimmick going on, a melodic pattern. Then a couple of weeks later Frank said to do one on 'That Old Black Magic,' which he was going to use in a picture called *Meet Danny Wilson,* and he said to write it something like the way I had written 'Get Happy.'"

The original liner text to the *Swingin' Brass* LP constitutes a mass of misinformation: whereas the notes claim that Hefti picked ten of the twelve tunes, Neal told me that, like most Sinatra arrangers, his input was not solicited in the selection of the songs. They also state that "Sinatra had not been singing in some time" before these two April 1962 sessions. Sinatra does sound a little rusty here and there, particularly on the slowest tune, "Serenade in Blue," a composition whose bridge seems designed to exhaust a voice so that it sounds breathless, hoarse, and passionate; yet even here Sinatra finishes on a glorious low tone. Still, he had actually cut no more or no fewer than his usual quota of albums and singles in the previous few months. Lastly, the writer professes that "the two recording sessions were booked six weeks in advance, allowing Neal to get the town's best [side]men." Drummer Irv Cottler recalled, however, that he wasn't able to do the album because the call went out to musicians only two days before the date. Cottler would have been willing to give up an audience with the pope himself to work with Sinatra, particularly on a swing set with Hefti. Unfortunately, this time the drummer wasn't able to get out of a commitment he already had for that date.

Given the histories of both Sinatra and Basie, several tracks recall specific bands: "Don'cha Go 'Way Mad," the most lighthearted lyric on the topic of infidelity imaginable (a swinging "Guess Who I Saw Today"), looks ahead to the first *Sinatra-Basie* album. It points quite specifically to Hefti's work on that record as well as to his dozens of instrumental pieces for Basie both earlier and later, mounting to a marvelous climax in which Sinatra produces even more "babies" than Mother Dionne.

The brass bass-backed "Love Is Just Around the Corner" suggests the way Benny Goodman phrased the same melody as "A Smooth One," particularly in the way that Sinatra clips the ends of each line in the central (A) sections. The rhythmic phrasing also suggests Louis Prima's signature shuffle beat, as does the band's unison mock–Italian-American exclamation after the second bridge ("wow!"). "Ain't She Sweet" sounds like something that Jimmie Lunceford would have played in the 1950s (had he not died in 1947). A minimal 1920s "rhythm novelty," it bounces along to a two-beat feeling in an atomic-age update of what Lunceford and Sy Oliver achieved in "Margie" and "My Blue Heaven."

"I'm Beginning to See the Light" recalls both credited co-composers, Duke Ellington and Harry James, and in particular points to the trumpeter's evocation of the Duke in his 1944 hit rendition. Having Ben Webster, greatest of all Ellington tenor saxophone stars, on hand doesn't hurt. In his only solo on the date (trading fours with the ensemble on the instrumental break), Big Ben lustily deputizes as an official representative of "The Guv'nor"— his pet name for Ellington—with his full-throated, big-toned tenor sound, a voice surely as unmistakable as that of Sinatra himself. While Webster's instrument sounds like a human voice, the Chairman, conversely, makes his voice sound more like a horn by phrasing the central strains in harmony with a section of tightly muted trumpets. The move violates a central tenet of vocal orchestration (it was Gordon Jenkins, remember, who established the very worthwhile precedent for not doubling the melody behind a singer) but very evocatively suggests both Ellington and James. The piece ends unexpectedly on a 1-2-3 Basie tag, played on a celesta.

The album includes a number of songs that Sinatra had recorded as recently as the Capitol era, but the old standbys sound just as fresh as the virgin versions. "They Can't Take That Away from Me" and "I Get a Kick Out of You" find Sinatra channeling his wattage in ways that make them completely new. Sinatra had sung Cole Porter's "I Love You" frequently in the 1940s but never recorded it, even though he found time to wax two other tunes with the same title. Written (supposedly on a dare from Monty Woolley) in 1944 for the musical *Mexican Hayride*, "I Love You" finds Porter in the same vein of beautiful simplicity as the best of his colleague, Irving Berlin. Sinatra instills it with a perfect balance of romance and raucousness, as he does throughout the album, particularly on "Pick Yourself Up," which sports an especially syncopated second eight bars of the first chorus, where he deliberately leaves out the word "yourself" from two key lines. There's a hint of a contemporary go-go beat throughout here, as well as dissonant brass phrases, that, while totally tasteful, could only have been written in the early 1960s. "Pick Yourself Up" may be the most euphoric track on the album, but *Swingin' Brass* on the whole is saturated with contagious euphoria.

In Hefti's official capacity as producer for Reprise, he had cultivated a sturdy business relationship with Sinatra; with *Swingin' Brass,* the two proved that they could make beautiful music together as well. Hefti found Sinatra "easy, very easy" to work with, and Emil Richards recalled that Sinatra really enjoyed working with Hefti: "Frank's got a bunch of people he invited to the session [Benny Carter, Papa Jo Jones, Dinah Shore, and two juniors, Sammy Davis and Frank Jr., among others, were in attendance on the Basie date], and Neil was in the booth listening to a playback. He calls out, 'Frank, come on in! You're gonna cream in your pants when you hear this one!' Frank looks at me and says sarcastically, 'Do you believe this guy? Talking like that in front of all these people?' Frank was digging it!"

As was clear to all concerned, including Richards, Hefti was the logical choice to oversee *Sinatra-Basie: An Historic Musical First.* Hefti described getting an assignment from Sinatra in a "delivered package" that contained a stack of sheet music and instructions from Sinatra and Bill Miller. Sinatra was no longer providing his writers with as detailed a map as he had in the 1950s with Riddle; even so, the songs, keys, and tempos had already been determined. It was up to Hefti to flush out the details within the parameters of what Sinatra had already worked out. "I really didn't need to talk to him that much. Everything was fairly clear," said Hefti. "I had done enough charts with singers in my life to know what was going on, especially when he would pick the instrumentation or when he would say, 'We're going to do this with Count Basie's band.' If I was told it was going to be Sinatra and Basie, I knew they didn't want it to sound like Carmen Cavallaro."

As Sinatra announced at the start of the date, "I've waited twenty years for this moment." On another occasion, Sinatra declared the Basie band "the greatest orchestra at any time in the history of the world." He had followed the band since it exploded on the national scene in the late 1930s and had known the leader personally since the '40s. When introducing "Please Be Kind" in Las Vegas that December (a few months later), Sinatra said, "This is a marvelous Neal Hefti arrangement, and I recently recorded [it in] an album with Count Basie's band. . . . It's most exciting for me because I think most of the singers in the world today would like one shot at singing with the Basie band, and I was fortunate enough to be able to do it."*

---

* For all of his lifelong empathy (and support) of African American civil rights, Sinatra still had no qualms about evoking *Amos 'n' Andy* (then too, while some African Americans found the show to be offensive, the series was extremely popular in the black community during its long run on radio and then television). At the December 1962 Vegas show, as Sinatra

Earle Warren and Harry Sweets Edison, two longtime members of the great original Basie band of the 1930s, both told us that the Count and the Chairman (then still The Voice) were constantly hanging out together whenever they happened to be in town at the same time. "He liked to sit there with his arm around Basie," said Edison, to which Warren added, "Which Basie didn't mind because Frank was such a big star and always getting bigger." At some undetermined point, Sinatra also got to know the original Basie band's greatest apostle, the legendary Lester Young. "I knew Lester well. We were close friends, and we had a mutual admiration society," Sinatra told Arlene Francis. "I took from what he did, and he took from what I did." "If I could put together exactly the kind of band I wanted," as Young himself said to Nat Hentoff in 1956, "Frank Sinatra would be the singer." Prez added, "Really, my main man is Frank Sinatra."

(Robert Sherrick, the noted Sinatra archivist, tells a great story about working in a Midtown record store in 1955 when Lester Young came in and asked to hear the latest from "My man Frank." The two listened to Sinatra doing "When Your Lover Has Gone" from the new *Wee Small Hours*, and Sherrick could see that as Lester listened, he wasn't exactly crying, but "his eyes were getting, like, a little watery.")

As Warren and Edison indicated, Basie didn't consider himself merely a musician but a key player in the show business fraternity. "Basie was fascinated by anybody who had acted in the movies," Frank Foster confirmed. "He loved to be around actors and actresses. And he was totally in awe of talented singers if they had been in movies. He was really in awe of them. And of course Frank had been in a few movies."

Where *Swingin' Brass*—the song "Goody Goody," in particular—finds Sinatra phrasing more evenly, sacrificing some of his idiosyncratic rhythm accents for greater swing, like Jimmy Rushing or Joe Williams when they take on a fast rhythm number, he takes this idea to even greater extremes on *Sinatra-Basie*. "Nice Work If You Can Get It," for instance, has Sinatra maintaining the hard-swinging, even-toned, unfrivolous lines associated with blues vocal style.* Whatever the reason, Sinatra couches each line in a way

---

continues speaking, he starts approximating the voice of the Kingfish, "That's 'cause I'se de president of de record company, that's why I got it done! Now Smokey the Bear, that's Sammy Davis. Smokey, he's the vice president, he gonna get the second chance at Basie." (Sinatra fondly referred to Davis by that affectionate nickname because, even more than Sinatra, Davis was never without a cigarette in his hand. He would eventually die of throat cancer.)

* Alec Wilder reported that Sinatra had chosen an unfortunate moment to record the disc because that particular October the Dodgers had made it to the World Series. Sinatra yelled his head off at every game, and, said Wilder, "his throat really wasn't in any condition to

that's taut and unfettered, thus tapping into the paradox that is the central strength of the "New Testament" edition of the Basie band, an aggregation that's at once as tight as the clothes on a floozy and as loose as her morals. The band marches with tum-on-a-dime precision to better serve the cause of reckless abandon. Where Riddle and May (other than on *Come Dance with Me!*) often color their up-tempo ensembles with a dash of humor, Hefti and Basie are serious even when they're being whimsical. This is especially true of classic instrumentals like "Flight of the Foo Birds" and "Splanky." Billy Strayhorn might have showed us "The Majesty of the Blues," but Basie and Hefti make it clear that the blues can also be highly capricious as well.

More than any other bandleader, "Basie epitomizes the greatest kind of tempo for swing, in jazz" is how Sinatra described working with the great band (in a 1965 interview with Larry King). "It was a joy because all I had to do was just stay up on the crest of the sound and move along with it. It just carries you right through." Sinatra's appreciation of the nuances of rhythm come through during a run-through of "I Only Have Eyes for You" on the session tapes, when he asks the pianist (whom he addresses as Bill, which could mean either Miller or William "Bill" Basie), "Can you add a little more rhythm? It sounds like Shep Fields" (another novelty/sweet band leader of the 1930s—not all that different from Carmen Cavallero).

They were able to achieve this balance of tension and relaxation thanks to arduous rehearsals. Unlike what occurred on the Sinatra-Ellington dates five years later, "the day before the first date, we rehearsed all day, all night," said Bill Miller, officially serving as contractor. "Everybody also came in an hour before so we could go over them again." As Joe Bushkin, Sinatra's pianist pally from the Dorsey era, pointed out, "The Basie guys could read as well as any studio band," but to help them nail the charts even tighter (as they would with Ellington) Sinatra and Miller brought in ace lead trumpeter Al Porcino. Basie was a capable but not an expert reader, Miller continued, "and he was very slow to learn new tunes, so on a couple of the songs he said, 'You play it.'" It didn't hurt that Miller had already served as "Vice-Count" with Basie-worshiper Charlie Barnet's band, deputizing on such tributes as "The Count's Idea."

Of the ten tracks, only "The Tender Trap," the archetype of the Sinatra-Riddle style, fails to work as reimagined in the Basie mold.* "Learnin' the

---

make the album." (After several takes of "I Won't Dance," Sinatra refers, in the session tapes, to the "frog" in his throat.) Upon checking the record, the 1962 World Series did take place at the same time as the Sinatra-Basie sessions, but between the New York Yankees and the San Francisco Giants, not in Los Angeles. Of course, Sinatra could have still "yelled his head off" while watching the game on television.

\* Sammy Cahn told a story about how the original 1955 version of "The Tender Trap" worked

Blues," another item from the same idiom, functions more smoothly in the new setting. The first two numbers on the album, "Pennies from Heaven" and "Please Be Kind," sound even more like the Basie style at its absolute purest than anything on the Count's two contemporaneous instrumental albums for Reprise (*This Time by Basie!*, 1963, and *Pop Goes the Basie*, 1964).

"Pennies from Heaven," on which Miller plays piano, may be the disc's most successful cut. It's certainly a chart Sinatra kept alive for a long time, in which the tenor sax solo originated by Frank Foster continued to be played by a variety of tenor players (such as Bob Cooper in 1981). Here Sinatra is firmly entrenched in Basie's rhythmic groove and never deviates from it, to the point of using the last phrase of the bridge ("up-side-down") as a blues stop-time break. This approach also makes the second chorus of "Please Be Kind" swing with strong stresses and firm fermatas to delay the key phrase at the end of each line, giving the second bridge of that refrain over to an instrumental section. Most memorable is the heavenly ending of "Pennies": Sinatra swingingly repeats the final phrase, "For you and, for you and . . ." a mess of times before resolving it with the final note ("*me*"). Apparently, he concocted this classic coda on the spot; two previous takes have him merely holding the last note while the band plays the phrase over and over instrumentally.

Likewise, "I'm Gonna Sit Right Down and Write Myself a Letter" transforms the entire ensemble into a colossal rhythm section behind soloist Sinatra, beating out a pattern that suggests a hip Native American rain dance. Working around two booting tenor solos (Frank Wess or Frank Foster or both), the singer expediently drops all articles from the outchorus bridge ("write words . . . sweet . . . knock me off") to show that he's not going to let anything get in the way of his momentum, even the lyric. The comparatively capricious "Looking at the World through Rose-Colored Glasses" comes as close as the album ever gets to sheer, utter whimsy, recalling "Foo Birds," "Ducky Bumps," and some of Hefti's giddier pieces for Woody Herman.

On the other hand, "My Kind of Girl," the one current tune of the ten (a 1961 hit for British swinging lover Matt Monro, words and music by rising songwriter Leslie Bricusse), becomes the oldest-fashioned stylistically, opening with a closely bridled Sinatra atop sixteen bars of vintage Basie piano and sensitive drumming by Sonny Payne. Both this tune and "I Only Have Eyes for You" recall Basie's classic version of "All of Me" in that after a quietly elegant half chorus, the entire brass section comes crashing in like thunder on the bridge. "Nice Work If You Can Get It" delves into Sinatra's own musical

---

so well because he was there to goad Sinatra into hitting an impossibly high note at the end. "You have to hit that note because you're Frank Sinatra!" The 1962 version just doesn't have the same extramusical motivation.

past. Of the set's several remakes, "Nice Work" comes the closest to the original (on *Swingin' Affair*) yet is cast in a more frantic mode. Two trumpet solos recall the horn men closely associated with Sinatra, one using a tight mute à la Sweets Edison, the other (probably Sonny Cohn or Porcino) wide open and rich in Harry James–like vibrato. The medium-slow "I Won't Dance," another remake from *Swingin' Affair* (although not reiterating the "ring-a-ding-ding" line), effectively caps the program, showing how all the rehearsing paid off. The band works hard to follow the central player closely, and here the individual vernaculars of each of these two master auteurs become indistinguishable.

The finished album was an immediate sensation, ranking with *Ring-a-Ding-Ding!* and *I Remember Tommy* among the biggest sellers of the early Reprise era. Still, with two full-length triumphs under their belts (and several singles, including "Everybody's Twistin'," a memorable, go-go-style update of Rube Bloom's 1935 dance hit "Truckin'"), the Sinatra-Hefti relationship abruptly ended at this point.*

Despite his formidable success, Hefti always felt uneasy in the world of mainstream popular music. He was never enamored of the music business, and perhaps the very fact that he felt no great attachment to that world allowed him to negotiate with it more painlessly—unlike, say, Nelson Riddle, who seemed to care so intensely about every little move he made, every chart he wrote. Hefti didn't think much about what he was arranging while he was doing it, and never listened to his older works. "When I write anything, I try to put it behind me," he told me. "I was always a reluctant writer. I don't really like to write on call like that. I didn't mind doing a couple of tunes a year when I was with Woody's band, when I could do whatever I wanted and take as long as I wanted. But when you tell me, 'Do this and have it tomorrow and that's that,' I never liked that process. To me, it's like an order." Even though Hefti considered Sinatra about the best singer around as well as the easiest to work with, he "never wrote for another singer since that *Sinatra-Basie* album."

Both men did work again with Basie. A month after *Sinatra-Basie,* Hefti and the Count were on their way and shoutin' again in an all new Basie-Hefti album titled *On My Way & Shoutin' Again.* In 1964, Sinatra and Basie taped the second of their two studio collaborations, *It Might as Well Be Swing,* a program of ten charts put together by Quincy Jones. The sequel has a very different feel from the original. Even considering the absence of any material with prior Basie associations, *Sinatra-Basie* can be described as Sinatra retai-

---

* Sinatraphiles once circulated a story that Hefti left Reprise over a disagreement over the title of *Swingin' Brass*—it was rumored that the arranger insisted the album be titled *The Thin One and Hefti* or *Hefti Meets the Thin One.* When asked, Hefti remembered those titles being considered, but clearly he never would have demanded equal billing in such a fashion.

loring his approach to fit into Basie's idiom, whereas *It Might as Well Be Swing* takes it the other way around, with the Basieites accommodating their guest (even to the point of adding a string section).

Quincy Delight Jones first worked with Sinatra in a land far from either man's own home turf. On June 14, 1958,* Sinatra gave a special concert in Monte Carlo, which simultaneously promoted the opening of his film *Kings Go Forth* and raised money for a special United Nations charity fund for refugee children, a pet project of his *High Society* costar, Princess Grace of Monaco. Coming completely out of left field, Sinatra hired the twenty-five-year-old trumpeter-arranger-composer to assemble and direct his accompanying orchestra. "Somebody told me once that Ava Gardner had told him about me," Jones told me in the early 1990s. It seems more likely, though, that Sinatra had heard of Jones through his early work with Basie (the title of his first recorded composition, "Kingfish," indicates that he shared Sinatra's fascination with *Amos 'n' Andy*), Dinah Washington, and others.

Even before his tenure with Basie, Jones had toured in Lionel Hampton's orchestra from 1951 to 1953, and then actively freelanced all over New York. In 1956, he joined Dizzy Gillespie's big band for a continental tour, after which he elected to remain in Europe to work as the house musical director for Barclay Records in Paris and furthered his musical studies with two very prestigious "longhair" French musical icons, Nadia Boulanger and Olivier Messiaen. While working at Barclay, Jones presided over a studio orchestra that, thanks to the ensemble playing of the local musicians and the availability of American soloists (both visitors and expatriates), was the equal of any in Hollywood or New York.

"We used a regular fifty-five-piece orchestra in Paris," said the conductor. "It was pretty hot, you know. And it had Lucky Thompson, Don Byas, Stéphane Grappelli, Kenny Clarke, Zoot Sims—and a lot of people used to come through and play with us. Even the Double Six [of Paris] was the vocal group." Jones recalled that any number of these jazz legends could be present on the Sinatra Monte Carlo concert and recalled specifically that pioneering bebop drummer Kenny Clarke played on that show. (With that knowledge in mind, one can hear that the drum breaks on the Monte Carlo "Come Fly with Me" include a lot more bebop bombs than one would expect from Al Stoller or Irv Cottler.) "I remember we all went down to Monte Carlo by

---

* This was issued at last in the 2016 package *World on a String*. According to Marcucci and other sources, Sinatra and Jones may have given a second concert together at about this time in Monte Carlo as well.

train," said Jones. "I was scared to death. I was so in awe of him at the time that I hardly said a thing. Our first meeting was really quite brief."

Jones was rapidly establishing his bona fides as something other than a brilliant orchestrator for singers and jazz orchestras, as indeed Neal Hefti and Johnny Mandel (not to mention Riddle and May) were, but as a true bandleader and a general all-purpose musical factotum. He had no shortage of skill in terms of writing charts, but his true gift lay in setting out the overall trajectory of the band and the project; he was better at organizing a staff of the best arrangers in town and calling upon them for specific assignments than actually writing each chart himself.

"Quincy is an excellent writer, but he doesn't like to write much," as his longtime lieutenant Billy Byers told us in 1995. "He found a better and easier way to go. He's highly motivated and finds it tough to sit down. To be a great arranger, you gotta be a recluse. He's learned to give arrangers credit, since they're no longer a threat to him." Q was and is what we might call a big-picture man—he is a fox rather than a hedgehog (to quote Archilochus and Isaiah Berlin)—yet one who never neglected the details. In 1959, he was called upon to conduct the music for an American musical comedy in Paris titled *Free and Easy* (actually a revision of Harold Arlen and Johnny Mercer's *St. Louis Woman*). When the show closed abruptly, Jones, who had assembled another top-notch orchestra, decided to take the band on tour. This was both the start and the high point of Jones's career as a jazz maestro; the Barclay studio band, as Jones describes it, was one of the major big bands of all time because it was composed of the best musicians available to him, European or American, black or white. They toured most successfully as the accompaniment for Nat King Cole on a 1960 European tour.

By 1964 Jones was back in the United States, now established as the first major African American A&R man/producer at a major pop label, Mercury Records, after having collaborated very successfully with both Ray Charles and Peggy Lee (as well as masterminding hit singles for Lesley Gore and others). The total antithesis of his friend Neal Hefti, Jones relished the business side of the music industry and thrived it it. He also had become entrenched as Basie's frequent second-in-command, having put together several whole albums of charts for the band (*Li'l Ol' Groovemaker . . . Basie!* and *This Time by Basie!*, both 1963), which he also conducted.

It was in May of that year that Jones received his second call from Sinatra, and, coincidentally, once again the two were to work together far away from home. Sinatra was at the time camped in Hawaii, where he was on location for his 1965 film *None but the Brave* (a World War II epic he was not only costarring in, but also directing; the score was composed by the young John

Williams). The singer asked Jones to travel to Los Angeles to "pick up" Bill Miller; the two then jetted to Honolulu, where they spent a week working out the details of the second Sinatra-Basie set.

"I went over there, and he had a huge flag up over his bungalow in Hawaii," Jones recalled in 1994. "Only instead of an American flag, he had a flag up with his bottle of Jack Daniel's on it. And that's when we really first met. It was a great, great chemistry. He was finishing up his movie, and when it was wrapped up, we all went to Honolulu and took the top floor of a hotel. He took a bunch of us, I guess about twenty, twenty-five people, and we all had a great time. Then we came back, and when we were flying back home— we were on a commercial flight—we were calling [his daughter] Nancy and Tommy Sands who were down below us in a boat on their honeymoon. I'll never forget that."

They spent about a week working hands-on together, laying out the details of the album that would be released as *It Might as Well Be Swing*. Jones seems to have had more input than most Sinatra collaborators in terms of repertoire. "We started to talk about the tunes," said Jones, "and it's very funny the way songs come up. You'd suggest one and he'd suggest a couple, and you keep thinking them up and you just come up with a real nice mix."

The main difference between Jones and Sinatra's other co-adjutants was that he already had a team of arrangers working for him, his principal writer being Billy Byers. (Byers would arrange "I Wish You Love" on the studio album, and later also do "Where or When" and "The Lady Is a Tramp" for Sinatra and Basie.) Jones wrote the bulk of his own arrangements and worked out the other details while Sinatra continued shooting interiors for *None but the Brave*. "I moved in at Warner Bros. into Dean Martin's dressing room while Frank was next door, shooting the picture every day and editing and so forth. . . . I locked myself there for a week and just kept writing. I fell asleep late Sunday night, and then on Monday morning I looked up and there's Frank in a military uniform, asking me how I wanted my eggs. He was cooking breakfast!"

As with the 1962 sessions, the band rehearsed prodigiously before the recording, both with and without the star singer present. "I liked Sinatra's lithe, easy manner," tenor saxophonist Frank Foster pointed out. "He didn't get ruffled, and he didn't get all excited or anything. The band had been rehearsing with Quincy directing us in the studio and Sinatra walked in. When a star walks in, you think that he or she would [automatically take charge and start barking orders], 'Okay, let's try this or that.' But when Sinatra came in, Quincy asked him, 'What do you want to do, Frank?' Frank says, 'I don't know. What have we got?' And so from that point on, Quincy just said, 'Hey, let's do this.' And Sinatra said, 'Okay.'"

On June 9, 10, and 12, Sinatra and the Basie crew worked together in the studio (at the same time, the band was also finishing a run in Lake Tahoe and beginning one at Disneyland). Once again, "ringers" were brought in to make sure everything went smoothly, including two Stan Kenton veterans who were now top studio players, trumpeter Al Porcino (again) and trombonist Ken Shroyer. On three numbers (the last session), a small string section was added. But the instrumental star of the date was Harry Sweets Edison, the iconic trumpeter who had already enjoyed a long history with both Sinatra and Basie.

The two most famous tracks on the album are "Fly Me to the Moon" and "I Can't Stop Loving You," both of which were extensions, so to speak, of tracks on *This Time by Basie! Hits of the '50s & '60s*, a wildly successful 1963 Basie album produced by Jones for Reprise. Everyone had big hopes for "I Can't Stop Loving You"; Basie and Jones had just won a Grammy award for that arrangement. The team had glommed it from Ray Charles (on his own even more wildly successful 1962 album *Modern Sounds in Country and Western Music*), who himself had been inspired by the country music star Don Gibson, who composed and introduced the song on a hit 1958 single.

Perhaps because the Basie instrumental had been so successful, it was decided to simply annex Sinatra's voice onto the chart. The team would have done better to reconceive the song for Sinatra from the ground up. As it is, both song and orchestration are entirely unsuited to Sinatra, for all his cowboy contortions, such as a forced twang on "I've made up my *mi-ind*" and an artificially induced downward thrust on "(those happy) hours." Sinatra could have taken it out of tempo and transformed it into a saloon song, as he later did with Kris Kristofferson's "For the Good Times." He also did a marvelous, straight-up country song in 1975, "The Only Couple on the Floor." But hearing Sinatra and Basie trying to "go country" in this fashion makes one cringe in the same manner that watching his movie westerns (like *Johnny Concho* and *Dirty Dingus Magee*) does.

Conversely, "Fly Me to the Moon" was a sleeper surprise for all concerned. Sinatra had known composer Bart Howard for roughly a decade by 1964, having heard him play piano for Mabel Mercer and other cabaret headliners at New York's Blue Angel nightclub. Howard originally wrote the song as a slow waltz titled "In Other Words," but by the time it reached Basie and then Sinatra, it had been transformed into a fast 4/4 swing number now titled "Fly Me to the Moon." The song was widely recorded under its original title, including lovely readings by June Christy and Peggy Lee, and it was Lee who suggested the name change. The 1963 Jones-Basie instrumental, in which the melody is essayed mostly by flutes, sounds closer to the song as we know it, but the track is frustratingly tepid compared to the way it would sound in 1964 and later. (In fact, on the 1963 album, "This Could Be the Start of Something Big," the Steve Allen standard that opens the set, is considerably more swinging and exciting.)

When Sinatra decided to address it with the Basie-Jones combination, he recharged it into a straight swinger. "Frank changed the lyrics [and the song] so much," said Howard, "which normally would have annoyed the shit out of me—but didn't because it worked so well." Whereas the instrumental was merely novel and even cute, the Sinatra reading all but explodes with energy; the instrumental is a soft-shoe dance, and the vocal version is an out-and-out two-footed stomp. The same elements that sound quaint on the 1963 album—the gentle bass intro and the flute in the first chorus (which harmonizes with the muted trumpets on the instrumental and twitters behind Sinatra on the vocal)—fairly blast on the Sinatra version. In short, even the flute sounds aggressive on the Sinatra track, as do several extremely dynamic episodes of wildly plunging and soaring brass. Sinatra established the song so firmly as a *swingerlander* (as Sinatra's favorite deejay, WNEW's William B. Williams, used to say) that for the last thirty years singers feel that they have to get away from his definitive reading by putting the song back into ballad time. The fast 4/4 and slow 3/4 approaches could even be described as two entirely different songs, respectively, "Fly Me to the Moon" and "In Other Words."

The song immediately became one of the anthems of Sinatra's swingin' '60s; although never released as a single, it became de rigueur at Sinatra concerts and was frequently heard on the radio. Further, "Fly Me to the Moon" helped Sinatra become the first musician to gain an audience in outer space: as Buzz Aldrin told Jones, when the astronauts flew to the Earth's satellite for real in 1969 they brought a portable tape player, and Sinatra's "Fly Me to the Moon" became the first music ever heard on the moon (or at least the first human music that we know of).

In 1956, Bing Crosby had made an album called *Songs I Wish I Had Sung the First Time Around . . .* , a sampling of signature songs of other "boy singers"; Sinatra seems to have had much the same idea with *It Might as Well Be Swing* (although not as much so as on *Some Nice Things I've Missed*, from ten years later; that 1974 album really could have been titled *Other People's Money*). Then too, Sinatra might have been taking more inspiration from that smash 1963 Basie album; the working title might well have been *This Time by Sinatra: Hits of the '60s*. Nearly every track on *It Might as Well* is preassociated with a major male singer: Ray Charles ("I Can't Stop Loving You"), Jack Jones ("Wives and Lovers"), Steve Lawrence ("More"), Louis Armstrong ("Hello,

Dolly!"), and Tony Bennett ("I Wanna Be Around," "The Good Life," and "The Best Is Yet to Come").

"Wives and Lovers" would be the first of only two songs that Sinatra would record by one of the major hit-making teams of all time, Burt Bacharach and Hal David. "Wives and Lovers" was what publishers once deemed an "exploitational" song, written to promote, but not heard in, a 1963 comedy of that name starring Van Johnson and Janet Leigh. In the politically correct atmosphere of the last thirty years or so, the lyrics seem blatantly chauvinistic, although that bothered no one at the time (Jack Jones later addressed the issue by writing a second set of lyrics as a feminist response: "Hey, little boy, cap your teeth, get a hairpiece"). Where Jones's hit single was naively sweet in a "young married" kind of way, Sinatra's version is more mature, suggesting that there's more than PTA meetings going on behind closed doors in Suburbia, USA. But if the lyric reading is more grown-up, the change of time signature is profound. The melody as written by Bacharach and sung by Jones is one of the major jazz waltzes of the period, but since this was a rhythmic mode that both Sinatra and Basie were clearly uncomfortable with, he and Jones put the song into 4/4.*

Three songs on the album derive from Europe. "More" (famously the theme from the 1962 Italian documentary *Mondo Cane*) has Sinatra himself phrasing like Harry Edison, knocking out the song's single-note key phrase as if it were a Sweetsian "beep." This track also amounts to the single most successful annexation of strings to the Basie machine. Both "The Good Life" and "I Wish You Love" (arranged by Billy Byers) derive from the Gallic, and the latter acknowledges its roots when Edison reprises the muted-trumpet phrase ("all around the mulberry bush") that Thad Jones famously played on Basie's "April in Paris." "I Wish You Love" begins strictly in Sinatra ballad style with a rubato verse done entirely with strings and then leaps into a full-blooded rocker for the refrain, which Sinatra climaxes with an interjection of "Hot damn!"—if you'll pardon his French. (There's a moment on the session tapes where we can hear Sinatra telling "Quince" exactly where the strings should enter behind him on a certain phrase.)

"I Believe in You" and "Hello, Dolly!" come from Broadway (*How to Succeed in Business without Really Trying* and *Hello, Dolly!*), although as early as the mid-1960s it was no longer to be taken for granted that even a successful show tune would provide Sinatra with enough musical meat to chew

---

* Jones himself chalked it up to the band. As Bacharach related in an interview in the *Guardian*, "They did 'Wives and Lovers,' which is in 3/4 time, but they did it in 4/4. I said, 'Quincy, what happened?' He said, 'The Basie band can't play in 3/4.'" (And yes, following "Fly Me to the Moon," this is the second song on the album to be so dewaltzed.)

on. "Dolly" is that rarity, a respectful homage that swings. Sinatra does the first chorus as a rip-roaring romper, with only an exuberant Armstrongian trumpet solo to allude to the eternal inspiration of Pops. Then with a cry of "Hello, Satch!," Sinatra's second chorus becomes the most gracious piece of *noblesse oblige* that he has ever offered, beginning with a paraphrase of Satchmo's "This is Louis, Dolly" into "This is Francis, Louis" and bringing it home with a resoundingly Satchelmouthed, "Oh, yeahhhh!" The only regret is the absence of an iPhone camera to capture the lighting up of Louis Armstrong's face when he heard Sinatra's record.

"I Wanna Be Around" (words and music by Johnny Mercer, suggested to him by a Cincinnati housewife named Sadie Vimmerstedt*) and "The Good Life" were classic Tony, but not classic Frank, although they're certainly worthy of a place on the album. The first is slightly underinspired; one can't imagine that any woman could have been smart enough to break the middle-aged Sinatra's heart, so it requires a certain suspension of disbelief; but Sinatra hasn't invested enough time in fleshing out his interpretation. "The Good Life," a French song, is almost too animated; Bennett's record is a self-conflicting conundrum; it's deliberately vague what the speaker means when he talks about "the good life"—is it connection or freedom? The Sinatra-Basie version just avoids the question; it swings too hard to be looking for anything, particularly in the outchorus (which features a wailing tenor, probably played by Frank Wess). It's sung beautifully, but by Sinatra standards it's far from one of his deeper interpretations.

The third Tony Bennett number is "The Best Is Yet to Come," destined to become another all-time Sinatra signature, and, through a curious route, a song associated with both Sinatra and Bennett. In 1959, Cy Coleman (whose songs "Why Try to Change Me Now?" and "Witchcraft" had already become Sinatra classics) was commissioned by his friend, publisher and emerging entertainment mogul Hugh Hefner, to provide a theme song for his forthcoming television series *Playboy's Penthouse*, and Coleman composed an appropriately sensual, minor key instrumental titled "Playboy's Theme." (Hefner had instructed Coleman that he wanted something along the lines of "Like Young," André Previn's "beatnik" number.)

Not long after, Coleman and his longtime lyricist Carolyn Leigh added a lyric to "Playboy's Theme," which also started them thinking about a new song in that general style. That became "The Best Is Yet to Come," which was written more or less with Sinatra in mind. They submitted the song to Sina-

---

* In some accounts of how the song came to be written, it's said that Vimmerstedt was inspired to come up with the title and the idea by the Frank-Nancy-Ava love triangle.

tra; he liked it, but he had one request. As Coleman told me, "He wanted it longer. He said the song wasn't long enough, so we added another interlude." Coleman was happy to accommodate him, and he and Leigh then added the section with the lyric "Come the day you're mine, I'm going to teach you to fly. / We've only tasted the wine, we're going to drain the cup dry." Said Coleman, "and it was very nice, I mean, it worked out very well."

So far, so good; but a year later, Coleman was still waiting for Sinatra to record the song. Then, he said, "Tony Bennett called me, and said, 'Do you have something like "The Playboy Theme"?' I said, 'I do have a song called "The Best Is Yet to Come," but we've been waiting for Sinatra.' Well, Tony decided he would do it." Unlike Sinatra, who dragged his heels, Bennett pounced on the song, and cut his version the very next day. (The arrangement that Bennett commissioned was only half-finished, but fortunately Coleman was present and wound up rewriting the chart as well as conducting.)

When I asked him about it thirty years later, Coleman admitted that he could see the value of Sinatra having waited for the opportunity to record "The Best is Yet to Come" with Basie. Even though Bennett had introduced it and had the initial hit with the song, "I mean the Sinatra version is always important. No matter what."

Of the three songs here that were and remain associated with Bennett, Frank doesn't quite wrest "I Wanna Be Around" or "The Good Life" away from Tony; but "The Best Is Yet to Come" is second only to "Fly Me to the Moon" as the overall most winning performance on the album. After a characteristically aphoristic Basie piano intro, Sinatra ecstatically wails the lyrics against an antiphonal choir of muted brass, who throw it back to him like one of Fats Waller's asides to a vocalist—they seem to be saying, "Tell me about it!." Like "Fly Me to the Moon," "The Best Is Yet to Come" positively screams Basie-Sinatra from the gitgo. The Sinatra-Basie track wasn't the first recording or the biggest-selling one, but as Coleman told me, "A Sinatra performance is a wonderful thing, it's a badge of honor."

Although not as big a seller on its first release as *Sinatra-Basie*, *It Might as Well Be Swing* has been much more widely heard in the last thirty years. "Fly Me to the Moon," "The Best Is Yet to Come," and (for reasons I fail to understand) "I Can't Stop Loving You" have been omnipresent on every radio programming format oriented toward grown-ups and are being spun many times without mention of the Basie band. And it was remarkable for another reason: it was the first Sinatra concept album comprised entirely of recent songs. This was the last point in his career in which Sinatra could achieve something like this—to take contemporary hits and render them as big-band jazz. Even the title acknowledges this: although these songs were written long after the big-band era, Sinatra and Basie are telling us that they might as well be swing.

Then, in 1964–65, Sinatra made the decision that the Basie band would provide the catalyst that he was waiting for to prod him to finally release his first live album. In retrospect, it seems absurd that Sinatra was so late to this particular party: two of his favorites, Ella Fitzgerald (in Berlin in 1960) and Judy Garland (at Carnegie Hall in 1961) had already released blockbuster concert albums, and so too had many of his own disciples, including both Mel Tormé and Tony Bennett. But not until 1966 was a live album by Sinatra officially released; ironically, fifty years later, many earlier live sets by Sinatra have become legally available, but none of these were released until decades later. Sinatra had been having some of his shows taped for such a purpose at least as far back as the founding of Reprise, but none of them were deemed special enough by Sinatra that he wanted to be represented by them as his first live album—not even the excellent live recordings that existed of Sinatra and the sextet during the 1962 World Tour. Having failed to get there first, he now wanted to arrive with the most. And the Basie band, he decided, was the factor that would give him a leg up in this live-album arms race, so to speak.

He prepared extensively for the project; even though Sinatra and Basie had already done two studio albums together, he still decided to ascertain the band's "poker-playing habits"—to use Duke Ellington's term for musicians getting accustomed to working with each other—by bringing the band with him on tour. In November and December of 1964, they did a two-week run together at the Sands. Then in the summer and fall of 1965, even as he was preparing for his big fiftieth birthday, Sinatra and the Basieites played a series of dates across the country, nearly all of which were memorable for different reasons: in April, they played a prison outside of Washington, D.C. In July, they were filmed by a CBS News camera crew in Pennsylvania and Detroit for a documentary on Sinatra. On June 20 at the Kiel Opera House in Saint Louis, the band was present at the climactic appearance of the Rat Pack, when Sinatra reconvened with Sammy Davis Jr. and Dean Martin for what would essentially be the last time. On July 4, they played the Newport Jazz Festival—Sinatra's only appearance at that iconic event. (The Saint Louis Rat Pack show was filmed, and it was released on home video in the mid-1990s. Alas, the only tapes anyone has ever heard of the milestone Newport concert have inevitably been in substandard audio quality.)

Right after Newport, the Sinatra-Basie combination did three milestone nights in Forest Hills, New York, at a tennis stadium in Queens. This was almost the Woodstock of Sinatra; virtually every music lover I have ever met who had been born before 1950 claims to have seen Sinatra and Basie in

Forest Hills. On July 18, the combination played the Arie Crown Theater in Chicago (which resulted in another murky but listenable concert tape). But the first climax of the Sinatra-Basie tour was the *Hollywood Palace* television show broadcast on Saturday, October 16 (videotaped on September 26); the long-running variety show was ABC's answer to Ed Sullivan, with ever-changing guest-star hosts, and this week they donated almost half the show to Sinatra and Basie. (A remarkable show of faith, considering that they also had to fit in comic Fat Jack E. Leonard, the Peter Gennaro Dancers, high-wire walker Luis Murillo, and Alice and Ellen Kessler, a towering terp team of twins, as *Variety* would have said, from Berlin, who sang "Together" in German.) By now, the singer and the band were remarkably tight together, and the five numbers they perform (captured on beautiful color videotape and readily viewable) are a high point in the careers of both men.

Still, it was all merely a warm-up. Sinatra had been setting up the end of 1965 and the start of 1966—when he was going to turn fifty—as the big moment of the decade. This was the time of his first of five annual television specials (all but the last one on NBC), titled *A Man and His Music* (also the name of a double-disc retrospective album issued contemporaneously), as well as the CBS news documentary on Sinatra (*Sinatra Off the Record*) hosted by Walter Cronkite. To make things even better, his latest album, *September of My Years*, was yielding a new Sinatra standard in "It Was a Very Good Year." And at the absolute epicenter of this activity, the occasion that Sinatra chose to mark what he obviously regarded as the big moment in his career, was the month-long run of Sinatra and Basie at the Sands in Las Vegas.

As much work as they had done together from April to October, Sinatra and Basie preceded the January 9 opening at the Sands with yet two more days of rehearsals. Then Sinatra waited until their synchronicity was at its most simpatico, beginning January 26, whereupon he had the final five nights (two sets per night) recorded. He then culled from the ten sets to produce the seventy-six-minute double LP *Sinatra at the Sands*, released in August 1966. It was worth all the effort: *Sands* is one of those miraculous moments in American music that explain why so many of us become Sinatra fans to begin with.*

When I interviewed Byers in March 1995, he described the experience of arranging for stars like Sinatra and Basie as being "half psychologist and half tailor—and even then, the pants don't always fit." The brilliance of *Sina-*

---

* In 2006, Reprise Records released eighteen previously unheard tracks from the January 1966 sets as part of the boxed set *Sinatra: Vegas*; eight years earlier, the label had already released a whole disc of Basie instrumentals from the same sets under the title *Live at the Sands (Before Frank)*.

*tra at the Sands* is that everything fits perfectly. Sinatra and the band now "know" each other almost better than any other musical aggregation that he had traveled with, and they fit together in a way that is beyond tight. Sinatra has completely mastered the unique Basie beat; he has never been more perfectly and completely swinging. For their part, the Basie men have likewise perfectly adapted iconic Sinatra works, like Riddle's arrangement of "I've Got You Under My Skin" and May's "Come Fly with Me," and made them part of their own musical universe, aided largely by adaptations of those charts prepared mostly by Billy Byers and the rest of Quincy's crew. The result is a perfect hybrid of two outstanding musical idioms, a combination in which the two sides come together to produce an even greater whole.

"Now this man here, he's gonna take me by the hand, he's going to lead me down the right path to righteousness—and all that other mother jazz—*in the right tempo.*" Sinatra announces that, in a tone half Kingfish and half Pigmeat Markham, at the start of "Fly Me to the Moon" and he means it. More than on either of their previous studio albums, Sinatra and Basie himself now felt so comfortable together that Basie personally played on nearly all of the tracks. Bill Miller was present but happy to let Basie handle most of the piano work; the only numbers on the actual album that Miller apparently plays on are the ballads "One for My Baby" and "Angel Eyes," in which his signature keyboard style (starting with the intro) is immediately apparent.

From the opening announcement by William Conrad (already famous for *Gunsmoke* and *Rocky and Bullwinkle*) and the leadoff "Come Fly with Me," this is an album where everything is exactly right—the pants, the jacket, the entire ensemble—every note and every beat are supremely in place. Only one number, "Fly Me to the Moon," is repeated from either of the studio albums; the rest of the repertoire consists of Sinatra favorites mostly in new, Basie-specific treatments by Byers, like his in-the-groove interpretation of "Where or When," which is completely different from Sinatra's two previous recordings (from 1945 and 1958), both of which were ballads. Apart from "Where or When," there's also an excellent new chart on "Street of Dreams," and Byers outdoes himself with an ambitiously polyrhythmic treatment of "Get Me to the Church on Time" that captures the inner essence of both Basie and Sinatra in a single chart.

The synergy that Sinatra achieves with Basie's saxophone star, Eddie "Lockjaw" Davis, is representative of the whole project. Like Ben Webster, Davis was a gloriously schizophrenic player who could switch between the rapturously romantic and a highly aggressive, bearlike sound. Davis solos prettily on "Street of Dreams" in the Chicago concert, prompting Sinatra to exclaim, "Ah! That Tony Martin tone!" Sinatra reintroduced the vintage

Gershwin classic "I've Got a Crush on You" into his book for the occasion, even though that had never been a big live number for him (his classic 1947 recording with Bobby Hackett notwithstanding). As Davis plays a breathy, almost erotic obbligato behind Sinatra (crooning of "a cunning cottage we could share"), the singer (in what obviously was a routine that they perfected over the month) turns to the saxophonist and addresses him directly, saying, in a Don Rickles–like tone, "You wanna meet Monday and we'll pick out the furniture?" The wisecrack, which is not repeated in the alternate performance on the Vegas box, illustrates the easy, comfortable rapport that Sinatra and the Count's men enjoyed with each other.

The most atypical performance at the Sands is "The Shadow of Your Smile," which he introduces (in the alternate performance) as being "inspired by a marvelous record of Tony Bennett's." It's unique among the set's twenty or so songs in that he never addressed the Johnny Mandel melody (and Paul Francis Webster lyric) in any other context, studio or live. This isn't entirely surprising, as it's hardly a highlight, though not exactly a misfire either; for the ballads, Sinatra really needs the easy intimacy of Miller's piano. "September of My Years" is merely functional, but "It Was a Very Good Year" is an outright disaster; clearly it was impossible to capture the majesty of the Jenkins arrangement without a string section. Sinatra was unwise to even try, and even more so to actually put the track on the album. Mysteriously, "Luck Be a Lady," heard here in what must be its best performance ever, was inexplicably not on the 1966 LP but remained unheard until the 1998 CD. One major omission is "It's Easy to Remember," which is heard in the Newport concert and nowhere else; it's a very different chart, Basiefied and swinging, than Riddle's ballad version from the 1956 *Close to You* album, very much in the spirit of "Where or When" (also by the combination of Rodgers, Hart, and Byers).

"Basie and Frank always seemed to have a great relationship going on," said Frank Foster. "I know Sinatra always talked about being a saloon singer. [In shows he says things like] 'As soon as this set is over, I'm going to the saloon.' And I imagine Basie hit a few saloons with him."

*Sinatra at the Sands* was a bestseller, eventually certified "gold" (one million dollars in retail sales), an impressive feat for a double album. During the years of the Basie collaboration—the three albums and the tour—the singer also recorded and released *The Concert Sinatra, Sinatra's Sinatra,* and *Academy Award Winners,* his first albums for Reprise with Nelson Riddle, and in 1965 he cut *September of My Years* with Gordon Jenkins. In 1963 he had sold the controlling interest in Reprise. Sinatra and his new company had been considerably weakened by an economic and legal war with Capitol Records, which had dumped all his 1950s albums on the market at half price. Sinatra's lawyers were not able to get them to stop and had even less luck at convincing the courts that Capitol should be forced to "rescind ownership and restore the masters" to the artist himself.

In a multimedia package deal, Sinatra sold two-thirds of Reprise to Warner Bros. Records and his own services as an actor for a number of films to Warner Bros. Pictures, as well as some of his holdings in casinos and other ventures, for a reported $3.5 million. That was nearly twice what Sinatra had almost paid Norman Granz for Verve only four years earlier, and Verve's back catalogue (extending back to mid-1944) was considerably more valuable than that of Reprise. Essentially, Jack Warner seems to have wanted to buy Sinatra, and the rest of the Reprise assets were so much gravy.

Music business scholars still debate whether the initial four years of Reprise Records, the period when Sinatra owned the controlling interest, was a success or a failure. We know that Sinatra continued to sell a lot of records, even more as the 1960s progressed, as did the label's other two biggest stars, Dean Martin and Sammy Davis Jr. How does Sinatra stack up as a producer and a label head? We don't really know, because, as when Johnny Mercer part-owned and operated Capitol Records from 1942–48, he was never able to concentrate on being a "record man" full time. Still, Sinatra for his part had at last achieved what he had originally set out to do at Capitol in 1959: run his own subsidiary label where he could call the shots and yet let someone else sign the checks. And that's without considering the millions that went into his pockets.

Unbelievably, the label's most ambitious project, *The Reprise Musical Repertory Theater*, cost the company more than it earned in 1963. Sinatra conceived the series as a way of competing with the oldest established labels such as Decca, Columbia, RCA, and Capitol, all of whom had deep back catalogs of bestselling original Broadway cast albums. Sinatra picked four all-time classic musical comedies, *Finian's Rainbow, Guys and Dolls, Kiss Me Kate,* and *South Pacific,* and recorded all the songs from their scores with A-list pop and jazz stars, starting with himself.

This wasn't an entirely new idea—all the labels had released "cover albums," as collectors call them, of classic show scores—but Sinatra was doing it with a vengeance, and with more big names than any one label could previously muster: *South Pacific,* which may be the best in the series, features not only Sinatra himself (with his best-ever rendition of "Some Enchanted Evening," among others) but Jo Stafford, Keely Smith, Dinah Shore (doing some of the best singing of her career on "I'm Gonna Wash that Man Right Outa My Hair"), Sammy Davis Jr., Debbie Reynolds, and even Papa Bing

Crosby himself (sounding magnificent on "Younger than Springtime"); and instead of a conventional Broadway chorus, we have two vocal groups, the McGuire Sisters and the Hi-Lo's, stars in their own right. (And other albums feature Rosemary Clooney and Dean Martin—not too shabby.) It's hard to believe the releases were not a success (at least not when first issued), but the cost of assembling all this talent must have been prohibitive in terms of the venture making a profit.

Although Sinatra produced or coproduced virtually every record he made from 1943 onward, these four volumes were almost the only time he took credit in this capacity, thereby acknowledging the dictum of Irving Thalberg that "credit you give yourself isn't worth having." Not surprisingly, Sinatra makes as good a producer as he does a conductor; in working with Dinah Shore on "Honey Bun," for instance, he elicits from the songstress some of the best work of her career. Sinatra did not excessively feature himself; to the disappointment of fans, he rarely appeared on more than two or three cuts per disc, and often only one of these was a solo. He doesn't take any solos at all on *Kiss Me Kate*, thus automatically making it the weakest entry in the bunch. (*Kate* also wastes too much playing time on second-tier talents like Johnny Prophet and Lou Monte. However, balancing the scales in the other direction, Clark Dennis, a completely forgotten tenor from the Doris Day era, does a marvelous job on "More I Cannot Wish You" on *Guys and Dolls*.)

*Guys and Dolls* is singularly outstanding; this was Sinatra's opportunity to settle a score (literally) with Samuel Goldwyn, who cast him as the nebbish Nathan Detroit rather than the slicker Sky Masterson in the 1955 movie adaptation. Personally, I think Goldwyn was right: Sinatra plays the character like a musical Angelo Maggio (in *From Here to Eternity*), and Marlon Brando's singspiel renditions of the Sky Masterson ballads are precisely what composer Frank Loesser had in mind when he cast the original Broadway production with nonsinging character actors. Still, the Billy May arrangement for Sinatra of Masterson's climactic number, "Luck Be a Lady" is the highpoint of the whole four-album series and an instant Sinatra classic. Sinatra's "Luck Be a Lady"—both the 1963 recording and the countless times he sang it over the next thirty years—were so essential and profitable to the Sinatra oeuvre that the whole Reprise Repertory enterprise could have been subsidized by this one arrangement by itself. (In 1963 the four albums were issued together in a four-LP box, and then released individually to retail outlets. In 2000, Warner Bros. at long last issued the four albums complete for the first time on CD in a boxed set.)

The following year Sinatra also "conceived and produced" two deadly serious sets that he appeared on along with Bing Crosby and Fred Waring's

Pennsylvanians: *America, I Hear You Singing* and *12 Songs of Christmas*, as well as *Frank Sinatra and His Friends Want You to Have Yourself a Merry Little Christmas*, a somewhat lighter seasonal sampling.

*America, I Hear You Singing*, taped within six weeks of the assassination that shook the world, is a singularly beautiful album. Overall, it's somber—even Kate Smith herself never recorded anything so heavy—but nothing here sounds pretentious or pious. Above all, it's an album about a people coming together and putting aside their differences at a time of tragedy. As late as 1960, when Sinatra attempted to break the Hollywood blacklist by producing a movie written by "unfriendly witness" Albert Maltz, he was branded a pinko (or at least a dangerous liberal) by some of the more conservative political elements. Here, he balances the scales by singing with Crosby, a lifelong Republican. The collection features songs by left-leaning writers, like Woody Guthrie's "This Land Is Your Land," sung beautifully by Crosby, and Sinatra's most majestic recorded version of "The House I Live In," but also traditional Americana like John Philip Sousa's "Stars and Stripes Forever" and the African American spiritual "Let Us Break Bread Together."

And apart from all these albums, Sinatra continued to turn out singles, continuing his career-long policy of devoting this medium to newer songs with hit potential. He also used the format to try out new arrangers; there was such a surfeit of talent even as late as the 1960s that many of the better orchestrators he collaborated with never got the call to do an entire album. For instance, Torrie Zito, who would later go on to do great things with Tony Bennett, and Marty Paich, who had already written many masterful scores for Mel Tormé and Ella Fitzgerald (and, on Reprise, for Sammy Davis), were each assigned to score one ballad and one up-tempo for Sinatra. "He had his favorite arrangers," Paich told me, "but once in a while when he couldn't get them, then the rest of us would have a chance to slip in."

In 1965, Zito tackled "Ev'rybody Has the Right to Be Wrong (at Least Once)" and "I'll Only Miss Her When I Think of Her," both from *Skyscraper*, Cahn's and Van Heusen's most significant bid for a Broadway hit. (The show was shot down, according to showbiz lore, not just by the unwieldy length of the titles of its two key songs but by the unfortunate choice of the nonsinging Julie Harris as its leading lady.) Two years before, Paich had worked on "Here's to the Losers" (coincidentally cowritten by another Tormé collaborator, Bob Wells) and "Love Isn't Just for the Young."

"Apparently he heard something that he liked that I did, and called me to do these two things," Paich said. "So we went in with a large orchestra, and we just had this brief encounter. The whole thing was a little quick for me. I usually like to work a little slower. But the sides came out very nicely, very musical—and that was the last time I worked with him." Mel Tormé confirmed that Paich was rather finicky, the kind who insisted on endless rehearsals; whereas Sinatra, as we've seen, consistently tried not to over-rehearse for fear it would take the spontaneity and the joy out of his performances. Yet the two swingers in this batch, Zito's chart on "Ev'rybody Has the Right to Be Wrong" and Paich's "Here's to the Losers," came out especially well, showing both men to be keen students of the Sinatra-Riddle style: Zito dropped hints via Nelsonian trombones (the bass trombone in particular), and Paich had saxes and trumpets echo each other in round harmony on the central theme in the intro.

"Here's to the Losers," like "Ring-a-Ding-Ding!" and "Come Blow Your Horn" (a theme song for a Sinatra movie, put together around this time for the Chairman by Cahn, Van Heusen, and Riddle to a Neil Simon title), is a perfect piece of Sinatra philosophy, at once swinging and spiritual. If the payoff line had only been "Here's to the losers—bless *us* all," instead of "bless '*em* all," it would have given the text the ironic edge it needs to become an impeccable Sinatra set piece.* The charming "Right to Be Wrong" (which he sang on *The Hollywood Palace* with Basie) also suits Sinatra superbly. "I'll Only Miss Her" fares even better, setting Sinatra against a curtain of shimmering strings (sounding slightly Jenkinsian near the end) and flamenco-style Spanish guitar from both Laurindo Almeida and Al Viola.

One of the more curious singles of 1964 was a song called "Stay with Me," written by two Broadway and Hollywood vets, Carolyn Leigh (of "Young at Heart" fame) and Jerome Moross, as the theme for a spiritual drama titled *The Cardinal*. At the time, the movie itself was successful but the song didn't get any higher than number eighty-one on the charts. Yet fifty years later, "Stay with Me" became much more important to Sinatra fans when Bob Dylan included it in *Shadows in the Night*, his 2015 album of Sinatra songs. You can see why Dylan was attracted to it: it's a winding, sinewy melody and a conundrum of a text that sounds more like liturgy than lyrics—in all, it seems like one of the songs that Dylan himself might have written in his "Jesus period" in the late 1970s, like "Gotta Serve Somebody." (So props to Mr. Zimmerman for calling my attention to a unique Sinatra record that I had never really noticed previously.)

Reprise collected some of these singles onto two anthology "pick up" albums, titled *Softly, as I Leave You* and *My Kind of Broadway*. (The latter was a collection of recently recorded material, almost all previously released on various albums and singles, including a real rarity titled "Golden Moment"

---

* Blessed be they who ring-a-ding, for they shall be swinging, sayeth Pope Francis.

from a musical version of *Picnic* that had closed in Boston.) Other singles from the mid-1960s reveal Sinatra working harder and harder to capture the ever-shifting attention of the market. Don Costa's "I Can't Believe I'm Losing You" and Henry Mancini's "Dear Heart" sound vaguely like very mellow country and western music, while "Forget Domani" and "Softly, as I Leave You" (aka "Piano"), both originally Italian, belong to a genre of foreign songs, many associated with movies, that we might refer to as "Eurotrash."

But the elephant in the room was the youth market. As an artist, Sinatra's focus was now almost always fixed on the album, the medium that he virtually invented. Still, he wanted hit singles too; but over the course of his career, the only time when he consistently dwelt in the upper brackets of the pop charts had been in the 1940s. He only had a handful of big hits in all of the Capitol era, and in terms of singles he really didn't compete with Crosby, Cole, or the newcomer, Elvis.

Sinatra had already been making noises that sounded like rhythm and blues for decades, including "The Hucklebuck" in 1949 and his first "rock" record "Castle Rock," in 1951. They were followed by "Bim! Bam! Baby!" (1952) and "Lean Baby" (1953), and in the early Capitol era he cut a number of doo-wop singles, most infamously the 45-rpm pairing of "Two Hearts, Two Kisses" and "From the Bottom to the Top" (1955). Contrastingly, "Hey! Jealous Lover" (1956) was a more copacetic blend of youth pop (aka doo-wop) and the familiar Sinatra sound, thanks to the input of both Nelson Riddle and Sammy Cahn—and it was one of his major hits of the period.

By 1964–65, it was increasingly clear to Sinatra that he had to address this thing—whatever the hell it was that the kids were listening to—both as an artist himself and as the spiritual force behind Reprise. Beginning in mid-decade, his output would grow increasingly schizophrenic: he was continually raising the bar of popular music in masterpiece albums like *The Concert Sinatra* and *September of My Years*, but in terms of staying current in the market, he was obligated to sing whatever junk he thought would sell, as uncomfortable as that made him. Even as he was celebrating his own maturity (both musical and otherwise) during the year of his fiftieth birthday, he was also trying to reach the audience that was buying his daughter Nancy's hit singles; not only did one hand apparently not know what the other was doing, but the two hands almost seemed to belong to two different artists. (One man who keenly appreciated the irony was the songwriter Ervin Drake, who was responsible for both "Castle Rock" and "It Was a Very Good Year.")

It was in trying to extend his horizons beyond the world that he knew that Sinatra reached out to Jimmy Bowen, who may be the first producer he worked with whose tastes were not a direct extension of his own. In everything he had done with Voyle Gilmore, Dave Cavanaugh, Sonny Burke, or Quincy Jones, for instance, he often expanded his horizons but was never expected to completely leave his comfort zone. Bowen had started as a performer, a contemporary of Buddy Holly in the Texas rock and roll scene, most successfully with the Rhythm Orchids (he played bass and sang), a trio responsible for a number of top-ten hits in the era of Rockabilly, among them "Party Doll" and "I'm Sticking with You" (both written by Bowen and Jimmy Knox). "My problem was that I sang a little flat. I could hear it, but I couldn't do anything about it," Bowen told us in the early 1990s. "So I knew that [my career as a singer] was a short-term thing. And then after about two years, the girls quit screaming and they started listening. Then I knew I was in trouble. So I said to myself, 'I'd better find something else to do.'"

Over the next few years, Bowen built up a reputation as a composer and producer, primarily for a Los Angeles label called Chancellor Records. An associate there named Murray Wolf, who happened to know Sinatra, informed Bowen that Sinatra was looking for a producer who was more in tune with the contem-pop culture. "When Frank first started Reprise, he said, 'No rock and roll on this label,' but obviously that changed," said Bowen. He told Wolf he was interested, and "about five or six weeks later I get a call one night from Murray, talking softly. He said, 'Listen, you got the job. Hang on, Frank wants to talk to you.' Sinatra came on and said, 'James? Glad to have you aboard.' Click! That was it."

Bowen began by producing strictly rock-style hits for the label, such as Jack Nitzsche's 1963 "Lonely Surfer," which was, he said, "a hit wherever there was water." He would attain some of the label's biggest sellers by virtue of his concept of repackaging the star power of the biggest classic pop names in terms that the current audience could accept. Not having the nerve to approach Sinatra with this idea at first, Bowen initially asked if he could do a date with Reprise's crooner *numero dos*, Dean Martin. According to Bowen, many of the rockabilly pioneers had been Dino diehards since childhood, not least among them Elvis himself. (Presley was such a fan of the Italian crooners, especially Martin and Sinatra, that he actually recorded more Italian songs than Sinatra, and even christened his entourage "the Memphis Mafia.")

Bowen was already working extensively with orchestrator Ernie Freeman. "I had used other arrangers, but Ernie was my favorite," he said, "because we communicated so well. Ernie had the temperament to sit with me for a couple of hours while we went over things: 'I want this and I want that.' It was a give-and-take, and a lot of arrangers won't do that. Plus, I like simplicity with a big orchestra, and Ernie would do it for me. He was just an incredibly talented man." A veteran of Los Angeles's Central Avenue jazz scene of the

1940s, Freeman (born 1922) recorded with Dexter Gordon and singer Helen Humes. Throughout the 1950s, he starred on a long series of blues sides for Imperial Records, one of which, an R&B cover of the instrumental hit "Raunchy," made him a star under his own name.

In the 1960s, Freeman specialized in helping white teen idols like Bobby Vee and Paul Anka pass themselves off as rock 'n' rollers, and then pulled off a comparable caper in making Sinatra and Dean Martin palatable to teen audiences. "He'd been around a long time," said Bowen. "I first became aware of Ernie when he did Gene McDaniels and Johnny Burnette arrangements for Snuff Garrett at Liberty Records, a big hit called 'Dreamin'' by Johnny Burnette. I remember when I heard that, and I said, 'Whoa, is that wild? Strings on rock and rockabilly records!' So when I got the opportunity, I went right to him."

Bowen and Freeman made their presence known at Reprise with their updated production of Dean Martin's "Everybody Loves Somebody"—they took an old song, and an older singer, and made a new hit. "Since I was making hits for Frank's buddy, Frank said, 'Well, I should give the kid a try.'" Said Bowen, "He called me one day and asked if I'd come over for a meeting, and I grabbed a tune out of my good song file, that I knew Frank would just love." This was "Softly, as I Leave You," based on an Italian song titled "Piano" (referring not to the musical instrument but to the Italian term for "soft," meaning low volume), which had already been a top-ten hit for Britain's number-one traditional crooner (and honorary Italian), Matt Monro. "I took it over and we talked a bit, and he said, 'Listen, if you're going to produce some music for me, what would you do?' I said, 'Well, I wouldn't bastardize you. I'd change the music around you but keep you who you are.' He said, 'Well, that makes sense. What do you have?' Thank God I picked up that song. I played 'Softly,' and he said, 'Fine, let's do it.' So we went in a week or two later and recorded 'Softly as I Leave You.'"

Sinatra's first session with Freeman and Bowen took place in July 1964, when they layed down "Softly," and two other newish items with *Billboard* potential: "Then Suddenly Love" by veteran Roy Alfred (responsible for the lyrics to such crossover milestones as "The Hucklebuck" and "The Rock and Roll Waltz") and Sammy Cahn's "Available." If all three had been orchestrated in other eras, they might have proven traditional Sinatra material. Usually Sinatra insisted on his own rhythm section, but he gave Bowen a free hand to bring in his own players out of the Nashville/rock idioms, such as drummer Hal Blaine (of Wrecking Crew fame), keyboardist Leon Russell (later a major singer-songwriter), and concertmaster Sid Sharp, who knew how to get fiddlers "who didn't mind busting a string." Glen Campbell, not far away from his own breakthrough as a pop star, played rhythm guitar on numerous Bowen-Sinatra dates.

While Sinatra is superlative on all three, the quality of the finished product has less to do with the singing than the acoutrements: on "Softly" we hear monotonous rock drumming, a cloying choir, and the same kind of trite, nails-on-chalkboard string figures we know from, for instance, Belford Hendricks's charts for Dinah Washington and Nat Cole. The chorus and strings do the same for the other two songs, both of which, like Sy Oliver's charts, use a prominent baritone sax. Ten years earlier, "Then Suddenly Love" would have been the basis for a brisk Sinatra frolic à la "Ya Better Stop"; while it retains some deft touches (such as an Edisonian bleating in the coda), it remains a shotgun marriage between ring-a-ding-ding and yeah-yeah-yeah. Sinatra exclaims "Hot damn! I wish you love" (on the second Basie album) when singing to his own generation, but when trying to contact the now generation, he feels obliged to tone down his energy to a piddling "Hot dog!"

"When we finished cutting 'Softly,'" said Bowen, "we were listening to the playbacks and Frank said, 'Well, James, what do you think?' And I said, 'I think it's [only] about a number-thirty record, but it'll get us back on radio.' He looked at me like that didn't please him too much, and he left. And I think the record went to twenty-seven. But with Sinatra that would be important because your word is very important to him, and that's what I felt. We had a challenge to get Sinatra on top-forty radio when the Beatles were happening."

The Bowen-Freeman sessions suggest how later generations will regard the 1990s *Duets* discs: after their novelty and hit value have faded, we'll be wondering why anyone ever made such a fuss about them. One's joy in the fact of Sinatra returning to the charts is severely hampered by the sacrifices in the quality of his work that made these achievements possible. In the mid-1960s, the public obviously wanted countrypolitan cadenzas, a doo-wah choir, the ever-present sixteenth-note triplets, and strings that screech rather than soar. Freeman delivers these goods on such singles as "Somewhere in Your Heart," "Tell Her (You Love Her Each Day)," and "When Somebody Loves You."

"It's one of those things where you grasp the moment," said Bowen. "I had about a four- or five-year period where I had the feel of how to take these kinds of artists into the marketplace, to top-forty radio, at a time when top-forty radio didn't want to play them." "Forget Domani" and "Strangers in the Night" are typical 1960s movie music. "Domani," from the 1965 Rex Harrison film *The Yellow Rolls-Royce*, at least offers something in the way of camp value in the way it combines a Neapolitan mandolin sound with that of a discotheque. As Bowen himself clarifies, these sessions were never attempts to make classic Sinatra music for the ages (the Chairman continued to work with Sonny Burke on those projects) but were quick shots intended to move product in the moment. "We were just experimenting in all those sessions," he said. "If you listen to them, you can hear that. Basically, it was my idea of how I heard him in the marketplace at that time."

Bowen succeeded most spectacularly with "Strangers in the Night," the only one of these singles to have a long-lasting impact on the Old Man's career. (Yes, they were already starting to refer to him as the Old Man then, but not to his face.) "Strangers" originated as the title music of a then-upcoming James Garner spy comedy called *A Man Could Get Killed,* with a score by Bert Kaempfert. Considered the German giant of easy listening (sort of a Deutschlander Percy Faith, remembered by history as the first man to get the Beatles in a studio and as the composer of Nat King Cole's final hit, "L-O-V-E"), Kaempfert was a major player on the international pop music stage. Bowen first heard the tune when the composer's manager and American publisher, Al Fine, sent a song plugger to Bowen's house to demonstrate it. "I said, 'Man, get me the lyric on that, and I'll do it with Sinatra.' I'd never said that to anybody because, obviously, nobody knows what Frank is going to do till he says what he's going to do. [But] I knew that melody [would be a hit]. So they sent me a couple of lyrics I didn't like, but then finally they got me one that I thought was right. And we went in and did that song."

The biggest battle to land the hit, however, occurred after the recording. Sinatra had made "Strangers in the Night" on a Monday, but Jack Jones had recorded his version the previous Friday and immediately mailed out copies to the leading radio stations. Bowen quickly mixed the Sinatra performance, cut a few acetates, and thanks to obliging flight attendants and couriers racing to and from airports all over the country actually had the Sinatra record in the hands of disc jockeys hours before the competitor's product arrived.

Sinatra, as he has said at numerous concerts, didn't care for the song and had recorded it only reluctantly. (There are many live performances wherein he takes the line, "Love was just a glance away, a warm embracing dance away" and goofs it up as "a lonesome pair of pants away.") But the arrangement capitalizes on the strength of the central hook, which the singer exalts with an effectively forlorn sound and the arranger supports with a chinking rhythm guitar and effectively repetitive percussion pattern. Luckily, the string lines are several notches more bearable than those of the team's usual efforts, and Sinatra fades out with a surprisingly quixotic scat coda that quickly replaced "ring-a-ding-ding" as the crowning Sinatra-ism of the 1960s: "dooby-doo-by-do." (Sinatra had uttered his first documented "oo-bedoo-be" a year earlier as a spontaneous interjection on the *Hollywood Palace* performance of "Please Be Kind" with Basie.)

"Strangers" was an almost unprecedented, resoundingly massive hit—Sinatra's first number-one single since an entire generation ago—and it went on to provide the title and opener to his final album with Nelson Riddle, a set so beautifully done it almost seemed as if Sinatra were apologizing for the original track. As Bowen recalled, the remaining *Strangers* album had been originally intended for another project; Sinatra and Reprise annexed the material under the "Strangers" banner out of a quick need for an album to complement his megahit single.

Irv Cottler, Sinatra's longtime drummer, coined the phrase "ballad rock" to describe the singer's efforts in this area. He elaborated, "I don't know why they call it rock because it's not rock at all. It just has that contemporary feel."

After "Strangers," ballad-rock established itself as the dominant mode of Sinatra's singles and, eventually, his albums as well. When he turned "Strangers" into an album, it was subtitled *The Popular Sinatra Sings for Moderns*, and many of the songs for swinging moderns turned out to be the work of Johnny Mercer and Walter Donaldson. But when it came time to produce an album around the next Sinatra-Freeman-Bowen hit, "That's Life," instead of going again to one of his high-grade arrangers, the threesome contrived an entire set of material in the same general style as the title track.

Unlike "Softly" or "Strangers," Sinatra himself discovered "That's Life" (sometime in the summer or fall of 1966, he probably heard the record by soul singer O. C. Smith), which explains why it's a song that's so much better suited to him than the others—one that he actually enjoyed singing. He originally commissioned an arrangement from Nelson Riddle, which was both swinging and bluesy and utilized a Hammond electric organ (in the manner of "Summer Wind"), and introduced it in his 1966 television special, *A Man and His Music Part II*. Alas, he didn't bring this chart into the recording studio, but rather turned the song over to Bowen and Freeman. What they came up with sounds much more like a hit single of the period—which indeed it was—removing the organ and adding a gospel-style choir behind the Chairman.

The recording took place at a brand-new studio, and when Bowen walked into the session he was informed that most of the microphones weren't yet operational. Turning a liability into an asset, he did the date with only two working mics, one on Sinatra, the other on the rhythm section. Although a full contingent of horns, strings, and backup singers had been assembled, the producer concluded that it didn't matter: given the right performance by Sinatra, he could overdub the other elements of the track (including a keyboard part by Mike Melvoin*) at a later time.

---

\* A famous Hollywood keyboardist, his daughter Wendy Melvoin achieved greater fame as guitarist with Prince and the Revolution.

Sinatra arrived, went to work, and soon came up with a performance of "That's Life" that almost all present were sure was "the one." "We played it back, and Frank said, 'Boy! That's a hit, isn't it?' And I said, 'Well, no. If you want a hit, you're going to have to do it one more time.' Everybody got real quiet, and he gave me the coldest look an artist ever gave me. But he went right out, and instead of singing it *hip*—he was pissed now—he *bit* it! That's when he sang 'That's Life'!"

"That's Life" is Sinatra's most concerted effort to approximate a blues or a soul sound. The most important element is the attitude. Bowen realized that getting Sinatra pissed at him was actually key to him getting the right feeling for the song—the feeling that made it relevant to the era of Ray Charles, James Brown, and Aretha Franklin. "That's Life" is Sinatra's version of a Ray Charles number; Charles himself had already crossed over into the realm of standard ballads with strings (as in "Georgia on My Mind" and "Come Rain or Come Shine") and now Sinatra was meeting him halfway, even down to a background of pseudo Raelettes.

The Riddle arrangement of "That's Life" (which paid homage to Louis Armstrong with a descending paraphrase of the classic Satchmo coda "Oh, yeah!") had Sinatra getting merely sensually funky. The Freeman-Bowen treatment shows that he has come a long way from the semiclassical sound of the 1940s; now he gasps, growls, grunts, snarls, and all but spits at the audience: he does indeed sound, in Bowen's phrase, "pissed." Ladies and gentlemen, I give you *The Antisocial Sinatra.*

Bowen was determined not to repeat what he viewed as the error of the *Strangers in the Night* album, i.e., one contemporary hit and nine jazz standards. He told Sinatra, "We can't do just one thing that's modern and innovative for the times and then go back and do 'Wee Small Hours' for the other nine tunes." The rest of *That's Life* consists of orchestrations that are, admittedly, more brassy and less discothequey than other Freeman-Bowen-Sinatra items, although the songs themselves are the sort Sinatra would do had he deigned to portray a singing villain on *Batman.*

*That's Life* represents the first full album wherein Sinatra capitulates to commercial pressures, the first time he did an album filled with songs he hoped would sell rather than songs that he thought were great—and for the first time, there was a clear-cut discrepancy between the two goals. It's a unique combination of material from American, British, and French sources (Brazil would be next), some of which is quite excellent, such as Michel Legrand's "I Will Wait for You" and André Previn's "You're Gonna Hear from Me," two contemporary film songs that were both absolutely right for him in that particular moment.

The biggest surprise is "Somewhere My Love (Lara's Theme)" the Maurice Jarre number, and "Winchester Cathedral," a 1966 hit by the British novelty group the New Vaudeville Band. On both of these, you almost feel like Freeman and Bowen wanted to prove to Sinatra how hip they could be. Both arrangements are surprisingly swinging, with an obvious doff of the hat to Count Basie and Nelson Riddle. "Somewhere My Love" is particularly finger-snapping: all of a sudden "Doctor Zhivago" becomes "Doctor Chicago." Neither of these caught on, but "What Now My Love," by French singer-songwriter Gilbert Bécaud, became a concert perennial that Sinatra was still singing into the 1990s.

"The Impossible Dream," the climactic number from the hit musical *Man of La Mancha* (which was still running off-Broadway when Sinatra recorded it in November 1966) is a case unto itself. It's also a kind of template for the slightly later "My Way"—you certainly wouldn't need to hear both songs on the same concert. And like "My Way," Sinatra himself apparently couldn't stand it; according to collectors' gossip, he only included it on the album as a present for his new third wife, Mia Farrow, who adored it.

It's also been bruited about that Sinatra couldn't go through with singing the whole thing in one full take, and this turns out to be true. "We didn't cut it twenty-seven times or anything like that," said Bowen. "We broke it up into three or four sections. Then we just recorded the sections, and I edited it together. That was a crazy song to sing, plus he was not in great voice that particular week. I was afraid if we tried to get a whole take, it'd turn into agony, and he'd throw it out. He had promised somebody to do it, so he wasn't going to throw it out, but I didn't find that out until later." The impossible dream, indeed.

For a "commercial" album, *That's Life* still had plenty of moments—and is actually better than much of what he recorded later on in the immediate postretirement era. Even as late as 1967, there was still plenty of nourishing food on his plate: he would bookend that year with two classic albums with deliberately similar titles, *Francis Albert Sinatra & Antônio Carlos Jobim* and *Francis A. and Edward K.* While the first concluded the singer's 1960s cycle of one-shot collaborations, the two sets as a pair would unfortunately be regarded as the final two classic Sinatra concept albums for at least a decade.

The buzzword for much of 1960s pop was "the British Invasion," but the many mop-topped bands that invaded *The Ed Sullivan Show* in the wake of John, Paul, George, and Ringo are only a tiny fragment of the overall picture. As was happening simultaneously in the movie industry, pop music in the 1960s became a truly international scene; it was an era of multilingual maestros and singer-songwriters from all parts of the globe. Michel Legrand from France, Anthony Newley from England, "Strangers in the Night" composer Bert Kaempfert from Germany, even Manos Hadjidakis (whose theme to *Never on Sunday* was a blockbuster hit in 1960) from Greece; all had huge presences on the American pop charts, just like such homegrown heroes of the era as Henry Mancini and Burt Bacharach.

But perhaps the most influential force of the era—and in a very positive way—was the new Brazilian music known as bossa nova, as spearheaded by the Rio-born songwriter and performer Antônio Carlos Jobim. (To this day, his most famous number, "The Girl from Ipanema," is sometimes listed as the most recorded song of all time, a claim that can't be proven but does give some indication of the song's popularity.) To their credit, North American jazz musicians and traditional pop vocalists were among the first non-Brazilians to explore the sounds coming out of Rio, and it was the great saxophonist Stan Getz, more than anyone, who really put the music on the map of the Northern Hemisphere.

Bossa nova eventually made its widest impact worldwide as an additive, an element that interacted with better-established American genres, and was rarely presented in its pure form stateside. By the mid-1960s, jazz and pop stars as diverse as Miles Davis, Eydie Gormé, Gil Evans, Ella Fitzgerald, Zoot Sims, Mel Tormé, Vic Damone, Perry Como, Kenny Dorham, and Peggy Lee were all blaming it on the bossa nova.*

By the age of thirty-nine in 1967, Jobim had already composed virtually all of the music's trademark hits, including "The Girl from Ipanema," "One Note Samba" ("Samba de Uma Nota Só"), "Quiet Nights of Quiet Stars" ("Corcovado"), "How Insensitive" ("Insensatez"), and "Meditation" ("Meditação"). As the German arranger Claus Ogerman recalled, "Frank really liked these strong and famous songs by Jobim and wanted to do an album with them."

Famously, Sinatra then reached out to Jobim and found him, via an international phone call, in a bar in Rio; when he told the composer what he had in mind, Jobim accepted instantly. Not only would Sinatra be doing an album of Jobim's music, but he wanted the guitarist-pianist and occasional singer to participate as well. Ogerman "came along with Antônio," he told us, "because Frank had heard earlier albums I had done with Antônio and liked what I did."

---

* Even Elvis Presley found himself a "Bossa Nova Baby" in his 1963 movie *Fun in Acapulco*. The song was basically an R&B number, by Jerry Leiber and Mike Stoller, with a vaguely Latin backbeat and mariachi-style brass. Somehow it's hard to imagine Elvis singing "Desafinado" or "Corcovado."

Rather than tentatively dipping his toes into this particular lagoon, Sinatra elected to dive in headfirst. His rationale seemed to be that although other singers—notably Tony Bennett*—had gotten there first, he would get there with the most. No other American pop star would so thoroughly immerse himself in the world of bossa; he not only recorded two whole albums' worth of the stuff but sacrificed his signature stylistic devices in order to more seamlessly fit into the new vernacular. The two albums were *Francis Albert Sinatra & Antônio Carlos Jobim* (1967) and *Sinatra-Jobim* (1969), although the latter would never be issued as Sinatra had originally intended.

What did go through as Sinatra had planned was that Jobim himself is a prominent presence throughout; his distinctive nylon-string guitar can be heard on every track, often in the introductions and instrumental breaks. He also sings harmony lines, bass parts, or countermelodies, sometimes humming wordlessly, sometimes chanting the original lyrics in Portuguese; his actual credit on the album itself is "vocal support by Antônio Carlos Jobim." Sometimes he sings what amount to obbligatos, much the same way Sweets Edison does with his extremely vocalized trumpet on many a Sinatra classic. There's only one track, "Desafinado" (from the second album) where they sing together in full voice in what amounts to a true duet.

Jobim plays an even more important role as the composer of nearly all of the material, seven of the ten tunes on the first album and all ten of the second. Sinatra planned the arrangements in advance with Ogerman; he supplied him with a list of songs and the proper keys, and left everything else pretty much up to the arranger. The understanding was that the sound would be the same as the previous Jobin-Ogerman album, *The Composer of Desafinado Plays.* And in fact, when one listens to that record it sounds exactly like the 1967 album, only with Sinatra's voice removed—music minus one Frank.

The Jobim collaboration represents Sinatra's most successful foray beyond the body of music that he had done more than anyone to define as what became known as the Great American Songbook. What distinguished Jobim from the major North American songwriters was that Jobim's songs, unlike Berlin's or Porter's, are more rigorously set into certain specific modes of interpretation. You can rearrange Irving Berlin's "Change Partners" as a bossa nova, but it would be silly to try and interpret "The Girl from Ipanema" as anything but a bossa nova. If you were to remove the Brazilian rhythm, there would be nothing left worth playing or singing. Ogerman agreed: "In a way, the tempos are locked in on the Jobim songs. You can't do them faster or slower."

---

* Unlike Sinatra, Bennett discovered the new music while playing in Brazil, and was recording "Corcovado" and other bossa standards several years ahead of Sinatra.

Sinatra also commissioned Ogerman to orchestrate three American stan-dards—"Baubles, Bangles, and Beads," "I Concentrate on You," and "Change Partners"—in the bossa idiom. "At that time," said Ogerman, "there were not enough Jobim songs with good English lyrics. Antônio has about four hun-dred songs that are great, but most of them had no English words because Antônio is very hard to please in that respect. It's very hard to translate Antô-nio's Portuguese into decent English. Unless you can get it into the hands of a master like Johnny Mercer, you're almost lost. So Frank decided to do some Cole Porter and Irving Berlin in addition to Antônio's songs."

Whereas other aspects of Brazilian music have a harder edge to them, Sinatra uses bossa nova as the vehicle for the softest singing he had ever done—on a par with his original "chamber" sessions for *The Voice* album in 1945. As he says in the album's liner notes, "I haven't sung so soft since I had the laryngitis." All twenty bossa ballads feature Sinatra's sensual, supple, and super-subdued vocals atop sensitive strings, very understated brass (only the quietest of all brass instruments, a single trombone, played by Dick Noel, is audible), and gently undulating Brazilian rhythm, as laid down by Jobim on guitar and his "personal drummer," Dom Um Romão. The miraculous "Dindi" is so supremely soft that you almost have to listen twice to be sure that it's actually Sinatra.

As on the sessions with Duke Ellington, recorded that December, Sinatra offers his most uncharacteristically reverential singing here, devoid of Frank-ish interjections and the familiar swagger. When he throws in an extra beat on the end of "Baubles, Bangles, and Beads" on the phrase "I *have* heard," it derives both from the inherent playfulness of the Brazilian form and what was to become a signature Sinatra device in the latter part of his career, the expanded contractions. As with other arrangers, Ogerman was only given a pitifully brief time to write the ten charts, but he actually felt that this was a positive circumstance. "I had to write so fast that I didn't have time to put down millions of notes," he said, "so I left my arrangements extremely trans-parent, and that made it nice for the singer."

Throughout, Sinatra's lines display a startling flexibility and delicacy, as if they could be blown about by a soft breeze from the Amazon. It's not even surprising when Jobim joins him on the climactic phrases of "Girl from Ipanema," transforming his solo vocal into a harmony line. Likewise, Sinatra presents himself as a wide-eyed innocent here, which is the only way he could make "Girl from Ipanema"—lyrically, it's about a million miles away from "Angel Eyes"—work for him. He even utters an "ooh" that's entirely wor-shipful and not at all leering; he sounds like a teenage boy admiring teenaged girls, not like a fifty-something letch.

Sinatra is never at a loss for exactly what to do, even when the dynamic options span the gamut only from piano to pianissimo. His phrasing is about as far removed from the Basie albums as Rio is from Kansas City; yet Sinatra is no less of a jazz singer here, particularly when he subtly emphasizes the syllables "tall" and "tan" (dropping the "and" between them) in "Ipanema" and similarly stressing the "you've" and "in" (in the lines "*you've* been locked / *in* his arms") in "Change Partners." He so completely reconstructs this 1938 classic that despite Fred Astaire and *Carefree,* an entire generation has grown up unable to conceive of "Change Partners" as anything other than a bossa nova. In the twenty-first century, more people think it was written by Jobim than by Berlin.

Ogerman's elegant orchestrations indicate that he could have been the next great Sinatra collaborator. Jobim, who died in 1994, frequently observed that the most important element that the bossa nova shared with North American jazz was a pliant, malleable rhythm, which he distinguished from traditional European, and particularly Teutonic, music with its unrelenting *oompah.* Paradoxically, *FAS & ACJ,* the greatest of all bossa nova vocal records, was arranged by a Munich-based German orchestrator. Born in Ratibor (today Racibórz in Poland) in 1930, Claus Ogerman had played piano in the big bands of the swing-oriented Kurt Edelhagen (a sort of German Ted Heath, who himself was sort of a British Woody Herman) and the funkier Max Greger before immigrating to the United States in 1959. Ogerman had grown up with American jazz and pop, listening to it even during the Nazi regime. He had been a Sinatra fan since the Harry James days; Nelson Riddle was his favorite orchestrator, and for him, *In the Wee Small Hours* was "the pinnacle of everything in pop music."

Working extensively with producer Creed Taylor at Verve Records, Ogerman established himself as one of the few jazz-oriented orchestrators of the 1960s who seemed comfortable with contemporary developments in both rock and the new thing in jazz and yet remained relevant to what Sinatra called "the good pop music." In addition to arranging albums for Johnny Hodges, Donald Byrd, Jimmy Smith, Cal Tjader, and Bill Evans, Ogerman worked with Stan Getz on *Reflections* in 1963. In the same month as the first Sinatra-Jobim set, Ogerman taped *Voices,* a program of orchestrations originally intended for Wes Montgomery but reassigned to Getz when the guitarist switched label affiliations.

For Ogerman, working with Sinatra was a dream come true, and the reality of arranging and conducting for him was better than anything he had imagined. When Ogerman met Sinatra at his office at Warner Bros. to help pick the key for "Drinking Again," he sat down at the piano at one point and started noodling around with what he described as "very modern jazz harmonies." Sinatra then announced to all present, "Listen, this guy isn't from Germany, he's from Brooklyn. He's just faking with that accent."

That song, "Drinking Again" (previously recorded memorably by Dinah Washington with Don Costa) makes it clear that Sinatra and Ogerman should have moved on to other projects after completing the *Jobim* album. They taped this little-known gem of a Johnny Mercer lyric at the end of the first round of Jobim dates in 1967, with studio guitarist Al Caiola replacing the Brazilian. Ogerman had known the song's composer, Doris Tauber, in New York. "She worked for many years as a staff pianist and song demonstrator for [music publisher] Harms Inc., which is the job Gershwin had earlier. She was practically Gershwin's successor [at that firm]." Thirty years earlier, Tauber had also composed the all-time jazz standard "Them There Eyes."

For "Drinking Again," Ogerman crafted a light, shimmering background every bit as colorful and supportive as the best of Costa, bringing together Mercer's on-target lyric and Bill Miller's always welcome saloon piano to inspire a Sinatra performance that's stunning even by his own Olympian standards. The singer tempers his perfectly poised declamation with just the right balance of self-pity and self-consciousness, and with minuscule, never overtly noticeable tinges of the slightly sloshed phrasing of the inebriate. By the fadeout, in which—replete with self-crucifying humor—he inwardly intones "Look at me, I'm drinkin' again," Sinatra has concocted a perfect cocktail of tragedy and noir comedy, followed by a chaser of irony. The track was issued on an album called *The World We Knew*, in which it was a veritable buried gem, hidden among piles of inferior "ballad rock."

Sinatra would have done well to give Ogerman the call two years later for his second set with Jobim, though it's foolish to suggest that there was any room for improvement on the ten marvelous orchestrations arranged by Eumir Deodato and conducted by movieland veteran Morris Stoloff. While Ogerman, whom Jobim might have classified as coming from the country of the "oom-pah," wrote the softer set, the Brazilian Deodato (born in Rio in 1942) and Sinatra turn up the voltage for a brassier and more high-powered collection. "One Note Samba" and "This Happy Madness" have much more of a 4/4 swing groove to them, while "Wave" shows a much more pronounced use of trumpets and trombones.

"Drinking Water (Água De Beber)" gives us the extra kick of Sinatra singing several lines in Portuguese. On "Triste," he creates an ineffable sense of melancholy, refusing to let the mood be compromised by the unrelenting Brazilian dance beat. "Don't Ever Go Away (Por Causa de Você)" builds to a traditional Sinatra-type climax. They're all representative of an even more danceable album with a stronger beat than the first Jobim collaboration. However, "Wave" may well be the dramatic apex of the entire Sinatra-Jobim cycle, with Sinatra diving deep for a spectacular low note an entire octave beneath the tonic.

When Jobim guested on Sinatra's 1967 TV special (*A Man and His Music, Part III + Ella + Jobim*), the collaborators revised the arrangement of "Ipanema" slightly so that Jobim was more heavily featured; instead of merely offering "vocal support" on the television show, they were now singing a true duet. In 1969, they tried duetting on "Desafinado," with somewhat awkward results; on "Ipanema," it's clear that they're singing about a girl they both admire, but on "Desafinado" it almost could be mistaken for a homoerotic love song in which the two men are singing romantically to each other. (From what we know of Sinatra's personal life, this thought would have made him truly uncomfortable.) "Desafinado" originally became a hit in the States in 1962 thanks to an English lyric by jazz songwriter Jon Hendricks, however, Jobim was apparently never happy with that set of words, which is why he and Sinatra are here singing a newer text by Gene Lees. But where the television duet of "Girl from Ipanema" is sheer magic, the duet on "Desafinado" falls flat, and not just because Jobim's own voice is more than slightly out of tune. ("Desafinado" may be the weakest track in the collaboration, but I'm pleased to own it just the same.) Given more time to reconsider, Sinatra would have probably redone the song as a solo, with "Tom" in the background.

Two of the most beautiful numbers from the 1969 sessions are "Bonita" and "Song of the Sabia (Sabiá)." The former is a straightforward love song, while the latter is a soft, mystical piece on the order of "Dindi" from the 1967 album. "I'm not sure what was on his mind," said Milt Bernhart, who played on the dates. "He was unhappy because there were a couple of very difficult songs. These weren't just ballads, these were art songs that Jobim had written. He fought that one because it was very hard. It just was not reading right." However, the trombonist felt, and rightfully so, that the results justified the effort, and he named "Sabia" (a Brazilian bird) one of the most gorgeous things he ever heard Sinatra sing. It's indeed beautifully gnomic, revealing Jobim as a Brazilian Billy Strayhorn who intrigues without ever quite making explicit what's going on. "Bonita" and "Song of the Sabia" were, for decades, among the rarest of all Sinatra studio recordings, which is a shame.

The second Sinatra-Jobim album was wrapped up after three sessions (February 11, 12, and 13, 1969), resulting in ten usable masters. It was given a title (*Sinatra-Jobim*), and a cover was designed—Sinatra standing in front of a Greyhound bus (no, I don't get it either). It was about to be released, but then, all of a sudden, it wasn't. No one has yet provided a satisfactory explanation as to why, especially since the original 1967 project had made it to number nineteen on the pop album charts. (Sinatra, in the 1965 *Man and His Music* set, gives thanks to "DJs brave enough to give me equal time in Beatle land.") A few eight-track cartridges somehow made it into stores, and that was it for *Sinatra-Jobim*. Seven of the ten tracks were issued on an oddball LP titled *Sinatra & Company* in 1970; but, thankfully, the whole kit and caboodle was at last issued in 2010 on a glorious twenty-track CD titled *Sinatra/Jobim: The Complete Reprise Recordings.*

It was forty years in coming, but worth it. The Jobim collaboration represents Sinatra's final truly great work for a long spell that lasted at least a decade, until his late career reprieve with *Trilogy* and *She Shot Me Down.*

It was a growing problem: Sinatra was worried that he was increasingly irrelevant to changing tastes in popular music. And not only was the game constantly changing, but the stakes were growing, to quote the title of his first starring movie, ever higher and higher. In the 1960s, the record industry was steadily expanding, keeping pace with the national economy. There was also expanding globalization of the media: in 1965 it was much more possible for an American pop star to sell records in India or the Philippines or anywhere else in what was then referred to as "the free world" than it had been in 1955 or 1945. And it all added up: for whatever we think of the artistic value of Jimmy Bowen's productions (and it must be said that Bowen himself doesn't necessarily defend them), all three of the core Rat Pack members—Sinatra, Sammy Davis Jr., and Dean Martin—sold more records in these years than in any other period of their careers (that's in terms of sheer quantity of records sold as well as chart positions).

Sinatra had achieved artistic success and respectable sales with the Jobim and Basie records (even as he had with the great 1960s collaborations with Riddle, May, and Jenkins) and commercial success with the Bowen singles: "Strangers in the Night" (number one on the *Billboard* hit singles chart), "That's Life" (number four), and "Somethin' Stupid" (number one again). But he yearned to find a balance between the two, music that he genuinely loved that would also sell in quantities to satisfy him. That was the goal, to achieve both ends at the same time.

Other singers he respected, like Nat King Cole and Tony Bennett, had long utilized the process of building an album around a hit single, which Sinatra had done with his 1960 *Nice 'n' Easy*. This was now the dominant practice, as with *Strangers in the Night*, *That's Life*, and the last full collaboration with Bowen and Freeman, *The World We Knew*, which, as we noted at the beginning of this chapter, was the follow-up to "Strangers in the Night" by the Sinatra-Kaempfert-Bowen-Freeman combination.

*The World We Knew* album was in the same general vein as the *That's Life* LP. When the new Kaempfert song came along, Bowen recalled, "Sinatra used to laugh at me. I think he was just challenging me to see if we could do it or not. And he used to laugh because Kaempfert's melodies were always testy. 'Strangers in the Night' is not easy to sing. And 'The World We Knew.' . . . Oh God, what a hard song to sing!" The song did make it to the singles charts, but only up to number thirty. Bowen's artistic sensibility pervades the proceedings, although Sinatra sings with conviction throughout, on the good numbers and even, as we shall see, on the bad.

The prevailing mode of the album was deeply serious, highly earnest pop anthems like the similarly titled "This Is My Love" and "This Is My Song." Both songs fit the mood of the era, but both have deep pedigrees—the second especially. The first had originally been recorded by Sinatra as a Capitol single in 1959 as "This Was My Love"; although both versions were arranged by Gordon Jenkins, the 1967 one is superior: Sinatra's vocal cuts deeper and the song and the chart suit the era more. "This Is My Song," the theme from Charles Chaplin's final film, *A Countess from Hong Kong* (written, directed, produced, and composed by Charlie himself), is pleasant and memorable, more so than the movie itself.

"This Is My Love" and "This Is My Song" are the lightest cuts on the album; the latter, in particular, sounds more like Don Costa than Ernie Free-man. The high Bowen-Freeman style kicks in with "Don't Sleep in the Sub-way" (the Petula Clark hit, and sound advice as well), particularly in the use of a chiming choir that's continually surrounding Sinatra with "come on baby, come on baby"—it's like "That's Life" all over again. The fascinat-ing thing about that track is that rough session tapes exist without the choir (which was added later via overdubs), and it sounds much better that way, particularly on the alternates. Here, we can hear Sinatra trying to get the stu-dio orchestra to swing it in more of a 4/4 Basie style. The choirless alternate is far superior to the issued take, but that version was much more "commercial" by 1967 standards.

Film themes predominate. In addition to "This Is My Song" and John Barry's "Born Free," there's "You Are There" (both Jenkins again) from Sina-tra's own movie, *The Naked Runner*. This strongly Chopinesque melody is credited to Harry Sukman, who had played the classical piano solo on Sina-tra's classic 1958 track of "Only the Lonely." "This Town" is from *The Cool Ones*, and more than his other records, it sounds like the Old Man is going after his daughter's audience here—it's almost a kind of pop music pedophilia.

"This Town" was composed by Lee Hazlewood and arranged by Billy Strange, two of Nancy Jr.'s most dependable collaborators. Bowen commissioned Strange to orchestrate Hazlewood's tune because "Billy did the best arrangements of Hazelwood songs—he did 'These Boots Are Made for Walkin' with Nancy. So I hired him to do 'This Town' with Sinatra." The number is funky and bluesy, even more so than "That's Life," and features prominent harmonica by Belgian master Toots Thielemans. (The track was recorded in New York, and features a number of East Coast studio all-stars, such as guitarist Bucky Pizzarelli and bassist Milt Hinton.) In Bowen's opinion, "I didn't think it ever quite came off, but the idea was good on paper." Yet to me, it's one of Sinatra's more successful approximations of blues feeling; it's more listenable than "Strangers in the Night," if not quite as essential to the Sinatra canon as "That's Life." Okay, it may not be classic Frank, but at least it's got a beat and you can dance to it.

The album is marked by its extremes, two songs by iconic songwriters. The high point is Johnny Mercer's "Drinking Again"—as we've seen, recorded in the middle of the Jobim sessions with Claus Ogerman. The low point is an unbelievably ghastly arrangement of what should have been a Sinatra triumph, H. B. Barnum's arrangement of "Some Enchanted Evening." On the session tapes (those that have been circulated), the amazing thing about hearing them is that Sinatra could get through this horrific chart in complete takes, with all the grandiose mock-classical tempo changes and without barfing—not only because the chart is so bad, but all those stops and starts would be enough to give somebody whiplash. It's hard to believe Sinatra or Bowen or anyone could have greenlighted this: it truly trashes the melody, and goes a long way toward explaining why Richard Rodgers didn't want anybody messing with his music. The arrangement liberally rewrites the tune, in a way that must have made Rodgers cringe; but what's worse is that Sinatra sounds completely uncomfortable with the new melody (particularly in the lines "once you have found her, never let her go"), like he's struggling to keep up with it. It's surely a candidate for the worst thing Sinatra ever recorded, along with "Mama Will Bark," which at least qualifies as an honest mistake, where he did the best he could with a terrible song; here it's the other way around. But man, does he ever go for the gusto in terms of his personal commitment; he doesn't do anything halfway—even when he's driving off a cliff, it's full speed ahead.

On the session tape for "Some Enchanted Evening," we hear Sinatra saying, "long as we're flower children, let's act like it!" If a little child shall lead them, Sinatra's two finest moments in this immediate period were both in the company, at least metaphorically, of his firstborn: one is completely of the period, in the best possible way, and the other is timeless. In September 1967, a few weeks after the *World We Knew* dates, Sinatra taped an absolutely stunning reading of "Younger than Springtime," which was dedicated to Nancy and performed as his guest spot in her 1967 NBC-TV special, *Movin' with Nancy*. (It was also included in the younger Sinatra's Reprise album of the same title.) The arrangement, by Billy Strange, and the singing are so sublime that Sinatra almost seems to be apologizing directly to Rodgers for the atrocity he had committed with "Some Enchanted Evening," the other big love song from the *South Pacific* score, a short time earlier.

"Somethin' Stupid," however, would represent the pinnacle of Sinatra's collaboration with Jimmy Bowen. The singer-songwriter Carson Parks wrote it as a duet for himself and his wife, Gaile Foote, and they included it on an album for Kapp Records (apparently the Carson version was never issued as a single). Bowen didn't quite remember how the song reached the Sinatras, saying, "I don't know if Nancy found it, or Frank found it." In retrospect, it seems like Parks, who was part of the Los Angeles folk music scene, would have been more likely to try and reach out to Nancy Sinatra. However, Nancy's producer, Lee Hazlewood, said that Frank was the one who played the Parks record for him; upon hearing the track, Hazlewood told Sinatra, "If you don't record that with Nancy, I will."

In contrast to such overwrought angst from that tumultuous era as the title song for "The World We Knew" and such sheer horrors as the 1967 "Some Enchanted Evening," "Somethin' Stupid" is remarkably simple and sweet—much more so than anyone would have thought the world-weary living legend could be at this point in his and the nation's cultural history. Sinatra is channeling his own younger, more innocent self through his daughter (much the same way he channeled different kinds of feelings through Peggy Lee when he produced and conducted *The Man I Love* album with her in 1957). It's so innocent that no one gave a second thought to a father and daughter ending a song with the words "I love you," though it's clearly meant in a romantic way—the lyrics describe a boy and girl on a date, not a parent and child. James Kaplan, in his excellent bio of Sinatra, says that "Somethin' Stupid" became known as "the incest song," but I respectfully disagree. That's how it would be perceived in the more cynical twenty-first century; but 1967, although times were a-changing, was still a more innocent era, and the Frank-Nancy recording harkens back to a time even more innocent than that. Importantly, they're not portraying themselves as father and daughter, they are embodying other roles here.

Bowen's description of the recording session captures the sweetness of the scene. "We had two microphones set up in the studio, and they were singing side by side. It should have been filmed. It would have been a great TV spot."

It's two minutes and twenty seconds of pure charm. Not to mention pure gold—the single went to number one on the *Billboard* Hot 100, and thus counts as one of the biggest records of the career of either Sinatra.

"Somethin' Stupid" was taped in February 1967, before the rest of the *World We Knew* sessions. This makes me wonder why the album wasn't titled *Somethin' Stupid*, since that song was a much bigger hit than "The World We Knew," unless it was because the singer didn't want to go to market with an album titled *Frank Sinatra: Somethin' Stupid*. He would go on to do several other single duets with Nancy (although "Life's a Trippy Thing" and "Feelin' Kinda Sunday" aren't worthy of discussing here) as well as television shows and concerts; but, as mentioned, it was Sinatra's last big moment with Jimmy Bowen.

"Frank was pleased with the results of 'Softly,' 'Strangers,' 'That's Life,' and 'Somethin' Stupid.' I don't know about the other things," Bowen very astutely said of the sessions he produced for Sinatra, which totaled parts of four albums (not including two packages of *Greatest Hits*) and many singles over three years. "A lot of the other things we did together were not nearly as wonderful as what he did when Sinatra was in charge of Sinatra. My guess would be that it was just something he was doing at that time in his life." The producer added that the one thing he saw him really "get into" was not a Bowen project at all but a more traditional Sinatra taping he attended strictly as a guest, namely the *September of My Years* album.

After *The World We Knew*, Jimmy Bowen left to start his own independent label in 1968 (this was Amos Records, which, among things, produced Bing Crosby's pop-rock album, *Hey Jude/Hey Bing!*, in 1969). Now the decade was coming to an end, and Sinatra was still trying to come up with new ways to create both art and pop at the same time. He was still looking for the hook.

After *The World We Knew*, and the various projects involving both Nancy and Bowen, Sinatra wound up the year with the Duke Ellington album, *Francis A. and Edward K.*, taped in the days around his fifty-second birthday in December 1967. He didn't enter a studio again until July; eight months is a long time between sessions in the life of Sinatra. When he came back, it was to begin work on a new album, *Cycles*, with a new/old collaborator, Don Costa. The album they created together, *Sinatra & Strings*, back in the long-gone days of the world we knew (i.e., 1961) was a beautiful set worthy of comparison with Riddle or Jenkins. But that wasn't what Sinatra needed in 1968–69.

For the next three years, until the start of his retirement in March 1971, Sinatra worked most consistently with Don Costa: they would make two full albums of timely tunes, *Cycles* (1968) and *My Way* (1968–69); half of *Sinatra*

*& Company* (1969–70); and all of Sinatra's most extreme concept album, *A Man Alone* (1969), as well as a slew of singles. The Sinatra on these records is closer to the Sinatra of "Somethin' Stupid" and the Jobim albums—a kinder, gentler Sinatra, as opposed to the harsher, more transgressive Sinatra on "That's Life" and the Bowen sessions in general, or the swinging Sinatra on the Basie and Ellington albums.

*Cycles* was recorded between July (the first date in New York) and November 1968, with arrangements by Don Costa but conducted by Bill Miller, since Costa famously preferred to sit in the control booth while someone else conducted. The album pivots on two songs by Gayle Caldwell: the title song, "Cycles," and "Wandering," both in waltz time. Caldwell (1941–2009), a singer-songwriter from Eugene, Oregon, had been part of the hugely popular folk group the New Christy Minstrels before becoming half of the pop duo Jackie and Gayle (not to be confused with the popular comedian Jackie Gayle). She wrote the song for herself, she said in an interview (available on YouTube), but her publisher thought it sounded more like a "guy" song; so they recruited one of the baritones in the Christy Minstrels to sing the demo, which the publisher then sent to the Sinatra office.

"Cycles" is a beautiful, simple song, which Sinatra sings as softly and subtly as the piece demands. The lyrics start with a pessimistic pronouncement (beginning with "So I'm down, and so I'm out, but so are many others" and going on with "My gal just up and left last week / Friday I got fired"), which is matched by the low-glam image of Sinatra on the album cover—he looks like a man who's just been handed a parking ticket. However, the melody takes its cue from the title, utilizing a cyclical feeling, which is supported by the 3/4 time signature. What he's trying to tell us is that things may be bad, but this too shall pass—bad times don't last any longer than good times: it all comes and goes in cycles.* With Miller conducting, Ernest Hayes plays the prominent piano part, which is very much in the distinctive style of Nashville keyboard virtuoso Floyd Cramer.

"Wandering" is another worthy song about winding up back where you started, which Sinatra sings with a wide-eyed sense of wonder. Since both tracks are, in a sense, about the same thing, it would have made perfect

---

* Longtime Sinatra fan and friend Bill Boggs admits to a special fondness for "Cycles," which Sinatra continued to sing in his concerts into the 1970s. He tells a story about going to see a Sinatra show at the Garden State Arts Center in the summer of 1975 with a lady friend who had recently lost her job, and how they both found the song especially moving under the circumstances. Boggs sent a note to Sinatra to that effect. That Labor Day, Boggs spoke with the singer at the Jerry Lewis telethon, and Sinatra asked him, "How's your friend doing? The one who got fired?"

sense to begin the album with "Cycles" (the title song, after all) and end with "Wandering."

The biggest mistakes on the album are an inferior song, "My Way of Life," and a superior one, "Both Sides, Now"; the latter is a major missed opportunity. "My Way of Life" is the third Bert Kaempfert–Sinatra anthem; it's more overblown power balladry/German Sturm und Drang/true Eurotrash. It seems like a leftover from the Bowen-Freeman period, and it's precisely the same kind of big belter then in fashion, the kind of number that Dusty Springfield would sing. Elvis was much better at this sort of thing (i.e., "You Don't Have to Say You Love Me"). "Moody River" and "Pretty Colors" aren't great songs either, but at least they sound like they belong on the album.

Joni Mitchell's contemporary classic "Both Sides, Now" would have potentially been a great choice for Sinatra, but unfortunately he and Costa completely misread it in this 1968 recording. He approaches it like "Somethin' Stupid": quick and folksy and unpretentious, extremely sing-songy—a minor throwaway.* The song deserves better; in fact, when the composer herself returned to her song in 2000, she stretched it out and extracted a considerable amount of drama and wisdom—almost like a companion piece to "Send in the Clowns." Mitchell's own later middle-aged version was everything Sinatra's should have been but wasn't.

So far the score is two winners and two losers. There are three lesser-known songs here, "Rain in My Heart," "Moody River" and "Pretty Colors"; they're all rather insignificant, somewhere closer to bad than good. "Moody River" was a 1961 hit for Pat Boone; Costa seems to have been striving for a deliberately inappropriately cheerful arrangement for a rather dire song about a river that "took my baby's life." "Rain in My Heart" is more grandiose, power pop by Teddy Randazzo, composer of the hit "Goin' Out of My Head"; while "Pretty Colors," by folkster Chip Taylor (brother of Jon Voight), has an attractive hook. But overall, none is a good fit for Sinatra.

The remaining three songs were all huge pop/rock/folk hits in their day and are now considered classics, all three having been recorded by Glen Campbell, the session guitarist (who had played on several Sinatra dates) who by 1968 had become a hugely popular star singer by combining pop, rock, folk, and country. Bobby Russell's "Little Green Apples" is about sustaining commitment—keeping the music playing, as it were—while John Hartford's "Gentle on My Mind" (winner of four Grammy Awards) is about avoiding

---

* He also got the title wrong: for some reason the track is titled "From Both Sides, Now" on the *Cycles* album. Famously, Judy Collins had introduced the song on her 1967 album, *Wildflowers*, and Sinatra actually recorded his version before the composer recorded hers, on her 1969 album *Clouds*.

it and Jimmy Webb's "By the Time I Get to Phoenix" is about ending a relationship. As with "Both Sides, Now," they're all from well outside of Sinatra's
wheelhouse; but unlike the Joni Mitchell song, he goes out of his way to find
ways to make them all work for him.

He sings them all in the same sing-songy folk voice, with vastly understated dynamics. There are none of his usual range of louds and softs; he's
meeting the songs halfway between the way we expect them to be sung in this
era and Sinatra's more typical delivery. In "Little Green Apples" he revels in
the details of an ongoing marriage, "puppy dogs and autumn leaves and BB
guns," whereas in "Gentle on My Mind" he praises the woman of his dreams
for leaving her door open and her "path . . . free to walk," and not trying to
"shackle" him with "forgotten words and bonds." He sounds like a dog that
wants to run around in more than one yard, but he makes himself seem sympathetic just the same.

The underappreciated gem of the album might be "By the Time I Get
to Phoenix," one of several excellent songs Sinatra sang from the catalog of
Jimmy Webb. Sinatra approaches it like an Arizona torch song, an "Angel
Eyes" for a later era. And what makes it really remarkable is the compassion
he shows for the woman he's leaving behind: even though he knows that he
can't stay with her, he still seems to be showing more concern for her feelings
than he is for his own. That's perhaps the key strength of the song: he never
tells us why he's leaving, or what he's thinking; the only information he shares
with us is the way he imagines her day and, subsequently, her life will be like
without him. Much more than the bombastic "Strangers in the Night" or the
overdone "My Way," Jimmy Webb's song is about as close as we get in this era
to truly classic Frank.

The last session for *Cycles* was in November 1968; a few weeks later, on the
night before New Year's Eve, he recorded "My Way." It's not a particularly
good Sinatra record—there, I said it!—but it proved to be a career milestone
nonetheless. The implications of "My Way" wouldn't be fully realized until
the years following Sinatra's return from retirement, so we shall discuss it in
the next chapter. But the rest of the album, taped in February 1969 (after the
second batch of Sinatra-Jobim sessions in January) belongs to the immediate
preretirement period. And for the most part, *My Way* is as good an album as
it was possible for Sinatra to make in 1969.

As an album, *My Way* probably has more classic Frank music on it than
*Cycles*, but fewer chances are taken and less new ground is broken. Unlike
*Cycles*, or for that matter, *A Man Alone* and *Watertown*, it's a stretch to call *My
Way* a concept album; it's more like a hodgepodge of tracks clustered around

a hit single, in the manner of the *That's Life* and *The World We Knew* albums. *My Way* boasts several examples of what might be classified as "bonus tracks," i.e., the only major Brazilian song he ever sung apart from the Jobim projects ("Manhã de Carnaval" by Luiz Bonfá, already a huge international hit as a theme from 1959's *Black Orpheus* and known in English as "A Day in the Life of a Fool"), his first lyric by Rod McKuen (to Jacques Brel's "If You Go Away"), and the first of only two Beatles songs he would ever record (Paul McCartney's "Yesterday").

He also covers some "old ground" very rewardingly, specifically a new reading of "All My Tomorrows," the Cahn and Van Heusen main-credit theme for *A Hole in the Head*—one of Sinatra's best movie roles and movie songs. The 1969 reading is a full minute longer and ten years darker and deeper than the classic 1958 original; when Sinatra gets to the high note on the phrase "arms that *cling* at all," he makes that last word into an incredibly potent, not to mention *clinging*, verb in this heartfelt vocal.

"Didn't We" is probably the best of the four songs Sinatra recorded by Jimmy Webb—perhaps even better than "By the Time I Get to Phoenix." By 1969, Webb had developed a special technique for pitching his songs to stars of the Sinatra era, and to the Old Man himself in particular. "If I may say so, I used to be damn good at it," said Webb. "I didn't think of myself as much of a performer or a singer, but I did think that I was a hell of a pitcher! In fact, we used to deliberately sing songs in a kind of half-assed way, because we knew that the ego [not only of Sinatra but other stars who sang Webb's songs] we were dealing with was so huge, that their frustration level would build to the point that they would say 'Oh shut up! Let me sing this song! Just get out of here and leave me the lead sheet, I'll sing it!'" "Didn't We" illustrates both Webb's increasing maturity (he was only twenty-two when he wrote it in 1968) and shows just how well Sinatra could interpret a song from the contemporary era; Webb's music is equal parts pop, folk, and country, and Sinatra doesn't sing it like a musical genre but rather as a painfully slow torch song. He stretches a single chorus over three minutes, revealing his trust for the audience to take their time with him, and in his accompanist (probably Lou Levy),* for providing rock-solid yet unobtrusive support.

"All My Tomorrows" and "Didn't We" are the two major highlights of the album, the rest of which consists of worthy experiments, Sinatra assimilating the songs and, to a degree, the styles of the Beatles (on "Yesterday")

---

* The authoritative Sinatra discography *Put Your Dreams Away* by Luiz Carlos do Nascimento Silva (Greenwood Publishing Group, 2000) lists Costa as conductor for the session and both Bill Miller and Lou Levy as being present. From the sound of the piano, I would guess it's Levy playing, and Miller is likely conducting.

and Ray Charles ("Hallelujah I Love Her So"). Coincidentally, McCartney was also twenty-two when he wrote "Yesterday" in 1965. His rendition is also considerably slower than the famous string quartet version by the Fab Four; the fifty-three-year-old Sinatra sounds like he's got a great many more yesterdays behind him than the songwriter himself did. McCartney's yesterdays seem more vague and symbolic when he sings about them, compared to Sinatra's yesterdays, which are tangible and concrete—you can actually feel their weight. But then, that's what a great interpreter does.

Sinatra also goes after the Tony Bennett audiences on two Tony staples, "For Once in My Life" and "Watch What Happens"; I don't think either are up to Bennett's definitive versions (the first was also widely sung by soul stars of the era like Stevie Wonder), but they're both valid attempts. All the numbers associated with contemporary pop acts—the Beatles, Ray Charles, and Simon and Garfunkel, on "Mrs. Robinson"—find Sinatra trying to make peace with the younger generation, trying to see what works from the music of the era that he can use to make himself "feel at home" (as Paul Simon's lyrics go).

"Mrs. Robinson," the pop classic introduced in *The Graduate*, is a special case. Sinatra's and Costa's inspiration may well have been Ella Fitzgerald, who had set a precedent for swinging contemporary numbers like the Beatles' "Can't Buy Me Love" and "Savoy Truffle." She sang the latter, in particular, like scatty nonsense, in the approximate tradition of her classic improvisatory extravaganzas like "Flying Home" and "How High the Moon." Sinatra and Costa seem to be aspiring for a similar vibe here, but "Mrs. Robinson" is a curious song to use as a starting point: the lyrics strike a crucial salvo in the war of the generations, in which the twenty-three-year-old Simon fires a shot at the establishment by turning meaningless bureaucratic clichés into anarchic nonsense lyrics: "We'd like to know a little bit about you for our files / We'd like to help you learn to help yourself." In other words, Simon is telling us, all of it is just so much "yeah, yeah, yeah," typical of the gobbledygook spouted by the older generation. Simon says as much in the line, "Where have you gone, Joe DiMaggio?" which seems to imply that the former gods and idols of our parents' era are no longer around to help us. Lord only knows what Sinatra thought, especially since DiMaggio had been a close friend of his. If Simon is sticking it to the older generation, Sinatra is himself zinging Simon back by turning it into a 4/4 swing number set in a Basie template and with a lusty tenor solo, probably by Nino Tempo. Where Simon is irreverent, Sinatra is even more so—especially when, in Simon's famous reference to Jesus in the second line, Sinatra substitutes the name of his most famous lieutenant and aide-de-camp, Jilly Rizzo. "Here's to you, Mrs. Robinson, Jilly loves you more than you will know." Bam! You got served.

Was *My Way* a "concept album"? It's difficult to say; the songs don't have anything to do with each other, except that virtually all of them were already very well known to record buyers of both generations in 1969. It could be that Sinatra's implicit concept was, "I know you've heard all these songs before, but now you're going to hear them my way." But there's no ambiguity in Sinatra's next two albums, both also recorded in 1969 (a surprisingly busy year for the Chairman), *A Man Alone* and *Watertown*: they are perhaps the most clearly-defined "concept" albums that Sinatra ever created.

Those two albums are also the defining parameters of what we might call "alt-Sinatra" music, which is to say that the vast rank and file of casual and even very committed Sinatra buffs don't care for them—they're not high on anybody's list. But they are increasingly appreciated by new generations of more eclectic listeners; in 2017, there is even an entire website devoted to *Watertown*. They are what we might call "cult albums," although in this case, I prefer the term "alt-Sinatra." (The most extreme example of this is, infamously, *The Future*, the third disc of *Trilogy*, and even that has its defenders and champions.)

First, a thought or two about what a "concept" album is. Sometimes Sinatra's classic albums like *In the Wee Small Hours* and *Songs for Swingin' Lovers!* are described as "concept albums" even though they're not driven by programmatic concept so much as mood and tempo. *Moonlight Sinatra*, in which all the songs have the same subject matter, might come closer to an actual concept album according to some definitions. But in the wake of *Sgt. Pepper's Lonely Hearts Club Band, Pet Sounds, The Dark Side of the Moon, What's Going On*, and the other breakthrough rock-pop albums of the late 1960s and early '70s, the term was increasingly understood to refer to albums that were conceived and composed from the ground up, with entirely original words and music, as programmatic packages. In that definition, the first ever concept album was Gordon Jenkins's 1946 *Manhattan Tower*, and there were precious few until twenty years later. (A notable exception being Duke Ellington, whose many extended works—his famous "suites"—all double as true jazz concept albums.)

Sinatra recorded the album *A Man Alone* over three sessions in March 1969, but the album had its roots in a meeting four years earlier. In a video interview taped a few years before his death in 2015, poet-singer-songwriter Rod McKuen said that he and Sinatra first met in 1965. It's also reported that they met through Bennett Cerf, the legendary publisher, writer, television game show celebrity, and humorist, who was also the major literary figure in Sinatra's circle. Cerf, like a lot of Sinatra's old friends from New York, had been among the guests at Sinatra's Manhattan recording sessions in 1967–68 (for parts of *The World We Knew* and *Cycles*) and he invited Sinatra to a birthday party for McKuen in April 1968. (Of course, that could have also been a second meeting.)

However McKuen and Sinatra first met, or however Sinatra first discovered McKuen's work, the direct template for *A Man Alone* was *The Lonely Things*, by the folksinger Glenn Yarbrough.* Like *A Man Alone*, this 1966 RCA album consisted of a solo male vocalist doing a combination of songs and spoken poetry recitations, all on top of a string background—in Yarbrough's case, arranged and conducted by Mort Garson. However, *A Man Alone* is three years later and three years better; Sinatra is clearly the more compelling and dynamic performer (not to take anything away from Yarbrough, who was a major force in the folk music world, both as a key member of the Limeliters and in his five-decade-long solo career), and McKuen's 1969 songs are better as well, as are Costa's arrangements. Then too, they all had learned more about how to put an album together by then. The 1969 record is much more clearly focused, with a stronger narrative, as evidenced by such touches as the way that *A Man Alone* ends with a reprise of the title song, which makes us feel more like we've been listening to a coherent story rather than just a random collection of lyrics and poetry.

As McKuen told Leonard Feather (around the time of *A Man Alone*), "I had tried for years to reach Frank; wrote songs with him in mind, but could never get to him." The first McKuen lyric that Sinatra sang was his adaptation of "If You Go Away" by the iconic French singer-songwriter Jacques Brel, on the *My Way* album, and it seems likely that he and McKuen and Costa were already planning the *Man Alone* album by that point. McKuen continued, "When we finally met, instead of just offering to do just one or two [of my songs], he promised me an entire album, which he'd never done before for any other composer. It was incredible."

Incredible indeed. To the cynical (including myself at one point), it may seem like Sinatra was drawn to the work of Rod McKuen for purely economic reasons. In the *Laugh-In* era, McKuen had established himself as the most pecuniarily successful poet-songwriter of all time: three books of his poetry had sold a million copies by 1968, plus two million LPs of those verses spoken and sung in that year. It won't do to chalk his success purely to Herculean promotional skills, both his own and that of his publisher; whatever one thinks of his work, there's no arguing that McKuen perfectly captured the zeitgeist of the era. The sheer numbers of his success prove that it wasn't just the flower children (and would-be flower children) who supported his

---

* Thanks to Chuck Granata for bringing this album to my attention.

work, but older generations as well. Naturally, Sinatra wanted to grab a piece of that action, but like Miles Davis's increasing immersion in electronic and rock-oriented music at precisely the same time, there was more to it than that. He was still looking for the perfect market fit, as they say, between what he could sing comfortably and what could sell.

The anticipated outcome was that "Sinatra + McKuen = blockbuster," a logical summation, considering that "Somethin' Stupid" was a number-one hit for Sinatra only two years earlier (admittedly, those two years made quite a bit of difference) and that McKuen's own books and albums were also selling in huge quantities. And after all, this had been the basic logic that worked out so successfully for the Sinatra-Basie and Sinatra-Jobim collaborations. Yet in terms of sales, *A Man Alone* wasn't eagerly snatched up by fans of Sinatra or McKuen. A few Frank followers appreciated it right away, but for the great majority it took a while for the album to grow on us.*

The three most salient factors of the album are McKuen's songs, the very different style of singing that Sinatra affected for them, and Costa's arrangements. In all of these aspects, the album might well have been titled *A Man in Transition* or *A Man Caught Between Two Worlds*. In the broad outline of his career, McKuen, like Jimmy Webb, was a transitional figure between what Webb would describe as a "pure songwriter" (a term that Jimmy uses to characterize most pre-1964 songwriters, from Rodgers and Hart to the Brill Building) and the singer-songwriter era. McKuen was a part of the era of brand-name maestros like Henry Mancini and Burt Bacharach—musical auteurs who were better as songwriters than singers, but still name-above-the-title celebrities, unlike, say, Sammy Cahn and Jimmy Van Heusen (from the era when most songwriters were completely anonymous). No less than Dylan and Lennon and McCartney, writer-performers such as Webb, Bacharach, and McKuen helped usher in the era when songwriters like James Taylor and Joni Mitchell, not to mention Michael Jackson and Prince, would be superstars.

McKuen's music also seems completely congruent with more traditional forms of pop as well as the folk music movement, which had been completely

---

* One Frank fan, Burton Kittay of Texas, met McKuen at an AIDS benefit late in the poet's life. "I told him, 'Mr. McKuen, I am a Sinatra lover.' He turned around and I said that of all of Sinatra's recordings, my favorite without question is *A Man Alone*. He started to cry and walked over and said 'That is the nicest thing anyone has ever said to me in my life. Can I give you a hug?'" Granted that this is a rather extreme opinion, but it illustrates the degree to which the album has risen in the general estimation. At the time of Sinatra's death, most Sinatra fans could barely tolerate it; in 2016, I'm no longer surprised to learn that some actually consider it their favorite.

upended when Bob Dylan made the jump from singing traditional folk songs to writing new ones in the same style. So too is Sinatra's singing: his softer vocals here (again, a complete turnabout from the harsher, more aggressive style of "That's Life") are a direct extension of the Jobim sessions, "Somethin' Stupid," and *Cycles*. As you may recall, he likened that style of singing to having laryngitis, but it was a valid attempt to modulate his music for a new era, much as he had changed in going from the 1940s to the 1950s. Costa's arrangements also split the difference between a more traditional Sinatra sound and that of the classier, more purely musical pop acts of the day, like, say, the Carpenters or even the later works of the Beatles, who were still together as a band in 1969. There's even a lovely pure instrumental, following the recitation of "Out Beyond the Window," a rare moment on a Sinatra album that just doesn't need words.

*A Man Alone* (and, as we'll see, *Watertown*) have both grown in reputation over the years; in listening to it in 2017, I fail to see what I found so objectionable in 1991. Nearly all of the songs are lovely, and at least two (or maybe even three), are first-rate Frank. The album is a success at the very least for the title song, "A Man Alone"; "The Single Man"; "Lonesome Cities"; and, especially, the album's best-known song, "Love's Been Good to Me." The recurring theme of the album is loneliness. In songs like "In the Wee Small Hours" or "One for My Baby," Sinatra seems to be dealing with the immediate aftermath of a relationship, i.e., what do you do the morning, or even the next few hours, after the gal that got away gets away? In other words, short-term loneliness. McKuen's songs deal with loneliness and the solitary state as a long-term proposition. Ironically, even though Sinatra and McKuen were both trying to appeal to the youth market, he sings with the pervasive outlook of a middle-aged man.

One of Sinatra's greatest fears was being alone; he preferred to be in the company of an entourage, his friends, his longtime valet and companion George Jacobs, and women. Don't forget that Sinatra created the Rat Pack, the first pop music supergroup, and that Elvis deliberately modeled his Memphis Mafia in the image of what he imagined Sinatra's posse to be like. Yet throughout *A Man Alone*, Sinatra completely convinces us that he has accepted loneliness not just as a temporary condition—an interlude between broads—but rather as a lifestyle. And for Sinatra, of all people, to be able to do that, is remarkable; in fact, it's probably the very last thing we ever expected from him.

He sets the ground rules with "A Man Alone," and throughout, McKuen's songs allow Sinatra to create those emotional gradations, the many emotional shades, the microtonal points of feeling that he had already pinpointed so brilliantly in his interpretations of Cole Porter and the Gershwins. "The Beautiful Strangers" and "Love's Been Good to Me" are an old stud's warm, nostalgic recollections of all the girls he's loved before—yet he sings of them so warmly and affectionately that we have to step back a bit to see, in perspective, that some might describe these relationships as one-night stands, or, as they say on Tinder, hookups. "Love's Been Good to Me" is an extraordinary song, much like Ervin Drake's "It Was a Very Good Year" that uses a form derived from traditional folk music, including an ABABAB melodic structure. In "Very Good Year," Sinatra actually makes us believe that he had been a small-town boy in pursuit of small-town girls; here Sinatra makes McKuen's passing reference to "October Hill" sound like a real place, or an incredibly vital symbol of one. Listening to him, you feel like *you* used to go a-courtin' along October Hill as well.

The poetry readings aren't quite as successful; there are times when one's reaction echoes that of that imminent scholar, Walter Burns (in *The Front Page*), "Tell him his poetry stinks and kick him down the stairs!" And yet there are moments when it works. "Empty Is" progresses very nicely from spoken (poetry) intro to sung (main chorus), and "Out Beyond the Window" finds Sinatra—or rather this incarnation of Sinatra—and McKuen perfectly on the same page. "Some Traveling Music," referencing a phrase from the sainted philosopher Jackie Gleason, finds McKuen putting thoughts in his mouth that Sinatra might have actually thought. ("One day, I'm gonna find me an island, a think place / Go there with a mess of records and a ukulele. / Just sit strumming, I might even do some thinking.") Where Mike Shore, in the famous 1963 *Playboy* interview, served as Sinatra's ghostwriter, McKuen has here become his ghostthinker—it's not a stretch at all to imagine Sinatra saying these things to himself.

One collateral benefit from the project was that Sinatra incorporated parts of *A Man Alone* into his 1969 television special, the fifth and last of his annual "Man and His Music" shows, titled simply *Sinatra*. Sinatra had included a ballad segment in all five shows, and the 1969 one is a stunner. Presented as a lonely man in an apartment (it looks like a soap opera set) and a turtleneck sweater, he begins with the spoken words of "Out Beyond the Window" (the best of McKuen's poems on the album), then sings "A Man Alone," which leads to Webb's beautiful "Didn't We" and Teddy Randazzo's "Forget to Remember," which Sinatra had recorded as a memorable single and is here elevated by the company it keeps. This is exactly what Sinatra was going for: a sequence of songs that's at once classic and contemporary.

*A Man Alone* ends with a reprise of the title song that states the whole premise of the album ("Never talk to strangers, someone might be kind / And muddle up your mind") even more successfully than the opener, and caps the whole project brilliantly. To my surprise, in 2017, I find myself wishing that Sinatra had sung more songs by McKuen.

If it's difficult to picture Sinatra as a moody, philosophical loner, it's even tougher to imagine him as a small-town father, trying to raise his two sons by himself in the wake of his wife's departure, while at the same time working through his feelings over her. It's the kind of a notion that one would expect to find in one of Sinatra's dramatic films (as opposed to his movie musicals), although even there it was more customary to find Sinatra as a soldier, a detective, or even a cowboy—nothing so mundane as a divorced dad.

Even more than *A Man Alone*, *Watertown* is a true rock-'n'-roll–era concept album, even more so, perhaps, than *Sgt. Pepper* or *Pet Sounds*. While the mid-1960s albums of Bob Dylan and the Beatles are certainly all-original, it's debatable to what point they too can be described as concept albums, since relatively few try to sustain a consistent mood and even fewer tell a coherent story from beginning to end. (And certainly none of these were as ambitious as Jenkins *Manhattan Tower*.)

By the end of the 1960s, pop and rock stars had found a common concept that was inspiring most of their songwriting: social protest and commentary, a carryover from the folk music boom of the early 1960s. There were legitimate things to protest about: the war in Vietnam, civil rights for minorities (as well as women), and, soon enough, pollution and the environment, even if a lot of the songs of the period sound like kids whining about their parents and complaining about the older generation in general. The poetic anarchy of many Dylan lyrics from the period (i.e., "Subterranean Homesick Blues") was understood to be its own kind of social protest, but there were literal societal objections as well.

Released in January 1969, *The Genuine Imitation Life Gazette* was a major departure for the Four Seasons. At the start of the group's career, in 1962–64, when they were continually on the singles charts, they were one of the more family-friendly rock acts, the last of the great doo-wop quartets. It was clear that lead singer Frankie Valli was steeped in the old school, that he owed as much to Sinatra as to Elvis; the group even recorded "I Can't Give You Anything but Love" in homage to the Fats Waller disciple Rose Murphy. With their indisputable musicianship—the solid songwriting and Valli's indisputable technical vocal skill—one can't imagine anybody's parents getting annoyed at their kids for listening to the Four Seasons.

Thus *Imitation Life Gazette* was a formidable turnaround; it begins with "American Crucifixion Resurrection"—a far cry, no pun intended, from "Big

Girls Don't Cry." All ten songs were, if not a full protest, a genuine social statement offering criticisms or observations regarding contemporary mores. There was even a song called "Saturday's Father," all about little girls and their divorcé dads. ("See him always smiling, full of games to play / Fun to have a daddy every Saturday.") The album, notably, was not a hit—Four Seasons fans didn't flock to it—but people noticed; both Harry Belafonte and folksinger Chad Mitchell recorded the title song. (The Four Seasons' version incorporates a background vocal chant that sounds exactly like that on the Beatles' "Hey Jude," although it's difficult to ascertain which one was released first.)

By 1969, there had evolved such a distinct thing as rock concerts. Live performances from earlier in music's history were more like the old movie theater "stage shows" of the big-band era. Even the Beatles shared their live appearances with other bands, rarely playing more than a thirty- to forty-minute set. But longer concerts by individual bands led to something more like concert music, much as Paul Whiteman had begun to conceive jazz-influenced "concert music" forty years earlier. In 1969, the Who's *Tommy* was perhaps the first work to be dubbed a "rock opera" (although there haven't been many since), and certainly the first widely successful rock/pop work to tell a single story over the course of an entire album; even more ambitiously, it was a double album. *Tommy* was released a month before the recording of *Watertown*, thus it probably wasn't a direct influence; but the notion of using pop music to convey more complex narratives and ideas was definitely in the wind. *Tommy* was successful enough to be adapted into a film and a Broadway musical, and was a half step away from works like Andrew Lloyd Webber's 1970 *Jesus Christ Superstar*, which seems to have been conceived from the get-go for all three media: rock concept album/musical theater piece/ movie. (Webber followed it with *Evita* in 1976.)

Thus it appeared that two disparate sets of interests were coalescing on a single point. Sinatra was looking for a way to reach the younger g-g-generation and still be true to himself, while the singer-songwriters of that era, such as Bob Gaudio of the Four Seasons, were trying to find ways to bring their music up to the next level—the same level where Sinatra had already dwelt for decades. If the number one Season was Frankie Valli, whose distinctive, piercing falsetto gave the group its distinctive musical muscle, number two was Gaudio, who wrote most of the quartet's hits. As the other Seasons came and went, the lynchpin of the group was always Valli and Gaudio; they were even more the fundamental core of the band than Lennon and McCartney were of the Beatles.

There were two other two major contributors to the *Watertown* project: Jake Holmes had come up during the coffeehouse era, and had also been a comedian (at a time when folk groups like the Limeliters and the Smothers Brothers brought comedy and folk music together) in a trio called Jim, Jake, and Joan, in which the latter was the equally young Joan Rivers. He attracted some attention with his debut album, *"The Above Ground Sound" of Jake Holmes* (1967), which included his two most famous songs, "Genuine Imitation Life" (the one that led to the Four Seasons album) and "Dazed and Confused," which famously inspired a similar song by Led Zeppelin. (Whether it was inspiration or plagiarism is a dispute that continues to daze and confuse the United States legal system.) Charles Calello was a bassist, vocalist, composer, and arranger who had been part of Valli and Gaudio's inner circle since the early 1960s: he had been a member of Valli's earlier group, the Four Lovers, and later rejoined the Four Seasons as bassist and vocalist. For Gaudio and Calello, especially, it was an honor to work with Sinatra, who had long been held up as a symbol of Italian-American achievement, and not just among Jersey Boys.

Valli was not directly involved in *Watertown* except in one key way: it might not have ever happened had it not been for him. In fact, the genesis of *Watertown* begins with Valli, who, as Calello described him, "had this uncanny ability . . . or the balls, really, to go up to and talk to anybody. But anyway, Frankie had a lot of confidence in my ability, and he also had a lot of confidence in Gaudio's ability. So he told Sinatra they had all these hit records because Bob Gaudio wrote and produced all their songs. And Sinatra said, 'Well, could he write some songs for me?'"

The story of their initial meeting—when Valli introduced Sinatra to Gaudio and Holmes—is at least as entertaining as anything on the album. In July 1969, the four of them had lunch at the Waldorf, where Sinatra was staying; at the end of the meeting, Gaudio invited Sinatra to his home in Jersey for a pool party the following weekend. Sinatra said he'd love to, and walked off, at which point Valli reminded Gaudio that he had just moved and that his new house did not, in fact, currently have a pool. Rather than disappoint the Chairman, they proceded to call every contracting *paisano* in Jersey and somehow managed to get a swimming pool installed within seven days. Or so they thought; there was a long storm in the days leading up to the party that not only made swimming a moot point but nearly destroyed the semiconstructed pool. Sinatra signed his name in the still-wet concrete, as if it were Grauman's Chinese Theatre; later, when Gaudio moved, he ripped out the 110-pound slab of cement and carried it with him.

Gaudio and Holmes went to work writing songs for Sinatra. Calello said, "I think they wrote about four songs, and Sinatra liked them. And then Gaudio laid on him the concept of doing it as the *Watertown* album." Eventually Gaudio came up with the idea of putting Sinatra "in a small town"; as the songwriter told Frankophile Ed O'Brien, "having a small-town approach and taking it down as much as we could to basic life in middle America." Gaudio also recalled that Sinatra initially thought the team was merely preparing an album's worth of individual songs for him; he didn't realize until he heard all the demos that he was getting a concept album, with a coherent narrative that flowed from start to finish.

Gaudio had gotten to know Sinatra personally some months earlier by hanging out with him for a few weeks between shows in Las Vegas; but Calello, who was conducting, did not meet him until the first session. "Came the night of the date, he was supposed to be there at seven o'clock. Three minutes after seven, the orchestra is playing, and Frank walks in the back door. As he walked in, I felt the air in the studio change—evidently the musicians caught him walking in because they started to play with an entirely different intensity. My back was to him, so he walked towards the orchestra as I was conducting on the podium. He taps me on the leg, because I was elevated, and says, 'You Calello?' [I] turned around to go shake hands with him and say hello, but nothing came out of my mouth. Literally, nothing came out, I was so intimidated!"

The orchestra laid down tracks for eleven numbers over four dates in New York (longtime NYC studio reed maven Phil Bodner is unmistakable on the title song) in July 1969; it's not known how many of them Sinatra recorded vocals for at this time. He felt he could do better in terms of his singing, and not wanting to hang around the East Coast (Calello remembers somebody was trying to serve him with some papers at the time), he decided to overdub new vocal tracks in Los Angeles. "He didn't know the songs well enough," said Calello. "One of the things I found out about working with him is that it took him a long time to learn a song. But I had spoken to Sammy Cahn about that. I asked him, 'How long does it take you to teach a song to Sinatra?' He said, 'Well, Frank doesn't like to speed-learn a song. He takes his time so he can really get it, to appreciate the value of the song. Sometimes it takes him a good week before he gets it under his belt.' So for him to learn all originals for a new album was a major task." Along the way Gaudio substantially remixed the orchestrations from the original tracks taken down by engineer Frank Laico; Sinatra also produced his own backings to several verses, employing Al Viola and his acoustic guitar.

*Sgt. Pepper*, undisputedly the touchstone concept album of the rock epoch, had been a collection of whimsical psychedelia, while other famous thematic packages, such as the Who's *Tommy* and, later, Pink Floyd's *The Wall*, addressed the issue of adolescent alienation. Sinatra's "rock concept" set deals with more mature themes; while the songs never spell out a crystal-clear narrative, the lyrics repeatedly suggest such issues as divorce in a small town, custody of the children, and a man and woman who grow up together only to grow apart. The cover artwork, depicting a train station where much of the action (such as it is) transpires, as well as a montage of marriage memorabilia (a photo album, anniversary cards, dolls) on the inside of the gatefold, delineates at least as much of the narrative as the texts. (For that matter, so does an inserted poster that shows a 1960s-casual Sinatra in a windbreaker, standing by those selfsame railroad tracks.) Overall, the mood is halfway between the Beatles' "She's Leaving Home" and virtually every country-western song ever written. In both attitude and its Costa-like orchestrations ("I was always a fan of Don's," said Calello. "Don was my all-time favorite."), *Watertown* could be called *By the Time I Get to Phoenix: The Album.*

Many issues are at play in *Watertown.* The standard mode of most music-driven storytelling, such as opera and musical theater, had long been established: convey the specific action itself in spoken dialogue, but then use music to depict the characters' reactions to the plot developments; for all the murders and suicides committed in grand opera, very little of the action is carried by the music itself. Even in the more serious works of American musical theater, Pore Jud doesn't attack Curley in a middle of a song and Billy Bigelow doesn't fall on his knife as he's about to hit a low F. Most numbers in contemporary Broadway shows aren't necessarily about communication between characters but about revealing their inner lives to the audience. Operatic arias, show tunes, and even rock 'n' roll power ballads are for the contemplation of plot developments, the reaction rather than the action. It makes sense that twenty-first century honks like *Spring Awakening, American Psycho*, and especially *Hamilton* have had to essentially devise an unconventional musical style all their own, the same as Gershwin and Sondheim had done, decades earlier, in *Porgy and Bess* and *Sweeney Todd.*

And this too is what Gaudio and Holmes did for Sinatra in *Watertown.* It doesn't sound like anything Holmes or the Four Seasons had done previously, and it certainly doesn't sound like anything from Sinatra's history—and certainly not like the rock-oriented projects he had undertook with either Bowen or Costa. *Watertown* is something very new for everybody—and in many ways, it's more like *Hamilton* or *Sweeney Todd* than it is like *In the Wee Small Hours, A Man Alone,* or even *The Genuine Imitation Life Gazette.*

The musical language of *Watertown* is unique: it follows the structure of some of the more adventurous rock writing, away from either the AABA form of most Sinatra songs or the ABAB of most folk music. And there is a genuine attempt to tell the whole story, all the dramatic action, in words and music. And yet it's different too, from *Tommy* or *Jesus Christ Superstar*, in that it's all told through the eyes of a single character and a single performer. (In other words, not like a contemporary one-man show where a single actor might play several roles, like Terry Teachout's *Satchmo at the Waldorf* or Alan Cumming's one-man *Macbeth*.) Barbra Streisand found her own way to this format in the 1983 film *Yentl*, a movie musical with a large cast but in which the only singing (thinking in words and music) is done by Streisand's central character.

*Watertown* opens with the title song, which sets the scene: a small town where "no one's goin' anywhere / Livin's much too easy there." It's an affectionate though hardly laudatory portrait of the place, with no specific characters or relationships indicated. At one point, there were vague plans to develop the work into a television special (or made-for-TV movie), and Holmes told O'Brien that this would have been heard behind the main titles and presumably the opening shot, a pan down the main streets of the town in question.

However, the next song, "Goodbye (She Quietly Says)," takes us right into the heart of the story. As recounted by the Sinatra character after the fact, he tells us how he and his wife were eating in a coffee shop when she quietly and suddenly said goodbye. We are never told explicitly why; it's left to us to infer that it's because she's just tired of life in this tank town. What's ingenious in this scene is that the lede, as we say in journalism, is deliberately buried. The team conveys the action very subtly, as the lyrics describe the scene ("There is no string ensemble / and she doesn't even cry"). We're kind of awestruck by the way such a devastating piece of news can be delivered without opera or Broadway theatrics.

And scene.

First scene: establishing the setting; second scene: action. Most of the rest of the work is contemplation and reflection, bringing us closer to the world of *In the Wee Small Hours* and *A Man Alone*. He continues to refer to his departed wife in the second person (i.e., addressing her as "you"), indicating that he's talking directly to her, although in some cases it's understood that this is merely in his own head. The third song, "For a While," is all about how life is fine, sometimes for long stretches here and there, until he stops and remembers how devastated he is.

The fourth track, "Michael & Peter," is an exceptional slice of musical storytelling that is sometimes considered the highlight of the work. It's written in the form of what we are led to believe is a letter from the man to the departed wife—the musical equivalent of an epistolary novel—and should be divided into two distinct songs. The first is talking about their two boys, and which one takes after which parent. ("Michael is you, he has your face / he still has your eyes. . . . Peter is me, 'cept when he smiles.") Then the tempo shifts gears and the letter continues, talking about other subjects and conveying that some time has passed. ("This spring we had some heavy rain / by summer it was dry again.")

"I Would Be in Love (Anyway)" has our hero thinking to himself, but still addressing the departed "her" as "you." It's a very sweet song, full of admirable and well-expressed sentiment ("If I knew that you'd leave me, / if I knew you wouldn't stay, / I would be in love anyway.") This is the most Frankish vocal on the work, with Sinatra using his famous dynamics, his loud louds and soft softs, that were such an influence on so many singers (especially Tony Bennett), his voice rising and surging on exactly the right dramatic moment (in a way that was also a major influence, especially on Sammy Davis Jr.).

Side two begins with "Elizabeth," more contemplation and very lovely, this time identifying his wandering wife by her first name. By now there has been a lot of contemplation in proportion to a relatively small amount of action, but it isn't over yet. "What A Funny Girl (You Used to Be)" is reflection in the form of a flashback, describing the wife as a little girl, thus showing us indirectly that these two small-town lovers go back a long time together. "What's Now Is Now" brings the contemplation back up to the present day; Holmes said that this is where he hints that she left because "somebody else" was in the picture, but again it's highly cryptic and understated.

After a lot of contemplation, we finally get some action, but again the lede has been buried. "She Says" is a deliberately bizarre and unsettling track—talk about being dazed and confused—delivered in parlando, very close to spoken word. We hear what sounds like a Japanese samisen (a stringed instrument that resembles a banjo, sonically, but this might be guitarist Vinnie Bell playing what Gaudio has identified as a *bellzouki*) and a combination of flute and repercussive percussion reminiscent of Ennio Morricone's spaghetti western themes. While a children's choir also participates, this is far from "High Hopes"—you could call it "Low Hopes." But it's here, finally, that we get a response from the wife, apparently in the form of a letter. (At long last he refers to her as "she" rather than "you.") It builds to a quiet, but dramatic conclusion: "She says / She's coming home."

It's hard not to be moved by the final track, "The Train"; yet Holmes and Gaudio refuse to let us enjoy a conventional happy ending. Our hero is standing on the platform, waiting for her train to arrive (in the rain no less, as if it were a country song), and thinking how happy he's going to be when she gets there. Spoiler alert: "The train is slowly moving on / But I can't see you anyplace / And I know for sure I'd recognize your face." Which is more disturbing: the idea that she might not have come at all, or that she's been gone so long that he might not remember what she looks like? (He even repeats to himself, "And I know for sure I'd recognize your face.") Holmes has said that, in his intention, this means what it sounds like, that she's never coming home. But to me, the ending is up for grabs—sometimes when I listen to it, there seems to be a chance that she's there but he hasn't spotted her yet. Or that she missed this train (she's always catching colds and missing trains) but is on the next one. Or something. The point is that the ending is ambiguous. But still, it is an ending.

And curtain.

Whatever we think of *Watertown*, nearly fifty years after the fact, the most salient point regarding the album was that it was not, by any commercial standard, a success—though that could at least partially be blamed on the failure of Warner Bros. Records, which now owned Reprise, to sufficiently advertise and promote the album. Several of the individual numbers were issued on 45s and at least two dented the *Billboard* Adult Contemporary charts: "What's Now is Now" reached number thirty-one and "I Would Be in Love (Anyway)" made it all the way to number four. For an industry leader such as Sinatra, this was indeed a disappointing result. This was the last of the major Sinatra albums to make it to CD: it wasn't heard in the digital era until very late in Sinatra's life, in 1994.

One collateral benefit from the project is the song "Lady Day," originally written by Gaudio and Holmes for the *Watertown* suite. Sinatra eventually decided the number would make an interesting tribute to Billie Holiday, even though that was not what the authors had intended. "Gaudio didn't know they referred to Billie Holiday as Lady Day," said Calello. "It was a coincidence, because Gaudio was not a jazz lover, and he didn't really know who Billie Holiday was." Sinatra rerecorded "Lady Day" a few months later with a more opulent orchestration by Don Costa, and it eventually wound up on the *Sinatra & Company* package.

Some of *Watertown* is beautiful, but its overall problem is that for a narrative work, there isn't much narrative. The story suffers from a distinct and deliberate lack of dramatic incident; in this it hardly compares to *Superstar* or *Tommy*. Gaudio and Holmes created a scenario that is ultrarealistic, perhaps to a fault; and, as in reality, nothing much happens. In the opinion of many, that's a good thing, it makes the whole piece more true to life, especially since it's bereft not only of a happy ending but even a clear-cut, easily understandable conclusion. It would likely have made a very dull television special, eminently believable but not very interesting. It doesn't help that Sinatra was not in his best voice; he sounds somewhat strained in spots, even though the instrumental tracks were recorded first (in New York) and Sinatra had all the time he wanted to add his vocal parts. Still, the songwriters might have felt that his relatively rough-sounding voice (by Sinatra standards) contributed to the anguished sound of the character and enhanced the work. Ultimately, *Watertown* is a fascinating work of art, albeit a flawed one.

In 1985, Sinatra was attacked—that's the only word for it—by cartoonist Garry Trudeau in the comic strip *Doonesbury*. In the larger context of the Sinatra Saga, Trudeau seems hopelessly naive, in that he regarded it as despicable and heinous that the singer's company was sought out both by presidents (as in presidents of these United States) and mob bosses, and that Sinatra didn't shirk from either association. Sinatra himself was dumbfounded by the cartoons; that was, after all, the way it had always been. As he had learned growing up in the shadow of his mother in Prohibition-era Hoboken, politics and organized crime were not flipsides of the same coin, but rather they both resided side by side on the same side of that coin.

Trudeau could have even more easily gone after Sinatra in 1971–72. Within a span of about fourteen months, he was presented with the Jean Hersholt Humanitarian Award, at the forty-third annual Academy Awards ceremony (handed to him by friend Gregory Peck), yet before he knew it, he was flying to Washington to appear before the House Select Committee on Organized Crime. Trudeau would not have been alone in finding it inconceivable that anyone could be heralded as a great humanitarian (which indeed he was) while at the same time being called upon to discuss his alleged connection to the Mafia.

Both of those events received massive media attention in those years, and so did a statement Sinatra issued on March 23, 1971: "I wish to announce, effective immediately, my retirement from the entertainment world and public life." The era would end as it had begun, with silence, only a greater and longer one. Twelve years earlier, when he was forming Reprise Records, he had begun with a one-man strike against Capitol, refusing to enter a studio until they could come to terms; this time, he announced, he was through with performing altogether.

Sinatra acted like he didn't know how to cope with a changing world. In interviews, he railed against the "protestations" of young people marching in opposition to the "establishment." No one seems to have realized that the major cultural sea change had already come and gone, that the onetime counterculture now was the establishment; by 1971, Sinatra was now the guy fighting the status quo, or, in the parlance of a still-later generation, raging against the machine. Yet he was unable to process this new topsy-turvy reality in which he was no longer the mainstream, he was now the niche—albeit a gigantic one. In 1971, Sinatra was where, say, Pete Seeger had been twenty years earlier. "Sinatra music," as Jimmy Bowen calls it, had assumed the position of an alternative expression, guys in long hair and bell-bottoms, playing guitars and shouting had become the mainstream.

Disenchanted with the dissipated Camelot he had helped create, Sinatra began a gradual switch to the GOP (that's the way things go), embracing Nixon, Agnew, and Reagan—a serious turnaround for one who had once pledged allegiance to the Roosevelts and even the highly "progressive" Henry Wallace. At least one part of his audience suspected that this was strictly for shock value; in 1945, as the political landscape was growing ever more conservative, Sinatra was at his most liberal, preaching tolerance and civil rights. Twenty-five years later, when he wanted desperately to reach the kids who were marching on the campuses, he perversely rebelled against the rebellion. He was just as determined to upset the apple carts of those who thought they could predict his next move as he had been when he made waves in the Truman years.

And he was not only physically tired, he was mentally exhausted from what now seemed like this unending search for the hook, the Shangri-La–like balance between artistry and marketability. It came so easy to him all the way up to the mid-1960s that he never even bothered to think about it. Now it seemed to be beyond his grasp.

What was left for him? Nightclubs were closing and changing—the 500 Club, the Copacabana, the Persian Room—and the live music biz was heading in a whole new direction (one whose implications he would fully fathom later on). He also burned several bridges in Las Vegas, getting into a tiff (talk about an understatement) with a casino manager at Caesars Palace that left him vowing never to return to Nevada. He also seemed to have lost his mojo where television was concerned, and let his generally brilliant *Man and His Music* specials end with the fifth installment in 1969; there was no Sinatra special in 1970. (Perhaps that was what *Watertown* was supposed to have been.) His film work had also been increasingly marginal: there were only two truly classic movies in all of the 1960s, the politically infused dramatic thriller *The Manchurian Candidate* (1962), and the musical comedy *Robin and the 7 Hoods* (1964). (The latter is admittedly more of a fan favorite than a critic's choice, perhaps.)

And yet, looking at Sinatra's recorded work from the perspective of the next century, the well seems to be far from dry in this period. Remarkably, 1969 was one of his all-time most productive years: between *My Way*, *A Man Alone*, *Watertown*, and the second Sinatra-Jobim album, Sinatra had cut four full albums in that year. The major disappointment regarding his decision to retire in 1971 is that Sinatra was, in his mid-fifties, generally in excellent vocal condition: his singing (with the exception of *Watertown*) was at a remarkably high level that, arguably, he never quite achieved again, at least not as consistently, in the postretirement period.

The last album, *Sinatra & Company*, is a double-sided mystery. The A side consists of seven tracks from the intended second collaboration with Jobim, the dates with Eumir Deodato's arrangements (conducted by Hollywood veteran Morris Stoloff), and the B side is seven contemporary pop songs done with Don Costa. Why didn't he go through with the release of *Sinatra-Jobim* (as it was to be titled);* and for that matter, what were those Costa tracks originally intended for? Those answers apparently died with Sinatra, Jobim, and Costa.

The Costa arrangements, taped over four sessions in October 1970 (except "Lady Day," from November 1969), may well have been intended for a follow-up to *My Way*, in that a fair share of the songs were already well-known (and, though no one knew it at the time, a few would also become hits later on for other artists). These seven tracks might be described as an adult version of the so-called sunshine pop that his daughter Nancy was already well-known for: the sound is, overall, contemporary, and optimistic, if not necessarily upbeat in a rhythmic sense. ("Lady Day" is somewhat melancholy, but hardly the epic tragedy we expect from Billie Holiday's own later years.) Sinatra's much-professed difficulties with keeping in step with the times don't seem to trouble this music at all; four to five decades later, these tracks represent the very best that the period had to offer.

There are two numbers by Henry John Deutschendorf Jr., more familiarly known as John Denver, that charted for other artists: "My Sweet Lady" (later a hit for Cliff DeYoung) is suitably sweet and tender in a way that recalls the best of the *Cycles* tracks. "Leaving on a Jet Plane" (the last big hit for Peter, Paul, and Mary) is marvelously and convincingly cheerful, stressing the return rather than the departure. If I had known Sinatra was only going to record two songs by Burt Bacharach, I'm not sure I would have picked "Close to You" (the other was "Wives and Lovers," with Basie) but he does an excellent job with it; again, Costa's arrangement helps make it completely credible for the Chairman.

The other songwriter represented with two songs is one Paul Ryan, responsible for "Sunrise in the Morning" and "I Will Drink the Wine." In his Royal Festival Hall concert of November 16, 1970 (second show), Sinatra

---

* I've always had a sneaking suspicion that the strangely homoerotic nature of "Desafinado," his most fully realized duet with Señor Jobim, had something to do with it.

describes Ryan as a young English songwriter, and the son of some "very dear friends." (Ryan's mother was Marion Ryan, a popular singer and star of early British television.) The former is an annoyingly redundant title,* but the song itself brings out the warm and engaging side of Sinatra, and takes him back to the realm of dance music. "I Will Drink the Wine" is musically copacetic, although Ryan's lyric can be read as a somewhat mean-spirited attack on the flower child mentality of the era ("I'll give you back your flowers / and I will take the land"); Sinatra was, briefly at this time, friendly with Spiro Agnew, and this sounds vaguely like something that the soon-to-be-disgraced vice president might bark to legions of nattering nabobs.

"Bein' Green" is a harbinger of the future, being the first song he would sing by Joe Raposo, a major songwriter in the immediate postretirement period. Written for Kermit the Frog to sing on *Sesame Street* (and later *The Muppet Show*), Sinatra internalizes Raposo's lyric from "It's not easy bein' green" to "It's not easy bein' *me,*" recognizing that the song's message has nothing do with skin, or fabric color (Kermit was the original velvet frog). Yet he stays true to the author's juvenile aesthetic, singing the piece with a confined, naive quality. By abandoning his dynamic range, Sinatra sounds at once folkish and childlike, more effectively than any of his earlier folk-influenced works (with the exception of "Somethin' Stupid"). He doesn't even put the expected emotional accents on phrases like "big like an ocean" or "tall like a tree."

He was continuing to work toward the creation of a new Sinatra aesthetic that's also reflected in some of the final singles before his retirement. In 1969 he recorded two songs by pop songwriters. "Goin' Out of My Head" was a respectable Sinatrafication of a 1964 hit for doo-wopper supreme Little Anthony and the Imperials (most jazz fans are more familiar with the instrumental hit version by guitar giant Wes Montgomery), although the 1969 single isn't as good as his 1967 television duo with Ella Fitzgerald. The other, "Forget to Remember," is as good a performance as Sinatra would give in this era. He sings it in his "big" voice—the same basic voice as anthems like "Ol' Man River"—not quite belting, but loud and full of authority. Just as he was working toward new ways to sing soft, folklike, and childlike songs, such as "Somethin' Stupid" and "Bein' Green" (apparently the apostrophe replacing the G was a signifier of something—or somethin'), he was also formulating new ways to sing big songs, those rock-era power ballads.

---

* I can hear the voice of Sammy Cahn in my head saying, "When else would it be?" But then again, let us not forget that it was Sammy himself who wrote "in the evening, when the day is through" in "Time After Time" as well as "each little small café" in "Only the Lonely."

In the middle of the *Sinatra & Company* sessions, he called a date with two numbers conducted by Lennie Hayton, another music and movie industry veteran—a very close, very longtime friend of both Sinatra and Bing Crosby (and probably best known to history as Lena Horne's husband and musical director)—that resulted in another pair of curate's eggs. As McKuen wrote (in a 2012 blog post), Sinatra had admired Hayton's writing since they had worked together at MGM twenty years earlier; he had not found an opportunity to collaborate with him since, but now it was clear that both Hayton's health and his marriage were unraveling, and Sinatra realized that the time to bring him in on a project was sooner rather than later.

McKuen remembered that Sinatra had Hayton rewrite the "I'm Not Afraid" arrangement three times, but that he was correct to do so: the chart kept getting better and better until at last Sinatra and McKuen were both satisfied. "I'm Not Afraid" is a follow-up to "If You Go Away" (on *My Way*), another Jacques Brel perennial with English text by McKuen; the track steadily grows in volume, tempo, and anxiety, from small and controlled to big and anarchic. I must confess that Sinatra kind of loses me by the end of it, but it's an exciting journey nonetheless. Brel was kind of the French equivalent of Alec Wilder in that his songs are almost invariably dark and depressing, but this was still another worthy avenue for Sinatra to explore. "Something" is the first of two versions of the George Harrison ballad that Sinatra would attempt, and on hearing the Hayton track it's clear why Sinatra commissioned a new and much superior chart (by Nelson Riddle) in 1979 (for *Trilogy*).

Other follow-ups were less impressive. In November 1970, he called what he then thought would be his final session. Here, he tried to make "stupid" magic happen again with two additional duets with his daughter Nancy: "Feelin' Kinda Sunday," cocredited to the pop saxophone star Nino Tempo (who had played on numerous Sinatra dates), and "Life's a Trippy Thing," by Howard Greenfield, Neil Sedaka's longtime partner. The two Sinatras do the best that they can, as does arranger Don Costa, who employs a vocal chorus in vain hopes of making the two songs sound like more than they are. Alas, both songs are trippy (not to mention hippy-dippy)—beyond the pale even for what was only intended as the frothiest possible pop music. They're so lightweight and fluffy that they make "Somethin' Stupid" look like the "Soliloquy" from *Carousel* by comparison.

And yet there was a worthy postscript; after the two duets, there came a solo, "The Game Is Over," the third song he would record by John Denver. (There would be two more later in the decade, as well as two memorable team-ups on television specials.) "The Game Is Over" is a much quieter number: no Nancy, no choir, very little brass, mostly Sinatra, in his soft voice, guitar, and rhythm. It's also short (two and a half minutes) and deliberately modest. Knowing the way Sinatra was feeling at this moment, one can't help but assume that he's singing to his collective audience, as anthropomorphized in the form of a woman, a departing lover. "Time, there was a time you could talk to me without speaking, / You would look at me, and I'd know all there is to know." The underlying message is that he and the pop music audience are no longer relating to each other like they used to. "The Game Is Over" meant ending with a whimper rather than a bang, but he couldn't have chosen better; it's an understated gem, especially from a period when grandiose bombast seemed to be the coin of the realm.

As the title indicates, the game was indeed over. This was November 1970; his remaining performances were guest shots on television with old friends (Jack Benny, Danny Thomas, and a rather amazing New Year's show with Dean Martin). The final live appearances were all benefit concerts: for the Ronald Reagan gubernatorial campaign and other political causes, a Songwriter's Hall of Fame dinner for Richard Rodgers (he sang two songs; we don't know what they were, but it's an even bet that neither was the 1967 H. P. Barnum arrangement of "Some Enchanted Evening"), and a benefit for the comic Frank Fontaine.

A big surprise was an appearance in Madison Square Garden on March 8, 1971—not as a singer, but as a photographer, covering the boxing match between Muhammad Ali and Joe Frazier. Sinatra a paparazzo? The world was indeed turning topsy-turvy. He was there for *Life* magazine, which published his photos in the March 19 issue. For his efforts on the magazine's behalf, *Life* gave him a double-edged reward: they made the news of his retirement the cover story of the June 25 issue, "Sinatra Says Good-by and Amen." It was a knowing reference to a Sinatra classic (Cole Porter's "Just One of Those Things"), but the cover picture itself was anything but flattering: he looked much older than his fifty-five years. He seemed puffy and wrinkly, like a Halloween pumpkin in January. If there was any doubt why he was retiring, this photo made it clear.

The last big appearance, the "retirement" concert, occurred on Sunday, June 13, 1971; there were actually two shows, and Sinatra was singing until well past midnight. To complete the feeling of a testimonial in which all his old friends were saying goodbye, Rosalind Russell, a movie star from Sinatra's generation, made a speech that began:

*This assignment is not a happy one for me. Our friend has made a decision. A decision we don't particularly like, but one which we must honor. He's*

*worked long and hard for thirty years with his head and his voice and espe-
cially his heart. But it's time to put back the Kleenex and stifle the sob. For
we still have the man, we still have the blue eyes, those wonderful blue eyes,
that smile—for one last time we have the man, the greatest entertainer of the
twentieth century.*

Auntie Mame's speech was sentimental in a way that Sinatra's performances had never been, but no one could question the sincerity of those
words or, indeed, their veracity. More important, Nelson Riddle himself was
at the podium, just to make it a proper "farewell and amen" indeed. And the
music itself was anything but sentimental: with the exception of "My Way"
and "That's Life"—two very successful and relatively recent songs that perfectly fit the occasion—all twelve songs performed at the Ahmanson Theatre
that night were indisputable Sinatra classics. "This was the beginning," he
said, over the vamp to "All or Nothing at All"—yet it was also up-to-date,
since they launch into Riddle's 1966 treatment of Sinatra's earliest hit.

The forty minutes of music he offered were indeed Sinatra's finest. There
was, as he put it, "Cole Porter's shining hour and Nelson Riddle's brilliant
arrangement," "I've Got You Under My Skin," and another high-octane Riddle swinger, "The Lady Is a Tramp." He went back more than thirty years,
to 1940, with "I'll Never Smile Again" (the Gordon Jenkins arrangement,
however) and to World War II with "Nancy." There was a big but amazingly intimate "Ol' Man River" with just Bill Miller, and an even warmer
and more personal "Try a Little Tenderness" with only Al Viola's guitar. "Fly
Me to the Moon," the Basie-Quincy-Byers 4/4 chart, was another relatively
recent swinger that he absolutely nailed. And although neither "My Way" nor
"That's Life" (bereft of both chorus and electric organ) were Riddle's charts,
he and Sinatra made them sound better than on the recordings.

In contrast to most of his concerts of the 1970s, "My Way" was not the
climax or the closer. After "Tramp," he concluded with the absolute perfect
moment of farewell and amen in which, Roz to the contrary, no Kleenex
was necessary. He sang "Angel Eyes," taking us gradually to the climax with
the aid of a visual equivalent of a diminuendo: as the song winds down and
gets quieter, the spotlight on Sinatra grew smaller and smaller, until it was
little bigger than a pin spot. He was accompanied only by Bill Miller and a
cigarette, and it was as if he had somehow willed the smoke to engulf him, to
cover more and more of him, even as the spotlight continued to recede.

Finally, just as Sinatra uttered the last line, "'Scuse me while I disappear,"
the stage went black. And he was gone.

# 10

# "OL' BLUE EYES IS BACK"

## *The Concert Years, 1973–1994*

*On the day I decided to put my youth behind me, I immediately felt twenty years younger. You'll say the bark of the tree has to bear the ravages of time. I don't mind that—the core is sound and the sap goes on doing its work, as in the old apple trees in my garden: the more gnarled they grow, the more fruit they bear.*
—GEORGE SAND to Gustave Flaubert

In the final phase of his career, Sinatra was widely recognized as the most famous old guy who was still out there on the road, working steadily. Thus, it was a very big deal when he made the headlines twice in one week in March 1994, both times for not exactly flattering reasons. The first incident occurred at the annual National Academy of Recording Arts and Sciences awards ceremony, held on March 1, when he received the Grammy Legend Award. In his acceptance speech, the seventy-eight-year-old Sinatra starting rambling, and then babbling, and gradually started getting less and less coherent. It was decided by the show's producers and, supposedly, Sinatra's own "people" (all of whom were, apparently, terrified of any moment smacking of genuineness), to abruptly cut to a commercial while the Old Man was still talking. Let's just say it didn't look good. Then on March 6, at his first engagement after the Grammys, he was halfway through his second night at the Mosque theater in Richmond, Virginia, when he overheated and then blacked out for a few seconds and collapsed in the middle of "My Way."

If there's any song that would inspire Sinatra to pass out, it would be "My Way," for reasons both physical and emotional. It's a physically demanding song that calls for a lot of lung power and concentration, a lot of high, loud, and sustained notes. And then too, there was his long and complicated history with "My Way." Is it a great song? No. But it is a Sinatra classic, much as he professed to dislike it. And it is almost unquestionably the definitive song of the final chapter of his career, the postretirement period, aka "the concert years." "My Way" was his recurring mantra, his idée fix, his leitmotif—or, as he puts it in his 1974 Main Event concert, "We're about to sing the national anthem, but you needn't rise."

Long before the coming of the modern singer-songwriter, there already was a highly personal strain in pop music that had its origins in the idea that performers were telling their own stories. Prominent songwriters would tailor specific songs for specific performers: Irving Berlin could tailor a certain song for Al Jolson and another for Bing Crosby (often for movie roles), even though they both could sing each other's songs as well, and that was well before Rodgers and Hammerstein and Lerner and Loewe fully developed the idea of using songs to delineate character in the modern musical theater. In the 1940s and 1950s, songwriters began to craft songs for the general characters of larger-than-life artists like Billie Holiday and Edith Piaf. Most of the signature numbers of these divas (even though they both were accomplished songwriters themselves) were written in this fashion, by professional songwriters who were often close friends, who understood the way they thought. The relationship of Sinatra with his own in-house songwriters, Sammy Cahn and Jimmy Van Heusen, was perhaps even closer, since Van Heusen not only expressed the Sinatra persona in song, he had helped create it. Unlike, say, Michael Jackson or Prince, Sinatra didn't have to write his own songs, because Cahn and Van Heusen captured his own inner essence more than anything he could have wanted to write himself.

When Paul Anka wrote the English lyrics to "My Way," he was aligning himself with that tradition, and also of others. More than any other artists of their period, Piaf and Holiday transmuted their personal lives into their professional careers, but in very different ways. In most of Holiday's songs, she comes off like a victim, beaten down not only by abusive lover men but by the world itself, as in "My Man." (Ironically, this was originally a French song, "Mon Homme," but not one that Piaf would ever sing.) Piaf's trials and tribulations were also well known to her public, including various addictions, widely publicized love affairs, and a string of near-fatal automobile accidents. Yet the type of songs she chose to represent her were very different: instead of being beaten down, Piaf was more often triumphant, and typically sang about how she fought against seemingly impossible odds and yet somehow came out on top. Her signature number in her final years wasn't "La vie en rose," which was her best known song in the USA, but rather "Non, je ne regrette rien," which became known in English as "I Regret Nothing." The piece had come to her in late 1959, the work of Charles Dumont and Michel Vaucaire, two young composers who had never written for her previously but nonetheless strove to capture her essence in song.

"Non, je ne regrette rien" became the archetype for a whole other kind of song, one that had scarcely been written or even dreamed of before 1960: the reflective self-aggrandizing anthem. After the French, the idea spread westward to the English-speaking world, and the next stop was Great Britain. In 1961, the team of Leslie Bricusse (who wrote most of the words) and Anthony Newley (who did most of the music, and also starred) created a classic work of the musical theater, and a huge hit, titled *Stop the World—I Want to Get Off*. It was an allegorical show glorifying the common man, in which the leading character, played by Newley, was named "Littlechap." Many of the songs, especially "What Kind of Fool Am I?," "Gonna Build a Mountain," and "Once in a Lifetime" (all sung by Littlechap) were all about reflection, self-examination, and, ultimately, self-celebration.

The Newley-Bricusse songbook crossed the pond to America thanks to Sammy Davis Jr., who apparently had a direct pipeline to the team; he recorded "What Kind of Fool Am I?" and "Gonna Build a Mountain" a few weeks before *Stop the World* opened in London, and almost a year and a half before the premiere of the New York production. Davis was a Reprise artist by then, but Sinatra would have paid attention to what he was singing anyhow. As Newley once told me, even though the Newley-Bricusse songs were widely successful in the States (to many, this was the actual start of the British invasion), that Sammy was singing them on his label was enough for Sinatra.

Sinatra realized that for Sammy to sing songs of self-glorification was a whole other thing—rarely if ever before in history had a black man proclaimed so loudly and clearly about being proud to be who he was. In Sinatra's estimation, for him to have to sing the same song would have been pure musical egomania, and that was just not his thing. Steve Lawrence arrived at the same conclusion when he encouraged Davis to sing "I've Gotta Be Me" in 1968; for Davis to sing such a self-affirming text would serve a larger purpose, much more so than if a white man sang it. "I've Gotta Be Me" was only one of many self-aggrandizing show tunes of the era, such as "Don't Rain on My Parade" and "The Impossible Dream," songs that were impossible to imagine in musicals only ten years earlier. (In the classic Rodgers and Hammerstein shows, songs like "A Puzzlement" and "Soliloquy" are about trying to conquer self-doubt, not patting oneself on the back.)

As the 1960s were about to turn into the 1970s, the mood was changing: the youth movement was driving us from a collective culture to a nation of individuals in the so-called "Me Decade," and old notions of community were increasingly vilified as "conformity." This was the mood that Paul Anka caught when he wrote the English lyrics to "My Way." Anka was one of many transitional figures in pop music who seemed to belong to multiple generations and eras, an early rock-pop teen idol who was also steeped in the music of the generation that had come before him. He was born in Ottawa, Ontario, in 1941 to Syrian and Lebanese parents, leading Sinatra to refer to him frequently as "that little Arab." He was only twenty-seven when he wrote "My Way" in 1968 but already had many years of experience in many aspects of the music business. Anka came to New York and landed a number-one hit in 1957 with his own song, "Diana," making him one of a growing number of early singer-songwriters. His path to Sinatra was through Don Costa, who, in addition to being Sinatra's primary musical director in the late 1960s and '70s, was also a publishing mogul during the Brill Building era.

Anka happened to hear the French song "Comme d'habitude" (written by Claude François, Jacques Revaux, and Gilles Thibaut) while in Paris early in 1967. "I thought it was a shitty record, but there was something in it," he said in an interview (in the London *Daily Telegraph* in 2007); through his publishing connections, he optioned the English-language rights to the song, but didn't do anything with them until two years later. He thought about the tune again in 1969 after having dinner in Florida with Sinatra and several men he described as "a couple of mob guys. Frank drops a bombshell—he says, 'I'm quitting the business. I'm sick of it, I'm getting the hell out.' I was floored by this—no more Frank."

A few nights later, back in his home in New York, he put it all together in the form of a song for Sinatra. His master stroke was uniting all the various strains, starting with the "Comme d'habitude" melody, the idea of a self-glorifying anthem, and the notion of Sinatra quitting. The song (the title of which translates into "As Usual") was originally about a pair of lovers fighting and breaking up, but the lyric that Anka had in mind for Sinatra was more along the lines of "Non, je ne regrette rien"—a quasi-autobiographical text through which Anka captured his vision of Sinatra. "At one o'clock in the morning, I sat down at an old IBM electric typewriter and said, 'If Frank were writing this, what would he say?'" He had essentially combined two French songs together, the melody of one and the basic conceit of the other (although the French hardly had a monopoly on self-aggrandizement). It was also heavily informed by the conversation at the dinner, specifically the way the "mob guys" talked. "I used words I would never use: 'I ate it up and spit it out.'" (It's also been pointed out that lines like "I saw it through without exemption" are not grammatically correct.)

At five AM, Anka had finished and was ready to play it for Sinatra, whom he immediately called in Las Vegas. Sinatra showed no hesitancy in agreeing to record it, in contrast to his later protestations to singing it live in concert. Don Costa was the logical man to orchestrate the song, and on December 30, 1968, he cut "My Way" with Bill Miller conducting and Lou Levy playing piano. Milt Bernhart, on seeing that there was a single piece of music on the stand—indicating that they would finish quickly and go back to celebrating the holidays—remarked to the rest of the band that here was a Christmas present indeed. "Bud Brisbois played the lead trumpet on that," the trombonist recalled. "It was a Maynard Ferguson–type thing, and it wasn't easy." The band and Sinatra ran through two takes, and the whole process was completed in less than half an hour. Bernhart feels that the familiar performance—issued and reissued on numerous singles, LPs, and CDs all over the world (and mimicked by many)—is actually a composite of the two takes, noting a change in vocal quality. The only obvious splice in the track occurs right before "I've loved, I've laughed and cried," where Sinatra cuts down instantly from a really big voice to a small voice in less time than he or anyone else could do naturally. The transition just doesn't sound natural, and he never sang it quite exactly that way in live performance.

In its first release as a single, "My Way" didn't chart as high as "Cycles" and, in fact, was not an instant sensation in concert. When *Variety* attended one of the earliest shows to include the anthem, the reviewer noted that Sinatra referred to both "My Way" and "Cycles" as intended "for the kids." He also pointed out that those two tunes received polite applause but nothing compared to the tumult that greeted "The Lady Is a Tramp" and "I've Got You Under My Skin." But early in the new year, Sinatra decided to make it the title song of his next album, released in March 1969—surely a vote of confidence.

The combination of Sinatra and the song gradually snowballed. Musically, this is a highly repetitive melody that contains five nearly identical stanzas, each consisting of a string of deliberately monotonous fournote phrases. (Small wonder that as he gradually lost his memory and his ability to concentrate, this is the song that Sinatra most frequently got lost in.) Yet the manner in which he transforms this unpromising source material takes him beyond alchemy and into the realm of sheer magic. In short, another, more melodically complex melody would get in the way of Sinatra, or at least his ego—or more accurately, this perception of his ego.

Put another way, the song is not about a musically profound tune or witty words—no one was looking for Cole Porter—but a compelling frame for the Sinatra persona. It was up to Sinatra to pump up with the grandeur of an operatic aria what might have seemed like a five-minute exercise in self-indulgence—except that it wasn't, it was a version of the "self" that his audiences relished seeing him indulge in. It starts quietly, even intimately, and ends enormously. It became the centerpiece of Sinatra's act when he took to playing rock venues, eighteen-thousand-seat amphitheaters and sports stadiums, rooms that were a mite too spacious for "Try a Little Tenderness." In a sense, "My Way" became both a self-fulfilling and a self-inflating prophecy: Sinatra gradually grows bigger and bigger on stage, starting off life-sized but quickly getting much bigger than that, until he's larger than the giant levitating head of the Great and Powerful Oz.

There's no room for irony—in fact, irony would have been the knife to poke a hole in the balloon and let all the air out—except in the obvious point that fans perceived this as the "real" Sinatra when, obviously, it was just another construct, one perhaps significantly less real than "All the Way" or "High Hopes" had been. In fact, the central irony regarding "My Way" might be that we probably see more of the authentic, actual Sinatra—whatever that may be—in "Angel Eyes" or "You Make Me Feel So Young." We hardly need the pretense of a text created with biographical/autobiographical relevance to get a glimpse of the real Frank. Like Mike Shore did with the 1963 *Playboy* interview, Anka was effectively ghostwriting Sinatra's autobiography, with a considerable number of dramatic embellishments. Anka supplied Sinatra with not just a song, but a script for a remarkable piece of one-man theater. Even for all my cynicism, every time I saw Sinatra sing it in concert, I too leapt to my feet and began applauding hysterically. How can you not stand up and cheer at the sight of a man who can, at will, grow to be ten stories tall?

Whenever he introduced the song, Sinatra tried, over and over, to tell us how much he hated the damn thing; in retrospect, it seems like these protestations were a tip-off that the song wasn't really about him. When Bill Boggs asked Sinatra, in 1975, why he bad-mouthed the song so consistently, Sinatra pointed to his own nose—meaning that it was too "on the nose"—that it depicted a character that everyone assumed was his real self. He also couldn't have enjoyed the opening line, "And now, the end is near / and so I face the final curtain." In 1969 Anka had meant that literally, that Sinatra was about to retire and therefore face an actual final curtain. But postretirement, the phrase was taken metaphorically, as if Sinatra were about to shuffle off this mortal coil.

More important, Sinatra was simply uncomfortable singing about self-love. He was the unequivocal master of singing about love for another human being and thereby revealing his own soul in the process. "My Way" was the transitional song that opened the floodgates for multiple generations of self-glorifying pop stars, mostly uberdivas like Barbra Streisand, Bette Midler, and Celine Dion, whose entire act would seem to be standing in the middle of a stadium and telling you, at the very top of their lungs, how great they art.

At the center of it all was "My Way," the ultimate victory-lap song. The relatively unimpressive sales of "My Way" as either a single or an album were entirely beside the point. The most important thing, especially as Sinatra came out of retirement in 1973 and embarked upon a concert career, was that millions of people were willing to pay a lot of money to see him sing it in person.

In 1962, when Sinatra performed at the Royal Festival Hall (as part of the World Tour), it was such a notable occasion that the BBC sent a camera crew to interview celebrities on their way inside. One of them was the British pop star Shirley Bassey, who, when asked if she had ever experienced Sinatra in concert before said, no, she had only seen him live in Las Vegas. To those watching this footage today, this response is rather puzzling. The casino show rooms of Las Vegas were and are huge airy spaces, holding hundreds if not thousands of attendees. Why wouldn't an appearance in Las Vegas count as a concert? Because it wasn't the size of the room that mattered: a concert hall, of which Royal Festival and New York's Carnegie were the gold standard, was a sacrosanct space for the performance of serious music—symphonies, chamber works, operatic recitals, and the like. A casino showplace was where high rollers and wannabees could indulge in drinking, smoking, chasing chippies, and enjoying boozy entertainers like Sinatra's hero, song-and-joke man Joe E. Lewis. No, Caesars Palace and The Sands shouldn't be considered concert halls, any more than it's possible to play the slot machines at Carnegie.

The idea of the pop concert was still a new concept in 1973–74 when Sinatra came back to work again. Pop singers and jazz bands played in nightclubs, not concert halls; those were the exclusive province of symphony orchestras and opera singers giving recitals. All the early appearances in Carnegie by jazz and nonclassical artists in the hall, like Benny Goodman (in 1938), Paul Whiteman (also 1938), Duke Ellington (1943), and John Hammond's "From Spirituals to Swing" concerts (1938 and '39) were auspicious occasions and much remarked upon by the media. In 1943, Sinatra was one of the first popular singers to give a formal concert tour, when he played a string of large-scale venues, like Lewisohn Stadium in New York with Max Steiner and the New York Philharmonic (on August 3; 7,500 people attended) and the Hollywood Bowl with Morris Stoloff and the Los Angeles Philharmonic.

But in general, the biggest rooms that Sinatra played were the larger supper clubs, like the Copacabana in New York and the 500 Club in Atlantic City, and the high-toned ballrooms converted into nightclubs in the tonier hotels and other hostelries across the country, like the Wedgwood Room at the Waldorf Astoria and the Fontainebleau in Miami Beach. Other singers made it to Carnegie, like Billie Holiday in 1956, Joni James in 1959, Harry Belafonte (for multiple years), and Tony Bennett (1962); Judy Garland created an absolute sensation in Carnegie for one night in 1961. (The success of her double album at Carnegie undoubtedly inspired the production of Sinatra's own double live album, *Sinatra at the Sands* with Count Basie.)

Before Vegas, Sinatra's basic bread and butter derived from what were then called "stage shows"—appearances in movie theaters in package productions that were centered around the popular orchestras of the swing era. The main attraction was always the name band: Tommy Dorsey and Glenn Miller were among the "top draws," as *Variety* would say, playing their hits as well as accompanying a variety show–type lineup of singers, comics, jugglers, acrobats, adagio dance teams, or whatever. You saw an hour-long stage show, in addition to a full program of newsreels, shorts, cartoons, and a feature; for bands it meant playing five or six of these shows a day, starting before noon and going until close to midnight. (But at least it meant they got to stay in one place for as long as a week or two; even six shows a day was easier than playing every night in a different city.)

The movie stage shows were the intermediate step, the missing link between vaudeville and video (i.e., the television variety shows). In fact, when Ed Sullivan launched on CBS in 1948, the stage shows were in their waning years. In 1956, the Dorsey Brothers even hosted a weekly variety series titled *Stage Show*.

The drummer Alvin Stoller, who would play on most of Sinatra's classic albums of the 1950s, first worked with the singer at New York's Capitol Theatre in 1945. He remembered those performances vividly: "The orchestra would play his theme song, 'Night and Day,' the stage would come up and the orchestra would rise, and he'd be standing on top of the piano, with everything lit from underneath. Frank was the act, he was *it*, he was the whole show. The Will Mastin Trio [the only other act on the bill] gained recognition [at that engagement]. Sammy [Davis Jr.] was hoofing and doing imitations and all that stuff. But the Mastin Trio was only out for maybe ten minutes [as an opener], and the whole rest of the show was Frank."

While that was unusual for the period as a whole, according to Stoller, it was typical of Sinatra's theater appearances. "Every show was a Sinatra concert," as the drummer put it, "and the place used to be jampacked with people." Incidentally, despite Sinatra's bringing in more bobby-soxer business than anyone could compute, he did not consistently break his own box-office records because theaters found it impossible to eject fans between shows.

"The theater tries to book as inferior a movie as possible to complement Sinatra," The *New Yorker* observed in 1946, "hoping (vainly) that the recurring flashes of mediocrity on the screen will discourage fans from waiting around for the next show."

In some instances, as on several occasions in Atlantic City (particularly on the Steel Pier), theater owners dispensed with the movie altogether. "[I used to do] eleven shows a day," Sinatra reminisced in the middle of a show in the same city around 1983.* "In those days they used to run people in and out so fast that you barely had time to turn around between shows. . . . I remember one day I had just gotten a bottle of soda and a sandwich, and I was still up on the stage; the curtain had come down. I was hungry. So I'm there, munching on this sandwich, and I turn around to say something to somebody and up goes the curtain. They were so fast that they had brought in a whole new audience, seated them and everything. The band starts up, and I'm expected to sing with a sandwich in my mouth. Well, I finished that sandwich. Believe me, I needed it. It was brutal then. But let me tell you something: I treasure those days. We did it—we got the job done."

The stage show appearances and movie theater tours took up the majority of Sinatra's time throughout the Columbia Records years; indeed, he made considerably more money from accompanying pictures than he did from starring in them, even such blockbusters as *Anchors Aweigh* and *On the Town.* This tradition continued into the 1950s: in 1951, Sinatra used his CBS-TV series to hawk his May appearance at New York's Paramount (doing one show with the full cast of that revue, including the virtuosic Joe Bushkin, the vivacious Eileen Barton, and the indescribable Dagmar).† However, television would gradually put an end both to the big bands and to the movie business as it had been. Sinatra made his final movie theater stage show, fittingly, at the Paramount—the "home of swoon" as press wags dubbed it—working with the Dorsey Brothers and his own current picture. (This was the lamentable *Johnny Concho*; it was almost as if Sinatra wanted to apologize for the movie by being there in person.)

Movie theaters were never a perfect venue for Sinatra to begin with, but the end of the stage shows left him with one fewer option. "The problem was, we could never find places that were big enough," said Sinatra aide-de-camp

---

* As quoted in *Philadelphia* magazine, September 1983.
† As we mentioned in chapter five, in 1951, one of Sinatra's stage shows at the Paramount Theatre in New York was broadcast via shortwave over French radio (complete with a French announcer throughout). This twenty-minute segment, which costars pianist Joe Bushkin and *le magnifique Dagmar*, has only recently surfaced, and it is virtually the only recording of a movie theater stage show that is known to exist.

Frank Military. "There was no Carnegie at that time; they weren't doing that then. So we worked at places like the Cow Palace in California. I remember one time in El Paso when we played some kind of bull arena, and occasionally large concert halls, like in Saint Louis, before Frank started doing stadiums." Sinatra regularly worked the Copacabana in New York and the 500 Club in Atlantic City, even though these places were hardly large enough to accommodate everyone who wanted to see him. "You couldn't get anyone in with a shoehorn," added Military, explaining why Sinatra had to do so many shows a night. The young Bill Boggs, future television host and producer, was so anxious to see Sinatra at the 500 Club that he infiltrated the boîte by buying a waiter's uniform and entering through the service entrance; he stood around during the show, trying to look busy, hoping nobody would notice him.

With cinemas no longer an option, Sinatra worked much less in live appearances for much of the 1950s and '60s, other than hotels in Miami and casinos in Vegas; recordings, film, and television were keeping him busy enough in any case. Bill Miller remembered that he and Sinatra spent so much time on location and in the studios that "we hardly ever worked [on the road] in those days."

While Sinatra was occupied elsewhere, the remnants of the former stage shows were evolving: in the early 1950s, enterprising impresarios like Morris Levy and Teddy Reig, of New York's Birdland (and later Roulette Records) were putting together stage show–like productions and sending them on the road, where they would play concert-type venues rather than movie houses. There would be touring "packages" with names like "The Big Show of 1952" that would generally be built around an orchestra like Stan Kenton or Duke Ellington and feature several additional instrumental stars and at least two or three well-known vocalists, like Nat King Cole or Ella Fitzgerald. (Kenton toured with Charlie Parker and Dizzy Gillespie in 1954; there was a famous Birdland All-Stars tour with Count Basie, George Shearing, Sarah Vaughan, Stan Getz, and Lester Young that crossed the Midwest in 1955.)

Thus the stage shows were becoming package tours, and there were other changes as well. The earlier all-star package tours were jazz and big band–oriented (the most famous was Norman Granz's Jazz at the Philharmonic series), but quickly the tours became increasingly oriented toward younger audiences and the nascent rock 'n' roll style. (At the same time, the jazz packages evolved into festivals, like the Newport Jazz Festival that began in 1954, the Monterey Jazz Festival in 1958, and the Playboy Jazz Festival in Chicago in 1959.) The dawn of the rock era was dominated by package tours for well over a decade, in fact nearly all of the Beatles' so-called "concerts" in America were not really concerts at all, in the sense that Judy Garland at Carnegie Hall was a concert, but package tours; even at Carnegie and the Hollywood Bowl, the Fab Four were never more than one of numerous acts on the bill, who each played for only thirty to forty minutes at most.

It was the enormous popularity of the Beatles and other rock bands that opened up the largest existing venues for musical shows—the sports arenas, like Shea Stadium and Madison Square Garden. George Wein, who had launched the Newport Folk Festival in 1958, watched his idea burgeon into the Monterey Pop Festival in 1967, then Woodstock (more formally the Woodstock Music and Art Fair) and the disastrous Altamont Speedway Free Festival (at which four people were killed and many more injured), both in 1969.

All the while this was happening, both the undisputed king and prince of pop—Frank Sinatra and Elvis Presley—were gazing down from on high, taking note at what their royal subjects were up to. The two monarchs had arrived at roughly parallel points in their careers: Sinatra hadn't hit the road extensively (excepting Vegas and some political benefits) since the 1962 World Tour, and Elvis had barely performed live since being mustered out of the service in 1960. Presley had spent the entire decade making movies that were generally considered, even by his fans (especially by his fans, in fact) to be so bad that they made the worst of Sinatra's cinematic bombs look like *Gone with the Wind* by comparison. In 1969, Presley resumed giving live appearances, starting with a triumphant series of runs at the International Hotel in Las Vegas, and by 1970 he was playing sports stadiums like the Houston Astrodome, the Oklahoma State Fair Arena in Oklahoma City, and the Denver Coliseum.

Just as Elvis had followed Sinatra into the casinos, when Sinatra made the decision to come out of retirement in 1973, he knew he had to follow Elvis into the stadiums. And yet even as he was emulating the rock stars and the youth movement professionally, he was even more solidly aligning himself with the conservatives politically. Sinatra's modulation from the left to the right was the most notable of any publicly visible American figure since Ronald Reagan, who, like Sinatra, had started as a New Deal–type FDR-era Democrat. In 1962, he could barely force himself to shake the hand of Richard Nixon when he ran into the former VP at Toots Shor's (the incident was reported by Earl Wilson), and as late as 1968 he gave fundraiser concerts for Nixon's democratic challenger, Hubert Humphrey. But around the time of the retirement, he drew closer and closer to Vice President Spiro Agnew and eventually to Nixon himself. His only performances in 1972 were a few numbers here and there sung at events in support of Agnew. (Although it should be noted that Elvis Presley, Sammy Davis Jr., and, even more so, James Brown, all shocked many of their fans when they came out as Nixon supporters around the same time.)

Then in April 1973, Sinatra performed at the White House, at the invitation of President Nixon in honor of the prime minister of Italy, Giulio Andreotti; Nelson Riddle, who had been at the podium at the retirement concert in June 1971, conducted the United States Marine Band. Considering this was Sinatra's first full concert in two years, he sounds remarkably good—although this is unmistakably the "later" Sinatra voice, the deeper sound of the postretirement period, not the lighter and more flexible sound of 1971 and earlier.

It's at this concert that Sinatra is said to have reconsidered his decision to forsake the limelight. After observing the thirty-seventh president serve as cheerleader in a standing ovation, Riddle remarked to the singer, in his usual dry martini fashion, "You can't do much better than that." Ironically, just as Agnew and then Nixon were forced to resign, Sinatra unresigned from his voluntary retirement. (For the old-guard lefties that my parents hung out with at the time, the disgraced ending of the Nixon-Agnew administration was even better news than the return of Ol' Blue Eyes. Not for me, of course.)

For some time to come, Sinatra would be asked about the retirement and the subsequent "unretirement." I remember watching one of his first postretirement appearances on *The Tonight Show*; when host Johnny Carson posed that question, he responded with an answer that he had obviously thought long and hard about beforehand. As Sinatra told Carson, he had been getting a lot of mail from fans, and they would make suggestions like, "We know you don't want to make live appearances anymore. But won't you consider doing us, your fans, a favor by making a new album?" "So," he continued, "So I began to think about recording, and then I gradually came around to the idea of touring again."

Given these statements, one would conclude that after Sinatra returned to performing he would make recording his primary activity and touring only a secondary consideration. And by May 1974, Sinatra had recorded two entirely new albums. But this turned out to be a false spring; the situation worked out in exactly the opposite way. The Voice, now known as Ol' Blue Eyes (a moniker dreamed up by publicity man Lee Solters), continued to thrill millions—but now almost exclusively in concert.

There were realities that had to be faced. "What most of these [prerock] artists really didn't understand was that as the record business changed, the way of selling music also changed," arranger Charles Calello (who had worked with Sinatra on *Watertown* in 1969) observed in the early 1990s. "The record-buying audience is from an age of, let's say, ten years to about twenty-six. Then after you get out of college and get on your way, start your life, the chance of your running into a record store or really being interested in music is sort of limited, based on your romantic attachment. And after people start their adult lives and their families, then the new generation of people start to come in and buy their own generation. So if you go to see Sinatra, the audience will be a bunch of blue-haired people. If you go see the Four Seasons, you'll see a bunch of Italian-looking guys with mustaches and polyester clothes. And so Sinatra's record-buying audiences dried up. It wasn't so much that he needed to change his product, he needed to change his marketing."

The major individual responsible for helping Sinatra to "change his marketing" was promoter Jerry Weintraub. "When Frank came out of retirement and started doing stadiums, he didn't know if he would draw," recalled guitarist Al Viola. "He was going to have to pull in fifteen thousand or eighteen thousand people every place he went. But Jerry Weintraub handled the promotion and booking when he started to tour. Jerry was involved with rock groups. [The most important of these rock acts was, famously, Elvis.] He knew all the stadiums from one part of the country to another, and he knew what he could sell. But in 1974, neither Frank nor anybody else had any idea what he could actually do in a room where they sold hot dogs."

The concert years would last a full two decades, until Sinatra made his last appearance before a paying audience in 1994. For the entirety of that time, he was one of the world's strongest concert attractions; how many acts from 1974—let alone 1944—were still on the top of the heap in 1994? For the first time, anybody could buy a ticket and see him, without having to know somebody who knew somebody—or without having to buy a busboy uniform and sneak your way in through the back door of the 500 Club. Now, all you had to do was scrape up the dough and wait on line all night for a ticket.

All of a sudden, concerts were the main event, although there would still be occasional television appearances (which mainly served to promote the concerts) and, less frequently, albums (and even rarer than that, theatrical film roles). His life became an unending blur of stadiums, sports arenas, limos, and airports.

He was also increasingly distanced from his sidemen. "He stayed more aloof from the musicians," percussionist Emil Richards explained. "He no longer called me 'Dag' [short for 'Dago'], he would just say 'hello' and never call me by name. Don't get me wrong, he was always friendly. It just was a whole different bag. He was rubbing noses with the Republicans and stuff. Now it was time to make some heavy bucks, and he started to do concerts. I think that the musical integrity suffered a little bit from then on."

Richards's observations should be placed in context. "Frank's entourage treated him like God and, in a sense, he was," said arranger and trombonist Billy Byers. "He'd been exalted so long he didn't act like he was just another guy in the band anymore. But he was still terrific. He was way above the usual kind of guy you work for—who treats you like a waiter, like you ought to come in through the servants' entrance."

It's a recurring theme in Sinatra's career—how much he appreciated musicians, treated them royally, and even coveted the best ones. During his movie theater stage show years, he preferred to work with an established big band; those guys who played together all the time could be counted on to be tight and dependable as a band, to always hit their mark. In 1945, he played cinemas up and down the East Coast with Jan Savitt's Top Hatters, an unconventional but swinging orchestra originally from Philadelphia. Thirty years later, during the Main Event tour, he did the same thing with Woody Herman and his Young Thundering Herd, adding his own rhythm section and several different groups of string players based on location; the band served as both accompaniment and secondary attraction (i.e., opening act).

Getting the right musicians was paramount; the problem was that most musicians of the caliber he wanted preferred not to go on the road and were generally able to land enough studio work so as not to have to. As we've seen, having to fight with the Copacabana house orchestra in 1950 contributed greatly to the vocal breakdown Sinatra suffered during that engagement, and the locals hired to accompany him in Atlantic City that September weren't any better. "We [Sinatra's rhythm section] went up and rehearsed the band," drummer Johnny Blowers recalled. "The stage band was pretty bad. They were good guys, but they didn't give a damn. They sloughed off a lot of things, and you don't slough off with Frank! So when he got there, he called me and said, 'How's the band?'

"I was trying to think what kind of an answer to give him, and I didn't answer right away. Then he said it a little strongly: 'Alright, did you hear? I said, how is the band?'

"I said, 'Well, it's *comme ci, comme ça.*'

"He said, 'What the hell does that mean?'

"I said, 'Well, I think you'd better hear it.'

"Well, we barely got through the first show and—whew!—they were pretty bad." At this point, Sinatra did what situations like this occasionally forced him to do. "After we finished that first show, he said, 'Fellows, we won't use the band anymore. Just have them come in on the closing chords.'"

When Sinatra began playing Las Vegas the following year, he similarly dreaded dealing with local players. "In the beginning, in Las Vegas, they didn't have enough musicians to go around," explained Milt Bernhart. "It was still a small town in the '50s, and believe me, Frank's standards were high. So after a rehearsal prior to opening night, there would be a call out in Hollywood for players that he wanted, to come to Las Vegas in a hurry. And money was paid; he paid very handsomely. It was almost a regular event. If he was going to open in Vegas, I almost expected it. And a couple of trumpet players, trombone players, and several fiddle players, and a fiddle section for sure, and maybe a saxophone—it depends on the band. But usually the local band just couldn't handle his music, not to his satisfaction. He'd even go so far as to rehearse with them. But the orchestra there never satisfied him."

From 1974 onward, Sinatra's primary accompaniment was the "New York" band assembled for him by contractor and concertmaster Joe Malin, who lasted until virtually the end (he died in 1994). This ensemble would travel with Sinatra to any gigs that happened to be closer to New York than Los Angeles, often including Europe, Africa, and South America. The permanent rhythm section would travel with the singer everywhere. In putting it together in 1973, he started with as many of his old stalwarts as he could get; Bill Miller was first (although he and Sinatra would part company for a few years), Al Viola would grace the guitar chair until he tired of the road not long after Miller left (Miller's sabbatical was only temporary, it turned out), to be replaced by another tristate Italian, Tony Mottola. For a time, Emil Richards traveled with the unit on vibes, until Sinatra's accountants convinced him that a permanent mallet man was not necessary. Charles Turner also traveled with all editions of the Sinatra band for many years as the Chairman's preferred lead trumpeter (and frequent soloist). Ralph Peña, bassist with the '62 sextet, had been killed in a tragic accident in Mexico in the mid-1960s, so Gene Cherico played bass with the group for roughly a decade, until he retired.

But the rock of the Sinatra rhythm section during the concert years was always Irv Cottler. Sinatra depended so completely on the drummer's ultra-reliable rhythm patterns that they became a veritable road map to the singer; he could practically pass out and then wake up in the middle of any number and know exactly where he was and what he had to do. Cottler's unswerving solidity gave Sinatra the support he needed to continually take chances, to improvise and crawl out on whatever limb happened to catch his musical fancy. "Irv was a great big-band drummer. I mean, the tempo really didn't move—it stayed where it was supposed to be," observed engineer Lee Herschberg, himself a former drummer and a lifelong percussion connoisseur. "He really was a dictator of tempo. Once he set it down, that was where it stayed. And he knew what was going to be sung and where to put in the crashes of cymbals and stuff like that. He was really excellent at that."

Emil Richards told a similar story. The vibraharpist and Cottler worked together frequently on variety shows, for television and elsewhere, in which they were required to play for all sorts of dancers. As the vibist recalled, "The dance acts would come up to Irv and say, 'Faster! Faster! I want it faster!' Irv would then stop playing. Then they'd say, 'What are you doing? Keep going, only faster!'" Cottler would then glare at the hapless terpsichoreans and inform them, in no uncertain terms, "'Don't tell me to play faster or slower. You show me where you want it, and I'll put it there and I'll keep it there!' Irv had a metronomic mind as far as knowing where the beat was, and Frank always depended on him. Frank would go into a song and just bring his hand down, and Irv would take up the tempo. Irv was right every time!" Speaking not long after Cottler's death in 1989, Richards added, "He would lock into the tempo that he knew Frank wanted, and I think that's what Frank misses about Irv the most. I don't think there's another drummer anywhere who could do what Irv did as far as knowing the tempo that was gonna make it really cook for Frank."

Cottler's predecessor, Johnny Blowers, felt that of all the instruments the drums were the ones Sinatra empathized most with; he described the singer as "a frustrated drummer," like many show business icons (including Bing Crosby, Johnny Carson, and Bill Cosby). "Drums are very important to Frank," said Blowers, "because he digs time and he likes rhythm. Yes, Frank was strong on drums. So was [Bunny] Berigan. So was Goodman. So was Dorsey. They all were. The heart of the band is the drum. If you've got a good drum, you've got a good band. If you've got a bad drum, you've got a bad band."

Between 1956, when Cottler first appeared on a Sinatra date, and 1971, the drummer and the singer worked together frequently if not religiously. On most of his studio sessions, Sinatra's first call was the more flexible Alvin Stoller. Both were firmly rooted band-pushers in the Buddy Rich manner; yet while Stoller knew more different ways around the beat, on the road Cottler was Sinatra's man.

As for his personality, Cottler represented the opposite of Bill Miller, his partner of roughly forty-five years (off and on) in the Sinatra rhythm section. The Old Man himself, who at times described himself as a manic-depressive, could have discerned his own reflection in each of the two men. At certain times Sinatra identified with a retiring loner like Miller; other times he saw something of himself in the always aggressive, occasionally hotheaded Cottler.

As Miller put it, "Oh, Irv hated to be told what to do." For instance, there's Billy May's favorite Irv Cottler story, about a date that the arranger conducted for Bobby Darin. "We called Irv 'Grump'—because he was so congenial, see? Anyhow, the first date we did started out with some bright tune, and it had a big fat introduction, and Irv had a drum break in bars seven and eight of this introduction. So we played the introduction, and Irv played the drum break. Then Darin, who was a smart asshole kid, stopped the band and walked over to Irv and said, 'Now I'll tell you how I want this played.' Oops! And Irv stood up and stared him down and said, 'You sing the songs, I play the drums, see? Don't fuck with me.' That was the end of it. There was no trouble after that. Irv was wonderful! I think he'd even tell Frank where to go if Frank ever pulled that shit."

While neither Sinatra nor Cottler was known to pull his punches, they got along famously with each other. "He's beautiful," the drummer said in 1979. "I worked a lot of shows with a lot of singers, and I've never seen anything like him. You could never get bored with Frank. You could do the same songs day in and day out with him, but each time there's a different level. And I'm talking about twenty-five years here!

"In the music business," he said, "I got my four biggest thrills with Red Norvo, Claude Thornhill, Tommy Dorsey, and Frank Sinatra"—listing said thrills in chronological rather than quantitative order. Cottler was first inspired to play the drums by the great African American big-band drummers. "The first drummer I ever saw play was Chick Webb," he said, "and then Jo Jones, the original drummer with the Basie band. I'll never forget the first time Basie came to town. He and Jo opened everybody's eyes with a new sound and a new approach." Talking about other percussionists he had been inspired by, Cottler continued, "Sid Catlett was a beautiful drummer. Shadow Wilson played with Basie a little later; he died at an early age, but he was a dynamite drummer."

But Cottler reserved his greatest praise for Buddy Rich: "He *is* a genius. He's something else! When you talk about drummers, you put him on the side, then you start with the rest. He's a fine man and a beautiful human being. Buddy's like Frank, they're both perfectionists, they're great musicians. Hell, they're geniuses! I hope Buddy goes on forever because the young kids who are coming up should make it their business to see him, to know what the drums are. It's not the sixteen tom-toms that they've got going and all that bullshit. There are a couple of [good] young drummers around, but for the most part it's amateur time!"

Stoller himself had recommended Cottler to Sinatra. "My dad was sick in New York," he recalled not long before he died in 1992, "and I went back for a day. I sent Irv in to sub for me." Cottler first appeared with Sinatra in 1955 on half of the tracks used on the album *Songs for Swingin' Lovers!* From that point on, Cottler turned up occasionally on Sinatra Capitol albums, although Stoller played on the bulk of the sessions. Cottler placed himself at Sinatra's disposal more often in terms of appearances outside the Los Angeles area. "When I didn't want to travel," said Stoller, "Irv jumped in because he wanted the job." Cottler made the famous 1962 World Tour with Sinatra, the first occasion that the two men had to get to know each other well; but as Cottler noted, "I never got to play the 500 Club [in Atlantic City] with Frank because we were all too busy in the studios."

The music industry itself was going through a severe shake-up around the time of Sinatra's retirement. The studio scene of the 1940s and '50s was quickly being superseded by developments like rock 'n' roll (in which being a traditional musician became a liability) and electronics. Many musicians, even those whose skills had been as in-demand as Cottler's, panicked. "Irv had gotten very panicky," said Milt Bernhart. "Frank wasn't working, and the record dates were slowing down. Everybody was looking around for something else to do. So Irv bought a liquor store, and he lost everything he had on it." (Bernhart had better luck with his own postmusic venture, a travel agency that he operated successfully for more than thirty years.)

When Sinatra began to plan for his reemergence in mid-1973, he and Cottler decided to commit to each other full-time. "In the early days," he said, "I couldn't get away from the studios often enough to go on the road. But then the studios became a real drag to go into, music-wise. So when Frank came out of retirement, I said, 'Forget it, I'm gonna have a ball!'"

For roughly fifteen years the routine was the same: Sinatra's regular men would rehearse with the locals, and the star himself would do only the actual show itself with the full contingent. In the earlier part of the concert years, Sinatra would run through at least part of the program with all the players. "The band would rehearse one day without Frank just to run down a chart," said Cottler. "He doesn't like to over-rehearse, which I agree with. When Frank walks in and he does rehearse, it becomes a different band. We have the same guys, but it sounds different. The minute he walks in, everybody just goes up a level, even two levels. The rehearsals are like a performance on stage."

Throughout the greatest part of the 1970s and '80s, Cottler was the primary force that propelled the Chairman and his board. It wasn't always "a ball": In the '70s, Cottler made no secret that he detested playing the rock-oriented numbers that Don Costa had arranged, even though Costa had done them, obviously, at Sinatra's request. Cottler, who occasionally rankled follow sidemen as affable as Miller and Viola, was bound to butt heads with the more assertive Frank Sinatra Jr., who began conducting the band in 1988. Cottler hardly kept it a secret that he didn't get along with the Old Man's son. "Junior took years off Irv's life," as one veteran sideman (who preferred to remain anonymous) put it. Cottler was also considerably demoralized by the death of Buddy Rich in 1987. "Irv felt as if he and I were the only two drummers in the world," said Alvin Stoller. "He would always say, 'There are only two of us left.'"

"Irv worked with the Old Man so long that he just couldn't stop," said drummer Sol Gubin, who played with Sinatra many times in the 1960s and eventually succeeded Cottler. "Irv had arthritis very badly in his hands, and that's why that thing got to be that constant backbeat and pounding and shit. Irv really didn't have any chops left, and I knew he didn't like his own playing anymore, and I was really sorry. As a matter of fact, I ran into him a couple of times, and he said he wanted to quit and he wanted me to take the job. At the time I said I really didn't know if I wanted to go back on the road again."

He died in 1989. The loss of Cottler was one of several factors responsible for the occasionally erratic quality of Sinatra's performances in the 1990s. He went through over a dozen drummers in the early 1990s in what other sidemen described as a continual search for another Irv Cottler. "He'll never find one," pianist Lou Levy said. "No way. Irv fit him like a glove. But there's only one glove, and he had it!" Not for nothing did Sinatra regularly introduce Cottler as "the best drummer I ever worked with in my entire career."

In the big picture of Sinatra's career, the concert years might be considered a disappointment, in the sense that he recorded so infrequently: from 1974 to 1979, Sinatra would venture into the studios only sporadically. All of a sudden, in terms of productivity, even 1969 seemed like a golden era by comparison: in that one year he had recorded almost as much as he would (four albums) in all of the mid- and late-1970s (five albums, but only if one counts *Trilogy* as three albums).

Still, these were the years in which most of us got in to see Sinatra—those of us who weren't well-heeled enough to bribe the headwaiter or maître d'hotel at the Copa. For most of us, our memories of seeing Sinatra in person are from the years 1974–94.

As we've mentioned, Sinatra's voice was never fully what it had been in 1971 and earlier (the voice is particularly resonant on the 1971 sessions heard on *Sinatra & Company*), but for most of the subsequent years he worked very hard to keep his chops in the best shape possible. In 1975, he gave one of his rare extended television interviews to Bill Boggs—who had sneaked into the

500 Club fifteen years earlier—for his WNEW-TV program *Midday Live*. The issue of how he prepared for his concerts was very much on his mind.

Speaking after having recently wound up a triumphant two-week run at the Uris Theatre in New York, he told Boggs, "When you saw me, after the so-called retirement, I was struggling, I was really fighting my way out of the doldrums. Because when I quit, I let everything go, and it all fell down. It's like somebody who lifts weights and they stop it for a while, or a football player. I was having a tough time at the time, vocally, trying to do what I wanted to do."

He also talked about his preparation immediately before each concert. "I keep thinking to myself, am I warm enough? Am I really ready to pitch? Or, we've got ten minutes, should I run into the dressing room with Bill Miller and do four or five minutes of exercises? And at times, even if I don't need it, it gives me a sense of security, I'll go up to an F, and hit it once or twice and know that I will never use it, but it's there if I need it." He added, "Then what I do is I go over in my head as quickly as possible, 'Am I shy any lyrics? Am I unsure of a couple of words here and there?' Which sometimes can happen if we do something new in the book. And then the usual things of fixing your tie and so on and so forth." And so forth.

Apart from the evolving voice, the major sonic element that distinguished the 1970s from earlier decades was the presence of Don Costa, who had become increasingly important to Sinatra's music in the years leading up to the retirement (1968–71), and even more so afterward. Nearly six months before the official end of the retirement in 1973, Sinatra began taping his comeback album, *Ol' Blue Eyes Is Back,* which dovetailed with a television special broadcast in November with the same title. The four most notable tracks were all arranged by Gordon Jenkins (namely the three best—"You Will Be My Music," "Send in the Clowns," and "There Used to Be a Ballpark"—and the absolute worst, though no fault of Jenkins, "Noah"), but the dominant instrumental voice both here and throughout the next album, 1974's *Some Nice Things I've Missed,* was that of Don Costa.

Sinatra might not have even come out of retirement if not for Costa—or someone like him—whose great strength was outfitting the Chairman with suitable arrangements of contemporary songs. He felt that in order to fill the stadiums he had to be able to convincingly sing current material as well as "The Lady Is a Tramp" and "I've Got You Under My Skin." Sinatra articulated this in the Boggs interview in reference to a mention of his son, Frank Jr., who was at that time touring as a singer. "I argue with him about some of the material that he does. He keeps talking to me about Cole Porter and Rodgers and Hart and I say fine, but there is also Bacharach and Jimmy Webb and a whole bunch of other guys that are writing good things. And he says, 'No I want to do this stuff,' and I said, 'Yeah but they're not buying that now—not always buying it. You've got to mix it in some way.'" That was Sinatra Senior's intention: to mix it in some way.

As Al Viola put it, "Don had helped Paul Anka get started, and he had an ear for that kind of music. Nelson didn't. Billy May didn't. Gordon Jenkins didn't. But Don Costa did. He had that extra talent. He was also younger." But like Cottler, Viola was also less than happy about all the contemporary-style songs that were increasingly prominent in the band "book." "Unfortunately, that [style] didn't fit with what Irv Cottler and I wanted to do, and though I liked Don personally, both Irv and I agreed that it didn't fit Sinatra." Charles Calello elaborated: "Don supplied Sinatra with contemporary arrangements that were musical enough for him to sing, which was good. The market had changed to such a degree that when it came to picking the new songs that would have any kind of longevity, he really needed someone who had some [modern] song sense."

Sinatra and Costa first met when the latter, born in 1925, was in his early twenties and working with a local theater band in his native Boston. As the singer told the story, when they first met, Costa was much more intimidated by meeting Axel Stordahl than he was by Sinatra. "Axel and I were doing a theater date in Boston, and we used a local orchestra and Costa was the guitarist. And that's when we first met," as Sinatra related to Sid Mark, by far his favorite deejay, not long after Costa's untimely death. "And Don later told me that he was terrified because he was such a big fan of Axel's. Don was thinking about writing and orchestrating in those days, and he finally met with Axel who was his idol. And Don was shaken when he met him and the great New York musicians we had brought up."

Costa worked with dozens of singers (including Paul Anka), but he first entered Sinatra's radar as the arranger-conductor for Eydie Gormé and Steve Lawrence at the time the two singers hit the national scene, both individually and as a professional team. As Lawrence said, "The three of us—especially Eydie and Don—kind of grew up together musically." Sinatra and Frank Military had known Gormé and, subsequently, Costa and Lawrence since the late 1940s when Sinatra's Barton Music office was down the hall from her first agent, Ken Greengrass, in the Brill Building. Said Billy May, "Don did a lot of wonderful things for Steve and Eydie before he went to work for Sinatra." May added, only half kidding, "For a guitar player, he turned out really good."

"Actually," said Gormé (who was also known as Mrs. Lawrence), "I first heard of Don when I was singing with Tex Beneke's band in 1950 because he was sending in original arrangements, as were a lot of other arrangers, for the band to play. And I kept seeing his name on these charts. He kept calling them things like 'Costa's Last Stand,' 'Costa's Retreat,' Costa's this, Costa's that . . . and the stuff was wonderful, I mean, really wonderful. Unfortunately, Tex never used any of Don's charts because they really weren't Tex's style." (Slightly earlier, Costa and Bucky Pizzarelli had played tandem guitars on Vaughn Monroe's hit "Riders in the Sky.")

In the early 1950s, Gormé and Lawrence, many years away from marrying, were singing here and there around the New York studios, on various radio and television shows and whatever: WPIX-TV, Coral Records, etc. "Don said, 'Hey, can I do some charts for you?'" recalled Gormé, "And I said, 'Sure.' And we started to do a record here and a record there." Within a few years, Costa had become not only their musical director but their producer and A&R man as well. This is important: more than Riddle or May, Costa had his eye on something beyond the purely creative end of music-making (i.e., conducting, arranger, composing): he was also attracted toward the business side—publishing, production.

Costa found opportunities for Lawrence, Gormé, and himself with two different film conglomerates that were launching record labels during the LP boom that began in the mid-1950s, first ABC-Paramount Records and then United Artists Records. "Don really was the chief cook and bottle washer," said Lawrence. "He ran artists and repertoire, he signed new artists and did the orchestrations, and he searched for songs written by other composers, hired other producers. Where the other guys basically were orchestrators— and did that miraculously well*—Don had a greater thirst for knowledge and a greater, wider, broader gift than that of arranger. He orchestrated, composed, produced, and had a knowledge of electronics and studios and soundboards. Don really was very, very inventive, and ahead of his time." (Costa also recorded his own albums for these labels, such as *Music to Break a Sub-Lease* by "Don Costa's Freeloaders.")

Costa was only four years younger than Riddle—almost to the day—but musically, he seemed to belong to a later generation. As we've seen, he also came up in the tail end of the big-band era (Vaughn Monroe, Tex Beneke), yet he was much more immersed in the burgeoning rock-pop movement. He became a full-scale music mogul during what pop music historians have called the Brill Building era; his office was at 1650 Broadway on the corner

---

\* Costa came up with one of the wittiest and most Billy May–like arrangements ever recorded by that Frankenstyle funster Steve Lawrence on his 1961 album *Lawrence Goes Latin*: On the song "Small World," the key word of the lyric is "funny," and whenever Lawrence hits it, Costa has a female choir in the background chant "ha! ha! ha!" as if it were "cha-cha-cha!"

of Fifty-First Street (two blocks away from the more famous Brill Building), where just as many publishers and producers were based. He published hundreds of ephemeral rock-pop songs, and even had hits of his own (like the American instrumental version of the Oscar-winning "Never on Sunday") even as he was starting to work for Sinatra.

One of the dozens of aspiring songwriters under contract to him was Cary Hoffman, a lifelong diehard Sinatra fanatic (and future producer, artist manager, and vocalist). "We were all sitting in little cubicles, churning out all these cheesy little pop tunes while Don was in his office, just a few feet away from us, creating those magnificent orchestrations like 'Night and Day' and 'Stardust' on *Sinatra & Strings*," said Hoffman. Cary also remembered that he lobbied, unsuccessfully (to put it mildly), to be invited to the *Strings* recording session.

One thing Costa didn't like to do was conduct. "Don just wasn't very good at conducting, and he didn't like to do it," said Lee Herschberg. "He liked to be able to sit in the control room and listen to what was going on. Don was a big help with a lot of things, particularly on arrangements of his that were fairly intricate, that might be balanced in different ways. He wanted to hear all the specifics, things that a lot of the other writers didn't worry too much about. He felt that his contribution would be more in the booth than in conducting an orchestra he had already written." Costa would carefully rehearse his musicians, who hardly required a conductor to begin with, and then pass the baton to a specialist like Nick Perito (who later became Perry Como's musical director), or Joe Guercio in the United Artists period, or Sonny Burke or Bill Miller on the Sinatra sessions.

The last arrangement that Costa wrote for the Lawrences was "Again," which Steve introduced at Carnegie Hall in the early 1980s. While the band rehearsed the chart in the main auditorium, Costa sat in one of the sub-basements, hundreds of feet below, poring over a pile of musical manuscripts. What was going on upstairs reached his ears only as a muffled morass of noise, yet when he finally emerged he informed the conductor exactly which string player hit precisely which note flat in which specific measure.

"You know, Don never used a piano," recalled fellow guitarist Tony Mottola. "If you were sitting next to him and had your radio on, you're listening to some rock and roll station, Don could still write an arrangement. He would be oblivious. No matter what was going on in the room, he could sit there and score an orchestration." Billy Byers described Costa as "the Puccini of pop," adding that Costa's orchestrations are "seething with melody" as opposed to those of Riddle, whom Byers felt used comparatively little melody in the arrangements themselves, primarily supplying background harmonies (and, as we've seen, contrapuntal melodic figures) while the soloist up front assumed most of the melodic responsibility.

Why and how did Sinatra decide to give Costa a shot? As with everyone else he worked with, from Stordahl onward, as Military explained, "he heard something by Don that he liked." As Lawrence answered the question, only semi-sarcastically, "Frank stole Don from us!" Costa seemed to be the perfect musical director for the postretirement Sinatra: Jimmy Bowen and Ernie Freeman could help him make pop hits but, as Bowen said, he never would have attempted making traditional "Sinatra music" with the Chairman. Riddle and May could make high-class music, but their textures weren't what was selling in the disco and leisure-suit era. Costa, Sinatra hoped, could help him do both. "Don brought all these songs to him, and there were others he turned away," agreed pianist Vincent Falcone. "But most of what Sinatra did were things that the two of them agreed upon. He trusted Don's taste far more than you would believe."

Also, in using Costa, Sinatra would not be wed to any one particular sound. Nelson Riddle sounds completely different on *Swing Easy!* than he does on *Moonlight Sinatra,* but in both cases he was making an automatically identifiable Sinatra-Riddle kind of music. Costa's sonic signatures were never as obvious as Riddle or May at their most extreme, and especially not as much as Jenkins; but versatile as he was, Costa had a clear-cut style of his own. Falcone felt, "Harmonically, Costa was probably the most inventive and aggressive of them all." As Lawrence added, "Costa had everything the other writers had, and he wrote in a way that was very identifiable to me. However, I think probably most listeners wouldn't recognize his work—not like you could Gordon or Billy. Don was a lot more flexible and versatile than some of the other guys. They seemed to have gotten locked into their own identities early on. Costa had much greater horizons that he was exploring. He didn't settle into a niche."

Costa not only followed Stordahl and Riddle as Sinatra's central arranger-conductor, he also replaced Sonny Burke as Sinatra's main producer. He joined Jimmy Van Heusen and Sarge Weiss (who looked after Sinatra's own publishing interests following his break with Hank Sanicola) as a member of Sinatra's intimate business and music circle. "Don loved the Old Man to the point where he would sit like a dog at his master's knee," one member of the touring group recalled. "Great man that Don was, when he was around Sinatra he was a puppy dog." In both capacities, Costa was responsible for most of the production and arrangements of the two immediate "comeback" projects, *Ol' Blue Eyes Is Back* and *Some Nice Things I've Missed.*

Costa's contributions to *Ol' Blue Eyes* start with two songs that seem like "My Way" all over again; "Winners" is another attempt at a victory-lap lyric, while "Let Me Try Again" is another grandiose French anthem ("Laisse moi le temps"), this time with words by both Paul Anka and Sammy Cahn. Teddy Randazzo's "You're So Right (For What's Wrong in My Life)" is excruciatingly forgettable, something you could never say about the same author's "Goin' Out of My Head" (perhaps the only song done memorably by both Little Anthony and the Imperials and Sinatra), and his superior "Forget to Remember." Paul Williams's "Dream Away" (from the film *The Man Who Loved Cat Dancing*) recalls the "soft" folksy Sinatra voice of *Sinatra & Company*, while the song itself is a well-crafted folkish tune superior to anything on *Cycles*. It was barely noticed at the time—you can see how it would be overshadowed by "There Used to Be a Ballpark" and "Send in the Clowns"—but today resonates as Costa's standout contribution to the album.

Jenkins received the lion's share of the honors on *Ol' Blue Eyes*, but on *Some Nice Things I've Missed*, Costa arranged most of the ten songs (which left primarily David Gates's "If" and the Johnny Mercer–Jimmy Van Heusen gem "Empty Tables" for Jenkins). The concept of the album was that these were songs that had been introduced during the years of the retirement and that they might have been hits for Sinatra had he been making records at that time. Admittedly that's a stretch of a premise, but, it actually is the same unspoken connecting point that unites all the songs on the 1964 *It Might as Well Be Swing* with Sinatra and Basie: other people's hits.

After not having seriously listened to the whole album in many years, I found upon reevaluating it in 2016 that it seems like it doesn't matter what the purpose of the original songs might have been—a good song is a good song. "I'm Gonna Make It All the Way" and "Satisfy Me One More Time" are by Floyd Huddleston, a longtime veteran in the army of Tin Pan Alley, who had hits and some memorable tunes (usually in collaboration with former Rhythm Boy Al Rinker), but never quite created anything like a standard. His two numbers here seem to be attempts to come up with something rockish and funky that Sinatra could swing, but they don't really satisfy either end of the equation. Fortunately, it gets better than this.

Conversely, Neil Diamond's "Sweet Caroline" and the Tony Orlando hit "Tie a Yellow Ribbon 'Round the Ole Oak Tree" are at least good songs, and although they're not exactly right for Sinatra, one can understand why he wanted a piece of this particular action. In the case of the latter, the Sinatra-Costa arrangement seems rather like an attempt to cook a three-course dinner out of bubble gum. (They beef up the track with what French experimental composers might call a slice of *musique concrète*, the sound effect of a crowd cheering as if at a ball game.) Jim Croce's "Bad, Bad Leroy Brown" seems like a desperate move, although the Sinatra track will perhaps be better enjoyed by anyone born after 1970 who didn't have to suffer through the song's omnipresence as a youngster.

None of the five Sinatra/Costa up-tempo numbers here is completely embarrassing, and although Cottler was correct in observing that Costa was not a jazz writer (as Riddle and May were), they all swing, lightly but convincingly. They weren't trying to create a full-blooded, high octane, firing-on-all-cylinders swinger like Benny Goodman doing "Sing, Sing, Sing," but something light and graceful, something inspired by the lighter side of Count Basie and Neil Hefti, or even the heartbeat tempo of Sinatra and Riddle. (In fact, "You Are the Sunshine of My Life" seems to have been based directly on the template of "The Way You Look Tonight" from *Academy Award Winners*.)

Regardless of how you feel about these songs, or even the idea of Sinatra singing them, you can't deny that your foot is patting up and down, whether you want it to or not. The one that works by far the best is Stevie Wonder's "You Are the Sunshine of My Life." The voice, the tempo, the chart, and the words all make sense—it's the opposite of "Leroy Brown," and the least embarrassing up-tempo here. In its own way, Costa's arrangement is quite radical—the time feel is completely different from Wonder's number-one hit single from 1973. Essentially, Costa replaces Wonder's relaxed but funky backbeat with straight ahead, 4/4 swing; it could be any of the better swing bands of the late 1940s, say, Les Brown and his Band of Renown. (Costa could have arranged it in exactly this fashion for Tex Beneke.) More than any other tune on *Nice Things*, this is the one that would stay in Sinatra's working concert "book" for decades to come.*

Even so, the ballads were Costa's strength, and here he comes up aces. "You Turned My World Around" is the last and best of the Bert Kaempfert anthems, and though it's somewhat over-the-top (winningly so) Sinatra and Costa reign it in to keep it from becoming bombastic. But there are also two

---

* Sinatra was not the only one so enamored of the song: in all of the vast Stevie Wonder songbook, this is the one number probably most performed by jazz and traditional pop artists: Ella Fitzgerald, Carmen McRae, George Shearing, Monty Alexander, Dick Wellstood, Dick Haymes, Irene Kral, Al Grey and Jimmy Forrest, Mel Tormé and Buddy Rich, Anita O'Day, Perry Como, Andy Williams, and even Jim Nabors, among others. (Even though it is a marvelous song, to employ Sinatra's favorite adjective, one line, at least, is somewhat awkwardly written: "You must have known that I was lonely / Because you came to my rescue." The way the notes and the syllables are arranged, the last word of each of those lines is stretched out, as if they were hyphenated, and while "lonely" sounds perfectly acceptable as "lone-ly," "rescue" sounds amateurish and awkward as "res-cue." Even Sinatra, master phraser that he is, can't come to the res-cue of this line.)

additional ballads by another European composer, and these take us right to the beating heart of Sinatra's music at its best.

The most important songwriting team of the 1970s and '80s, as far as artists of Sinatra's genre and generation were concerned, was the combination of composer Michel Legrand and the lyricists Alan and Marilyn Bergman. Sinatra had gone way back with both halves of the equation: he had sung lyrics by the Bergmans from their partnership with composer Lew Spence, going back to the 1958 "Sleep Warm" (and had recently revived their 1960 "Nice 'n' Easy" with guest Gene Kelly on his 1973 TV special). He had also earlier sung melodies by Legrand with English words by others, such as "I Will Wait for You" and "Watch What Happens," both of which were satisfying but hardly magical performances.

Jenkins's chart on "The Summer Knows" and, even more so, Costa's on "What Are You Doing the Rest of Your Life?" show us how good Sinatra's music could be at this point in his life, even as he was pushing sixty; performances of songs like this were enough to justify his coming out of retirement. The team of Legrand and the Bergmans achieved a spiritual synergy well above and beyond what they had been able to realize with others. The best of the Bergman lyrics were perfectly suited for veteran singers (and they were done by all of the better jazz and traditional pop stars, from Sinatra and Bennett on down) in that they were about love in the long haul; not concerned with falling in love but sustaining it over a lifetime; not starting the band but keeping the music playing. Just as Cahn and Van Heusen were the perfect team to capture Sinatra's mood in the 1950s and '60s, the Bergman-Legrand combination totally nailed Sinatra's late-life worldview, his inner leitmotifs, in this stage of his development.

All five of the participants concerned have sufficient experience under their belts: Costa, both Bergmans, Legrand (the youngest, being only forty-two in 1974), and especially Sinatra, who sings slowly and deliberately, letting the tension and drama mount and build around him while raising his voice only microscopically. As always, Sinatra is all about the details: there's a whole different tone of voice as he goes over the items in the Bergmans' lyrical laundry list of "indicators"—"All the seasons and the *times* of your days," "nickels and the *dimes* of your days," "reasons and the *rhymes* of your days." Every note, every syllable, he sings is full of purpose, and that purpose is clearly all about taking the still-blossoming later stages of a relationship nice and easy. Sadly, the five-way collaboration, between Sinatra, Costa, Legrand, and the two Bergmans would produce only one more track, the even more magical "Summer Me, Winter Me" (on 1979's *Trilogy: The Present*).

One wishes that there had been a whole album of Sinatra and Costa doing Legrand-Bergman songs—surely it would have been more impressive than *A Man Alone* or *Watertown*. It would have been a challenge, though, in that Legrand and the Bergmans wrote nearly all of their classic songs as main title themes for movies, so they're meant to be heard one at a time, not as part of an extended score like those of Frank Loesser or Richard Rodgers. The songs are almost too consistent; they're not necessarily all alike melodically or even lyrically, but they're nearly all based on the same idea conceptually, and it might have been a challenge finding enough variety in that song catalog.

Finding songs continued to be an issue. Vincent Falcone, who came on board a few years later as Sinatra's musical director, remembered. "Frank would listen and find out whoever was the hot writer at the time. Peter Allen, Carole Bayer Sager, they were all hot at one point. Most of those songs were forgettable." So forgettable that most of them never even made it into the studio, surviving only on privately circulating concert recordings.

As on *Some Nice Things I've Missed*, throughout the concert years he had an easier time of finding worthwhile new ballads than he did with up-tempo numbers. It was difficult making rock swing, and as talented as Costa was, it rarely worked as well as it should have. Said Cottler, "He's a fine musician, and I wish I had his knowledge of music. If I were a singer and I wanted a ballad, I would definitely have Costa write it. For instance, 'Lady Day' [on *Sinatra & Company*] is a beautiful chart. But he's just not a jazz writer! He overwrites. His jazz writing is like trying to push a Mack truck with four flats uphill. Unlike Nelson, he doesn't know what to leave out."

Ted Nash, Sinatra's primary saxophone soloist of the 1950s and '60s, said of Costa, "Well, he was more commercial. He never did anything outstanding *musically* that the musicians could relate to, but he did a good job and came up with nice backgrounds, and Frank seemed to like the way he wrote. But it was sort of all the same. He just didn't have that much imagination." Or, to be more charitable, the circumstances didn't allow Costa to function at his best. Costa did little with Sinatra after 1961 that's as good as even the routine albums of standards he turned out for Steve and Eydie in the '50s. Judy Tannen, the Lawrences' manager for more than fifty years, may have been biased toward her clients when she said, "As good as Don's work was for Sinatra, he did his best charts for Steve and Eydie." However, she is, in fact, correct. Still, there are some absolute gems buried in the Sinatra-Costa output of the 1970s and '80s.

Sinatra's live shows were almost always fantastically successful, with the only major exception being the infamous debacle of Australia in July 1974.

For most of the previous year, he'd primarily worked in Las Vegas, including several long stretches at the Circus Maximus in Caesars Palace (which, interestingly enough, were conducted by Gordon Jenkins; another run there costarred Ella Fitzgerald and Count Basie). There also was an East Coast tour in the spring, which included a memorable concert at Carnegie. His first postretirement engagement overseas was therefore going to be a big deal, and it was announced he would tour the Pacific Rim: first Budokan Hall in Tokyo on July second and third, then several cities in Australia. There was also a fascinating concert given on the fifth of July on the USS *Midway*, anchored at Yokosuka Naval Base. Fortunately, the performance was captured by a single video camera, and the surviving tape shows Sinatra in a blue denim leisure suit, singing with what could be the 1974 edition of his World Tour sextet (Miller, Viola, Cherico, and Cottler plus, on some numbers, Bud Shank on alto); he is loose and funky and in marvelous spirits.

The first Australian concert was scheduled for July 9; in addition to the quartet, he had brought along three horn-section leaders, Marvin Stamm on trumpet, Billy Byers on trombone, and Shank on lead alto. "In Britain there's a yellow press, and in Australia the press is eight shades yellower," as Byers recalled the incident. "Sinatra had a chauffeur who was supposed to let us off at a rehearsal hall at the top of a hill. But the press paid off the driver to let us off at the bottom of the hill where the reporters were waiting. So here's Sinatra, who was no longer a young man, on a brick road running up a steep hill away from the reporters. Naturally, he got very angry and called one of them a whore. The minister of labor got wind of what happened and said Sinatra had insulted all Australian workers." Byers felt the whole catastrophic incident was a scheme concocted by an unscrupulous politician to get his name in the headlines by provoking and then counterattacking Sinatra.

Then, at the concert of July 9, Sinatra exploded at some length, offering his inflammatory opinion of the local press; and the entire collected force of Australian labor unions decided to boycott him. Without organized electricians and stagehands, Sinatra had to postpone his remaining appearances; the airport workers refused to sell him fuel or fill his tanks, so he couldn't even leave the continent. "Believe me when I say Frank was one hundred percent right," insisted Cottler, who was unabashedly biased in favor of his boss and friend. "The people, the public, were marching in the street in Sydney with cards and signs printed that said, 'We want Sinatra! Down with the press!' Naturally, they didn't put pictures of that in the papers or on the air." While Sinatra never formally apologized—not in so many words—for his statements, he did make a peace offering to the Aussie media by doing a television appearance "on the house."* Whatever the case, Sinatra's tirades were not only keeping him on the front pages, they ensured his continued status as an inciter of international incidents. "Or, as they say in Australia," Blue Eyes jokes in his Madison Square Garden show a few months later, "Ol' Big Mouth is back."

Clearly, a new live album would be the perfect way to inaugurate the Concert Years; in the middle of the sessions for *Some Nice Things I've Missed*, he played his first major solo concert at New York's Carnegie Hall, which was recorded for possible release on Reprise. (As it turned out, it was released thirty-five years later as part of the boxed set *Sinatra: New York*.) Some tracks are everything we want them to be—he's never sung "You Will Be My Music" better than he does here at Carnegie. But this live recording (from April 8, 1974) is also, overall, much more rough than the subsequent concerts would be: he gets completely lost during "I Get a Kick Out of You" for instance ("Where the hell am I?") and some moments are other than G-rated: during that same Cole Porter song, he sings of "the cocaine from Spain." (My personal favorite Frankism is the way he shows his disdain for "My Way" by introducing it as a melody by "an eighteen-year-old French songwriter whose name was Jacques Strappe.")

He returned to the live album idea that fall as he prepared a tour of the Northeast, making two major changes, one practical and the other conceptual. The first was that he recorded multiple nights and ultimately culled the album together from songs as performed on four different shows: Boston, Buffalo, and two different nights in New York City.

In fact, the whole enterprise—the ongoing tour, the live album, and a television special as well—would hinge upon the three shows in New York, October 12 (Saturday), 13 (Sunday), and 14 (Monday). Rather than following in the tradition of Holiday, Belafonte, Garland, and Bennett, he elected to go where only Elvis had gone two years before in doing a live album from Madison Square Garden—but he went further than Presley in that this would be a television special as well. And more than Presley, Sinatra, who was a fight fan, would capitalize on the idea of boxing metaphors and terminology, starting with the album title, *The Main Event—Live* (he likely had gotten the inspiration sometime after March 1971, when he attended the Ali-Frazier fight at MSG, ostensibly as a photographer). The phrase "Main Event" refers to the climactic match in an evening that includes more than one fight, and the boxing concept is further reflected in the cover photo, which shows

---

* The incident was effectively dramatized in the 2003 Australian feature film, *The Night We Called It a Day*, with Dennis Hopper as Sinatra and Melanie Griffith as Barbara Marx.

Sinatra posing like a heavyweight champ (in one of his speeches, he refers to himself as a former flyweight and current middleweight) complete with a towel around his neck. The show is also introduced by the most famous sports announcer of the day, the obsequious Howard Cosell (not for nothing was he dubbed "the mouth that bored" by none other than the legendary sports journalist Oscar Madison). The first words Sinatra utters, after riveting renditions of "I Get a Kick Out of You" and "The Lady Is a Tramp," are "I am happy to be back in New York and delighted to work here. I've had some of my greatest fights here." Yes, he means it on multiple levels.

The second change from the Pacific Rim tour was to make the entire project even more exciting by bringing on one of the great big bands still operating, Woody Herman and the Thundering Herd. Herman's big band, then comprised of mostly younger musicians (road bands were almost always younger musicians, generations younger than Frank and Woody), would be the opening act (although, as usual, there were also comedians on the bill, like Red Buttons and Pat Henry). When Sinatra came on, the Herd would be supplemented by strings and would use Sinatra's own rhythm section, with Miller conducting.

Sinatra also added at least three other players to the Herd, lead alto saxophonist Jerry Dodgion, who had last worked with Sinatra as a member of the Red Norvo Quintet in 1960; the outstanding veteran trombonist Urbie Green (who takes the famous solo on "I've Got You Under My Skin"); and percussionist David Carey. "I hadn't seen [Frank] in about fourteen years when I got the call to tour with him and Woody," said Dodgion. "Anyhow, at the rehearsal he came right up to me and said hello. That kind of shocked me. We had only worked together briefly much earlier."

The album released as *The Main Event—Live* was primarily taken from the October 13 concert, although songs were also used from Boston, Buffalo, Philadelphia, Pittsburgh, and one number ("I've Got You Under My Skin," which he again introduces as "Cole Porter's finest hour") is from October 12. (The complete October 12 concert was also included on *Sinatra: New York* in 2009.) The telecast of the October 13 Sunday-night show was broadcast live at 9:00 PM EST on the ABC network. As Dodgion remembered, the concerts other than the televised Sunday show were considerably more fun for everyone. "On a normal concert, Frank establishes his own rhythm in how he builds from song to song. But at the Garden, every time he was ready to go into a song, the director had to stop him and say, 'Oh, no, hold that.' He couldn't build up his usual momentum because of the TV crew. Anyway, that's why the special isn't as good as it should be. I know his performances were really a lot better on all the other concerts."

Even so, all of the commercially released documents of the *Main Event* tour—the album, the live television performance, and the "bonus" Saturday night concert—capture Sinatra at his best, and the video is especially thrilling. Even with the painful *interuptus* described by Dodgion, Sinatra is electric from beginning to end, and he's created a format where the best of the traditional Sinatra standards, like "Skin" and "Kick" and "Tramp," can meaningfully exist with new material like "You Are the Sunshine of My Life" and "Let Me Try Again."

In fact, the new songs, especially "Sunshine" and even "Leroy Brown," are much livelier here than on the studio album; "Sunshine" is sunshine-ier and even "Bad, Bad" (enlivened by a Louis Prima–style mock-Italian gag) is almost good. Sinatra reprises a number of classic Nelson Riddle charts, like "Skin" (with a spontaneous insertion of "That Old Black Magic"), and at least two of the old-timers are heard in newly minted charts: Billy Byers's hard-swinging "Lady Is a Tramp" and a souped-up revamp of "My Kind of Town" by Riddle himself that even inspires an arena full of hardcore New Yorkers to cheer for Chicago. The new "Tramp" had come out of Sinatra's tour of the Pacific Rim the previous July, introduced in Australia. "Frank said he needed a 'hipper' arrangement," Byers recalled, "although he said, 'Make sure that the last two bars are the same because I have my choreography.' He used to like to give a little kick with his foot at the end."

"I don't care how long you've been in this business, there's nothing like singing to live people," Sinatra says after "Angel Eyes." Pastiche that it may be, the sequence builds beautifully in excitement and intensity, making it the most worthwhile project he had done since the retirement, and possibly even going back as far as Jobim and Basie. In his intro to "Angel Eyes," he tells the crowd, "I have never felt so much love in one room in my whole life." Even better than the album, the video captures the back and forth outpouring of love between Sinatra and the 14,876 people present, ranging from celebrities like Carol Channing, Robert Redford, Walter Cronkite, Rex Harrison, and William Conrad to two hot young blondes Lindy Hopping to "Leroy Brown" and blue-haired former bobby-soxers in "Frankie" T-shirts.

After New York, the *Main Event* tour continued until he wound it up with a concert at the Dallas Memorial Auditorium on October 29. By that point, he had only been out of retirement for roughly sixteen months; yet in that time, he had produced two studio albums, two very successful television specials, and one exceptional live album (something he'd done only once before). And yet he seemed not to know what to do next, other than constantly touring. (It's a shame that he didn't, at the very least, choose to go forward with additional live albums; it seems like it would have been a no-brainer to do a *Main Event 1975*, a *Main Event 1976*, and so on, each mixing Sinatra standards and new songs.)

It would be a long time between albums—almost six years between *Some Nice Things I've Missed* and *The Main Event—Live* in 1974 and *Trilogy: Past Present Future* in 1980. He was in there pitching, looking for worthwhile new songs and new avenues to explore. Between 1975 and 1977, he recorded over a dozen songs for singles release—easily enough to fill an LP by 1975 standards—all of which were collected on the *Complete Reprise Studio Recordings* (the "suitcase" package) in 1995.

Clearly, he would have liked to follow the successful path of the years 1966–69, with "Strangers in the Night," "That's Life," "Cycles," and "My Way": each of those singles had been so successful that he was able to build an album around it. That wasn't happening with any of the fifteen 1975–77 singles tracks, alas, although they're all certainly better than "Satisfy Me One More Time" and "I'm Gonna Make It All the Way" on *Some Nice Things I Missed*. But indulge me: if there were such an album, it could have been titled *Some Nice Things That Everybody Missed*.

The most prominent feature of this imaginary album is that the two best songs are also the two worst tracks: these represent Sinatra's headlong foray into the disco craze of the 1970s. "When disco became popular, he decided to do two disco tunes," as Cottler recalled. "I think he was talked into it by Don Costa. But when he mentioned the idea of doing two of the standards that were associated with him, I mentioned 'Night and Day,' and 'All or Nothing at All.' It sounded like a great idea at the time. That was the only time I ever suggested any tunes to him."

The idea may have been Costa's, but clearly Costa was out of his depth here, so they turned to a guitarist and composer named Joe Beck. Beck's specialty at that point was bridging the gap between jazz and rock, and his biggest credential was having been the first musician to play an electric instrument on a Miles Davis session. (This was on a 1968 date that served as a precursor to Davis's jazz-rock fusion blockbuster *Bitches Brew*.)

The disco date went down at the conclusion of this sequence of sessions, in February 1977. Many Sinatra fans would list them as the all-time nadir of the Sinatra canon, and Irv Cottler agreed. When Sinatra fan and researcher Rick Apt asked Cottler his opinion of the two tracks and Beck's work, the drummer motioned to the tape recorder and responded vehemently: "You want it on tape? I'll put it on tape! I think he's the worst writer I ever heard in my life! He's not a writer, he's a bricklayer. If it were up to me I'd ban all [that music] and ship it to an island!" In the opinion of Vincent Falcone, who joined the Sinatra entourage a few months later, "They were just horrible. I don't understand how Sinatra ever got hold of Beck, but he did. Those charts were my nemesis! I kept beating on the Old Man to get rid of them. And finally, one day in a rehearsal at Caesars Palace, we were doing the thing, and I made some kind of face. And he stopped the band and said, 'Throw it on the floor!' And we never did those disco things again. We got the old 'Night and Day' back out!" They have a point, but honestly, these charts aren't particularly horrible by the standards of the music—even though there are precious few disco arrangements of standards to compare them to. (They're certainly better than those on the infamous *Ethel Merman Disco Album* of 1979.) Beck did exactly as Sinatra had asked, and likely no one could have done a better job—this was truly a thankless task in every sense of the word.*

Or maybe someone could have: on the same session (February 1977), Sinatra also recorded "Everybody Ought to Be in Love" a Paul Anka song in an arrangement by Charles Calello—he of the Four Seasons, who had orchestrated the *Watertown* album in 1969. This isn't exactly full-out disco, but it is definitely 1977-style club dance music, a single (it was, in fact, the flip of the disco "Night and Day") that would not be unwelcome in Studio 54. It's actually one of the best things Anka ever wrote, a warm and sincere slice of sunshine pop—and Calello boosts Anka's melody with several inspired modulations—emblematic of all the good things of the have-a-nice-day decade. ("Everybody Ought to Be in Love" is a vast improvement on the hopelessly wishy-washy "Anytime (I'll Be There)" from 1975, not a highlight of the Sinatra-Anka-Costa triumvirate.)

Overall, there's no way Sinatra could have wrapped these fifteen tracks into an album, because they all sound so different from each other—disco tracks, hillbilly songs, Christmas carols, and even a few classic show tunes and traditional-style American standards; yet many are excellent in their own way. "Everybody Ought to Be in Love" belongs in a discotheque, and "The Only Couple on the Floor" belongs rather literally at a barn dance, which is to say that it's first-class country-and-western music. "The Only Couple" was the work of John Durrill, who as a guitarist was best known for being part of the highly successful instrumental rock group the Ventures, and who as a songwriter worked very rewardingly with the pop and country producer Snuff Garrett. Costa did the excellent arrangement for Sinatra, resulting in a country piece that's totally credible for him; it's more hardcore country—and better—than say, anything on the *Cycles* album. At various points, Sinatra was

---

* How committed was Sinatra to these disco tracks? Not very, apparently. Only one of the two ("Night and Day") was released at the time as a 45 rpm single, and neither was available in any other format until the 1995 *Complete Reprise* suitcase.

said to have been considering a full-length collaboration with Garrett, and "The Only Couple on the Floor" makes me wish that they had gone ahead with that. It's much better than the flip side, the nondescript and forgettable "I Believe I'm Gonna Love You," although that, ironically, is the song that charted (but not very highly, at number forty-seven).

This batch of singles includes three new Christmas songs, all of them excellent—although it's a personal call whether one of these might be considered a Christmas song, even though it is about Christ. Considering that Sinatra had only done one solo holiday LP—and that was twenty years earlier—a new Christmas album would also have been appropriate. "Christmas Memories" is a very traditional holiday song, very much in the spirit of "The Christmas Song" and "The Christmas Waltz." The music is by Costa himself, as is the chart, and the Bergmans' lyrics, a loose collage of holiday images, are up to standard; but it's hardly a classic.

Yet the other two songs, both by modern-day singer-songwriters and recorded by Sinatra in 1975–76, are something very different indeed. Both John Denver's "A Baby Just Like You" and Neil Diamond's "Dry Your Eyes" tap into the same zeitgeist that inspired the last hurrah of Sinatra's original role model, Bing Crosby. In 1977, the great crooner capped his career on a very high note (you might say that Bing went out with a bang), when, in his final television special (aired after his death), he sang a duet with 1970s rock avatar David Bowie, a medley of the familiar Christmas song "Little Drummer Boy" and the new "Peace on Earth" (by Larry Grossman, of Broadway and *The Muppet Show*). Over the last forty years, this twilight performance has become Crosby's best known to contemporary audiences, and when the duet was released as a single in 1981 it became one of the bestselling discs of both singers' careers.

"A Baby Just Like You" and "Dry Your Eyes" are clearly predecessors to the Crosby-Bowie medley; all three are very serious, even somber, post-Vietnam kinds of Christmas songs—not about trees and gift-wrapping and chestnuts roasting on an open fire, but about the spirit of peace pervading the planet, for just a few weeks at least. Like "My Way," "A Baby Just Like You" would seem to be autobiography written for him by someone else. On May 22, 1974, Nancy Sinatra's first child, Angela Jennifer Lambert (today formally known to almost everyone as "A. J.") was born, and at multiple moments in the Main Event concerts, he consistently kvells over the thrill of becoming a grandfather. The song, written by Denver* and Joe Henry, starts with Sinatra

---

* Denver and Sinatra exchanged guest shots on each other's television specials around this time, and Denver served as Sinatra's opening act at Caesars Palace in September 1967.

singing directly to the new baby (we even hear children's toy instruments in the background), telling her of the wonders of "the Christmas time when I was young / the magic and the wonder," describing her as a "little angel" (that is, in fact, her name). The second verse has grandpop likening her to "the savior king" who was born on Christmas, who was "a baby just like you." The message is blissfully optimistic: all babies have the possibility to be Jesus and save the world. It's a highly original song, one of Denver's best, combining the autobiographical with the spiritual and the universal; the capper comes when he mentions the baby girl by name: "Merry Christmas, little Angela, Merry Christmas everyone."

Neil Diamond's "Dry Your Eyes" might be considered a Christmas song, although it's about the death of Jesus rather than the birth (perhaps it's more Easter than Christmas). When we talk about this particular song, another issue comes up. In decades past, when Sinatra sang a song by Cole Porter, for instance, he could take a number written as a ballad, like "I've Got You Under My Skin" and completely rearrange and reinterpret it as a swinger. Now that he was singing Neil Diamond and John Denver, however, the paradigm had shifted: he wanted to sing songs that the kids would know, so what was the point, he reckoned, of radically reinterpreting them? In songs such as "Dry Your Eyes," "Stargazer," and "Like a Sad Song," he felt compelled to sing them more or less in the same arrangements that the original songwriters had used.

Recorded in New York in 1976, Denver's "Like a Sad Song" is more folksy Frank, but absolutely beautiful, miraculously understated both lyrically and vocally, with a marvelously subtle arrangement by another returning friend, Claus Ogerman. Ogerman focuses on Sinatra and guitar,* with the strings only as very appropriate window dressing. This was a singularly beautiful record and a successful Sinatra performance; but, overall, his musicians found it frustrating and limiting. As Al Viola elaborated, "We were essentially doing a copy of what Elton John or some other rock guy had done, which didn't make sense to me. That's what really upset Irv, because he had to play all the same drum breaks that the original rock drummer played."

In that sense, Sinatra was valuing the recognition factor of these songs above their inherent musical worth—why change them up so that the kids won't recognize them? Then again, Diamond and Denver, unlike Porter and Berlin, were not writing songs designed to be reinterpreted in different styles, tempos, and moods. Say what you like about "That's Life," "My Way," and

---

* There are three players listed, Al Viola, Jay Berliner, and Bucky Pizzarelli. I would like to think that the very prominent guitar voice we hear echoing Sinatra is New Jersey guitar legend Pizzarelli, making his most prominent contribution to a Sinatra record.

"Strangers in the Night"; they may have kowtowed to the kiddie crowd, but at least they weren't mere covers of other people's hits. As Cottler put it, "He's a leader, not a follower." Unfortunately, as Vincent Falcone reminded us, "by the late '70s the market for our kind of music was just completely gone. Nobody could make a record that didn't have 'Song Sung Blue' on it. You couldn't turn a radio on without hearing that thing forty-five times a day!"

One gets a sense of Sinatra and Costa trying to solve this problem—of "interpreting," rather than merely "covering," i.e., just sticking Sinatra's voice on a contemporary number. Obviously, it worked better when the song was suitable for him, and he heard two such songs in "Stargazer" and "Dry Your Eyes" on Diamond's 1976 *Beautiful Noise*; in these cases, both of these songs are inspired, to a degree, by existing pieces of music. Diamond clearly heard Johnny Mercer's lyric to "Lazybones" before he wrote "Stargazer" (the last line is very similar) and "Dry Your Eyes" is a direct revamp of the folkloric anthem "Battle Hymn of the Republic."

In "Dry Your Eyes" (cowritten by Robbie Robertson of The Band, who was the producer of *Beautiful Noise*), Costa starts with the mood of the original, at once militaristic (the snare drum and march tempo) and spiritual (the choir, way in the background). Sinatra's voice is even treated with reverb to make him like a preacher—or even God Himself.* The Sinatra performance is very powerful, making this a far more moving religious folk-rock anthem than virtually anything in *Jesus Christ Superstar* or *Godspell*, and it also anticipates any number of the songs that Dylan would write in his own spiritual period a few years later—the time of his Confession.

"Stargazer" is especially interesting in that it was one of the few new songs that Sinatra rendered as a swinger. (Another reason why "You Are the Sunshine of My Life" seemed like such a godsend. "The Best I Ever Had" sounds like a leftover from *Hee Haw* or a rejected chase theme from a *Smokey and the Bandit* movie.) On *Beautiful Noise*, "Stargazer" is already something special: Diamond intended it as sort of a fusion of old-timey hillbilly music and Dixieland jazz, with prominent banjo, clarinet, and tuba. Again, Sinatra does Diamond one better; he retains the two-beat feeling as well as the banjo and tuba; but instead of the clarinet he adds in Sam Butera, the lusty, big-toned tenor saxophonist best known for his years of service with Louis Prima. Even though it's in 2/4 time, he takes the whole thing at a much more exciting tempo. Where Diamond tells his band, "Look out son," Sinatra shouts to Butera, "Jump on it Sam, get all over that!" This is one of the few numbers in

---

* One is reminded of comedian Jackie Gayle's line: "Frank was very nice to me. He even took me to see the manger where he was born."

this batch that Sinatra liked enough to do in concert and on television (on the Jerry Lewis telethon), in a modified arrangement that sounds like the work of Billy Byers; for part of 1976, Butera toured with Sinatra's group (he's heard with the Chairman on a Chicago concert from that year), empowering him to shout "Sam Butera! I hear you behind me. Blow, you mother, blow!"

By all rights, "Stargazer" should have been a hit: it was an exciting song in the tradition of the best Sinatra swingers, and it was a credibly contemporary song—Sinatra had actually made Neil Diamond jump, swing, and blow like crazy, even if it was in two-beat tempo. And he dutifully promoted it in concert, singing it at dozens of shows. But it only made it to number twenty-one on the Adult Contemporary chart. Sinatra had griped on some of his 1974 concerts that his songs must be on a label called "Secret Service Records," because they were so hard to find—in other words, the suits and the hippies who had succeeded him at his own company, Reprise Records, were doing a lousy job of distributing and promoting his music.

He also covered a pair of items recorded by Barry Manilow, although in these two cases he worked harder to wrest the songs from their sources, and both also have autobiographical relevance in a vaguely "My Way"-ish fashion. You can see how a song that begins with the lines, "I've been alive forever / And I sang the very first song" would appeal to Sinatra in 1976, a few weeks after his sixtieth birthday. "I Sing the Songs" had already made the rounds as "I Write the Songs," written by Bruce Johnston of the Beach Boys and recorded by the Captain & Tennille and then David Cassidy (all of whom, now that I think of it, were second-generation pop stars) before Manilow landed his hit record with it. Costa's arrangement again sticks close to Manilow's; Sinatra is more inherently honest, telling everybody that he sings the songs (Manilow, who composed most of what he recorded, was bothered enough by this that he later wrote a song called "I Really Do Write the Songs"), but he can't quite make it work for him—he's defeated by the "hook" ("I sing the songs that make the whole world sing / I sing the songs of love and *special* things"); the way the notes are written forces Sinatra to syllabicate that word as "spe-e-cial," which sounds awkward and defeats any naturalness the song might have had. (To Manilow's credit, that phrasing sounds fine in his original single.*)

"(Why Don't You) See the Show Again" is an actual Manilow melody and a much better arrangement by Calello. In "It Was a Very Good Year," Sinatra seems to become us, turning Ervin Drake's song into our own collective

---

* Sinatra sang "I Sing the Songs," in a leisure suit, on *The Tonight Show* of November 12, 1976, in which, at one point, he fixed the phrase "special things" to "pretty things," which works better for his phrasing. (Later that same day he recorded "I Love My Wife.")

autobiography; in "See the Show Again" he does just the opposite: he brings us all into his persona, letting us see the world through his eyes. A singer on a stage is telling a woman in the audience to stick around after his late show, and while it could sound like a tawdry pickup, he makes it into something marvelously tender, using the slightest and subtlest emphasis on the key words: "and *you*, you're pretty as a picture, and *I* don't even know your *name.*" Unfortunately, he released "I Sing the Songs" as a single but didn't record "See the Show Again" at all. (It survives in various concert performances and, very memorably, on *The Tonight Show* of November 14, 1977, which the singer guest-hosted.)

There were other songs he tried in this period that he didn't commit to wax, which were often better than the ones he did—Neil Sedaka's "The Hungry Years," Elton John's "Sorry Seems to Be the Hardest Word," and Eric Carmen's "Never Gonna Fall in Love Again." Trombonist Dick Nash remembered several sessions with Costa that "never came to fruition. I think they threw them out because Frank wasn't in great voice. That happened a lot, too. You know, he'd have a session all planned and set up, and he'd show up and go for about an hour, whatever, and the scratches would come in, and he'd say, 'Thanks a lot, guys, but this ain't it tonight.'"

The last thing left to try was a pair of traditional Sinatra songs: on February 5, 1976, after "I Sing the Songs," Sinatra had Bill Miller stay while the rest of the orchestra left and recorded two amazingly intimate readings of songs he had cut earlier with Jenkins, "Empty Tables" and "Send in the Clowns," the latter prefaced by a spoken intro. The 1973–74 string arrangements of these two are just fine, thank you very much, but these two Sinatra-Miller duets are even more marvelous; both are saloon songs to compete with "Angel Eyes" and "One for My Baby." They're heartbreakingly personal, Sinatra's chops are at their eleventh-hour peak, and Miller is no less perfect in his touch, his harmonies, his very presence. The Mercer–Van Heusen song uses a barroom metaphor and the Sondheim takes place in an old-world setting; thus Miller is saloony in the first and lightly baroque in the second. Even in those moments where Sinatra isn't singing, it sounds like pure Frank.

From the vantage point of forty years later, it seems especially frustrating that Sinatra's music of the mid-1970s sessions is, overall, much better than the singles and "pop" material he was cutting ten years earlier in the Bowen period, yet none of it seemed to get him anywhere as far as the charts were concerned—obviously Bowen knew something that no one else did. Throughout the 1974–79 period he was singing especially well, and he was playing to tens of thousands of people practically every night; there was more than sufficient demand for the right Sinatra recording. He was trying frantically to find a new path, even as the existing ones seemed to be disappearing—or leading nowhere. He still loved the old songs, and started at least two albums of standards: in 1974 he cut new versions of the Dorsey-era classics "Just as Though You Were Here" and "Everything Happens to Me" with Jenkins (the latter was redone in 1981 for *She Shot Me Down*), and in 1977 he and Riddle put a lot of effort into an uncompleted album of songs inspired by girls' names; but there was little that came out at the time in terms of the classic songs that had done so much for Sinatra, and vice versa, over the years. Quite the nicest track of the era that anyone actually heard was "I Love My Wife," a Cy Coleman song (from a Broadway show of the same name) that he also cut with Riddle (it would have fit perfectly onto the aborted *Here's to the Ladies* album).*

Why had he come back to "Empty Tables" in 1976? He was probably aware that Johnny Mercer was suffering from a brain tumor—he would be gone in June—and would write no more saloon songs for him. Likewise, Jimmy Van Heusen, even more of an unstoppable iron man than Sinatra himself, had gotten married (for the first time) a few years earlier and gradually retired from songwriting, although he still was around when Sinatra needed him. "Empty Tables" and the lackluster "Barbara" (1977) would be the last new Van Heusen songs Sinatra would sing. (He also brought two classic Burke and Van Heusen songs briefly back into the concert book in 1975–76, "But Beautiful" and "Imagination," neither of which was recorded, alas.) This was fast becoming an era of goodbyes: "I Love My Wife" and "Something" (in 1979) would be the last notable new charts he would sing by Nelson Riddle.[†]

---

* That was further than other projects got—Sinatra also pondered a country album with Snuff Garrett and a Latin album with Tito Puente. "We talked about it several times," El Rey del Mambo told me in a brief phone interview, "but we never got around to making it. We both were always on the road, and we never could get together." The rumor mill of the period also had talk of Sinatra collaborating on full-length projects with both Michel Legrand, which seems like a natural, and, less expectedly, George Harrison. Burt Bacharach said that Sinatra called him once to talk about an album, but he wanted to do it immediately, and the composer wasn't available right at the moment. "He hung up the phone. There's no regret there. We've been talking about how I drive singers crazy. I've seen him record. He comes in. The band are ready. One take, two takes, done. I don't know how to do that. And my songs are not easy. I would have lasted maybe one hour with Sinatra before he said, 'Let's forget this whole thing.' But hey. It was great to be even asked. Flattering" (the *Guardian*, May 21, 2015).

† There was also one new association: in 1976, he married his fourth and final wife, Barbara Marx (née Blakeley), a onetime showgirl who had met Sinatra through her second husband, Zeppo Marx, the youngest of the Marx Brothers. Not long after the wedding, one of his longtime musicians, trombonist Dick Nash, went to play at a recording session, and

The saddest thing of all was the departure of Bill Miller. After roughly four years of especially intense touring from 1973 to '77 (preceded by twenty years of working together from about 1951–71) the two had built up a marvelous simpatico synergy—perhaps the closest singer-pianist relationship ever. The closest point of comparison would be the way that Nat King Cole accompanied himself, in that the piano and the voice are fundamentally extensions of the same soul, expressing itself on two instruments simultaneously. The partnership had reached the point where Miller's touch at the keyboard was as much a part of Sinatra's signature sound as the singer's voice itself. But they also reached the point, as the pianist told us (recounted in chapter one), where they were taking each other for granted and getting on each other's nerves.

The upside was the split with Miller opened the door for a new Sinatra collaborator, who would help achieve yet more new artistic pinnacles over the next ten years or so. Vincent Falcone first began playing with Sinatra occasionally during the mid-1970s, a point at which Miller was still in the entourage, now conducting rather than playing. A native upstate New Yorker, Falcone was born in 1938 and was attracted to the piano early on. Although he studied for many years with the intent of becoming a "legitimate" (Falcone's word) concert soloist, he discovered contemporary jazz piano purely by accident in the mid-1950s, progressing from Stan Kenton to Erroll Garner, Horace Silver, Bobby Timmons, Art Tatum, and Hank Jones, as well as "every jazz piano record I could get my hands on."

Falcone went to college and then played around his native Syracuse, his career interrupted by a stint in the army (he saw Sinatra perform in Paris during the 1962 World Tour). He briefly played in Las Vegas but grew frustrated with the music scene and, for a few years, supported his growing family with a steady nine-to-five job selling pianos. By the time he was thirty-two, Falcone had moved up the retail ladder to the point where he managed a multimillion-dollar chain of music stores. "But I was afraid that the next morning I would wake up and be fifty and never have done what I really wanted to do," Falcone said. "So I chucked it all. Nobody could believe that I would give up that kind of financial security, but there was just no choice as far as I was concerned. I packed up my stuff, packed up my family, and moved to Las

---

he brought a young and attractive friend named Jeannie with him. He introduced her to Sinatra, "'Frank, I'd like you to meet a friend of mine.' On the road, guys would bring girls to Frank. If you know what I mean." Nash continued, "and you know, she's a pretty girl, I guess in her mid-forties. Anyway, he shook her hand, looked her right in the eye, you know, with those steely blue eyes, and she was kind of turning whatever....He looked at me, and he says, 'You know I'm married now.' Yeah, she enjoyed that. Anyway, it was cute."

Vegas, with no job, no place to live, nothing." He soon began playing in the lounge of the Thunderbird Hotel, which turned out to be, he said, "absolutely the worst musical experience I ever had in my life! After six months of that, I was really ready to blow my brains out."

Things started looking up when he switched to the Dunes and then Caesars Palace. Shortly after starting at Caesars in 1973, the first act he was called upon to accompany was Frank Sinatra. Falcone later learned that one of his mentors, Nat Brandwynne, who had conducted for Sinatra at the Waldorf Astoria in the mid-1940s, was enthusiastically talking him up to the Old Man. Over the next five years, Falcone's playing at Caesars justified his rabbi's recommendation. The Sinatra people began hiring him with increasing frequency, not just to work in Vegas but for traveling gigs as far as London.

Falcone took advantage of a unique opportunity to impress his new boss when Sinatra came up with a medley based on two classic charts by Nelson Riddle that he had recorded nearly twenty-five years earlier: "The Gal That Got Away" and "It Never Entered My Mind." Costa pieced the two together, taking the most liberties with the Riddle treatment of "Never Entered" in that he arranged it so that the full orchestra could either stay or drop out entirely, leaving only a solo piano behind Sinatra. To everyone's surprise, Sinatra chose to use the piano version, especially after he heard Falcone play it, and it became a regular feature of the concerts.

In July 1978, Falcone was even more astounded to receive a call from Costa informing him that Sinatra wanted him to conduct, for the first time, on a recording session. He flew from Vegas to Burbank for the date and ran down three Costa charts with Sinatra and a typical fifty-piece orchestra of highly venerated Los Angeles studio musicians who had never heard of him. When, halfway through the date, the air-conditioning system broke down, Falcone was already perspiring so much from sheer nervousness that he never noticed the difference. "I was sweating so heavily on the podium that the drops of perspiration were blotting the music!" he said. "Of course, Sinatra told me later that the whole recording session was bogus; he just set it up to test me out. The Old Man decided that he wanted to see what I could do."

Falcone flew home to Vegas that night wondering what Sinatra had thought of his work and perplexed that Bill Miller hadn't been there. The next time Sinatra played Lake Tahoe not long afterward, things were back to normal: Miller was conducting, and Falcone was at the keyboard. Then, a week after Tahoe, Sinatra's business manager, Mickey Rudin, notified Falcone that Sinatra wanted him as his permanent conductor, beginning in four days at Radio City Music Hall. Falcone accepted only after being assured that Miller had left of his own accord. "That was a hell of a place to open!" he said. "Talk about starting at the top. It's one thing to break in in Grand Rapids, Michigan, and quite another to open at Radio City. And I don't think I could ever have explained to anybody what a feeling it was when opening night came and Sinatra said to me, 'Are you ready, Vincenzo? Let's go!' And I realized, as I walked out on that stage, that there was no turning back, there was no stopping the orchestra if you didn't get something right. I mean, this was it, pal. This would either be a feather in my cap or the end of a very promising career. Fortunately, it went very well."

A few months later, after Falcone had been conducting for Sinatra for a few months, he and the Old Man happened to be doing another recording date. He doesn't remember what songs they were working on, only that the whole date was scrapped after Sonny Burke went into the booth and suggested something called *Trilogy* to Sinatra. "Sonny explained it to Sinatra. He had it all laid out, he showed it to him," said Falcone. "And at that point, if my memory serves me correctly, Sinatra was so taken by Sonny's project that he ended that recording session right then. He said, 'We will not do another thing until we do this.'"

When it was finally released in 1980, *Trilogy* was a smash hit, going gold in a matter of weeks (meaning that it sold a minimum of 500,000 units or a million and a half individual LPs), which at twenty-one dollars a pop added up to a lot of lettuce. That price becomes all the more exorbitant when one considers that, at the time, most hardcore Sinatra fans were really paying for just one record, *The Past*, the disc that was arranged and conducted by Billy May. Most listeners could get through only a track or two of *The Future* and probably played *The Present* all the way through once or twice; but *The Past* was the disc that rated as essential Sinatra, worth reprising again and again. But thirty-five years after its release, well, *The Future* doesn't sound any better (or worse) than it did in 1980, but *The Present*, with the exception of a few missteps (one in particular), now seems like the best album that Sinatra could have made in this period.

*The Present* is in the same tradition and general mode as *Some Nice Things* and *Ol' Blue Eyes Is Back,* but is overall an improvement because the parameters of what it included were wider and the pickings not necessarily so slim. Covering the entire rock era, the material goes back as far as the 1956 Elvis Presley hit "Love Me Tender." (It seems churlish to cavil that a song from 1956 could be regarded as "The Present." "Love Me Tender," the oldest song on *The Present*, is actually only two years newer than "All of You," the oldest song on *The Past*—older still when one realizes that "Tender" has its roots in a Civil War–era folk song.)

*The Present* works better than the 1973–74 studio albums not only because the material is better—there's only one song on the whole thing that I have to skip whenever I play it—but because greater care was taken with it. Where some of *Some Nice Things* seems to have been ground out, many of the *Present* arrangements, like those for "Summer Me, Winter Me" and "New York, New York," had been in the concert book long before the sessions. Sinatra had been working on them, fine-tuning them before live audiences, honing them to perfection.

By this point, Sinatra has adapted and seems to be working with the contemporary rhythmic feeling rather than fighting it. Normally, he used Cottler and bassist Gene Cherico, who were perfect on swing material but no more used to the 1970s-time feel than the Old Man was; for *The Present,* Costa insisted on employing a more flexible bassist and drummer in George Duvivier and Jimmie Young. While the brilliant jazz bassist would have been aghast to learn he got the gig because of his capacity for rock rhythms, the flexible Duvivier (who was also skilled on the electric Fender bass, although he much preferred the traditional upright acoustic) could handle anything.

All three of the bouncier numbers on *The Present* (all the work of powerhouse singer-songwriters)—"Just the Way You Are," "Song Sung Blue," and "Isn't She Lovely"—were taped in New York on the same date, August 22, 1979. All three are good illustrations of the modified groove, somewhere between the backbeat-driven sound of the original record (and most 1970s pop) and Sinatra's familiar 4/4 swing. "I couldn't stand 'Song Sung Blue' at the time, and I still hate it!" said Falcone. "The only thing that made it worthwhile was Don's chart. But you just couldn't do much with that song." Sinatra's version is certainly catchy—you can't help humming and patting your foot to it—but "Isn't She Lovely" (not released until the digital era), a 1976 Stevie Wonder song, is stronger, both emotionally and musically. It's a considerably more convincing swing number, using electric keyboard and a Basielike *whomp!* at the end. Wonder's lyrics (except for several trivializing and out-of-place references to the Deity) fit into the tempo nicely, and the piece has the same feeling as any of those marvelously ephemeral rhythm singles that Sinatra cut for Capitol. He also turns it into another paean to his grandchildren.

Billy Joel's "Just the Way You Are,"* from his bestselling 1977 album *The Stranger*, is possibly the newest song on the album. Costa originally planned to arrange the first piece in the same medium-slow fashion as on *The Stranger*

---

* Although I first heard it as sung by Bob Hope's wife, Dolores, numerous times on her husband's television specials of the period—that shows you where *my* head was at.

until Falcone demonstrated to Sinatra how it could work in a swing tempo. Sinatra then instructed Costa to about-face and revamp it into a Basielike dance pattern. "Don was already fifty percent into the chart," said Falcone, "and he got a little angry with me because I caused him to have to redo the whole thing." Sid Cooper, who was part of the saxophone section when Sinatra recorded "Just the Way You Are" in August 1979, opined, "I Thought 'Just the Way You Are' was a wonderful arrangement, although nobody ever made much of it. I liked the way the saxophones were written there. It was one of the few times that we could swing a little bit."

Of the ballads, "For the Good Times," written by Kris Kristofferson, had been a huge hit in 1970 for the country crooner Ray Price and was also a concert staple for Elvis Presley; it ranks as a noble effort for the Chairman, and still whets one's appetite for a Sinatra country album. (Although I have to say that I still prefer "We Were the Only Couple.") With its clever use of soprano Eileen Farrell as a counterpoint voice (replicating the use of vocal harmony on the aforementioned versions), what we have here is a legendary popular singer and a great opera singer venturing together into what is unusual territory for either one of them. Lines like "lay your warm and tender body next to mine" are sort of like watching your parents making love—and for a five full minutes at that. But like the best Sinatra ballads, it has an ineffable air of sadness and inevitability. (I actually prefer any number of concert performances, which don't use the secondary voice, to the studio version.)

Around the same time, Kristofferson had also written a pop-country classic inspired by a line from Sinatra's 1962 *Playboy* magazine interview (a piece of expository writing by Reprise copywriter Mike Shore), namely his 1970 hit "Help Me Make It Through the Night." One wishes that Sinatra had chosen "Help Me Make It Through the Night" for *Trilogy* instead of "That's What God Looks Like to Me," even though the latter song also seems to reflect some of the ideas expressed in the *Playboy* interview: it's better philosophically than musically, and, as in "A Baby Just Like You," it gives Sinatra a chance to find God in young children. The story goes that it was the work of two unknowns (it's credited to Lois Irwin and Lan O'Kun), who, according to the urban legend, walked in off the street and anonymously submitted it to Sinatra's office. When the content of "That's What God Looks Like" was explained to Billy May, his reaction was a simple "Oh, shit!" (It's so much easier to avoid this track in the digital era, but even in the LP days it was nonetheless worth getting up and walking across the room to lift up the tone arm from the vinyl.)

But it gets better. *The Present's* opener, "You and Me" (the only song Sinatra ever recorded by either Peter Allen or Carole Bayer Sager), and "MacArthur Park" are further examples of Sinatra turning other people's songs and other people's stories into thrilling autobiography; "MacArthur" could be an "answer song" to Jimmy Webb's haunting "Didn't We" of ten years earlier. "MacArthur Park" merits attention as an offbeat experiment, one that was certainly worth trying. This ambitious art-rock aria, written by Webb (supposedly on Buddy Greco's piano, or so the latter consistently claimed), had been a most unlikely hit (and a Grammy winner) for nonsinging actor Richard Harris in 1968. Following the example set by Tony Bennett in his 1969 version, Sinatra elects to tackle only a brief excerpt from this seven-minute pop epic. (It was perhaps the single most ambitious pop-rock song of its generation, a precursor to Queen's "Bohemian Rhapsody.") "MacArthur Park" might be construed as a psychedelic answer to "Lush Life"—except it's a much better song for Sinatra. Where Strayhorn's parted lovers jet off to Paris for jazz and cocktails, Webb's boy and girl enjoy their romantic rendezvous in a rather seedy Los Angeles public park, where they dine on cake made soggy by liquid precipitation. Sinatra eliminates those very lengthy passages of the elegy that explain the narrative and cuts to the heart of it, finding autobiographical relevance in lines such as "I will win the worship in their eyes / and I will lose it."

Like "There Used to Be a Ballpark" on *Ol' Blue Eyes*, "MacArthur Park" represents a rare occasion when, in this world of contemporary pop tunes, Sinatra took the highest of high roads. One wishes that Sinatra had bitten off the entire seven-minute work (give props to Vic Damone for trying that) just to see what would happen. Conversely, "Love Me Tender"* is the simplest tune in the lineup, and compared to such long and complex tunes as "MacArthur Park" (not to mention all of *The Future*), there's absolutely nothing wrong with something as simple, direct, and unassuming as a folk song. Costa backs Sinatra with a guitar and choir, then adds very subtle strings.

Thus *The Present* has its share of swingers, as well as folk and rock-type tunes, nearly all of which are successful; yet there are also three tracks here that qualify as all-time Sinatra classics, starting with two relatively contemporary ballads from 1969, "Summer Me, Winter Me" (Costa) and "Something" (Riddle). He was drawn to the second lyric for its ambiguity, the first for its abundant specificity. Both pieces use a very classical string orchestra bereft of brass, reeds, or anything resembling a jazz big band, with Costa hearkening back to *Sinatra & Strings* and Riddle to *Moonlight Sinatra*. Sinatra doesn't

---

* "Love Me Tender" appears once previously in the Sinatra saga: in 1960, on a television special costarring Elvis Presley, it was part of a duet medley by the two colossi in which Sinatra finger-snapped a Nelson Riddle–style swinging treatment of "Love Me Tender" and Elvis gyrated a hillbilly version of Sinatra's hit "Witchcraft." Both performances were rendered with a copious amount of tongue-in-cheek and self-mocking humor.

exactly make "Something" out of nothing, but he greatly embellishes the two melodies with his characteristic rising and surging through mountains and valleys of emotional crescendos and decrescendos, flowing in and out of tempo, sometimes only for a few bars at a time, before drifting to a whole new melodic current. Sinatra sang both frequently in concert, but these are rare cases when nothing topped the definitive studio recordings (at least, comparing them to the concert tapes that I've heard).

"Summer Me, Winter Me" (from the 1969 movie *The Picasso Summer*, starring Albert Finney) is a sequel, more or less, to the 1974 track "What Are You Doing the Rest of Your Life?," with the same cast of creators: Sinatra, Costa, Legrand, and the two Bergmans. Both songs derive from the same central idea, about love in perpetuity; but then again, nearly every song the Bergmans wrote dwells on that theme. "'Summer Me' was an exciting, marvelous arrangement," said lead saxophonist Sid Cooper. "Costa really entwined himself in that arrangement, and we had played it for a year before we recorded it. Oh, it's fantastic, just fantastic."

Falcone explained why this well-received piece was so infrequently performed after the release of the album: "It was magnificent, but to this day [circa 1992] nobody really knows how to perform that chart. The orchestral application is just missed. That chart takes two hours of rehearsal and a great deal of explanation before it gets performed the way it's supposed to be. But it is a masterpiece." Sinatra uses the Bergmans' deliberately repetitious nursery rhyme of a lyric (which also has elements of a Cole Porter–style "list" song) to express deep and profound romantic sentiments, making the most of the lyricists' handy way of turning nouns into verbs, i.e., "I'll wrap you up and *ribbon* you, *rainbow* you." To Alan and Marilyn, "summer me, winter me" is a poetic and highly Bergmanesque way of saying "love me forever."

By contrast, "Something" (which Sinatra had first recorded in a very different, inferior arrangement in 1970) isn't at all poetic or profound in that sense. The strength of George Harrison's lyric is its very directness; like most songwriters of his tradition, the Beatles' lead guitarist was writing and singing out of what was essentially a folk music tradition, where the profundity emerges from keeping everything as simple as possible. Most people remember "Something" as the second track on the classic Beatles album *Abbey Road* (1969). Harrison, who famously visited a Sinatra session around 1968, sings it in what is essentially a monodynamic vocal. He may use the occasional pause for emphasis ("Something in the way ... she moves... / attracts me like ... no other lover"), but he keeps it on a very even dynamic level. Sinatra, as is his wont, employs a wide range of dynamics and even of different voices, from loud, brash, and confident to trembling and trepidatious.

Post–rock-era wisenheimers will sometimes use Sinatra's misattribution of the song's authorship as proof that he didn't really understand "Something"—and they also decry his substitution of the Frankism "Jack" in place of "now" in the line "You stick around now it may show." Yes, it's true that on at least one concert, he introduced the song as by Lennon and McCartney, and also that he said it was "the greatest love song of the last fifty to a hundred years." He was wrong in the first assertion, but correct in the second: it's not only a great love song, but it's classic Frank. Riddle, as always, deserves as much credit as Sinatra, and the strength of the chart is that here, unlike in Sinatra's readings of John Denver or Neil Diamond songs, no one is afraid to wreak great changes on the melody, harmony, and general feel of the song, to make it into something wholly different and even bigger than it was.

Where the Bergmans unleash a virtual torrent of words in "Summer Me," a veritable Websters of synonyms and antonyms (well beyond summers and winters, rainbows and ribbons), Harrison makes a point of saying as little as possible. In fact, he refuses to say what it is about this woman that moves him like "no other lover" (a phrase he uses twice in the text), it's just a certain intangible "something." Again, it's quite the polar opposite of the Bergman libretto. It's what the song doesn't say that makes it so profound. As Sinatra often pointed out in concert (for instance, at the September 27, 1979, Egypt show released on *World on a String*), "it never once says 'I love you,'" and that makes perfect sense since he's communicating his feelings to a third person—in his world, it's probably a bartender—not to the object of his desire. It's a song about "her" and "she" rather than about "you." Sinatra transforms the piece into what he would call a saloon song, but remember that the more accurate definition of that expression is not that it's necessarily sad or about a departed lover, but a song in which Sinatra literally positions himself in a saloon, talking to a bartender or someone else in the bar.

As in "Angel Eyes" and "One for My Baby," we are overhearing one side of a conversation, a notion that becomes especially clear in the bridge (the existence of which also underscores that the song is in something like an AABA format, which also makes it structurally similar to most of the songs in the Sinatra oeuvre). In the line, "You're asking me, will my love grow," he is clearly talking to someone, even if he has to restate the question for clarification. And it's the lack of a specific answer, even repeated for emphasis ("I don't know, I don't know") that speaks more, in this case, than any actual words can say. "Something" became an absolutely classic vehicle for Sinatra in that it gave him another text through which he could offer a highly rarified level of empathy. Stick around, Jack, it may show.

By far the most commercially successful number in all of *Trilogy* wasn't an ambitious art-pop exercise like "MacArthur Park" or a cover of a major rock and roll anthem that had already been a huge hit, but what amounts to an old-fashioned show tune. It's also part of the long show business tradition of a classic song emerging from a flop production, no less than "All the Things You Are" from *Very Warm for May* or "Guess I'll Hang My Tears Out to Dry" from *Glad to See You*.

"Theme from *New York, New York*" was brought to Sinatra's attention by Frank Military, who had been part of the FS entourage (a principal employee of Barton Music) in the 1950s. In later years, he took considerable pride for two things regarding his former boss and lifelong friend: that he was one of the few Sinatra business associates who parted company with him on good terms (the same thing cannot be said, for instance, of longtime manager—and whatever—Hank Sanicola) and that he was the first to steer Sinatra to "New York, New York."

Sinatra had been familiar with the remarkable collaboration of John Kander (mostly music) and Fred Ebb (mostly words): they had worked on his 1973 television special *Ol' Blue Eyes Is Back*, and he had also sung their "Maybe This Time" (originally written for Kaye Ballard during their tenure on *The Perry Como Show* and later incorporated into the film version of *Cabaret*). "I sent him the song, and he said he would listen to it," Military told us in 1991. "I kept calling Dorothy [Uhlemann, Sinatra's secretary] to find out what was happening, and she said, 'It's on the turntable. He's getting to it.' It took him a while, but he finally got to it, and now it's probably the most popular thing he's ever done."

Written for Liza Minnelli in Martin Scorsese's unfortunate 1977 musical of the same name, "New York, New York" marked the second show-type tune of that title to be associated with Sinatra (the first was from his 1949 film *On the Town*). In some early concert performances, Sinatra opened with the Leonard Bernstein–Betty Comden–Adolph Green song to lead into the soon-to-be familiar John Kander–Fred Ebb introductory vamp. Sinatra began doing the new "New York, New York" in concert in October 1978, in the period when Miller left and Falcone was becoming increasingly important. Initially, "New York, New York" was used as an opening number. "We were rehearsing up at NBC, and he brought the sheet music up to the piano and said, 'Here, play this for me,'" the pianist recalled. Around that time, Sinatra commissioned Costa to assemble an instrumental "overture" medley of New York songs for the Radio City engagement, which would include "Autumn in New York" and "Sidewalks of New York" and conclude with the now internationally known vamp to "New York, New York." The Chairman would enter the boardroom on top of the riff, the audience would begin applauding, and Sinatra would, to coin a phrase, start spreading the news.

"After that engagement," Falcone continued, "he said to me, 'Man, this thing is getting big. We have to take it out of the overture.' So I wrote a new ending for Don's overture. And then he said, 'We gotta put this further down in the show.' So it went down about halfway into the program because 'My Way' was still the closer. But 'New York' just kept getting bigger. Of course, all during this period, all during that year, he started to grow with the song, and he started to put it into the shape that it eventually took. It didn't start out being as dramatic at the end as it is now, with a much, much slower tempo. That's why he likes to do a song on stage for several months before he records it; he feels that he develops the song. And he doesn't want to record it too early because then he figures he'll change it." Once a record was released, Sinatra usually became locked into the rough form of the arrangement. (Of course, he might decide a number of years later to start all over again with a completely new treatment.)

Sinatra had originally recorded "New York, New York" in New York, appropriately, in August 1979, along with most of the rest of *The Present*. Between August and September of that year, however, he felt his take on the tune had so improved that he should remake the number, doing it on the same date that he was also tackling part of the Billy May portion of the package. Said Falcone, "The Old Man didn't like the way it came off in New York. He wasn't satisfied with the way he did it. He had kept growing with that song, and by the time we were recording in Hollywood, it had grown that much more. So he said, 'The hell with it. I want to do it over again.' So I conducted it and [veteran West Coast jazzman] Pete Jolly played piano."

By 1980, when *Trilogy* finally came out, "New York, New York" was a bona fide hit—one that now concluded every Sinatra concert. Released as a single, "New York, New York," together with the entire *Trilogy* package, marked Sinatra's biggest record triumphs in a decade, and a double whammy at that. For the final fifteen years of his touring career, he could be counted on to bring the house down with "New York, New York" at virtually every show, particularly those in the New York City area. Prior to Sinatra, the song was just another show tune, with a vaudeville ending and a slowed-down climax that was more representative of Judy Garland's idiom (hence the connection to Minnelli) than Sinatra's. In fact, the obvious inspiration for "New York, New York" is undeniably Garland's production number presentations of such major metropolitan anthems as "Chicago" and "San Francisco," both performed definitively by her at Carnegie Hall in 1961. That's no coincidence:

like "My Way," "New York, New York" is a song for Sinatra to sing in concert halls, not clubs; a song for Carnegie and Radio City, not the 500 Club.

In the hands—or tonsils, rather—of Sinatra, "New York, New York" exemplifies the anger and the optimism, the ambition and the aggression, the hostility and the energy, the excitement and the excrement that is New York. And that also is Sinatra. By the time he reaches the outchorus and the modulation that occurs with the second time he sings "those little town blues," the excitement of the crowd is impossible to contain. Even as "My Way" became the Sinatra signature for the 1970s and the Me Decade, "New York, New York" became not only the definitive Sinatra anthem for the 1980s and '90s but a rallying cry for a city that was just beginning to claw its way out of the abyss.*

By 1980, Sinatra was on a roll again: he had switched to a new policy, one that was in step with the age of movie blockbusters like *Star Wars*. In the 1950s and '60s, top pop and jazz artists turned out three or four albums a year (in his case, nearly all of them masterpieces); in the blockbuster era, you created a huge massive album that people waited around the block to buy, one that probably made even more than two or three years' worth of albums put together from the old days—remember, Michael Jackson's *Thriller* was just a few years away. There was more anticipation regarding *Trilogy* than any other album I can remember; even the gap between the final preretirement release, *Sinatra & Company,* and *Ol' Blue Eyes Is Back* was only two years. (Which is another reason why everyone hated *The Future*—the expectations were so disproportionately high.) There was some discussion as to how the whole thing would be packaged, which also delayed the release; "I would buy the damn thing if they put it out in a brown paper sack," said William B. Williams of WNEW, Sinatra's favorite deejay on Sinatra's favorite station, at the time. The singer also was happy with synergy with the big album and the hit single: where "Strangers in the Night" and "That's Life" were hit singles that he then spun into albums, *Trilogy* was a highly successful album that gave birth, very organically, to an unforgettable song.

Sinatra was inspired by his new relationships. He was happy in both his marriages: the one at home in Palm Springs with Barbara, and his other marriage, the professional one, on the road with Falcone and the rest of his

---

* In the 1990 horror comedy *Gremlins 2,* when the army of furry little killers are about to invade Fun City en masse, their head honcho cheers them on by donning a trench coat and fedora and breaking into "Start spreading the news. . . ."

touring group. *The Trilogy–She Shot Me Down* years, the early 1980s (the singer's mid-sixties), were possibly the last great Sinatra era, wherein he was working hard—even with a concert virtually every night, he took the time to warm up before every show, and was often challenging himself to learn new songs (although relatively few of these made it into the recording studio) and producing great results.

How to follow *Trilogy*? For a while there was talk of going back to work on the *Here's to the Ladies* album; he even briefly considered expanding it into another three-LP box, this one containing thirty-six songs.* Falcone recalled that Sinatra occasionally mentioned the *Ladies* project in the early 1980s, thinking that this certain song would be perfect or that that one should go into it, but it never went any further than that. It didn't help that he and Riddle were, for the time being, not on speaking terms.

But while one wishes that he had finished *Ladies*—in any iteration, three discs or one—the project he did concentrate on was precisely the right one for the time. Rather than an epic miniseries of a package covering all time periods and moods, *She Shot Me Down* would focus on what Sinatra did best: an intimate and sad set of torch and saloon songs. With *Trilogy*, Sinatra was trying to conquer the world and prove that he still had that old Frank magic. With *She Shot Me Down*, Sinatra was making an album just for his old fans. As we've seen, the desire to cut this final set with Gordon Jenkins also grew out of Sinatra's desire to vindicate the aging arranger after the trouncing that *The Future* had received.

While *Shot Me Down* was primarily Jenkins's show, Costa made the next most significant contribution. He received credit as producer, he arranged the opening track (Stephen Sondheim's "Good Thing Going"), composed the song "Monday Morning Quarterback," and assembled the closing medley of "The Gal That Got Away" and "It Never Entered My Mind" from vintage Nelson Riddle charts. "Monday Morning Quarterback" is that rarity, a tune composed by Costa and arranged by someone else. Although it's Costa's tune, it's top-drawer Sinatra-Jenkins, featuring one of the most movingly morose string arrangements ever written by "Lefty" and a real in-your-gut interpretation by Sinatra. It is one of the most gloriously emotional performances in the collection.

Costa wrote the arrangement of the Sondheim song (from *Merrily We Roll Along*, not a hit on Broadway but considered a classic show nonetheless)

---

* What a bonanza that would have been—a mitzvah even—since it would have, out of necessity, been mostly standards. One yearns to hear what Sinatra would have done with Barry Manilow's "Mandy," Bob Dylan's "Sara," or John Lennon's "Dear Prudence."

on an airplane as the Sinatra entourage returned from Rio (circa January 1980). The most lightweight entry on the set, "Good Thing Going" may deceive first-time listeners into thinking they're going to get another elevator-rock session. Compared to the increasingly moody Jenkins scores that follow, it may seem like opening a wine-tasting event with a bottle of Snapple. However, it just takes us a while to realize how truly deep Sondheim's text— and Sinatra's interpretation thereof—actually are; the cheerfulness is only on the surface. (Other than "Clowns," this is the only time Sinatra ever sang a Sondheim melody.)

Like *The Present, She Shot Me Down* concentrated on new songs that would be completely unknown works to the practiced hands in Sinatra's circle. As with *The Present,* Sinatra made the decision to tape the bulk of the album in New York. At the time, he let it be known that he was far from happy with the recording studios in Fun City. "There are maybe three decent studios in all of Manhattan that you can work in, and they're not the best," he told interviewer Arlene Francis. "The sound is not good, they're old, and they've been tinkered with and fooled with. The walls have been changed. They've been ruined, actually." Coincidentally, Sinatra happened to film his last movie, *The First Deadly Sin* (released in 1980), in New York at around the same time; it costarred Francis's husband, Martin Gabel, and featured a score by Gordon Jenkins. (Sinatra also talked about a new partnership with real estate baron Harry Helmsley to build a state-of-the-art studio, to his specifications, on some "property behind Lincoln Center that's owned by the *New York Times.*")

But the glories of recording with the "New York band" made up for his dissatisfaction with the facilities. "We had been working a lot together at the time," said Sid Cooper. "We had just come back from Africa and also played Rio de Janeiro, Argentina, São Paulo, and then did some things in New York. So the band was very tight. And Frank loved that particular band, he was really very enamored of it. He spent a lot of time with us, did a lot of rehearsing, a lot of conducting, in his own fashion. He made very specific demands in terms of dynamics and things that he enjoyed hearing in back of him. And he was very much a part of the orchestra at that time."

Cooper may be understandably partial toward the New York band, whose sax section he led for seventeen years (1974–91), but his claims are more than supported by Falcone, who conducted for all of Sinatra's orchestras. "The New York group was by far the best band ever!" Falcone averred. "Los Angeles had great musicians, but those guys never learned how to 'band' together, and that was the problem. Too many egos, too many players who have reputations that certainly are deserved. They never learned that New York attitude of burying one's ego in favor of the finished product. And although you'll hear the bands in L.A. sound wonderful, when you're actually inside a band and hear the intricacies of an orchestra when it's playing together to make everything work, there's just no comparison between the New York guys and the L.A. guys."

The decision to do *The Present* and *She Shot Me Down* in New York was foremost an economic one. "As I always say," Cooper added, "the bottom line, as far as management was concerned, is what it would cost. And that band was ready to go. We could go in and do anything in one take. If we went to California, they would sit down and make six takes, and take three hours to do one number, and we would do six numbers in three hours. It made more sense just to fly Gordon in."

Falcone said, "These guys are close friends of thirty and forty years, and they think nothing of saying to one another, 'Hey, this isn't right,' 'You better do that again,' and 'Watch this over here.' I mean, there's nothing personally connected, no egos. The section leader has the responsibility. And Sid Cooper is, in my view, probably the greatest lead alto player that ever lived. Sid would run the saxes, and all the guys in that section were stellar people, all stars in their own right. Yet when Sid said, 'Do it this way,' they did it that way. If you tried to do that in L.A., they'd just look at you out of the comer of their eye. The New York band was just the rompin' stompin' band of all time." Cooper concluded, "I remember, on a number of performances that were really unusually great, that Frank came up to me and kissed me!"*

By the early 1980s, more changes were occurring in Sinatra's musical relationships: now it was the end of the road for Jimmy Van Heusen; those long years of working hard, partying harder, and carousing had caught up with him. He lived until 1990, but his final years, in which he was confined to a wheelchair, were less than glorious. In 1980, Al Viola, who had worked with Sinatra since the 1940s and been his regular guitarist at least since the 1962 World Tour, left the road for complicated professional and personal reasons. Yet other old friends came back: for a brief period, Sinatra renewed his relationship with Jules Styne, and Tony Mottola became Sinatra's guitarist for a decade or so.

Sinatra and Mottola went back together to 1932 when, as teenaged hopefuls, they performed together on Jersey City radio station WAAT. They

---

* Trumpeter Chris Griffin, who had last recorded with Sinatra in New York in 1951, was also on one of the early 1980s dates. "I hadn't seen Frank in years, but he came right up to meet and shook my hands, asked about my wife and kids, everything." The punch line for the story came sometime after the session, when Griffin was told by another musician, possibly contractor Joe Malin, that Sinatra had said to him, "Isn't it great the way that Chris still remembered me after all these years?"

crossed paths frequently in the studios in the 1940s and early '50s, most famously on "S'posin'," "We Just Couldn't Say Goodbye," and the immortal "My Cousin Louella." Released as by Frank Sinatra and the Tony Mottola Trio, these 1947 sides represent the best of Sinatra's early attempts to assimilate the style of the King Cole Trio.

In 1980 Mottola, who was then sixty-two, considered himself retired. Though he held on to his home in Denville, New Jersey, he stayed in Florida most of the time and hadn't actually touched a guitar in several years. Then to his surprise he received a call from Joe Malin. The contractor informed Mottola that an old friend of his wanted to work with him again—and Mottola thought that Malin was kidding when he said it was Sinatra. Malin assured him that he wasn't. It seems that Al Viola had left Sinatra's group, and Sinatra wanted Mottola to fill in for a week at Resorts Casino Hotel in Atlantic City and then another week at Carnegie Hall. Sinatra told him, "It's been a long time. Listen, now that I got you here, I want you to do a spot in the show." Mottola responded, "With you, like we used to do on *Vimms* [Sinatra's 1944 CBS Radio series], just the guitar and voice? 'Yeah,' he said, 'but I want you to do a solo spot, too.'"

When Rudin made Mottola an offer to go on the road with the Sinatra group, Mottola agreed, with the stipulation that he could bring his wife, Mitzi, with them. "It was great when Tony came along," said Falcone, "and, if you'll pardon the observation, in my humble view, Tony was the quintessential guitar player for Sinatra. Not that Al wasn't, of course; they had two different styles." Viola is unbeatable as a jazz rhythm master, after the fashion of Freddie Green in Count Basie's band, whereas Mottola was celebrated as a virtuoso soloist. Before long, Mottola was enjoying two featured spots in each concert, one a feature for himself (such as "Guitar Concierto de Aranjuez," a Spanish classical feature for solo guitar, or "Manha de Carnaval") and the other a duo between himself and Sinatra, such as "September Song" or "As Time Goes By" (which Sinatra also performed as a duet with Teddy Wilson, no relation to Dooley Wilson, in a 1979 TV tribute to *Casablanca* star Ingrid Bergman), in the tradition of the 1962 Sinatra-Viola "Night and Day."

Sinatra and Mottola had done a number of different tunes on the road, but when they went into a studio together in 1983, they recorded an entirely new piece, "It's Sunday" by Jules Styne. During the years when Styne was collaborating with lyricist Sammy Cahn, he had been Sinatra's "house" composer for most of his movie musicals at RKO and MGM. Then, in the post-*Trilogy* era, the songwriter became a presence in Sinatra's music again, in songs with lyrics both by Cahn and his new collaborator, the talented young lyricist Susan Birkenhead. (At one date in 1983, Sinatra ran down three new Styne songs a row.) Styne was pushing eighty at the time but nonetheless was tire-lessly turning out new songs and shows (which, among other things, helped to subsidize his gambling habit).

"Hey Look, No Crying" had been one of the saddest and most moving numbers on *She Shot Me Down*. "Love Makes Us Whatever We Want to Be" is a bouncy show-type tune in 2/4; it could have come from *Bells Are Ringing* or *Do-Re-Mi* (and actually sounds melodically reminiscent of Van Heusen's "Ev'rybody Has the Right to Be Wrong" from *Skyscraper*). "Searching," which Sinatra most famously sang at his pinnacle *Concert for the Americas* in 1982, is a rangy melody and a vague lyric, the reach of which exceeds its grasp. "Searching" doesn't quite know what it's looking for, but is a valid search nonetheless. The charming "Only One to a Customer" from 1986, with lyrics by Carolyn "Young at Heart" Leigh is a solid swinger arranged by Billy May that, both rhythmically and philosophically, could have been a Capitol single from the "Tender Trap" era.

But the gem of the bunch is "It's Sunday." In 1926, Styne's first successful song had been the jazz standard "Sunday," and now the calendar had rolled all the way around again. Sinatra's first thought had been to commission an orchestral arrangement from a new collaborator, Peter Matz, who had never worked with the Chairman before, although he had written no end of won-derful orchestrations for Tony Bennett, Barbra Streisand, and many others. Said Mottola, "We ran the arrangement down, but Frank didn't seem too pleased with it." Sinatra and Company happened to be in Vegas at the time, and since Costa was handy, as always, Sinatra asked him to write a chart for "It's Sunday." "We ran it down again," Mottola said, "and again Frank wasn't happy with it. He said, 'You know, you're missing the whole point. I want this to be a very intimate thing. Let me do it with Tony for a little bit to show you what I mean.' So I played it, and he said, 'That's the kind of intimacy I want.' So Don wrote yet another chart! We were going to do it at the next record date, which was going to be in New York. However, we didn't have a chance to rehearse that one." Sid Cooper described Costa's chart as "a big orchestration. We recorded it with the orchestra, and Frank said, 'Tony, why don't we just dismiss the band and see what happens with the two of us?' And that's the way it came out—just wonderful."

At last, in February 1983, Frank and Tony went to the Warner Bros. recording studio without the rest of the orchestra. "And it turned out beauti-fully," the guitarist commented. "It's what I call a love song for mature people, not teenagers. I mean, like older people in love, people talking about things: 'It's Sunday morning, I wake her up with a rose, bring her breakfast in bed.' It's a very difficult song to sing. In the first couple of bars there's something like eight words in every measure! It's the first time that he's ever recorded anything with a solo guitar, and it makes me very proud. And it's a beautiful song and a beautiful rendition." It's a remarkably intimate song for a bombastic era; this is a period when everybody's most successful numbers were loud and over the top, a sweet and mature love song in an era of belty, juvenile anthems. It's actually a "Sunday kind of a love" kind of song, expressed so simply and directly in both the vocal and the accompaniment that it becomes almost monumental in its vivid exaltation of homely virtues. Sinatra not only sees the big picture—as in "Ol' Man River" or "Lost in the Stars"—but finds God in the details.

"It's Sunday" was clearly worth all the effort, although it took at least three sessions and two full-scale orchestrations before they finally nailed it, which shows how difficult it was becoming for Sinatra to get something exactly the way he wanted it. There were two other singles from the approximate period, both of which might be considered propaganda of a sort, in the same way that "New York, New York" can be considered a propagandistic jingle for Fun City. Arranged by Joe Parnello, who took over as Sinatra's conductor a few years later, "Here's to the Band" reprises all the Garland-Minnelli–type vaudeville shtick from "New York, New York"; this time it's a rah-rah rallying cry on behalf of professional musicians, right down to its half-time climax.

From the title, one might hope that "Here's to the Band" would contain some kind of metaphoric conceit in the same vein as Irving Berlin's "Let's Face the Music and Dance" or Abbey Lincoln's "You Gotta Pay the Band" (not a bad song for Sinatra, now that you mention it). But no. Three otherwise unknown Jerseyites, Sharman Howe, Alfred Nittoli, and Artie Schroeck, conceived "Band" as a vehicle for Sinatra to pay homage to the members of the American Federation of Musicians. Sinatra is never given the opportunity to go beyond the jingoistic message and tap into something deeper, the way he does on "New York, New York." It's a solidly crafted song (by three unknowns), sung with great feeling by the Chairman, but it's hardly surprising that it didn't catch on.

Joe Raposo and Hal David's "To Love a Child" was written as the theme for First Lady Nancy Reagan's Foster Grandparent program; it could have also been the theme song of the children's charities chaired by Barbara Sinatra. The song brings us a side of Sinatra that we haven't seen in a long time: the paternal, avuncular jokey guy that Little Nancy and Tina knew, the Sinatra we remember from "High Hopes" and "Pocketful of Miracles." Costa's arrangement of "To Love a Child" is kind of *Trilogy* all by itself—the past, the present, and the future. It's a song for those who believe that children are the future (speaking personally, I have my doubts), and to that end costars the arranger's nine-year-old daughter (and future pop star), Nikka Costa; but it's also a song of farewell, in that it's the last important work in the Sinatra canon by either Costa or Raposo. (At the same session, Sinatra would record, but never release, a Costa chart on Raposo's *Sesame Street* number "Sing"—what I wouldn't give to hear that.) "To Love a Child," with words by Hal David, has the formulaic feeling of one of those songs in musical versions of *A Christmas Carol* or *How the Grinch Stole Christmas* where the grumpy old geezer becomes a warm and cuddly old geezer. Yet even though my intellectual mind knows that full well, I can't stop myself from kvelling each time I hear it. There aren't many classic Sinatra performances that one would describe with the adjective "charming," but this is one of them.

Sinatra was again underrecorded—there were only a handful of singles between 1981 and 1984—but he and his musical entourage hit a genuine peak in the early '80s. The only thing missing in those years was the familiar sound of Bill Miller's soft chords emanating from the keyboard; it would have made sense to keep both Falcone and Miller on the payroll, alternating in the roles of pianist and conductor where appropriate. Miller would play on the saloon songs and classic 1950s and '60s arrangements; Falcone was just right for the more contemporary material and items that required more of a modern jazz sensibility.

Surprisingly, such things were beginning to turn up in his repertoire. "When I left Tommy, we went with the full [string] orchestra at all times," Sinatra said in a 1980 interview, "and now I'm thinking of going the other way, going with a good jazz band, a Basie-type band and stay with that for a while. And if something soft has to be done, we would use a rhythm section, just a piano, drums, guitar, and bass, and do all the ballads quietly." For a time Sinatra put the emphasis on hard swing by dropping his string section and whittling his accompaniment into what he called "the hot band." As he told Sid Mark, "The people [in the audience] are excited by the sound. I can see their faces from the stage. And I am excited by it. It really pushes you along when you are up there on a stage and the band is blowing away behind you. So I feel that we made the right move."

Encouraged by Falcone, Sinatra exhibited more of an interest in jazz than he had since the Basie collaboration; in these years, he made the bold move, for him, of occasionally keeping the orchestra quiet while he swung standards with only the rhythm section: "Lover, Come Back to Me," which he had never performed before; yet another new variation on "Night and Day"; and "I Get a Kick Out of You." (This latter piece was done with just the rhythm section, as on the 1981 *The Man and His Music* television special, and with the addition of Al Klink's golden-toned tenor on at least one concert recording.) Where we expect to hear Sinatra with the familiar sound of Miller's playing, which comes out of the era of Teddy Wilson and Earl Hines, here he was singing on top of pianistic underpinnings closer to Wynton Kelly or Sonny Clark.

But what really made the *Trilogy/She Shot Me Down* era so special was that, all these years after the unretirement, Sinatra himself had reached a new peak. The idea that he was getting older may actually have been a blessing, because it made him work all the harder to remain in top condition. "I first met him when he was fifty-nine years old, and by that time he was already starting to suffer some vocal deterioration," said Falcone. "But it didn't matter because he worked so hard at keeping his voice in shape in those days. He got excited about what we were doing and began to do vocal exercises again. We used to spend several hours every day in vocal exercises. I'd meet him every afternoon, and we would spend a couple of hours going over scales and arpeggios, et cetera. And then later, for at least an hour immediately prior to every performance, he would do still more exercises.

"These were the kind of exercises that had been taught to him by classical singers over the years. I even went with him one time when he went to visit Pavarotti. We were doing a concert with him in New York, and we went to his apartment because the Old Man was having a particular problem with something and wanted to discuss it with him. Robert Merrill was another one whom he'd always go to for advice about the use of the voice and so forth. He knew that they didn't know how to do what he did, but he knew that they knew about the voice and how to maintain the equipment." Sinatra went so far as to temporarily quit smoking (except to use a cigarette as a prop in "The Gal That Got Away") during this period. He also refused to drink when he had a show coming, knowing that whiskey was bad for the throat, and even kept tea in his glass on stage. Falcone emphasized, "I mean, he really toed the line."

Falcone's conducting also served to bring up the quality level of the concerts. Sid Cooper, who traveled with Sinatra through four orchestra leaders, described Falcone as the most "serious" of the bunch. "Vincent was probably the one who cared the most about the position he had. He was always trying to make Frank happy. He made himself available all the time. He would leave messages about where he was in case the Old Man wanted him. He really cared for his position." Falcone explained that his philosophy on conducting had been imparted to him by Gordon Jenkins, who taught the young musician to watch Sinatra like a hawk. "Sinatra never got away from me," he said. "He's done this with other conductors over the years. He absolutely demands that you stay with him on every phrase that he makes, every breath, every movement. He wants that orchestra deadlocked to him. It used to get to be a game between him and me, where he would actually try to get away from me, and he couldn't because I had learned how to keep up.

"I think that was one of the things that kept me in his good graces all those years. He knew that he didn't have to worry about changing a phrase here or there, or if his voice wasn't quite up to par on this particular night and he didn't want to hold a note as long as he might have held it the night before. He didn't have to worry about having to let me know about anything like that because he never told you anything. He just went out and did it. Gordon taught me to watch his mouth, to watch his chest when he breathed so I would know when he was going to do what he was going to do. As a tip, it was priceless. Gordon told me many other things, but that's probably the most important thing that he ever laid on me."

The rapport between Sinatra, at the top of his form vocally, and his team was perfect, and the performances were extraordinary. They took chances together: in 1982, Sinatra and Falcone experimented with an eight-minute *Porgy and Bess* medley, using only voice and piano.* But it was all too good to last. There was bad feeling between certain members of the group who were jealous when any of the others received any attention, one in particular. Eventually it became unbearable for Falcone, who left at the very end of 1983 after playing for Sinatra as occasional pianist and then conductor for a total of ten years. Falcone was only the first to go as the team gradually broke up; next was bassist Gene Cherico, then lead trumpeter Charlie Turner, then Mottola. "And unfortunately," said Falcone, "when that group disbanded, the replacement musicians were a considerable step down." Finally, in 1989, Irv Cottler died.

That was the other problem: when *Trilogy* was released, all of the people Sinatra counted on to make music with were still active. It was bruited about at the time that all the tremendous effort required to produce *Trilogy* took years off of the life of Sonny Burke, but at least he had lived long enough to be aware of its success when he died at age sixty-six in May 1980. Then, they all started checking out: Don Costa died in 1983, Gordon Jenkins in 1984, and Nelson Riddle in 1985. Ironically, Riddle succumbed to cancer just as the breach between him and Sinatra was mended, and he was starting work on a new album for the singer.

The death of Costa, only fifty-seven, hit Sinatra particularly hard. Those close to the late arranger are too protective of him, even in death, to tell any

---

* That *Porgy and Bess* is most vividly documented in a singularly excellent concert from Buffalo, New York, on May 8, 1982, which will hopefully someday be issued commercially.

outsider what killed him, though one gets the impression that had he been blessed with another kind of personality, he might have saved himself. But then, he might not have been what he was. "Don's heart was bad," said Sid Cooper, "and he was a very stressed guy, a very tense guy, and I don't think he took care of himself. He had marital problems [he had children with two different wives], and this and that. He was not a drunk by any means, and he wasn't on drugs, outside of his medicines. He just didn't lead the kind of life you lead if you want to hang around for a while."

By 1981, said Cooper, Costa's health was bad and getting worse. "Don was conducting a number for Frank in Rio, and he really didn't want to do it. At that time he already wasn't feeling that well. And he came to the end of the bandstand and looked over to me and said, 'Would you finish up?' So I stood up, and he walked offstage, and I conducted till the end of the show. In other words, he just wanted to get off there as soon as he could. And he liked [being able to leave] so much that we did it that way on every show."

The last project he and Sinatra worked on was an album the singer produced and conducted for his old friend, cabaret legend Sylvia Syms, taped in April 1982. Costa did the charts but was already too sick to attend the sessions; during the recording, Sinatra would occasionally phone him and hold the receiver up to the proceedings so he could hear how everything was going down. Costa held on for another eight months, and after undergoing multiple bypass surgery died in January 1983.

Yet the decline of the Sinatra road company was hardly immediate, and they would have many spectacular nights yet. On August 20, 1982, Sinatra performed in the Altos de Chavón amphitheater in the Dominican Republic at a festival titled the Concert for the Americas. This event was Sinatra's first foray into new media; it would be shown on cable TV (or as it was called at the time, "pay TV") and released on home video. They couldn't have picked a better show: Sinatra and the classic lineup of his "concert years" ensemble (Falcone, Cherico, Mottola, Cottler, and trumpeter Charlie Turner) and the Buddy Rich Orchestra are all at the absolute peak of their game. Sinatra and Mottola do what might be the best version of "Send in the Clowns" yet, and he also resuscitated the 1961 Neal Hefti–Count Basie "I Won't Dance," to swinging effect. According to Sid Cooper—who, like Sinatra, had worked with the "super drummer" in the Tommy Dorsey days—Rich's band was exciting as an opening act, but the reed section couldn't cut Sinatra's charts. "Steve Marcus was a good [saxophone] soloist, but he couldn't play the clarinet to save his ass," said the saxist. "They couldn't play the flutes, and they couldn't play the woodwinds. So they called me out, and I stayed a week with them and taught the guys how to do it."

Cooper was miffed, however, that after providing the Rich sax section with such brilliant tutelage, he was not invited to join them on that South American tour. (I saw the Sinatra-Rich tour when they played the Nassau Coliseum, and the response to "New York, New York"—so close to Manhattan—was even greater than in the Dominican Republic.) Joe Parnello, conductor, pianist, and arranger, took over from Falcone in January 1983. His three years with Sinatra are best summed up by Cooper: "Joe Parnello was somebody who was used to other singers, and his writing was good, although it wasn't in the same class [as Riddle, Jenkins, Costa, and so forth]. Joe seemed a little frightened most of the time. He didn't seem to have the confidence that was necessary, and you had to have that around Frank. If he sensed that you were insecure, he could lay a number on you! But Joe was good. He worked very hard, and he did a very good job." Parnello, who contributed a red-hot treatment of "Change Partners" (very different from the 1966 Jobim version) left in 1985; he too died very young, not long after.

Parnello's pinnacle achievement as Sinatra's conductor may have been the amazing concert that was videotaped at the Nippon Budokan in Tokyo, on April 18, 1985. Gaining on his seventieth birthday, Sinatra was in fantastic shape, as was the mostly Japanese orchestra now conducted by Parnello. One is tempted to describe Sinatra and his musicians as functioning like a well-oiled machine, and indeed they are; but the metaphor sells Sinatra's music short. Who's to say that machines, no matter how well they may be oiled, have such a monopoly on perfection? Sinatra's playfulness at times borders on the maniacal: throughout the 1970s, he would often affect a Daffy Duck–like lisp on "You Make Me Feel So Young" and in the 1980s, he got into the habit of singing "The Lady Is a *Tramp*" with a country-like twang on the last word of that phrase, inspired by Elvis, Cher, or both. Here, in front of a room full of Japanese fans, he even sings "*Ruck* be a *Rady*." Politically correct he wasn't (even if he had been the first celebrity to crusade for equal rights for all Americans, regardless of skin color, racial background, or immigrant status), but hot and swinging he was. Throughout the mid-1980s, he was on an unbelievable high; still, it was clear even then that nothing lasts forever.

In August 1984, Sinatra released his next album, *L.A. Is My Lady*. As we've seen, he was in something of a Basie mood off-and-on in the early 1980s, and Basie himself made his first appearance on a Sinatra television special on the 1981 *The Man and His Music*. The idea of Basie-style swinging was appealing to him: as excellent as he was sounding, it was inevitable that his vocal resources would start to diminish, and the Basie style doesn't require a lot of long sustained notes but rather the ability to cut them off in a tight, swinging fashion—in fact, those Basie style cut-off notes are the very quintessence of what swing is. The Count himself checked out in April 1984, and it made sense anyhow for Sinatra to work again with Quincy Jones, who had served an apprenticeship, so to speak, with both Basie and Sinatra.

More than anyone else in Sinatra's world, even Costa, Jones had enjoyed staggering success in the world of youth-oriented pop music; he had produced the all-time blockbuster of the late twentieth century, Michael Jackson's *Thriller*, and the collected total sales of singles and albums produced by "Q" would surely number in the billions. A year after *L.A. Is My Lady*, he would produce "We Are the World," one of the most successful singles of all time. And even more than Costa, Jones's roots were in authentic jazz. In a sense, Quincy Jones had started in the same place as Sinatra—the big-band era—and he had long since transitioned over to where Sinatra wanted to be, a world where record sales were measured in multiples of millions.

Born in 1933, Quincy Delight Jones had effected that transition in 1964, when he became one of the first African American executives at a major record label; at Mercury, Jones not only produced albums with his own big band (one definitely in a Basie-esque mold, but very contemporary at the same time) but began crafting hit singles by pop stars such as Leslie Gore. Even while he was busy running Mercury, he took time out to essentially conduct and produce the second Sinatra-Basie album, *It Might as Well Be Swing*, and stayed with the Chairman and the Count through the long road tour of 1965 into early '66 (which culminated in the classic *Sinatra at the Sands* double album). By the time of *Thriller* in 1982, Jones had become the virtual godfather of pop music, the combined equivalent for that industry of what George Lucas and Steven Spielberg represented for the movie business—a magnate of middlebrow culture whose empire still extends well beyond music and into film and television production.

He had only briefly been a jazz orchestrator: he just did that job long enough to learn how it was done. There was considerable precedence: decades earlier, Ray Noble was a first-rate dance band arranger who toiled anonymously for a few years until he became famous enough to lead his own big band. But when Noble became a bandleader, he largely stopped writing charts himself but instead supervised the work of other arrangers, and his principal orchestrator was Glenn Miller. Like Noble, Miller worked behind the scenes as an arranger before he too launched his own band, and then Miller also stopped writing charts himself but commissioned, organized, and edited the works of others. Jones followed in the same tradition: once he became a bandleader and conductor, he realized that his time was better spent delegating than writing out every note for the third trombone and the bari sax. Although he is credited as arranger on those two Sinatra-Basie albums, he actually did more supervision than actual arranging, a fact that he has never tried to conceal.

Rosemary Clooney once told me, "It's impossible to pick out a Quincy Jones arrangement," which isn't necessarily because he never had a signature sound as identifiable as Riddle or May, but because we don't actually know which arrangements are by Jones himself. When I interviewed him, around 1993, Jones was very quick to deprecate his own work as a writer; but the late Frank Foster, his Basie colleague, felt that he deserved more credit in that respect. "When people compare me to him, they say, 'Hey, man, you got a whole lot more on the ball than Quincy,' and I say, 'Well, I don't really think so.' Quincy was really a wonderful arranger. He just put it all aside to do something else, to come into the contemporary era. He took it somewhere else. When he wrote for the Basie orchestra, you couldn't exactly tell [which charts] were Quincy's; all you could tell was that they were very good. With his own band he seemed to have more of an individual trademark. When people hear things like 'The Midnight Sun Will Never Set,' 'Nasty Magnus,' 'Rat Race,' and 'I Needs to Be Bee'd With,' they say, 'Man, those are dynamite charts. Who did them?'"

Quincy's number-one arranger and lifelong friend was the brilliant Billy Byers (1927–1996), who had started as a trombonist. "Quincy was an excellent arranger, but he doesn't write anymore," he said about the same time as I interviewed Jones. "He found a better and easier way to go. Quincy is highly motivated and finds it tough to sit down long enough to write a whole chart. You've got to be a recluse, like Nelson was, to do orchestrations. Quincy would much rather be up front with the clients, doing what I call his 'floor show.'"

Jones seems to have reattracted Sinatra's attention through his work with another showbiz legend whom Sinatra had long admired, Lena Horne. Jones had produced the hit album of her 1981 one-woman Broadway show, with its Sinatra-inspired title, *The Lady and Her Music*, and the success of the disc cemented the success of that Horne "comeback." Around 1982, Sinatra was discussing the idea with both Jones and Horne. Long a supporter of the lady in both her music and her liberal politics, Sinatra had employed both Horne and Eleanor Roosevelt in his 1960 television special *Here's to the Ladies*, a bold gesture even at the dawn of Camelot.

Like the aborted album that shared the same title of *Here's to the Ladies*, the Lena Horne project at one point expanded into a three-disc set in the wake of *Trilogy*. In a 1983 interview with Washington, D.C., deejay Ed Walker, Sinatra reported, "We were ready to do the album about two months ago, and she had a vocal problem, a nodule that grew on a vocal chord or something, and she had to get off the road with her show. Consequently, we didn't do the album with Quincy Jones. That's quite an undertaking, by the way, with thirty-eight songs involved in it. He thinks he's gonna do it in two weeks. I say if we do it in four months we're lucky!"

If Jones and Sinatra had been able to stick to a small-scale scenario, a one-disc set of duos, they might have been able to pull it off. As it was, they kept expanding the project until it was set to become another super-spectacular. "We were planning on a really big extravaganza there," Jones told me. "It was going to be an incredible mixture of jazz musicians and duets. We had Lionel Richie involved and Michael Jackson, Cynthia Weil and Barry Manilow, and lots of people." In addition to the duets, the set was supposed to include a number of solo selections, on which Sinatra would sing numbers associated with Horne and vice versa, climaxing in a gala medley. "If we had been able to pull it all together, it would have been a great album."

There was one other relevant factor: Once upon a time, Sinatra and Horne had been close friends. In 1960, she was a guest on his ABC-TV special *Here's to the Ladies*, and the pair sang a delightful Harold Arlen medley together with obvious, sincere affection. But a few years later, a rift developed between them. Horne had married one of Sinatra's dearest friends, the conductor and composer Lennie Hayton (a daring move, when so-called interracial marriage was illegal in most of the country); but after twenty years, that marriage was unraveling. Friends took sides, with Sinatra siding with Hayton; and like so many other things, he griped about it in concert. He spent a lot of the 1970s bitching about Horne on stage, without ever explaining why. (Whenever I heard him complain about her in concert, I had no idea what was going on—thankfully it was explained in Jim Gavin's biography of Horne, *Stormy Weather*.) As an unfortunate result, it seems highly unlikely that the two would have actually wanted to work together in 1982.

Jones and Sinatra were able to get the *L.A. Is My Lady* project done for precisely the opposite reason: they came up with the idea, struck while the iron was hot, and crafted a perfectly respectable release well before it could be bogged down in over-planning. This album began with a song, "L.A. Is My Lady," credited to Jones and his wife, Peggy Lipton (an actress who had costarred on television's *Mod Squad*). Jones had written the piece for a civic celebration in Los Angeles that involved the city's mayor, Tom Bradley. (Bradley was only the second African American to be elected mayor of a major American city, and Sinatra was a very enthusiastic supporter.) Although the Bergmans received credit for the text, Jones said that the song wasn't written specifically for Sinatra or anyone else. "They might have written a different song if they had known that at the time," he said.

Jones said that he wasn't the one who passed the song on to Sinatra directly, only that the singer had somehow heard it and then called him suggesting that they use it as the title track for an album. "His mind was focused on the project, and he wanted to do it right then, you know?" said Jones. The two then set out to select the repertoire, Sinatra picking "How Do You Keep the Music Playing?," among others, and Jones's suggestions including "Mack the Knife." As producer and conductor, Jones assumed responsibility for "casting" four arrangers on various tracks, including two fellow Basieites, Frank Foster and Sammy Nestico, plus Torrie Zito (who had scored a single for Sinatra some twenty years earlier and then worked more extensively with Tony Bennett) and Sinatra's current musical director, Joe Parnello. Jones also provided for the set to be released on his Warner Bros. subsidiary, Qwest Records.

In its abstract form, *L.A. Is My Lady* suggests the same outline as *Strangers in the Night*: Sinatra and Jones start with a new potential hit, rendered in the contemporary style. They use this to lead off an album of standards that Sinatra had not previously recorded, rendering the whole package in swinging dance tempos. Even the ballads have a beat. Whereas Tony Bennett treats "How Do You Keep the Music Playing?" as a dramatic showstopper (in crawl tempo with a roof-rattling closer), Sinatra keeps his danceable. The only thing wrong with this plan is that the title track failed to materialize as the hit that Sinatra and Jones hoped for. They were clearly looking for a Lotusland follow-up to "New York, New York," but the obvious geographic hook tended to work against the song rather than for it. Then, too, the disco-y nature of the melody and the arrangement, while considerably better than the 1977 treatment of "Night and Day," is the kind of thing that might have hit for Sinatra and Jones in the '70s but seemed a beat behind the times in 1984. To make it more in step with "New York, New York," "L.A. Is My Lady" builds to a Judy Garland—style "slow down" climax, which serves to make the track sound like a misguided attempt to please everybody.

As a piece of music that was neither especially good (nor, it must be admitted, particularly bad) nor a pop hit, the title track unfortunately served to drag down the entire set in the minds of most listeners. As an album, *L.A.* lacks the abject profundity of the classic swing sets by Riddle and May, among them *Strangers in the Night*. Still, it's bright and brassy and a ball to listen to.

Although Jones corralled a quartet of ace arrangers, the biggest star recruited to operate behind the scenes was Phil Ramone. He had long since established himself as a hitmaking producer and a pop music icon (his name had long since inspired the Ramones, the most famous of all punk rock bands in the 1970s), but he had begun his career as a recording engineer and had, in fact, served in that capacity on the New York session for Sinatra's 1967 *The*

*World We Knew.* To work with Sinatra again, Ramone volunteered to be temporarily demoted from calling the shots to twisting the dials. "Quincy and I have been close friends for a long time," said Ramone, "and he called me and said, 'Would you like to be involved in [this album]? You know how to make a band holler on tape.' I said, 'If you want me to fix microphones, that's where I'll be! I don't care, I just want to be there.'"

Jones assembled an all-star aggregate of the hottest New York players. Selecting the cream of the city's studio giants, he leaned toward veterans of the bands of Basie, Hampton, Herman, and Goodman. He also enticed a number of players who had formidable careers as recording stars in their own right, such as Randy and Michael Brecker and George Benson (who solos on "It's Alright with Me," a Sam Nestico chart on a classic Cole Porter piece that dovetails nicely with Billy May's "All of You" on *The Past*)—not to mention jazz legend Lionel Hampton himself. This provided Sinatra with yet another of his great recording bands.

Fortunately, the session tapes of the album have been circulated among collectors (we don't have any other session outtakes since the mid-1960s), and they reveal that Sinatra was still an active participant in matters well beyond his actual vocals themselves. For instance, on "Body and Soul" (arranged by smooth-jazz giant Bob James in his only work for Sinatra) we hear the singer instructing Jones to dispense with the orchestra in the opening measures. "Do it with piano and voice," he says, "make it sound like a saloon in front." It's a worthy performance of a great standard that Sinatra hadn't recorded since 1947; but alas, it didn't meet his own standards—admittedly, his throat sounds a bit scratchy—and therefore didn't make it to the finished album. (Perhaps Sinatra felt that overall it sounded too saloony; the mood here is considerably more melancholy than any other song in the collection, and the chart quotes the 1941 ballad "I Think of You," recorded by Sinatra and Dorsey.)

As we have seen, the idea was to do for Los Angeles what Sinatra had previously done for New York, New York.* Apart from the title song, there are only two other pieces that come from what Mel Tormé deemed "the RRP—Relatively Recent Past," namely "How Do You Keep the Music Playing?" by

---

* City songs were indeed a remunerative avenue for singers to pursue; Sinatra had not only found big-city gelt with "New York, New York" but also "My Kind of Town (Chicago Is)" in 1964, as had Tony Bennett with "I Left My Heart in San Francisco" in 1962. Fred Astaire, in his guise as an avocational songwriter, had also provided Bennett with a better L.A. song at around this same time, "City of the Angels," released in 1986. Neither Quincy Jones nor anyone else apparently noticed back then that "New York, New York" had been recorded in Los Angeles while "L.A. Is My Lady" was taped in New York.

the Bergmans and Michel Legrand, and "The Best of Everything" by John Kander and Fred Ebb, apparently not written for a show but specifically for Sinatra. "How Do You Keep the Music Playing?" isn't bad, except when compared to the amazing profundity Sinatra (and Legrand and the Bergmans and Don Costa) extracted from "What Are You Doing the Rest of Your Life?" in 1974 and, even more so, "Summer Me, Winter Me" in 1979.* "The Best of Everything" isn't up to the level of the best songs by Kander & Ebb, but it works well on the album—although I have difficulty picturing Sinatra getting excited over "skateboards with style and speed."

This 1984 album is the last in which Sammy Cahn had any kind of a presence. He could have certainly written a better "Los Angeles Rah Rah Rah" title song than Jones (no matter if his partner were Van Heusen, Styne, or anyone else), but he graciously settled for writing special new lyrics for Sinatra to sing on two of his vintage classics, "Until the Real Thing Comes Along" (one of his earliest hits, based on an older number from Kansas City) and "Teach Me Tonight" (with Gene DePaul), both new to the Sinatra canon. On "Teach Me Tonight" arranger Zito deploys Riddlesque flutes, while "Until the Real Thing Comes Along" finds the Chairman really zinging it to us via his emphasis on the rhyme on "sigh" and "cry" in the second chorus. Cahn adds extra sauce to the mix via his new verbiage, expanding the original texts in a racy, midnight-in-Vegas fashion. "Teach Me Tonight" enhances the original's classroom metaphor with a triple rhyme ("graduate," "articulate," and "matriculate") that rates as a characteristically ingenious Cahn job. Frank Foster, who himself had written some additional lyrics as part of his chart to "Mack the Knife," recalled, "I had thought the words that I added to 'Mack' were pretty out there, but Sammy's (on 'Teach Me Tonight') were really 'hell-ified!' Yeah, they were pretty risqué."

New lyrics also figure on Foster's arrangement of "After You've Gone," on which both Benson and Hampton solo. Foster explained that he approached the song "as sort of a departure. It was. There were no other charts in the whole production that were quite like that. I was just trying to put a heavy personal Frank Foster touch on it. I try not to borrow from anybody else. I just went down into my own arsenal of licks and said, 'I'm just going to make this a bad motherfucker!' I liked the challenge of writing the up-tempo

---

* The most significant collateral benefit from Sinatra's performance of "How Do You Keep the Music Playing?" (from the 1982 film *Best Friends*) occurred during a concert, when after he sang it, he announced to Tony Bennett, who was sitting in the audience, "Tony, you should sing this song." He was right: it proved to be a major song in the Bennett canon for many years thereafter, something it never had been for Sinatra.

arrangement. I didn't know how it would be accepted, but I thought, if it goes out strong, they can't turn it down."

Sam Nestico's arrangement of the jazz standard "If I Should Lose You" (from the 1936 film *Rose of the Rancho*) also goes out strong, with Sinatra giving out with the opening phrase (and the first line of each A section) in a well-timed orchestral rest. Nestico also provided two slightly slower pieces, the bluesy ballad "Stormy Weather" and the shuffle-rhythmed "A Hundred Years from Today" (with a trombone part by Benny Powell), which utilizes an effective ritard in the coda.

Sinatra's third official version of Harold Arlen's "Stormy Weather" may well have been a holdover from the aborted Lena Horne project. It finds Sinatra in a searingly slow tempo, the roughness of his sixty-eight-year-old chops not only very much in evidence but contributing to the intensity of the piece. There's more than a hint of a swing feeling to it, and Sinatra doesn't try to get anywhere near as dark as he does on Arlen's "Blues in the Night" or as deep as he does on his "Come Rain or Come Shine." "Stormy Weather" was originally cut in New York on April 17, 1984 (right after "Teach Me Tonight"), but while listening to the playback, Jones and Ramone realized after the date that the orchestra was a half step higher that it ought to have been, so the whole thing had to be redone. According to Ramone, the original vocal was "beautiful. He sang his ass off." They rerecorded the whole thing a few weeks later (this was the only track on the *L.A.* album actually recorded in L.A.) after Sinatra had returned home to the West Coast; alas, said Ramone, "when he recut it, it was not as great."

Then there's "Mack the Knife," which up to then had been the greatest Sinatra record that never was. The song was a groundbreaking hit for Bobby Darin in 1959—very deliberately modelled on the Sinatra-Riddle *Swingin' Lovers* template—probably the biggest single of the era. It propelled Darin from youth-directed jukebox singles to the more respected and lucrative world of adult popular standards, in which he used a singing style very much informed by Sinatra and an orchestration heavily influenced by Riddle and May.

It was Q's idea for Sinatra to tackle "Mack," and Sinatra didn't consent right away; for him to sing it after Darin already had stamped his Sinatraesque personality all over it seemed somewhat redundant. This left Sinatra in a strange relationship with the Weill-Brecht theater piece. He had never gone near it, and yet in a certain sense a lot of people seemed to think they had already heard him sing it. Jones recalled that when he suggested "Mack the Knife" to Sinatra, "He said, 'Louis [Armstrong] and all of them did it so well, what the hell can we do with it?'" Further, unlike "It Had to Be You" or "After You've Gone," "Mack" is a very specific theater piece, being Kurt Weill's dramatic/musical introduction to *Die Dreigroschenoper* (*The Threepenny Opera*), which details the bloodthirsty deeds of the ubercriminal Macheath. Originally written in a medium-slow drone, the piece assumed a new life when Louis Armstrong swung it and brought it into the realm of American pop and jazz; then Darin and Ella Fitzgerald also recorded classic versions. However, Jones insisted to Sinatra, "I still think you can do a version that would be distinctively yours."

"So Frank Foster wrote [that] into the lyrics," Jones added, "to acknowledge that all these other great singers had done such a great job with it and now he was trying 'Mack.'" Upon commissioning Foster to do "Mack the Knife," the producer gave the arranger only three words of instruction: "Make it funky." Foster complied. Whereas the 1959 Darin version, arranged by Richard Wess, incorporates a shuffle beat (associated with both Louis Jordan and Louis Prima) the Sinatra-Foster version is pure swing à la Basie. "I made it as funky as possible," stresses Foster. "I stole some licks from Lionel Hampton's 'Flying Home,' and I just put a whole potpourri of stuff in there [as countermelodies]. When the band played it, it was swinging so hard and so was Frank, and when he got to the end of it, he was so delighted with it, he threw the whole arrangement up in the air!"

The great film director Billy Wilder once said that Frank Sinatra "is beyond talent. It's some sort of magnetism that goes in higher revolutions than that of anybody else in the whole of show business. There's a certain electricity permeating the air. It's like Mack the Knife is in town and the action is starting." (When this statement was repeated to Sinatra, the singer's characteristic response was, "I think that Wilder's a drunk for saying such things!") Louis Armstrong once said that he related to the song because it reminded him of some of the more sharkish types he observed—from as far away as possible—in the gang-ridden New Orleans of his childhood. Sinatra, who had also known his share of Macks the Knife with no necks and broken noses, could also relate.

Foster's supplementary libretto (heard at the song's end) reflects on Armstrong, Darin, and Ella Fitzgerald. Sinatra's version not only discusses all three earlier singers but goes on to drop the names of the "bad cats" in the band backing him up. (Foster justifiably included his own name in the list, although he preceded it with trumpeter Joe Newman, so less informed listeners might think Sinatra is referring to a single "cat" named "Newman Foster.") Since Sinatra has always been mindful to give credit to his accompanists, the song provided a perfect vehicle for him in concert to introduce Bill Miller, Irv Cottler, Frank Sinatra Jr., and the other members of his regular company.

"Mack" went over so well in concert that Sinatra kept singing it until, after two and a half years, he felt he was doing it much better than in the original 1984 session and decided to remake it. He laid down a new vocal track on top of the original orchestral track (which opened with bassist Major Holley bowing-and-humming after the fashion of Slam Stewart) in 1986. The Foster arrangement of "Mack the Knife" had already become a classic part of Sinatra's concerts, even though the record itself had never meant much. (The new 1986 vocal was apparently recorded directly for the CD edition of the album.) Whatever the reason, it's a stunning improvement. By now Sinatra has come up with that especially winning tag in which he informs his audience, "You better lock your door / and call the law" in anticipation of the dreaded yet revered Captain Macheath.

While neither the single nor the album *L.A. Is My Lady* qualifies as an RIAA-certified chart hit, "Mack the Knife" became an instant perennial in Sinatra's own terms. It outlived the rest of the set by a considerable length of time, particularly the album's title track, and it never failed to, in Sinatraian terms, knock the crowd on its collective ass. It was the last in the series of rock-era showstoppers that he paraded since "Strangers in the Night" and "That's Life" in the late 1960s. Still—and I'm not sure if this constitutes irony or not—by the time of the nation's centennial, no one was any longer associating "Mack" with Sinatra. I don't think I heard it at any of the dozens of 2015 Sinatra tribute shows I attended, yet it was an essential part of his concerts in his last decade on the road. He never succeeded in wresting "Mack" away from his own disciple; but to be fair, he wasn't trying to—he was only seeking to have some fun with it, and in this, he succeeded. Even though Sinatra was inspired to sing it by an artist who was originally doing what amounted to a Sinatra impression, "Mack the Knife" became the final, important "new" song to join the essential Sinatra canon.

Following the release of *L.A. Is My Lady* in August 1984, Jones became one of many members of Sinatra's inner circle who was determined to get him back in the studio. As Jones told me in 1991, "He has my number, and I'll be there anytime he wants me." Charles Calello, who had last worked with Sinatra in 1978, told the same story: "I tried many times to get Frank interested in making more records, but he said to me, 'You know, I really don't sing so good anymore. I don't feel my voice can handle being with the strings. [This was perhaps one reason they weren't used on *L.A.*] I really don't want to make records.'" The singer's son—by then his conductor—Frank Sinatra Jr., also tried, also in vain.

In 1985, Joe Parnello left the entourage and Falcone returned, staying for only a year. "It didn't work out too well with Joe," said Falcone (adding that there were no hard feelings; he and Parnello remained friendly up to the latter's death), "and they asked me to come back. But when I did, there were so many things that needed to be fixed. Also, I knew when I went back that I could never put my future completely in the hands of one client."

It seemed as if Sinatra was reinstating his accompanists in reverse order: from Miller to Falcone to Parnello to Falcone back to Miller. At the age of seventy-one, Bill Miller went into his own unretirement and back on the road with Sinatra. From 1986 to 1988, he conducted while a number of capable hands sat in the keyboard chair. Among them were Bernie Leighton, one of the most recorded pianists of all time (a top New York studio man, he seems to have played on at least ten sessions a week in the 1950s and '60s), the prodigious Russ Kassoff, and Mike Renzi, an exceptionally gifted virtuoso who seemed to be playing for Peggy Lee, Mel Tormé, Jack Jones, and Lena Horne all simultaneously in the 1980s. (More recently, Renzi was Tony Bennett's regular pianist for about five years until illness forced him off the road in 2016.) On several occasions, such as an April 1987 engagement in Las Vegas, astute audience members even spotted the legendary Lou Levy on the bandstand. One of the most revered accompanists of all time—a first choice of Peggy Lee and Ella Fitzgerald—Levy had already worked with Sinatra occasionally (as on a 1958 televison show with Fitzgerald and on the 1969 "My Way" session).

In 1988, Frank Sinatra Jr. (1944–2016), then forty-four, began conducting for his father. For his entire career thus far, the younger Sinatra had decided he wanted to follow in his father's footsteps as a jazz-pop singer. He was certainly as talented as many singers who made it, and less derivative of Sinatra Senior than many (although, unlike Gary Crosby, he never went out of his way to avoid sounding like his famous father). Unfortunately, there was no room for a singer in the general mold of Sinatra (even one with a famous name) in the mid-to-late 1960s and afterward. Even Bobby Darin, who had achieved huge success as a basic Frankentype in 1959–60, was singing a very different tune a decade later.

Junior's career had also been damaged in the aftermath of his kidnapping in 1963, when at the ensuing criminal trial, the defense manufactured a totally fictitious countercharge that the Sinatra family had staged the crime to stir up publicity for the young singer's career. During the trial, he told the *Los Angeles Times* that he feared the kidnapping had nurtured "a seed of doubt about my integrity that will stay with me for the rest of my life." "I've never been much of a success," he once told the *National Enquirer*, "but I'm still in the running." At the time he began conducting for his father,* one of his managers, Andrea Kauffman, told one paper, "I see him as an opening act. He'll never say, 'I wanna be a superstar.' He opened for George Burns at Caesars. I see him opening for Buddy Hackett, Alan King."

As a singer, Junior didn't have the resources of his father, either vocally (he lacked the richness of tone that Sinatra Senior had) or emotionally (another area where Junior came up short, to put it mildly). Unlike Senior, however, Junior was a formally trained musician who was a skilled pianist and sightreader. "He is a fine pianist and has a sense of composition," Sinatra said of his son in 1977. "I would like to see him achieve status as a composer, for movies or TV more than anything else, rather than [singing]." Junior eventually assembled his own jazz orchestra, which worked primarily in the lounge showrooms of Las Vegas, doing shows that were a mixture of instrumentals and vocal numbers. He established his new identity as his father's conductor over the course of two tours that received a lot of attention even by Sinatra standards: the Ultimate Event tour of 1988–89, and the Diamond Jubilee tour of 1990–91. The first had originally been conceived as the Together Again tour with Sammy Davis Jr. and Dean Martin, which would have been a major event, not least because the Rat Pack had never formally toured as a unit to begin with during their hey-hey-heydays of twenty-five years earlier; alas, although Martin was not yet an old man (he was eighteen months younger than Sinatra), his touring days were behind him, and he withdrew from the plan early on. When Liza Minnelli was brought in as the third member, the Together Again package became the Ultimate Event. For the Diamond Jubilee tour, celebrating Sinatra's seventy-fifth birthday, the opening act was old friends Steve Lawrence and Eydie Gormé.

Gradually, Sinatra Jr. began replacing the men who left the classic New York band of the early 1980s with musicians who had served in his Vegas band. "I hesitate to bad-mouth anybody, so the only thing I can say is when [Sinatra Jr.] first came with the band," said Sid Cooper, "he didn't know his ass from his elbow. We carried him for a couple of years until he learned. And then, once he learned how to do what he had to, he started bringing in the Vegas guys that played with his band out there."

The most radical personnel change resulted from a higher authority than either Sinatra. While at the home of his daughter in 1989, drummer Irv Cottler, then seventy-one, died of cardiac arrest. The choice to replace him was obvious. "I think Sol Gubin is the best drummer that Sinatra could possibly have had," opined Falcone. "In my view Sol should have been with him all

---

* The first date was April 19, 1988, at the McCallum Theatre in Palm Springs.

those years. To me, there's just no comparison. He was the best drummer that ever played for Sinatra, the quintessential Sinatra drummer." Although younger than Cottler, Gubin was also a veteran of the swing era, having played with such bandleaders as Charlie Barnet, Sonny Dunham, Elliot Lawrence, Hal McIntyre, Stan Kenton, and Count Basie. He had worked for Sinatra on East Coast dates throughout the late 1950s and the '60s. Gubin recalled that the two Frank Sinatras were so anxious to have him get started that Junior presented the drum parts to him at Cottler's funeral. "I loved Sol," said Cooper, speaking for the band. "He played the book the first time in Atlantic City as if he had been playing it all his life."

That rosy glow of enthusiasm quickly faded, however. Junior and Gubin seem to have taken an instant dislike to each other from the first time they worked together. They tolerated each other for sixteen months, which might be described as Sinatra's last stand—regarded by some as the final opportunity the Old Man had to work with a drummer who gave him exactly what he needed.

Yet even at the start of the 1990s, Sinatra was still in consistently good shape and frequently performed at a higher level than anyone was expecting. Gubin recalled one show in Sweden where, even though Sinatra had been using teleprompter monitors for several years (as a crutch to lean on when necessary), on this one particular evening he dispensed with the monitors entirely. "We worked in an outdoor arena, and he jumped off the stage and went down on the track and mingled with the people. And then he got an ovation [that even for him] was incredible. In fact, he cried after the show. He cried on the plane coming back to the States. He just couldn't get over the ovation and how these people loved him. To me, every time I worked with him, I just enjoyed the hell out of it."

"The power had to be in Junior's hand, not the new drummer," said one member of the band. "If he beat it off the wrong tempo, Sol would play the right tempo." Gubin charged that Junior waited for him to ask for a raise and when he did, used that opportunity to fire him. Gubin sued for breach of contract, and though he eventually won a financial settlement, he didn't get the prize he wanted, which was to keep playing for Sinatra. Both Bill Miller and Falcone took exception to the breakup. Miller, while admitting that Junior acted like a "cement head," felt that Gubin's "big mouth did him out of the job. And he's a good player, you know, but a constant complainer." (Anyone would seem like a kvetch compared to Miller's own Zenlike tranquility.)

Falcone felt that Gubin was no more or less difficult than most creative people and that the drummer was worth special handling. "Sol has a temperament like every musician has a temperament. The challenge for the leader is to learn how to take these temperaments and meld them together into a team that works out. You don't have to eat dinner with him, you don't have to sleep with him, you've got to play with the guy. When he gets on the stand, if he kicks the hell out of the band, that's all you've got to care about as the leader. You don't care whether the guy parts his hair on the left side, you don't care whether the guy's a pain in the ass. You care how he plays the show! That's what the primary consideration is. You get your problems solved off the bandstand, and you take care of business. The guy who plays the show the best, that's the guy who sits in my drum chair. And to me, to not have Sol Gubin playing for the Old Man these days is a travesty!"

After Gubin, the Sinatras went through drummer after drummer. At one point, Alvin Stoller replaced Cottler, who, ironically, had been the one who took his place to begin with. Stoller, who hadn't played with Sinatra since the 1960s, also had his difficulties with the younger Sinatra ("He talks like a colonel in the Marine Corps!" the drummer correctly observed). The real problem, though, was that the veteran percussionist was simply too old and too sick to play. "I told Junior, 'Let's try Alvin,'" Bill Miller recalled. "[In his prime] Alvin could have done it, but he wasn't well. Alvin was just *old* up there." This was an ironic observation, considering that Miller was himself ten years older than Stoller. The pianist continued, "It might have worked out, but the timing was bad. So he was out." Not long after, "I had to stop," Stoller told us in July 1992. "Doctor's orders are that I can't play. I have to sit back and get well, so that's what I'm doing. I don't even listen to anything." Stoller died a few months later in October 1992. The best choice—after Cottler, Stoller, and Dubin—was the excellent and considerably younger drummer Gregg Field, who lasted longer than anyone else in the twilight years of the Chairman's career. (Before and after his tenure with the Sinatras, Field enjoyed considerable success not only as a studio musician and bandleader but as a producer of artists including his wife, singer Monica Mancini, daughter of Henry Mancini.)

If finding a suitable drummer was one of Sinatra Jr.'s major problems, his greatest ambition as musical director was to make a new record with his father. "All the years that I've known him" said Gubin, "he's been talking about trying to get the Old Man into the studio again." Across a ten-year period, from 1984 to 1993, Sinatra participated in only four known sessions, two items of which have been heard: on the October 1986 date in which he redid the vocal track on "Mack the Knife" he also sang Jule Styne's "One to a Customer" and the only song he would ever do by Jerry Leiber and Mike Stoller. Although best known as the kings of early rock and roll songwriting (via "Hound Dog" and "Jailhouse Rock"), in their later years they often turned out lovely, mature songs for mature singers like Peggy Lee and Sinatra. "The Girls I've Never Kissed" is another end-of-life summation song, though just the opposite of a victory-lap anthem like "My Way" (rather, it's an aria of regret); in Sinatra's hands, it's a thing of beauty. In introducing it in Vegas in December 1986, he enthusiastically compares it to "September Song."

In June 1988, several standards were attempted, including two Billy May charts; "My Foolish Heart" was deemed releasable a few years later when it was issued on the *Complete Reprise Studio Recordings* suitcase. Sinatra sounds just fine, and it's indeed easier for him to do a number in swing time, even a romantic song such as this Victor Young–Ned Washington classic, than a slow ballad with lots of sustained notes. This was followed by "Cry Me a River," an even better idea for a Sinatra–Billy May number, but alas, he didn't complete an issuable take. (There's one surreptitious recording that survives, of Sinatra rehearsing the song, barely audibly, without his vocal mic being turned on—it makes one wish he had gone through with it.) These two tracks reveal that Sinatra was doing exactly what he should have been doing: jazzy and bluesy treatments of standards. May's chart of this 1953 Julie London hit swings considerably harder than the bulk of *L.A. Is My Lady.* Like "Mack," it would have been a perfect song for Sinatra to add to his book at this point in his career. Three years later, he entered the studio in August 1991 to cut a track of the traditional carol "Silent Night, Holy Night" with just piano, for a Christmas charity album.

The most fascinating of these late orphan tracks is "Leave it All to Me," a Paul Anka song (and, according to some sources, a Torrie Zito arrangement), taped in January 1988. "Leave it All to Me" is a surreal psychedelic work in a late-1960s style that sounds like a crazy European carnival scene, with clowns in pantaloons and funhouse mirrors distorting everything. There are echoes of a number of sources: Jacques Brel's "Carousel," Jerry Herman's français-style melodies in the show *Dear World*, Kurt Weill, Kander and Ebb, and even the Beatles' hallucinogenic circus song, "Being for the Benefit of Mr. Kite!" It's a real departure for Sinatra (and Anka too) and he embraces it enthusiastically. Frankly, he sounds great; the problem is not with the singer but with the song. Anka had a worthy idea—it's kind of a production number in search of a Broadway musical—but he never seems to have finished it. And unlike the "Carousel"/carnival songs of Brel and Herman, "Leave it All to Me" is *all* relentless repetition; among other things, it lacks an ending. (The composer would later repurpose the song into a jingle for a radio commercial promoting Atlantic City, where no ending was necessary.) Clearly that was the reason that Sinatra chose not to issue it, but "Leave it All to Me" offers a tantalizing hint of a new direction that his music might have taken.

By the aftermath of the seventy-fifth birthday tour (which brought him back to Madison Square Garden for the first time since 1974), Sinatra had become a self-fulfilling prophecy. For the most part, the concerts maintained a consistently high level, and great multitudes of fans shelled out ever-increasing ticket prices to be there. Some loss of chops was inevitable, he didn't seem to have kept up the regimen of vocal maintenance exercises that he was so committed to in the Falcone era, and there was some mental deterioration as well. Tina Sinatra has charged that Sinatra's wife was messing with his medication to make him more confused and docile; but even if so, this affected his concert work surprisingly little. It was never by rote; every concert was a new and exciting experience, with everything communicated from Sinatra to each individual audience member directly from the inside out. But he had given so many thousands of shows by the early 1990s that he instinctively knew what to do on stage; it wasn't automatic pilot so much as following the well-worn mental pathways.

There were, in fact, some shows where he messed up the lyrics, and wasn't able to correctly follow the teleprompter. He thus became a reluctant pioneer of yet another upcoming trend: he was the first aging entertainer to spark a debate about mandatory retirement (or, in his case, reretirement), which started when some *Newsday* hack happened to see a subpar show at the Westbury Music Fair, and then wrote a piece demanding that Frank pack it in. In recent years, the debate has raged again with regards to both B. B. King and Bob Dylan, among others. (Admittedly, setting this precedent is not the kind of accomplishment Sinatra's fans and family can point to with pride.)

Then, in late 1993, *Duets* was released, and the tone of the media changed—sort of. To some, it seemed like Sinatra's presence as a force in the music industry was revitalized, an opinion supported by the numeric evidence of its sales. To others, this was a rather melancholy final walk around the garden before, in the memorable phrase of W. C. Fields, the man in the bright nightgown was due to escort him off to the next world. It was, in fact, something of both.

The pioneer of the pop music duet was Sinatra's original inspiration, Bing Crosby, who enjoyed "crossing a cadenza" with his fellow vocalists and vocalistas on many a radio show and Decca disc in the 1930s and '40s. The early days of the LP saw full-length collaborations by Crosby and Rosemary Clooney, as well as Louis Armstrong and Ella Fitzgerald, Billy Eckstine and Sarah Vaughan, and others. Then in more recent years, there had been megahits like "You Don't Bring Me Flowers" (1978) by Barbra Streisand and Neil Diamond (lyrics by the Bergmans) and "To All the Girls I've Loved Before" (1984) by Willie Nelson and Julio Iglesias; note that all four of these stars were recruited for the Sinatra project. (Sinatra himself had recorded duets in all phases of his career, from the Dorsey years onward, if hardly as frequently as Crosby.) But the pioneer of the modern duet album was unquestionably Ray Charles. In 1984 he launched a new series of country albums with *Friendship*, a set of duets with his Nashville peers (Hank Williams Jr., the Oak Ridge Boys, Willie Nelson, Johnny Cash) that, as the title promised, included a countrified reading of Cole Porter's "Friendship."

The 1990s saw the coming of the "electro-duet," a specific kind of technologically driven cadenza-crossing in which a contemporary star sang with a legendary one, living or otherwise. Natalie Cole launched this trend in 1991 with "Unforgettable," in which she teamed with her father, Nat King Cole, who had died in 1965. In the world of electro-duets, sales are not amplified incrementally but exponentially, following the model of not only "Unforgettable" but the 1982 single release of the Crosby-Bowie "Little Drummer Boy"/"Peace on Earth" duet; the idea was to appeal to two generations at the same time. Sinatra's first indirect involvement in such a project was a 1992 release by Cyndi Lauper dubbing her voice over Sinatra's 1947 Columbia record of "Santa Claus Is Coming to Town."

Clearly, Sinatra's *Duets* originated as a means for the Sinatra organization to pick up a piece of the "Unforgettable" action. Phil Ramone, who produced the album, never took credit for the concept; he told us it was one of the ideas raised when he first started talking with the "Sinatra people," including Sinatra general manager Eliot Weisman, EMI North America CEO Charles Koppelman, and EMI VP for A&R Don Rubin in 1991. Although Ramone had worked as a senior recording engineer on *The World We Knew* and *L.A. Is My Lady*, he was better known as a top-flight producer, often referred to as "The Prince of Pop." (Ramone shares one compliment—of sorts—with Sinatra: both have had punk and new-wave rock bands named after them: the Ramones, the Trashcan Sinatras, Frankie Goes to Hollywood.)

Originally, Ramone had an entirely different idea in mind. "I went to Frank and said to him, 'I know it's impossible, but conceptually what I'd love to do is a *Wee Small Hours* kind of album with just a rhythm section and maybe a string quartet and a couple of great soloists.' I had all these grandiose ideas of doing Sinatra easily." Sinatra was unsure that he could still pull that idea off, and dragged his feet. "And then about three months later we talked again, and the concept of other artists singing with him came to the table, and I said, 'Jesus, I want to be there. I want to make sure we make this album because I feel that if I can convince him that he will be in and out of that studio, we'll do it.' It took another six months of dialogue back and forth."

After several months of discussions, primarily with Weisman, Ramone had another opportunity to talk it over with the Old Man himself. "I went down to Palm Beach, Florida, where he was playing and I really faced him head-on and talked it through. And although he was quite enthusiastic at that point, he kept checking it over as to why anybody would want to sing these songs, why they would want to sing with him, and how he would match these modern-day artists." The project went to Capitol Records; by then the connections to Warner Bros. had withered away, like water under a bridge that had itself burned down years ago, as had his old animosity toward Capitol. EMI actively "pursued" the project, Ramone reported, promising not only a generous budget for production but considerable promotion, which they more than delivered.

Ramone, with his background in engineering, was an ideal producer in that the overall concept for *Duets* was based primarily in technology and might more accurately be described as a set of ground rules. First, as the title implies, Sinatra would sing with other artists. Second, they would be stars of comparable drawing power—which automatically eliminated virtually every other performer in Sinatra's general genre—artists who sang the traditional songbook. Third, the material would basically consist of very familiar Sinatra standards and hits. Fourth, because of the logistics of getting the Old Man into the studio, Sinatra would lay down his vocal tracks (in some cases on top of orchestral parts that had already been recorded), and the other singers would overdub their parts of these electronically created "duets" at convenient intervals. Pat Williams, a veteran television incidental-music writer whose credits include *The Mary Tyler Moore Show* (and who had also arranged such terrific pop LPs as *Steve & Eydie Together on Broadway*), served as musical director, conducting and occasionally revising familiar Sinatra charts.

After one aborted attempt in early 1993 (Ramone described the first date as a "total disaster"), the producer and the singer tried again in July. Recording at night, when Sinatra was used to working, the first two summer sessions were also unsuccessful in that Sinatra was uncomfortable and complained of a sore throat. According to some stories, on at least one occasion he forgot the purpose of the tracks he was creating and wondered aloud why he was rerecording pieces he had done so often before (why, indeed?). Finally, on the third night (July 1), coproducer Hank Cattaneo got the idea to set the studio up like a concert stage, complete with a wireless, handheld microphone.

That was the night that Ol' Frank magic started to happen. When Sinatra arrived, said Ramone, "he put me through hell for about ten minutes while the orchestra waited, asking why we were doing this again, why we would subject ourselves to this kind of possible ridicule, what would happen if it didn't work. And I said to him, 'You know, you have the final say on everything we're doing here. The most important thing is that if it's musically not there, we're not putting it out. If the duets don't work, nothing's going to happen.' And he said, 'All right, we'll try one, but you'd better be right.' I went into the control room. We did a take of 'Come Fly with Me,' played it back, and you could see the eyes start to light up. That's because the band was smokin'. They were right next to him. He said, 'All right, we'll do one more.' Well, we did nine more tunes. And, you know, that's the historic night. We had the best time with each other."

Some of the vocals he laid down justified the harshest criticism of the *Newsday* reviewer; others (particularly "One for My Baby") were among the most remarkable things Sinatra recorded in his entire career. Still, the major economic value was not only in what they laid down on that night or any other, but in the way these tracks were electronically manipulated to include other artists. When the rumor first began to circulate among the Sinatra constituency that *Duets* was happening, many of us couldn't quite believe he was going to sing with the likes of Bono (from the Irish rock band U2). *New York Times* technology writer Hans Fantel later contended that the "duets" on *Duets* weren't "true duets" at all but what Fantel labeled "sonic collage." "I think it's a little scary that this technology exists," as even Nancy Sinatra admitted (to Michael Musto in the *Village Voice*). "They can pair Dad with Newt Gingrich. He wouldn't have to know about it until it's too late."

However, Tony Bennett responded (to me at least) that the producers weren't just taking two random pieces of tape and sticking them together; he worked to make his vocal fit in very specifically with the one Sinatra had given him to work with. On one selection, "They Can't Take That Away from Me," with the original electro-duetist, Natalie Cole (who had sung with Sinatra on a 1977 television special), the two voices match so closely you might think the singers actually were in the studio together. Yet on most tracks, the shortcomings of the process are immediately evident—namely that the rapport between the two costars is lost, a failing particularly evident on the sequel, *Duets II.* Many of the partners insisted on acknowledging their ghostly collaborator (referring to him as Francis or Frank, as if they had ever met him or had ever been within a hundred feet of him), and these asides seem especially disingenuous.

In some of the early promotion for *Duets*, the label tried to turn an obvious liability into an asset by ballyhooing the idea that the *Duets* weren't real duets and promoting the set as a technological achievement. A year later, their tune had changed: they were no longer playing up the techno angle, the fiber-optic phone lines, and the digital multitracking. The liner notes to *Duets II* and the 1994 CBS Thanksgiving-weekend television special *Sinatra Duets* completely skirt the issue and rather dishonestly lead listeners and viewers to believe that the artists were actually singing in tandem with Sinatra.

There is nothing wrong with using available technology. Perhaps you've heard of an art form known as the movies, where performances are made up of zillions of tiny fragments edited together; no one claims that Laurence Olivier can't act because it's on film. As Johnny Mandel has pointed out, technology is generally used in contemporary pop music as a substitute for talent and technique, but who is to say that major artists like Bennett and Sinatra should not be allowed an occasional technological indulgence to enhance what they do?

When Sinatra finally warmed up to the *Duets* concept, said Ramone, the Chairman's first question was "How is Ella [Fitzgerald] doing?" The First Lady of Song had apparently hung up her microphone for the last time, but other great artists in Sinatra's bailiwick were more than available, for instance Peggy Lee, Joe Williams, Rosemary Clooney, Margaret Whiting, Mel Tormé, Barbara Cook, Nancy Wilson, Ray Charles, Julie Andrews, and Jack Jones. Yet the *Duet* partners were chosen not for reasons of taste or talent but strictly because of the balance sheet.

To their credit, the majority of the *Duets* costars were "legacy" artists: Aretha Franklin, Barbra Streisand, Patti LaBelle, Willie Nelson, Neil Diamond, Carly Simon, Gladys Knight, George Strait, Bono, Stevie Wonder, Jimmy Buffett, and the late Luther Vandross; none of these were fly-by-night stars of the moment; they're all just as celebrated in 2018 as they were in 1993–94. And to be fair, the producers also thought to include at least a few artists who came from Sinatra's world: Tony Bennett, Liza Minnelli, Lena Horne, and Steve Lawrence and Eydie Gormé.

The talent and the long-term value of the costars isn't the problem. Rather, it's the very concept of the project and the approach: Luther Vandross and Aretha Franklin both sing wonderfully on their tracks, "The Lady Is a Tramp" and "What Now My Love." Obviously, Sinatra recorded his tracks as solos, with no knowledge of who would be added later on. But the crime is that they're not really singing *with* him either: both Vandross and Franklin in particular are singing *around* him. A lot of these singers have no particular skill in negotiating the traditional American songbook, but that isn't even the point. When Elvis and Sinatra sang together in 1960, Elvis had probably never heard of Cy Coleman and Sinatra was only barely familiar with the folk-song tradition of "Love Me Tender"; but that was a classic duet because they were truly in it together, relating to each other and to the moment. The 1993–94 electro-duets seem to be lost in time; they don't exist in any real "space."

The duets with those partners who really know how to sing this material are, not surprisingly, the best: Natalie Cole ("They Can't Take That Away from Me"), Liza Minnelli ("I've Got the World on a String"), Willie Nelson (even granted that "My Way" was a terrible choice for the two of them*), Tony Bennett ("New York, New York"), and especially Steve Lawrence and Eydie Gormé ("Where or When"). The latter is especially ingenious—the team had the idea to weave words around the voice of The Voice and the Billy Byers orchestration, much like Lambert, Hendricks, and Ross had done with classic Basie charts generations earlier.

By the same standard, some of the others are especially horrible for the same reasons—there's no earthly reason why "Summer Wind" (with the highly inappropriate Julio Iglesias) should be a "buddy" song. The Bono duet on "I've Got You Under My Skin" is particularly painful, especially given that the rock star and philanthropist led the charge in his generation for rock-'n'-rollers to appreciate Sinatra. Bono's introduction of Sinatra at the 1994 Grammy awards was heartfelt and moving—which is precisely what *Duets* isn't. At one point in "I've Got You Under My Skin," Bono addresses him as "you old fool," which is particularly uncharitable, considering that the old fool wasn't even there in the room with him at the time and thus unable to defend himself.

Billy Byers was one of the arrangers whose work was utilized (along with Riddle, May, Costa, etc.) on the two *Duets* albums; he wrote the charts for two Rodgers and Hart classics, "Where or When" and "The Lady Is a Tramp." He offered some frank opinions on the subject: "On 'Tramp,' the tempo is wrong, the band ain't swinging, and on most of the album, you don't even hear the drums. They're just not rhythmically convincing." Like most of us, he agreed that the second album was an improvement (and added that he was flattered by Steve and Eydie's adaption of his 1966 "Where or When" arrangement), but Byers had reservations regarding the whole concept. "Phil is a smart guy and Pat is excellent, but I'd rather hear Sinatra do some new stuff. I think everybody's getting a free ride: everybody's doing the same concept, *somebody* with *somebody else*. It's just a way to get all the names on one CD cover." (Several other arrangers expressed similar opinions, but asked not to be quoted.)

A few years later, a bootleg CD titled *Solos* began to circulate, containing sixteen of Sinatra's 1993 vocals unaltered (as God intended), and it is indeed far superior to the commercially released tracks. As the recording industry proceeds on its march to oblivion over the last twenty years, the "Duets" format has proven a reliable formula for reversing these negative fortunes.

---

* Why in the world is this a duet? It doesn't even make sense logistically: it should be "Our Way."

Ray Charles did another duet set, the 2004 *Genius Loves Company*; as it had been for Sinatra, it proved to be the opportunity for Brother Ray's own last hurrah. Tony Bennett has released at least four albums of all-star duets, not to mention a full-length collaboration with millennial superstar Lady Gaga. Fortunately, he learned from the mistakes of the Sinatra team; say what you will about Gaga, but at least she and Tony are really singing together, in the same room at the same time. In a way, the more simpatico duets on the Sinatra albums are the most disappointing—especially "Fly Me to the Moon" with Jobim, who would die (in December 1994) just as the second volume was being released, because we know that when Sinatra and Jobim were really working together, the results were magical.

And that's the reason that the *Duets* project is easily the greatest disappointment in Sinatra's canon: whatever he is, good or bad, he's always real, and *Duets* just isn't. Even when he sang "Mama Will Bark" or "Bad, Bad Leroy Brown," he was being honest (in those cases, making an honest mistake), and *Duets* is anything but. It's the worst kind of a cheat, simultaneously self-conscious and dishonest. It darn well knows that it's not fooling anybody.

The two *Duets* albums served the purpose of moving Sinatra back into the national spotlight: CBS-TV gave him his first special in years when *Duets II* came out at Thanksgiving, 1994, and he had already been on the Grammy telecast a few months earlier. Viewed from that perspective, the project was a success. While the brouhaha was over *Duets* in 1993 and then *Duets II* in 1994, the big deal in fall 1995 was Sinatra's eightieth birthday; there was another special (produced by George Schlatter for ABC-TV), this time an all-star concert tribute. More important, Capitol released a new live album, *Sinatra 80th: Live in Concert* (drawn from concerts in 1987 and '88), which amid the birthday festivities sold enough CDs to be certified gold by the RIAA.

His whole team wanted him to make a new album: Frank Jr., Phil Ramone, even Bill Miller, hardly a cockeyed optimist, who felt that if Sinatra were to really put the effort in, learning and recording one new song at a time, he could do it in a matter of weeks or months. But it never happened, and Capitol was wise to draw from the increasing stockpile of excellent live performances to create some sort of eightieth-birthday package.

Learning new songs seemed like a bridge much too far in the 1993–94 period; on certain shows it was hard enough for him to get through the familiar songs he'd been doing for decades. By now, he was highly dependent on the teleprompter; in Miller's opinion, the reason he still occasionally loused up the lyrics was because of his declining eyesight. The intonation had suffered to a slight degree as he approached the eightieth, but even without Irv

Cottler he could almost always find his way around the beat. There would be nights when he would coast; sometimes he just seemed to be going through the motions. Ironically, it was on the shows when he wasn't trying to dig too deeply that he got through it without incident. But it was on those occasions when he took chances and invested himself more emotionally in the material that he was most likely to blow his concentration.

And yet there would always be nights when he was incredible, even as he was approaching the end of that long, long road. April 1994 at Radio City was solid, but in these final seasons he was at his best in the comparatively smaller casino showrooms of Las Vegas and Atlantic City. The relative intimacy of these venues and the familiarity of the casino-saloon setting give him warmer vibes than an enormous, antiseptic stadium. He performed so well at these venues that at the time the fans kept wishing he would just confine himself to the gambling houses and perhaps one or two big cities and cut down on the constant touring that was clearly wearing him down.

Sol Gubin told us about a concert in Salt Lake City where the crowd was even more overwhelmingly enthusiastic than usual. "The people were screaming and yelling and throwing flowers at him and everything," but a short time later, as the company was flying away, "the Old Man was very sad about it. He turned around and said, 'Jesus, these people make me feel as if they're coming to see me for the last time.'" He had learned the wisdom of a famous line from the classic 1937 film *Stage Door,* that "one should always listen closely when people say goodbye, because sometimes they're really saying farewell."

Frank Foster, who shared the stage with Sinatra as part of the Basie orchestra on many occasions (he was the leader during the April 1994 Radio City run), put it this way. "After all these years, his voice is going, and at seventy-eight what do you expect? But he still has the same charisma, the same ability to stir a crowd that he had years ago. It may seem like a shame that they have to have four monitors on stage to flash the lyrics in front of him and that he makes heavy use of them. Hey, man, if you're still going professionally at seventy-eight, it's no disgrace to use whatever props are necessary, especially when you can still fill Radio City Music Hall for an entire week."

Three Sands shows from 1992, 1993, and 1994 are among the most sensational Sinatra sets I've ever experienced; to be sure, I was also present at more than one disappointing show, but the good far outweighed the bad. On the opening night of one run, November 11, 1993, he had only one embarrassing moment, when he got lost in the out-of-tempo verse to "I've Got a Crush on You," a notoriously sing-songy horse that has thrown many a younger rider. In a misguided attempt to offer aid, one fan in the house yelled "Get Barbra, Frank!" Sinatra thought the guy meant his wife, Barbara, and responded—pretty much to himself—"I wish she were here. We'd be havin' a drink right now," making it obvious that he was oblivious to the fact of having made a record of "Crush on You" with (in absentia) Barbra Streisand.

Yet for the rest of the evening, Sinatra was totally on target. His "For Once in My Life," which usually suits Tony Bennett much better than him (FS originally encouraged Bennett to do this 1965 song), was practically the best performance he has ever given of it, displaying a more potent combination of tenderness and bite than any other documented Sinatra reading. In place of "One for My Baby" in this particular show, his big saloon song was "Guess I'll Hang My Tears Out to Dry," and it was every bit as moving as Sinatra has ever sung it.

Not all of his later performances were this successful. According to several accounts, the August 1994 concert at New Jersey's Garden State Arts Center found Sinatra momentarily singing into the wrong end of his handheld wireless mic. Yet October and November appearances in Chicago and at the Sands were spectacular. At the Sands, however, Sinatra was so sure of himself he even had the chutzpah to poke fun at his own memory and/or vision problems by daring the audience to remember the words to "All or Nothing at All." (Around this time he was also singing Pat Williams's lovely new revision of "My Funny Valentine," happily shorn of "How Do You Keep the Music Playing?")

Overall, his last years on the road were triumphant ones, in which he still, for instance, refused to ever do the same ending twice on "Mack the Knife"; there was always some sort of extra twist in the windup that would be created in the heat of the moment. As always, even in the very big rooms, "Come Rain or Come Shine" remained defiant and triumphant. "My Way," with its so-hard-to-remember and so-easy-to-forget melodic line, occasionally made him lose his bearings, once during an otherwise excellent set in March 1992. Yet in May 1994, he delivered one of the best renditions of his career. Haughty, arrogant, aggressive, and irresistible, it was everything that Frank Sinatra singing "My Way" ought to be.

Throughout the final shows, it was never a case of the audience just pulling for Sinatra to make it through the set without too many screwups, without anything really terrible happening. It would have been a mistake to think of the Sinatra of 1994 as a diminished version of the Sinatra of 1974 or 1954 or 1939. The *Duets*-era Sinatra was a vastly different artist, even from the one who had come out of retirement twenty years earlier. He was dealing with an all-new set of considerations, and he was reacting to what the current crowd was feeding back to him, not limiting himself to what he did decades ago. He was always beholden to the moment, even if, apparently, as soon as he got off stage he had no idea what moment it was.

In the fall of 1994, as *Duets II* was being released, Sinatra kept working steadily through Thanksgiving; he also filmed a cameo appearance in *Young at Heart*, a television movie produced by his daughter Tina. After taking a few weeks off around the time of his seventy-ninth birthday, he resumed touring on December 19 with two nights at Fukuoka Dome in Japan. But somehow, something was different. He should have been rested—for most of his seventy-nine years, he had been blissfully free of jet lag—but suddenly it was all catching up with him. He was tired and incoherent; he could barely get through any songs without badly and obviously losing his way. The two concerts were somehow edited together for a Japanese video release, but it was clear that the singer had, finally—to reprise the title of his 1961 album—passed the point of no return.

It was decided by "his people" to pull him off the road. He only gave one more "concert," a charity event mounted by Barbara Sinatra in Palm Springs on February 25, 1995, at which he sang six songs and was in generally terrific shape. Then there was the eightieth birthday concert at the Shrine Auditorium in Los Angeles (held on November 19, 1995); he only came on stage at the finale, escorted by Tony Bennett, looking at once pleased at receiving so much love and attention and yet also at least a little annoyed that everyone but him was getting a piece of his own action as he rather defiantly joined the company in "New York, New York."

He lived on for almost two and a half years after that, mostly in a wheelchair, during which time he was visited by his kids and by a few old friends such as Steve Lawrence and Eydie Gormé and Italian-American crooner Jerry Vale (whom he had affectionately nicknamed "Jerry Fail"). Frank Sinatra, age eighty-two, died on May 14, 1998.

On that day, as such dramatis personae as Angelo Maggio or Nathan Detroit might have put it, he bought the farm. Or as Clarence Doolittle or Frankie Machine or Ben Marco might have said, he kicked the bucket. As Alan King once told me, the standard slang for Broadway touts, showbiz-type insiders, guys and dolls, and hanger-arounders was to "take a cab." ("What happened to Louie?" "He took a cab." "Oh.") As another famous carouser, Lord Byron, would have put it, he would go no more a-roving, so late into the night. In the words of still another literary character, he had reached the undiscovered country from whose bourn no traveler returns.

Yet he left the world a very different place than the one he had entered in 1915. He had completely changed the way we listen to music, in particular the role of singers and the songs they sing, and with it the relationship of both songs and singers to the audience. He changed the way we hear songs, he changed the way songs are sung and the way those performances are presented. In short, there was virtually nothing left of the original world that he knew; the world he began life in and the world he left behind were two completely different places.

In his perfection of the art of singing barroom ballads, Sinatra tapped into the same truths that Elwood P. Dowd espoused in *Harvey*. Speaking not just of six-foot rabbits and icemen who cometh, he tells us how those who frequent public establishments invariably talk about "the big terrible things they've done, and then they talk about the big wonderful things they'll do. . . . Because nobody ever brings anything small into a bar."

Over the course of a career that lasted wholly six decades, Sinatra proved himself a thousand times over. Beyond his singing and acting, he often captured our imagination with his extramusical activities, which involved close associations with the movers and shakers of Hollywood, Washington, and the underworld. It seemed like Sinatra insisted on doing all of his "big terrible things" in full public view; he hardly ran and hid when someone took a picture of him with this or that mob boss (or, for that matter, Nixon and Agnew); and when he wanted to punch someone, it was a columnist, for Pete's sake. Yet most of his big wonderful things—the benefit concerts, the subsidy of hospitals and great philanthropic works, usually for children— were often anonymous. This would seem to be the way that he wanted it.

I personally would like to think that he did a lot more good than he did harm; but let's just say, for the sake of argument, that "the big terrible things" he has done were ultimately canceled out by "the big wonderful things" he has also done. His acting career too, leaves his account at zero; there were probably more lousy movies than good, but he appeared in more than his share of classics, from *Anchors Aweigh* and *On the Town* to *From Here to Eternity*, *The Man with the Golden Arm*, and *The Manchurian Candidate*.

That only leaves his music with which to remember him. From "Frankie" to "The Voice" to "The Chairman" to "Ol' Blue Eyes," he was, at every point in his development, never anything less than the definitive voice of the American experience and the twentieth century. It's time again to recall the words of his friend, the film director Peter Bogdanovich, who said, "His songs are not only his biography but ours as well."

Frank Sinatra kept singing until he couldn't anymore, until he had given all that was his to give, and then some, and then he left us a relatively short time after that. As it was in 1995, there is no better way to conclude than with what was Sinatra's favorite toast in the latter part of his career: Raise your glasses, please, ladies and gentlemen: may we all live to be 150 years old, and may the last voice we hear be his.

# POSTSCRIPT

As the year of Frank Sinatra's centennial dawned, I could name two women who still walked among us who had known Sinatra when he was a young man. One, famously, was the former Nancy Barbato, who since 1939 has been known as Mrs. Frank Sinatra. At the time of her own hundredth birthday (March 25, 2017) "Big Nancy," as she is also known (all five feet of her), was still cooking enormous Sunday-night dinners for her children and grandchildren, and recently, her great-granddaughter.

The other was the legendary supper club chanteuse Julie Wilson, who had turned ninety in October 2014. I had seen Julie in performance many times and interviewed her more than once, specifically on Sinatra. I knew the usual stories she told: how Frank came to see her in London in 1950, while he was still married to Big Nancy, but on a very public tryst with Ava Gardner; how Frank and Ava heard her sing "London by Night," written by a friend of hers named Carroll Coates; how Ava, who had great taste in music, liked the song and told Frank he should sing it; how Frank thanked Julie for introducing him to the song (and, parenthetically, that's at least partially why Sinatra recorded "London by Night" so often—because it always reminded him of the great love of his life). One of Julie's favorite stories involved a piece of advice that Sinatra had given to her: "You're a great gal," he said, "but you sleep with all the wrong men." (At Julie's memorial concert in 2015, singer-entertainer Sidney Myer piped up, "To think that I have something in common with Julie Wilson!")

In March 2015, I was enjoying a visit from the great love of my own life. Patty always made a point to check up on Julie whenever she was in town, to take her to lunch and spend quality time with her. Together, we had interviewed Julie more than once: about the Persian Room, about the Playboy Club and television show, and other aspects of her long career. But Patty had the idea of talking to Julie about the Copacabana, which we had never done, and she asked me if I wanted to come along. Of course I did. My principal motivation was to spend a little more time with Patty, but I also welcomed the opportunity to pay a call on

Julie again. Then too, I knew that Julie's close companion and virtual kid sister, the charming Debbie Dampiere, would be with us, which was another good reason to go. (With all that femininity around—in that multitude of pulchritude—I could easily pass out from an overload of estrogen.)

So I had plenty of reasons to visit with Julie at her son Holt's apartment on West Fifty-Fifth Street, but, frankly, I wasn't actually expecting to learn anything new. I was in for a surprise. We asked her about the Copa, and unexpectedly, it turned out to be a road that led back to Sinatra.

In 1946, Julie, age twenty-one, was working at the Copa. She looked like a chorus girl, but she was in fact part of the vocal ensemble, the choir that backed up the headliners. And she was also starting to be given the occasional solo part. The first time she met Sinatra was during the run of the spring show, when he came in to hear Joe E. Lewis, already one of his heroes. (Interestingly, she remembered Lewis primarily as a "great singer" rather than a comedian.) This was the nightclub revue that introduced "The Coffee Song," and that was where Sinatra first heard it (he would record that song more than once as well).

A few months later, the act slated to headline the fall 1946 show was the comedy team of Phil Silvers and John Lee Morgan Beauregard "Rags" Ragland. For most of his lengthy career Silvers was a single, but he was always funniest when he worked with someone, and Rags was a perfect foil. Where Silvers was a fast-talking, highly verbal comic, Ragland's style was contrastingly slower and more physical. They fell into the familiar vaudeville pattern of a sharpie and a stooge, and they were, by all reports, dynamite together, what *Variety* might describe as a surefire "socko" comedy act.

A lot was riding on the team's September 1946 opening at the Copa, but to everyone's horror, Ragland died suddenly of uremia only about two weeks prior. Silvers had decided to go on as a solo act, but was nervous and frightened without his partner. He asked his longtime friend Frank to help out, but Sinatra was contractually obligated to stay in Hollywood, where he was supposed to be filming his latest MGM movie, titled *It Happened in Brooklyn* (despite the title, it was actually being shot in Culver City, California). Then at the last minute, Sinatra, who was already perpetually in trouble with MGM for acting like he had a mind of his own (in those days, the movie studios essentially owned all the actors they had under contract, who never questioned the orders they were given), suddenly decided to play hooky from Hollywood. He unexpectedly hopped a plane to New York, and presented himself to Phil Silvers—on the afternoon of the opening—as the funnyman's new stooge.

Louis B. Mayer was horrified at first, but Sinatra's selfless act of pitching in and helping out two pals, one living and one departed, was a bonanza of positive publicity—the whole country was buzzing about Silvers and Sinatra at the Copa. Most of these details are recounted in several biographies of Sinatra, including James Kaplan's excellent *The Voice*. (Even the dreadful Kitty Kelley had to acknowledge it.) Yet somehow none of us realized that Julie Wilson had been right there, smack dab in the middle of the entire incident.

Ah yes, she remembered it well. "And then, it came the opening night for Phil Silvers, and Rags Ragland died, and Sinatra flew in and didn't tell anybody—showed up to be his sidekick. Isn't that nice? I was there. And Frank said, 'C'mon Julie, we're going to do a song together, the three of us.' It was Phil Silvers, Frank, and I was the girl singer. I still remember the song." At this point in the interview, Julie started singing to us, "I've flown around the world in a plane. . . . I can't get started with you." She added, "I was so thrilled I could hardly talk."

Julie later guest starred on Silvers's *Sergeant Bilko* television show and would cross paths with Sinatra again more than once, including that London encounter. But that was the only time she ever sang with him. "He was a very nice guy, you know? He'd show up when people were in need. So I felt very lucky—yeah, I got to do that *one* song with him."*

Even at ninety, with her soul slowly leaving her body, Julie was still an amazing storyteller and even though she could barely remember names or lyrics at that point, for an hour or so she had transported all three of us—Patty, Debbie, and myself—back to the Copacabana, 1946. Then, she was finished with her story. All of a sudden, we were back in the apartment once more, not even ten blocks away—but seventy years away.

Patty and I couldn't have known then that this was the last time we would ever see Julie, that she would die a few weeks later on Easter Sunday. But even then it felt like a transcendent moment.

And the last words that Julie Wilson ever said to me were about Sinatra. "He was such a kind man." Then, to make sure she wouldn't be misunderstood, she took my hand in hers and pulled me closer to her, looked me straight in the eye, and repeated it, for emphasis. "He was a kind, kind man."

*And scene.*

—WILL FRIEDWALD
Harlem, New York, 2016

---

* The late Jean Bach told me a similar story regarding Sinatra's unexpected kindness: in the mid-1960s, she went into a small piano bar on New York's Upper East Side. The pianist was Walter Gross, who had earlier been an important keyboardist and conductor on network radio and who, as a songwriter, had composed the music for the popular standard "Tenderly." That night Sinatra came in, stayed for a few minutes, and asked Gross if he could sing "Tenderly." He did, and Gross accompanied him; the pianist was too drunk to have any consciousness of what he was doing or who was singing, but he was able to play the melody by rote. When Sinatra finished, he dropped a hundred-dollar bill into the tip jar, and left.

# A NOTE ON SOURCES

All unattributed quotes come from interviews conducted (with the kind folks listed in the acknowledgments) by me and Mr. Granata. Only two individuals I wanted to talk with directly turned me down: Mo Ostin of Warner Bros.–Reprise Records and Frank Sinatra himself. In the case of Mr. Sinatra, it probably wasn't such a loss as I might have imagined: with him, the past was past. It's well known that he loved to talk about his "salad days" with Tommy Dorsey, but other than that, he rarely thought about, for instance, how he created his classic albums after the fact. I also have been extremely fortunate to excavate a series of interviews (never published in print form) with the singer going back to the mid-1940s. Because it's been a kind of Sinatra tradition for those around him to put words in his mouth (such as the 1963 *Playboy* interview, which is actually an inspired piece of creative scriptwriting by Mike Shore), I have tried my best to stick with radio interviews in which he's clearly speaking for himself.

The most substantial new Sinatra interview that I've been able to use for the new (2017) edition of the book was with Bill Boggs, conducted on September 22, 1975, for his WNEW-TV program *Midday Live*. (This was broadcast on a special edition of the program titled *A Conversation with Frank Sinatra*, on December 1, 1975.) Special thanks to Bill for making this available to me, since it has never been published or included in any other book.

Herewith is a list (in roughly chronological order) of the interviewers and approximate dates, and, in some cases, the subject matter:

Dave Garroway, from late 1945, mostly on Glenn Miller.

Jack Ellsworth, New York, July 11, 1949.

Ben Heller, Atlantic City, Labor Day weekend, 1950.

Larry King, 1965.

Paul Compton, KGIL radio, San Francisco, June 5, 1970, and December 30, 1973.

Bill Boggs, WNEW-TV studios New York, September 22, 1975. (Thanks very much to Mr. Boggs for allowing me to cull from the complete, unedited interview for the revised edition of this book.)

William B. Williams, U.S. Army Reserve recruiting program, syndicated, July 1976.

*Suzy Visits Ol' Blue Eyes and Ol' Brown Eyes* (television show, also referenced in some places as *Suzy Visits the Sinatras*), May 25, 1977.

Arlene Francis, WOR radio, New York, January 10, 1977, September 24, 1980 (with Martin Gabel), and September 15, 1981.

Sid Mark, September 1981.

William B. Williams, WNEW-AM radio, New York, November 13, 1981.

Ed Walker, WMAL radio, Washington, DC, April 19, 1983.

Sid Mark, taped November 1983 (mostly on Don Costa).

Sid Mark, April 28, 1984, backstage in Philadelphia (mostly on Gordon Jenkins).

Sidney Zion, one-on-one "seminar," conducted before a small audience of students at Yale University, April 15, 1986.

Jonathan Schwartz, WNEW-AM radio, New York, on Irving Berlin's one-hundredth birthday, May 11, 1988.

Larry King, CNN television interview, 1988.

Other interviews consulted (other than my own) include Nelson Riddle (with Robert Windeler and Jonathan Schwartz), Gordon Jenkins (with Wink Martindale), Irv Cottler (with Richard Apt), and Alan Freeman (with Stan Britt).

# CONSUMER GUIDE AND COMPACT DISCOGRAPHY

In 1990–95, I drew on many sources of discographical information, perhaps most frequently on *The Sinatrafile Part 2, Commercial* (second edition) by John Ridgway (John Ridgway Books, Birmingham, UK, 1991) and *Sinatra: The Man and his Music. The Recording Artistry of Francis Albert Sinatra, 1939–1992* by Ed O'Brien and Scott P. Sayers (TSD Press, Austin, Texas, 1992).

In 2016–17, however, I relied on two more recent and authoritative studies. The first is *Put Your Dreams Away: A Frank Sinatra Discography* (Greenwood Press, 2000) compiled by Luiz Carlos do Nascimento Silva, a Brazilian scholar who managed to gain access to the files of all the various labels Sinatra recorded for as well as, more amazingly, the files of both the Los Angeles and New York musicians' local unions. Garcia concentrates on the actual recording sessions, as well as any other live (concert, radio, film) material that had been commercially issued by 2000.

The other is *Where or When: The Definitive Sinatra Database*, by three European researchers, Giuseppe Marcucci (Italy), Dick Schwarz (Holland), and Ed Vanhellemont (Belgium). In the text, I simply refer to this as either "Marcucci" or *Where or When*. In preparing this edition, I referred to the sixth edition, issued as a CD-ROM in 2006. The goal of this trio was nothing less than to chronicle where Sinatra was every day of his life, so his listing is an enormous itinerary consisting of every concert, every broadcast, whatever days he was on the set of whatever movie—the whole *megillah*.

I found both of these works to be extremely reliable, each containing information that isn't in the other but almost never contradicting each other.

It's with both delight and dismay that I update the basic discography in 2017. The first because so much Sinatra material has been either reissued or issued for the first time since the dawn of the digital era; but the second because a great many of the more valuable sets (like Rhino Records' *Frank Sinatra in Hollywood 1940–1964*) have been allowed to go out of print. Hopefully Frank fans have found some sympathetic friend to share the tracks with them—better that than having to go to the price-gougers on Amazon or eBay.

In any case, my goal here is to list all the worthwhile Sinatra material that has been issued over the last thirty years or so (the digital era—the years of CDs, then MP3s, digital downloads, and streaming); but be mindful that some essential works are no longer available, neither as physical offerings nor paid downloads, nor even from the streaming services, alas.

A note regarding unauthorized releases, sometimes referred to herein as "bootlegs." In this listing, I'm including everything I believe to be of musical value, taking under consideration the performance, the sound quality, and the singularity of the material (i.e., whether the performances are unique or something available on other releases). The moral and legal aspects of these releases is not my concern here. As a general rule, you can assume that most of the releases on labels other than RCA (BMG, Buddha), Columbia (Sony), Capitol (also including Blue Note, and now part of Universal Music), or Reprise (Warner Bros.)—or such legitimate licensors as Rhino Records, Artanis, and Shout Factory—have not been sanctioned by Frank Sinatra Enterprises. The most difficult aspect in collecting Sinatra "boots," the vast majority of which were issued in the 1990s and early 2000s, is that even when they were new, most of them were not easy to find. Now, with the digital diaspora firmly in place, I can't offer any advice as to where you can track them down. (Maybe there's an Apple Music for bootlegs somewhere? I'm just sayin'.)

## THE UTMOST ESSENTIAL SINATRA

If for some reason you've decided to limit your Sinatra purchases to a minimum few sample packages, fortunately there are multiple sets that present a good cross section of the best of what Sinatra recorded during the three most important label affiliations of his career.

*A Voice in Time (1939–1952)* (**eighty tracks on four CDs, Legacy 88697096692 or Legacy 716124**). Produced by our pal Chuck Granata in 2007, this four-CD set is the best summary so far of the origins of a legend. We start in 1939 with "All or Nothing at All" and end with "I'm a Fool to Want You" and "Why Try to Change Me Now?" from the final Columbia session. Along the way, we hit all the high spots of The Voice's early career: the big-band work with Harry James and Tommy Dorsey, the first phase of Sinatra hysteria during the war and immediately after, and then all the in-between years of the late 1940s and early 1950s. Housed in an attractive package with a beautiful booklet, this is a highly recommended package even if you happen to already own the complete works. (*The Best of the Columbia Years: 1943–1952*, Legacy C4K 64681, which contains ninety-three of The Voice's key classics from that era on four CDs with a sixty-eight-page booklet, is also recommended but in general has been superseded by the *Voice in Time* package.)

*The Capitol Years* (**seventy-five tracks on three CDs, Capitol C2-94777**). A bargain, with the most tracks crammed onto the fewest discs, this 1990 set is offered for the Sinatraphile who has everything—containing one brand new Sinatra–Billy May discovery, major album tracks, and lots of singles as well—and nothing, with many classic cuts selected for benefit of the neophyte who wants to sample the classic Capitol "concept" albums before buying all of them. Again, trust me, you will eventually want them all. Maybe not today, maybe not tomorrow, but soon—and for the rest of your life. However, even then this sampler will still contain some goodies unavailable anywhere else.

*The Reprise Collection* (**eighty-one tracks on four CDs, Reprise 7599-26340-1**). As with *The Capitol Years,* it's a very listenable mixture of the rare and the familiar. Another seventy-fifth-birthday compilation, the most interesting and unusual material, surprisingly, comes from the 1970s, making the point that this was a much more rewarding era in Sinatra history than the regularly released tracks from these years would lead us to believe.

*Frank Sinatra in Hollywood 1940–1964* (**182 tracks on six CDs, Reprise/TCM Turner Classic Movies Music 8122-78285-2**). Not a sampler, but an absolutely essential compendium of Sinatra's singing from the long peak years of his career—from the Dorsey years (*Las Vegas Nights*) to the Rat Pack (*Robin and the 7 Hoods*). The six discs contain virtually every vocal that The Voice recorded for his appearances in films, the bulk of which (at least as represented here) were movie musicals. All the big highlights are here, such as the songs from his blockbuster hits like *Anchors Aweigh*, *On the Town*, and *Guys and Dolls*, as well as such lesser-known "cult" favorites as *It Happened in Brooklyn, Double Dynamite,* and *Meet Danny Wilson*—not to mention extreme rarities and gems like the songs from the unproduced animated musical version of *Finian's Rainbow.* This was essentially produced by Rhino Records (more specifically by Chuck Granata and Didier C. Deutsch) for Reprise, with a major assist from Michael Feinstein (don't let my liner notes stop you). No longer officially available; if you can't get or borrow a copy, perhaps Robbo and his Merry Men could procure one for you.

Also worth noting: in conjunction with the rather silly 1992 television miniseries *Sinatra,* Reprise issued an unusual double-disc sampler that contains tracks from all of Sinatra's myriad periods, from Tommy Dorsey on up to "My Way." The full title is *Sinatra: Soundtrack to the CBS Mini-Series* (two CDs, Reprise 9362-45091-2).

Another double, the recommended *Sinatra Saga* (thirty-nine tracks on two CDs, Bravura CD2-104) offers concert highlights from the 1950s to the '80s, covering many stages of Sinatra's career evolution.

## THE NEARLY COMPLETE WORKS

Corresponding with the outline of this book as a whole, this section is organized by either collaborator or period, whichever seems the most sensible. Reprise albums with more than one arranger, such as *Trilogy,* will usually be found in the "general" sections for the 1960s ("Looking for the Hook" ) and 1970s-'80s-'90s ("The Concert Years").

### With Harry James

Sony's *Harry James and His Orchestra featuring Frank Sinatra* (CK 66377, issued in 1995) is the number-one document of the James-Sinatra tenure. It features twenty-one songs, including seven radio performances from 1939, as well as all the master recordings and alternate takes.

Hindsight's *All or Nothing at All* (HCD-263, issued in 1995) features seventeen airchecks by the 1939 James band, nine with Sinatra vocals.

### With Tommy Dorsey

The recommended, complete package of the Dorsey-Sinatra collaboration is *The Song Is You* (121 tracks on five CDs, RCA 07863 66353-2), which offers all the master takes complete, in excellent sound, with a ninety-page booklet and a bonus disc of previously unheard live radio performances.

Those radio performances are explored at much greater length in three CDs released individually by BMG in 1999 and 2004. The emphasis is on rare and unrecorded songs, which sometimes leads to a preponderance of the amateur songs written for the *Fame and Fortune* songwriting contest, but there are some great performances here nonetheless, and the audio fidelity is excellent:

*Learn to Croon* (Buddha Records 99601 or BMG 74321691732).

*It's All So New!* (Buddha Records 99600).

*Young Blue Eyes: Birth of the Crooner* (BMG/Sony Music Entertainment 771174, or RCA 60283, or Bluebird RCA 82876602832). This is the disc that features the highly unusual "East of the Sun" with a mysterious "double vocal" by Sinatra.

Other live performances by the Dorsey orchestra, with occasional vocals by Frank Sinatra, can be heard on the following unofficially released discs:

*The Tommy Dorsey Orchestra Volume 2 Featuring Frank Sinatra* (Echo Jazz EJCD 09).

*Tommy Dorsey 1940* (Tax CD 3705-2, issued in Denmark).

*1942 War Band Broadcast,* featuring "Blues in the Night" (Jazz Hour JH-1013).

*Palladium Nov. 26-1940—Raleigh Show Jan. 6-1943* (Jazz Hour JH-1035).

*The All Time Hit Parade Rehearsals*, including a 1944 Sinatra-Dorsey reunion (Hep CD 39, issued in Scotland).

*This One's for Tommy* (Voice V-CD-1103) features the 1955 reunion, a 1958 FS-TD tribute, and other rarities.

Not to forget: *I Remember Tommy* with Sy Oliver (Reprise 45267) from 1961. Also, sessions and other extra material on the privately issued *Inside Tommy* (Artisan 606-2).

## With Axel Stordahl (1943–52)

### Studio

I'm understandably prejudiced by having worked on it, but I don't think many Frankophiles would disagree with the assertion that *The Columbia Years 1943–1952: The Complete Recordings* (approximately 285 songs on twelve CDs, Columbia Legacy CXK 46873) ranks as one of the great achievements of the modern recording industry. Including the master take of every song Sinatra recorded for Columbia in the best possible sound, the set contains scores of rarities, among them dozens of selections that were either previously only issued on 78 or not at all, with a 140-page booklet. I can't recommend this set too highly.

Following the release of the "big blue box" in 1993, the various corporate descendants of Columbia Records (Sony Music, Sony-BMG, Sony Legacy, etc.) have released several individual volumes containing new and different material; all of these offer at least a few new items—alternate takes and/or radio performances—not on the twelve-CD set:

*Christmas Songs by Sinatra* (CK 66413).

*The Columbia Years 1943–1952: The V-Discs* (two CDs, C2K 66135). A godsend for collectors, this double-disc package contains radio performances and an original session as mastered for the GI audience during World War II. Be aware that while the performances are often fascinating and even revelatory, the sound isn't always up to the commercial masters.

*Sinatra Sings Gershwin* (Legacy/Columbia CK-61057 or Sony Music Distribution 5078782).

*Sinatra Sings Cole Porter* (Legacy/Columbia CK 61058 or Sony Music Distribution 5078772).

*Sinatra Sings Rodgers and Hammerstein* (Legacy/Columbia CK 64661).

*Swing and Dance with Frank Sinatra* (Legacy/Columbia CK 64852). This last "bonus" title is particularly valuable as a summary of Sinatra's early jazz work as well as of the artistry of the great missing link of Sinatra collaborators, George Siravo.

### Live and Radio

*A Voice on Air 1935–1955* (107 tracks on four CDs, Columbia/Sony Music 88875099712). Along with the *Sinatra in Hollywood* box, this centennial package is one of the two most worthwhile releases of Sinatra music issued since his death. An absolutely essential survey of Sinatra's career on radio, from the first Major Bowes appearance in 1935 to the remarkable *Perfectly Frank* series in 1955. The young singer is, for the most part, in even better voice and spirits than on his commercial Columbia sessions, and the guest stars, such as Benny Goodman and the King Cole Trio, are amazing. I might even recommend it even more highly than the 1993 "big blue box" (the *Complete Columbia* package), and it's a lot easier to find. (Knowing the track record that the major labels have for keeping important works in print, I would recommend that everyone go out and grab this 2015 package before it becomes a collector's item.)

*Lost & Found* | *The Radio Years* (Smithsonian/Columbia/Legacy 88875147142). This is a single-volume addendum to the four-CD box listed immediately above, also produced by Chuck Granata, in which the performances are every bit as good.

As far as noncommercial material goes, the 1940s is the most prolific period of Sinatra's career, considering that Sinatra had a weekly radio slot and then television show going straight for nearly a decade. For two seasons, in fact, Sinatra even did two shows at once, as well as dozens of pro bono appearances on the Armed Forces Radio Network. Numerous unauthorized releases were issued in the early days of the compact disc medium; of those, the following are worth owning, though many are ridiculously impossible to find.

JR Records of England, which specializes in highly recommended compilations of unrecorded songs gathered chronologically, produced the following:

*Your Hit Parade 1944* (JRR-144-2).

*Songs by Sinatra 1945* (JRR-145-2).

*Your Hit Parade 1947* (JRR-147-2).

*Your Hit Parade 1948* (JRR-148-2).

*Your Hit Parade 1949* (JRR 249-2).

*Light Up Time 1949* (JRR-149-2).

The VJC series also concentrates on rare songs and performances:

*The Unheard Frank Sinatra Volume 1: As Time Goes By* (VJC-1004-2).

*The Unheard Frank Sinatra Volume 2: The House I Live In* (VJC-1007).

*The Unheard Frank Sinatra Volume 3: Long Ago and Far Away* (VJC-1030).

*The Unheard Frank Sinatra Volume 4: I'll Be Seeing You* (VJC-1051).

*The Songs of Sammy Cahn and Jule Styne* (VJC-1045).

Additional 1940s radio collections, also recommended:

*Portraits from The Past* (Bravura BCD-101).

*Frank Sinatra "The Voice" 1943–1947* (Decade DCD-102).

*The Rarest Sinatra* (Decade DCD-103, which is true to its title).

*Live Duets, 1943–1957* with Bing Crosby, Nat Cole, Louis Armstrong, etc. (Voice V-CD-1101).

*Frank Sinatra Live 1942–46 Complete Songs by Sinatra Shows* (Jazz Hour JH-1020).

*Frank Sinatra Hit Parade Shows April 30–May 28 1949* (Jazz Hour JH-1036).

*Frank Sinatra 1946 Old Gold Shows* (Jazz Hour JH-1040).

*1949 Lite Up Time Shows* (Jazz Band EBCD 2116-2, British), featuring several tracks with Bobby Hackett.

*Young Frank Sinatra: In the Blue of Evening* (Natasha Imports NI-4007).

*A Treasury of Sinatra Vomume 1* [*sic*] (JRR 001-2) commemorates the fortieth anniversary of the Sinatra Music Society with many rare radio and television broadcast items, including the 1943 FDR sixty-first-birthday tribute version of "Night and Day."

*In Celebration* (Exclusive EXC101) includes the complete October 17, 1945, *Songs by Sinatra* show, with twelve other songs from various radio shows.

*Frank Sinatra & Friends* (Hallmark 300022, British) includes twenty-one duets, mostly radio, taken from Voice 1101.

*There'll Be Some Changes Made (The Rarities 1950–51)* (Voice V-CD-1102) comes from early television tracks.

*Sinatra: The Radio Years 1939–1955* (six CDs, Meteor CDMTBS 001, British) Even twenty years ago this was a tough one to find, and the audio is just as bad as the music is rare, but there's some fascinating material on here. (Good luck snagging it.)

## CAPITOL RECORDS, 1953–62

In 1992, EMI gathered all sixteen of the classic original Sinatra albums originally produced for Capitol Records into an imposing wooden box that they titled *Concepts* (Capitol 7 99956 2). Eight years later, the set was reissued in a somewhat more modest but no less attractive package (Capitol 23004). Both of these include the otherwise hard-to-find instrumental set, *Tone Poems of Color*, but not the singles compendiums, which fortunately were reissued in 1996, as well as a booklet of notes by me. Either way, it's a convenient (though not necessarily inexpensive) way to obtain all of the masterpiece Sinatra Capitol albums in one fell swoop.

The worthy companion to the above set is this 1996 package of *The Complete Capitol Singles Collection* (eighty-nine tracks on four CDs, Capitol 38089 or Capitol/EMI Records 0724383808953), which features everything that Capitol released on a 45 rpm disc in these years, along with a few rarities that were not. Considering that Sinatra did some of his best work (and created some of his biggest hits and signature songs) in the singles medium, this one is also fairly indispensable.

Then, not to be outdone, in 1998, following Sinatra's death, the British branch of EMI issued *The Capitol Years* (FRANK1-21). Not to be confused with the American three-CD package of the same title, this is a highly ambitious twenty-one–disc set that includes the sixteen "Capitol Concept" albums, plus five albums of singles compilations and miscellaneous tracks. This megabox contains both the most of Sinatra's output for Capitol and, in the general agreement of audio specialists like Chuck Granata, in the best possible sound quality. (There are still a few tracks left out that can be found on the *Complete Capitol Singles Collection*.) Between the enormous boxes offered by Sony (Columbia), Capitol, and Reprise, when you buy these Sinatra products you're not merely acquiring software, you're investing in furniture.

However, almost all of the original Capitol theme albums are also available individually. I'm not going to attempt to keep track of all the CD-era reissues of the classic Capitol and Reprise albums, but let's just say that most have been issued and reissued, mastered and remastered, more than once. Many of the Capitol albums have had singles added as "bonus" tracks, a practice I don't always approve of (and neither would Sinatra, who planned his albums very carefully), even though more Frank is generally better.

The individual albums are listed below.

### With Nelson Riddle

The classic, original Capitol albums:

*Songs for Young Lovers* and *Swing Easy!* (on one CD, CDP-748470-2).

*In the Wee Small Hours* (CDP-746571-2).

*Close to You* (CDP-746572-2).

*Songs for Swingin' Lovers!* (CDP-746570-2).

*A Swingin' Affair!* (CDP-794518-2).

*Frank Sinatra Sings for Only the Lonely* (CDP-748471-2).

*Nice 'n' Easy* (CDP-791149-2, now including "The Nearness of You").

*Sinatra's Swingin' Session!!!* (CDP-746573-2).

The Reprise albums:

*The Concert Sinatra* (FS 1009-2).

*Sinatra's Sinatra* (FS 1010).

*Sinatra Sings Days of Wine and Roses, Moon River, and Other Academy Award Winners* (FS 1011-2).

*Moonlight Sinatra* (FS 1018-2), *Strangers in the Night* (FS 1017-2).

## With Billy May

On Capitol:

*Come Fly with Me* (CDP-748469-2).

*Come Dance with Me!* (CDP-748468-2).

*Come Swing with Me!* (CDP-794520-2).

On Reprise:

*Sinatra Swings/Swing Along with Me* (FS 1002-2).

*Francis A. & Edward K.* with Duke Ellington's Orchestra (FS 1024-2).

## With Gordon Jenkins

On Capitol:

*The Sinatra Christmas Album* (originally released as *A Jolly Christmas with Frank Sinatra*) (CDP-748329-2).

*Where Are You?* (CDP-791209-2).

*No One Cares* (CDP-794519-2).

On Reprise:

*All Alone* (927022-2).

*September of My Years* (FS 1014-2).

*She Shot Me Down* (FS 2305).

## Miscellaneous 1950s Live and "Noncommercial" Material

*Concerts:*

*Melbourne, 19 January, 1955* (JRR 155-2). A surprisingly disappointing concert that probably won't be issued anywhere else.

*Sinatra '57 in Concert* (Artanis ARZ-101-2). An authorized release of one of the most spectacular Sinatra concerts ever, both in terms of the performance, with Nelson Riddle conducting, as well as the sound quality. From the Seattle Civic Auditorium, June 9, 1957, issued in 1999. (This was also reissued as a bonus disc with the compilation *Best of the Best* in 2011.)

*With the Red Norvo Quintet: Live in Australia, 1959* (Blue Note 37513, issued in 1997). Ditto and perhaps even more so.

*Broadcasts and Other Rarities:*

> *Perfectly Frank.* Unique small-group tracks done for radio, 1953–55 (Bravura BCD-103).

> *The Television Years.* Late 1950s, that is (Bravura BCD-105).

> *From the Vaults* and *From the Vaults Two and More* (Archive 2201 and 202). These were two volumes of session outtakes from the Capitol years, some of the rarest and most valuable material that's ever been bootlegged; the second volume also includes ten rare broadcast tracks from the 1950s.

> *Frank & Bing* (Boardwalk 503) collects both Bing Crosby shows from March 1954 guest-starring Sinatra, from immediately before and after the Oscar ceremony, along with a 1953 transmission of Sinatra in Italy.

> *FS After Hours* (Artistry ART 3001) offers thirty-three more cuts from the *To Be Perfectly Frank* show: fifteen ballads and the rest with rhythm section.

## LOOKING FOR THE HOOK: THE REPRISE YEARS

In honor of the big eightieth birthday in 1995, Reprise entered the luggage business with *Frank Sinatra: The Complete Reprise Studio Recordings* (Reprise 46013-2), a limited edition, twenty-disc package. The CDs, carrying 452 songs (among them eighteen never-before-released titles), came in an overdone suitcase package (putting new meaning to the term "traveling music") but with a rather minimal booklet and, unfortunately, without the magnifying glass necessary to follow the track listing. It's not the way I recommend hearing these tracks, especially since most of the albums were broken down into recording sequence rather than the actual album sequence that Sinatra intended; but while it was available, it was the quickest way to acquire 99.9% of FS's issuable Reprise master takes in one fell swoop. (Also for the eightieth: Reprise issued a single-CD collection, *Everything Happens to Me* (Reprise 9 46116-2), purportedly programmed by The Man himself. The very dark 1981 reading of the title cut is the highlight here.)

In 2010, in honor of the fiftieth anniversary of Reprise Records, the company's UK division issued *The Reprise Years* (currently listed with a catalog number of Universal Music 2751376). This set contains all thirty-five studio albums (both the 1965 *A Man and His Music* and the 1980 *Trilogy* are on two CDs each) on thirty-seven CDs. What's missing are the live albums and the singles; the two volumes of *Greatest Hits* are not included. Plus, there's a bonus DVD containing the first three *Man and His Music* television specials.

Reprise and other 1960s albums (other than those with Riddle, May, and Jenkins). All of these are on Reprise, except where indicated.

> *Ring-a-Ding-Ding!* with Johnny Mandel (9 46933-2).

> *Point of No Return* with Axel Stordahl (Capitol CDP-748334-2).

> *Sinatra & Strings* with Don Costa (9 46970-2).

> *Sinatra-Basie* arranged and conducted by Neal Hefti (9 47241-2).

> *Sinatra & Sextet: Live in Paris* (45487-2).

> *Sinatra Sings Great Songs from Great Britain* with Robert Farnon (9 45219-2) (also *Inside Great Songs*, Artisan ART 605-2, though the complete issued album and some of the session material is included in the *Sinatra: London* boxed set).

> *Sinatra and Swingin' Brass* with Neil Hefti (9 27021-2).

> *It Might as Well Be Swing* with Count Basie, conducted by Quincy Jones (1012-2).

> *Softly, as I Leave You* with Riddle, May, Ernie Freeman, Marty Paich, etc. (1013-2).

*My Kind of Broadway* with Torrie Zito and others (1015-2).

*A Man and His Music* with various arrangers (two CDs, 1016-2).

*Sinatra at the Sands* with Count Basie, conducted by Quincy Jones (two LPs on one CD, 9 46947-2).

*That's Life* with Ernie Freeman (1020-2).

*Francis Albert Sinatra & Antônio Carlos Jobim*, arranged and conducted by Claus Ogerman (1021-2).

*The World We Knew* with Ernie Freeman, Gordon Jenkins, and others (1022-2).

*Cycles* with Don Costa (1027-2).

*A Man Alone* with Don Costa (1030-2).

*Sinatra & Company* with Don Costa, Eumir Deodato, Antônio Carlos Jobim (1033).

*Greatest Hits Vol. 1* (2274-2).

*Greatest Hits Vol. 2* (2275-2).

*My Way* (1029-2).

*Watertown* (45689-2).

*The Sinatra Christmas Album* (45743-2). A recommended 1994 compilation, primarily drawn from *12 Songs of Christmas* (1964) and *The Sinatra Family Wish You a Merry Christmas* (1968).

## IT'S SINATRA'S WORLD, WE JUST LIVE IN IT: THE GEOGRAPHICAL BOXES

Over a ten-year period, from 2006 to 2016, Sinatra Enterprises has released four ambitious boxes of live performances. Although they seem to have been programmed by Google Maps, all four are highly recommended and contain a treasure trove of audio (and even video) being issued legitimately for the first time.

*Sinatra: Vegas* (issued in 2006 as Warner Bros./Reprise/Rhino 8122740752, and more recently given a new catalog number in 2014 as Signature Sinatra/Universal B 002035902).

Sands Hotel, November 2, 1961.

Sands Hotel, January–February 1966 with Count Basie and His Orchestra, and Quincy Jones (part of the same pool of material as *Sinatra at the Sands*).

Caesars Palace, March 1982.

Golden Nugget, April 1987.

DVD: Caesars Palace, May 5, 1978.

*Sinatra: New York* (issued in 2009 as Reprise R2 520602 in the USA, and 8122-79734-2 in Europe).

Manhattan Center, February 3, 1955, with Tommy Dorsey and His Orchestra.

The United Nations, September 13, 1963, a fascinating and revealing concert with Skitch Henderson on piano.

Carnegie Hall, April 8, 1974.

Madison Square Garden, October 12, 1974.

Carnegie Hall, June 1984.

Radio City Music Hall, June 1990.

DVD: Carnegie Hall, June 25, 1980.

*Sinatra: London* (issued in 2014 as Universal Music 4703568).

*Great Songs from Great Britain*, plus spoken introductions to the individual songs recorded for the BBC.

Session material and outtakes from *Great Songs from Great Britain.*

BBC Studios, a live performance for the BBC *Show Band Show*, July 16, 1953.

Royal Albert Hall, September 21, 1984.

DVD: Royal Festival Hall, June 1, 1962, with the Bill Miller Sextet, as part of the famous 1962 World Tour.

DVD: Royal Festival Hall, November 16, 1970 (the second show that night).

*Sinatra: World on a String* (issued in 2016 as Universal 5708090).

Sporting Club, Monte Carlo, June 14, 1958.

Rome, Italy. *RAI Radio Club*, May 20, 1953.

Sydney Stadium, Australia, December 2, 1961.

Giza pyramid complex, near Cairo, Egypt, September 27, 1979.

Altos De Chevón, La Romana, Dominican Republic, August 20, 1982.

This time, the DVD consists of video entirely from the 1962 World Tour:

Hibiya Park, Japan, April 21, 1962.

*Frank Sinatra With All God's Children*, 1962.

*Sinatra In Israel*, 1962.

Perugina Chocolate Commercials, 1962.

## Additional Live Concerts from the 1960s

*Saloon Singer* from the Sands, 1961, and Chicago, 1962 (Encore ENCD-1001).

*Frank Sinatra, Dean Martin, Sammy Davis Jr. at Villa Venice, Chicago, Live 1962, Volume One* (Jazz Hour JH-1033) and *Volume Two* (Jazz Hour JH-1034); the same material was condensed down into one CD on *Live & Swingin': The Ultimate Rat Pack Collection* (Reprise R9 73965, issued in 2003).

*Cole Porter—You're the Top: A Testimonial* (Viper's Nest VN-180) contains the audio recording of a panel discussion, University of Southern California (February 12, 1967) hosted by Alan Jay Lerner in honor of the dedication of the Cole Porter Library, including Ethel Merman, Fred Astaire, Gene Kelly, Jimmy Stewart, and screenwriter Garson Kanin, with occasional songs accompanied by pianist Roger Eden. Sinatra sings five songs, among them a rare ballad/solo-with-piano version of "I've Got You Under My Skin."

*Sinatra in the Sixties* (Virtuoso 5001) collects live songs from Vegas; several television shows; the 1961 Inaugural Gala; concerts from Sydney, Saint Louis, and Oakland; and the 1963 United Nations concert.

One package well worth finding is *Live & Swingin': The Ultimate Rat Pack Collection* (Reprise R9 73965). It contains both an audio CD of the 1962 Villa Venice show listed above and a DVD of a later concert that's the last spectacular gasp of the Rat Pack, recorded live at the Kiel Opera House in Saint Louis on June 20, 1965, costarring Sammy Davis Jr. and Dean Martin, as well as Quincy Jones conducting Count Basie and His Orchestra. It's not only the single best document of the Rat Pack but one of the all-time most exciting Sinatra performances.

*The Lost London Concert* (Esquire 2200): this is the first show from Royal Festival Hall, November 16, 1970 (the second of which has been released on DVD in the *Sinatra: London* package).

### 1960s TV Soundtracks

*Christmas in California* (Fremus SAS CDFR 0500, Italian) containing the 1967 *Dean Martin Show* episode costarring Sinatra and featuring the children of both Sinatra and Martin.

*Sinatra: The Classic Collection: A Man and His Music* (Fremus CDFR 0503, Italian), the 1965 NBC special.

### Other 1960s Session Material

The following are all very underground: *Sinatra Sessions* (Decade DCD 100); *On the Inside Volume 1* (Artisan ART 601-2); *On the Inside Volume 2* (Artisan ART 602-2); *Inside Brass* (Artisan ART 603-2); and *Inside Basie* (Artisan ART 604-2).

## THE CONCERT YEARS

*Ol' Blue Eyes Is Back* with Gordon Jenkins & Don Costa (2155-2).

*Some Nice Things I've Missed* with Don Costa & Gordon Jenkins (2195-2).

*The Main Event—Live* with Woody Herman and the Young Thundering Herd (2207-2).

*Trilogy: Past, Present, Future* with Billy May, Don Costa, and Gordon Jenkins (two CDs, 2300-2).

*L.A. Is My Lady*, produced and conducted by Quincy Jones (Qwest Records 9 25145-2).

*Frank Sinatra Duets* (Capitol CDP 077778961123).

*Frank Sinatra Duets II* (Capitol CDP 7243 8 28103 2 2).

Also: *Sinatra 80th: Live in Concert* (Capitol CDP 7243 8 31723 2 0) comes from two sources: the Dallas Reunion Arena concert of October 1987, which also featured Sammy Davis Jr. and Liza Minelli (not heard on the Capitol disc), and a show from the Fox Theatre in Detroit in December 1988. A well-made conglomeration of two fine concerts, but for some reason the producers felt compelled to stick a particularly heinous electro-duet of "My Way" by Sinatra and Pavarotti at the end.

## MISCELLANEOUS

*The White House, 17 April 1973* (JR Records JRR 173-2).

*The Sinatra Saga Volume 2* (Bravura BRCD 7107).

*For the Good Times*, Resorts International 1979 (Boardwalk 501).

*A Swingin' Night at the Sabre Room,* with Dean Martin, Chicago 1977 (MAC 200).

*A Jumpin' July 4th* (MAC 2100) features a complete concert (July 4, 1986) from the Golden Nugget in Atlantic City.

The limited edition *See the Show Again* (Boardwalk 502) is well worth finding, featuring twenty-four mostly unusual songs (many he never recorded, such as the title tune by Barry Manilow) from the mid-1970s, in varying quality.

*Sinatra and Sammy: North Country Concert* (Matdant 586) features the March 22, 1988, Bloomington, Minnesota, Met Center concert, taped just after Dean Martin dropped out of the Together Again tour.

When *The Last Performance* was released, the title seemed rather pessimistic, but alas, it turned out to be correct. From the Frank Sinatra Golf Tournament in Palm Springs on February 25, 1995.

Two additional boots featuring a wide array of studio rarities, in highly variable audio quality: *The Unissued Sinatra* (Tyrecords TY D100) is mostly in fairly mushy sound; *Sinatra Unreleased* (Getzel #1) also offers Reprise rarities that didn't make the big suitcase, including the intriguing "Leave It All to Me."

And yet more: *The Sinatra Songbook Live* (Artistry 3002), a well-curated amalgam of 1970s and '80s live tracks, and *Francis Albert Hall* (Melcone 401).

## GREAT SONGS FROM GREAT BATONS

The following CDs feature Sinatra in his alter ego as conductor and producer:

*Frank Sinatra Conducts the Music of Alec Wilder* (Sony Music Special Products A 4271).

Dean Martin: *Sleep Warm* (Capitol CDP 7243 8 37500 2 3).

Peggy Lee: *The Man I Love* (issued at last in the United States on DRG CD 94783 in 2009). This is easily the best of Sinatra's conducting jobs and one of the all-time great vocal albums.

The 1983 album *What's New* by trumpeter Charles Turner (and conducted by Sinatra) has been issued on CD along with *I've Got You Under My Skins* by Irv Cottler, from the same year, both together on Big Band Archive BBA111.

The Sylvia Syms album *Syms by Sinatra* (Reprise 9 23724-1) has apparently not been issued anywhere in any digital format—more's the pity.

## VIDEO AND DVD

Frank Sinatra: *Concert Collection* (Shout! Factory 12220) is a seven-DVD package issued in 2010 that contains virtually all of the television and concert material that has been authorized for release by the Sinatra family. That includes all the *Man and His Music* TV specials and an assortment of filmed concerts, such as the classic *Concert for the Americas* (from the Dominican Republic, 1982) and a lesser-known but equally marvelous concert from Budokan Hall, Tokyo, in 1985. The set is both easy to find and inexpensive.

At the time of the centennial, and into 2016 and 2017, Eagle Rock released some of the most important Sinatra videos and television specials (most of the material owned by the Sinatra estate) on a series of DVDs (this includes virtually all of the material from the earlier Shout Factory package):

*The Timex Shows Vol. 1*: contains *The Frank Sinatra Timex Show* (October 19, 1959) and *An Afternoon With Frank Sinatra* (December 13, 1959) (EREDV1278).

*The Timex Shows Vol. 2*: contains *To The Ladies* (February 15, 1960) and *Welcome Home Elvis* (May 12, 1960) (EREDV1279).

*Happy Holidays With Frank & Bing* and *Vintage Sinatra* are on EREDV1243. The first is a vintage TV special first aired on December 20, 1957; the second is a welcome compilation of outstanding numbers, mostly from the singer's ABC-TV series of 1957–58.

*A Man and His Music* (1965) and *A Man and His Music Part II* (1965) are on EV307639.

*A Man and His Music + Ella + Jobim* (1967), *Francis Albert Sinatra Does His Thing* (1968), and *Sinatra* (1969) are all on EV307649.

*Ol' Blue Eyes Is Back* (1973) and *The Main Event* (1974) are on EREDV1241.

*At The Royal Festival Hall* (1970) and *Sinatra In Japan* (1985) are on EV307709.

*Sinatra and Friends* (1977) and *The Man and His Music* (1981) are on EV307659.

*Concert for the Americas* (1982) is on EV307669.

However, even though I wrote the notes (along with Chicago writer Bill Zehme) for the Shout Factory package, I still find it disappointing that none of these vintage videos has been "restored" or "remastered" in any way; these are fundamentally the exact same copies that were being sold in the VHS era thirty years ago. The time is well-nigh to revisit the original master tapes and extract some improved video and audio quality for what are essentially Sinatra's finest moments on television. (And while we're at it, I'd also like to see a lot more of Sinatra's two weekly series, on CBS 1950–52 and ABC 1957–58, get an official release on home video.)

For additional information, the reader is referred to the Sinatra family website (http://sinatrafamily.com). There are also, of course, many Sinatra discussion groups on Yahoo and Facebook.

# INDEX